THE BLOOMSBURY HANDBOOK
TO AGATHA CHRISTIE

THE BLOOMSBURY HANDBOOK
TO AGATHA CHRISTIE

Edited by

Mary Anna Evans and J.C. Bernthal

BLOOMSBURY ACADEMIC
LONDON • NEW YORK • OXFORD • NEW DELHI • SYDNEY

BLOOMSBURY ACADEMIC
Bloomsbury Publishing Plc
50 Bedford Square, London, WC1B 3DP, UK
1385 Broadway, New York, NY 10018, USA
29 Earlsfort Terrace, Dublin 2, Ireland

BLOOMSBURY, BLOOMSBURY ACADEMIC and the Diana logo are
trademarks of Bloomsbury Publishing Plc

First published in Great Britain 2023
Paperback edition published 2024

A catalogue record for this book is available from the British Library.

A catalog record for this book is available from the Library of Congress.

Library of Congress Control Number: 2022939313

ISBN: HB: 978-1-3502-1247-3
         PB: 978-1-3505-0277-2
         ePDF: 978-1-3502-1248-0
         eBook: 978-1-3502-1249-7

Series: Bloomsbury Handbooks

Typeset by Integra Software Services Pvt. Ltd.
Printed and bound in Great Britain

To find out more about our authors and books visit www.bloomsbury.com
and sign up for our newsletters.

To Catherine Brobeck (d. 2021), who helped popularize Agatha Christie scholarship, and who is greatly missed.

CONTENTS

LIST OF ILLUSTRATIONS

FIGURES

TABLE

FOREWORD

VAL MCDERMID

Agatha Christie was my gateway drug into crime fiction. That revelation makes me far from unique. Whenever I say as much in front of an audience, there is invariably a murmur of recognition. Lee Child has said, "When you read one of my books, you go straight on to read two or three." But with Christie, when you're smitten with one, only the entire canon will do.

I was eight or nine years old when I read *The Murder at the Vicarage* for the first time. I used to spend a lot of time at my grandparents' house in a mining village with no library, and the library books I'd brought with me generally didn't last as long as my stay. My grandparents were not readers; they only possessed two books. One was a copy of the Bible which had very thin, fragile pages which filled me with a terror of what clumsy fingers could do. The other, for reasons nobody has ever been able to explain, was *The Murder at the Vicarage*. I can only imagine that a visitor had left it behind at the end of their stay.

Linguistic scientists tell us that Christie's vocabulary and sentence structure are such that they are comprehensible to someone with a reading age of nine. I was a precocious reader, so I suspect the reading itself held few stumbling blocks for me. Where I was probably a little at sea was with the underlying currents of emotional entanglements, of which there are plenty in this, Miss Marple's first outing.

I couldn't have told you then what it was that I found so captivating about this strange little book. I recognized the world it was set in—a charming English village with cottages and well-tended gardens—for it was also the world of Enid Blyton's *Famous Five* and *Five Find-Outers and Dog* series, which I'd devoured since first I could read. But the characters were entirely alien to me.

Retired colonels, curates, artists, and spinsters with herbaceous borders were, on the surface, completely outwith my experience. But what I did recognize—sometimes through a glass, darkly—was human behavior that made sense, both from my own experience and from reading Nancy Drew and the Hardy Boys.

But that in itself is insufficient to explain the hold *The Murder at the Vicarage* took on my imagination. From what I know now, I suspect that a large part of its fascination is one to which we are generally oblivious. That's because it is about the technique buried below the surface of the narrative.

I consider myself fortunate that the first Christie I encountered is one of a dozen or so where she is at the absolute peak of her powers. What distinguishes *The Murder at the Vicarage* from so many of its contemporaries (and Christie's successors and imitators) is the layered complexity of its storytelling. There is an overarching central mystery (who killed Colonel Protheroe) but beneath it lies a series of intersecting story arcs, each comprising set-up/development/payoff. We never have occasion to grow bored and skim read, because Christie sets another hare running to distract us when there is a lull in the main action. Some of those subplots cast light on the central story, but that's not their principal purpose. They're there to keep us engaged, to draw us into "just one more chapter."

Christie seems to have had the natural storyteller's gift for shaping a narrative, but she honed that skill in the early years of her career on magazine short stories. She produced dozens of these, usually to a tight deadline. When it came to writing novels, it almost feels as if her subplots grew out of her understanding of those compact and satisfying nuggets of narrative that act as boosters to the main tale.

Certainly, there's no evidence from her own words that the construction of her novels was a deliberate architectural plan. She said that plots came to her suddenly, often when she was out walking, "when suddenly a splendid idea pops into your head." Often, it was nothing more than an ingenious idea for a murder method. Then she'd work out whodunnit, why, and how. Only then would she invent the rest of the cast of characters, plant her clues, and strew her red herrings. And then, "There is no agony like it. You sit in a room, biting pencils, looking at a typewriter, walking about, or casting yourself down on a sofa, feeling you want to cry your head off."

Remarkably, she pulled it off time after time. *And Then There Were None* has sold more copies than any other novel in history. *The Mousetrap* is the longest running play in the world. She was given the coveted Grand Master award by the Mystery Writers of America. *The Murder of Roger Ackroyd, Murder on the Orient Express,* and *The ABC Murders* still confound new generations of readers with their unforeseen twists. She invented the psychopathic serial killer in *4.50 From Paddington.* She gave us permission to experiment and because she did not always succeed in what she attempted, she gave us permission to fail. And yet there have always been detractors who sneer at her work, deride her fictional world, and sniff at her success.

I can't believe she was unaware of this criticism, but it seems never to have put her off her stride. Nevertheless, I think she would have been astonished to find herself the subject of scholarly study. That there is now a sufficient body of academic work devoted to her output to justify a collection such as this would, I suspect, have been a cause for self-deprecating mirth.

But there is good reason why her work attracts the interest of researchers. Crime fiction is the most widely read genre in modern times. I've come across many readers who consume two or three or even more crime novels every week. At its best, it stands shoulder to shoulder with any other kind of fiction. It is the place we go to read about how we live now. As we turn to Dickens to understand Victorian England, so will readers a century hence turn to the likes of Sara Paretsky, Peter Temple, and Henning Mankell to discover how our societies functioned—or dysfunctioned!

Without Christie, it's questionable whether that would be the case. Even crime writers who are snooty about her work—"cardboard characters, racism, anti-Semitism, bourgeois sensibility" are among charges regularly leveled with some justification but without any regard for the mores of the times—owe her a debt. She is the monument in the landscape, whether we learn from her or react against her. The craft with which her plots are composed, the ingenuity she brings to the often banal act of murder, the cunning knitting together of disparate elements—all of these are still key elements of the genre we read today.

I would not be the writer I am today had I not stumbled across *The Murder at the Vicarage* as a child. From Agatha Christie, I learned how to turn a plot that would grip my readers. I've learned many different things from other writers, but without that fundamental understanding, I couldn't have done any of it. There's a lot to learn from Agatha Christie. I hope you'll find many of these lessons right here.

Val McDermid

PART ONE

Agatha Christie, the Woman and the Writer

FIGURE I.1 Agatha Christie at work, *c.* 1950. Close inspection of the notebook on her lap shows that she was making notes for *They Do It with Mirrors*. Courtesy of The Christie Archive Trust.

Introduction, and a Chronology

MARY ANNA EVANS AND J.C. BERNTHAL

It is no overstatement to say that Agatha Christie was the most influential crime novelist of the twentieth century. "A puzzle worthy of Agatha Christie" has become a cliché describing problems that appear utterly insoluble, until they are not. To be called a real-life Miss Marple or Hercule Poirot is to be told that you are shrewd enough to tackle one of those insoluble problems routinely solved by her two most iconic detectives. If crime fiction can be considered the literature of justice, a body of narratives that investigates questions of good and evil, then critical attention to the work of the woman synonymous with crime fiction is natural. Such attention came late, largely beginning after Christie's 1976 death, with most scholarly work on her *oeuvre* written since 1990.

Now, over a century after *The Mysterious Affair at Styles* launched the career of the best-selling novelist of all time, scholarship on her work has grown to such an extent that it is necessary to pause and consider the varied conversations in context with each other and with our era. It is time to take stock of what Agatha Christie accomplished and what she contributed to crime fiction and literature as a whole. In fact, it is past time. It is also time to consider her widespread and enduring popularity, which is arguably a contributing factor to the scholarly community's long delay in granting her work serious attention. It is time to give Agatha Christie her due.

The first sustained English-language evaluation of Christie's work was Gordon Ramsey's *Mistress of Mystery* in 1967. Christie thanked Ramsey with the lukewarm compliment that she could not understand a word he had written and that she valued the work chiefly for its exhaustive bibliography, which helped her publishers catalogue her books (Morgan [1984] 1997: 350). Christie herself considered the only valid criticism of her work to be that which assessed its entertainment value, rather than anything analytic: "detective novels," she once wrote, "were excellent to take one's mind off one's worries" (in Haycraft [1941] 1974: 129). However, after her death, fairly detailed "appreciations" which nonetheless insisted that they were not "academic" started to appear. These include H.R.F. Keating's *Agatha Christie: First Lady of Crime* in 1978, Robert Barnard's *A Talent to Deceive: An Appreciation of Agatha Christie* in 1980, and Charles Osborne's *The Life and Crimes of Agatha Christie* in 1982.

Christie was in many ways an innovator, which partly explains critics' keenness to analyze her work even when the idea of "serious" scholarly attention was unthinkable. As her publishers consistently remind the world, she has been outsold only by the Bible and Shakespeare, with sales figures exceeding two billion copies, and she has been translated into more languages than any other writer. As Barnard wrote shortly after her death, "she not only bridges national and generational gaps; she seems to appeal equally to all class and intelligence brackets" (11). Christie's universal appeal also underlies her many "firsts": she was the first mystery novelist published by the Bodley Head; she was the author who inspired the iconic Penguin series of paperbacks; her groundbreaking novel *The Murder of Roger Ackroyd* became the first-ever audiobook, produced by the Royal National Institute of the Blind in 1935; she became the first woman to have three plays running in the West End at the same time, including *The Mousetrap*, which has broken every longevity record since it opened in 1952 and is still going; and the movie adaptation of *Murder on the Orient Express* broke box office records in 1974, as did the heavily Christie-inspired *Knives Out* in 2019.

An international phenomenon and the seldom-challenged "Queen of Crime," Christie herself was a remarkable individual. Intensely shy and withdrawn, she embodied the archetypal image of demure, unostentatious "Englishness" that pervades her books. Famously, when arriving at a party to celebrate the tenth year of *The Mousetrap* in 1962, she was turned away at the door by a member of staff. Instead of reminding them who she was, Christie left and came back later (Christie [1977] 2011: 116–17). At the event, Christie was presented with a gold-covered *Mousetrap* script and toasted. Asked to give a speech, she rose, said, "This is awful," and spoke of her disbelief while downplaying her achievement: "If I were writing a book, it wouldn't be a person like me who'd written a play" (BBC). But beyond this self-deprecation, she saw and understood the world, being actively involved in two world wars, experiencing two eventful marriages, and traveling extensively, with her first husband on a tour promoting the British Empire Exhibition and with her second husband as part of an archaeological team. She was a trained pharmacist, a competent surfer, and a shrewd businesswoman who was approached (and refused) at least twice to write propaganda. The complex political and emotional journeys that were the backdrop to her life form the very heart of her literature.

THE MYSTERY OF THE MISSING SCHOLARSHIP

As we edited this volume, the first specifically academic companion to contemporary scholarship on Christie's work, one thing became apparent: almost everyone thinks they know Christie. Of course, they think so. When an author is widely considered the best-selling novelist of all time, with billions of copies in print, while also having authored the longest-running play of all time and inspired a plethora of film and television adaptations, it is difficult to find anyone who is not in some way aware of her work. However, when that author produced more than seventy novels, more than one hundred and seventy short stories, more than fifteen plays, two volumes of poetry, assorted poems published singly, two memoirs, and a trove of never-published manuscripts residing in private archives, a vanishingly small fraction of people have even read all of her work. So, while nearly everyone thinks that they know Christie, it is more correct to say that they are acquainted with part of an *oeuvre* so vast that it is easy to make false generalities based on a fraction of her work, misremembered.

This can be true of sources that have been widely cited as authoritative. Julian Symons wrote the following passage in his 1985 revised version of *Bloody Murder, From the Detective Story to the Crime Novel: A History*, which has long been considered a key text in crime fiction studies. We cite it here to analyze not only the mistakes Symons makes about Christie's life and work, but also how his reading, far from uncommon, reflects a dominant critical attitude. The impact of such approaches is not negligible.

Symons, who succeeded Christie as president of the Detection Club and could reasonably be considered a major authority in his field, wrote:

> Agatha Christie (1890–1976) was brought up by her widowed mother and had no formal education, either at school or at home. After writing two or three novels which she says were "long and confused" and were rejected by publishers, she decided to try her hand at a detective story. The influences working on her were "the pattern of the clue" and "the idiot friend," as developed in the Holmes stories. She worked during the First World War in a hospital and so obtained some knowledge of poisons, which she put to use in the story written in odds and ends of leisure time over a period of eighteen months. John Lane then agreed to publish the book, which sold about 2,000

copies. She made £25 out of the British publication and had to wait for ten years before it appeared in the United States.

(1985: 91)

This passage is not just factually wrong; it has the distinction of being wrong, or at least misleading or confusing, in every sentence. While Symons was not an isolated case, and some of his errors are understandable in the context of what material was available, the book continues to be cited extensively by both Christie scholars and students of crime fiction. Thus, it is instructive to take this quote sentence by sentence as an illustration of the danger of thinking that one "knows Christie."

Sentence One: "Agatha Christie (1890–1976) was brought up by her widowed mother and had no formal education, either at school or at home."

The error here is partially understandable, as Symons wrote the first version of *Bloody Murder* in 1972, before Christie's autobiography and first estate-authorized biography had been published in 1977 and 1984, respectively. In 1972, short of speaking directly to Christie, his best available sources would have been her rare published interviews and Ramsey's *Mistress of Mystery*, where Christie presented herself consistently as a woman who "never went to school," although she did clarify in interviews "that Mrs. Miller (Agatha's mother) tutored Agatha at home" (Ramsey 1967: 13). Ramsey also speaks directly to her formal education outside the home and to her mother's home tutelage when he quotes Christie as saying, "You went to Dancing Class—Swedish Exercises—Art School—Piano Lessons—Singing Class—Cookery Classes, etc. All I escaped was a resident governess and certainly my mother was much better fun" (1968: 13). There is no way Symons could have known, without original research, that Christie did go to school, for a year and a half, in Torquay, and then to a series of French boarding schools (Christie [1977] 2011: 150–1) because she chose to present herself as lacking in formal education. That he chose not to revise this statement when ample evidence was available is another matter, but mainly of interest is that he takes the *implications* of Christie's statement that she "never went to school" at face value, and extends it into "no formal education, either at school or at home," thus sidestepping other available information about home tutelage.

Christie was not raised entirely by a widowed mother, but lived for eleven formative years with a father who evidently impacted her childhood and adult career significantly. In her autobiography, Christie credits her father for their "happy house," writing that he was a "very agreeable man" who had a "simple and loving heart" (15–16). She writes that he had "no meanness in him, no jealousy, and he was almost fantastically generous" (16). It is also evident from archived materials and biographies that both Christie's parents were highly involved in developing her as a storyteller, writing and sharing stories as a family (Thompson [2007] 2008: 15–16). In fact, it was Christie's father who "said that, as I could read, I had better learn to write"; she describes her writing practice in "copybooks full of pothooks and hangers" and "lines of shaky B's and R's" (Christie [1977] 2011: 26). Later, her father said that she "might as well start arithmetic, and every morning after breakfast, [she] would set to at the dining-room window seat" then, "proud and pleased" with her progress, he promoted her to a more challenging math text called *Problems* (26). These passages contradict both the intimation that her father's death erased him as an influence on his daughter and the statement that she received no formal education at home.

The image of herself that Christie chose to present is one of a conventional English housewife who happened to be a writer, whose youth was happy and "fun," and who therefore was not trying or expecting to be inducted into any kind of literary canon or tradition: "I don't know why people would want to write about me," she told Nigel Dennis in an influential 1956 interview for *Life*. "I specialize in murders of quiet, domestic interest" (Dennis 1956: 91, 88). Symons took this at face value, and his essentializing statement about her receiving no formal education is understandable, while also reflecting a conscious decision not to dig beyond the surface, as he could have done. Later scholars have problematized this lack of curiosity in scholarship—what Marty S. Knepper has called "inaccurate [...] truisms" and "dubious assertions," which extend to discussions of the texts themselves (1995: 34)—and have sought to show Christie as a writer whose cultivation of a traditionally "middlebrow" persona was strategic, commercially shrewd, and itself worthy of study (Bernthal 2016b: 25–74).

Sentence Two: "After writing two or three novels which she says were 'long and confused' and were rejected by publishers, she decided to try her hand at a detective story."

This statement about the writing of her first book is unsourced and is puzzling, as we know of no record of Christie describing her pre-publication work in this way, and we know of no published source in which she claimed to have written more than one novel, the novella-length *Snow Upon the Desert*, before her crime debut. This was not "nearly long enough for a novel," and she describes in her autobiography her efforts to "finally" bring it to "the requisite length" (Christie 1977: 144).[1] Perhaps if analysis of Christie had been considered worthy of a proper referencing system in 1972, or in time for the 1985 and 1992 revisions, this mystery could be cleared up.

---

[1]She had also at this point written an experimental story, "Vision," which she later expanded into a very short novel for the Bodley Head, which rejected it, during a contract dispute (Morgan [1984] 1997: 111).

The phrasing "long and confused" may suggest efforts at wordiness and so-called "literary" prose that, it follows in this vision of Christie, were beyond her. The idea that she glibly "decided to try her hand at" genre fiction suggests that she took an easy option or settled into it. In fact, we know at least one incident that prompted her to begin writing in this genre. She is very clear in the autobiography that she was inspired by a conversation with her sister Madge in which she said that she would like to try writing a detective story. Madge's response was that they were difficult to write, and the conversation ended with her saying, "Well, I bet you couldn't." Christie's response to that bet was: "At the back of my mind [...], the idea had been planted: *some day I would write a detective story*" (210–11, emphasis original). This is the origin story that appeared on multiple editions of that novel, and also appears in the *Life* interview (Dennis 1956: 92). Symons's version, though, presents Christie as something of an industrious workman, writing easily to satisfy public taste, rather than to communicate or innovate.

This understanding held sway in some critical circles throughout the twentieth century, with the idea of Christie's books as "trite and slight," with clever puzzles "[b]ut that was about it" (Bowen 2021) persisting in some quarters to this day. It reinforces the image Christie promoted of herself, and which Symons and others have echoed: that she created games and mental exercises; what Francis Wyndham called "animated algebra" (1966: 25) that need not be taken too seriously. If Christie is dismissed, reducing the genre she helped shape "to the level of a board game or an intelligence test" (Rankin 2003: 7), it follows that there is nothing to see here; no use or value in studying or even seriously remembering her work. However, that view has been successfully challenged several times, with an early influential take on Christie's relevance as a social commentator and novelist of ideas coming in 1991, when Alison Light's *Forever England: Femininity, Literature and Conservatism between the Wars* positioned her as a writer who understood and engaged with "the appeal and the dangers of security" with her handling of crime (Light 1991: 99).

Sentence Three: "The influences working on her were 'the pattern of the clue' and 'the idiot friend,' as developed in the Holmes stories."

Symons does not source the quotations in this sentence, which is typical of early genre scholarship. The use of unreferenced quotations, which other scholars take up, often without attribution and often slightly changed in the process, can lead even the most casual researcher down endless rabbit holes. The reference to "the idiot friend" evokes a common expression for the detective's sidekick, and echoes Christie's own description of Captain Hastings as Hercule Poirot's "stooge assistant," "in the Sherlock Holmes tradition," in her autobiography (282), as well as in several interviews. However, the idea of "the pattern of the clue" risks rewriting the genre's history, positioning

Christie as a pure imitator of Arthur Conan Doyle. While she clearly modeled the eccentric detective, witless sidekick, and bumbling Scotland Yard policeman (Inspector Japp) on Doyle's Holmes, Watson, and Lestrade, her plotting was never like Doyle's. While Doyle and many of his imitators were content to entertain with stories of their detective reaching, then rationalizing, apparently fantastic conclusions, Christie set out in her fiction to present clues to the reader as and when they appear to the detective, allowing the reader, the detective, and the author to engage in a kind of competition.

This aspect of detective fiction was already so ubiquitous by the time Symons was writing that it might seem inevitable to apply it to the Holmes stories, but it is much more Christie's domain—and contribution—than Doyle's. Symons nearly acknowledges that in his next paragraph, damning Christie with faint praise when he notes that her first detective novel was "original in the sense that it is a puzzle story which is solely that," adding that it "permits no emotional engagement with the characters" (Symons 1985: 92). While the editors of this volume would take issue with the idea that it is impossible to engage with Christie's characters, that has been a dominant cliché against which other crime writers have positioned themselves as socially engaged, critiquing Christie's characters and settings as so two-dimensional as to be "an insult to cardboard" (Ruth Rendell in "Quote Unquote"). The critique is often pithy but seldom extensively evidenced—again, there is a dominant sense that we *know* Agatha Christie and her work without having to read or examine it.

Sentence Four: "She worked during the First World War in a hospital and so obtained some knowledge of poisons, which she put to use in the story written in odds and ends of leisure time over a period of eighteen months."

It is hard not to read this statement as a deliberate diminution of both Christie's accomplishments as a wartime nurse and apothecary's assistant and of her labor in creating a book that Symons himself claims heralded as the beginning of the Golden Age. While it suits an image of an author who writes and is read purely for pleasure, it belies both the labor of writing and the professional, real-world experience underscoring Christie's work. Even at this date, multiple readers and even scholars are surprised that Christie had more than "some knowledge of poisons." As Kathryn Harkup writes in *A Is for Arsenic: The Poisons of Agatha Christie*, "[f]ew other novelists can claim to have been read by pathologists as reference material in real poisoning cases" (10), while Christie was formally tutored—and examined—"in practical, as well as theoretical, aspects of chemistry and pharmacy" (11).

Christie served as part of the Voluntary Aid Dispatch (VAD) during the First World War. She took to nursing, despite the gritty realities of the profession like death, bedpans, vomit, lice, urinals, and amputations, and she claims in her autobiography that she would have trained as a "real hospital nurse" had she not married (230). When a dispensary was opened at the hospital, she began working there and stayed for two years. Her work required her to study subjects including chemistry and to pass an examination before she could dispense for a medical officer or chemist. Ramsey gives more detail, stating that she took First Aid and Home Nursing Certificates (1968: 14). She prepared medicines including ointments, suppositories, lotions, and tonics that required precise calculations and measurements, and errors carried with them the risk of harm or death to the patient. She returned to work in dispensaries in Torquay and London during the Second World War.

As for the statement that *The Mysterious Affair at Styles* was written in "odds and ends of leisure time," this too seems dismissive and also arguably incorrect, as it suggests a lady of leisure who uses her spare time for writing. Instead, Christie describes in her autobiography working on the novel during slow periods at the dispensary, interspersing her meditations on the characters and plot with time spent making up "a couple of bottles of extra hypochlorous lotion so that I should be fairly free of work the next day" (255). She mentions devising characters while people-watching on a train and basing Poirot on Belgian refugees in town. She describes walking down the road muttering to herself about her story, and she recalls being absent-minded at home. Saying that she was encouraged by her mother to go away for a fortnight and focus on her writing, she writes of traveling to Dartmoor and alternating time at the typewriter with long-brainstorming sessions spent walking on the moor. The first draft of the manuscript of *The Mysterious Affair at Styles* was completed during her time at Dartmoor. While she does write that her story rattled around in her head in "leisure moments," the scenario that comes to mind when reading this passage is that of a young woman with a demanding job and many home duties who is fighting for time to write her book (254–9).

Sentences Five and Six: "John Lane then agreed to publish the book, which sold about 2,000 copies. She made £25 out of the British publication and had to wait for ten years before it appeared in the United States."

By the time Symons was writing, it was well known that *The Mysterious Affair at Styles* had been rejected several times before publication. Indeed, it is mentioned in Symons's likely sources, the *Life* interview and the Ramsey. That he transfers the rejections in his construction to the imaginary previous novels indicates a lack of attention to detail that has pervaded scholarship surrounding writers of genre fiction. The sum of £25 Christie received for *The Mysterious Affair at Styles* did not actually represent royalties paid for the book's publication in the UK but was instead her share of the payment for serialization in a newspaper (Christie [1977] 2011: 280). It is a small point, but again speaks to partial information presented without confirmation—and popularized, for this is a very common observation about Christie, fueled in part by her own statements—as the whole picture. Symons's statement that Christie had to wait for ten years before it appeared in the United States is inarguably in error, as it was published in book form in the United States in 1920, even before it was published in book form in the UK.

What are we to make of Symons's inaccuracies? Do a few mistakes in a book published fifty years ago matter now? We believe that they do, but we also believe that the carelessness and the dismissive tone in which the errors are presented matter more. The carelessness plays into the presumptions of people who think that they know Christie and, thus, that they do not need to confirm their presumptions. The dismissiveness has led, we contend, to the critical neglect that has dogged the most widely read novelist of all time. As evidence of this neglect, we offer the book in your hands, the first of its kind. Christie has been dead almost a half-century, and a full century has passed since her first book was published. It should not have taken so long for her work to receive this level of serious attention.

Why has it taken so long? We offer as evidence the dismissiveness of generations of critics, including Symons himself, who elsewhere dismissed her popularity as "the comfort of the familiar" (1980: 29). Symons's sneer was a descendant of Edmund Wilson's famously devastating critique of her prose as mawkish and banal in a way that he considered "literally impossible to read" (1945: 59). Twenty-one years after Wilson's slam, Francis Wyndham called her work "animated algebra." Fourteen years after that, Robert Barnard called her skill in plotting "merely a trick, a childish ingenuity beneath serious consideration" (1980: 44).

Symons's carelessness in describing Christie's life and his failure to take her expertise in the dispensary seriously are part and parcel of this worldview that consigns her and her work to a cozy pigeonhole where they do not fit. Describing her as merely a "puzzle maker" (Symons 1980: 1) ignores the literary novels she wrote as Mary Westmacott. It erases her spy thrillers, her poetry, her stories of the uncanny, her stories for children. Intimating that she was a woman of leisure who spun tales in her spare time invites us to forget that she began her writing career while a hardworking woman who made time for her art when she had little time to spare and who practiced it for the rest of her life, long past the point where continuing to write was a financial necessity. Belittling, even infantilizing, narratives such as Symons's have persisted because they have been often repeated, and they have done their damage, but they are inaccurate and it is important to refute them. It is important, in this case as in all cases, to seek the truth.

WHY AGATHA CHRISTIE? AND WHY NOW?

Seeing beyond the puzzle in an Agatha Christie novel is a surprisingly recent trend. Alison Light brought widespread attention to the "conservative modernism" of Christie's work in her seminal volume, *Forever England*, in 1991. As crime fiction scholarship itself started to move beyond the hardboiled genre, Christie received some critical attention, including in such monographs as Susan Rowland's *From Agatha Christie to Ruth Rendell* in 2001, Merja Makinen's *Agatha Christie: Investigating Femininity* in 2006, and R.A. York's *Agatha Christie: Power and Illusion* in 2007. These generative monographs consider Christie from a variety of angles which have now become established bases from which to analyze her work.

Rowland's 2001 monograph examines Christie as part of a lineage of six prominent female crime writers, seeking "a more nuanced consideration" of their lives and work (Rowland 2001: 1) and aiming "to provoke debate, in particular by moving away from the stale conception of these writers as unproblematically conservative" (114). Makinen's study, five years later, was prompted by an "awareness" on the author's part that what she found in Christie's texts, as a reader, was vastly "at odds with much of the criticism of her, particularly when it came to gender" (Makinen 2006: 1). Aiming to move beyond the tone of earlier criticism outlined above, and to "allow a new consideration based on what is actually present in the texts" (3), Makinen argues that Christie is a socially engaged writer whose discussions of femininity can be read easily alongside those of established social commentators and feminists who were her contemporaries. Taking a different, but complementary, tack, York looks at the mechanics of disguise and deception in Christie's work, but unlike more conservative scholarship positioning the puzzle as the dominant—or only—part of a Christie novel, York contextualizes his observations. These monographs, published in the first decade of the twenty-first century, evidence a shifting approach to Christie, with clear moves to problematize easy stereotypes about what she wrote and why and to engage with the texts beyond what we think we already know about them.

Still, attention to her work in critical circles was slow in gathering steam; the first academic edited collection focusing solely on Christie's life and legacy, J.C. Bernthal's *The Ageless Agatha Christie* (2016b), was not published until 2016. Meanwhile, scholarship on Christie's work has developed beyond literary studies, with current work being done in the fields of adaptation (Aldridge 2016), language and semiotics, in which *The Murder of Roger Ackroyd* is often a key text (Emmott and Alexander 2019), cultural studies (Appignami 2016), medicine (Harkup 2015), information science (Kazmer in the present volume), and even religious studies (Blyth and Jack 2019).

Christie has also enjoyed something of a cultural re-evaluation. While eternally popular, with adaptations never far from television schedules, Agatha Christie Limited's rebranding efforts in the mid-2010s, complemented significantly by a new series of dark, brooding television adaptations, were particularly impactful. With Christie reimagined as a worldly woman via a much-promoted photograph of her surfing in 1922, the BBC positioned its 2015 version of *And Then There Were None* as an adaptation of "the first sort of slasher thriller ever written [and] the template of modern-day horror movies" (Karen Thrussal, in Hastings 2015). Scholarship of the late 2010s and early 2020s has moved toward examining the darker and more cosmopolitan themes in Christie's literature. For example, between 2019 and 2021, the flagship journal *Clues: A Journal of Detection* printed five articles specifically on Christie, each highlighting themes and contexts traditionally ignored in nostalgic interpretations of Christie as too artificial and removed to be socially relevant. These include the darker side of tourism (Mills 2019), presentations of legal justice (Bernthal 2019), xenophobia and antisemitism (Brown 2020), subversive femininities (Evans 2021), and the ethics and legality of food consumption after the Second World War (Yiannitsaros 2021). It is, in short, high time for us to take stock of the state of Christie scholarship and consider its future avenues, and that is our purpose here.

A TREASURE FROM THE ARCHIVE REMINDS US THERE IS MORE TO LEARN

Christie Studies is, as a field, blessed in several important ways. Agatha Christie was a celebrity for most of her fifty-plus-year writing career. That half-century of fame began during the early twentieth century at a time when established media like books, newspapers, and magazines were building on past successes and new media like radio and film were beginning an astronomical expansion. Television and its possibilities were on the horizon. Archives were available when the time came to curate and maintain the material generated by the various media that documented Christie's career. Driving the media machine generating the materials held by today's archives was her prodigious output. The volume of material—photos, correspondence, business files, manuscripts, tear sheets, media coverage, and more—that is available for study is hard to grasp. While this can be a challenge for researchers, it is an obvious blessing. It can also be the source of pleasant surprises.

In a July 2012 post to the blog of the University of Pennsylvania Museum of Archaeology and Anthropology, commonly known as the Penn Museum, Amanda Ball wrote of an unexpected find. Ball, at that time an intern at the museum's archives, was sorting through correspondence and photographs related to the Joint Expedition to Nippur. This archaeological project, funded by a partnership between the University of Chicago and the Penn Museum, began excavation in 1949, but the partnership was fraught with conflict between the two institutions and their on-site liaisons, and it only lasted three seasons. Three seasons, while a brief interval in the life of an archaeological expedition, can generate many photographs and documents for later interns to catalog. This is what Ball was assigned to do, sixty years after the fact.

Ball writes that "sorting photos by number can get pretty tedious," but friction evident in correspondence between the two organizations, both powerhouses in archaeology, "made for some pretty enthralling reading." She describes excavation members complaining "about power plays, budget constraints and even whose letterhead was being used" (Ball 2012). Conflict escalated to the point that the Penn Museum left the partnership in 1953, but not before a photo interesting to readers of this book was taken and then filed away where it remained unnoticed until Ball began her work.

Although Agatha Christie's autobiography describes her 1928 and 1930 visits to Leonard Woolley's excavations at Ur during a period when those excavations were being funded jointly by the British Museum and University of Pennsylvania, there are no known photos of her on that site in the Penn Museum's archives. Because of Ball's work, however, we know that a photograph of her does exist in those archives in a less-expected place, the files of the Joint Expedition to Nippur. During the 1949–50 season, she and her husband archaeologist Max Mallowan visited Nippur, and an image of that visit survives. Ball noticed that its caption mentions "Mrs. Mallowan" and showed it to Senior Archivist Alessandro Pezzati. He recognized Mrs. Mallowan for who she was—Agatha Christie.

Christie, wearing a hat and sunglasses, stands on the far left, one of a group watching a worker named Halaf coat a tablet with wax. She is a participant in a slice of everyday archaeological life of that time, around 1950. The group is surrounded by ancient walls. Implements, presumably Halaf's, rest in the foreground, providing an intriguing glimpse of the day-to-day details of mid-twentieth-century archaeology. Max Mallowan is front and center, as the Director of the British School of Archaeology in Iraq should be, deep in conversation and dressed in a suit, tie, sweater, and hat. In front of him, Halaf is bent over his work. Flanking him are Donald E. McCown and Richard C. Haines, towering figures in the history of Nippur archaeology who would publish *Nippur I* in 1967 and, with others, *Nippur II* in 1978 (Oxford Biblical Studies Online n.d.). Haines is in the act of lighting a cigarette and another of the party, Mohammed Ali, holds a cigarette between his lips. Unnamed individuals are barely in the frame to left and right, giving a sense of activity surrounding the vignette photographed. Standing next to Christie is Barbara Parker, identified as "Miss Parker" in the Penn Museum archives, whom Mallowan would marry after Christie's death.

The photograph gives us a glimpse of Agatha Christie Mallowan, the enthusiastic participant in her husband's archaeological world. This is the woman who wrote so lovingly of the hardships and joys of life on a real-life archaeological dig in *Come Tell Me How You Live* and about crime on a fictional dig in *Murder in Mesopotamia*. She was a public figure for so long that other treasures like this one likely rest in the archives holding records of her professional life, but we must remember that she was not acting as a public figure for every second of that long life. More images of Mrs. (or Lady) Mallowan living her everyday life probably lurk, like the fugitives in her books, in archives and private collections. Moreover, articles, letters, interviews, and even works of fiction are continually being "discovered." In the 2010s alone, stories such as "The Incident of the Dog's Ball" and "The Man Who Knew" were published for the first time (Curran 2011), while essays such as "Murder and the Sporting Instinct" and "The *Crime Passionnel*" have not been printed since they appeared in periodicals in the 1920s (Bernthal 2022). Undoubtedly, more treasures are waiting for us to hone our detective skills and, like Ball, find them in their hiding places and bring them into the light.

FIGURE I.2 Agatha Christie and Max Mallowan at archaeological dig at Nippur, Iraq, watching tablet being coated with wax, 1949–50. Left to Right: Agatha Christie Mallowan, Barbara Parker, Irene Haines, Halaf, Carl Haines, Max Mallowan, Don McCown, Mohammed Ali. Courtesy of the Penn Museum, image #49024.

CONVERSATIONS IN THIS BOOK

In this book, we aim to set aside the false and misleading narratives that cling to the image of Agatha Christie, bringing together a diverse group of scholars who are among the most significant voices in the field, so that they can present the current state of research on her work and to point the way forward. All the voices in this volume look ahead to work yet to be done, as Christie's *oeuvre* and legacy enters its second century. The sheer volume of her output and the substantial archival holdings held in collections around the world ensure that there will remain much to say about the Queen of Crime for a very long time.

Under the heading *Critical Approaches*, we offer eight chapters at the vanguard of current critical conversations surrounding Christie. In **The Middlebrow Woman Detective Writer**, Rebecca Mills places Christie firmly *in situ* as both an author of middlebrow women's fiction and a modernist. In **Christie's Clues as Information**, Michelle M. Kazmer uses the tools of information science to take on Christie's handling of information in the construction of her plots, an aspect of her work process that was essential to her groundbreaking approach to the play-fair mystery. Mary Anna Evans's **Reading Christie with a Feminist Lens** addresses some of the most written-about topics in Christie studies: her portrayal of women, their lives, and their relationships with a patriarchal society. J.C. Bernthal's **Queer Clues to Christie** challenges scholarship that, too often, falls back on oft-repeated narratives that presuppose an unengaged unreality in her work, a presupposition that he suggests is itself disengaged with reality.

Susan Rowland's **Christie Does Ecocriticism**, which addresses the urgency of ecocritical approaches in the Anthropocene age, offers an earth-centered reading that shows Christie to be an important historian of the earth and our relations to it. Sarah Martin contributes **Psychogeography and the Flapper Sleuth**, which investigates the ways that Christie used space, especially for her female characters, as more than physical, as they clothed, walked, and inhabited the public and the private, as well as metaphysical, cultural, and gendered, space. Closing this section, Nadia Atia's **Christie's Contemporary Middle East** on Christie's representation of the Middle East in her novels recognizes the shadow of empire on her work, using the memoir of Christie's friend, Palestinian writer and translator Jabra Ibrahim Jabra, to expand our knowledge of her relationship with an important part of the world and its people.

The next section is titled *Christie and Society*. It features seven chapters rich in context, so often sorely lacking in previous decades, and analysis. J.C. Bernthal's **Christie and the Carnage of War** highlights the impact of two world wars on the body of work created by a woman who lived through them, nursing wounded and dying soldiers, preparing medications to treat them, and sending off two husbands to serve in them. Meta Carstarphen's **Of Race, Law, and Order: Colonial Ghosts** explores the troubling history of minstrelsy, counting rhymes, and blackface performance behind the problematic original title of the best-selling crime novel of all time. Mary Evans's chapter, **Christie and the State,** gives a sociologist's perspective on the relationship between Christie's work and the state that made the laws transgressed by her villains and enforced by her detectives and their society.

Brittain Bright's **House and Home: The Country House** reorients our perception of Christie's fictional settings as uniformly upper-class country homes, showing that her concern was more on houses as homes, a topic that Christie herself emphasized as important when she said that they were "where people *live*" (in Wyndham 1966: 2, emphasis original). Mary Anna Evans contributes **Agatha Christie, the Law, and Justice,** examining Christie's treatment of justice in her work and reflecting the overarching concern of crime fiction with justice and society's attempts to achieve it. Bernthal returns with **Christie and Christianity,** which considers the role of Christie's faith in her life and work, presenting a case study of a story from her little-discussed volume of religious tales, *Star Over Bethlehem.* Katherine Harkup, author of *A Is for Arsenic,* rounds out this section with **Poison in Golden Age Detective Fiction** on the use of poisons in Christie's work, recognizing the author's hard-won expertise, gained through years of work done during, and research persisting beyond, two world wars.

Our final part, *Beyond the Crime Novels,* opens with Merja Makinen's **Hiding in Plain Sight: Mary Westmacott,** on the little-written-about novels Christie wrote pseudonymously, as Mary Westmacott, investigating approaches through the lens of life-writing analysis, but also considering the novels as important works of modernist middlebrow feminine fiction in their own right. In **Christie's BBC Radio Broadcasts, 1930–55,** Vike Martina Plock investigates an aspect of Christie's work that was in danger of being forgotten, delving into the archives of the BBC for traces of this part of her professional life. Benedict Morrison uses his chapter, **Christie and the Theater,** to foreground Christie's career as a playwright which, though often overshadowed by the number and success of her novels, was marked by milestones that include her status as the first, and thus far only, woman to have three plays playing simultaneously in London's West End and, of course, her status as the playwright responsible for the longest-running play of all time, *The Mousetrap.* Mark Aldridge explores in **Film and TV Adaptations of Christie** the phenomenal success of the adaptations that continue to introduce her work to wide audiences of people who have never opened one of her books.

Framing the critical heart of the book are narratives contributed by people whose lives were directly affected by Christie. Her grandson, Mathew Prichard, has contributed **My Grandmother, Agatha Christie,** a tender remembrance of his grandmother and her relationships with her loved ones. He describes the shared experiences of a lifetime, from the stories she told to him as a child to the love of artistic expression that they shared as adults. Barbara Peters, a Raven Award-winning editor who founded the globally influential Poisoned Pen Bookstore and co-founded Poisoned Pen Press, introduces **Legacies**, an exploration of Christie's influence on today's crime fiction, including contributions from four crime novelists now working in the field: Martin Edwards, Rhys Bowen, Ragnar Jónasson, and L. Alison Heller. These contributions have ensured a thoroughly interdisciplinary perspective in the volume that will be useful to crime fiction readers and creative writers in addition to students and researchers. They also highlight a range of perspectives on the world's best-selling novelist, often unflinching, and not always in agreement. No truly influential figure unites opinion. Notably, Peters and, to an extent, Edwards refer to the Queen of Crime as "Agatha," showing the sense of kinship that we described at the start of this chapter, a kinship that leads readers—and Christie's professional successors—to feel in a variety of ways that they know her.

It is our earnest aim for this volume to serve as an introduction to those readers who are new to the discussions and debates in this still-emerging field of study, while providing a reference for researchers active in the field and mapping out future directions of inquiry. It is the first critical companion to Agatha Christie scholarship, but it is just part of a dynamic, multivalent, and ever-evolving conversation.

A CHRONOLOGY

With an author as productive and impactful as Agatha Christie, a conventional chronology risks running the length of a volume in its own right. For this timeline, the editors have chosen an accessible decade-by-decade approach to Christie's life events, placing them in the context of related major national or international developments and in the context of her reception in scholarship and media, especially in the UK and the United States. For each decade, also listed are the first publication dates of major Christie books published by her main UK and US publishers (The Bodley Head/John Lane, Collins/HarperCollins, Dodd, Mead, and Doubleday) and those from Geoffrey Bles, Odhams, Putnam's Sons, and Heineman later picked up by her regular publishers, as well as UK and US cinematic adaptations. For collections of stories, poems, or plays, the contents and original publication or West End performance details are footnoted.

1890s

With the British Empire extending further than ever before, growing nationalism and mobilization across the globe would result in the Anglo-Boer War (1899–1902), between the empire and the South African republics of Transvaal and the Orange Free State.

Agatha Mary Clarissa Miller (AM) was born in Torquay, England on September 15, **1890,** the third child and second daughter of Frederick Alvah Miller and Clarissa (Clara) Miller, née Boehmer. Against her mother's wishes, AM taught herself to read aged four. While her older sister Margaret (Madge) received a school education, AM was tutored at home by her mother, who had changed her opinion on the appropriateness of young girls being educated outside the home. During the war, her brother Montgomery (Monty) fought for the British Empire.

1900s

Great Britain's Queen Victoria, the first Empress of India, died on January 22, 1901, and Britain entered the Edwardian era, a decade marked by class distinctions and concentrated leisure for the upper classes and increasing leisure and literacy across the country.

Aged ten or eleven, AM published her first poem, concerning electric trams, in an Ealing newspaper. Her father Frederick died in November **1901,** having a profound effect on her. In **1905,** Clara sent AM to Paris, where she was educated in music and briefly explored becoming an opera singer. Around **1908,** AM wrote her first stories that would later be revised and published, including "The House of Beauty," inspired by May Sinclair. Her first novel (unpublished but surviving), *Snow Upon the Desert,* was declined by several publishers and her eventual literary agency Hughes Massie, but it led to informal mentorship from novelist Eden Phillpotts. She also read a great deal of detective fiction, including Arthur Conan Doyle's Sherlock Holmes stories and Gaston Leroux's *The Mystery of the Yellow Room.*

1910s

The First World War, or Great War, lasted from July 28, 1914, to November 11, 1918, and was responsible for approximately 20,000,000 deaths. The 1918 influenza pandemic (misleadingly known as "Spanish flu," 1918–20) was responsible for up to 50,000,000 more.

Although she had "come out" at 17 in Cairo, AM did not consider many of the men she met marriage material. However, she later became engaged to Captain Reginald (Reggie) Lucy before meeting Archibald (Archie) Christie in October **1912.** He was seconded to the Royal Flying Corps in April **1913** and proposed marriage, which AM accepted. Archie fought in the war in France, and the couple wed while he was home on leave on December 24, **1914,** in Bristol. Now known as Agatha Christie (AC), AC joined the

Red Cross's Voluntary Aid Detachment (VAD) and became a qualified pharmacist. She wrote her first detective novel, *The Mysterious Affair at Styles*, in **1916** after a bet with her sister. The novel, which introduces Hercule Poirot, was rejected by six publishers but accepted with revisions by John Lane of the Bodley Head in **1918**. During this period, Christie published poetry as A.M. Miller. The Christies' only child, Rosalind, was born on August 5, **1919**.

1920s

This decade was marked by recovery from the ravages of war and societal perceptions of decadence, especially among the young. Despite the conspicuous consumption in upper socioeconomic classes in the UK and the United States that is reflected in the term "Roaring Twenties," it was a time of economic conflicts across Europe that saw the rise of fascism in Italy and Germany. A general strike in the UK in response to depleted supplies of coal lasted nine days in 1926. In October 1929, the Wall Street Crash marked an end to the decade's heady optimism.

AC's debut novel was serialized in *The Sunday Times* and published in the United States in **1920** before being published in book form in the UK in **1921**. AC quickly became a popular novelist, with frequent short story commissions and enough success to switch to a more lucrative publishing contract with Collins, after averaging a book a year, in **1926**. During this decade, she also created most of her recurring detectives, including Tommy & Tuppence Beresford, Superintendent Battle, and Miss Marple.

AC's mother, Clara Miller, died on April 5, **1926**, two months before the publication of *The Murder of Roger Ackroyd* catapulted AC to global celebrity. That August, Archie asked for a divorce, so that he could marry secretary Nancy Neele. AC suffered a mental breakdown and disappeared for eleven days, prompting a media sensation and national manhunt. The incident engendered a deep mistrust of journalists in AC's later life. She recovered with a trip on the Orient Express and joined Leonard and Katherine Woolley on an archaeological dig at Ur in **1928**, the year Michael Morton's *Alibi*, an adaptation of *The Murder of Roger Ackroyd*, was staged. The next year, at Ur, she met her future husband, Max Mallowan (MM).

Novels:

- 1920 *The Mysterious Affair at Styles*
- 1922 *The Secret Adversary*
- 1923 *The Murder on the Links*

- **1924** *The Man in the Brown Suit*
- **1925** *The Secret of Chimneys*
- **1926** *The Murder of Roger Ackroyd*
- **1927** *The Big Four*
- **1928** *The Mystery of the Blue Train*
- **1929** *The Seven Dials Mystery*

Collections:

- **1924** *Poirot Investigates* (UK edition)[2]
- **1925** *Poirot Investigates* (UK edition)[3] *The Road of Dreams*[4]
- **1929** *Partners in Crime*[5]

UK/US films:

- **1928** *The Passing of Mr Quinn* (dir. Leslie S. Hiscott and Julius Hagen)

1930s

The British Empire was losing its influence and stability, something evidenced by the independence of Australia in 1931 and the "Year of Three Kings" in

---

[2]Stories originally published in *The Sketch*, April to October 1923 ("The Adventure of the Western Star"; "Tragedy at Marsdon Manor"; "The Adventure of the Cheap Flat"; "The Mystery of Hunter's Lodge"; "The Million Dollar Bond Robbery"; "The Adventure of the Egyptian Tomb"; "The Jewel Robbery at the Grand Metropolitan"; "The Kidnapped Prime Minister"; "The Disappearance of Mr Davenheim"; "The Case of the Missing Will").

[3]Stories originally published in *The Sketch*, April to December 1923—as above, plus "The Chocolate Box"; "The Veiled Lady"; "The Lost Mine."

[4]Poems, of which two had been published in *Poetry Today* in 1919 ("Dark Sheila" and "World Hymn, 1914"), one had been published prior but is untraced ("Harlequin's Song"), and others appear for the first time (*A Masque From Italy*; "The Ballad of the Flint"; "Elizabeth of England"; "The Bells of Brittany"; "Ballad of the Maytime"; "The Princess Sings"; "The Dream Spinners"; "Down in the Wood"; "The Road of Dreams"; "Beatrice Passes"; "Heritage"; "The Wanderer"; "The Dream City"; "A Passing"; "Spring"; "Young Morning"; "Hymn to Ra"; "A Palm Tree in Egypt"; "Easter, 1918"; "In a Dispensary"; "To a Beautiful Old Lady"; "Wild Roses"; "Love Passes"; "Progression"; "There Where My Lover Lies"; "Pierrot Grows Old").

[5]Adapted stories originally published in *The Grand Magazine* in December 1923 ("The Clergyman's Daughter"; "The Red House"), *The Sketch* from September to December 1924 ("A Fairy in the Flat"; "A Pot of Tea"; "The Affair of the Pink Pearl"; "The Adventure of the Sinister Stranger"; "Finessing the King/The Gentleman Dressed in Newspaper"; "The Case of the Missing Lady"; "Blindman's Buff"; "The Man in the Mist"; "The Crackler"; "The Sunningdale Mystery"; "The House of Lurking Death"; "The Ambassador's Boots"; "The Man Who Was No. 16"), and *The Illustrated Sporting and Dramatic News* in December 1928 ("The Unbreakable Alibi").

1936, when George V died and his son Edward VIII was forced to abdicate in favor of his brother, George VI. Following the 1929 Wall Street Crash in the United States and spreading throughout the world, the Great Depression contributed to a rise in entertainment consumption, including mystery novels, new "talkie" films (developed in 1929), radio and, for some, television. Political tensions escalated across Europe, resulting in Britain's declaration of war with Germany on September 3, 1939.

AC and MM married in Edinburgh on September 11, **1930**, with AC retaining the Christie surname that she had continued using professionally and personally after her divorce. Her first professionally performed play, *Black Coffee*, debuted in London on December 8 the same year. This decade was Christie's heyday in terms of productivity and perceived quality. It was also the decade in which adaptations of her work started to take off, with the first Poirot films, starring Austin Trevor, released between **1930** and **1934**, and Christie's own radio and television scripts broadcast in **1934** and **1937**.

Novels:

- **1930** *The Murder at the Vicarage*; *Giant's Bread*
- **1931** *The Floating Admiral* (collaborative novel); *The Sittaford Mystery* (AKA *Murder at Hazelmoor*)
- **1932** *Peril at End House*
- **1933** *Lord Edgware Dies*
- **1934** *Murder on the Orient Express*; *Unfinished Portrait*; *Why Didn't They Ask Evans?*; *Three-Act Tragedy* (AKA *Murder in Three Acts*)
- **1935** *Death in the Clouds* (AKA *Death in the Air*)
- **1936** *The ABC Murders*; *Murder in Mesopotamia*; *Cards on the Table*
- **1937** *Dumb Witness* (AKA *Poirot Loses a Client*); *Death on the Nile*
- **1938** *Appointment with Death*; *Hercule Poirot's Christmas* (AKA *Murder for Christmas*, *Holiday for Murder*)
- **1939** *Murder is Easy* (AKA *Easy to Kill*); *And Then There Were None* (AKA *Ten Little Indians*)

Collections:

- **1930** *The Mysterious Mr. Quin*[6]

---

[6]Stories originally published in the *Grand Magazine* between March 1924 and March 1929 ("The Coming of Mr. Quin"; "The Shadow on the Glass"; "At the Bells and Motley"; "A Sign in the Sky"; "The Dead Harlequin"), *The Story-Teller* between January and May 1927 ("The Soul of the Croupier"; "The Voice in the Dark"; "Face of Helen"; "The World's End"; "Harlequin's Lane"), and *Britannia and Eve* in 1929 ("The Man from the Sea"), or appearing for the first time ("The Bird with the Broken Wing").

- **1932** *The Thirteen Problems* (AKA *The Tuesday Club Murders, Miss Marple and the Thirteen Problems*)[7]
- **1933** *The Hound of Death* (UK only)[8]
- **1934** *The Listerdale Mystery* (UK only);[9] *Parker Pyne Investigates* (AKA *Mr Parker Pyne, Detective*)[10]
- **1937** *Murder in the Mews* (AKA *Dead Man's Mirror*)[11]
- **1939** *The Regatta Mystery* (US only)[12]

UK/US films:

- **1931** *Alibi* (dir. Leslie S. Hiscott); *Black Coffee* (dir. Leslie S. Hiscott)
- **1934** *Lord Edgware Dies* (dir. Henry Edwards)
- **1937** *Love from a Stranger* (AKA *A Night of Terror*—dir. Rowland V. Lee)

---

[7]Stories originally published in the *Royal Magazine* from December 1927 to May 1928 ("The Tuesday Night Club"; "The Idol House of Astarte"; "Ingots of Gold"; "The Blood-Stained Pavement"; "Motive v. Opportunity"; "The Thumb Mark of St. Peter"), *The Story-Teller* from December 1929 to May 1930 ("The Blue Geranium"; "The Companion"; "The Four Suspects"; "A Christmas Tragedy"; "The Herb of Death"; "The Affair at the Bungalow"), and *Nash's Pall Mall Magazine* in November 1931 ("Death by Drowning").

[8]Stories originally published in the *Grand Magazine* from June 1924 to February 1926 ("The Red Signal"; "The Fourth Man"; "The Mystery of the Blue Jar"; "S.O.S."), *Flynn's Weekly* in January 1925 ("The Witness for the Prosecution"), the *Sunday Chronicle Annual* in December 1925 ("Wireless"), and *Ghost Stories* in November 1926 ("The Last Seance"), or appearing for the first time ("The Hound of Death"; "The Gypsy"; "The Lamp"; "The Strange Case of Sir Arthur Carmichael"; "The Call of Wings").

[9]Stories originally published in the *Grand Magazine* from February 1924 to September 1926 ("The Listerdale Mystery"; "Philomel Cottage"; "The Girl in the Train"; "The Manhood of Edward Robinson"; "Jane in Search of a Job"; "Swan Song"), the *Novel Magazine* in August 1924 ("Mr Eastwood's Adventure"), *Red Magazine* in July 1926 ("The Rajah's Emerald"), the *Daily Mail* from August 1928 to August 1929 ("A Fruitful Sunday"; "The Golden Ball"), the *Sunday Dispatch* in September 1929 ("Accident"), and the *Illustrated Sporting and Dramatic News* in December 1929 ("Sing a Song of Sixpence").

[10]Stories first published between August 1932 and April 1933 in *Cosmopolitan* ("The Case of the Discontented Soldier"; "The Case of the Distressed Lady"; "The Case of the Discontented Husband"; "The Case of the City Clerk"; "The Case of the Rich Woman," between June and July 1933 in *Nash's Pall Mall Magazine* ("Have You Got Everything You Want?"; "The Gate of Baghdad"; "The House at Shiraz"; "The Pearl of Price"; "Death on the Nile"; "The Oracle at Delphi"), and in October 1932 in *Women's Pictorial* ("The Case of the Middle-aged Wife").

[11]Novellas originally published in the *Strand Magazine* in May 1936 ("Triangle at Rhodes") and *Women's Journal* in December 1936 ("Murder in the Mews"), or expanding on other stories ("The Incredible Theft"; "Dead Man's Mirror"). The US version lacked "The Incredible Theft" until 1987.

[12]Stories originally published in *Ladies' Home Journal* from January 1932 to June 1935 ("The Mystery of the Baghdad Chest"; "How Does Your Garden Grow?"), the *Strand Magazine* from November 1935 to July 1937 ("The Regatta Mystery"; "Problem at Pollensa Bay"; "Yellow Iris"), *Collier's Weekly* in July 1934 ("In a Glass Darkly"), the *This Week* in January 1936 ("Problem at Sea"), and the *Saturday Evening Post* in October 1937 ("The Dream"), and a radio transcript from the BBC's National Programme in May 1934 ("Miss Marple Tells a Story").

1940s

The Second World War grew to dominate the global stage, with the Allied Powers (led by the UK, Soviet Union, and the United States) against the Axis Powers (led by Germany, Japan, and Italy). Responsible for up to 85,000,000 fatalities, it remains the deadliest war in human history, with technology advances increasing its force and threat. Mandatory conscription meant a shortage of men on the home front. An Allied victory in 1945 led to the fall of Nazi Germany, and countries involved were plunged into a period of reconstruction, leading to the creation of the United Nations. Britain depended on economic assistance from the United States to recover economic stability.

During the war, AC volunteered at University College London, and leased her holiday home, Greenway in Devon, first for evacuated children and then for American military personnel. In **1940**, her daughter Rosalind married Major Hubert de Burr Prichard. Their son, Mathew Prichard, was born on September 21, **1943**. On November 12, **1944**, Hubert Prichard was killed in action in the Battle of Normandy. Rosalind married Anthony Hicks, a lawyer, in **1949**.

AC's London residence was bombed in May **1941**. MM served with the Royal Air Force Voluntary Reserve in North Africa. AC wrote prolifically throughout the war, and began adapting her books for the stage, with success, with a version of *And Then There Were None* in 1943. Nostalgic for archaeological digs with her husband, AC completed her first memoir as "Agatha Christie Mallowan" in **1946**. In **1949**, AC was exposed as the person behind "Mary Westmacott," her pseudonym for semi-autobiographical literary fiction.

Novels:

- **1940** *Sad Cypress*; *One, Two, Buckle My Shoe* (AKA *The Patriotic Murders*)
- **1941** *Evil Under the Sun*; *N or M?*
- **1942** *The Body in the Library*; *Five Little Pigs* (AKA *Murder in Retrospect*)
- **1943** *The Moving Finger*
- **1944** *Towards Zero*; *Absent in the Spring*; *Death Comes as the End*
- **1945** *Sparkling Cyanide* (AKA *Remembered Death*)
- **1946** *The Hollow*
- **1948** *Taken at the Flood*; *The Rose and the Yew Tree*
- **1949** *Crooked House*

Collections and other:

- **1946** *Come, Tell Me How You Live* (memoir)

- **1947** *The Labours of Hercules*[13]
- **1948** *The Witness for the Prosecution* (US only)[14]

UK/US films:

- **1945** *And Then There Were None* (AKA *Ten Little Indians*—dir. René Clair)
- **1947** *Love from a Stranger* (AKA *A Stranger Walked In*—dir. Richard Whorf)

1950s

Though often viewed nostalgically in the twenty-first century, Britain in the 1950s was negotiating tense reconstruction efforts in the wake of war and anticipating social change. Increased birth rate resulted in the "baby boomer" generation during the rock and roll era, while the United States and the USSR were engaged in the Space Race, as well as a nuclear arms race. The coronation of Britain's Queen Elizabeth II helped increase domestic television ownership. Wartime rationing continued in the UK in various forms until 1954.

AC was elected a Fellow of the Royal Society of Literature in **1950**. In November **1952**, her record-breaking play, *The Mousetrap*, opened at the Ambassadors Theatre, London, starring married couple Richard Attenborough and Sheila Sim. In **1953**, AC became the first female playwright to have three plays in the West End at the same time. AC received the Mystery Writers of America's (MWA) first Grand Master Award and *Witness for the Prosecution* received the MWA's Edgar Award for best play, both in **1955**.

---

[13]Stories originally published in *This Week* between September 1939 and March 1947 ("The Lernaean Hydra"; "The Arcadian Deer"; "The Erymanthian Boar"; "The Augean Stables"; "The Stymphalean Birds"; "The Cretan Bull"; "The Girdle of Hippolyta"; "The Flock of Geryon"; "The Apples of Hesperides"; "The Capture of Cerberus") and the *Strand Magazine* between November 1939 and June 1940 ("The Nemean Lion"; "The Horses of Diomedes").

[14]Stories originally published in the *Grand Magazine* from June 1924 to February 1926 ("The Fourth Man"; "The Mystery of the Blue Jar"; "Philomel Cottage"; "The Red Signal"; "S.O.S."), the *Novel Magazine* in August 1924 ("The Mystery of the Spanish Shawl"), *Flynn's Weekly* in January 1925 ("The Witness for the Prosecution"), the *Sunday Chronicle Annual* in December 1925 ("Where There's a Will"), the *Sunday Dispatch* in September 1929 ("Accident"), and the *Illustrated Sporting and Dramatic News* in December 1929 ("Sing a Song of Sixpence"), and *The Strand* in July 1932 ("The Second Gong").

AC was appointed a Commander of the Order of the British Empire (CBE) in 1956, after some debate as to whether she should be considered for damehood. In September 1957, *The Mousetrap* became the longest-running play in British history. It became the West End's longest-running show of any kind in April 1958 and took the world record shortly later. The death of Dorothy L. Sayers in 1958 meant AC took over as president of the Detection Club, although she insisted on a co-president, the third Baron Gorrell, to assist with public speaking.

Novels:

- 1950 *A Murder Is Announced*
- 1951 *They Came to Baghdad*
- 1952 *Mrs. McGinty's Dead*; *They Do It with Mirrors*; *A Daughter's a Daughter*
- 1953 *After the Funeral*; *A Pocket Full of Rye*
- 1954 *Destination Unknown* (*So Many Steps to Death*)
- 1955 *Hickory Dickory Dock* (*Hickory Dickory Death*)
- 1956 *Dead Man's Folly*; *The Burden*
- 1957 *4.50 from Paddington* (*What Mrs McGillicuddy Saw!*)
- 1958 *Ordeal by Innocence*
- 1959 *Cat Among the Pigeons*

Collections:

- 1950 *Three Blind Mice* (US only)[15]
- 1951 *The Under Dog* (US only)[16]

UK/US films:

- 1957 *Witness for the Prosecution* (dir. Billy Wilder)

---

[15]Stories and a novella originally published in *The Sketch* in October 1923 ("The Adventure of Johnnie Waverly"), *Flynn's Weekly* in October 1926 ("The Love Detectives"), *Hutchinson's Adventure and Mystery Magazine* ("The Third Floor Flat"), *Collier's* in November 1940 ("Four and Twenty Blackbirds"), *This Week* in November 1941 ("Strange Jest"; "Tape-Measure Murder"), the *Chicago Sunday Tribune* between July and September 1942 ("The Case of the Perfect Maid"; "The Case of the Caretaker"), and *Cosmopolitan* in May 1948 ("Three Blind Mice").

[16]Stories originally published in *The Sketch* between March and December 1923 ("The Plymouth Express"; "The Affair at the Victory Ball"; "The Market Basing Mystery"; "The Lemesurier Inheritance"; "The Cornish Mystery"; "The King of Clubs"; "The Submarine Plans"; "The Adventure of the Clapham Cook") and *Mystery Magazine* in April 1926 ("The Under Dog").

1960s

The "Swinging Sixties" was a decade marked by increased self-expression and civil rights movements, especially in the United States where the assassination of Martin Luther King, Jr. in 1968 and the Stonewall riot in 1969 pushed racist and homophobic injustices into the forefront of public consciousness. The UK saw the rise of the "teenager," a generation of youth that had not been forced into conscription, and the rise of the Beatles and pop music.

AC received an honorary degree from the University of Exeter in **1961**. Her first husband Archie died in December **1962**. In her seventies, AC continued to go on excavations with MM, including to Iran, Kashmir, and Iraq in **1962**. MM authored *Nimrud and Its Remains*, his defining archaeological text; he was knighted in **1969**. In **1965**, AC completed her autobiography, which would be published posthumously. AC sought to keep up-to-date with youth culture and drug references in her prose and in her reading matter, but this was viewed as a charming relic by the general public. She continued to write plays, but without the success of the 1950s. A disagreement with MGM over jokey, trivializing films ended in **1966**, when the contract was terminated.

Novels:

- **1961** *The Pale Horse*
- **1962** *The Mirror Crack'd from Side to Side*
- **1963** *The Clocks*
- **1964** *A Caribbean Mystery*
- **1965** *At Bertram's Hotel*
- **1966** *Third Girl*
- **1967** *Endless Night*
- **1968** *By the Pricking of My Thumbs*
- **1969** *Hallowe'en Party*

Collections:

- **1960** *The Adventure of the Christmas Pudding* (UK only)[17]

---

[17]Stories originally published in *Mystery Magazine* in April 1926 ("The Under Dog"), *The Strand* in February 1938 ("The Dream"), *Collier's* in November 1940 ("Tour and Twenty Blackbirds"), and the *Daily Mail* in December 1956 ("Greenshaw's Folly"), and two expansions of previous stories ("The Adventure of the Christmas Pudding"; "The Mystery of the Spanish Chest").

- **1965** *Double Sin* (US only)[18]
- **1965** *Star Over Bethlehem*[19]

UK/US films:

- **1960** *The Spider's Web* (dir. Godfrey Grayson)
- **1961** *Murder She Said* (dir. George Pollock)
- **1963** *Murder at the Gallop* (dir. George Pollock)
- **1964** *Murder Most Foul* (dir. George Pollock)
- **1965** *Murder Ahoy* (dir. George Pollock); *Ten Little Indians* (dir. George Pollock); *The Alphabet Murders* (dir. Frank Tashlin)

1970s

This decade was marked in the West by the rise of neoliberalism, and further afield by the spread of decolonization and increased tensions in the Middle East. Key social movements of the 1970s include widespread awareness of political corruption, antiwar protests, the sexual revolution, and the Second Wave feminist movement.

AC slowed down considerably, infirm and struggling to write. She was created a Dame of the British Empire in **1971**. Wooed by Lord Louis Mountbatten, she agreed to let *Murder on the Orient Express* be filmed by Sidney Lumet; the film in **1974** was a global box office hit, and it led to a lucrative franchise. Its royal premier was AC's last public appearance. Her last-authored novel appeared in **1973**. The last Poirot novel, *Curtain*, written in the 1940s for posthumous release, was published in **1975**. AC died in Oxfordshire, England, on January 12, **1976**. Her autobiography was published posthumously in **1977**. MM remarried and died on August 19, **1978**.

---

[18]Stories originally published in *The Sketch* in December 1923 ("The Double Clue"), *Ghost Stories* in November 1926 ("The Last Séance"), the *Sunday Dispatch* in September 1928 ("Double Sin"), the *Daily Mail* between November 1928 and December 1956 ("Wasp's Nest"; "Greenshaw's Folly"), *This Week* in September 1954 ("Sanctuary"), *Star Weekly* in October 1958 ("The Dressmaker's Doll") and *The Adventure of the Christmas Pudding* in 1960 ("The Theft of the Royal Ruby").

[19]Religious stories and poetry first published in the *Women's Journal* in December 1946 ("Star Over Bethlehem") or appearing for the first time (stories: "The Naughty Donkey"; "The Water Bus"; "In the Cool of the Evening"; "Promotion in the Highest"; "The Island"—poems: "A Greeting"; "A Wreath for Christmas"; "Gold, Frankincense and Myrrh"; "Jenny by the Sky"; "The Saints of God").

Novels:

- **1970** *Passenger to Frankfurt*
- **1971** *Nemesis*
- **1972** *Elephants Can Remember*
- **1973** *Postern of Fate*
- **1975** *Curtain*
- **1976** *Sleeping Murder*

Collections and other:

- **1971** *The Golden Ball* (US only)[20]
- **1973** *Akhnaton* (play)
- **1973** *Poems* (UK only)[21]
- **1977** *An Autobiography* (memoir)
- **1978** *The Mousetrap and Other Plays*[22]
- **1979** *Miss Marple's Final Cases* (UK only)[23]

---

[20]Stories originally published in The *Grand Magazine* between February 1924 and September 1929 ("The Listerdale Mystery"; "The Girl in the Train"; "The Manhood of Edward Robinson"; "Jane in Search of a Job"; "Swan Song"; "Next to a Dog"), *Royal Magazine* in March 1926 ("Magnolia Blossom"), *Red Magazine* in July 1926 ("The Rajah's Emerald"), the *Daily Mail* between August 1928 and August 1929 ("A Fruitful Sunday"; "The Golden Ball"), and *The Hound of Death* in 1933 ("The Hound of Death"; "The Gypsy"; "The Lamp"; "The Strange Case of Sir Arthur Carmichael"; "The Call of Wings").

[21]Edited reproduction of *The Road of Dreams* (1924), plus poems previously published in "Star Over Bethlehem" ("Jenny by the Sky") or appearing for the first time ("Beauty"; "The Water Flows"; "The Sculptor"; "A Wandering Tune"; "Ctesiphon"; "In Baghdad"; "An Island"; "The Nile"; "Dartmoor"; "To a Cedar Tree"; "Calvary"; "Count Ferson to the Queen"; "Beatrice Passes"; "Undine"; "Hawthorn Trees"; "Lament of the Tortured Lover"; "What Is Love?"; "To M.E.L.M. in Absence"; "Remembrance"; "A Choice"; "My Flower Garden"; "Enchantment"; "From a Grown-up to a Child"; "I Wore My New Canary Suit"; "Racial Musings"; "Picnic 1960").

[22]Plays (West End debuts in parenthesis): *And Then There Were None* (November 1943); *Appointment with Death* (March 1945); *The Hollow* (June 1951); *The Mousetrap* (November 1952); *Witness for the Prosecution* (October 1953); *Towards Zero* (September 1956); *Verdict* (May 1958); *Go Back for Murder* (March 1960). Later split into two volumes, *The Mousetrap and Selected Plays* (1994) and *Witness for the Prosecution and Selected Plays* (1995), then recombined in 2011.

[23]Stories originally published in *Collier's Weekly* in July 1934 ("In a Glass Darkly"), *This Week* between November 1941 and September 1954 ("Sanctuary"; "Strange Jest"; "Tape-Measure Murder"), the *Chicago Sunday Tribune* between July and September 1942 ("The Case of the Caretaker"; "The Case of the Perfect Maid"), and *Star Weekly* in October 1958 ("The Dressmaker's Doll"), and a radio transcript from the BBC's National Programme in May 1934 ("Miss Marple Tells a Story").

UK/US films:

- **1972** *Endless Night* (dir. Sidney Gilliat)
- **1974** *Murder on the Orient Express* (dir. Sidney Lumet)
- **1974** *And Then There Were None* (AKA *Ten Little Indians*—dir. Peter Collinson)
- **1978** *Death on the Nile* (dir. John Guillerman)

1980s

A decade of renewed conservatism, marked by nostalgia for the 1950s and reactions against the advancements and self-expression of the 1960s and 1970s. The Cold War, which had started in the 1940s, neared its conclusion; the Berlin Wall, which divided East Berlin from West Berlin, fell in 1989.

Agatha Christie Limited was run by AC's daughter, Rosalind Hicks, who maintained tight control over her mother's legacy but permitted some carefully selected television adaptations. The 1980s saw Christie established as a British and American television staple, with *Partners in Crime* (1982), *Miss Marple* (1983–91), and *Agatha Christie's Poirot* (1989–2013), as well as various "modernized" CBS adaptations premiering in this decade. Popular scholarship in earnest began emerging in the 1980s, including the first Christie volume published by a university press, Earl F. Bargainnier's *The Gentle Art of Murder* in **1980**.

Collections:

- **1983** *The Scoop & Behind the Screen* (collaborative novellas)[24]

UK/US films:

- **1980** *The Mirror Crack'd* (dir. Guy Hamilton)
- **1982** *Evil Under the Sun* (dir. Guy Hamilton)
- **1985** *Ordeal by Innocence* (dir. Desmond Davis)
- **1988** *Appointment with Death* (dir. Michael Winner)
- **1989** *Ten Little Indians* (dir. Alan Birkinshaw)

---

[24]Originally published in *The Listener* between June 1930 and April 1931.

1990s

The New Technology Age reflected an increasingly globalized and more multicultural world. The Soviet Union dissolved in 1991, and the 1990s saw the introduction of such developments as domestic internet use. The "dot-com" bubble of 1997 reflected massive technological advances and opportunities at a time when the probed limits of human knowledge were tested in ethical debates around issues such as gene therapy and identity politics.

AC's legacy remained fueled by nostalgia, and her appeal was largely reflected during this period in television adaptations, with no authorized English-language cinematic adaptations and only one new stage adaptation, which flopped, premiering in **1993**. AC's publishers released "new" collections of short stories sourced from magazines in **1991** and **1997**, and authorized Charles Osborne to adapt the first of three plays he would eventually develop into novels, which are published as part of the canon, in **1998**.

Novelizations:

- **1998** *Black Coffee* (by Charles Osborne, from the 1930 play)
- **1999** *The Unexpected Guest* (by Charles Osborne, from the 1958 play)

Collections:

- **1991** *Problem at Pollensa Bay* (UK only)[25]
- **1997** *The Harlequin Tea Set* (US only)[26]
- **1997** *While the Light Lasts* (UK only)[27]

2000s

During this decade of globalization, communication and social media expanded exponentially, while emerging economies developed considerably. Following

---

[25]Stories originally published in the *Royal Magazine* in March 1926 ("Magnolia Blossom"), *The Story-Teller* in December 1926 ("The Love Detectives"), the *Grand Magazine* in December 1929 ("Next to a Dog"), the *Strand Magazine* from July 1932 to July 1937 ("Problem at Pollensa Bay"; "The Second Gong"; "Yellow Iris"; "The Regatta Mystery"), and *Winter's Crimes* 3 in 1971 ("The Harlequin Tea Set").

[26]Stories originally published in *The Novel Magazine* between May 1923 and April 1924 ("The Actress"; "While the Light Lasts"), the *Royal Magazine* between October 1925 and July 1926 ("The Lonely God"; "Within a Wall"), *Sovereign* in January 1926 ("The House of Dreams"), *Pearson's Magazine* in February 1927 ("The Edge"), the *Daily Dispatch* in May 1930 ("Manx Gold"), *The Adventure of the Christmas Pudding* in 1960 ("The Mystery of the Spanish Chest"), and *Winter's Crimes* 3 in 1971 ("The Harlequin Tea Set").

[27]As above, but without "The Mystery of the Spanish Chest" or "The Harlequin Tea Set" and with "The Mystery of the Baghdad Chest" and "The Love Detectives."

a 2001 terrorist attack, the United States launched the "War on Terror," with the UK joining to invade Iraq. Globalization and an ever-increasing carbon footprint led to an intense focus on climate change and renewable energy that would gain urgency over the next decade. The US housing crisis in 2007 led to a global recession.

Rosalind Hicks died on October 28, 2004, and the estate passed to her son, AC's grandson Mathew Prichard. A media deal with Chorion saw Agatha Christie Limited seek to attract younger readers, with a string of video games, while new UK television adaptations (especially episodes of *Agatha Christie's Marple* from **2004**) emphasized or inserted gay and lesbian content. A range of jaunty adaptations, including animation, appeared in Japan and France from **2004** and **2005**, respectively. In **2009**, John Curran published the first of two volumes revealing Christie's notebooks and including previously unpublished stories.

Novelizations:

- **2000** *Spider's Web* (by Charles Osborne, from the 1954 play)

Collections and other:

- **2009** *Agatha Christie's Secret Notebooks* (by John Curran)[28]

2010s

Beginning in the midst of a global financial crisis, the 2010s saw significant progress for LGBTQ+ rights with the introduction of same-sex marriage in several countries including the UK and the United States. In parallel, the decade saw a significant rise in right-wing politics and culture wars, with regular discussions of terrorism and neonationalism. In 2016, the British public voted to withdraw from the European Union.

Mathew Prichard continued as an active leader of Agatha Christie Limited, editing and publishing his grandmother's correspondence from the 1922 British Empire Exhibition Tour in **2012**. He was awarded the Prince of Wales Medal for Philanthropy the same year. In **2014**, he stepped down from chairmanship in favor of his son, James Prichard. A new rebranding effort to position Christie as "canonical" involved Poirot continuation novels from Sophie Hannah, biennially starting with *The Monogram Murders* in **2013**, a series of dark BBC/Amazon miniseries, starting with *And Then There Were None* in **2015**, and the first cinematic franchise in nearly forty years, with Twentieth Century Studios releasing *Murder on the Orient Express* **2017**. Attention has also been

---

[28]Previously unpublished material: notebook extracts and two stories ("The Capture of Cerberus"; "The Incident of the Dog's Ball").

brought in this period to Christie's playwrighting credentials, with over a dozen unpublished plays "discovered," staged, and published for performance.

Novels:

- **2014** *Hercule Poirot and the Greenshore Folly* (novella)

Collections and other:

- **2011** *Murder in the Making* (by John Curran)[29]
- **2012** *The Grand Tour* (collected correspondence)
- **2019** *The Last Séance*[30]

UK/US films:

- **2017** *Crooked House* (dir. Gilles Paquet-Brenner)
- **2017** *Murder on the Orient Express* (dir. Kenneth Branagh)

REFERENCES

Aldridge, M. (2016), *Agatha Christie on Screen*, London: Palgrave.

Appignami, T. (2016), "Murder and Emancipation: Agatha Christie and Critical Qualitative Methods," *IAFOR Journal of Cultural Studies*, 1 (2), September 30. Available online: https://iafor.org/journal/iafor-journal-of-cultural-studies/volume-1-issue-2/article-1/ (accessed November 1, 2021).

Ball, A. (2012), "Mystery in the Stacks: A Discovery Is Made in the Museum Archives," *Penn Museum Blog*. Available online: https://www.penn.museum/blog/collection/archival-practice/mystery-in-the-stacks-a-discovery-is-made-in-the-museum-archives/ (accessed November 1, 2021).

Barnard, R. (1980), *A Talent to Deceive: An Appreciation of Agatha Christie*, London: Collins.

Bernthal, J.C. (2016a), *The Ageless Agatha Christie: Essays on the Mysteries and the Legacy*, Jefferson: McFarland.

Bernthal, J.C. (2016b), *Queering Agatha Christie: Revisiting the Golden Age of Detective Fiction*, London: Palgrave.

Bernthal, J.C. (2019), "Killing Innocence: Obstructions of Justice in Late-Interwar British Crime Fiction," *Clues: A Journal of Detection*, 37 (2): 31–9.

Bernthal, J.C. (2022), *Agatha Christie: A Companion to the Mystery Fiction*, Jefferson: McFarland.

Blyth, C. and Jack, A. (2019), *The Bible in Crime Fiction and Drama: Murderous Texts*, London and New York: Bloomsbury.

---

[29]Previously unpublished material: notebook extracts and two stories ("The Case of the Caretaker's Wife"; "The Man Who Knew").

[30]Nineteen stories available in other anthologies plus "The Wife of the Kenite," first published in *The Home* in September 1922.

Bowen, R. (2021), "Those Golden Age Ladies Weren't So Hot!," *Jungle Red Writers*, August 17. Available online: https://www.jungleredwriters.com/2021/08/those-golden-age-ladies-werent-so-hot.html (accessed November 1, 2021).

Brown, S. (2020), "'Scoring Off a Foreigner?' Xenophobia, Antisemitism, and Racism in the Works of Agatha Christie," *Clues: A Journal of Detection*, 38 (1): 70–80.

Christie, A. ([1936] 2001), *Murder in Mesopotamia*, London: HarperCollins.

Christie, A. ([1977] 2011), *An Autobiography*, London: HarperCollins.

Curran, J. (2011), *Agatha Christie's Murder in the Making: More Stories and Secrets from Her Archives*, London: HarperCollins.

Dennis, N. (1956), "Genteel Queen of Crime," *Life Magazine*, May 14, 87–102.

Emmott, C. and Alexander, M. (2019), "Reliability, Unreliability, Reader Manipulation and Plot Reversals: Strategies for Constructing and Challenging the Credibility of Characters in Agatha Christie's Detective Fiction," in R. Page, B. Busse, and N. Nørgaard (eds), *Rethinking Language, Text and Context: Interdisciplinary Research in Stylistics in Honour Of Michael Toolan*, 177–90, New York and Abingdon: Routledge.

Evans, M.A. (2021), "Killing Bluebeard: Claiming Subversive Femininity in Agatha Christie's 'Philomel Cottage' and *The Stranger*," *Clues: A Journal of Detection*, 39 (1): 104–14.

Harkup, K. (2015), *A Is for Arsenic: The Poisons of Agatha Christie*, London: Bloomsbury.

Hastings, C. (2015), "What HAS the BBC Done to Agatha Christie? Christmas Viewers Will Be Stunned by Controversial New Adaption Featuring Drugs, Gruesome Violence and the F-word," *Mail On Sunday*, December 13. Available online: https://www.dailymail.co.uk/tvshowbiz/article-3357749/What-BBC-Agatha-Christie.html (accessed November 1, 2021).

Haycraft, H. ([1941] 1974), *Murder for Pleasure: The Life and Times of the Detective Story*, New York: Biblo and Tannen.

Keating, H.R.F. (1977), *Agatha Christie First Lady of Crime*, New York: Holt, Rinehart and Winston.

Knepper, M. (1995), "Reading Agatha Christie's Miss Marple Series: *The Thirteen Problems*" in M. DeMarr (ed), *In the Beginning: First Novels in Mystery Series*, 33–57, Bowling Green: Popular Press.

Light, A. *Forever England: Femininity, Literature, and Conservatism between the Wars*, London and New York: Routledge.

Mallowan, A.C. ([1946] 2012), *Come Tell Me How You Live*, New York: William Morrow.

Makinen, M. (2006), *Agatha Christie: Investigating Femininity*, Basingstoke: Palgrave Macmillan.

Mills, R. (2019), "'I Always Did Hate Watering-Places': Tourism and Carnival in Agatha Christie's and Dorothy L. Sayers's Seaside Novels," *Clues: A Journal of Detection*, 37 (2): 83–93.

Morgan, J. ([1984] 1997), *Agatha Christie: A Biography*, London: HarperCollins.

"The Mousetrap Tenth Anniversary Celebrations" (2019), *BBC Archive*, June 10. Available online: www.bbc.co.uk/archive/the-mousetrap-tenth-anniversary-celebrations/zbfsqp3 (accessed November 1, 2021).

"Nippur." in Eric M. Meyers, Richard L. Zettler (eds), *The Oxford Encyclopedia of Archaeology in the Near East. Oxford Biblical Studies Online*.

Available online: http://www.oxfordbiblicalcstudies.com/article/opr/t256/e780 (accessed October 24, 2021).

Osborne, C. (1982), *The Life and Crimes of Agatha Christie*, London: Collins.

"Quote Unquote" (1983), *Independent*, April 3. Available online: http://www.independent.co.uk/voices/quote-unquote-1453120.html (accessed November 1, 2021).

Ramsey, G.C. (1968), *Agatha Christie: Mistress of Mystery*, New York: Dodd, Mead.

Rankin, I. (2003), "Why Crime Fiction Is Good for You," in B. Turner (ed), *The Writer's Handbook Guide to Crime Writing*, 3–14, London: Macmillan.

Rowland, S. (2001), *From Agatha Christie to Ruth Rendell: British Women Writers in Detective and Crime Fiction*, Basingstoke: Palgrave.

Symons, J. (1980), "Puzzle Maker, Review of *A Talent to Deceive* by Robert Barnard," *Inquiry*, November 24: 29–30.

Symons, J. (1985), *Bloody Murder, from the Detective Story to the Crime Novel: A History*, revised ed., New York: Viking.

Thompson, L. ([2007] 2008), *Agatha Christie: An English Mystery*, New York: Pegasus Books.

Wilson, E. (1945), "Books: Who Cares Who Killed Roger Ackroyd?: A Second Report on Detective Fiction by Edmund Wilson," *The New Yorker*, January 20, 59.

Wyndham, F. (1966), "The Algebra of Agatha Christie," *The Sunday Times*, Weekly Review supplement, February 27, 25–6.

Yiannitsaros, C. (2021), "Delicious Death: Criminal Cake in and beyond Agatha Christie's *A Murder Is Announced*," *Clues: A Journal of Detection*, 39 (2): 107–17.

York, R.A. (2007), *Agatha Christie: Power and Illusion*, Basingstoke: Palgrave Macmillan.

FIGURE 1.1 A young Mathew Prichard with his grandmother, Agatha Christie, in the 1950s. Courtesy of The Christie Archive Trust.

CHAPTER ONE

My Grandmother, Agatha Christie

MATHEW PRICHARD

I was delighted to be asked to contribute to this *Bloomsbury Handbook to Agatha Christie*, who was my grandmother. Actually, I used to call her Nima, which I presume was my first rather inaccurate attempt at Grandma, but in any case it became adopted as the family name. *The Bloomsbury Handbook to Agatha Christie* contains a wealth of essays concerning her work and its various connotations, whose scholarship I could not even begin to match. (Nima herself may perhaps have been surprised, flattered, and even slightly bemused at the length and breadth of researchers assembled to discuss her and her work.)

Since Nima died in 1976 the research into her work has grown, particularly in the last twenty years. Thanks to archives and libraries within academic and commercial institutions, an array of material has become much more widely available than it was in her own lifetime. Nima's own correspondence between publishers, producers, friends, and much other comment on other aspects of her archive, together with analysis of her texts themselves, have promulgated many more thoughtful interpretations of her work. Nima herself would not have known much of the existence of this. Writing as she did from early in the beginning of the twentieth century, her work and its adaptations across developing media such as radio and television undoubtedly provides a helpful lens through which to consider the media developments since her Victorian childhood.

I do not know the extent to which Nima might be surprised at the continued appetite for adaptations on the new platforms of the twenty-first century or the opportunities for scholarship that are still being found. I have certainly learned much more about the context of her early life and work through close studies that have been written of her notebooks, her life in the theater, and her television and film adaptations, to name just three examples. What I thought might assist with this project is to try and give a brief sense of the family life we had together and how that, and her strongly held belief in the family unit, managed to fit in with the other achievements of her remarkable life.

When Nima realized that other people sought to write about her life and work she began work on her autobiography. I think this was partly a defense mechanism and born of an anxiety to tell her own story—though she enjoyed it too! It took her some time to write and I think she felt she convincingly committed to paper what she felt she wanted to say about her beliefs, values, and appreciation of life. I believe her family life was as important to her as her work as an author, and as her contributions to her husband Max's career as an archaeologist. Indeed, she once said that when asked to describe her profession, she unhesitatingly used to reply "married woman." I believe that some of the attributes she displayed as a wife, mother, and grandmother help to understand her as one of the most natural, accomplished, and influential women of the twentieth century.

I was born during the Second World War in 1943 when Nima was over 50 and was well established as a detective fiction writer with a burgeoning play writing career, spending very happy periods working on archaeological sites in Syria and Iraq with her second husband, Max Mallowan. My father, Hubert, was killed in action in 1944 and I was largely brought up by my mother, Rosalind, and Nima. My mother and I went to live in my father's house in South Wales after he died whose rural location was far removed from the exigencies of life in London during the war.

Earlier in the war, with Max posted to North Africa with the Air Ministry, Nima, who had resumed her dispensing career at University College Hospital, decided to carry on living in a small studio flat in the modernist Isokon building in Lawn Road, London. Nima chose not to write about her experiences of the war as she believed others would do it better than her, but for her writing it was an extraordinarily intense period of her life. Throughout her life she was a prolific and thoughtful letter writer and some of those that survive from this time demonstrate how her curiosity, enthusiasm for life, and imaginative powers only seemed to be heightened by the cultural and physical excitements of a single life in London.

The extraordinary breadth of her work at this time is well documented. Suffice to say she found it possible to write some of her most taut and psychologically complex detective novels, a highly charged Mary Westmacott novel and a touching memoir of her life in the Middle East, alongside managing the trials and tribulations of plays coming in and out of London's West End. Although she was no longer able to travel abroad, she was deeply involved in her play rehearsals, traveling to places like Dundee for premiers as well as finding time to attend lectures, theater (from Shakespeare to new contemporary plays), and cinema around London, undertaking all of this while keeping up with old friends and making new ones.

And then she would come to South Wales often to fend off some domestic crisis or just be another pair of hands. Her patience and loyalty to my mother in the time of her bereavement were unquestioning. They and my father's dogs were my life. My mother and I had suddenly inherited my father's rural life in Wales which was far removed from Nima's own, not to mention my mother's. It was clear that Nima wholeheartedly supported my mother in trying to give me the sort of upbringing my father would have wanted.

My father was a passionate countryman and soldier who loved his Welsh home and dogs in equal measure. One of the significant memories Nima had of my parents was meeting them in a hotel in London with my father with a puppy peeking out of his army coat. Nima, who had a huge affinity to dogs throughout her life, I feel sure would have found this very reassuring and certainly very amusing when she found out about the havoc it had caused in their hotel bedroom. At least five or six hours from London (there was no bridge over the River Severn to Wales at this time), my father's relatively remote family home was surrounded by rolling farmland with food either being grown in the garden or rather chaotically acquired direct from kind local farmers. I can still smell the gas that dimly lit the rooms and caused such difficulty for the cantankerous stove. Electricity had not yet arrived, so any food was cooked and cooked again to ensure the maximum value was achieved out of every animal part when it was available.

Although Nima was well used to wartime rationing, I think she found our existence quite precarious, yet if extra nappies or other essential household items were required, it was Nima who was the organizing and enthusiastic hand. She threw herself into every domestic chore helping out with the imaginative handling of offal delicacies as they presented themselves and would return exhausted to London for a rest. Without my father to introduce us to local friends and neighbors, it was a challenging period for my mother to settle into her newfound home, but Nima's easy, self-deprecating humor and endless resourcefulness helped us all to adjust to our new lives. I recently found the copy of *The Times* with the announcement of my father's death that Nima had kept. It simply had the number of her flat at the Isokon on and yet it spoke volumes to me of the life she had left to come to us when we needed her most.

Nima herself wrote in her autobiography a very shrewd appreciation of my father.

"And I think, too, that there had always been something about Hubert—not exactly melancholy, but that touch or look of someone who is not fated for long life. He was a dear person [...] with I think a great vein not exactly of poetry but something of that kind in him" (Christie 1977: 502). This was a good example of Nima's spirituality and generous judgment of the people she loved best.

As I grew up, Nima's unselfishness and passionate interest in me were a beacon of light in what might otherwise have been a constricted life. I find it difficult to find the words to adequately convey the impact of her on my life. Even in the first ten years of my life, I think I sensed some of the characteristics that had already propelled her to her status as a full-time storyteller. Her curiosity at all my mad games and flights of fancy showed (perhaps unwittingly!) her own depths of invention and imagination. She never complained about being woken early for a further installment in the life of Flutt and Butt, my toy elephants, who were our rich source of entertainment. When they went missing on a trip to Wells Cathedral in Somerset, Nima was in Nimrud in Iraq with Max. Having been informed of the traumatic loss by my mother, Nima immediately wrote, vividly recalling a similar event with my mother as a child. She suggested the elephants had taken a flight from Glastonbury to Nimrud as she thought she had seen a peculiar aircraft around about that time thereby uniting two enigmatic worlds in one leap of consoling faith and imagination. Sadly, none of our stories were ever recorded, but there did not seem a need to as they flowed effortlessly between us.

When I began to read, even at an early age and particularly when I went to school, she instilled in me the importance and joy she herself attached to reading. She herself read and reread fiction, nonfiction, and poetry—from the classics such as Shakespeare, Dickens, and Sherlock Holmes, to contemporary detective fiction, but above all to books which appeared to have no connection or use of immediate relevance. She always asked about my reading and was not particular about its nature. She even suffered in silence for my enthusiasm for Biggles, a fictional pilot, created by W.E. Johns. I firmly believe that part of her success can be explained by the enthusiasm she had for reading from childhood right through her life.

She famously taught herself to read and did not have a formal education. On the bookcases at Greenway, her home in Devon, now owned by the National Trust, it is still possible to see the wide range of books she read when she was young. In an entry in her family's Victorian Confessions Album, written at age 13, she recorded her favorite occupations as Reading and Singing with Jo from Louise May Alcott's *Little Women* being her literary heroine. Her passion for reading grew, and especially with her relationship with Max her continuous quest for knowledge and understanding was a sustaining and nourishing part of their life together. Their letters during his absence during the war show how vital discussions of the books they were reading or recommending to each other were. In one where she is imagining their ideal future life together, she suggests it might be to live simply by the sea in Greece with a house filled with books.

When I would later spend time with them at Greenway during the summers of the 1950s, I saw the anticipation she had for her weekly package of library books coming from London wrapped in brown paper and string. Then if she had exhausted them, she would find newspapers and magazines or even go down to Dartmouth on the River Dart on the ferry to pick up extra supplies. I have sometimes sensed in her writing that she was always on the side of the reader. Perhaps her own experience as a reader was one of the reasons she found she was able to communicate so directly to her own readers, contributing to the sense of immediacy and timelessness while strengthening the bond that persists in her own books.

And yet the energy and curiosity she had for literature manifested in so many other aspects of her life. Her love of singing and music was also a major source of enjoyment throughout her life as was her restless and boundless appetite for travel. She was an accomplished singer and pianist but was too shy to perform in public, so she was a regular attender of concerts and opera throughout Europe. I cannot emphasize enough the value of growing up in the company of such a dynamic and vital person. Sometimes a parent (who is by definition also responsible for discipline!) is not able to be the person to communicate this kind of enthusiasm, but the presence and unqualified support of my grandmother were unquestionably one of the defining characteristics of my childhood. She found a way of gently introducing me to aspects of culture that she sensed I might be susceptible to and allowed me to develop my own interests and passions.

I realize that being an only child of an only child meant that I was lucky enough to attract and enjoy an inordinate amount of love, time, and resources from those closest to me. During this time, I was not able to witness the process of my grandmother writing as she did that privately and very professionally. But what I did gradually begin to understand was her enthusiasm and her natural instinct for other people's lives, her initial shyness with strangers, and her phenomenal gift for friendship that so quickly established itself. She was a normal and loving grandmother who loved food and sharing it through entertaining and conversation. Although she did not drink alcohol or smoke herself, she did not mind it when others did and sitting around a table she was always absorbed by the discussions of any nature around her. Perhaps it is only now when the sheer scale of her letter writing has become clear to me with more and more of her correspondence emerging from a number of quarters that I realize the scale of her commitment to friends and family. I have always said she was the best listener I have ever known and there was never a period of her life when she did not write from wherever she was in the world to let her family know she was thinking of them, wrapped up in humorous anecdotes and observations.

When I began to develop my own friendships, she generously included my friends in our frequent trips to concerts or opera. When I traveled by car across Europe with a couple of college friends, we were lucky enough to join Nima and Max at the Salzburg Festival in July 1963. Although we were holed up in the local campsite, Nima remained unfazed by our rather chaotic appearance and timetable. Sitting with her in a concert or opera halls such as this, I felt her total absorption in the live performance experience. Without her, I know that this introduction would not have been available to me and music would not occupy the importance it does for me to this day. For young college students discussing experiences of this nature with an elderly writer of a certain sort of fiction, it would be easy to understand that they might harbor slightly prejudged impressions of how the conversation might go. Nima was patient in her listening, and, as she unraveled her invited thoughts and observations, she often quietly challenged and provoked their expectations.

After I left university and had worked for Allen Lane at Penguin, it was a natural step that a member of the family would begin to work with the business side of her literary work. Nima, who had maintained a deep work ethic throughout her working life, had begun to slow down when the physical effort of writing books increased, especially in her 70s. I observed her keen sense of duty to provide what had become known as a "Christie for Christmas" which was eagerly anticipated by her readers. I have always believed that the first and most important aspect about her work was that it was written to entertain. For a very shy person she was actually conscious of her ability to provide entertainment and this continuing desire, combined with her undaunted determination to always challenge herself, helped to overcome many of the difficulties of age.

Naturally, being such a close-knit family, who gradually became involved in Nima's working life, there were sometimes tensions, particularly as Nima got older and my mother was keen for her to slow down. Perhaps the best illustration I can give of this is to expand on her lifelong and genuine love of theater and how despite numerous setbacks with her own plays she had an extraordinary ability to occasionally ride the rough with the smooth. I saw all her plays with her, and witnessed her undying enthusiasm for the theater, and her fascination with the challenge of adapting whodunits to deceive a live audience without the protection of a book cover. I witnessed her modesty, her excitement when things went right, and her patience and short-lived disappointment if she experienced a rare failure (which *Verdict* was to start with). I also witnessed her frustration with other family members who tried to persuade her to give up writing plays!

Since the death of my mother in 2004, I have become involved in conserving some of the material she retained from some of the working aspects of Nima's life. When I look at her notebooks and manuscripts, carefully filed, I am conscious that this was not how they looked when Nima created them. She often said herself she was messy and disorganized and to see elements of her working life carefully preserved must inevitably remove some of her own impulsiveness from them. Friends who knew her well often observed how she would suddenly whip a notebook out of a capacious handbag when she was desperate to capture a thought. Certainly, the notebooks are disparate and chaotic with fragments of life squashed alongside excitements of budding plots she never had any difficulty conjuring up.

Perhaps one of the biggest surprises has been to find some negatives of photographs she had taken as early as 1922 when she traveled around the world with her first husband, Archie, or of their beloved dog, Joey, sat in my mother's pram where her indefatigable sense of fun and humor shine through. Thanks to digital processes, and the format of the negatives themselves, it has been possible to unlock a great deal of the saturated detail of the subjects she captured. Photography had been another enduring interest in her life, and she often developed and printed relatively small prints herself. It has been a strange experience to be able to appreciate them more clearly and to get a greater sense of the atmosphere of the time in which they were taken than perhaps she was able to do herself.

So, I know there are still things to find out about her life and work. I hope that my wholly partial glimpse of her helps to demonstrate how I believe that in the same way as there is a great author there is a great grandmother, and to me Nima was both. She once said, "Family? Family life is the best life there is, much more fun than any other kind of life. The more maddening one's family is, the more one seems to like them." My favorite memories of her as a small boy to the ones I have of the strangely restful two days I spent with Max after her death (with Nima in an open coffin next door) are the family ones and I remain immensely grateful for the private time I had with her.

It is perhaps unorthodox to have a family member contribute to a critical survey of this nature. If you are coming to Agatha Christie for the first time, I hope I have transmitted aspects of her nature that are helpful to your line of inquiry and inform your further debate. When I consider what she achieved in her lifetime I sometimes find it hard to believe there was time for the family life we had and yet there was. They were entwined and enriched each other and perhaps help explain the fascination that her work and life story inspire. I know it because I feel it embedded in her books and on the look on the faces of her readers I meet. I have always been an admirer of enthusiasm, and I think Nima had it in abundance, and somehow it is always visible to her audience.

REFERENCES

Christie, A. (1977), *An Autobiography*, London: Collins.

PART TWO

Critical Approaches

CHAPTER TWO

The Middlebrow Woman Detective Author

REBECCA MILLS

INTRODUCTION

A short story by prolific English author W. Somerset Maugham (1874–1965), "The Creative Impulse," hinges on the decision of a distinguished lady author known for "an imagination so delicate and a style so exquisite" ([1926] 2009: 122) to turn her attention to writing "a good thrilling detective story" when her husband, a currant merchant and an avid but secret fan of the genre, leaves her for their cook. It is, in fact, the cook who suggests Mrs. Albert Forrester's career shift from "slender volumes" (121) of Latin-titled verse and prose aimed at "serious students of literature" (121); she demands: "Give me a lady in evening dress, just streaming with diamonds, lying on the library floor with a dagger in her heart" (147). While Mrs. Albert Forrester is at first indignant at the thought of lowering her sights to genre fiction—"I could never hope to please the masses" (147)—she reassures herself that Edgar Allan Poe, who influenced "the Symbolists" and "Baudelaire and all that" (149), had written detective stories, and decides to elevate the genre: "I am going to raise the detective story to the dignity of Art" (150).

Her debut detective novel, *The Achilles Statue*, follows, resulting in far more commercial success than her critically acclaimed poems and essays combined. As Albert Forrester tells his wife, "If you can give the masses a good thrilling story and let them think at the same time that they are improving their minds you'll make a fortune" (147). Concomitantly, he notes, "Give the highbrow the chance of being lowbrow without demeaning himself and he'll be so grateful to you, he won't know what to do" (147). In Maugham's story, then, detective fiction begins below stairs and behind closed doors—in the province of the cooks and guilty nocturnal reading for pleasure—and ends out in the open, between classes and brows, with a reminder of the genre's highly regarded progenitor Edgar Allan Poe and his influence on avant-garde writing. The liminality, popularity, and mobility of the genre described here are reflected in the varying positions and perceptions of middlebrow Golden Age detective fiction texts and authors, and particularly in Agatha Christie and her work.

"The Creative Impulse" was first published in *Harper's Bazaar* in August 1926, three months after Agatha Christie's *The Murder of Roger Ackroyd* came out. It is not inconceivable that "Achilles" alludes to "Hercule"; indeed, both Mrs. Albert Forrester's title *The Achilles Statue* and the name of Christie's detective suggest that detective fiction, though written for the masses, could employ classical allusion effectively. Albert Forrester's recommendation that his wife "play fair" (147) with the reader reflects a shared understanding among readers, writers, and critics of the emerging rules of the "clue puzzle" fiction— rules which Christie, as a member of the Detection Club, helped to codify but also happily parodied, broke, and subverted. Maugham's narrator's sardonic commentary on the fame and fortune found by a lady detective author as opposed to the small income and niche prestige of the highbrow author could be inspired by the commercial success of Christie and her peers in the 1920s— success which was regarded dubiously by highbrow modernist authors such as Virginia Woolf who famously commented:

> The middlebrow is the man, or woman, of middlebred intelligence who ambles and saunters now on this side of the hedge, now on that, in pursuit of no single object, neither art itself or life itself, but both mixed indistinguishably, and rather nastily, with money, fame, power, or prestige.
>
> ([1930] 1942: 115)

Woolf's comment here is often used by scholars such as Nicola Humble and J.C. Bernthal as an example of dismissive attitudes toward the "middlebrow" by modernist authors and critics—attitudes which were maintained long into the twentieth century and hindered the scholarship of this mode, as well as hindering recognition of its artistic value and significance as social commentary. The dismissal of the middlebrow in literary scholarship overlapped with the exclusion of many women writers by critics of 1920s and 1930s literature, as Humble observes in her influential *The Feminine Middlebrow Novel, 1920s to 1950s: Class, Domesticity, and Bohemianism*, going on to point out that

Convenient literary fictions like "Modernism", the "Auden generation", "the angry young men" leave little space for writers like Rosamund Lehmann, Rose Macaulay, Elizabeth Bowen and Elizabeth Taylor, and none at all for their more frivolous contemporaries such as Stella Gibbons, Dodie Smith, and Nancy Mitford. Yet these are the writers the majority of people read.

(2001: 2)

Humble is a scholar of middlebrow writing and readers; her work has extensively influenced interwar detective fiction and Christie criticism; considering the Golden Age women writers as middlebrow offered a way out of the dead-end of the critical perception of the formulaic "clue-puzzle" of minimal creative merit or social and political engagement. Middlebrow scholars, and critics who employ this scholarship to examine gender, class, politics, sexuality, and national identity in Agatha Christie's writing are to some extent engaged in a project of recovery. Maugham's story, then, offers a microcosm of the tension between serious literature and detective fiction that resonates throughout criticism of Christie's work, and suggests that detective fiction exists within a productive liminal space between *salon* and servants' hall where this tension can be not only resolved but also generate a creative impulse as well as a response to financial necessity.

Maugham's treatment of detective fiction as a mobile and liminal genre with a readership that crosses genders and classes is echoed in scholarship of detective fiction texts, authors, and readers; as Humble remarks, "the middlebrow is never a fixed category: [...] texts move in and out of its bounds according to who was perceived to be reading them" (2012: 92). While she goes on to remark that an association with women and middle-class readers, particularly between the wars in England, tends to encourage the situation of texts within this category, she notes that detective fiction, however, was "ranked high as it was the preferred leisure reading of men, particularly intellectual ones" (2001: 13). The genre, then, potentially transcends both gender and class demographics, as suggested by Maugham's story, as well as reaching across "brows."

The "middlebrow" has no single or comprehensive definition or canon, or indeed stable readership; it comprises multiple genres and reading communities. At its most basic, the term refers to a midway point between the lowbrow and the highbrow, supporting the scaffolding of a hierarchy of perceived cultural and artistic value. Humble comments on the problems of the term as follows:

Defining the parameters of the fictional middlebrow is clearly problematic. The broad working definition I employ throughout this book is that the middlebrow novel is one that straddles the divide between the trashy romance or thriller on the one hand, and the philosophically or formally challenging novel on the other: offering narrative excitement without guilt, and intellectual stimulation without undue effort.

(2001: 11)

Focusing on a slightly different time period, Kate MacDonald and Christoph Singer, in the introduction to their essay collection *Transitions in Middlebrow Writing 1880–1930,* locate the beginnings of the British middlebrow when "in the early years of the twentieth century the increase in modernist and avant-garde writing displaced realism in literature from its previous position, in Bourdieu's sense, as the only 'legitimate' form of culture" (Macdonald and Singer 2015: 2). Macdonald and Singer go on to characterize the formation of the brows as follows:

It began to be noticed that cultural production was no longer a dyad (solid, worthy, respectable; versus low, sensational, disposable) but tripartite. In the literary domain, "lowbrow" had the clearest lineage: emerging from serialized sensation fiction and the penny dreadful periodicals of the nineteenth century, [...] "Highbrow" meant texts that required intellectual effort, challenged established mores and ideals, and demanded close attention. "Highbrow" authors modified existing forms in pursuit of a new expression, and appeared in design-led media that paid little attention to commercial survival, being focused on aesthetic or radical projects. The third member of this grouping, "middlebrow", did not emerge from nowhere, but was also not simply a downgraded version of the classical realist Victorian novel. Middlebrow fiction was driven first by the economics of a new readership rather than a literary impulse, emerging as established ways of selling stories changed from hefty and high-priced three-volume books, to the cheap edition and the multiple edition sold at different prices for a range of readers.

(3)

Humble's "broad working definition" and MacDonald's and Singer's summary are worth quoting at length in order to draw attention to key points relevant to this chapter: the liminal space of the middlebrow, the commercial imperative of middlebrow fiction, the significance of consumption patterns and reading habits of the period, the perceived distinction between the intellectual nature of the highbrow and the entertainment value of the lowbrow—which is viewed in different ways by different Christie scholars, as discussed later—and the crucial observance that not all fictional detective narratives are regarded as middlebrow. Indeed, the "lowbrow" mode of "trashy" lurid and sensational thrillers remained popular on both sides of the Atlantic throughout the twentieth century, in different formats.

CHRISTIE AMONG THE MIDDLEBROW SCHOLARS

The terms "popular" and "middlebrow" are considered by some scholars to be overlapping, if not identical, categories—the "middlebrow" inherently suggests a broad appeal, or popularity, as opposed to the selective appeal of the highbrow. In "The Reader of Popular Fiction," cited above, for instance, Humble includes middlebrow reading communities and the wide dissemination of middlebrow fiction via lending libraries and book clubs—and a brief note on Christie's *The Hollow* (1946)—in her discussion of popular fiction readers (2012). Similarly, Clive Bloom includes Agatha Christie, as a wildly and enduringly popular writer, in his monograph *Bestsellers: Popular Fiction Since 1900* (2008), taking the term "popular" to mean quantifiable commercial success while suggesting that this success challenges the qualitative hierarchies and authorial intentions. Bloom notes: "At the end of the twentieth century the two leading popular genres were the same as at its beginning and still commanded the greatest sales: detective fiction and women's romance" (2008: 36), commenting later that "[m]uch emphasis has been placed on the serious intellectual study of the novels of Agatha Christie which conveniently combine the best features of the middlebrow romance (with its emphasis on economic home-making) and the puzzle mystery" (2008: 377*n.*); he refers to this combination as "genius" (191). Bloom's emphasis is on analyzing the features and consumers of commercially appealing work, so it would follow that his use of the term "genius" here suggests Christie's capacity for creating bestsellers by catering to her audience.

While Bloom and Humble seem to take the middlebrow nature of Golden Age detective fiction and Christie's work for granted, the very popularity of the genre causes Melissa Schaub to briefly question this conflation of mode and genre:

> Whether detective fiction should be included in the category of middlebrow is slightly less clear. Detective fiction was certainly popular and bestselling, and it is entirely possible that for this reason [Virginia] Woolf [...] would have happily discussed them over tea with her imaginary lowbrow friend.
>
> (2013: 13)

Schaub goes on to solidify the position of detective fiction among the middlebrows, however, noting, "But while the brow level of Christie, Sayers, and Heyer is debatable, they certainly did not '[make] of style a fetish', and the middlebrow is the best available context in which to set their class and gender politics" (13). Other critics, however, incorporate Christie's style and narrative strategies *within* their classification of her work as middlebrow and discussion of gender; Kathy Mezei, for instance, opens "Spinsters, Surveillance, and Speech: The Case of Miss Marple, Miss Mole, and Miss Jekyll" as follows:

Agatha Christie's *The Murder at the Vicarage* (1930), E.H. Young's *Miss Mole* (1930), and Ivy Compton-Burnett's *A House and Its Head* (1935) are inter-war, middlebrow, domestic and detective novels characterized by narrative ambiguity and illusion. In contrast to the more radical and overt modernist experiments of Katherine Mansfield, Virginia Woolf, and Dorothy Richardson, these three novels covertly query power and gender relations while simultaneously upholding the status quo.

(2007: 104)

Here, the middlebrow is in direct contrast to the modernist, but still afforded a political point of view and sense of narrative complexity. As will be discussed later, other scholars inch Christie's narrative style toward modernism. Although Bloom notes the "serious study" of detective fiction (as indeed he should, as editor of Palgrave MacMillan's *Crime Files* series!), and agrees with Humble that "detective fiction has always had cachet" (2012: 37),[1] the serious study of Christie's work as literature rather than genre fiction was rare *before* her writing was considered *as* middlebrow by Humble and Alison Light. Examining the middlebrow, then, has afforded scholars a liberating vantage point for exploring thematic concerns beyond identifying structural elements and evaluating the mechanics of the genre itself.

Virginia Woolf's view of middlebrow text as being neither one thing nor the other, a negative space of absence and uncertainty rather than rich ambiguity, with a passive pedestrian audience limited in cultural taste and intellectual inquiry, if not numbers, was not the only perspective on the middlebrow at the time, but its general sense, coupled with the association of interwar middlebrow women authors with a conservative middle class and feminine readership, has cast a long shadow. Rather than absence and uncertainty, however, it is precisely a rich and complex ambiguity that Light assigns to the middlebrow: "If Agatha Christie is to be understood not as the doyenne of country house fiction but as queen of the 'middlebrows', then we need to remind ourselves just how modern a conservative creature the middlebrow was" (75). Light goes on to examine the domestic settings and communities of Christie's novels, proposing that it is

[m]isleading, then, to take the fiction at face value, and imagine that Agatha Christie never addresses any sense of social disturbance: on one level her writing speaks to nothing else. Far from suggesting a world in which every person knows their place, and in which values are firm and fixed, the fiction explores the difficulty of social belonging in a modern world in which the very idea of social status has something theatrical and impermanent about it.

---

[1]Clive Bloom is the editor of academic publisher Palgrave Macmillan's *Crime Files* series.

[This leads to] the unsettling implication that "it is the middle classes who are the murdering classes", and their victims are their own selves.

(97)

Light's identification of Christie's challenges to fixed values, coherent subjectivity, and the sense of belonging in the modern world, as well as the English class has inspired her successors to examine gender, sexuality, and politics within middlebrow Christie.

In *Middlebrow Feminism in Classic British Detective Fiction: The Female Gentleman* (2013), Schaub explicitly relates the middlebrow to the heroines of Christie, Sayers, Marsh, Heyer, and other interwar women detective writers who behave in a "gentlemanly" fashion—"cool, restrained, and ironic" (56), and functioning as comrades rather than conquests to the men in the stories, even if these men are romantic interests. Building on Humble's discussion of men "damaged" by the war, and the concomitant role reversals (2001: 197; in Schaub 2013: 61), Schaub observes that "the middlebrow female characters of these interwar years display the same courage and honor that the men do, since a man cannot relate to a woman as a comrade or equal without speaking the same language and sharing the same basic assumptions" (61). Schaub's main example of this dynamic from Christie's oeuvre is Tuppence, whom she describes as "insouciant and 'not sentimental,' and her 'gamin element' [*sic*] gives her an affinity for young boys, whom she is clearly meant to resemble" (76). Tuppence "insists on taking the 'joint' nature of [her and Tommy's] venture seriously" (76), and eventually persuades him to do so as well (76). The transgression—or transfer—of gender roles embodied by the "female gentleman" recalls Light's comment about Christie's sense of "social disturbance" (97) but, as Schaub reflects, the term "gentleman" has class connotations that to some extent uphold the charges of snobbery and conservative worldview often aimed at the authors she discusses. Nevertheless, she concludes that as well as affording these women professional lives and equality with the men in the stories, "The word 'gentleman' carried connotations in 1930 that made it useful to appropriate for the defense of individuality from fascism; middlebrow writers were able to use the influence of past values to authorize their modern concepts of human equality" (136).

Megan Hoffman also applies Light's and Humble's articulation of middlebrow social commentary to a variety of detective fiction authors, including Christie, in *Gender and Representation in the Gender and Representation in British "Golden Age" Crime Fiction* (2016). The middlebrow context is particularly relevant in her discussion of the "companionate marriage," which runs along somewhat similar lines to Schaub's conceptualization of the "female gentleman" as a step toward equality between the sexes. Noting that Humble "points out that ambivalence about what constitutes an ideal romantic relationship was not uncommon in women's middlebrow fiction of the period" (in Hoffman 2016: 75), Hoffman positions the drive toward equal romantic partnerships in interwar detective novels as a counter to contemporary psychological discourses regarding gender roles; psychologists Havelock Ellis (1913) and Wilhelm Stekel (1926), for instance, argued that "unequal power relations in relationships were natural," and indeed desired by the woman (Hoffman 2016: 76). Hoffman claims Christie's Tommy and Tuppence as a key example of the companionate marriage, noting that although their narrative pauses while Tuppence is a mother, they reenter detection together: "Neither is ever the sole detective figure; their partnership in both life and detection stands as the most ideally equal among golden age detective couples" (105). Interrogating domesticity and gender roles is a crucial concern of middlebrow literature, as Humble has demonstrated; applying this lens to Golden Age detective fiction has enabled both Schaub and Hoffman to find and develop fruitful case studies of modern and nuanced romantic relationships and gender roles in a genre and period often considered to lack both; as Knight observes, "Contemporary commentators were largely against romance in the clue-puzzle, some implying it is hostile to the rational tone, others pointing out that this feature tends to remove people from the suspect list" (2003: 79).

Schaub and Hoffman employ the middlebrow to examine heterosexual relationships and challenges to binary gender roles in detective fiction; scholars including Charlotte Charteris, Christopher Yiannitsaros, and J.C. Bernthal invoke the middlebrow in investigating queer characters and spaces in Christie's detective fiction. Humble's emphasis on the role of the home in the middlebrow (2001: 108–49) and Light's observation of "a modern sense of the unstable limits of respectability [...] portrays a society of strangers whose social exchanges have become theatrical and dissevered from a sense of place" (1991: 61–2) in Christie's work have led Charteris to reevaluate the country house, usually considered to be merely setting or symbol of snobbishness. Discussing *The Mysterious Affair at Styles*, *The Secret of Chimneys*, and *Peril at End House*, in "A Strange Night in a Strange House: The Country House as Queer Space in Interwar Mystery Fiction," Charteris challenges scholarly associations of "the rise of the country-house mystery to reactionary nostalgia and middlebrow sentimentality" (2017: 92), drawing on Humble's articulation of the "ambivalent space" of the middlebrow home (Humble 2001: 63) to propose that as a result of the First World War, in which a number of direct male heirs to properties were killed, "[t]he encroachment of strangeness into the formerly closed, domestic space of the country house radically reconfigures it as a queer space in narrative terms" (Charteris 2017: 95). In his PhD thesis *Deadly Domesticity: Agatha Christie's "Middlebrow" Gothic, 1930–1970* (2016) Yiannitsaros similarly reevaluates the home (in terms of buildings but also communities) in Christie's work, not merely applying a middlebrow lens but helping to articulate the category of the "middlebrow Gothic" as a literary category and critical field of enquiry. Yiannitsaros identifies the following types of Gothic: "the haunted house narrative, the Gothic village, Gay Gothic, Post-World War II Gothic, and Brontë Gothic," and seeks to "problematise Alison Light's famous characterization of Christie as a 'modernist [...] iconoclast' whose fiction nonchalantly shatters 'Victorian images of home, sweet home'" by examining Christie's textual relationship with nineteenth-century literary culture (6). The intertextuality of the middlebrow, then, is key to Yiannitsaros's reading, while he continues the project of reevaluating settings often taken for granted or regarded as clichéd in Christie's work that has dominated the 2010s; his chapter on the village, for example, examines the sinister side of surveillance in Miss Marple novels *Murder at the Vicarage* (1930) and *The Moving Finger* (1943), while he echoes Charteris's interest in queering the countryside in his chapter "'There will be gay doings in the Witches' Meadow tonight': Homosexuality, Monstrosity and the Sexual Geography of Murder is Easy."

J.C. Bernthal's *Queering Agatha Christie: Revisiting the Golden Age of Detective Fiction* (2016) is also a significant part of the current "re-evaluation" generation of scholars. Bernthal contributes a methodology for including a queer perspective within middlebrow studies, employing Humble's "theorization of detective fiction as something to be read, not merely 'in terms of the history of the genre,' but also as part of a 'middlebrow' twentieth-century movement, 'established through a complex interplay between texts and self-images of their readers'" (in Bernthal 2016: 14). This articulation of the middlebrow allows Bernthal to argue that "There is queer potential in these texts, as questions are raised about the ways in which normality, deviance and essential identity are perceived at the time Christie was writing" (2016: 14). Rather than identifying Christie's characters or their relationships as lesbian or homosexual, then, Bernthal's focus is on the interplay, perception, and production of identities—not merely among characters in Christie's fiction, but in terms of Christie's authorial persona and adaptations of her work as well.

CREATING AND CONSUMING MIDDLEBROW DETECTIVE FICTION

While the term "middlebrow" was not widely available in 1926, what Maugham's Mrs. Albert Forrester proposes is essentially middlebrow detective fiction, texts that offered the escapism of lurid and sensational crime stories, lucid but not simplistic language, and intellectual engagement. For some readers, however, even middlebrow detective fiction remained a guilty pleasure: "The same people who spent their days with Joyce were reading Agatha Christie at night" (Holquist 1983: 164). Indeed, some *writers* of detective fiction felt ambivalent, even guilty, about their own work; as Victoria Stewart points out in "Defining Detective Fiction in Interwar Britain," the porousness between the highbrow and the middlebrow could lead to unease. Anglo-Irish poet (and Poet Laureate 1968–72) C. Day Lewis (1904–72) displays a "strand of mild self-hatred" regarding the detective fiction he produced under the pseudonym Nicholas Blake; she quotes a letter from Day-Lewis to modernist poet Stephen Spender: "I've been trying to write commercial prose [...] I am horrified but secretly fascinated at the ease with which I can write good, window-box, bloody awful entertainment stuff" (in Stewart 2013: 109). This attitude echoes Woolf's contempt for "good" fiction with commercial appeal (as opposed to her enjoyment of straightforwardly lowbrow commercial fiction), but it was by no means shared by all modernist writers or detective fiction writers. Stewart contextualizes her discussion of how Day-Lewis/Blake and Dorothy L. Sayers (1893–1957) "show how anxieties—and indeed certainties—about the boundaries and continuities between the modernist and the middlebrow were worked through within detective novels themselves" (104) within a period and community of critics and authors who also blurred the boundaries of the brows, with a sense of curiosity if not appreciation: T.S. Eliot wrote on "Wilkie Collins and Dickens" (1927), Sayers herself wrote on "Aristotle on Detective Fiction" (1935) and set *Gaudy Night* in an Oxford College (1935), and Blake himself inflected his crime novels with "literary allusions of a more or less obscure kind, with Jacobean tragedy featuring in *Thou Shell of Death* (1936) and a surrealist poet making an appearance in *There's Trouble Brewing* (1937)" (113).[2] Stewart's examples, then, serve to reinforce Humble's argument that the middlebrow is an "essentially parasitic form, dependent on the existence of both a high and a low brow for its identity, reworking their structures and aping their insights" (2001: 12).

Like Sayers and Blake, Christie also inflected her work with literary and cultural references, but she offers a wider range than these novelists, from across brows and genres—including but not limited to children's nursery rhymes, Shakespeare's plays, Milton's epic poem *Paradise Lost* (1667), the Bible, Gothic tropes, and texts from her fellow middlebrow and detective fiction authors. This is in line with Humble's articulation of the feminine middlebrow:

> There is a determined intertextuality about this literature: novels continually refer to other novels, with the effect that an intricate network of connections is built up between texts. This has a number of consequences [...] the reader is introduced to other books that promise similar pleasures to that she is

---

[2]Outside Stewart's interwar period, W. H. Auden continued the trend of modernist poet ambivalent interest in detective fiction in his essay "The Guilty Vicarage: Notes on the Detective Story, by an Addict" (1948).

currently enjoying; it also allows the feminine middlebrow to establish its conventions, and direct the reader's expectations.

(2001: 47)

Managing the reader's expectations is, of course, a key feature of detective fiction. Middlebrow intertextuality in Christie's work offers clues to mysteries of crime and character; a crucial clue in the Miss Marple short story "The Affair at the Bungalow" ([1932] 1997: 201) lies in a reference to Maugham's play *Smith* (1909), suggesting not only mutual familiarity between the authors but also a shared audience—at the time, if not in the twenty-first century. In the Poirot novel *Murder in Mesopotamia* ([1936] 2016), narrator Nurse Leatheran reflects that she had considered a suspect to be "rather more like a P.G. Wodehouse book than like a real live young man" (129). In her chapter "Christie and Conservative Modernity," Alison Light proposes that "Christie is here as clearly 'post-realist' as any other modernist, deliberately playing with the assumptions of an earlier literary form, and working in pastiche" (1991: 96); the border between the modernist and the middlebrow is porous. Other textual clues to character in *Murder in Mesopotamia*, however, reinforce the essential middlebrow nature of the text; Nurse Leatheran reads *Death in a Nursing Home*, an allusion to Ngaio Marsh's *The Nursing Home Murder* (1935), and comments on its lack of realism. Poirot interprets the reading material of the victim, Mrs. Leidner (one of the few Christie characters based on a real person, further complicating the notion of "realism" here),[3] as clues to her character and thereby her murder:

> In her bedroom I noticed the following books on a shelf: *Who were the Greeks?*, *Introduction to Relativity*, *Life of Lady Hester Stanhope*, *Back to Methuselah*, *Linda Condon*, *Crewe Train*. She had, to begin with, an interest in culture and in modern science—that is, a distinct intellectual side. Of the novels, *Linda Condon*, and in a lesser degree *Crewe Train*, seemed to show that Mrs Leidner had a sympathy and interest in the independent woman— unencumbered or entrapped by man.

(241–2)

These books are evidence that Mrs. Leidner had been more than "a woman whose main preoccupation was to attract the opposite sex" (241); indeed, Humble describes Rose Macaulay's *Crewe Train* (1926) as "concerned to challenge, or at least to ironize, the growing assumption that middle-class women should find the meaning of their existence in actively caring for

---

[3]The description of Katharine Woolley in Christie's *Autobiography* has a number of parallels to that of Mrs. Leidner in the novel.

their home" (2001: 128). The novel has further resonance with *Murder in Mesopotamia*; the main character Denham's mother-in-law is herself an adventurous woman who travels to archaeological digs, but, despite her modernity, ultimately helps to trap Denham within the role of "cultured, domestically responsible Victorian wife" (Humble 2001: 129). Christie's novel is set on an archaeological expedition, dedicated to excavating a past civilization; Mrs. Leidner dies at the hand of her own husband as a consequence of wanting to leave her stifling marriage.

Not only did Christie frequently invoke Sherlock Holmes, only to challenge the narrative conventions established in Arthur Conan Doyle's stories, but she also wrote an entire series of stories featuring Tommy and Tuppence in the styles of her predecessors and contemporaries in the genre. As Merja Makinen observes, Christie's pastiches in *Partners in Crime* (1929)

> highlight the lack of feminine models generically within classic detective fiction. [...] Tuppence's gender blindness in adopting detective personalities highlights the absence of female fictional detectives. Also, in ignoring gender specificity, Tuppence's deployment points to a destabilising, subversive potential, offering alternative models of female subjectivity.
>
> (Makinen 2006: 34)

Christie's creative impulse tends toward "reworking," then, rather than merely imitating the lowbrow and the highbrow; the broad spectrum of influences and intertextual references within her work serve to enhance and enrich her thematic concerns, rather than attempt to disguise her commercial appeal, as in Blake's novels, for instance.

If Macaulay, Wodehouse, and Maugham are invoked to provide clues to direct the reader's attention, intertextuality is also employed in the service of misdirection. In *Hallowe'en Party* (1969), for instance, the reader may be so distracted by the comic gothic horror tropes of children's parlor games and superstitious rituals that they miss the clues that point to the real evil in the village—beautiful young man Michael Garfield's creation of a sunken garden, an Eden for fallen angels. At their last encounter, Poirot realizes that he is a murderer, but more by instinct for the way Garfield fits into one of the most ancient narratives in the Christian tradition than rational deduction:

> How did you come to suspect Michael Garfield?
> "He fitted," said Poirot simply. "And then—the last time I spoke to Michael Garfield, I was sure. He said to me, laughing—'Get thee beyond me, Satan. Go and join your police friends.' And I knew then, quite certainly. It was the other way round. I said to myself: 'I am leaving you behind me, Satan.'"

"A Satan so young and beautiful as Lucifer can appear to mortals ... "

([1969] 2010: 228, ellipsis original)

Christie refers to Jesus Christ's response to the temptations of the devil here: "And Jesus answered and said unto him, Get thee behind me, Satan: for it is written, Thou shalt worship the Lord thy God, and him only shalt thou serve" (*KJV*, Luke 4:8). But the notion of Lucifer/Satan as beautiful is also drawn from Milton's *Paradise Lost* (and was previously invoked by Christie in *They Came to Baghdad* (1951)). Not for nothing is Garfield's accomplice Rowena Drake, with Drake being an old word for "serpent." In this novel, then, a familiarity with Christian tradition and the Bible may have yielded clues for highbrow or devout readers, but excluded others—Hercule Poirot then becomes an interpreter and mediator not only of plot and motive, but also foundational myth. It is, perhaps, no coincidence that Ariadne Oliver, a detective author created by Christie, appears in this novel; in Greek myth, Ariadne helped Theseus find his way out of a labyrinth.

In other Christie novels, the detection obscures the precursor. One might read *The Murder of Roger Ackroyd* (1926) multiple times before noticing that the country house family relationship dynamics and class and power structures echo Jane Austen's *Emma*; the narrative trickery and breaking of detective conventions blind the reader to the parallel between Emma's flirtation with Frank Churchill even as he is secretly engaged to well-born, but poor, Jane Fairfax, and Ralph Paton's engagement to his cousin Flora while secretly married to parlor-maid/girl of good family in reduced circumstances Ursula Bourne. What Frank and Ralph possess in charm they lack in backbone; both Emma and Flora end up marrying much older men who offer security. These parallels anchor Christie's work within the tradition of the English country house and village novel. George Grella, for instance, has argued that "[t]his posh and pedigreed society, remote from criminal reality, often irritates detective novel readers, but it offers social forms for the novelist of manners and, within those forms, the observable clues to human behavior by which the detective hero can identify the culprit" (1970: 39), while Raymond Williams has suggested that "the true fate of the country-house novel was its evolution into the middle-class detective story" ([1973] 1975: 249). As well as adding an element of the satirical comedy of manners—and a subversion of the country house tradition, as demonstrated by more recent scholars Bernthal, Charteris, and Light—Christie's echoes of Austen can also be read as a sly comment on canonicity itself; during her lifetime, and for long afterward, Austen's work was dismissed by students of serious literature as light romance.

Significantly, although comparisons with Austen have been invoked elsewhere in studies of Christie's work, commentary on the specific influence of *Emma* on *The Murder of Roger Ackroyd* is easier to find in blogs and reader forums than in academic journal articles. "Griselda" notes the connection between Jane Fairfax and Ursula Bourne in a comment on an Agatha Christie community discussion board (June 2016), for instance, while Diane Reynolds's Jane Austen blog not only comments on these character parallels (which she finds almost "too obvious to state") but also suggests that "a more important parallel emerges from the way both writers tell a story through conscious omission, misdirection, euphemism, and understatement as well as the use of the throwaway comment" (2017). Maugham's sense of the middlebrow readership as broad, intelligent, and active demonstrated in Albert Forrester's and Mrs. Bulfinch's shared awareness of detective fiction conventions and plot suggestions, and the middlebrow author as creative and versatile, then, resonates with contemporary scholarship on both middlebrow texts and readers of popular fiction, as well as today's active online reading communities. As Humble observes, for instance, although "popular reading is repeatedly rendered through tropes of danger, passivity and lack of control," a closer investigation demonstrates "a more subtle, nuanced, critical engagement with texts" (2012: 86).

Maugham's story gestures toward the tropes of "trashy" escapist fiction, associating it with appetite of "the masses" for consuming sensation via unrealistic scenarios. When Mrs. Bulfinch the cook exclaims, "Give me a lady in evening dress, just streaming with diamonds, lying on the library floor with a dagger in her heart, and I know I'm going to have a treat" (147), the word "treat" here reinforcing the idea of consumption. Christie herself frequently playfully invokes a lowbrow mode of thrilling crime stories, particularly in what she called "the light-hearted thriller type" ([1977] 2010: 413). In *The Man in the Brown Suit*, for instance, heroine Anne Beddingfield enjoys "The Perils of Pamela," an episodic adventure film series in which Pamela and the hero have wild adventures and foil the elaborate plans of the "Master Criminal of the Underworld" ([1924] 2017: 12). In a nod to the bodily and imaginative effects of sensation fiction, Anne would leave the cinema "in a delirious whirl" (13). Eventually she is caught up in her own adventure and passionate romance, but Christie does not simply replicate the pulp fiction mode. Rather, as Bernthal observes, a more formally sophisticated approach is evident:

> Since Anne develops her identity as a woman through engagement with popular culture alone, she runs into contradictions and has to confront inadequate binaries. *Brown* is not a radical piece of feminine writing, but it draws attention towards popular texts' limited gendered paradigms, decoding a popular form and indicating a need for innovation through parody and some commentary.
>
> (2016: 47)

Similarly, in a 1942 Miss Marple novel, Christie provides her public a young woman's body in a library, making her engagement with the "lowbrow" even more explicit. In her "Foreword" to *The Body in the Library*, she writes:

There are certain clichés belonging to certain types of fiction. The "bold bad baronet" for melodrama, the "body in the library" for the detective story. For several years I treasured up the possibility of a suitable "Variation on a well-known Theme". I laid down for myself certain conditions. The library in question must be a highly orthodox and conventional library. The body, on the other hand, must be a wildly improbable and highly sensational body.

(n.p.)

As Bernthal points out, this cliché is also mentioned by Christie's contemporary and acquaintance, and fellow middlebrow detective author, Dorothy L. Sayers, in *Strong Poison* ([1929]2012: 58), furthering the sense of a collective imaginary of detective tropes during this period, which did (and still does) lead some critics to accuse the interwar detective writers of producing formulaic rather than innovative texts. Christie, however, elevates the cliché to the "dignity of Art" à la Mrs Albert Forester in her reworking of this trope. The body in her library is "[t]he flamboyant figure of a girl. A girl with unnaturally fair hair dressed up off her face in elaborate curls and rings. Her thin body was dressed in a backless evening-dress of white spangled satin" ([1942] 2010: 12), serving up Mrs. Bulfinch's "treat." Rather than the luxury suggested by the diamonds of the body in the library proposed in Maugham's story, however, the overall effect here is "cheap, tawdry" (12), in contrast to the "solid old-fashioned comfort of Colonel Bantry's library" (12). Here we see, perhaps, a rejection of the lowbrow sensation for the solidity of the middlebrow, with its legacy of Victorian realism. The fact that the body in question turns out to be that of an unfortunate innocent schoolgirl disguised as a parody of a *femme fatale* not only disrupts the reader's assumptions about genre and gender, but perhaps implicitly criticizes those who would view the dead girl as a precursor to a "treat."

Christie's middlebrow reworking of literary and cultural allusions from the classics and the penny dreadful mode is not limited to specific texts. Humble observes—correctly in the case of Agatha Christie at least—that "It is certainly true that the middlebrow fiction of the interwar years is keen to annex aspects of the high cultural—the bohemian, the avant-garde, the experimental—but it does so almost invariably with a tongue-in-cheek knowingness and a clear sense of superiority" (2001: 95). Humble gives *The Hollow* ([1946] 2015) as an example, noting the attitudes of a sociable country house family toward avant-garde sculptor Henrietta Savernake. Indeed, *The Hollow* also serves as an example of the slipperiness of the middlebrow text. While Humble observes a "combination of familiarity with and slight contempt for the effortful intellectual attitudes of the highbrow" (2001: 21), she finds the Angkatell family's respect for Henrietta and her abstract sculptures to be emblematic of a wider middlebrow awareness and appreciation for highbrow creative art, if not intellectual theorizing, a reading with which Stewart agrees (2013: 110). Other scholars, however, have perceived a more conversational, even confrontational, relationship between the brows in Christie's work. Merja Makinen, in "Agatha Christie in Dialogue with *To the Lighthouse*: The Modernist Artist," suggests that *The Hollow* offers a direct challenge to literary hierarchies. Makinen considers *To the Lighthouse* as a precursor (using Harold Bloom's term) to the Mary Westmacott novel *Giant's Bread* (1930), which she views in turn as a preliminary working-through of idea(l)s of artistic creativity and single-minded dedication, which are then developed, via Harold Bloom's theory of "anxiety of influence" in *The Hollow*. Makinen analyzes *The Hollow*, then, as Christie's response to Woolf's depiction of single-minded—and therefore single—avant-garde painter Lily Briscoe:

> In *The Hollow*, Christie takes Woolf's representation of the modern flawed marriage and crafts it into a workable ménage a trois, as a direct resolution to Lily's abstemiousness. While Bloom's theory reveals a tension between the Mary Westmacott persona, experimenting with form in ambitious "middlebrow" literary novels and the popular Christie detective fiction, it also demonstrates that both genres are deemed viable to contradict the modernist vision of Virginia Woolf.
>
> (Makinen 2016: 26)

As well as asserting the value of Christie's work and chosen modes of expression here, Makinen slightly reconfigures Christie's place in terms of the lowbrow-middlebrow-highbrow framework. In contrast to the scholars who define Christie's detective fiction as middlebrow, Makinen juxtaposes the "popular" detective fiction with the "middlebrow" Mary Westmacott novel, thus emphasizing the differentiation of the Christie and Westmacott authorial personas, and antagonism rather than cheerful incorporation toward modernism. Margaret Boe Birns and Nicholas Birns, however, include *The Hollow* in their discussion of modernist features and concerns in Christie's detective fiction, particularly after the Second World War, noting the "hollowness of heart in her characters, a sense of emotional isolation" (127) that exemplify Christie's "fractured yet resonant selves" (134). Both the modernist and the middlebrow, then, are flexible categories that can be used to highlight different aspects of Christie's work, style, and themes.

A DETECTIVE IN SEARCH OF AN AUTHOR

Perhaps Christie's most subversive authorial act is to embody each brow within a writerly persona in her work, coalescing abstract concepts into characters—text made flesh. Stewart suggests (in relation to Blake's and Sayers' author characters):

> To include a character within a detective novel who is an author of detective fiction is a strategy each uses to continue the debate about the nature of the form that is begun in their critical writing. The reader is invited to measure the work s/he is reading against the paradigm presented within the work itself, and, simultaneously, the author displays self-consciousness about the task of writing. (A similar self-consciousness, and the inclusion of a writer or other artist as a protagonist, can also be found in many modernist works, of course.)
> (Stewart 2013: 110)

As the presence of the author figure belongs to both detective fiction and modernism, this is perhaps also Christie's most middlebrow act. Although, like Sayers and Blake, a detective writer appears in some of her novels, Ariadne Oliver is not her only creation. Ariadne Oliver is Christie's most middlebrow literary figure, who bears some resemblances in persona and output to Christie herself. While Bernthal proposes that "The fiercely lowbrow 'Mrs Oliver' begins as a parody of stereotypes surrounding popular women writers and evolves into a strategic self-portrait through which Christie promotes an image of herself as a conventionally feminine professional amateur" (2016: 15), her similarity to the parodic, but self-deprecating, narratives of other middlebrow women writers such as E.M. Delafield in *The Diary of a Provincial Lady* ([1930] 1991) suggests rather that Mrs. Oliver is fiercely middlebrow. As Humble remarks, "when women writers are represented in the feminine middlebrow, they are invariably highly professional, very successful, and extremely modest about their work" (2001: 35).

Salome Otterbourne in *Death on the Nile* ([1937] 2010) is a flamboyant novelist. The blurb on her novel *Under the Fig Tree* "spoke enthusiastically of the superb courage and realism of this study of a modern woman's love life. 'Fearless, unconventional, realistic,' were the adjectives used" (53). Realism is mentioned twice here, perhaps attempting to evoke D.H. Lawrence's scandalous but critically acclaimed *Women in Love* (1920). Nevertheless, the image on the cover shows a woman "in the traditional costume of Eve" (nothing but a fig-leaf?) under "a tree with the leaves of an oak, bearing large and improbably coloured apples" (52). The cover design, then, has no relation to realism—the emphasis is on the female body and sexuality. While at first the reader may take Otterbourne at her own evaluation as a highbrow novelist, it becomes apparent that she in fact fits into the "trashy romance" of the lowbrow. Her daughter later tells Poirot that Otterbourne's books are no longer in demand as "People are tired of all that cheap sex stuff" (58). The lowbrow is associated with ephemerality and cliché; in another instance of Christie seamlessly matching literary allusion with plot point, Salome Otterbourne is also ephemeral, shot by the murderer she is about to expose.

Christie's main modernist/highbrow author, recurring in several Miss Marple stories and novels, is Miss Marple's nephew Raymond West, who "writes these very modern books all about rather unpleasant young men and women" ([1979] 1991: 231). Their relationship is one of mutual fond condescension; West views Miss Marple as "hopelessly Victorian" (231), and is determined to shield her from the seamier side of modern life that he represents in his books; Miss Marple is unflappable, shocking him with her astute insight into human nature and problems. In "Ingots of Gold," for instance, she says, "I do think you ought to be more careful how you choose your friends. You are so credulous, dear, so easily gulled. I suppose it is being a writer and having so much imagination" (46). West's and Miss Marple's conflict is a mini "Battle of the Brows"; their dynamic suggests Humble's remark that "middlebrow fiction laid claim to the highbrow by assuming an easy familiarity with its key texts and attitudes, while simultaneously caricaturing intellectuals as self-indulgent and naïve" (29). Miss Marple's domestic concerns, sensitive understanding of class, and Victorian inheritance of realism lend themselves to the middlebrow; West, despite his insistence on being a highbrow, means well.

BEYOND THE MIDDLEBROW

Humble and Light, then, not only demonstrate the validity and value of the middlebrow—and by extension Christie and her work—as objects of academic enquiry, but also carry out a project of recovery for women writers from the first half of the twentieth century who had been to a great extent understudied and undervalued. Christie's popular success endures, aided via adaptations and the continuing popularity of the detective genre; Humble and Light usefully recover the voices, achievements, and anxieties of Christie's contemporaries that allow her texts to be illuminated from different angles, beyond the study of her chosen genre; this chapter has fleetingly offered an insight into the opportunities afforded by close-reading and contextualization. The middlebrow as a category, however, remains porous. This fluctuation and recategorization does not only depend on contemporary framings of the text by publicists and reviewer and reader responses; in retrospect, authors, particularly women and genre fiction writers between the wars, slip in and out of this midway point, even as their relationship with the modernist avant-garde, and the popular lowbrow, is reevaluated and renegotiated by scholars. This work is by no means finished.

REFERENCES

Austen, J. ([1815] 2014), *Emma*, London: Vintage Books.

Bernthal, J. C. (2016), *Queering Agatha Christie: Revisiting the Golden Age of Detective Fiction*, London: Palgrave Macmillan.

Birns, N. and M. Boe Birns (1990), "Agatha Christie: Modern and Modernist," in R. G. Walker and J. M. Frazer (eds), *The Cunning Craft: Original Essays on Detective Fiction and Contemporary Literary Theory*, 120–34, Macomb: Western Illinois University Press.

Bloom, C. (2008), *Bestsellers: Popular Fiction since 1900*, 2nd ed., Basingstoke: Palgrave Macmillan.

Charteris, C. (2017), "A Strange Night in a Strange House: The Country House as Queer Space in Interwar Mystery Fiction," *Clues: A Journal of Detection*, 35 (2): 89–99.

Christie, A. ([1924] 2017), *The Man in the Brown Suit*, London: HarperCollins.

Christie, A. ([1926] 2007), *The Murder of Roger Ackroyd*, London: HarperCollins. [Kindle Edition]

Christie, A. ([1932] 1997), "The Affair at the Bungalow," *in Miss Marple: The Complete Short Stories*, 188–205, London: HarperCollins.

Christie, A. ([1936] 2016), *Murder in Mesopotamia*, London: HarperCollins. [Kindle Edition]

Christie, A. ([1937] 2010), *Death on the Nile*, London: HarperCollins. [Kindle Edition]

Christie, A. ([1942] 2010), *The Body in the Library*, London: HarperCollins. [Kindle Edition]

Christie, A. ([1946] 2015), *The Hollow*, London: HarperCollins. [Kindle Edition]

Christie, A. ([1969] 2010), *Hallowe'en Party*, London: HarperCollins. [Kindle Edition]

Christie, A. ([1977] 2010), *An Autobiography*, London: HarperCollins. [Kindle Edition]

Grella, G. (1970), "Murder and Manners: The Formal Detective Novel," *NOVEL: A Forum on Fiction*, 4 (1): 30–48.

Griselda (2016), Comment on "90 years of The Murder of Roger Ackroyd," *The Agatha Christie Community Forum Archive*, n.d. Available online: https://community-archive.agathachristie.com/discussion/854/90-years-of-the-murder-of-roger-ackroy

Hoffman, M. (2016), *Gender and Representation in the Gender and Representation in British "Golden Age" Crime Fiction*, Basingstoke: Palgrave Macmillan.

Holquist, M. (1983), "Whodunit and Other Questions: Metaphysical Detective Stories in Postwar Fiction," in G. W. Most and W. W. Stowe (eds), *The Poetics of Murder: Detective Fiction and Literary Theory*, 149–74, New York: Harcourt.

Humble, N. (2001), *The Feminine Middlebrow Novel, 1920s to 1950s: Class, Domesticity, and Bohemianism*, Oxford: Oxford University Press.

Humble, N. (2012), "The Reader of Popular Fiction," in D. Glover and S. McCracken (eds), *The Cambridge Companion to Popular Fiction*, 86–102, Cambridge: Cambridge University Press.

Knight, S. (2003), "The Golden Age," in M. Priestman (ed), *The Cambridge Companion to Crime Fiction*, 77–94, Cambridge: Cambridge University Press.

Light, A. (1991), *Forever England: Femininity, Literature, and Conservatism between the Wars*, London: Routledge.

MacDonald, K. and C. Singer (2015), "Introduction," in K. MacDonald and C. Singer (eds), *Transitions in Middlebrow Writing 1880–1930*, 1–13, Basingstoke: Palgrave Macmillan.

Makinen, M. (2006), *Agatha Christie: Investigating Femininity*, Basingstoke: Palgrave Macmillan.

Makinen, M. (2016), "Agatha Christie in Dialogue with *To the Lighthouse*: The Modernist Artist," in J. C. Bernthal (ed), *The Ageless Agatha Christie: Essays on the Mysteries and Legacy*, 11–28, Jefferson: McFarland.

Mezei, K. (2007), "Spinsters, Surveillance, and Speech: The Case of Miss Marple, Miss Mole, and Miss Jekyll," *Journal of Modern Literature*, 30 (2): 103–20.

Maugham, W. S. ([1926] 2009), "The Creative Impulse," in *Collected Short Stories Volume 2*, 121–50, London: Vintage. [Kindle Edition]

Milton, J. ([1667] 2009), *Paradise Lost and Paradise Regained*, London: Vintage Books.

Reynolds, D. (2017), "Jane Austen and the Murder of Roger Ackroyd," *Jane Austen & Other Writers*, May 5. Available online: http://janeaustenandotherwriters.blogspot.com/2017/05/the-murder-of-roger-ackroyd-and-jane.html (accessed November 1, 2021).

Sayers, D. L. ([1929] 2012), *Strong Poison*, London: HarperCollins.

Schaub, M. (2013), *Middlebrow Feminism in Classic British Detective Fiction: The Female Gentleman*, Basingstoke: Palgrave Macmillan.

Stewart, V. (2013), "Defining Detective Fiction in Interwar Britain," *The Space between: Literature and Culture, 1914–1945*, 9 (1): 101–18.

Williams, R. ([1973] 1975), *The Country and the City*, Oxford: Oxford University Press.

Woolf, V. ([1930] 1942), "Middlebrow," in *The Death of the Moth and Other Essays*, 113–19, London: The Hogarth Press.

Yiannitsaros, C. (2016), *Deadly Domesticity: Agatha Christie's "Middlebrow" Gothic, 1930–1970*. PhD thesis, University of Warwick.

CHAPTER THREE

Christie's Clues as Information

MICHELLE M. KAZMER

INTRODUCTION

This chapter takes the perspective of "clue as information object" to explore the use of clues in Agatha Christie's mysteries. Clues have been approached in the literature from disparate directions that include as semiotic identifiers, abductive fodder, fixed objects, red herrings, and scientific data. But clues are also "information objects," by which I mean items that can be used to change the understanding of the person who perceives them, in context (Kazmer 2016). Like the approach to "clues," definitions of "information object" range from the technical to the metaphorical depending on discipline. As information objects, clues manifest and work through informing the primary detective; mis-informing the other detectives in the story, including the police; and dis-informing the reader to the extent required to make the story work. Each of these concepts is explored in detail in this chapter. This chapter outlines the literature of clues and the literature of information, using primary texts to demonstrate how they overlap. It explores the use of clues as information objects in four short-form Christie stories that involve gunshots.

The four Christie texts are "The Second Gong," "Dead Man's Mirror," "The Market Basing Mystery," and "Murder in the Mews."[1] All four stories feature

---

[1] These four texts are a closely related quartet comprising two pairs: short story "The Second Gong" (1932) which was expanded and substantively revised into the novella "Dead Man's Mirror" (1937); and short story "The Market Basing Mystery" (1923), which shares a key plot device and overall plot outline with the novella *Murder in the Mews* (1936). All four feature Poirot, with the presence of co-solvers who are separate from the actors in the mystery itself. These co-solvers include familiar figures Hastings, Inspector Japp, and Mr. Satterthwaite, four pairs of police inspectors and surgeons, and some constables, fingerprint men, and photographers.

a death by gunshot that is either murder made to look like suicide, or suicide made to look like murder (Maida and Spornick 1982: 54). In none of the four cases is scientific forensic analysis (Thomas 2000), such as microscopic ballistic examination, used definitively to solve the crime, although fingerprint analysis is used in a supporting role to exclude the possibility of random outsiders being present (see also Dormer 2021). Nor are the clues generally concealed, as "Christie famously hides clues in plain sight" (Crescentini 2019: 114). Instead, the detectives gather readily seen clues and interpret their information to unravel mysteries. Despite a long and disparate list of ancillary investigative characters (Kinnell 2010), it is Poirot who is centered throughout the puzzling of clues, and Poirot who reveals the culprit through an interpersonal confrontation in the reveal scene in each story.

The paired nature of these stories was key to their selection for this analysis because the pairings demonstrate how "the same" clues can be used differently, and how "different" clues can be used for the same purpose. In "Dead Man's Mirror" and "The Second Gong," "the same" clues of the position of the body with respect to the French window, desk, and mirror; the shivering of that mirror; and an extra toll of the gong in the hall come together to incriminate different killers with different roles in the household and different motives (a difference oddly unnoted in Leitch's 1983 exploration: 478–9). Comparing "The Market Basing Mystery" and "Murder in the Mews" shows different sets of objects serving an identical informative purpose across the two stories: the purpose served parsimoniously by a handkerchief in the former is served extravagantly by an expensive watch on a moiré strap and a flamboyant emerald green quill pen—unused—in the latter.

Of course, some clues are "the same" across the story pairings and serve the same purpose. In "Dead Man's Mirror"/"The Second Gong," a key locational/temporal clue (from which room in the house someone emerges at a critical moment) is the consistent fact that points to the culprit. In "The Market Basing Mystery"/"Murder in the Mews," a large number of smoked cigarette stubs in the room with the body appear in each story with similar information for Poirot.

In all four stories, the physical clues (objects) play a key role in the solution. The first step in a clue fulfilling this role is for it to be noticed, by detective and reader (York 2007: 104–5). Noticing does not only mean seeing; these clues use senses in addition to the visual to do their work. We are accustomed to visual clues such as the presence of a weapon, the placement of an accessory such as a handkerchief or a writing pen, footprints in a flower bed, or a tiny object on the floor such as a minuscule fabric flower or the fragment of an enamel cufflink (Render 2015). While Symons wrote of Christie that "the central clue in almost all of her best books is either verbal or visual" (33 in Keating), these stories also feature significant clues that use other sensory channels (Stewart

2019). These include kinetic clues which rely for their information on motion that occurs at a specific time, such as someone stooping to retrieve something from the floor, or stiffening and stopping breathing upon the opening of a closet door. Another type of sensory information is offered through olfactory clues such as the odors of cigarette smoke and of oranges. The sense of hearing is also inherently vital in these stories, where the solutions develop in part through the processing of audial clues, such as an overheard conversation or the toll of a gong.

The addition of senses beyond sight to the ways a detective receives clues is intrinsic to the definition of "clue" and its distinction from related concepts such as "evidence." While etymological explorations of concepts we seek to define are typically useless-approaching-naïve, in this case, such exploration is mildly useful. "Evidence" shares an etymological root "weid" [to see] with "witness," visual, and so on, and its operational or connotational definition, even in everyday conversation, is tacitly shaped by Anglo-American jurisprudential definitions of what counts as evidence in legal proceedings (Bernthal 2016: 38; York 2007: 108). "Clue," on the other hand, comes from Proto-Germanic "kliwjo"—to gather into a mass, such as a ball of yarn—and subsequently from the unraveling of that yarn through symbolic use in translations of the myth of Theseus as being the guide out of the labyrinth. At the same time, our vernacular use of "clue" is not restricted even tacitly by any legal definitions. In detective fiction, clues are both gathered and unraveled as a guide to truth, and are explicitly unrestricted by the sense of sight. A clue can be anything; its definition as a clue emerges through its being acted on (gathered) and its own actions (guiding).

CONCEPTUALIZING "INFORMATION"

In this way, clues manifest multifaceted definitions of information. To approach "clues as information" requires not only approaching a working definition of "clue" as above but also exploring definitions of "information." Full treatments of the definitions of information are available (Bates 2006; Bateson 2015; Bawden and Robinson 2017; Belkin and Robertson 1976; Buckland 1991; Case and Given 2016; Floridi 2010; Losee 1997; Ritchie 1991; Shannon 1948), and aspects of these definitions salient to this argument are offered. One common (albeit not very useful, practically or theoretically) way of positioning information is on a "continuum" from data to information to knowledge to wisdom; there are no satisfactory empirical or philosophical proofs of this continuum, but its ubiquity requires brief acknowledgment. Another, more salient, way of thinking about information is to look at significant inflection points in its conceptualization from the advent of the computing age (toward the end of the Golden Age) until now.

Claude Shannon (1948), the "father of information theory," did not define information. He refined a process for reducing uncertainty when sending digital messages, slicing them into pieces so small that the entropy of moving each piece of information was reduced enough that one could be mathematically certain that the message received was equivalent to the message sent. Information in Shannon's formulation is a placeholder that holds a message just long enough to be chopped up into sufficiently small pieces, transported, and re-formed into the message. Shannon demonstrates that the received meaning of a message can differ from that intended by the creator, by the normal entropy occurring while the information is transferred.

Two decades later in the cybernetics age, Gregory Bateson (1970) also chopped information into increments, just small enough that each increment conveys enough difference for a change in state (of matter, being, belief, or mind) of the recipient. "Information" can be reduced to the smallest amount of messaging that will cause the recipient to change; Bateson has added a behavioral aspect to what was, for Shannon, a mathematical exercise in which the nature of the message was immaterial. Bateson expands the context from Shannon's computational setting into the lifeworld, noting that increments of information sufficient to change our state can be apprehended through multiple senses.

Another two decades on, in the information age, Michael Buckland (1991) expressed one of the most influential typologies of information per se—a typology *of* information, not a typology that *includes* information—by creating three categories: information-as-process, information-as-knowledge, and information-as-thing. Drawing on Briet's (1951) defining a document as any form of evidence, Buckland argues that while humans engage in information-as-process (similar to words such as digestion or observation), and while information-as-knowledge is more theoretically interesting, information-as-thing is more practical because the practice of information science requires a thing to act on. Only by thinking of information-as-thing can we proceed to the work of organizing, storing, preserving, retrieving, and using it. Buckland scopes his category of information-as-thing broadly, to include data, text, documents, objects, and events.

Luciano Floridi's (2010) work offers a definition of information that reintroduces the concept of meaning but embeds meaning into well-formed data to create information. "Meaning," for Floridi, asserts that the data offered must align with the semantics of the context, but the definitional context here does not require that the recipient exists or acts. Meaning can be intrinsic to the information object and made visible, and its effects obvious, once the recipient has apprehended the meaning within a specific semantic context.

CONSIDERING "CLUES"

Considering clues as information objects similarly requires a sketch of how clues have been treated in analyses of detective fiction in general and Christie's work in particular. Direct, detailed treatment of clues per se is surprisingly limited. Jesper Gulddal asserts this fact in his book chapter on clues, saying, "crime fiction scholarship [...] has rarely [...] made the clue an object of analysis in its own right" (2020: 194), an assertion supported by the slender bibliography of that chapter. This lack of focus is especially odd given P.D. James's statement that presence of the clue is the sole factor that changes a "story" into a "mystery story" (2009: 4). But limited does not mean absent, and in addition to the works woven through the close reading that follows, some other analyses show relevance here.

Clues have concrete and prosaic roles to serve; they are fundamental tools of the mystery form. From the earliest days of "rules" for detective fiction (Knox 1929; Van Dine 1928), clues have been seen as basic elements of the detective story but at the same time ill-defined; as the thing to be stated, described, gathered, analyzed, lighted on, or produced, a clue does not have an active role other than to "point" or "lead." Caroline Marie, in her discussion of transmodal self-adaptation, frames clues as objects that occur within the text and "point to a narrative of truth to come" (2014: 53). Marie also demonstrates that these objects function in fundamentally different ways across works that Christie self-adapted from story to play or vice versa, "playing on the reader's or audience's modal expectations" (51) to succeed in their work.

Clues as concrete objects are also the subject of analysis that proceeds beyond perception. Because of the intrinsic nature of the body of literature about forensic analysis in detective fiction in general, and Christie in particular, that literature tends to focus on everything except clues *qua* clues. This is not a failing, but is the nature of the work. Bardell's (1984) essay on Christie's dispensary work discusses poisons used in many Christie works and their connections to Christie's chemical expertise and does not address the poisons themselves as pointing objects (clues). Similarly, Gerald's (1991) treatment of physicians and pharmacists in Christie's works focuses on their activities and characteristics. Almost incidentally, a key point about poisons-as-clues can be inferred on page 37: rarely is the poison itself a clue. Instead, the presence or absence of a container or label, or a manifestation of a symptom in a victim, serves as the clue/sign. Dormer's (2021) book examines "era appropriate science" (EAS) and its focus is largely on the process of scientific analysis and the ways (and reasons) EAS was intentionally marginalized in detective stories.

Gulddal (2020) moves from clues as concrete objects, containers that either have a correct reading or are "ontologically soft," to clues as semiotic actors, as linguistic signs operating in a transcendent epistemological realm. The semiotic role of clues has been addressed by Umberto Eco (Eco and Sebeok 1983) and subsequently by writers such as Franco Moretti (1988) and Carl Malmgren. When mystery is considered a "plot-dominant form" (Malmgren 2001: 22), clues are often left underexamined. When clues' semiotic role is framed as the experiencing of a series of "wrong interpretations" (16) only to "finally be deciphered" (15), clues lose their semiotic resilience. Following the semiotic arc, Moretti argues that the solution of a crime requires the detective to "reinstate the univocal links between signifiers and signified" (146). Returning to Eco's theory of semiotics, however, restores a needed complexity with the reminder that "clues are seldom coded, and their interpretation is frequently a matter of complex inference rather than of sign-function recognition" (Eco and Sebeok 1983: 224). An example from Christie's "Dead Man's Mirror" clarifies this neatly. A burst bag smelling of oranges remains equally a sign of there being in the house a bag that once contained oranges—the bag does not lose that facet of its informativeness while simultaneously signifying a homely device that can be used to mimic the sound of a gunshot.

The linear nature of clues as having a "correct" meaning that must emerge among multitudinous incorrect interpretations is reflected in many additional analyses. Eliot Singer (1984) positions clues as one piece of an overall scheme of "alternative solutions" that must be rejected, and his analysis expands to a consideration of clues as part of information systems called "block elements," drawn from the field of riddle scholarship. "Block elements" serve to close or "block" the reader's mind from the solution. Cohen (2000: 28) argues that "the truth must be readable by means of signs"; clues are correctly interpreted only when they lead to the truth, and otherwise the reading of them is wrong. Catherine Aird (2020: 217) avers that "there are just two sorts of clue admissible in the detective genre": straightforward clues and red herrings. Similarly, York (2007) offers a binary division between "real" and "fake" clues. These relatively linear and binary approaches to clues leave space for a more flexible analysis.

CLUES AS INFORMATION OBJECTS

One way of approaching such a flexible analysis is to return to the definitions of information to shape an examination of clues-as-information within a discussion that is tightly tied to Christie's texts while continuing to discuss the existing literature of clues. This analysis is flavored by key aspects of information from the definitional offerings earlier. These key aspects are:

1. Information carries a meaning by way of a message
2. The meaning of the information can be changed through alterations in the message
3. Meaning, to a recipient, should cause a change in understanding

4. Meaning can be intrinsic to the information object, but the recipient's change in understanding will be shaped by their own context

5. An information object can be acted on in many ways

The clues in the four texts analyzed here represent a heterogeneous array of items and methods of sensory appreciation. These clues are "information objects," by which I now mean flexible items whose multiple layers of meaning and signification can be used to change the understanding of the person who perceives them, in context and not always in a linear way.

To be able to act on an information object requires enumerating its attributes. Attributes are characteristics of an information object; formal organization systems for information objects typically capture attributes of the same kind about every object. For example, every book in a library might have an attribute of Title, to which is attached the title of the book; every artifact in a museum might have an attribute of Acquisition Date, to which is attached the date it was acquired by the museum. When operating in the world, we tend to interact with information objects according to the attributes most salient to our context, instead of the same attributes for every object, and those attributes tend to be tacit rather than explicit (see also Mills 2016: 29). While this may seem like the object changes its meaning (Sills 2014), considering how attributes and their perceived salience shift, based on context, is a more appropriate way to think about this phenomenon (see also Beehler 1988).

Consider the use of clues in detective fiction: detectives interact with clues according to the information attributes most salient to the context at hand, but rarely make explicit those attributes, especially to the reader (Toker 1993; Weiss 2014). In "The Market Basing Mystery," Poirot and Hastings notice and discuss the handkerchief in Protheroe's coat-sleeve. Poirot immediately grasps that the salient attribute of this handkerchief is its location in Protheroe's right coat-sleeve. In the real world, "location" is not a usual attribute when we discuss handkerchiefs independent of context; one might talk about fabric, color, laundering procedures, monograms, and so on, but only in a specific context-of-use would "location" be salient. In the detective story, Hastings examines the handkerchief and struggles to identify the attribute that is important in this context: he thinks through attributes of decoration ("plain"), fabric ("cambric"), color ("white"), and cleanliness ("no mark or stain"), drawing no conclusions. When they discuss the handkerchief again, Poirot draws attention to the salient attribute of location ("up his sleeve"), but Hastings interprets that according to his own knowledge and relates it to the fact that sailors carry their handkerchiefs in their sleeves. Only in the post-exposure explanation does Poirot stress to Hastings the correct interpretation in context: the location in the *right* sleeve indicates that the dead man was left-handed. The "mental and emotional flexibility" (Gainor 2013: 4) required to make these determinations of salience in information objects distinguishes Poirot's ability as a detective from those around him (Eco and Sebeok 1983). One can proceed similarly with the green quill pen in "Murder in the Mews." In the real world, when we think about pens, typical attributes include style, ink-color, cost, and ease of writing. In Bardsley Garden Mews, however, for Poirot in the context of investigating the death of Barbara Allen,[2] salient information attributes of a pen include location left or right of the blotter, and indications of use: "innocent of ink" versus "ink-stained."

I have been referring to clues as "information objects" and using the word "object" in its sense of "material thing." Shifting to thinking about the word "object" in its sense of having action directed *to* it opens another avenue for analysis. Clues as information objects both "are" and "are acted upon." Clues are acted on (moved, organized, hidden, retrieved, described) by characters and by the author.

This shifting of clues between objects-as-indicators and objects-acted-upon is not unique to my analysis; a similar back-and-forth is demonstrated in Van Dine's (1928) Twenty Rules, where clues are things to be "stated and described," "gathered," and "analyzed," by others, but are also themselves capable of "pointing at the culprit." Knox's (1929) ten commandments only invoke the term "clue" once, but treat clues as objects-acted-upon in three ways within a nineteen-word sentence: detectives can "light on them," the writer must "produce" them, and the reader may "inspect" them. The codification of the form of detective fiction, in other words, explicitly called for clues to simultaneously signify and be manipulated (Glover 2000: 38).

Rarely do we find in Christie clues that are static and only interacted with once (see Sargent 2010: 302). More frequently, Christie's clues are: experienced through multiple senses; used to abduce multiple meanings depending on individual contexts; and both indicative objects and objects of action (Brown 2000: 192). As information objects in their role as indicators (rather than things-acted-upon), clues demonstrate a spectrum from inscribed and intentional information content (a letter, a label, a will) to information coming from the materiality of the object itself (a footprint, a spent match). This is a spectrum because many clues offer both types of content simultaneously: the content of a letter may be informative as is the color of ink used to write it, or the letters on a label from a vial of medicine may be informative as is the amount of dust on the label.

As information objects, clues have four dimensions needing further analysis: clues are mutable (intrinsically changed through use); clues are malleable (subject to intentional manipulation); clues offer information, mis-information (erroneous), and dis-information (intentionally misleading); and clues act as

---

[2]When taking on an alias, perhaps don't use the name of a popular culture figure who dies?

boundary objects (anchors of shared meaning or use across contexts). In the following discussions, the weight of explanation is shouldered synecdochally, through specific examples from Christie's stories, rather than through conceptual language. The reader is encouraged to think through similar examples and counterexamples to extrapolate an individually meaningful abstraction of each concept.

First, clues as information objects are mutable. When we think of information, we often think of "facts"—fixed handfuls (or bits, per Shannon) of truth that can be organized, stored, retrieved, and applied. But a clue as an information object is not stable; it changes through typical use. Mutability is defined here as changes in the information status of a clue that are not intentional with respect to the crime, but that may provide clues to solving the mystery.

One example of mutability is the paper bag in "Dead Man's Mirror." When Poirot and the reader first see the paper bag, it is in the wastepaper basket in the drawing room, crumpled and smelling of oranges. The bag did not originally smell of oranges, but came to carry this olfactory information intrinsically through its use by the Carpenter and Sons Fruiterers; it was not originally crumpled, but became so by way of an as-yet-unknown action; it did not from the beginning carry the location information "wastebasket," but was placed there by a human who acted as one typically would act with a used and crumpled paper fruit bag.

Another example of a clue as a mutable information object is offered by the ashtrays of smoked cigarette stubs in "The Market Basing Mystery" and "Murder in the Mews." A recurring theme in the Poirot stories is that he disdains grubbing for physical clues such as footprints and cigarette ash, and particularly disdains the "foxhound" type of sleuth who sniffs the ground like a dog. Christie has made another of her signature inside jokes by having Poirot sniff the air inside a locked room in these cases, where each room contains not a mere trace of cigarette ash but emphatically large quantities of cigarette stubs.[3] The ashtrays of smoked cigarette stubs demonstrate mutable information objects serving as clues. Cigarettes turn into stubs through their normal use; it does not require anything unusual to have happened. Yet, a smoked cigarette stub—or as many as twenty—tidily collected in a large ashtray or placed in the fireplace grate is a substantively different clue from twenty unsmoked cigarettes. This specific mutability, not an intentional piece of misdirection, is key to the information gleaned from this clue.

Second, clues as information objects are malleable; malleability of the information-bearing of an object means it is changeable through the intention of being changed, rather than incidentally through use. One example is the broken cuff-link in "The

---

[3]This is similar to her intentional move in *Hercule Poirot's Christmas*, where instead of tiny blood traces to analyze, Poirot is confronted with an entire room sloshed with blood.

Market Basing Mystery," which is remarkably informative for something so small and common. Its information is changed multiple times. Chronologically in the life of the cufflink (not the order in the narrative), the cufflink has been: broken; picked up by the housekeeper; dropped near a dead body; seen near the body and pounced on by Inspector Japp; shown to the housekeeper, who denies recognizing it; identified by another woman as belonging to her husband; and shown to the husband, who denies owning it. Each of these willful actions causes a change to the information afforded by this singular small clue.

Another example of malleability is the location of the bullet(s) in "The Second Gong" and "Dead Man's Mirror." In "The Second Gong," the bullet is found by the doctor "near the wall below the mirror," that is, where it would have fallen after it passed through the head of Hubert Lytcham-Roche and struck the mirror, based on the position in which the body was found. Poirot has seen someone stoop to pick up something from the floor; it was the murderer retrieving the bullet from where it actually landed in the hall outside the study. Unseen, the murderer "threw it under the mirror" and that is where the doctor found it. This bullet is also so malleable that, for a time, it "turns into" a matchbox and then a tiny fabric rosebud. No, the bullet does not turn into a rosebud, but the unknown item that Poirot saw a man stoop to retrieve is first explained away as being a matchbox with the goal that Poirot will be convinced it really was a tiny fabric rosebud (since the man has worked so hard to distract Poirot with the matchbox, the rosebud is all the more convincing, but is only as true as Romaine Heilger's second testimony in "Witness for the Prosecution," which is forced on the jury in the same way). In "Dead Man's Mirror," the bullet as clue demonstrates malleability as well as an adaptive shift from story to story similar to Marie's (51) shift of clues from story to play. Here, Poirot similarly finds the bullet on the floor under the mirror near the body, from where it is later retrieved by the doctor. Poirot has seen someone stoop to pick up something from the floor; it was the murderer retrieving the bullet from where it landed in the hall outside the study. Unseen, the murderer "dropped it by the mirror" and that is where Poirot, and subsequently the doctor, found it. This bullet is also so malleable that, for a time, it "turns into" a pencil-made-out-of-a-bullet—again, while the bullet itself does not change, the "object picked up by a person in the hall" is explained away as being the bullet-shaped pencil instead.

The third of the four dimensions associated with clues as information objects is that they offer information, or "truth"; they offer misinformation, which arises from error, through erroneous presentation or erroneous interpretation; and they offer dis-information, which results from a deliberate falsehood (Ecker, Lewandowsky, Cheung, and Maybery 2015; Hernon 1995; Rubin 2019).

This is a logical place to show that the dimensions are not mutually exclusive; the location of the bullet in "The Second Gong"/"Dead Man's Mirror" is malleable and also dis-information; the paper bag in "Dead Man's Mirror" is mutable and also mis-information. Clues mutate, clues are malleable, and clues' relationships to "truth" are dynamic rather than static.

Most clues-as-information-objects in detective fiction are used for (or as) dis-information and information. Misinformation is rarer within published stories; true errors are edited out of well-crafted stories, and too many intentional errors may (in the hands of a writer less deft than Christie[4]) detract from the narrative. For Christie, misinformation is generally found in the impressions of Hastings; if anyone erroneously interprets a clue, it is likely Hastings.[5] In the four stories of focus here, Hastings only appears once and his "erroneous interpretation" of a clue (the location of the handkerchief, discussed earlier) *is not wrong at all.* It is a glimpse of Protheroe's true identity, and simultaneously a refutation of Stewart's assertion that alternative interpretations of a clue exist "only in order for these alternatives to be dismissed when the solution is finally revealed" (Stewart 2019: 174). While that may typically be the case, the use of "only" in Stewart's argument unnecessarily flattens the potential of clues as information objects. An alternative interpretation may be true and *not* dismissed, while also not the interpretation that leads directly to the solution.

One example of information per se offered by a clue is the extra sound of the gong in "The Second Gong" and "Dead Man's Mirror." In each case, one character, the guest in the house whose bedroom is nearest overhead to the gong outside the study below, races downstairs in a panic upon hearing "the second gong." The man of the house is fanatical about everyone in the house being on time for dinner. Arriving downstairs after the second gong is bad enough for a family member and, for a guest, ensures that they will never be invited to the house again.

In "Dead Man's Mirror," the scene in which the guest (Susan Cardwell) races downstairs at hearing the "second gong" is recreated retrospectively throughout the novella, as Poirot investigates the death of Sir Gervase Chevenix-Gore (Weiss 2014). Apparently, the first gong sounded at 8:08 p.m., a "shot" was heard immediately after (causing much conversation but no concern, as everyone concluded it must have been a champagne cork, or outside, and perhaps a car backfiring), and the second gong sounded at 8:15 p.m. Concern about Chevenix-Gore only arose at 8:15, when he violated his own rule and was late to dinner. Poirot speaks with every member of the household and finally with Miss Cardwell, who mentions that she ran downstairs at 8:08 thinking she had heard the first gong. No one else notes an "extra" gong and Poirot passes over it at the time. Only in his summation does he elevate the information offered

---

[4]*A Murder Is Announced.*

[5]An exemplar of this type of misinformation occurs in another work, *Murder on the Links*, where Hastings's (admittedly infatuation-clouded) interpretation of two clues, a knife and a photograph, is so erroneous that Hastings goes to the extreme of physically assaulting and restraining Poirot.

by this single audial clue to being "very important"—because it was the sound of the murder bullet passing through the dead man's head and striking the gong across from the study door. The note of the gong forced the murderer to re-stage the death scene, turning the body and smashing the mirror with a bronze figure, thus creating another key clue: a fragment of glass on the bronze figure.

In "The Second Gong," the extra gong is presented in the first few paragraphs via dialogue; the reader is confronted with an extra gong, the "first" gong, the sound of a shot and the ensuing argument about its source, and the "second" gong. The guest in this case, Joan Ashby, duly reports the phantom "first" gong to Poirot, who again recognizes its true informative value and uses it as a primary clue in unraveling the case.

These audial clues appear in both stories: a phantom "first gong" heard by one guest, and a "shot" heard between the actual (sounded by the butler) first and second gong, and discussed by the house party. The forced sound of a shot between the butler's first and second gong is dis-information: the murderer intentionally makes a gunshot sound when the murder did not occur, and relies on the difficulty people have in identifying the directionality of a single sound to hide its location and their own identity. The phantom "first" gong is only heard by one houseguest, and is dismissed by the rest of the house party as being an explicable misapprehension by a young woman anxious to make a good impression by not being late to dinner. Encouraged in this perception of misinformation, the reader again hears about the phantom "first" gong, alongside Poirot when he questions the young woman. Poirot uses the phantom gong as the information (not misinformation!) it is, and combines it with other clues to solve the mystery.

A simpler example is the attaché case in "Murder in the Mews."[6] Jane Plenderleith uses the attaché case in the closet under the stairs as dis-information for the detectives, needed because she knows they have noticed her tense reaction (kinetic clue) to their search of the closet. The experienced Christie reader attends closely to the attaché case because it follows a list of items, and the presence of a list of items is usually a meta-clue to the reader. Japp and Poirot both refuse to be dis-informed by the dressing case, stressing its clear un-relation to the case based on its contents: among other items, there are four-month-old magazines, indicating the case has not been used recently. But Plenderleith foregrounds it insistently, stressing the dis-information object by "sneaking" off to throw the case (emptied) into a lake from which it is immediately retrieved by police. Poirot's refusal to engage with this disinformation and his connection of other items in the closet to clues in Barbara's sitting room allow him to solve the mystery.

The fourth dimension of clues as information objects is that they serve as boundary objects. As boundary objects, they are used by multiple communities,

---

[6]"Mystery of the Dressing Case" was used as a title of the novella when it was published in *Woman's Journal*.

groups, or individuals, for their own disparate needs, simultaneously, with variable levels and types of shared meaning; "Boundary objects are both adaptable to different viewpoints and robust enough to maintain identity across them" (Star and Griesemer 1989: 387). Boundary object theory has been applied to the conception of real-life policework; a functional boundary object should "facilitate the interaction of criminal investigators, analysts, unit heads and crime scene investigators" (Eppler and Pfister 2014: 833). This dimension, like the others, is not mutually exclusive to other dimensions, and is also best explained synecdochally with examples rather than abstractly.

One example of clues as boundary information objects is in the position of the gunshot wound on the body and the body in the room, in all four stories examined here. The information offered to each observer by these positions is different, although the gunshot wound and the body—at least after the detectives have accessed the room—do not actually move. To Inspector Japp ("The Market Basing Mystery"), a gunshot wound in the head, apparently self-inflicted, signifies that the deceased had difficulty with "debt, or a woman." To Dr. Giles ("The Market Basing Mystery"), the same wound is a sign of impossibility and a source of puzzlement: in his role as police surgeon, he cannot resolve the setting (a locked room) with the physiological reality of a gun in the right hand and a wound entering the left side of the head. For Constable Pollard, the position of the wound is a cause for action: hearing from Dr. Giles about the conundrum and remembering that Japp is in Market Basing, Pollard is impelled to find Japp and seek his help. For Japp, the position of the wound is a thing to hear about and then to observe firsthand, rather than taking the word of others. For Poirot, it is a thing to ignore; in examining the corpse, he focuses on the handkerchief in the coat-sleeve and not on the gunshot wound. For Miss Clegg, the position of the wound is an opportunity for retribution against the people she held responsible for the death. The gunshot wound in "Murder in the Mews" is a similar boundary object for the parallel players in the novella.

In "The Second Gong"/"Dead Man's Mirror," the gunshot wound on the body and position of the body in the room similarly serve as boundary objects. While the position of the gunshot wound in "The Market Basing Mystery"/"Murder in the Mews" offers a key actor the opportunity to re-stage a suicide as a murder, the "through-and-through" head wound in "The Second Gong"/"Dead Man's Mirror" is an unexpected event that causes the phantom "first gong" and requires the murderer to re-stage the scene for the death to appear a suicide. Similarly, the position of the wound is, to the doctor, an oddity: here, it means that, for the bullet to have followed its apparent trajectory, the dead man must have leaned at an unusual angle before firing the gun.

A second example of a clue as a boundary information object is the French window in "Dead Man's Mirror"/"The Second Gong." The French window is an apt boundary object because even outside the context of a detective story, it is a boundary object of two kinds: a boundary between two locations (indoors and outdoors; or two rooms indoors), and a boundary between two types of object, a window and a door. Within these stories, the French windows continue their boundary object role. For the domestic staff, the French window is something over which a curtain must be drawn. For the police, the French window is locked and therefore confirms the death as suicide. For Poirot the French window in "Dead Man's Mirror" is an opportunity to distinguish himself from the British police as having had "a pleasant chat with a burglar." This pleasant chat affords Poirot a unique context in which to read the French window's information as a clue: he sees that it can be locked from the outside without a key. In "The Second Gong" the burglar-as-informant context is absent, but even so, Poirot uniquely sees the French window as a door that can be locked from the outside without a key.

CONCLUSION

I conclude with a note about the synecdochic use of examples in this chapter and suggestions for future examinations of "clues." This chapter has used detailed analysis of specific instances of clues in a tiny portion of the Christie canon comprising four short-form stories. This choice was made intentionally—deep meticulous examples help (they do not ensure, but they help) the analysis avoid broad generalizations and overly simple categories. This choice also lays the chapter explicitly open to criticisms of narrowness and "what-about-ism"; the Christie *oeuvre* is so large and heterogeneous that one can often find a counter example against any general statement made by even the most knowledgeable scholars, and the statements within this chapter are open to critique. Also, the examples used here exclude important extremes: they omit the quintessential Christie crime method (poison); they omit a significant Christie crime method (stabbing, significant because it is central to two of her most influential works— *Murder on the Orient Express* and *The Murder of Roger Ackroyd*—as well as appearing in many others); and they omit the more esoteric methods (quern to the head from the roof; strangling by ukulele string; etc.) used elsewhere. Instead, this chapter intentionally viewed perhaps the most prosaic approach to death—a gunshot wound to the head—and uses that unremarkableness[7] and homogeneity across four works to draw out concepts that *do* reflect difference: boundary objects connecting disparate contexts, misinformation vs. disinformation, multiple sensory uptakes of clues, and how clues both act and are acted-upon in a reflection of nuanced definitions of information per se, rather than in their roles as narrative tools.

---

[7]See *Death on the Nile* to be assured that this method of murder is neither prosaic, unremarkable, nor even homogeneous.

This chapter takes an information science orientation to clues as *information objects*; in doing so, it fills some conceptual blanks left by analyses offered from different disciplinary epistemologies. And, while an exploration of existing analyses of clues has been included, for a complete understanding of clues and the way the concept of "a clue" serves as a boundary object among many disciplines (criminology, English, medicine, Modern Languages, creative writing, philosophy, and more) it behooves a reader to explore broadly in the literature and to think through and acknowledge, but not be restricted by, the offerings in this chapter. It is meant as a piece in a puzzle, not a stand-alone treatment.

Within information science, the path forward is clear: there is a small, but established, thread of research applying theories of information behavior to the actions of characters in detective fiction (Gainor 2013; Kazmer 2016; Sørensen, Thellefsen, and Thellefsen 2017). This chapter offers a nascent approach to applying concepts of information-as-thing to clues-as-objects in detective fiction. The obvious next step within information science is to address how characters in detective fiction interact with clues-as-information-objects as part of their information behaviors. Outside information science, as well as interacting with it, the need for transdisciplinary examinations is clear; each individual study of clues in detective fiction has been largely monodisciplinary, and that siloed approach leaves a lot of ideas unexplored.

REFERENCES

Aird, C. (2020), "Snakes and Ladders," in M. Edwards (ed), *Howdunit: A Masterclass in Crime Writing by Members of the Detection Club*, 217–21, London: Collins Crime Club.

Bardell, E. B. (1984), "Dame Agatha's Dispensary," *Pharmacy in History*, 26 (1): 13–19.

Bates, M. J. (2006), "Fundamental Forms of Information," *Journal of the American Society for Information Science and Technology*, 57 (8): 1033–45.

Bateson, G. (2015), "Form, Substance and Difference [1970 Alfred Korzybski Memorial Lecture]," *ETC: A Review of General Semantics*, 72 (1): 90–104.

Bawden, D. and L. Robinson (2017), *An Introduction to Information Science*, London: Facet.

Beehler, S. A. (1988), "Close vs. Closed Reading: Interpreting the Clues," *The English Journal*, 77 (6): 39–43.

Belkin, N. J. and S. E. Robertson (1976), "Information Science and the Phenomenon of Information," *Journal of the American Society for Information Science*, 27 (4): 197–204.

Bernthal, J. C. (2016), *Queering Agatha Christie: Revisiting the Golden Age of Detective Fiction*, London: Palgrave Macmillan.

Briet, S. (1951), *Qu'est-ce que la Documentation?* Paris: EDIT.

Brown, J. C. (2000), "Bleeding the Thriller: Alain Robbe-Grillet's Intertextual Crimes," in W. Cherniak, M. Swales, and R. Vilain (eds), *The Art of Detective Fiction*, 188–200, London: St. Martin's Press.

Buckland, M. K. (1991), "Information as Thing," *Journal of the American Society for Information Science*, 42 (5): 351–60.

Case, D. O. and L. M. Given, eds. (2016), *Looking for Information: A Survey of Research on Information Seeking, Needs, and Behavior*, 4th edn, Bingley: Emerald.

Christie, A. (2013 [1923]), "The Market Basing Mystery," in *Hercule Poirot: The Complete Short Stories*, e-book edn, New York: William Morrow.

Christie, A. (2013 [1937]), "Dead Man's Mirror," in *Murder in the Mews: Four Cases of Hercule Poirot*, Epub edn, New York: Harper.

Christie, A. (2011 [1936; 1937]), "Murder in the Mews," in *Murder in the Mews: Four Cases of Hercule Poirot*, Epub edn, New York: Harper.

Christie, A. (2012 [1932; 1948]), "The Second Gong," in *The Witness for the Prosecution and Other Stories*, Epub edn, New York: William Morrow.

Cohen, M. (2000), *Murder Most Fair: The Appeal of Mystery Fiction*, Madison, NJ: Fairleigh Dickinson University Press.

Crescentini, F. (2019), "'There Are Things One Doesn't Forget': The Second World War in 'Three Blind Mice' and 'The Mousetrap'," in R. Mills and J. C. Bernthal (eds), *Agatha Christie Goes to War*, 109–123, London and New York: Routledge.

Dormer, M. E. (2021), *The Fiction of Forensics and Professionals in Detective Stories*, S.l., s.n.

Ecker, U. K. H., S. Lewandowsky, C. S. C. Cheung, and M. T. Maybery (2015), "He did it! She did it! No, she did not! Multiple Causal Explanations and the Continued Influence of Misinformation," *Journal of Memory and Language*, 85: 101–15.

Eco, U. and T. A. Sebeok, eds. (1983), *The Sign of Three: Dupin, Holmes, Peirce*, Bloomington: Indiana University Press.

Eppler, M. J. and R. A. Pfister (2014), "Best of Both Worlds: Hybrid Knowledge Visualization in Police Crime Fighting and Military Operations," *Journal of Knowledge Management*, 18 (4): 824–40.

Floridi, L. (2010), *Information: A Very Short Introduction*, Oxford: Oxford University Press.

Gainor, R. (2013), "The Relevant Clues: Information Behaviour and Assessment in Classic Detective Fiction," *Proceedings of the Annual Conference of CAIS*.

Gerald, M. C. (1991), "Agatha Christie's Helpful and Harmful Health Providers: Writings on Physicians and Pharmacists," *Pharmacy in History*, 33 (1): 31–9.

Glover, D. (2000), "The Writers Who Knew Too Much: Populism and Paradox in Detective Fiction's Golden Age," in W. Cherniak, M. Swales and R. Vilain (eds), *The Art of Detective Fiction*, 36–49, London: St. Martin's Press.

Gulddal, J. (2020), "Clues," in J. Allen, J. Gulddal, S. King, and A. Pepper (eds), *The Routledge Companion to Crime Fiction*, 194–201, London and New York: Routledge.

Hernon, P. (1995), "Disinformation and Misinformation through the Internet: Findings of an Exploratory Study," *Government Information Quarterly*, 12 (2): 133–139.

James, P. D. (2009), *Talking about Detective Fiction*, New York: Random House.

Kazmer, M. M. (2016), "'One Must Actually Take Facts as They Are': Information Value and Information Behaviour in Agatha Christie's Miss Marple Novels," in J. C. Bernthal (ed), *The Ageless Agatha Christie: Essays on the Mysteries and the Legacy*, 114–29, Jefferson: McFarland.

Kinnell, H. (2010), "Agatha Christie's Doctors," *BMJ*, 341 (7786): 1324–5.

Knox, R. (1929), "Ten Commandments for Detective Stories," in H. Harrington and R. Knox (eds), *Best Detective Stories of the Year (1928)*, London: Faber and Faber.

Leitch, T. M. (1983), "From Detective Story to Detective Novel," *Modern Fiction Studies*, 29 (3): 475–84.

Losee, R. M. (1997), "A Discipline Independent Definition of Information," *Journal of the American Society for Information Science*, 48 (3): 254–69.

Maida, P. D. and N. B. Spornick (1982), *Murder She Wrote: A Study of Agatha Christie's Detective Fiction*, Bowling Green, OH: Bowling Green State University Press.

Malmgren, C. D. (2001), *Anatomy of Murder. Mystery, Detective, and Crime Fiction*, Bowling Green, OH: Bowling Green State University Popular Press.

Marie, C. (2014), "When Page Won't Go to Stage: Adaptation-Resistant Embryos of Theatricality in Agatha Christie's 'Three Blind Mice' and 'Witness for the Prosecution'," *Adaptation*, 7 (1): 47–61.

Mills, R. (2016), "England's Pockets," in J. C. Bernthal (ed), *The Ageless Agatha Christie: Essays on the Mysteries and the Legacy*, 29–44, Jefferson: McFarland.

Moretti, F. (1988), "Clues," in *Signs Taken for Wonders. Essays in the Sociology of Literary Forms*, 130–56, London: Verso.

Render, A. J. (2015), *The Adaptation of Clues in Agatha Christie's Poirot*, Utrecht University Faculty of Humanities Bachelor's Thesis.

Ritchie, L. D. (1991), "Another Turn of the Information Revolution," *Communication Research*, 18 (3): 412–27.

Rubin, V. L. (2019), "Disinformation and Misinformation Triangle: A Conceptual Model for 'Fake News' Epidemic, Causal Factors and Interventions," *Journal of Documentation*, 75 (5): 1013–34.

Sargent, N. C. (2010), "Mys-Reading the Past in Detective Fiction and Law," *Law and Literature*, 22 (2): 288–306.

Shannon, C. E. (1948), "A Mathematical Theory of Communication," *Bell System Technical Journal*, 27 (3): 379–423; 27 (4): 623–56.

Sills, H. (2014), *Saussure and Sherlock, Derrida and the Detective: A Semiotic and Deconstructive Interpretation of the Classic Detective Fiction Genre*. Vanderbilt University English Department Honors Thesis.

Singer, E. A. (1984), "The Whodunit as Riddle: Block Elements in Agatha Christie," *Western Folklore*, 43 (3): 157–71.

Sørensen, B., T. Thellefsen, and M. Thellefsen (2017), "Clues as Information, the Semiotic Gap, and Inferential Investigative Processes, or Making a (Very Small) Contribution to the New Discipline, Forensic Semiotics," *Journal of the International Association for Semiotic Studies*, 215: 91–118.

Star, L. S. and J. R. Griesemer (1989), "Institutional Ecology, 'Translations' and Boundary Objects: Amateurs and Professionals in Berkeley's Museum of Vertebrate Zoology, 1907–39," *Social Studies of Science*, 19 (3): 387–420.

Stewart, V. (2019), "Objects, Things and Clues in Early Twentieth-Century Fiction," *Modernist Cultures*, 14 (2): 172–92.

Thomas, R. R. (2000), *Detective Fiction and the Rise of Forensic Science*, Cambridge: Cambridge University Press.

Toker, L. (1993), *Eloquent Reticence: Withholding Information in Fictional Narrative*, Lexington, KY: University Press of Kentucky.

Van Dine, S. S. (1928), "Twenty Rules for Writing Detective Stories," *The American Magazine* (September).

Weiss, J. (2014), *Clue, Code, Conjure: The Epistemology of American Detective Fiction, 1841–1914*. CUNY Academic Works. https://academicworks.cuny.edu/gc_etds/126

York, R. A. (2007), "Clues," in *Agatha Christie: Power and Illusion*, 100–13, London: Palgrave Macmillan.

FIGURE 4.1 Agatha Christie aboard the RMS *Kildonan Castle*, setting off from Southampton on a world tour in January 1922. Courtesy of The Christie Archive Trust.

CHAPTER FOUR

Reading Christie with a Feminist Lens

MARY ANNA EVANS

FEMINIST READINGS: A HISTORICAL OVERVIEW

Literary criticism came late to Agatha Christie. Little scholarship was done on her work for decades, although Edmund Wilson's famously devastating 1945 critique—"Her writing is of a mawkishness and banality that seem to me literally impossible to read"—prefigured the decidedly half-hearted commentary of many critics to come (59). In 1966, Francis Wyndham equally famously called her mysteries "animated algebra," written to a formula that was "a basic equation buried beneath a proliferation of irrelevancies" (25). In 1975, John Leonard riffed on the mathematics theme, writing that her plots were "elegant, as a balanced equation is elegant. Who complains about the x or any other quantity, in an equation?" (60–1). Soon after, Julian Symons dismissed her popularity as "the comfort of the familiar" (1980: 29) and Robert Barnard wrote that "[t]he surprise at the end of a really good Christie" is "a childish ingenuity beneath serious consideration" (1980: 44).

There is, in addition to their uniformly condescending (or worse) tone, a commonality to these early critics. They are all men. Most literary critics and scholars of the time were. This is not to say that all male scholars of the late twentieth century were as dismissive of Christie's work. H. Douglas Thomson and Howard Haycraft, writing in *Masters of Mystery* (1931) and *Murder for Pleasure* (1941) respectively, cited Christie as a major crime novelist, although they did retain the focus on her puzzle plots rather than grappling with other aspects of her work. While Gordon Ramsey's *Mistress of Mystery* (1967) was an early, and perhaps the first, serious academic study of her work, he continued the trend of focusing less on her books as literary texts and more on what he called "the well-made plot" (6).[1] Written in 1980, the same year that Symons faintly praised her as comfortably familiar and Barnard declared that she was beneath serious consideration, Earl F. Bargainnier's *The Gentle Art of Murder*, notable as an early work on Christie that was published by a university press, provided an insightful book-long analysis that is worth noting precisely because he did not engage in the dismissiveness of so much earlier criticism as he considered her entire body of work. Instead, he noted "her brilliance in plotting" (Bargainnier 1980: 145), and compared her to Jane Austen (167). Charles Osborne wrote in the preface to *The Life and Crimes of Agatha Christie* (1982: vii) that he, too, set out to examine "not only the crime novel, but also everything that Agatha Christie published." Osborne wrote that his "qualifications for the books are slender," based solely on enjoying her work, on having acted in one of her plays, and on having met her once. Symons and Barnard also were specific in making no claim to a scholarly treatment of her work, but their rationale for this position was that detective fiction as a genre does not warrant it.

Occasional commentary on Christie written by women was published before the early 1980s, notably reviews by Dorothy L. Sayers published between 1933 and 1935 for the *Sunday Times* and five of the thirteen essays published in H.R.F. Keating's *Agatha Christie: First Lady of Crime* (1977),[2] all by fellow crime writers, but scholarship on her work written in that time period by women remained rare, as was serious analysis written by writers of any gender beyond discussions of her popularity and her plotting prowess. Patricia Maida and Nicholas B. Spornick's *Murder She Wrote: A Study of Agatha Christie's Crime Fiction*, co-written in 1982 by a man and woman and published by an academic press, was perhaps emblematic of the contemporaneous increase in

---

[1]Ramsey devotes a chapter to the idea that the lasting value of mystery writers might be that their work will be useful to future social historians. While this is an intriguing idea that speaks to their works' value to fields like feminist criticism that are concerned with social issues, it does not speak to their literary value (or lack thereof).

[2]The female authors represented in this volume are Christianna Brand, Emma Lathen, Elizabeth Walter, Celia Fremlin, and Dorothy B. Hughes. Brand's "Miss Marple—A Portrait" is a sentimental portrait of one of Christie's most popular characters. Lathen's "Cornwallis's Revenge" focuses on her books' popularity in America, acknowledging with a tongue-in-cheek passage that "an English reader may boggle at palpable absurdities" in her descriptions of English life, while avoiding the sneering tone of Symons and others. Walter's "The Case of the Escalating Sales" focuses on Christie's success in the marketplace and her professionalism. Fremlin's "The Christie Everybody Knows" adds to the commentary about her popularity while tracing the varying responses of critics over her career. Hughes' "The Christie Nobody Knew" is a rare essay on the Westmacott books, calling them "six unusual books, six fine books, six books which encompass some of the best of Christie's writing" (123). None of these five writers adopts the dismissive tone of the writers described in the first paragraph of this essay.

serious attention to Christie's work by both female and male scholars that has continued to the present.

Perhaps it is not coincidental that the rise of serious interest in Christie's work in the 1980s was coincident with landmark works of feminist criticism like Elaine Showalter's *A Literature of Their Own* (1977), Sandra Gilbert and Susan Gubar's *The Madwoman in the Attic* (1979), and bell hooks's *Feminist Theory: From Margin to Center* (1984). Both Showalter's and Gilbert and Gubar's books were ambitious, sustained readings of works by women, with Gilbert and Gubar considering Victorian-era authors who were already widely read, including George Eliot and Charlotte Brontë, and Showalter addressing a longer time period (1840s through 1930s) and including less well-known authors like Charlotte Yonge and Eliza Lynn Linton along with Eliot, Brontë, and Virginia Woolf. Both volumes set out to reclaim what Gilbert and Gubar called "a distinctively female literary tradition," committing what Kate Flint called in her re-evaluation of Showalter "a major act of canon-busting" in the process (Flint 2005: 289).

While Showalter, Gilbert, and Gubar questioned the patriarchy, hooks did the same while also questioning them and other White feminist writers of the time, opening her book with a preface pointing out that "[m]ost feminist theory emerges from privileged women who live at the center, whose perspectives on reality rarely include knowledge and awareness of the lives of women and men who live in the margin. As a consequence, feminist theory lacks wholeness" (1984: x). The centering of white upper- and middle-class people in Christie's work resonates with hooks's critique, calling attention to characters from outside that racial and social group who do appear in her work—among them *Ordeal by Innocence*'s (1958) Tina Argyll, born to a sex worker and an Asian seaman,[3] and *A Caribbean Mystery*'s (1964) Victoria Johnson, a Black hotel employee—and are notable for their rarity.

It is almost surely not coincidental that the flowering of feminist thought in Christie studies beginning during the 1980s came on the heels of burgeoning female participation in literary criticism as a whole during feminism's Second Wave, as evidenced by the rise in female candidates earning PhDs in English literature in a single country, the United States, from less than 23 percent in 1966 to parity at 50 percent in 1980 (AAAS). It took time for feminist theorists who came of age during this era to turn from considering canonical works to popular fiction, and thus to Christie. While it cannot be stated unequivocally that serious consideration of the best-selling novelist of all time was delayed because of her gender, it is true that Christie scholarship grew in volume during

---

[3]Tina Argyll is repeatedly called a "half-caste." Her parentage is said to be uncertain, but her father is referenced as a "Lascar," a sailor from India or Southeast Asia (105). Her mother was presumably White.

and after the 1980s when the wave of women who entered the field in the late 1960s, 1970s, and early 1980s were in the early to middle stages of their careers. When they were well-established and ready to look beyond canonical and often male authors, some looked to Christie. As an example, this shift in focus can be seen in the career of Merja Makinen, who wrote her first book in 1989 on a male literary writer, Joyce Cary, then published work in the 1990s on a female literary writer, Angela Carter, before turning her attention in the twenty-first century to Agatha Christie.

In 1983, Marty Knepper published a generative paper with a title that asked a key question for scholars of women's writing: "Agatha Christie—Feminist?" (389–406). She laid out the central problem in evaluating an author as feminist or anti-feminist, which is that the evaluation is subjective. To address this subjectivity, she presented her definition of a feminist writer, which is worth quoting in full:

> a writer, female or male, who shows, as a norm and not as freaks, women capable of intelligence, moral responsibility, competence, and independent action; who presents women as central characters, as the heroes, not just as "the other sex" (in other words, as the wives, mothers, sisters, daughters, lovers, and servants of men); who reveals the economic, social, political and psychological problems women face as part of a patriarchal society; who explores female consciousness and female perceptions of the world; who creates women who have psychological complexity and transcend the sexist stereotypes that are as old as Eve and as limited as the lives of most fictional spinster schoolmarms.
>
> (389)

Based on these criteria, Knepper argues that Christie's work showed feminist leanings at times when society was more open to it, while portraying women in more stereotypical ways during periods when anti-feminist thought was more prevalent.

Knepper's relatively brief paper prefigured work like Gillian Gill's 1990 literary biography and Alison Light's chapter on Christie in her *Forever England: Femininity, Literature and Conservatism between the Wars* (1991: 61–112), both of which continued the trend toward assessing Christie's *oeuvre* as literature worth considering outside the detective fiction genre, placing its origins within the modernist movement of the early twentieth century. Gill goes beyond the crime novels by giving Christie's more literary novels written under her Mary Westmacott pseudonym the attention that they merit on their own terms, while perhaps investing too heavily in them as autobiographical fiction that can be plumbed for aspects of Christie's life that are otherwise undocumented.[4] She speaks against dismissive interpretations of Christie's work when she writes: "When Miss Marple comments quietly on the evil that exists in a small village, she is not simply making a justification for her creator's particular brand of escapist fiction. She is also making a statement about human nature, evil, and crime" ([1990] 1992). Light, too, resists the tendency of earlier critics to confine Christie to the detective fiction genre, considering her side-by-side with such writers as Ivy Compton-Burnett, Daphne du Maurier, and Jan Struther, none of whom are generally categorized as "genre writers," as Christie was. Light credits Christie with "a modernist spirit," calling her "an iconoclast whose monitoring of the plots of family life aims to upset the Victorian image of home, sweet home" (61).

Coincident with the release of Gill's book, Judith Butler's *Gender Trouble* (1990) developed the concept that gender is performative that they had proposed in their 1988 essay "Performative Acts and Gender Constitution: An Essay in Phenomenology and Feminist Theory." In these works, along with others including "Imitation and Gender Insubordination" (1990) and *Bodies That Matter* (1993), Butler had a transformative effect on gender studies that led directly to publications in Christie Studies that include Gill Plain's chapter "The Corporeal Anxieties of Agatha Christie" in her *Twentieth-century Crime Fiction: Gender, Sexuality and the Body* (2001). With this exploration of Christie's portrayal of women's lives as defined by their bodies, Plain joined the list of writers finding elements of feminism in her work as they also recognize that the word "feminist" might not fully apply. Plain recognized this ambiguity, stating that "[t]he extent to which the term feminist can be applied to Christie is uncertain—the epithet is an unstable one, and its categories are constantly evolving—but irrespective of Christie's opinions on the public forms of women's activism, the assumption underlying her interwar fiction is one of female agency" (47).

In 2001, Nicola Humble's *The Feminine Middlebrow Novel, 1920s to 1950s: Class, Domesticity, and Bohemianism* further explored Plain's theme of female agency, doing much to situate the feminine middlebrow as "a powerful force in establishing and consolidating, but also in resisting, new class and gender identities" (3), placing Christie squarely within the cadre of female interwar writers exploring gender roles in their era's rapidly changing class structure. It is worth noting that Humble does not set Christie apart as a genre writer, including her along with more mainstream authors like Angela Thirkell and Jan Struther, writing that "[t]heirs is not a fawning literature, but rather a subtle denuding of the aristocracy" as she credits "Agatha Christie's actresses and retired colonels" with "moving into and modernising the big country houses," describes Struther's "Provincial Lady and Mrs. Miniver laughing at

---

[4]Merja Makinen's chapter in this volume, "Hiding in Plain Site: Mary Westmacott," addresses Christie's six pseudonymous novels, filling a need for more scholarship on these often-overlooked works.

their aristocratic friends," and discusses Angela Thirkell's "professionalised gentry." In Humble's view, "all represent a middle class taking what it wants of aristocratic values and happily discarding the rest" (72). When considering works like these, Humble judges that "the feminine middlebrow adopts a positively triumphalist attitude to class" (72).

Susan Rowland's *From Agatha Christie to Ruth Rendell: British Women Writers in Detective and Crime Fiction* (2004) opens with a wistful note as she laments the "comparative neglect" by literary scholars, still ongoing seventeen years after Knepper's feminist salvo, of six female crime novelists: Christie, Dorothy L. Sayers, Margery Allingham, Ngaio Marsh, P.D. James, and Ruth Rendell. Rowland argues that the "lack of critical engagement with the profoundly influential work of all six writers is astonishing," stating that the aim of her book is "to remedy some of this neglect" (vii). In so doing, she places Christie in the key position as the female crime writer whose work preceded and presaged the others. Contradicting Symons's comment that "few feminists or radicals are likely to read" Christie, Rowland credits Christie's work in *The Murder of Roger Ackroyd* (1926) with the feminist approach that she "consciously problematises the detective as a masculine hero" (Rowland 2004: 27). Continuing Knepper's questioning of the definition of a feminist author, and also continuing the work of the other scholars mentioned above in distinguishing an author's personal politics from their work's feminist potential, Rowland concludes that

> [a] writer need not call herself a feminist nor be female for her writing to be concerned with "feminist" questions of power, gender and the social roles of women. Although of these six novelists, only the later writers would accept the label "feminist," all six authors, as professional women in a century of social change, are inevitably fascinated by tensions over female participation in society.
>
> (2004: 157)

This is an essential point in viewing Christie's work through a feminist lens, as she makes well-known statements in her autobiography to the effect that women had been foolish to begin earning their own livings, rather than seeking to retain a system—never in effect for all women—in which a husband financially supported a wife who "accepted as her destiny *his* place in the world and *his* way of life" (Christie [1977] 2011: 132). Her pronouncement on this change in women's status was that "[t]he position of women, over the years, has definitely changed for the worse" (131). However, it should be noted that, despite arguments that she was not a feminist based on statements like this one, her statement that women's lot in life was preferable when they were supported by their husbands should be weighed against the fact that she herself worked well into her eighties, long after it was financially necessary for her to do so.

The word "feminist" does not appear in either the autobiography or the autobiographical *Come Tell Me How You Live* (1946), but it does appear in the novels in reference to sympathetic characters. Ariadne Oliver, often noted as having similarities to Christie that ranged from her profession as an author of detective fiction to a predilection for apples, is described as "a hotheaded feminist" (1936: 9). Aimée Griffith is characterized in *The Moving Finger* by the narrator's statement upon meeting her: "I was taken aback, I had come up against the Feminist" (1943: 79, capitalization and punctuation original). In the ensuing conversation, she says to him, "It is incredible to you that women should want a career. It was incredible to my parents. I was anxious to study for a doctor. They would not hear of paying the fees. But they paid them readily for Owen. Yet I should have made a better doctor than my brother" (1943: 79). Aimée Griffith's very existence, dependent on the brother whom their parents chose to educate, speaks against Christie's declaration in her autobiography that the lot of women was better when they were dependent on men. Thus, any effort to declare her feminist or not-feminist is complicated by her own words, reflecting Rowland's observation that a writer need not declare herself "feminist" for her writing "to be concerned with 'feminist' questions of power, gender and the social roles of women" (2004: 57).

In 2006, Makinen published a feminist reading of Christie that succeeds in its ambitious aim, to "engage with the whole *oeuvre*" through an analysis that is "unashamedly textual in focus" (3). Her thesis that "Christie was writing during a period of intense gender renegotiation in relation to the modern world and that a political conservatism did not necessarily rule out a questioning and even subversive attitude to cultural gender expectations" (1) further investigates the position of Knepper, Gill, Light, and Rowland that feminist potential can exist in the work of a writer with conservative leanings. Makinen's *Agatha Christie: Investigating Femininity* is a key text for anyone seeking a feminist perspective, as well as anyone seeking one author's reading of all Christie's novels. She makes a point of mentioning Bargainnier and Gill as authors of works that were similarly comprehensive, but claims, justifiably, that *Agatha Christie: Investigating Femininity* stands apart from these in its focus on "the representation of gender across such a wealth of the novels" (Makinen 2006: 3).

It is important here to note Makinen's use of the word "novels." While she does not ignore the fact that Christie worked in other fictional and dramatic genres, it is necessary to make choices when addressing such an extensive body of work; the bibliography for *Agatha Christie: Investigating Femininity* includes just five of Christie's more than 170 short stories. Gill's bibliography mentions even fewer stories. While Bargainnier addresses most of them, his discussions are necessarily brief, as his discussion of Christie's entire body of work was confined to less than 250 pages. There is room in the literature for a thorough analysis of Christie's short fiction from a feminist perspective. Indeed, there is room for investigation of her body of as-yet-underconsidered short fiction from any number of perspectives.

The effort to disentangle an author's personal conservatism from the feminist aspects of in her work continued in 2013 with *Middlebrow Feminism in Classic British Detective Fiction: The Female Gentleman* by Melissa Schaub. Schaub considers both gender and class as she investigates her thesis that middlebrow novels of the modernist period, including detective novels, portrayed ideal characters as gentlemen, no matter their gender, "producing an ideological composite that was mildly conservative in its approach to social class, but progressive in its approach to gender" (vii).

In 2016, J.C. Bernthal published the first sustained queer reading of Christie's work, *Queering Agatha Christie: Revisiting the Golden Age of Detective Fiction*. It is also an important text for feminist scholars, considering as it does "Christie's manipulation, parodic innovation and ultimate exploitation of male-coded detective fiction conventions" (Bernthal 2016a: 15). As Bernthal points out, "queer studies has roots in a variety of feminist debates and activist projects surrounding gender and sexuality in the 1980s." His book engages with the work of gender theorists, such as Butler's explorations of gender identity and performativity, making the point that "everything about identity, and therefore identity politics, can be subverted" (2016a: 10).

While Bernthal's work has begun the work of addressing the critical neglect of queer issues in Christie's work, more attention to her often-problematic treatment of other marginalized groups is needed. hooks's criticism of Betty Friedan's work in *The Feminine Mystique*—"She ignored the existence of all non-white women and poor women" (hooks 1984: 2)—is a reminder to scholars of Christie's fiction that there is much work yet to do to remedy a historical failure to include all viewpoints. This volume includes scholarship that focuses on people identified by hooks as "in the margin" (ix). In particular, Nadia Atia's chapter continues her work on Christie's novels set in the colonial Middle East, and Meta Carstarphen's chapter considers the titles and subject matter of *And Then There Were None* from the point of view of a scholar of race and the media. Allendinger (2019: 60–4), Arnold (1987: 275–82), Brown (2020: 70–80), Lassner (2009: 31–50), and Linares (2018) have also published important scholarship on racism, colonialism, and antisemitism in Christie's work, but the literature is in particular need of more criticism from an intersectional feminist perspective that must not be neglected.

Within the past decade, many valuable shorter works on gender issues in Christie's fiction have built on the largely book-length analyses discussed above. Two notable articles on her female detectives appeared in the *Clues: A Journal of Detection*'s 2016 issue dedicated to Christie's work: "The Paradox of Miss Marple: Agatha Christie's Epistemology" by Kimberly Maslin (2016: 105–15), and "'This Isn't A Detective Story, Mrs. Oliver': The Case of the

Fictitious Author" by Françoise Grauby (2016: 116–25). Several essays from Bernthal's *The Ageless Agatha Christie*: *Essays on the Mysteries and the Legacy*, also published in 2016, address questions that remain important to the future of feminist scholars studying Christie's work. Merja Makinen takes on the literary establishment that excludes genre fiction from serious critical consideration in "Agatha Christie in Dialogue with *To the Lighthouse*: The Modernist Artist" (2016: 11–28). Sarah Bernstein considers transgressive images of women in the postwar period in "Queer Girls, Bad Girls, Dead Girls: Post-War Culture and the Modern Girl" (2016: 45–60). Gender performativity is at the heart of both Charlotte Beyer's "'With practised eyes': Feminine Identity in *The Mysterious Mr Quin*" (2016: 61–80), and J.C. Bernthal's "'The sumptuous and the alluring': Poirot's Women, Dragged Up and Dressed Down" (2016b: 81–97). These essays point toward the future of feminist Christie studies.

As I conclude this discussion of the status of feminist Christie studies, it is important to note that Christie's influence on literary scholarship extends beyond the study of her work, as it has influenced recent feminist crime fiction criticism that does not directly address her work at all. Julie Kim's *Murdering Miss Marple: Essays on Gender and Sexuality in the New Golden Age of Women's Crime Fiction* offers her as a foil to the writers featured, featuring Miss Marple in the book's title while asking whether Christie's death in 1976 "gave birth to a new generation of women writers freed at last from the influence of the long-established mistress of classic mystery genre" (Kim 2012: 2). In Heather Duerre Humann's *Gender Bending Detective Fiction: A Critical Analysis of Selected Work*, Christie is directly referenced only when Miss Marple is offered as a comparison to P.D. James's Adam Dalgliesh (Duerre Humann 2017: 73) and as a literary influence for Val McDermid (85), and yet she is there. More than forty years after her death, a female author born into Victorian England at a time when women's rights were few and their professional opportunities were fewer is still the yardstick by which modern-day mystery authors are judged.

FEMINIST POTENTIAL IN CHRISTIE'S EARLY SHORT STORIES: A CASE STUDY

As I have noted, the size of Christie's *oeuvre* and the long delay in its receiving attention have resulted in a focus in the literature on longer works to the detriment of the short stories, which have been overshadowed by the books' success and obscured by their own very number.[5] This is a particularly significant omission in the study of her earliest stories, as they show evidence of her efforts to maintain her feminine self-expression when faced with formulaic demands

---

[5]An argument could be made that her short story output alone would be worthy of attention, even if she had never published a single novel. The same argument could be made for her career as a playwright.

of a male-coded genre and industry. Between her 1920 debut and the end of 1926, when the success of *The Murder of Roger Ackroyd* had removed any possibility that she was still an early career writer, she published six novels and an additional eighty short stories.[6] The intent of this case study of four stories published during this early-career period is to extend the existing feminist literature on her short works, pointing the way toward a sustained analysis of the stories as a body of work that considers their thematic relationships with the novels and their engagement with societal issues of their time.

This early period of Christie's career is bracketed by her debut novel, *The Mysterious Affair at Styles*, in which she explores the sexual desire of an elderly woman for a younger man and the struggles of an unhappy young wife, and the career-making book, *The Murder of Roger Ackroyd*, in which her interest in the complexities of women's emotional and sexual lives is also clear, although overshadowed by the experiences of the male narrator and victim. *The Murder of Roger Ackroyd* is of particular note for its depiction of a character, Elizabeth Russell, who is experiencing out-of-wedlock motherhood. Russell, who has worked for years to provide for her son's care, is a remarkably sympathetic unwed mother when one considers that Christie's society had only just passed the Legitimacy Act of 1925, a law that would improve the historically poor treatment of unmarried mothers and their children, albeit only somewhat and only for a small fraction of them that would not have included Elizabeth Russell and her son, who could only have been legitimized under this law if his parents eventually married.

Christie's clear interest in the story potential of the conflict between conventional sexual mores and women's self-fulfillment would continue after *The Murder of Roger Ackroyd*, evident in a long list of later novels that includes the Westmacott books, *Sad Cypress*, and *The Hollow*. The list of her short and long works that explore the conflict between societal norms, especially sexual norms, and women's self-determination is so long that I would argue that it was as much a hallmark of her work as the well-crafted whodunit plot. This theme is clearly discernible in many, but not all, of her early short stories. This variability in her approach to the feminist potential inherent in stories of women's sexuality is something that I wish to explore here.

While "feminist potential" is widely used, its centrality to this discussion dictates that I state my own definition. It is rooted in Rowland's statement that "[a] writer need not call herself feminist nor be female for her writing to be concerned with 'feminist' questions of power, gender and the social roles of women" and her investigation into whether a writer's "representation of the feminine suggests (perhaps without intending to) a feminist ethical attitude"

---

[6]This number can vary, depending on how one counts instances like "A Fairy in the Flat" and "A Pot of Tea," which were first published together, but eighty is a reasonable count.

(2004: 157–8). My position is that writers can and do explore feminist issues without considering themselves to be feminists and that Christie did so throughout her career. Thus, I define a text to have "feminist potential" when it explores—whether overtly, covertly, intentionally, or unintentionally—feminist questions of power, gender, and the social roles of women.[7]

These questions speak directly to the social milieu in which Christie began her career. It was a time of great social ferment in the lives of women, with a major contemporaneous milestone being recognition of the right of some of them to vote not long before publication of her first book. A feminist perspective is a useful approach for considering whether her response to this ferment was to write forward-looking stories that welcomed women's changing roles or whether it was to write fiction that looked backward at a time that had passed. It would be a mistake to focus this effort solely on the handful of novels she wrote during the early years of her career while neglecting the dozens of short stories from the same time period.

Christie's early stories include such tales of female subversion as a sympathetic portrayal of a woman fleeing her marriage to be with her lover ("Magnolia Blossom"), a lighthearted account of a proper lady who finds a way to start a romance with a man to whom she has not been properly introduced ("The Lonely God"), and a courtroom drama that asks the reader to sympathize with a perjurer desperate to save the man with whom she is living out of wedlock ("Traitor Hands"). Stories such as these meet my criterion for feminist potential in that they explore feminist questions of power, gender, and the social roles of women. What is more, they were written at a time when not all magazines would publish stories that dealt with sex and its impact on women's lives (Mullen).[8] Thus, Christie chose to limit her publication options when she consistently over time used her fiction to portray women who risked the condemnation of society by choosing their own paths in life. This approach to women's issues argues against the perception of some critics of Christie as a conservative voice speaking against women's new rights and freedoms through the voices of characters who "disapprove of Socialism, the modern woman, and contemporary literature" (Barnard 1980: 26) and who are "drawn from a tiny part of the complex class structure of between-the-wars Britain [...]: army men, clergymen ..., men from the colonies, country gentry, *successful* (or

---

[7]When conducting an inquiry from a feminist point of view, it is important at the time of this writing to note that the discussion incudes both cisgender and transgender women. Unless discussing a situation that requires distinguishing the two—for example, a twentieth-century law that would have barred a cisgender woman but not necessarily a transgender woman from jury service—the word "woman" should be understood to include all women.

[8]The R. D. Mullen essay cited here is an updated version of an essay published in *Science Fiction Studies*, Vol. 22, No. 1 (March 1995): 144–56.

long-established) doctors and dentists [a]nd of course, the women who depend on them" (Barnard 1980: 5, emphasis original).

Close reading of her earliest stories shows that, in many cases, Christie responded to her cultural and legal moment with a much more progressive approach than Barnard suggests, inviting an assessment of the feminist potential she created by crafting female characters who took advantage of a changing world. In the early 1920s, women in Christie's society began serving on juries. Their hair was shorter, and so were their skirts. They gained the right in 1923 to divorce on the grounds of adultery alone, a right that men already had and one that Christie was to exercise before the end of the decade. Laws passed during the 1920s gave married women more control over their own property. In 1925, a new law enabling some out-of-wedlock children to be legitimized was a step toward mitigating the harm done to women who rejected societal control of their sexuality, as well as the harm done to their children. Still, much was left to do. Even access to the most basic right as a citizen of the UK, the right to vote under the same rules applied to men, would wait until 1928.

How, if at all, did Christie portray these developments in her short stories, many of which were likely written quickly and submitted shortly before the magazine's issue went to print, thus potentially recording her response to societal change almost in real time?

The presumption that many of the stories were written shortly before they were published is based on common writing patterns in pulp writers of the time and on an extrapolation from what is known from her autobiography and letters. In her autobiography ([1977] 2011: 193), Christie mentions a few stories written prior to the publication of *The Mysterious Affair at Styles* in 1920—"The House of Beauty," "The Lonely God," "The Call of Wings," and a "grisly" story that was likely a version of "The Last Séance"—and her letters home from the 1922 around-the-world trip mention writing a story or stories in contexts that mention having been "rather idle" and having written "over the last few days," neither of which suggest a steady production of stories for future submission (Prichard 2012: 171, 178). Even considering Mark Aldridge's statement that the twelve or so stories intended for submission to The Bodley Head as a book-length collection had been written by January 1923 (Aldridge 2020: 18), this is a small fraction of the stories that appeared during the next two years; she published twenty-seven stories in 1923 and thirty-four in 1924. A trove of dozens more stories, ready to submit when the opportunity arrived, would seem worth mentioning in the context of those sources. No such trove of stories is known to have existed. Without one, publishing sixty-one stories in two years, while also writing her novels, would likely have required them to have been written quickly and shortly before publication.

Did her female characters' lives develop with the times, or were they mired in their author's Victorian childhood or Edwardian youth? For this discussion,

I have chosen four early stories, "The House of Beauty" (adapted into "The House of Dreams"), "The Wife of the Kenite," "Philomel Cottage," and "Magnolia Blossom," that did reflect the changing times as her female characters seized opportunities for self-determination that were newly available to real-life women.

Christie's first story, "The House of Beauty" (1926), was written prior to the First World War (Christie [1977] 2011: 193) and revised before its publication as "The House of Dreams" (Christie 2008: 199–211). In a discussion of feminist potential in her work, "The House of Dreams" is notable for its portrayal of a woman in a difficult situation who does not depend on a man to resolve her difficulty. It is told from the point of view of a young man who meets and falls in love with a woman. He believes that she loves him, yet she rejects him. He learns that she is determined not to marry, because she fears her familial tendency toward insanity. Thus, her refusal to marry him was an act of strength, love, and independence. She could have kept the secret and married a man who would have been responsible for her care for the rest of her life, as it would be decades before insanity was grounds for divorce in the UK. Her familial insanity does manifest itself and she dies. The young man dreams of a house that is a metaphor for happiness with her,[9] and he too eventually dies, apparently from a broken heart, prefiguring Gilbert and Gubar's observation about persistent themes in literature of the confinement of women—"Women themselves have often been described or imagined as houses" (1979: 88).

Christie's first published story, "The Wife of the Kenite," appeared in an Australian magazine, *The Home*, in September 1922, before fading into obscurity for almost a century (in Morris).[10] "The Wife of the Kenite" describes a woman's vengeance on the former German soldier who murdered her child, introducing Christie's theme of vengeance enacted by bereaved parents and caregivers seen in later works including *Murder on the Orient Express* and *The Mirror Crack'd from Side to Side*. Comparing the story to my criterion that texts with feminist potential overtly, covertly, intentionally, or unintentionally question power, gender, and the social roles of women, it is clear that the Kenite's titular wife assumes power over the narrator. She can certainly be credited with Knepper's criteria of intelligence, competence, and independent action, and the story unquestionably addresses her characterization of a feminist writer as one who "reveals the economic, social, political and psychological problems women face as part of a patriarchal society" in its portrayal of the psychological state of a woman bereaved by war (1983: 389). "The Wife of the Kenite" is not a play-fair whodunit with clues, red herrings, and a logical sleuth;

---

[9]And, perhaps, for safety and the womb.
[10]It would have either been written prior to or during her 1922 trip. Her letters mention "a Grand Guignol sketch and a short story" on May 9 (Prichard 2012: 171) and "short stories" on May 18 (177).

it is a dark tale of revenge, perhaps the darkest of Christie's works, putting the reader into the point of view of the first-person narrator to share his experience of being poisoned and his anticipation of a gruesome death. "The Wife of the Kenite" contradicts the easy assertions of writers like Symons and Barnard that pigeonholed Christie's work as comforting and inconsequential puzzle stories.

After "The Wife of the Kenite," Christie published a series of Poirot stories for *The Sketch* with far less feminist potential, not least because they focus on the homosocial friendship between Poirot and Hastings. Does this signify that Christie lost interest in women's issues for all of 1923, after writing the women-focused stories described above? Centered on puzzle plots in the Holmes-and-Watson vein, the Poirot stories published in *The Sketch* are stories written for a specific market and with the presumed intent of exploring her ability to establish herself in the commercial marketplace. This is not to say that Christie displays a regressive attitude toward women in these stories; it is that women and their concerns are not centered. The *Sketch* stories differ so markedly from the stories written when Christie was not under a long-term contract that it is useful to consider whether the wishes of the contracting party might account for the difference.

The Sketch was a long-running (1893–1959) London-based weekly publication with a focus on high society (University of Pennsylvania), which was a desirable demographic for a new author building a readership. *The Sketch* introduced Christie as a promising new voice, publishing a photo spread and touting her as the "creator of the most interesting detective since Sherlock Holmes" ("Maker" 1923: 467). The *Partners in Crime* stories written for *The Sketch* co-star the intelligent, competent, and independent Tuppence Beresford, who is an equal partner with her husband, and thus they address feminist issues more than the Poirot stories written for the same publication do, but none of the *Sketch* stories plumb the female experience in the way that the bereavement of the titular character of "The Wife of the Kenite" does, nor do they reflect the socially prescribed confinement of women in the way that "The House of Dreams" does.

As we will see, Christie was publishing women-centered stories in other publications while she was writing for *The Sketch*, and she would continue to do so long after her contract with that magazine was complete. Thus, I argue that the shift away from stories laden with feminist potential was likely a response to the marketplace of the time, in which each magazine placed firm editorial restrictions on potentially problematic subject matter. A subset of such problematic stories fell under the moniker, "sex-problem story." R.D. Mullen defines the sex-problem story, not as erotica, but as "a story about such problems as are created by infidelity or pre-marital sex" (Pulp Magazine Project). This definition is clear and none of the stories Christie wrote as part of the *Sketch* series meets it, although stories she wrote for other venues during and after her *Sketch* contract do. This suggests an editorial bent at *The Sketch* toward less edgy fare that is supported by Aldridge's observation that it was a magazine that dealt "with the lighter edge of society and fashion." He goes on to state that "there was no expectation for weightier matters to be brought into the publication via these mysteries" (2020: 21).

Because so many of Christie's earlier and later stories do fall under the purview of the sex-problem story, and because my purpose is to examine this change, or evolution, in her subject matter by contrasting her weightier stories with the lighter *Sketch* stories, it is worth pausing to consider the sex-problem story at a time when a magazine's stance on sexual content was often explicitly stated. This promotional text from the 1921 debut of *Love Story Magazine*, aimed at a female audience, uses the sex-problem story to illustrate the kinds of stories that they would not publish, showing the clear restrictions made by some publications at the time Christie began her career on stories that interrogated cultural proscriptions surrounding sexuality: "*Love Story* is not just another of those sex-problem magazines that have done so much harm in recent years. *Love Story* is clean at heart, and its stories are written around the love of the one man and the one woman" (Mullen). As an example of self-descriptive text from a publication on the other side of the sex-problem question, *Spicy Detective*'s 1935 writer's guidelines allowed a "girl to give herself to a man [...] up to the actual consummation," advising writers to "leave the rest up to the reader's imagination." Complete nudity, both male and female, was forbidden, but a "nude female corpse is allowable, of course" (Collier).[11] This clear explication of permissible subject matter demonstrates that, well into the second decade of Christie's career, firm rules defined which markets were open to material that might be considered risqué, and they established limitations on how risqué they might be.

A few of the Poirot stories from *The Sketch* do touch on matters of passion, but these topics are so peripheral that designating those stories as sex-problem stories seems an overreach. "The Adventure of the Western Star" (1923) and "The Veiled Lady" (1923) are possible exceptions, but Christie is careful to specify in both cases that the affair in question went no further than indiscretion and, thus, presumably did not extend to sex. In "The King of Clubs" (1923), a well-known dancer appears to have murdered an impresario who may have been her lover, but he was actually murdered by a brother defending her virtue from the dead man's unwanted advances. In "The Cornish Mystery" (1924), a man attempts to seduce an older woman, but she hesitates to leave her husband for him and there is no indication that they carried on a physical affair. I would argue that the consistent insistence in these stories that, despite appearances, no premarital or extramarital sex actually occurred is evidence that she was

---

[11]Of course!

writing within editorial constraints. A Tommy and Tuppence story, "Finessing the King"/"The Gentleman Dressed in Newspaper," is an exception, as it does allude to a woman's transgressive sexuality when the murderer kills his adulterous wife, but her transgressive body remains essentially absent while living and it has already been punished, only serving in death as a catalyst to events in other people's lives.

To find early Christie short stories that more overtly explore the emotional lives of women, including their sexuality, it is only necessary to look beyond stories published in *The Sketch*, considering stories being published elsewhere at the same time. This clearly discernible difference supports my thesis that the stories in *The Sketch* were written to the specifications of a specific market and for a goal which they did achieve: exposure of her work to a large upper-class readership. Thirty years after the editor of *The Sketch*, Bruce Ingram, introduced her short stories to the world, Christie dedicated *A Pocket Full of Rye* to him in gratitude. *The Sketch* continued publishing until 1959, but none of her stories debuted there after the completion of the 1923–4 series.

In 1923 and 1924, Christie was publishing stories in venues other than *The Sketch* that dealt clearly with women's sexuality and thus were only publishable in certain markets. This expansion in her subject matter allowed a return to her earlier interest in women's personal lives. Nine of the twelve non-*Sketch* stories from this period appeared first in *The Grand Magazine*. In his survey of British popular fiction magazines between 1880 and 1950, Mike Ashley credits Alice Grant Rosman, who assisted editor Reeves Shaw, for *The Grand Magazine*'s status as "a major market for women writers" in the years after the First World War (Ashley 2006: 84). Ashley provides a long list of women who published in *The Grand Magazine* between the war and 1927, when Rosman left to write full-time, calling her departure the point at which the magazine lost its "predominance of women's fiction" (84). Among the stories published during Rosman's tenure is one of Christie's most famous explorations of an independent woman's choices, "Philomel Cottage" (1924).

Alix Martin, the hardworking, prudent protagonist of "Philomel Cottage" (2008: 95–113), easily meets Knepper's standards of "intelligence, moral responsibility, competence, and independent action," having spent fifteen years supporting her mother and herself as a shorthand typist. Despite her prudence, she breaks off her courtship with a diffident man when, "swept clean off her feet" (96), she marries another man within a week of meeting him. Her sexual happiness with her husband is shown when she remembers her husband saying, "Nightingales should sing only for lovers," and blushes happily "at the memory of how they had indeed heard them" (98). Christie is still more specific about her protagonist's motives for marrying a man she has just met in the later dramatic adaptation when she says that physical attraction, "the sex stuff," is nature's basis for marriage ([1932] 2018: 28). As the story progresses, its parallels to the Bluebeard story of a woman rendered horrifyingly vulnerable by marriage become clear, a theme I discuss in "Killing Bluebeard: Claiming Subversive Femininity in Agatha Christie's 'Philomel Cottage' and *The Stranger*" (2021: 104–14). Alix comes to understand that her attraction to her husband has clouded her mind, realizing that he is a serial killer who intends her to be his next victim. At the story's conclusion, her intelligence and agency come to the fore again as she outsmarts a hardened killer intent on adding her to his body count. This story of a working woman consciously choosing a relationship based on physical attraction, then extricating herself from it by her own wits, is an early example of the self-sufficient heroines who can be found at every stage of Christie's career, questioning women's social roles as they chart their own courses.

Christie's sex-problem stories during this period were not limited to publication in *The Grand Magazine*. One of her most sensitive portrayals of a woman willing to flout convention for love can be seen in the provocative "Magnolia Blossom" (1926), first published in *The Royal*. "Magnolia Blossom" is one of the purest portrayals in Christie's *oeuvre* of a woman embracing transgressive sexuality with the author's obvious approval, exploring "the complex identities of the feminine self in conflict and complicity with social expectations and pressures of the family" (Makinen 2022). Published during Christie's personally tumultuous year of 1926, "Magnolia Blossom" epitomizes her continuing efforts to branch out from the formulaic puzzle stories written for *The Sketch* and explore the women's topics that had interested her since she wrote her first story.

"Magnolia Blossom" follows a married woman, Theo, pursuing passion as she runs away with her lover. She has refused to pursue her new love in a way that would save face, such as seeking a "discreet divorce," consenting instead to run away with her lover "with no hesitations or protests, as though it was the simplest thing in the world that he was asking her" (Christie 2008: 226–7). Christie returns repeatedly to the physicality of their relationship, describing "the faint tremor that shook her at his touch," "the response of her fingers on his," and "the clinging of her body, the abandon of her lips" (228–9); when she suddenly leaves the man she loves and returns to her husband, Christie makes it evident that is not for a lack of passion in the new relationship. Her return is based on a sense of responsibility felt when she learns that her husband needs her to weather a time of great trouble, an action that taps directly into Knepper's criterion of moral responsibility. After her return, Theo learns that her husband would have been willing to trade her sexual favors to spare himself financial disaster and prison. Upon learning this news, she leaves him again, not for the lover she has lost but "to freedom" (239). Christie lays out the morality of the situation clearly:

In leaving you for another man, I sinned—not technically, perhaps, but in intention, which is the same thing [...] You sold me, your own wife, to purchase safety! [...] We all have to pay in this life, Richard. For my sin I must pay in loneliness. For yours—well, you gambled with the thing you love, and you have lost it!

(239)

Theo's actions anticipate the words that Christie would write later under her Mary Westmacott pseudonym: "If I loved a man I'd run away with him even if it was wrong. [...] But I'd do it *honestly*. I'd not skulk in the shadow and let someone else do the dirty work and play safe myself" (Westmacott [1934] 2009: 407).

These early short stories show that Christie's interest in grappling with the complexity of women's emotional lives began early and continued throughout the period considered here, 1920–6. This consistent interest over a span of years supports my argument that her stories for *The Sketch*, a coherent collection of stories that stand out because they do not address the women's issues that appear frequently in her other stories, were written for a purpose—to build an audience for her work—and to the specifications of a specific market, *The Sketch*, which might not have been open to stories with a more feminist outlook.

The early neglect of Christie's work by literary critics, followed by the dismissive commentary of her work by some of them as "childish" (Barnard 1980: 44) or as "animated algebra" (Wyndham 1966: 25) distinguished only by the "comfort of the familiar" (Symons 1980: 29), continued until the rise of feminist literary criticism brought her work long-delayed and overdue attention. Finally given serious consideration, Christie's fiction has been shown to be consistently focused on issues of critical interest to women, such as matters of independence, maternity, romance, vulnerability, and more. It lends itself to feminist analysis, and that analysis belies the common perception of Christie and her work as emblematic of a conservative suspicion of "modern women" who fail to depend sufficiently on middle-class English men (Barnard 1980: 26). As I have shown here, close reading of her earliest published stories reveals a cast of female characters that goes far beyond such clinging vines. These are women who are capable of making their own decisions, earning their own livings, and charting their own courses through life. The stories featuring these strong female characters exhibit feminist potential in their questions of power, gender, and the social roles of women. They reward analysis by revealing Christie's early and sustained interest in writing about the lives of self-sufficient women who make their own choices and live with them.

REFERENCES

Aldridge, M. (2020), *Poirot: The Greatest Detective in the World*, New York: HarperCollins.

Allendinger, B. (2019), "The Erasure of Race in Agatha Christie's *And Then There Were None*," *ANQ*, 32 (1): 60–4.

American Academy of Arts and Sciences. n.d. "Gender Distribution of Degrees in English Language and Literature," *Humanities Indicators*. Available online: https://www.amacad.org/humanities-indicators/higher-education/gender-distribution-degrees-english-language-and-literature (accessed June 20, 2021).

Armer, F. (1935), "Sex in Detective Fiction – Do's and Don'ts," *Spicy Detective*, reproduced in B. Collier (n.d.), "Beau Collier's 'Birth of the Girlie Pulps'", *Pulp Magazine Project*. Available online: https://www.pulpmags.org/contexts/essays/history-of-girlie-pulps.html (accessed August 15, 2021).

Arnold, J. (1987), "Detecting Social History: Jews in the Works of Agatha Christie," *Jewish Social Studies*, 49 (3–4): 275–82.

Ashley, M. (2006), *The Age of the Storytellers: British Popular Fiction Magazines 1880–1950*, London: British Library.

Atia, N. (2019), "Murder in Mesopotamia: Agatha Christie's Life and Work in the Middle East," in N. Atia and Kate Houlden (eds), *Popular Postcolonialisms: Discourses of Empire and Popular Culture*, 87–107, New York: Routledge.

Bargainnier, E. (1980), *The Gentle Art of Murder: The Detective Fiction of Agatha Christie*, Bowling Green, OH: Popular Press.

Barnard, R. (1980), *A Talent to Deceive: An Appreciation of Agatha Christie*, New York: Dodd, Mead & Company.

Bernstein, S. (2016), "Queer Girls, Bad Girls, Dead Girls: Post-War Culture and the Modern Girl," in J.C. Bernthal (ed), *The Ageless Agatha Christie: Essays on the Mysteries and the Legacy*, 45–60, Jefferson: McFarland.

Bernthal, J.C. (2016a), *Queering Agatha Christie: Revisiting the Golden Age of Detective Fiction*, London: Palgrave Macmillan.

Bernthal, J.C. (2016b), "The Sumptuous and the Alluring: Poirot's Women, Dragged Up and Dressed Down," in J.C. Bernthal (ed), *The Ageless Agatha Christie: Essays on the Mysteries and the Legacy*, 81–97, Jefferson: McFarland.

Beyer, C. (2016), "'With practised eyes': Feminine Identity in *The Mysterious Mr. Quin*," in J.C. Bernthal (ed), *The Ageless Agatha Christie: Essays on the Mysteries and the Legacy*, 61–80, Jefferson: McFarland.

Brand, C. (1977), "Miss Marple: A Portrait," in H. R. F. Keating (ed), *Agatha Christie: First Lady of Crime*, 193–204, New York: Holt, Rinehart and Winston.

Brown, S. (2020), "'Scoring Off a Foreigner?' Xenophobia, Antisemitism, and Racism in the Works of Agatha Christie," *Clues: A Journal of Detection*, 38 (1): 70–80.

Butler, J. (1988), "Performative Acts and Gender Constitution: An Essay in Phenomenology and Feminist Theory," *Theatre Journal*, 40 (4): 519–31.

Butler, J. (1990), *Gender Trouble: Feminism and the Subversion of Identity*, New York and Abingdon: Routledge.

Butler, J. (1991), "Imitation and Gender Insubordination," in D. Fuss (ed), *Inside/out: Lesbian Theories, Gay Theories*, 13–31, New York and Abingdon: Routledge.

Butler, J. (1993), *Bodies That Matter, On the Discursive Limits of "Sex,"* New York and Abingdon: Routledge.

Christie, A. ([1920] 2012), *The Mysterious Affair at Styles*, New York: William Morrow.

Christie, A. (1922), "The Wife of the Kenite," *The Home*, 28, 96. Available online via *Collecting Christie*: https://www.collectingchristie.com/post/wife-of-kenite (accessed August 15, 2021).

Christie, A. ([1926] 2020), *The Murder of Roger Ackroyd*, New York: William Morrow.

Christie, A. ([1932] 2019), *The Stranger*, New York: Samuel French.

Christie, A. ([1936] 2011), *Cards on the Table*, New York: William Morrow.

Christie, A. ([1943] 2011), *The Moving Finger*, New York: William Morrow.

Christie, A. ([1958] 2018), *Ordeal by Innocence*, New York: William Morrow.

Christie, A. ([1964] 2011), *A Caribbean Mystery*, New York: William Morrow.

Christie, A. ([1977] 2011), *Agatha Christie: An Autobiography*, New York: Harper.

Christie, A. (2008), *Miss Marple and Mystery: The Complete Short Stories*, London: Harper.

Collier, B. (n.d.), "Beau Collier's 'Birth of the Girlie Pulps,'" *The Pulp Magazine Project*. Available online: https://www.pulpmags.org/contexts/essays/history-of-girlie-pulps.html (accessed August 15, 2021).

Evans, M.A. (2021), "Killing Bluebeard: Claiming Subversive Femininity in Agatha Christie's 'Philomel Cottage' and *The Stranger*," *Clues: A Journal of Detection*, 39 (1): 104–14.

Flint, K. (2005), "Revisiting *A Literature of Their Own*," *Journal of Victorian Culture*, 10 (2): 289–96.

Fremlin, C. "The Christie Everybody Knew," in H. R. F. Keating (ed), *Agatha Christie: First Lady of Crime*, 111–20, New York: Holt, Rinehart and Winston.

Gilbert, S. and S. Gubar (1979), *The Madwoman in the Attic: The Woman Writer and the Nineteenth-century Literary Imagination*, New Haven: Yale University Press.

Gill, G. ([1990] 1992), *Agatha Christie: The Woman and Her Mysteries*, New York: New York Free Press.

Grauby, F. (2016), "'This Isn't A Detective Story, Mrs. Oliver': The Case of the Fictitious Author," *Clues: A Journal of Detection*, 34 (1): 116–25.

Green, J. (2015), *Curtain Up! Agatha Christie: A Life in the Theatre*, New York: Harper Voyager.

Haycraft, H. (1943), *Murder for Pleasure: The Life and Times of the Detective Story*, New York and London: D. Appleton-Century Company.

hooks, b. (1984), *Feminist Theory: From Margin to Center* Boston: South End Books.

Hughes, D. B. (1977), "The Christie Nobody Knew," in H. R. F. Keating (ed), *Agatha Christie: First Lady of Crime*, 193–204, New York: Holt, Rinehart and Winston.

Humann, H. D. (2017), *Gender Bending Detective Fiction: A Critical Analysis of Selected Works*, Jefferson: McFarland.

Humble, N. (2002), *The Feminine Middlebrow Novel, 1920s to the 1950s: Class, Domesticity, and Bohemianism*, Oxford: Oxford University Press.

Keating, H. R. F. (1977), *Agatha Christie: First Lady of Crime*, New York: Holt, Rinehart and Winston.

Kim, J. (2012), *Murdering Miss Marple: Essays on Gender and Sexuality in the New Golden Age of Women's Crime Fiction*, Jefferson: McFarland.

Knepper, M. (1983), "Agatha Christie—Feminist," *Armchair Detective*, 16 (4): 389–406.

Lassner, P. (2009), "The Mysterious New Empire: Agatha Christie's Colonial Murders," in R. Hackett, F. Hauser, and G. Wachman (eds), *At Home and Abroad in the Empire*, 31–50, Newark: University of Delaware Press.

Lathen, E. (1977), "Cornwallis's Revenge," in H. R. F. Keating (ed), *Agatha Christie: First Lady of Crime*, 79–94, New York: Holt, Rinehart and Winston.

Leonard, J. (1975), "I Care Who Killed Roger Ackroyd," *Esquire*, August: 60–1.

Light, A. (1991), *Forever England: Femininity, Literature and Conservatism between the Wars*, Oxford and New York: Routledge.

Linares, T. (2018), "Dis-Orienting Interactions: Agatha Christie, Imperial Tourists, and the Other," MA Thesis, Bowling Green State University, Bowling Green.

Maida, P. and N. Spornick (1982), *Murder She Wrote: A Study of Agatha Christie's Detective Fiction*, Bowling Green, OH: Popular Press.

"Maker of the Grey Cells of M. Poirot," *The Sketch*, Wednesday March 7, 1923, 122 (1571): 467.

Makinen, M. (2006), *Agatha Christie: Investigating Femininity*, New York: Palgrave Macmillan.

Makinen, M. (2016), "Agatha Christie in Dialogue with *To The Lighthouse*: The Modernist Artist," in J. C. Bernthal (ed), *The Ageless Agatha Christie: Essays on the Mysteries and the Legacy*, 11–28, Jefferson: McFarland.

Maslin, K. (2016), "The Paradox of Miss Marple: Agatha Christie's Epistemology," *Clues: A Journal of Detection*, 34 (1): 105–15.

Morris, D. (2020), "Christie's First Short Story, 'The Wife of the Kenite,'" *Collecting Christie*. Available online: https://www.collectingchristie.com/post/wife-of-kenite (accessed June 7, 2021).

Mullen, R. D. "From Standard Magazines to Pulps and Big Slicks: A Note on the History of US General and Fiction Magazines," *The Pulp Magazine Project*. Available online: https://www.pulpmags.org/contexts/essays/pulps-and-big-slicks. html (accessed August 7, 2021).

Osborne, C. (1982), *The Life and Crimes of Agatha Christie*, London: Collins.

Plain, G. (2001), *Twentieth-Century Crime Fiction: Gender, Sexuality, and the Body*, Edinburgh: Edinburgh University Press.

Prichard, M., ed. (2012), *The Grand Tour: Letters and Photographs from the British Empire Expedition 1922*, London: HarperCollins.

Ramsey, G. C. (1967), *Agatha Christie: Mistress of Mystery*, New York: Dodd Mead.

Rowland, S. (2004), *From Agatha Christie to Ruth Rendell - British Women Writers in Detective and Crime Fiction*, Basingstoke: Palgrave Macmillan.

Schaub, M. (2013), *Middlebrow Feminism in Classic British Detective Fiction: The Female Gentleman*, Basingstoke: Palgrave Macmillan.

Schwartz, A. (2016), "The Curious Case of Dorothy L. Sayers & the Jew Who Wasn't There," *Moment*, 41 (4): 34.

Showalter, E. (1977), *A Literature of Their Own*, Princeton: Princeton University Press.

Symons, J. (1980), "Puzzle Maker, Review of *A Talent to Deceive* by Robert Barnard," *Inquiry*, November 24: 29–30.

Thomson, H. D. (1931), *Masters of Mystery: A Study of the Detective Story*, New York: William Collins.

University of Pennsylvania. (n.d.), "The Sketch: A Journal of Art and Actuality," *The Online Books Page*. Available online: https://onlinebooks.library.upenn.edu/webbin/ serial?id=thesketch (accessed December 9, 2021).

Uzzell, T. (1938), "The Love Pulps," *Scribner's*, April: 36–41. Available online: *The Pulp Fiction Project*: https://www.pulpmags.org/contexts/essays/article-on-love-pulps.html (accessed August 7, 2021).

Walter, E. (1977), "The Case of the Escalating Sales," in H.R.F. Keating (ed), *Agatha Christie: First Lady of Crime*, 11–24, New York: Holt, Rinehart and Winston.

Westmacott, M. ([1930] 2001), *Giant's Bread*, in *Absent in the Spring and Other Novels*, 163–405, New York: St Martin's Minotaur.

Westmacott, M. ([1934] 2009), *Unfinished Portrait*, New York: St. Martin's Minotaur, 187–429.

Westmacott, M. ([1944] 2001), *Absent in the Spring*, in *Absent in the Spring and Other Novels*, 1–163, New York: St. Martin's Minotaur.

Westmacott, M. ([1948] 2001), *The Rose and the Yew Tree*, in *Absent in the Spring and Other Novels*, New York: St. Martin's Minotaur, 469–644.

Westmacott, M. ([1952] 2009), *A Daughter's a Daughter*, 3–183, New York: St Martin's Minotaur.

Westmacott, M. ([1956] 2009), *The Burden*, 433–617, New York: St Martin's Minotaur.

Wilson, E. (1945), "Books: Who Cares Who Killed Roger Ackroyd?: A Second Report on Detective Fiction by Edmund Wilson," *The New Yorker*, January 20: 59.

Wyndham, F. (1966), "The Algebra of Agatha Christie," *The Sunday Times*, Weekly Review supplement, February 27: 25–6.

CHAPTER FIVE

Queer Clues to Christie

J.C. BERNTHAL

INTRODUCTION

A Caribbean Mystery, Agatha Christie's offering for 1964, sees the pink-and-white Victorian spinster, Miss Marple, on holiday in the West Indies. Bored by a major, who believes he is telling her exciting stories, barely "fit for a lady's ears" (Christie 1964: 10), Marple recalls her worldly, Oxford-educated nephew, who paid for this trip.

Nephew Raymond has assured his aunt that her cottage is in safe hands. A writer friend of his will look after it: "He's very house proud. He's a queer. I mean—" and, in the recollection, Raymond breaks off. What becomes clear, though, is that "even dear old Aunt Jane [has] heard of queers" (10). In fact, she knows all kinds of things from her life in a small village:

> Plenty of sex, natural and unnatural. Rape, incest, perversions of all kinds. (Some kinds, indeed, that even the clever young men from Oxford who wrote books didn't seem to have heard about.)
>
> (9–10)

The most caustic remark here is parenthetical, even in the protagonist's own thoughts. What distinguishes Marple's generation from her nephew's, she reflects, is not a different understanding of sexuality, but different approaches to how one talks about it, if at all. The truth is Miss Marple has known all about "queers" for longer than Raymond has been alive; but the terminology and the conversations have been different.

The scene occurs early in the novel, a reminder to readers in the Swinging Sixties and beyond that, for all its outward conservatism, the Christieverse is anything but twee, and it is just as engaged with the concerns of real life as any gloomy kitchen sink drama. It may also be a joke at the expense of Christie's younger husband, Max Mallowan, and his writerly Oxford friend A.L. Rowse, who recalled chiding Max in the early 1960s for not letting "the homo side to public school life" into adulthood—"but not in front of Agatha, of course" (Rowse 1983: 100). She may have had better hearing than Rowse imagined.

In the third decade of the twenty-first century, Christie is being re-evaluated as both a writer and a woman. Owing much to a change in focus for television adaptations, and to a considerable rebranding effort by Agatha Christie Limited, Christie is now being understood as an author who reflected the darker aspects of the human soul, and as a woman who *lived*: who surfed, romanced, and had a strong sense for business. However, the overarching image of Christie and her work is one that was cultivated by Christie and her publishers during her career, influencing most critical approaches at least until the early 2000s. This is the vision of a conservative, nostalgic body of work, where the intricacies of life are reduced to simple problems and where an untroubled, chocolate-box-illustration version of village life is restored without question once the murderer has been caught.

"Few feminists or radicals are likely to read her," wrote Julian Symons in 1980 (29). Even at the time, Symons's comment reflected the problem with dominant Christie (and genre) scholarship: that, in order to make pre-decided arguments about the books' unengaged unreality work, the research itself deliberately disengages with reality. Christie has always had an appeal as close to universal as any author could get (Barnard 1980: 11–12). Her engagement with "radical" themes was sufficient to have her plays consistently fall foul of the Lord Chamberlain's censors for dealing overtly with homosexuality or sailing too close to the wind (Green 2015: 507–9). Whether or not the "perversions of all kinds" mentioned in *A Caribbean Mystery* are named, they are there.

THE MALE AND FEMALE GAYS

In a sense, the critical laziness of Christie scholarship in much of the twentieth century owed a great deal to models of conservatism she was apparently dismissed for espousing. Paradoxically, on the grounds of her extreme popularity, her voice and the attitudes of her readers were for many years amalgamated, excluding a range of queer and minority perspectives that have always consumed and accompanied her work.[1]

With the broadening of literary criticism in the 1980s to include more popular texts, feminist perspectives on Christie began to emerge, as outlined

---

[1]Anecdotally, noticing the disconnect between common observations that Christie was only read by conservatives and my own lived experience of her immense popularity in queer and other marginalized communities first led me to consider Christie from the angle of queer theory.

in Mary Anna Evans's contribution to the present volume, "Reading Christie with a Feminist Lens." As the best-selling writer since William Shakespeare and the best-known at least since Charles Dickens, Christie's work began during these years to be considered from a range of perspectives. A small branch of scholarship considered, initially, gay and lesbian themes in popular fiction, and Christie would be mentioned—but only mentioned—in discussions of homosexuality and detective narratives. These discussions tend to be partial overviews of characters who are presented according to codes largely taken for what sexologists called "sexual inversion"—the supposed condition of having a man's personality inside a woman's body, or vice versa, which was understood in the early twentieth century as the basis for homosexual behavior (see Bernthal 2016: 83–5).

The stereotyping in traditional readings of gay and lesbian themes and characters in mainstream crime writing, including Christie's, is twofold. First, it is based on stereotypes included by the author that are spotted and understood by the reader. Second, it is underscored by preconceptions about the authors', texts', and readers' attitudes to sexuality. Anthony Slide's *Gay and Lesbian Characters and Themes in Mystery Novels* (1993) looks mostly at mainstream crime fiction, acknowledging that "the most popular of mystery writers [...] kept relatively clear of gay and lesbian themes and characters" (Slide 1993: 1). Nonetheless, Slide identifies characters as "gay" or "lesbian" in *The Moving Finger* ("a harmless gay character"), "Three Blind Mice" ("a gay character"), *A Murder Is Announced* ("obviously a lesbian couple"), and *Nemesis* (describing "a crime of passion") (41–2).

Dennis Altman's 2009 article, "Reading Agatha Christie," based on his work in the 1990s with Dorothy Portman, looks at "coded" characters, suggesting that Christie was unable or unwilling to write openly about homosexuality, but that their presence in her texts indicates "another, less ordered world" beneath the surface of her nostalgic vision of English rural life (Altman). While clearly not agreeing with Symons, above, that "[f]ew feminists or radicals are likely to read" Christie, Altman nonetheless makes the same unchecked assumption that the books are the embodiment of "nostalgia for a lost Gilbert and Sullivan, pearl-necklaced, sherry-drinking middle England" (Altman). He is writing more in the tradition of Charles Osborne who, observing "sketchy" stereotyped characters, noted that "Christie never progressed beyond the most superficial descriptions of her homosexual characters" (Osborne 1999: 242).

Altman has a potentially radical way of reading the stereotyped characters, whom he nonetheless identifies as homosexual: as so over-the-top-grotesque that they perform a kind of unconscious literary drag act, exposing the ridiculous prejudices that underpin them. To achieve this conclusion, Altman skims over texts that he appears to have read long ago, includes no quotations, and notably mixes up the diminutive recurring detective Mr. Satterthwaite with the bombastic victim Mr. Shaitana in *Cards on the Table*, when asserting that "Sattherwaite [*sic*] is killed off [...], thus meeting the fate of almost all homosexual characters of his era" (Altman). In fact, we last meet Satterthwaite, pining after a romantic ghost but alive and well, in a 1971 short story. Judith A. Markovitz's *The Gay Detective Novel* (2005) is focused more on specifically LGBT-themed novels and authors.[2] Christie here is identified mostly as an "influence" on LGBT writers, in terms of plotting and the amateur/outsider detective setup (Markowitz 2005: 127). While the study identifies Christie and other "straight" writers as influential in the world of LGBT crime writing, there is an underlying assumption that the world of straight crime fiction, like Christie's, is sexless and uninterested in diversity: "I doubt Mrs. Christie would approve," states one author, quoted, in a discussion of his debt to her (127).

However, as Lucy Bland has shown, the concept of an identity based on sexual orientation was not widely available in common British parlance until well into the century (Bland 1998: 183–96) and, as Nicola Humble has shown, common "codes" such as long fingers or lisps in men and tweed skirts or telegrammatic speech in women could be taken for gendered nonconformity rather than sexuality signifiers at least until the 1940s (Humble 2001: 235). Understanding categories like "gay" and "straight" or "woman" and "man" as social constructs means recognizing that they are contextually contingent. A logical step from this is that contemporary understandings of "gay stereotypes" would not have been available in exactly the same way across the various points of Christie's long career—indeed, she makes a very similar point in *A Caribbean Mystery*, quoted above, when Marple reflects that she did not categorize "perversions" quite as the "clever young men" do.

The tradition of listing "gay" stereotypes as they appear in Christie's work continues, especially among scholars who subscribe to the conservative vision of Christie writing, in her own words, "the old Everyman Morality Tale, the hunting down of Evil and the triumph of Good" (Christie 1977: 437). The most sophisticated approach to this tradition is that of John Curran, cautioning in 2017 against reading too much into the stereotypes, but stating that "there is little doubt about the orientation" of ten characters in various plays, novels, and stories, while identifying a further three "ambiguous examples" (Curran 2017: 53). Notably, Curran uses the same stereotypes as others listed above—if a male character is called "ladylike" or calls men "my dear," for example, he makes the list—but labels the example "ambiguous" if the character also expresses any form of interest in a member of the opposite sex. There is a homo/hetero binary at play here, in the interpretation of "orientation" signifiers.

---

[2] I use "LGBT" (Lesbian, Gay, Bisexual, Trans) here because, while the book's title refers to "Gay and Lesbian Characters," it also discusses bisexual and trans characters and themes. However, there is no concept of "queer" or other identities in the book, so I am not here using the "LGBTQ+" acronym, which I would use in similar contexts.

An illustration of a typically identified gay male stereotype can be found in a light reading of her 1943 Marple novel, *The Moving Finger*. The book features Jerry Burton, an ironically named wounded pilot ("Jerry" being war slang for "German" and "Burton" being war slang for a British fighter destroyed or killed) trying to recover in an out-of-the-way village, where he and his sister, Joanna, stumble into a poisoned pen campaign and a series of murders. One of the villagers Jerry meets, and is fascinated by, is "an extremely ladylike plump little man," Mr. Pye (Christie 1943: 24). Pye, as Christie introduces him, owns and inhabits "a very exquisite house"; "hardly a man's house." He is "devoted to his petit point chairs, his Dresden shepherdesses and his collection of bric-a-brac" (24). There are two obvious "codes" here that have not gone unnoticed by generations of Christie readers and scholars. First, and most obvious, Pye's "ladylike" bearing, not to mention his fondness for gossip and his "falsetto squeak" (25), suggests sexual inversion. When the police inform Jerry and Joanna that the murderer is probably "a middle-aged spinster," Joanna responds that "Mr. Pye [...] *is* a middle-aged spinster" (106, emphasis original).

However, with his house resembling "a museum" (25), he is also a collector. This was—and to an extent still is—a kind of shorthand that could refer to male homosexuality, combined with other "codes"; Ronald Gregg has discussed in relation to 1930s magazine culture, how describing "an interest in interior decoration and collecting art and antiques" was intended to be taken to sufficiently worldly readers to denote male homosexuality (Gregg 2003: 90). When Jerry, growing uncomfortable, argues that Pye is "queer" and "perverse" he is referring not to anything the character has done—because all he has done is gossip hospitably—but to the discussed codes.

If one is looking for gay characters in Christie, Pye is an easy target. He is, in Slide's words, "what used to be termed euphemistically a confirmed bachelor" (1993: 41). Slide concludes that Pye is "intended to be a harmless gay character" (41), and Curran agrees that readers are "left in no doubt about Mr. Pye's sexuality": "the final nail in the coffin of Mr. Pye's heterosexuality [is] an Italian bedstead" (2017: 54). Curran points out, too, that Pye is never a serious suspect, while the murderer is one of the "relatively few" married (and undeniably heterosexual) men in the novel (54). Pye never actually expresses a sexuality or even any history of or desire for a partner. As a fictional character, sexuality isn't part of his make-up: his gender performance and the effect he has unsettling Jerry and Joanna Burton are all.

Pye's queerness is not about sexuality, then, but about identity codes. The vehemence with which the Burton siblings suspect and criticize him can also reflect in their own journeys throughout the novel: both are trying to heal and to find (heterosexual) love, which they end up doing. Jerry in particular is not a conventionally heroic hero, down to his punning name, and a fondness for tea and cakes that alarmed one reviewer at the time, who commented that Christie did not understand how men think (see Bernthal 2016: 243). It is as if he needs something—an unmanly man—to react against in order to confirm his status as a red-blooded manly man, who will go on at the end of the novel to get the girl.[3] Meeting Pye has been an important part of Jerry's character-development, from reckless injured pilot to calm, recovered family man: he recalls his time with Pye and the other villages as "one of the queerest times I have ever passed through" (Christie 1943: 159).

SEEING QUEERLY

As I introduce my own contribution to the field, it is worth taking a moment to explain my use of the word "queer." Starting out as a slur to refer to people who were not "straight," the word has to some extent been reclaimed, first by activists, then in scholarship and theory, and more recently in general parlance, where it is sometimes used synonymously with the umbrella term "LGBTQ+" or variations thereupon.

"Queer," though, does not have a universally agreed-upon meaning. In fact, its indeterminacy is what has made it attractive in queer theory and the field of scholarship known as Queer Studies. These, too, are multivalent and far from uncontested, with different strands of queer theory taking different stances on a range of questions, from whether sexuality is innate or constructed to the extent to which queerness is possible or achievable within a heteronormative social order. Academically, queer theory rises from activism of the 1980s and from feminist theory. A key presence in queer theory, although they have sometimes distanced themselves from it, is Judith Butler, whose 1990 work *Gender Trouble* asserts that gender is "a stylized repetition of acts" and that gendered identity is constructed and reinforced every time it is performed (Butler [1990] 2006: 34).

Gender Trouble follows the lead of significant historians of sex and sexuality, such as Michel Foucault, and identifies the concept of biological sex being a binary identity signifier as itself bound up in the performative nature of gender. It is the enactment of gender that gives this apparently innate binary its power. In the same year, Eve Kosofsky Sedgwick's *Epistemology of the Closet* rejected "the homo/heterosexual" binary in readings of numerous established British and American novels (Sedgwick [1990] 2008: xvi). Building on Butler's and Sedgwick's enormous influence, queer literary studies have explored texts from a range of perspectives, united by a rejection of the concept that heterosexual/cisgendered/normative is natural or right and that it has an opposite which is therefore unnatural or wrong.

---

[3] I use the word "girl" advisedly. Jerry ends up with the childlike Megan Hunter, and assertively gives her a makeover so that she can return to the village a glamorous young woman, who is his bride.

My 2016 monograph, *Queering Agatha Christie*, builds on and begins to synthesize work done in Christie studies, gay and lesbian studies, feminist theory, and queer theory. It considers some of the stereotypes Christie deploys in their historical context, without assigning gendered or sexual identities but reading them in terms of the nebulousness of "normality." Characters like Christopher Wren in "Three Blind Mice" and *The Mousetrap*, cited by all the Christie scholars named above, are suspected by other characters and the implied reader/playgoer of moral decrepitude and therefore of guilt. Wren is a prancing, lisping architect who intimidates other men by spending time in the kitchen and requesting chintzy décor. Like Pye, he is suspicious not because of whom they sleep with but because they are perceived to have failed to perform masculinity appropriately.

Therefore, paradoxically, Christie does not make these men guilty, because that would be too obvious—she needs to shock the reader, and, in the case of *The Mousetrap*, makes Wren a war hero while identifying the assertively manly police sergeant as the murderer. *Queering Agatha Christie* does not look for LGBTQ+ characters in Christie's work, then, but engages with Christie's handling of key themes like gender, sexuality, and identity. Outside of authorial intention, this shows that the texts have what I call "queer potential" (Bernthal 2016: 2). They display an awareness that respectability is a collection of codes and signifiers, which can and should be mocked and undermined.

Other studies around the same time have used a similar lens to explore the intricacies of identity in these apparently straightforward narratives. My monograph is limited by a temporal focus (up to 1952) and an emphasis on generic masculinity; thankfully, a range of approaches have navigated further elements of this complex terrain. Alistair Rolls's "An Ankle Queerly Turned, or the Fetishised Bodies in Agatha Christie's *The Body in the Library*" starts with an adaptation to make a point about various ways of rereading the texts. Rolls notes the way bodies are disguised and hidden or dressed up as other bodies in the novel, while desire is curtailed before it can be properly expressed. He observes that Miss Marple and the reader are invited to read against "the male detective gaze" (Rolls 2015: 830), seeing bodies as more contested than they might appear, via "a detective uncovering of a (new) truth behind the red herrings" (840).

Christie's only overt example of a same-sex couple, and the most widely discussed couple in the context of LGBTQ+ or queer conversations, is Miss Hinchcliffe and Miss Murgatroyd, two women who live together in *A Murder Is Announced*. The novel, another Marple case, was published in 1950, and it is set thoroughly in the changing world of the post-war countryside. Chipping Cleghorn is a village where everybody knows their neighbors, but no one really *knows* their neighbors: people have moved into the area after the Second World

War, with only their word that they are who they say they are. Ration books and identity cards abound, as do false identities and hidden connections.

Hinchcliffe and Murgatroyd live together in perhaps the most loving relationship the novel depicts. The characters, who live together on a farm, are only called "friends" (Christie 1950: 16) but, as Slide points out, their loving, romantic relationship becomes clear when Amy Murgatroyd becomes the third victim (Slide 1993: 41). Hinchcliffe goes "stiff and taut" as she cradles her lover's body, and says, "in a low, quiet voice," "I'll kill whoever did this" (Christie 1950: 202). As Gillian Gill notes in her feminist biography of Christie, the characters are drawn "sympathetic[ally]," and Christie conveys Hinchcliffe's "savage but largely silent grief" sensitively (Gill [1990] 1991: 1970).

The couple is drawn along conventionally gendered lines: Hinchcliffe adopts "a manly stance" (60), is "attired in corduroy slacks and battledress tunic," and sports a "short man-like crop" of hair (15), while Murgatroyd is "fat and amiable" and dresses in skirts (16). If clothes make the man or woman, they have made Hinchcliffe and Murgatroyd a conventional heterosexual couple, with the masculine/feminine codes here signifying that they have assumed those roles in their conventionally coded relationship. These are not subversive queer revolutionaries, but a straightforward loving couple, with whom the detective and the implied reader come to sympathize.

A code-spotting approach which seeks to "out" the couple as lesbians could reach two opposing conclusions. The most common approach is that of John Curran, who argues that the characters are not seen as bad for being "unequivocally 'different'"; that "[t]hey are treated in a totally matter-of-fact manner by Christie, by Miss Marple, by the police and, most significantly of all, by the inhabitants of Chipping Cleghorn" (Curran 2017: 55). In other words, they are afforded the dignity of being unremarkably in love—a positive case of representation. Curran attributes this to the upheavals of the Second World War making social change inevitable and to the fact that lesbianism has never been criminalized in the UK (55).

The other conclusion is negative. Because Murgatroyd is Hinchcliffe's "friend," their love remains one that dare not speak its name. The couple remains, in this reading, in a literary and socially mandated closet; they are "problematical lesbians" (Bradley 1960: 15). To this extent, it has been concluded that many, if not most, of Christie's contemporary readers would have missed the true nature of their relationship altogether (Shaw and Vanacker 1991: 42). This was the rationale behind having the couple kiss in the 2005 television adaptation—Christie's grandson, Mathew Prichard, said to the media: "If you read the books carefully, it's all there. This is just more overt" (in Bernthal 2016: 238). The approach is strategically useful for encouraging LGBTQ+ visibility, but risks homogenizing the past in which Agatha Christie wrote and set her work, as a static time of repression where the only reason the couple did not kiss in the book is because they are constrained by a literary closet.

A contextualized reading sees this couple in light of sensational newspaper reports in the late 1940s and early 1950s—immediate postwar Britain. As Alison Oram has shown, two types of tabloid journalism in these years reveled in lamenting the destruction of sacred matrimony: one type would highlight the rise in divorce, noting that "warring couples were now no longer locked together forever" (Oram 2012: 52), while the other would note that many marriages were not what they seemed. These stories, couched in terms of "psychiatric explanations and moral condemnation" (51), would detail couples who married during or just after the Second World War, which were in fact unions between two women. In these cases, one of the women would have dressed as a man for the ceremony and may at the time of the article be living as a man (Oram 2007: 131–57). The concept of transgender identity does not seem to exist in these narratives, which largely precede the early sensational case of Roberta Cowell's gender reassignment surgery in 1951.

These articles are of particular note, since Christie's novel opens and closes with newspapers—indeed, the murder of the title is announced in a newspaper—and as Christie's 1948 radio play, "Butter in a Lordly Dish," and subsequent Poirot novel, *Mrs McGinty's Dead*, show she was at this time engaging with Sunday magazine culture. The presentation of the couple along strict gendered lines, as "manly" and "amiable" and certainly as a rather stagey couple, reflects how women living together were described in these publications, and enables readers to draw a rather substantial inference about the nature of Hinchcliffe and Murgatroyd's living arrangement. However, the focus is not on sexuality but on affection. The couple has a playful, sparring relationship until Murgatroyd's murder unlocks Hinchcliffe's stoic, sincere emotion. "I'll kill whoever did this" is the reaction of a genuine, heartbroken spouse. In its quiet way, the novel counteracts the moralizing and sensationalism of contemporary journalism, identifying an emotional core to the relationship.

NORMALITY IN *NEMESIS*

A contextualized queer reading of Christie, then, can go beyond a "code-spotting" approach to examine deeper questions raised by and reflected in the texts. While the characters discussed above in relation to *The Moving Finger* and *A Murder Is Announced* are generally benevolent, Christie also features queer-coded characters who are uncontrovertibly negative presences. The most unsettling example of this occurs in a 1962 play, *The Rats*, which features Alec, a jealous "pansy type" whose entire bearing is "very artificial" and "stylish" (Christie 1963: 11). Alec traps a young heterosexual couple because he wants revenge on the woman, with whose first husband he was in love.

"You've only got to take one look at Alec to see what kind of devotion that was," says the hero (16), concluding that Alec is "mad—of course he's mad" (16). In fact, as Julius Green has shown in his history of Christie on stage, the script originally had Alec referred to as "obviously a homo," with revisions labelling him "obviously a queer," then "a bit feminine," before settling on the final wording (Green 2015: 508–9). Although Curran has claimed that this play is unsettling because Alec's crime is "directly attributable to [his] sexual orientation" (Curran 2017: 57), nobody has ever claimed that Jacqueline de Bellefort, who kills four people, including herself, out of love for a man in *Death on the Nile*, did so because she was heterosexual. The crime and the madness do not stem from homosexuality but from obsession. What is objectionable is the negative stereotyping, which undeniably links homosexuality to spite and sensibility.

This may, however, be splitting hairs. Alec is not an example of positive portrayal, and *The Rats* is little-known partly because it is a negative force in LGBTQ+ representation. Our final case study concerns *Nemesis*, the last-written Marple case, published in 1971, which Curran (2017: 57) cites as the only other example of Christie attributing murder to homosexuality. In this novel, Marple investigates the disappearance and murder of teenaged Verity Hunt, which occurred sixteen years prior to the events in the book. Proving Verity's wastrel boyfriend innocent, Marple reveals that she was killed by her guardian, Clotilde, a middle-aged woman who was in love with her. Confronting Clotilde, Marple reveals:

> You loved Verity too much. She meant everything in the world to you. She was devoted to you until something else came into her life. A different kind of love came into her life. She fell in love with a boy, a young man. [… S]he loved him and he loved her and she wanted to escape. To escape from the burden of the bondage of love she was living in with you. She wanted a normal woman's life. To live with the man of her choice, to have children by him. She wanted marriage and the happiness of normality. [...] Sooner than let her go, you killed her. Because you loved her, you killed her.
>
> (Christie 1971: 229–30)

This portrayal of same-sex desire ticks several boxes for stereotypes about homosexuality that had developed along with terminology like "lesbian." It can be, and has been, read as representing what Jessica Murray in another context calls "homophobic stereotypes of lesbians as predatory, dangerous, violent, deviant seducers of 'innocent' heterosexual girls" (Murray 2013: 122). Even Owen Emmerson's insightful analysis of the dangers of outing characters as gay or lesbian in screen adaptations refers, in passing, to *Nemesis* as "the only 'Marple' novel where lesbianism was originally suggested as a motive for murder" (Emmerson 2014). R.A. York summarizes the problematic nature of this solution for twenty-first-century readers: "the murderer is a Lesbian provoked by her beloved's preference for a natural—heterosexual—romance" (York 2007: 69).

Christie does not use the word "lesbian" here. In fact, she only used it once, in *Hallowe'en Party* (1969), in which a schoolboy tries and fails to impress Poirot by saying, "in a man of the world way," that one of his teachers may be a "[l]esbian" (Christie [1969] 2001: 221)—as in *A Caribbean Mystery*, the trendy terminology is faintly mocked as nothing particularly new or shocking. *Hallowe'en Party* was published two years after the Sexual Offenses Act 1967 decriminalized consensual same-sex activity between men in England, although the changes had been expected since the Wolfenden Report recommended them in 1957, and with wide-reaching political protests, language around homosexual identities was very much in the public domain at the time of *Nemesis'* publication.

Instead, it may be that lesbianism has nothing to do with *Nemesis*. The discussion of "the happiness of normality" certainly espouses heteronormative clichés about the moral supremacy of the conventional family unit: a husband, a wife, and children conceived in wedlock. However, while it is undoubtedly a conservative narrative, the voice of Jane Marple provides a commentary on sexuality in a general sense throughout the novel: there is, for example, an uncomfortable reflection on the word "rape" and a lack of clarity around informed consent. What Marple advocates as "normal" in this novel is a relationship between the young Verity and the "boy" or "man" who is on her level; a relationship between peers. The abnormality of Clothilde's and Verity's relationship could be argued to lie in the abuse of power that the former shows as a mother figure for the latter, which ends with Verity being destroyed before she can leave.

Context again helps elucidation here. I have argued elsewhere that *Nemesis* can be understood as a rewriting of *Sleeping Murder*, subtitled *Miss Marple's Last Case* in the first edition and published posthumously in 1976. Like *Curtain: Poirot's Last Case*, *Sleeping Murder* was written several decades before its publication. Like *Nemesis*, it concerns a young woman's murder, blamed on her partner, several years in the past. In both books, Marple reveals that the woman was killed by an obsessive guardian—in this case, her half-brother—who did not want her to move out for a "normal and harmless" life with a boyfriend or husband (Christie 1977: 217). Helen, the victim in *Sleeping Murder*, "couldn't meet young men in the ordinary normal way" because "her brother had a deep affection for her"; an "uneasy and unhappy" kind of affection (216, 217). She was, says Marple, "a perfectly normal young girl who wanted to have fun and a good time and finally settle down with the man of her choice" (217) but her brother "was not going to let Helen go and live happily with her husband"; "racked with love" and unable to let "Helen [...] escape him," he killed her (219).

The speeches Marple gives about the pursuit of normality are similar in both cases, even down to the language: "happily," "normal," "escape." The only key difference in the setups is that the perverted attraction is same-sex in *Nemesis* but that does not translate to any different kind of moral judgment. If this reflection on normality and abuse was always intended to close out Marple's career, it appears that that the genders of the victim and perpetrator were never the key points. Decentralizing heterosexual perspectives means not reading queer people as abnormal; instead, "normality" itself is portrayed as something aspired to, but never achieved—because, in Christie, it is respectable people who are hiding things. That is how, commercially, the shock value of an unexpected solution works.

BEYOND EASY ANSWERS

The work being done in this arena is far-reaching, extending beyond specific sexual identities and characters who conform to or challenge available stereotypes. Building on the work of Lee Edelman, who argues that queer theory should reject "reproductive futurity" (the pressure to continue the status quo, bound up in the image of the nuclear family; Edelman 2004: 14), Sarah Bernstein has looked at deviant children in Christie's post–Second World War works. These children might kill, as in *Crooked House*, or be killed, as in *Dead Man's Folly*. They are, crucially, resisting the pressure to grow up and conform, and represent in Bernstein's words "a source of anxiety [...] whose presence threatens social order" (2016: 57). Her theory-driven, contextualized look at these characters adds to the discussion around Christie as a social commentator, whose work can be mined for commentary on deviance and the destructive enforcement of normativity.

Charlotte Charteris has shown that queer readings need not apply only to characterization, presenting the country house in Christie's interwar fiction as a queer space. Punning on the concept of a "queer plot," Charteris notes that Christie's houses "shape and mould" the characters and their journeys (Charteris 2017: 92). Boundaries do not move in these spaces, though experiments and aesthetic change can alienate and isolate (94). Charteris invites further research into queering these spaces, noting that as country houses have developed throughout the twentieth century (and in attendant literature) "from domestic to hotel space," they have created an uncanny effect both in and out of their own times (98). These readings show that there is significant mileage left in approaching Christie from a queer, theory-informed, and contextualized perspective.

Contextualized readings of Christie from a queer perspective, then, can open up new ways of understanding diversity in her texts. The extensive and

QUEER CLUES TO CHRISTIE

multivalent approaches to the Christieverse that a queer lens can illuminate have only yet been glimpsed. This movement necessitates the introduction of context in readings of Christie's published work, which, after all, was written between 1916 and the 1970s. The passage of time alone suggests that her world was hardly the static, unchanging milieu commonly associated in scholarship with her works. In particular, more attention needs to be focused on Christie's later texts, especially those published during the 1960s and 1970s, when LGBTQ+ activism and the seeds of queer theory were prominent in the public psyche.

REFERENCES

Altman, D. (2009), "Reading Agatha Christie," *Inside Story*. January 5. Available online: https://insidestory.org.au/reading-agatha-christie/ (accessed September 19, 2021).

Barnard, R. (1980), *Agatha Christie: A Talent to Deceive*, London: Collins.

Bernstein, S. (2016), "Queer Girls, Bad Girls, Dead Girls: Post-War Culture and the Modern Girl," in Bernthal, J. C. (ed), *The Ageless Agatha Christie: Essays on the Mysteries and the Legacy*, 45–60, Jefferson: McFarland.

Bernthal, J. C. (2016), *Queering Agatha Christie: Revisiting the Golden Age of Detective Fiction*, London: Palgrave Macmillan.

Bland, L. (1998), "Trial by Sexology? Maud Allen, *Salome*, and the 'Cult of the Clitoris' Case," in L. Doan and L. Bland (eds), *Sexology in Culture: Labelling Bodies and Desires*, 183–98, Oxford and New York: Oxford University Press.

Bradley, M. Z. (1960), *A Complete, Cumulative Checklist of Lesbian, Variant and Homosexual Fiction, in English or Available in English Translation, with Supplements of Related Material, for the Use of Collectors, Students and Librarians*, Rochester: Marion Zimmer Bradley.

Butler, J. ([1990] 2006), *Gender Trouble: Feminism and the Subversion of Identity*, New York, Abingdon: Routledge.

Charteris, C. (2017), "A Strange Night in a Strange House: The Country House as Queer Space in Interwar Mystery Fiction," *Clues: A Journal of Detection*, 35 (2): 89–99.

Christie, A. (1943), *The Moving Finger*, London: Collins.

Christie, A. (1950), *A Murder Is Announced*, London: Collins.

Christie, A. (1964), *A Caribbean Mystery*, London: Collins.

Christie, A. ([1969] 2001), *Hallowe'en Party*, London: Collins.

Christie, A. (1971), *Nemesis*, London: Collins.

Christie, A. (1977), *An Autobiography*, London: Collins.

Curran, J. (2017), "'Queer in Some Ways': Gay Characters in the Fiction of Agatha Christie," in C. Evans (ed), *Murder in the Closet: Essays on Queer Clues in Crime Fiction before Stonewall*, 52–66, Jefferson: McFarland.

Edelman, L. (2004), *No Future: Queer Theory and the Death Drive*, Durham and London: Duke University Press.

Emmerson, O. (2014), "Queering Agatha Christie," *Headmaster Rituals or Barbarism Began at Home?* May 13. Available online: https://headmasterrituals.wordpress.com/2014/06/13/queering-agatha-christie-2/ (accessed September 19, 2021).

Gill, G. ([1990] 1991), *Agatha Christie: The Woman and Her Mysteries*, London: Robson.

Green, J. (2015), *Curtain up: Agatha Christie—A Life in Theatre*, London: HarperCollins.

Gregg, R. (2003), "Gay Culture, Studio Publicity, and the Management of Star Discourse: The Homosexualization of William Haines in Pre-Code Hollywood," *Quarterly Review of Film and Video*, 20 (2): 81–97.

Humble, N. (2001), *The Feminine Middlebrow Novel, 1920s–1950s: Class, Domesticity, and Bohemianism*, Oxford, New York and Auckland: Oxford University Press.

Markowitz, J. A. (2005), *The Gay Detective Novel: Lesbian and Gay Main Characters and Themes in Mystery Fiction*, Jefferson and London: McFarland.

Murray, J. (2013), "Stereotypes and Subversions: Reading Queer Representations in Two Contemporary South African Novels," *English in Africa*, 40 (1): 119–38.

Oram, A. (2007), *Her Husband Was a Woman!: Women's Gender Crossing in Modern British Popular Culture*, London and New York: Routledge.

Oram, A. (2012), "Love 'Off the Rails' or 'Over the Teacups'? Lesbian Desire and Female Sexualities in the 1950s Popular Press," in H. Bauer and M. Cook (eds), *Queer 1950s: Rethinking Sexuality in the Post-war Years*, 41–57, Basingstoke: Palgrave Macmillan.

Osborne, C. ([1999] 2000), *The Life and Crimes of Agatha Christie*, revised edn, London: HarperCollins.

Rolls, A. (2015), "An Ankle Queerly Turned, or the Fetishised Bodies in Agatha Christie's *The Body in the Library*," *Textual Practice*, 29 (5): 825–44.

Rowse, A. L. (1983), *Memories of Men and Women, American and British*, Lanham, New York and London: University Press of America.

Sedgwick, E. K. ([1990] 2008), *Epistemology of the Closet*, Berkeley, New York, London: University of California Press.

Shaw, M. and S. Vanacker (1991), *Reflecting on Miss Marple*, London: Routledge.

Slide, A. (1993), *Gay and Lesbian Characters and Themes in Mystery Novels: A Critical Guide to Over 500 Works in English*, Jefferson: McFarland.

Symons, J. (1980), "Puzzle Maker," *Inquiry*, November 24: 29–30.

York, R. A. (2007), *Agatha Christie: Power and Illusion*, Basingstoke: Palgrave Macmillan.

CHAPTER SIX

Christie Does Ecocriticism

SUSAN ROWLAND

INTRODUCTION

As proposed by Cheryl Glotfelty in *The Ecocriticism Reader*, ecocriticism is earth-centered readings of literature (Glotfelty 1996: xix). It reverses the convention of considering nature in narrative as metaphors for human matters. Rather, ecocriticism looks for the ways human characters are actually representing the life of the land. This approach also responds to the recognition that the marginalization of nature was bound up with human hegemonies of colonialism, ethnicity, race, and gender.

In the twenty-first century, ecocriticism has gained momentum as the climate crisis accelerates. Today, ecocriticism is a diverse field that takes part in multidisciplinary debates exploring, as Lawrence Buell puts it, the mutual construction of the physical world in which societies and technology have always been shaped by environment and, in turn, shape it (Buell 2001: 6). In such an interactive field of being and knowing, longtime dualities such as nature versus culture are revealed as fictions.

To put the new ecocriticism in Christie terms, consider the setting she helped to popularize, the country house as crime scene. Ecocriticism can explore the ways that the country house in mysteries stands for specific historical and environmental conditions. These are largely dependent upon a particular climate. How might the fascination with this kind of crime story actually reveal something about the re-creation of the natural? Indeed, the crime genre Agatha Christie did so much to crystallize can be shown to offer modes of control, blame, passion, and rationality that today are visible in ecological conundrums and climate activism. Despite this, Christie lacks specific ecocritical attention, except in important recent work that I shall explore, and in the archetypal perspective that I have previously published. Therefore, this chapter will explore largely twenty-first-century criticism that begins to show Christie as an important historian of the earth and our relations to it.

Ecocriticism today includes the notion of the Anthropocene (Ellis 2018). In a sense, the Anthropocene is both the antithesis and the product of ecology itself. Put simply, the Anthropocene signifies a new era on this planet, one where humans have so disturbed its innate processes that we are now planet-shaping beings. Perspectives from ecology have led to the recognition of the Anthropocene, confirming that humans threaten the sustainability of the ecosphere.

Given that the Anthropocene puts human activity at the center of planetary influences, and that ecocriticism is earth-centered, the Anthropocene is a moral as well as a practical problem for the ecological critic. Put another way, the Anthropocene is where we are because dominant societies have thought in terms of Anthropos, meaning a privileged group of humans called "Man," to be served by everything "other." Ecocriticism is starting to use the concept of the Anthropocene as a tool to read literature against the grain, against its overt ethos. Intriguingly, Anthropocene ecocriticism is vitally connected to a form of criticism that has been marginalized, which is that of archetypes.

The key link between Anthropocene and archetype is myth. The Anthropocene is another attempt at an origin story, a way of making sense of humans in their relationship to the planet. It is not surprising therefore that Anthropocene scholars recognize myth, such as James Lovelock's theory of Gaia (Ellis 2018: 18). His portrayal of the earth as an intelligent system able to reject invasive species like us is summed up in the ancient earth goddess. Another myth germane to the Anthropocene is cited by Ellis, that of Prometheus, who stole fire from heaven to empower human beings. Gaining fire is a particularly apt idea for the beginning of humans refashioning the planet.

One way of understanding the persistence of myths is that of archetypes as proposed by C.G. Jung (1968). He suggested that humans have evolved psychologically over millennia as well as physically. We all inherit inborn patterning energies that are formative, yet not determining, of images and meaning. Here, archetypal theory adds a psychological layer to the creative mutual reciprocity of humans with the natural world. The Anthropocene as an image for where we are can take its place alongside other mythical potentials. For crucial to Jungian psychology is that there is always more than one myth because the collective unconscious (archetypes common to all humans) is innately creative. Human psychic health depends upon a conscious creative interaction with the unknown psyche, a process he called individuation.

So, what do Anthropocene and archetypes have to do with Agatha Christie? One project for modern ecocriticism is a critical exploration of Anthropos, or the centrality of exclusively human concerns in connection to the biosphere. Do Christie's country houses contribute to climate change not just because of the production of paper but because they encourage a regard for the earth as only meaningful in relation to the Anthropos? More excitingly, could critical treatments of Christie show resistance and alternatives to anthropocentric attitudes? This chapter shows how myth and archetypal critical approaches to Christie uncover alternative stories to that of the Anthropocene itself. First of all, it is worth considering recent work on the detective genre from ecocritical perspectives.

DETECTIVE FICTION DOES ECOCRITICISM IN *GREEN LETTERS* JOURNAL

Introducing a special edition of *Green Letters* on crime fiction and ecology in 2018, Jo Lindsay Walton and Samantha Walton give a succinct account of the intersection of genre and ecocriticism. They map out directions for Christie criticism in the Anthropocene age. For example, the detective restores her world, a drive often integral to environmental criticism and action. Hercule Poirot and Miss Marple are unlikely eco-activists yet more than Miss Marple's gardening links them to ecology. How far is the detective's heroic assumption of expertise and authority implicated in anthropocentric notions of stewardship or dominance in relation to nature?

The Waltons show the nineteenth-century emergence of the sleuth as a transcendent figure capable of knowing that is separable from being. It is part of a discourse that treats nature as object, subject to human dissection. A different detecting is a different relation to the world in the instance of noir crime. This detective discovers that she is more and more implicated in the criminal activity she ostensibly investigates, similar to ecocriticism's developing understanding that it too is entangled with ideas and practices or discourses that degrade the biosphere.

Christie skirts the noir genre in the way that Poirot, in particular, comes to feel implicated, even compromised, in some of his cases. Also connected to Christie is the notion of "fair play" and rationality that haunt the frustrations of environmental discourses as well as the fiction. Moreover, the Waltons suggest that villainy in crime fiction can be linked to discussions of responsibility and guilt in questions of pollution and exploitation of nature. Is the greed and unfeeling selfishness at the heart of many Christie murders a dimension of such motives in the behavior of polluting industries, governments, and persons? I suggest that it is so, given the mythical currents in the Christie mystery that circle around the grail and the wasteland.

What is far-reaching in this introduction is the way that crime fiction becomes open to ecocriticism in ways beyond its depiction of nature. Here, the genre's focus on human concerns in murder is termed "anthropocentric plotting," to be studied for its capacity to unpack the assumptions of the Anthropocene as cultural, not inevitable. In particular, the Waltons show that crime fiction typically apprehends totality, makes a viable picture of a world. Especially true of Christie with her enclosed groups of suspects, such envisioning is important to ecology and ecocriticism. Even generic tropes used by Christie such as the crime scene, red herrings, locked rooms, the denouement, investigation, and false solution are all subject to eco-analysis.

Finally, the Waltons cite Katherine E. Bishop as saying that "one may suspect the butler but not his begonias," in showing the "turn" inherent in ecocriticism that decenters human agents (Bishop 2018). The introduction does not state that it is Hercule Poirot who suspects the begonias in *The Mysterious Affair at Styles* (1920). Captain Hastings is frustrated that his supposedly brilliant friend keeps asking about the new flower bed. It is a few pages before Poirot's preoccupation is linked to what the flowers reveal about recent human activity. So Poirot does suspect the begonias. Gardening is where human and natural actions meet in ways that are more complex in Christie than "Anthropocentric plotting" would suggest.

Of course, this special issue of *Green Letters* includes an essay on Christie's own specialized work with plants. Alicia Carroll examines the mysteries in the context of the expansion of herbalism between the First and the Second World Wars. Showing the significance for debates around biodiversity, the paper explores Christie's knowledge stemming from working as an apothecary's assistant. With hands-on experience in extracting both poisons and medicines from common garden species, Christie's murder plots can be understood as nuanced constructions of the agency of plants. It is time to look further at the shifts in focus on Christie in the context of ecocriticism.

CRITICAL SHIFTS: CHRISTIE ECOCRITICISM GOES MULTIDISCIPLINARY

Christie's nature and natural economies, whether centered on villages or country houses, also attract social historians in an example of multidisciplinary eco-analysis. For example, in the *Journal of Social History 2010*, K.D.M. Snell reads Christie for the ethos of villages in a particular historical moment (Snell 2010). Reading landscape in the novels as embedded with moral values and depicted through multiple viewpoints, Snell decides that Christie charts the decay of the country house rural economy. Her novels are valuable historical resources on how nature and culture interacted. Again, the novel does more ecocriticism than the critic. Accused of living in "a stagnant pool" (part of Snell's title), Miss Marple points out that stagnant water is remarkably full of diverse life. *She* will not miss the diversity or perversity of any species, human or not.

Another movement in Christie eco-implied criticism is movement from the construction of space to the materiality of place. An example of place-oriented criticism, a division of earth-centered ecocriticism, would be Rebecca Mills's insightful study of novels by Christie and Dorothy L. Sayers given seaside resort settings. In "'I Always Did Hate Watering Places': Tourism and Carnival in Agatha Christie's and Dorothy L. Sayers's Seaside Novels," Mills explores the ironies of setting murders in places traditionally associated with health and holidays. The novels reveal moral corruption juxtaposed with a socially constructed natural world devoted to rest and restoration. Place is ethos and cultural ideologies found wanting, rather than verisimilitude. Here is ecocriticism again as diagnosis of the human pretensions etched into the environment.

Other examples of ecocriticism by means of examining Christie on social history can be found in *Agatha Christie Goes to War* (2020), edited by Rebecca Mills and J.C. Bernthal. In a volume devoted to Christie's shaping of war, particularly the Second World War, the topic of psychogeography proves to be a valuable lens for Christie and place. In "Mapping War, Planning Peace," Sarah Martin and Sally West cite Guy Debord on psychogeography. Place is carved into psyche, although psychogeography concentrates on knowable consciousness as opposed to the unconscious explored later in this chapter.

Martin and West bring to Christie ecocriticism the different attitudes to maps during the Second World War between England and Germany plus the wartime constructions of the earth through surveillance photography from above. How might Miss Marple's powerful binoculars, ostensibly for birds, be linked to wartime magnifying lenses for grainy photographs? These critics contrast the introspective character of the rural village in *Murder at the Vicarage* (1930) with the postwar dis-locations of *A Murder Is Announced* (1950) in which foreigners and newcomers indicate a shifting population. No longer is the village a place where being (present, perhaps for generations) indicates knowing or being known.

By the time of *The Mirror Crack'd* (1962), Miss Marple's house is no longer the epicenter of the village. Rather, she is called upon to go "[w]ith the feeling of Columbus" to the new territory known as the Development (Christie [1962] 2011: 13). Here, the new world is the built world of postwar town planning where Miss Marple discovers the inhabitants living "like a flock of happy birds" (6). While the natural image on the one hand divides Miss Marple from this indigenous population of young mothers of the lower middle class, it does take the reader back to her penchant for ornithology. Miss Marple, Martin and West show, is able to adapt to the changing rural economy and detect a murderer who is a privileged newcomer taking the now outdated position of Lady of the Manor.

Returning to more overtly earth-centered ecocriticism, Sylvia A. Pamboukian's "In the Apothecaries' Garden with Agatha Christie" (2016) also cites Christie's own wartime apothecary service. Pamboukian particularly stresses how the novels reveal the ambivalence of plants as poisons and medicines. Within the crime story itself, the active plant agent is neither wholly natural nor completely cultural. Poisons appear as complexity in this twenty-first-century ecocriticism. It is time to go deeper into Christie's articulation of genre and form from the point of view of nature and the Anthropocene.

CHRISTIE AND ECOCRITICISM THROUGH FORM, GENRE, AND ARCHETYPE

A neglected aspect of ecocriticism that pertains to Christie is that of genre and form. Novels and stories are more considered in their specificity to the historical moment, rather than for what links detective fiction over time and between authors. There is a gap in approach here between the distinctiveness of each story and the generality of genre. It is the study of the way a particular form, the basic structure of the work, interacts with genre. Just how do the assumptions about this type of story develop over time and contribute to larger narratives about humans and nature? In the intersection of form and genre reside patterns of relation to nonhuman nature. For example, in "The Wasteland and the Grail Knight" (2010), I expanded W.H. Auden's famous essay, "The Guilty Vicarage" (1948).

Auden proposed that human patterns of relating to nature as Other are also spiritual narratives. For him, the fictional detective is so mesmerizing because he (and it is "he" for Auden) restores the Garden of Eden to the paradise before human inhabitants disobeyed the law. His detective arrives in a fallen world where sin has polluted a small community. By identifying and removing the killer, harmony is restored, an essentially religious pattern.

Taking my cue from Dorothy L. Sayers's Lord Peter Wimsey in *Strong Poison* (1930) stating that detectives are the equivalent of medieval knights aiming to do good deeds, I suggest that the sleuth is on a grail quest. In fact, the detective arrives in a wasteland. The land or community is sick because of the unsolved crime. Solving murder involves asking the right question as the grail knights discovered. The solution heals the wasteland just as finding the grail did. For the grail is the healing truth as well as the re-constituted community, which is also the wasteland rejuvenated. Nature and culture are one; the wasteland is human and nonhuman society, polluted and sick.

Of course, land and/or society restored is not how many detective fictions end. While Christie's detectives such as Hercule Poirot and Miss Marple are usually effective grail knights, the noir sleuth often ends sick herself with a complicity that cannot be eradicated. In fact, the noir detective's transforming discovery is that the wasteland or society *cannot* be healed. She is converted into another character from the grail story, the Fisher King, whose illness is an aspect of the land's. As the Waltons point out in the *Green Letters* Introduction above, the noir detective uncovers ineradicable complicity. Such a notion can be part of the narrative of ecological crime stories, or it can stand for the complicity of humans in nature, otherwise known as the Anthropocene.

My argument is also that these two related mythical structures, successful grail knight and conversion to Fisher King, are also prototypes of comedy and tragedy. The succeeding knight renews the world just as comedy enacts a death and rebirth, a fall into the ridiculous followed by the restoration of communal laughter. The Fisher King is distantly related to the tragic hero who becomes a kind of scapegoat, suffering for or as the community's sins. After all, one of the earliest detective stories is Sophocles's *Oedipus Rex*. Ignorant Oedipus thinks that he is on a heroic quest for truth to heal his wasteland-city of the plague. What he discovers is that he is the source of infection and the murderer in the death of the previous king, his father. The first literary sleuth is also the first murderer.

Looking at genre becomes another way to examine cultural attitudes to the earth. Moreover, these cultural attitudes often have religious antecedents. Notably the transcendence of the classical detective stems from the way the Bible was interpreted in Christianity to legitimize hegemony over nature. Humans modeled themselves as their God, separate from his creation. Creation myths are consciousness stories. Modernity's disastrous consciousness of exploitation of the other, including the other as nature, was instated by its monotheism.

Hence the argument that *other* myths, particularly myths with diverse relations to nature, can be valuable to ecocriticism. Indeed, it is more. Anthropocene studies have already recognized that myth is *already present* in ideas such as Gaia.

Also, Prometheus himself arises from the scientists and philosophers of the Anthropocene.

> In 1999 Hans Joachim asked the pivotal question of the Anthropocene. "Why should Prometheus not hasten to Gaia's assistance?" If humans are indeed transforming the earth, what is to be done? Or more humbly – what can be done? Can humans help to bend earth's trajectory towards better outcomes for both humanity and non-human nature?
>
> (Ellis 2018: 144)

All this may seem far from ecocriticism and Christie, yet the notion that myth inhabits genre and shapes consciousness suggests that such novels have a more dynamic part to play in relating to nature than is often assumed. First of all, it is necessary to consider just how stories, consciousness, and nature interact. For that, the new evolutionary science of complexity is important. Much work remains to be done in linking ecocriticism to genre and form, and this study of Christie can only touch on these areas.

THE REJUVENATING TRICKSTER

Arising initially from computer science, complexity theory argues that change occurs through the encounter of environments acting as complex adaptive systems, or CAS (Holland 1994). When CAS encounter each other, the resulting intermingling is too complex to map and the result cannot be predicted. Hence a complexity model of evolution suggests an inherent creativity in nonhuman nature. Building on evolutionary complexity, CAS have been perceived in human social systems where one culture encounters another or groups merge with one another (Wheeler 2006: 67–8).

The human brain also produces a complex adaptive system. Jungians have noted that complexity theory works for individuation, or the lifelong development of psyche by ever-greater integration with the mystery of the unconscious (Shulman 1997). Naturally, individuation complexity also describes humans meeting the complexity of nature. Archetypes as patterning energies in psyche and culture are revealed as engines of complexity evolution. Indeed, the Jungian theory of archetypes closely resembles complexity theory in modeling how human–nature interaction produces unpredictable meaning-making rather than total chaos. Today, complexity evolution is often termed "emergence" to name how culture, creativity, and meaning *emerge* from an unmappable synthesis of complex systems.

So, what does complexity theory mean for ecocriticism, detective fiction, and Agatha Christie? Of course, literature, as a whole and within its genres, is among the many complex adaptive systems of culture. After all, genres emerge from multiple non-determining precedents and change in ways that cannot always be predicted. Genres mobilize and materialize psychic creativity in writers. To be more precise, the archetypal myths and images that make up the texture of literary genres are not only psychically potent; they also communicate beyond the single psyche in the complex act of reading. In terms of ecocriticism, they do even more. If we look at the archetypal myths and images as organs of ever-fluid complexity, they act as portals to nonhuman nature.

To consider this in detail, it is worth turning to Jung's depiction of the psychic image when materialized in words. He called everyday words operating largely in rational consciousness "signs" (Jung 1922: para. 105). However, those words in which mystery was embedded, which served as intersections between conscious and unconscious, are symbols (Jung 1922). When such words are articulated in a story, the story's narrative articulates the psyche. It reveals and shapes the border between ego and unconscious and is known to Jung as a myth (Jung 1930: para. 152).

Strikingly, Jung was an avid reader of Agatha Christie. He also put detective stories into his category of visionary literature which meant so suffused with symbols and myth as to be the utterance of the psyche of an age, rather than the consciousness of its writer (para. 137). A visionary work is when a writer cannot give a rational explanation of the work. It "arrives" as a voice from beyond shaped by myth and energized by symbols, even if the myth is bestowed by genre.

Such an argument provides an ecocriticism because via archetypes and complexity theory, it suggests that symbols in literature are not "about" nature, they are a way to it. Via the complexity psyche, literary symbol and myth knit writer and reader into the complexity evolution of the planet. One initial way to understand such a countercultural idea is in the role of the mythical trickster in detective fiction. Shapeshifting, thieving, gender-fluid, sexually unruly; within the trickster is to be found the criminality of the detective villain, and also in the tricky ways that the sleuth must adopt to catch him.

The trickster lives in Hercule Poirot setting his trap for the real killer in *The Mysterious Affair at Styles* (1920) as well as in later books. Lewis Hyde considered that the archaic trickster taught humans hunting (Hyde 1998). Today, that trickster mobilizes every reader hunting the killer. Moreover, detective fiction is truly complex in possessing many mythical ecologies. In addition to the grail quest and the trickster, I will offer four further myths for Agatha Christie and show them in six novels.

MYTHICAL ECOLOGIES IN RESPONSE TO THE ANTHROPOCENE

I suggest that four independent goddesses—Hestia, Artemis, Aphrodite, and Athena—provide alternative ecologies, or rather show that earth systems are multiple, not just of one story. As archetypes of psyche, these figures represent energies that are gender-fluid and manifest in creative dialogue with history and culture. Artemis is the name most used in this culture for a wild feminine purity that is both protector of young women and a fierce hunter. Something of her lives in Miss Marple in her garden and in her determination to save or avenge young women in books such as *Sleeping Murder* and *A Pocket Full of Rye*. Such mythical underpinning undoes what is troubling about the very idea of Anthropocene, the inference that humans can only disturb, that we are not already inside wild nature and it in us.

Perhaps more noticeable for both Miss Marple and Hercule Poirot are their Hestia qualities for she is both the hearth fire and the guardian of it. She makes a home in a house and in the community. Furthermore, she is the planet as our home since the Greeks believed that there was an energizing fire at the center of the earth. Again, Christie's detectives are strongly oriented to protect the home and any strangers it collects. It is Hestia who consecrates the stranger at the hearth from harm. These detectives frequently save the foreigner or newcomer from being the scapegoat. Moreover, both Poirot and Marple promote marriages or save them as we will see.

Hestian ecology is very different to the Anthropocene because home can be a sacred aspect of planetary being, in contrast to Prometheus behaving irresponsibly. Hestian ecocriticism suggests that home-making and interiority are part of the nature of the planet too. In addition, the romantic tendencies of Poirot and Marple take them into Aphrodite territory. She bestows the beauty that arouses erotic love, in animals as well as human beings. Aphrodite is in the roses that adorn the bride and in the coupling of snakes. She also, I suggest, inhabits mysteries by being outraged at murder, for she is the body's joys and murder is an unnatural deprivation of them.

Aphrodite ecology is carnal and embodied. She is the exploration of the body's joys that will not be forced into society's convenience or the heteronormative. Finally for this Christie ecocriticism, I want to include Athena. Associated with fostering the city, Athena's capacity to be wily, to work within patriarchy for her own ends, is undervalued. Two related aspects reveal her presence in detective fiction: she is goddess of weaving and ceramics or *containing*, and it was she who saved Orestes from the Furies of endless revenge in *The Eumenides* of Aeschylus by being the goddess of wisdom and strategy (1966).

Athena persuaded the Furies to let go of Orestes and come and live inside the city as honored aliens. In effect, she *contained* the endless desire for blood by offering it a home inside the human world. The social structure that she created to do this was the law and its courts, which would replace blood feuds with a system of justice. I suggest that she also created detective fiction which contains the furies by solving the murder. For a city, community, or family cannot survive an unsolved murder. There must be a solution to dissolve the constellation of the furies that appear in the human soul and have the capacity to destroy all human communities.

Athena is part of the necessity that drives Hercule Poirot and Miss Marple. She is an ecology that insists that justice is essential and not just for human beings. Even the visceral powers of nature (that is also human nature) must be satisfied. It is time to look more closely at six key novels across Christie's career.

The Mysterious Affair at Styles

Arriving at Styles, Captain Hastings is struck by the contrast between the peaceful countryside and the thundering war in Europe. However, he soon detects tension in the household, particularly around the universally disliked Alfred Inglethorp, second husband to the matriarch of the Cavendish family. While her intentions toward her first husband's sons, John and Lawrence, are good, Mrs. Inglethorp has failed as Hestia. She does not "command love," only the lives around her (Christie [1920] 1989: 39). It takes Hercule Poirot to reinvigorate Styles. He does so by solving her murder in a very Hestian manner. He attends to the begonias (evidence that a gardener could be called to witness a new will) and housekeeping details such as a smashed coffee cup.

Poirot also rekindles the dying fire of John Cavendish's marriage and tends the flame of Lawrence's adoration of Cynthia, a young woman working in a hospital dispensary with plenty of access to poisons. Poirot insists upon the neatness of facts as he spins about the house. However, he also calls himself a pig or "miserable animal" and is likened to a mad bull when he realizes he has overlooked a clue (75).

For no human psyche is driven by just one myth. *The Mysterious Affair at Styles* compares intelligence and natural instinct (Athena and Artemis) that Poirot says often go together (128). John's wife Mary is Artemis enchained yet only able to fight "tooth and nail" when her husband is put on trial for the murder (161). Hastings sees her as "slumbering fire," and "a wild untamed spirit in an exquisitely civilized body" (9).

In fact, Styles, the house, works as a kind of Jungian symbol in which more and more meaning is unpacked. It remains a symbol as Poirot and Hastings leave, mainly because of the novel's evocation of instinct as that which cannot be explained or ignored. Instinct is married to beauty in Mary Cavendish, who takes over as a beloved mistress of Styles. What with the healthy begonias and the spreading sycamore under which the family gather for tea, Styles could be described as icon of the Anthropocene. Yet it is more precisely home to Artemis as protector and Aphrodite, the beauty who inspires love. Poirot secures them by restorying Hestia and proving also wily Athena. These goddesses are ecologies of humans finding home in multiple modes of nature.

The Murder at the Vicarage

Although the title of this 1930 novel suggests violation of one household, the plot focuses mostly on another, that of victim Colonel Protheroe, his unhappy wife Anne, and his sulky daughter, Lettice. The intrigue shifts from the house to the village with Miss Marple proving a worthy Athena in protecting the integrity of her city. Introduced as one of a cluster of gossiping elderly women, the plot reveals Miss Marple as the only one whose instincts and compassion are necessary.

The sleuth is Artemis also in her dogged pursuit of the truth of the wild nature that seethes beneath the apparent conventionality of St. Mary Mead. It goes without saying that the village name combines the Christian feminine with "mead" or meadow, fertile earth, suggesting pre-Christian antecedents. Miss Marple is also Artemis in guardian of young women, particularly around childbirth. She ends by guessing the pregnancy of lively Griselda, the vicar's wife.

One of Christie's most delightful characters, Griselda's name recalls the folktale in which Griselda was the phenomenally patient wife of an incredibly cruel husband. *The Murder at the Vicarage* begins with Griselda flouting her namesake. She is a poor housekeeper who seems mostly to tease her husband, the narrator. Later gossip about her and Lawrence Redding, actually lover of Anne Protheroe, reaches the narrator vicar. At the end, his wife is revealed as a modern version of "patient Griselda" after all.

The echo of folktale and pre-Christianity is part of rooting the novel in mythical ties to the land. Even more emphatically than in *The Mysterious Affair at Styles*, the problem is the divorce between instinctual nature, passion in love and in religion, and convention. Absent from the Protheroe marriage, Aphrodite is betrayed in Anne's affair with Redding because his lust includes her money if her husband dies. Humanitarian Dr. Haydock, who does not believe in capital punishment, is convulsed by "primitive rage" at the discovery of how a vulnerable curate was driven to suicide (217).

Fortunately, Miss Marple is wily Athena most of all. She is able to let loose ancient trickster energy in collaboration with authorities, to restore order, not disrupt it. As the vicar puts it, "[t]here is always some perfectly good and reasonable explanation for Miss Marple's omniscience" (Christie [1930] 1993: 205). Unlike Poirot, she does not claim superior powers even though she has them. Also unlike Poirot, Marple is here detecting on her home ground and will continue to involve herself where she is already involved, by some relationship or obligation. She is the embedded god, the sleuth who detects from her own garden, watching over her neighbors from the inside.

In this sense, *The Murder at the Vicarage* offers an ecology of gardening itself. It recalls that gardening is part of divine Aphrodite in the creation of beauty to inspire love and the body's pleasure. Marple's roses are well cultivated with their instinctual nature carefully trimmed and shaped. Human nature, by contrast, has become warped by too much severing from the instinctual and the wild. As an Artemis able to detect the untamed in St Mary Mead, Miss Marple models in her narrative a healthy multi-goddess ecology. She becomes the symbol that is portal to nature and human nature.

Death on the Nile

No longer is the country house ecology capable of right cultivation through detection. Linnet Ridgeway's names combine a shy bird with a prehistoric track. Yet she values neither wildlife nor history in her ruthless remodeling of the country house she has acquired. Even more ruthless is her decision to marry the fiancé of her once dearest friend, the impoverished Jacqueline de Bellefort. When Linnet is driven to ask Poirot for help, it is because Jacqueline is pursuing her on her honeymoon.

Desperate to escape, Linnet and Simon Doyle join Poirot on a Nile cruise. Jacqueline appears on the ship. After a drunken scene in which Jacqueline shoots Simon, Linnet is found dead the next morning. Poirot discovers the ship fully occupied with the wealthy bride's enemies. These include a young woman descried repeatedly as "dog-like" who was made poor by Linnet Ridgeway's speculator father.

Nature in this novel does more than provide what is sorely dysfunctional among the humans. Egypt supplies a "human cluster of flies" while the Nile is full of rocks like "vast prehistoric monsters" (Christie [1937] 1960: 31, 38). While there is colonialism in calling destitute children "flies," murder is located inside a society of Anglo-American wealthy tourists. The boat passes through a former civilization with the river evoked as ancient, fertilizing, and inexorable. One dimension of this story is that the characters become the evanescent flies compared to the epochs of Egypt.

When Linnet at last senses her danger, she sees it in terms of the nature she cannot subdue. In England, she could have trees felled and cottages moved. Now she sees that Egypt incarnates Artemisian wild, bringing inevitable death: "Monsieur Poirot, I'm afraid—I'm afraid of everything. I've never felt like this before. All these wild rocks and the awful grimness and starkness. Where are we going?" (66). Where before the nonhuman held the instinctual that was being perverted in the human community, here the wild is the bringer of death, reminding that death is part of nature. Linnet has ignored nature by trampling over it in human and nonhuman forms. She is a failed Hestia in stealing the hearth fire of her visitor, Jacqueline, who should have been her sacred stranger. She has violated the *home* (of her cottagers too) and therefore opened herself to her own hearth being broken by Jacqueline who has too much passion for Simon. With her overwhelming Aphrodite thwarted, Jacqueline is possessed by Artemis, as bringer of death.

Here, Poirot brings an Athena capacity to *contain* the instinctual riot that has led to Linnet's carefully planned murder. His detecting is not quick enough to stop two other murders, but he is able to balance his Artemis with Athena and Aphrodite to foster one marriage and make space for another. Through him, the two unhappy young women find spouses that contribute to Athenian order and future Hestian hearth fires. The ecology of *Death on the Nile* is that of the rightful place of death in nature, death that can be invoked by ignoring nature, something pertinent for the twenty-first century as well.

N or M?

Written and published during the Second World War, *N or M?* (1941) reveals the necessity of feminine as well as masculine powers. When Tommy Beresford is sent to Sans Souci, a boarding house on the south coast, to look for enemy spies, he is surprised to discover his wife has got there before him, also in disguise and on the same mission. Wisely, Tommy tells his intelligence contact that he and his wife work better together. In fact, their alliance, and Tuppence's identity as a mother, will prove crucial to identifying spies who murder.

Tommy makes a distinction between those who serve their country by spying behind enemy lines and those who betray their country by volunteering to hand over vital information to an enemy in wartime. These latter he seeks as N or M, respectively a man or a woman. Set in 1940 when invasion by the Nazis from France was expected, archetypal polarities are stretched to breaking point by war. Rather than the ambiguous loyalties of the trickster, deception is treason against the government, or motherland, that Tommy and Tuppence serve. On the other hand, Tommy and Tuppence also deceive on behalf of that government/motherland. Unlike N and M, however, they do not kill. N appears as bluff protector and M as a harmless single mother of a charming child, Betty.

It is the mother archetype that is ultimately at stake in the quest to save the motherland. Tuppence spots M because the so-called mother of Betty shoots dead a woman holding "her" child. The murdered woman was Betty's true mother and the Beresfords, true children of mother Britain, will become her new parents. Vital information about the traitors is to be found in Betty's books of nursery rhymes, particularly, "goosey, goosey gander" (200). These geese famously wander yet belong to the home (of the nation). Tommy and Tuppence restore the British hearth as home by leaving their own, and becoming tricksters in *Sans Souci*. The Beresfords incarnate Athena in their deception for protection and Artemis in their determined pursuit of truth as well as being those who bring death—to enemy spies.

Above all, *N or M?* happens on the coast, the edge of the nation with the nation on edge. Designed for vacations, the seaside town is a thin stretch of water away from an army waiting to invade. In a sense, the novel is prescient of the climate emergency with the all-too-likely chance of the sea invading the land. Written when Germany was an overwhelming enemy, *N or M?* is also indicative of facing the overwhelming powers of the unknown psyche, including known and unknown nature. One spy even tries to use Tuppence's children against her by calling himself a colleague of her daughter in a secret war department. All this is true: it is the intentions of this particular fascist agent that are false. The elemental nature of mothering in *N or M?* is embedded in Mother Earth as the Hestian homeland.

4.50 FROM PADDINGTON

Rutherford Hall, home of the Crackenthorpe family, is the country house economy in mortal decay. No longer the organizing focus of rural community, it is surrounded by the expanding town and almost cut off by a curving rail track. The land is overgrown and overseen by a disappointed old man who resents his sons because his industrialist father did not like his penchant for collecting art. Hence, Mr. Crackenthorpe is victim of his father's will that left the estate to his eldest grandson after the son's death. Since Edmund died in the war, it disturbs the family no end to discover that he may have married in France and produced an heir.

The question of the French wife, Martine, becomes pertinent because of the discovery of the strangled body of a woman in one of Mr. Crackenthorpe's Italian sarcophagi. Detecting this crime will lead to another death before the feminine in the form of Miss Marple, channeling Athena and Artemis, and her avatar, Lucy Eylesbarrow channeling Hestia and Aphrodite, will rejuvenate the family and the land. For Lucy is a college graduate who combines traditional home-making roles with shrewd business acumen. As cook, housekeeper, and carer for hire for short periods, she is a successful enough to impress Miss Marple. Fortunately, she proves interested in searching for a missing corpse.

Miss Marple takes on the Athena role, solving a murder to save a city when her friend, Mrs. McGillicuddy, arrives at her cottage and announces that she has witnessed a murder in an adjoining train. Unfortunately, the police can find no evidence. Calculating that the body must have been ejected onto the Crackenthorpe estate, Miss Marple arranges for Lucy to become temporary housekeeper. Immediately, Lucy sets about sorting out the family, as well. Like many a Hestia, she rekindles the hearth fire of feeling around food, which is particularly successful when grandson Alexander arrives with a schoolfriend. After Lucy finds the dead body and the police begin to investigate, the boys are enthusiastic about hunting for clues.

The fires of Hestia are so bright that they kindle Lucy's Aphrodite in the eyes of Crackenthorpe males, even Alexander, who decides she might be a suitable replacement for his dead mother. The Crackenthorpe unwed sons and their father want to marry her while the married son offers her a senior role in his business. At the end of the novel, it is the potential suitor of the put-upon Crackenthorpe daughter who is revealed as the killer. Long thought to be Martine, the body is actually the wife of the murderer who had refused to agree to a divorce. Miss Marple as Artemis the hunter re-stages the murder scene, thus provoking identification and revelation.

At the end of the crime story, Lucy and the land face two possible fates. With the Rutherford Hall estate being a valuable building site, Hermes-like trickster Cedric wants to marry Lucy and use the land for his schemes. By contrast, Brian Eastley, father of Alexander, wants to marry Lucy and turn the Rutherford Hall back into a family home. Lucy is tempted by both men, and the novel concludes with Miss Marple sure that she knows Lucy's choice and not revealing it to the reader.

In terms of archetypal energies, Lucy's strong Hestia is related to tricky Hermes in a sort of polarization. It is likely that the land will be rejuvenated by a marriage with the feminine as stronger, directing partner. The ecology of Lucy as Hestia and Artemis with Brian and Alexander suggests fertility restored to the land as she brings the house and environs back to life. The country house economy as it was at Styles is over. The detective restoring the wasteland of psyche and nature is not.

HALLOWE'EN PARTY AND A CONCLUSION

In this late novel, Poirot comes to the aid of Ariadne Oliver when a child is murdered at a Hallowe'en party. The child, Joyce, is unsympathetic and has unwisely announced that she once saw a murder. She is found forcibly drowned in the tub of water used for bobbing for apples with fateful overtones of Eden despoiled. Here also, the Pagan roots of the murder mystery surface with the setting on the night of the year when the dead are close. Over the course of the investigation, Poirot discovers many characters are drawn to a beautiful garden. Unfortunately, this is a corrupted Eden, a wasteland disguised as a magical place that demands human sacrifices. A second child is drowned and the slaying of a third is narrowly averted.

The killers did it for money to purchase a Greek island in order to create the ultimate garden. Their cultivation of nature requires human blood, the country house motif-turned-predator. In a sense, murder mysteries rest upon atavistic notions of human sacrifice that provokes the furies to ravage the human psyche and make it a wasteland. One could say that *Hallowe'en Party* represents anti-human ecology except that the killers are fueled by all-too-human lusts and greed. Rowena Drake kills for the power money gives her and to keep Michael Garfield, obsessive gardener identified by Poirot as Narcissus. He loves only his own beauty reflected in his creations.

With their murders of children, the novel emphasizes that the killers are sterile. Mrs. Drake is too old for children and Michael too self-adoring while not owning his child by another woman, the precocious Miranda. Death by apple bobbing reframes Genesis. Joyce's fatal bite is actually precipitated by a lie. Miranda, not she, witnessed an earlier murder. This naïve proto-Eve suffers death as a kind of expulsion from the garden of paradise. Determined to be creator of his own Eden, Michael is a crazed god, willing to sacrifice anyone. In fact, he personifies the pitiless drive to usurp natural powers that acknowledge limits and necessity. Gardening does not require human blood as Miss Marple would be first to point out. When Poirot first encounters retired Superintendent Spence, his companion on this case, he is vigorously fighting weeds in his fruitful garden.

In a sense, the entire novel is Hallowe'en, the night when the veil between the world of the dead and this one is most transparent. Poirot uncovers many crimes and acts as Athena in re-storying this troubled rural community. However, the woman at the hub of this community proves deadly, a maggot in the apple. Vulnerable child Miranda was enchanted by poisonous Michael to almost acquiesce in her own murder. While it is possible to see ancient myths precipitating murder in the narrative, it is also the roles of Poirot, Spence, and Ariadne Oliver to root out dangerous enchantments that occur when humans think they are above nature and human nature.

As in all of Christie, the true gardeners are the detectives who suffer and survive their cases. Such a notion points to further work on Christie and ecocriticism that would range beyond the depictions of the natural world. Her novels are ecologies treating the psyche and the community as gardens to be tended. The stories invoke many gods and their myths of nature and humans as one system. Ultimately, Christie's mobilization of mythic archetypes mitigates the Anthropocene. She connects nature and human nature to restore—or, perhaps more aptly, restory—the severing that is characteristic of modernity. By returning death to nature and, through crime, to human nature, the ecology of Christie returns us to the earth and makes us a part of it.

REFERENCES

Aeschylus. (2006), "The Eumenides," in *The Oresteia*, trans. Robert Fagles, 227–77, New York: Penguin Books.

Auden, W. H. (1948), "The Guilty Vicarage," *Harpers Magazine* Archives, May. Available online: https://harpers.org/archive/1948/05/the-guilty-vicarage/ (accessed November 1, 2021).

Bishop, K. E. (2018), "'When 'tis Night, Death is Green': Vegetal Time in Nineteenth-Century Econoir," *Green Letters*, 22 (1): 7–19.

Buell, L. (2001), *Writing for an Endangered World: Literature, Culture and Environment in the US and beyond*, London: Belknap Press.

Christie, A. ([1920] 1989), *The Mysterious Affair at Styles*, London: Fontana.

Christie, A. ([1930] 1993), *The Murder at the Vicarage*, London: HarperCollins.

Christie, A. ([1937] 1960), *Death on the Nile*, London: Fontana.

Christie, A. ([1941] 1962), *N or M?* London: Fontana.

Christie, A. (1950), *A Murder Is Announced*, London: Collins.

Christie, A. ([1957] 1969), *4.50 from Paddington*, London: Hamlyn.

Christie, A. ([1962] 2011), *The Mirror Crack'd from Side to Side*, New York: William Morrow.

Christie, A. ([1969] 2002), *Hallowe'en Party*, London: Fontana.

Ellis, E. C. (2018), *Anthropocene: A Very Short Introduction*, Oxford, UK: Oxford University Press.

Glotfelty, C. (1996), "Introduction: Literary Studies in an Age of Environmental Crisis," in C. Glotfeltyand H. Fromm (eds), *The Ecocriticism Reader: Landmarks in Literary Ecology*, xv–xxxvii. Athens and London: The University of Georgia Press.

Holland, J. (1994), "Complexity Made Simple," *The Bulletin of the Santa Fe Institute*, 9 (3): 3–4.

Hyde, L. (1998), *Trickster Makes This World: Mischief, Myth and Art*, New York: Farrar, Straus and Giroux.

Jung, C. G. (1922), "On the Relation of Analytical Psychology to Poetry," in H. Read, M. Fordham, and G. Adler (eds), *Collected Works, Volume 15: The Spirit in Man,*

    Art and Literature, trans. R. F. C. Hull, 65–83, Princeton: Princeton University Press, 1953–1991.

Jung, C. G. (1930), "Psychology and Literature," in H. Read, M. Fordham, and G. Adler (eds), *Collected Works, Volume 15: The Spirit in Man, Art and Literature*, trans. R. F. C. Hull, 109–34, Princeton: Princeton University Press, 1953–1991.

Jung, C. G. (1968), *The Archetypes and the Collective Unconscious, Collected Works, Volume 9*, Princeton: Princeton University Press.

Martin, S. and S. West (2020), "Mapping War, Planning Peace: Miss Marple and the Evolving Village Space," in Rebecca Mills and J. C. Bernthal (eds), *Agatha Christie Goes to War*, 11–27, Hove and New York: Routledge.

Mills, R. (2019), "'I Always Did Hate Watering Places': Tourism and Carnival in Agatha Christie's and Dorothy L Sayers's Seaside Novels," *CLUES: A Journal of Detection*, 37 (2): 83–93.

Mills, R. and J. C. Bernthal, eds. (2020), *Agatha Christie Goes to War*, Hove and New York: Routledge.

Pamboukian, S. A. (2016), "In the Apothecaries Garden with Agatha Christie," *CLUES: A Journal of Detection* 4 (1): 72–81.

Rowland, S. (2010), "The Wasteland and the Grail Knight: Myth and Cultural Criticism in Detective Fiction," *CLUES: A Journal of Detection* 28 (2): 44–54.

Rowland, S. (2012), *The Ecocritical Psyche: Literature, Complexity Evolution and Jung*, Hove and New York: Routledge.

Shulman, H. (1997), *Living at the Edge of Chaos: Complex Systems in Culture and Psyche*, Zurich: Daimon Verlag.

Snell, K. D. M. (2010), "A Drop of Water in a Stagnant Pool? Inter-war Detective Fiction and the Rural Community," *Social History* 35 (1): 1–50.

Walton J. L. and S. Walton (2018), "Introduction to Green Letters: Crime Fiction and Ecology," *Green Letters* 22 (1): 2–6.

Wheeler, W. (2006), *The Whole Creature: Complexity, Biosemiotics and the Evolution of Culture*, London: Lawrence & Wishart.

CHAPTER SEVEN

Psychogeography and the Flapper Sleuth

SARAH MARTIN

INTRODUCTION

For many of her readers, Agatha Christie's works are characterized by the landscape of the closed community in both rural and city settings. It is the dialectic nature of the physical space of the landscape or setting, and the figure detective (and often the criminal too), in Christie's fiction that interests psychogeographers, who study the impact of place and space on the human psyche. W.H. Auden, a contemporary of Christie, "confessed" his love for detective fiction through his analysis of it in his 1948 essay "The Guilty Vicarage." As part of this analysis, he outlined the importance of place and space as an integral part of an effective detective story, of which Christie's body of work provides supreme examples.

Auden highlights the essential nature of the closed community, asserting: "The detective story requires [...] a closed society so that the possibility of an outside murderer [...] is totally excluded; and a closely related society so that all its members are potentially suspect" (1948: 407). Auden's emphasis on the detective story "requiring" a closed society for its plot and structure emphasizes the key role of space within detective fiction, as well as the role the nature of space has over character, plot, and structure. That Auden discusses this type of detective story intentionally "excluding an outside murderer" reflects the focus on the "evil within," certainly the case for Christie. Importantly, Auden highlights the ritualistic nature of space: "The murderer uses his knowledge of ritual to commit the crime and can be caught only by someone who acquires an equal or superior familiarity with it" (408). The nature of the space and the intimate details and structure of performed social identity within the closed community locale are vital components in detective fiction, and therefore also vital to the role of the detective who must uncover the murderer's story.

This chapter engages with that discussion of space in detective fiction, and considers its relationship to gender, examining the psychogeographical nature of the female flapper as detective through focusing on Agatha Christie's Tuppence Beresford. There is a wealth of what we may term the "flapper girl detective" in Christie, such as the resourceful journalist Anne Beddingfield in *The Man in a Brown Suit* and Lady Frances ("Frankie") Derwent in *Why Didn't They Ask Evans?* both of whom also deserve closer examination. However, Tuppence Beresford, who dominates the pages of two significant Christie texts of the 1920s, *The Secret Adversary* and *Partners in Crime*, has not been the main focus of scholarship surrounding Agatha Christie's female sleuths. It is Tuppence's understanding of the culturally, socially, and temporally layered nature of physical space and her exploitation of the dialectic between physical and mental space that enables her detection. Her position as a female detective in *The Secret Adversary* and *Partners in Crime* affords readers access to specific spaces unavailable to more traditional middle-class detectives, highlighting the ways in which a woman can negotiate these restricted spaces integral to successful detection. By extension, then, the spaces which Christie offers us admittance to in these particular texts, through her female detective, allow us a deeper reflection on the possibilities and the position of women in society during the early twentieth century.

The chapter examines the ways in which Tuppence's detection is inherently psychogeographic and explores psychogeographic detection methods including clothing, walking, and inhabiting physical spaces of both the public and the private, as well as metaphysical cultural and gendered spaces. This chapter, then, observes space as more than the physical; it considers what Lefebvre proposes in *The Production of Space*: "We are thus confronted by an indefinite multitude of spaces, each one piled upon, or perhaps contained within, the next" ([1974] 1991: 8). In demonstrating the ways in which specifically female detection is inherently psychogeographic, this chapter will examine the various shifts in cultural and societal life owing to the First World War, which directly impact the lives of women and influence the practice of detection.

CONVERSATIONS IN PSYCHOGEOGRAPHY

Guy Debord in his "Introduction to a Critique of Urban Geography" describes psychogeography as "the study of the precise laws and specific effects of the geographical environment, whether consciously organized or not, on the emotions and behaviour of individuals" ([1955] 2006: 8). The very nature and practice of detection are inherently psychogeographic. The influence of physical space over the thoughts, feelings, and behavior of an individual can be exploited, manipulated, and subverted or as Debord observes "turned to account" (10) in order to aid the process of detection. Will Self, who did much to popularize psychogeography in the twenty-first century, writes on the figure of the psychogeographer: "We [...] are all disciples of Guy Debord, and those rollicking situationists who tottered, soused, across the stage set of 1960's Paris, thereby hoping to tear down the scenery of the society of the spectacle [...] there are still profound differences between us" (Self 2013: 11).

Self highlights the "differences" between each individual psychogeographer; indeed, the nature of psychogeography is inherently individual in practice, experience, and, moreover, application of theory. The boundaries between space and self are so complex and varying that to know either a space or an individual exclusively does still not guarantee the production of the same thoughts, feelings, and behavior within an individual or group of individuals. Yi-Fu Tuan suggests in "Space and Place: Humanistic Perspective": "the space we perceive and construct, the space that provides cues for our behaviour, varies with the individual and cultural group. Mental maps differ from person to person, and from culture to culture" ([1979] 2012: 388). As Tuan highlights, if different types and different individuals react to space differently, we can understand that each woman's experience of space is *also* different, and furthermore her "mental map" differs too. The culmination of what brings both space and person together creates an uncertain and varying mixture of outcomes. Moreover, psychogeography stresses the marriage of psyche and space.

"We are a fraternity," Self asserts, "dispiritingly." He continues: "I do believe that men are corralled in this field due to certain natural and/or nurtured characteristics, that lead us to believe we have [...] superior visual-spatial skills to women" (2013: 12). That Self "dispiritingly" claims himself to be a part of "a fraternity" of psychogeographers engages with, not the absent, but the *ever-ignored* presence of female psychogeographers both in contemporary society and historically, as well as highlighting the psychogeographic nature of gendered identities in (social) space. Evidently, a woman's freedom to traverse a space, whether city, country, suburban, or private, has been, and still is, an ever-evolving one. The hidden or *ignored* presence of different types of women reflecting on the psychological effects and influence of physical space is certainly not nonexistent, though. It is this which Tuppence Beresford, as a figure of female detection, emphasizes through her detection methods interacting so intimately with spatial influences. While any woman's agency in space has been historically limited and is still a developing one, this is not to say it is any less valuable or that it makes them any less of a psychogeographer when compared to the "tottering" and "swaggering" Self-proclaimed fraternity.

Through his suggestions of a "fraternity," Self highlights the way in which socially constructed gender identities impact on not only our feeling of belonging *to* or *in* a space or our experience *of* it, but also the way in which the label of psychogeographer is considered, culturally, an inherently masculine one. Importantly, Agatha Christie's female detectives contribute to dismantling this particular perception, if we only read her work psychogeographically. Laura Elkin addresses in *Flaneuse: Women Walk the City* the historical development of a woman's freedom to traverse a space, and the limited record of a specifically female experience of public space: "our most ready-to-hand sources for what the streetscape looked like in the nineteenth century are male, and they see the city in their own ways" (2016: 9). With the reconsidered position of women in society and culture at the start of the twentieth century owing to a conflation of factors (see below), we see the ways in which Tuppence Beresford negotiates space begin to address the way in which a woman experiences public and private space, which challenges patriarchal structures and reveals the emergence of, and previously unacknowledged, female psychogeographer through the vehicle of detection.

As Elizabeth Grosz argues: "The ways in which space has been historically conceived have always functioned to either contain women, or to obliterate them" (1995: 120). The act of Tuppence's female detection—and it is a uniquely female performance of feminine identity—becomes an act of rebellion against the enclosed nature of the domestic sphere and its imposed identity. The obliteration of women, or containment of them, is highlighted at the beginning of most of the texts in which Tuppence features. She is seen to be consistently seeking an active role in a world which tries to contain her: "Something to do, that is what I keep saying all day long" (Christie [1929] 2016: 2). However, Tuppence rejects a woman's place in the domestic sphere and demands she takes up physical, social, and cultural space, and, importantly, career-space. This inhabitation of other spaces by Tuppence reflects what Penny Tinkler and Cheryl Krasnick Warsh highlight; women are now "active in the public sphere." They continue: "in particular, paid work engaged women in public life and space" (2008: 113).

Christie, whose name is synonymous with "detective fiction," produces a phenomenological experience of 1920s space through her female detectives, who have to navigate space as *women*, as well as investigators. This particularly intimate navigation invites an examination of the texts through the lens of psychogeographic literary theory, exposing the inherent psychogeographic nature of detection within female detectives in the interwar period. Recent attention has been given to applying theories of space and place to crime fiction more generally, namely, Brittain Bright's very significant PhD thesis, *Beyond the Scene of the Crime: Investigating Place in Golden Age Detective Fiction* (2015), as well as Sam Goodman's spatial examination of spy fiction,

British Spy Fiction and the End of Empire (2015). However, beyond my own article "Psychogeography and the Detective: Re-evaluating the Significance of Space in Agatha Christie's *A Murder Is Announced*" (2018: 20–9), there are no other explicit applications of psychogeographic theory to specifically female detectives in the Golden Age. It is significant that cornerstone texts such as Merja Makinen's *Agatha Christie: Investigating Femininity* and J.C. Bernthal's *Queering Agatha Christie* provide examinations of gender and sexuality, addressing and examining the performative nature of femininity, but there is no publication that draws theories of gendered space together to examine the significance of the flapper girl detective in Christie's fiction.

Megan Hoffman in *Gender and Representation in British Golden Age Fiction* analyzes Tuppence as one half of a whole, observing that "Tuppence is the partner who spiritedly maintains the momentum in both [her and Tommy's] professional and personal lives, constantly pushing Tommy into modernity" (2016: 102). However, as Makinen suggests: "active femininity should not need to be explained by recourse to masculinity, especially an immature masculinity" (2006: 74). Similarly, Bernthal observes that "the self-conscious way in which Christie draws attention towards her characters' artificiality demands attention" (127). Moreover, it is more than what Bernthal calls "artificiality" in the performative gender binary when applying theories of psychogeography to the practice of detection. The ways in which femininity is "artificially" performative, then, exposes the spatially imposed nature of gender performances, and, indeed, further exposes what Grosz suggests: "space has […] always functioned to either contain women, or to obliterate them" (1995: 120). Tuppence finds agency within the boundaries of spatially imposed feminine performance and enacts this culturally imposed feminine "artificiality" as a significant *part* of her psychogeographic detection process.

TUPPENCE THE FLAPPER

In the post–First World War period, fashion designer Coco Chanel "gave women's bodies their freedom back" (Bolt 2007: 16); her revolutionary fashion designs for women shifted away from the sweating bodies packed "under all the showcase clothes, under their corsets, their underwear, their padding" (16), and toward more useful and liberating designs. In 1919, Chanel said she had "woken up famous" (in Wallach 1998: 29), and so, the emergence of women more publicly inhabiting cultural, social, and professional space is marked. The emergence of more enduring and popular female fashion designers such as Chanel followed the progression of women into more cultural public spaces, following the complex renegotiations of gendered roles in the war. We are facing a period where more recognized female fashion designers clothe the bodies of women: the ways in which women are perceived in social space transforms. Clothes, then, allow ease of access and movement in public, social, and professional space; the tailoring of clothing develops to match these newly and more frequently inhabited spaces by women, including that of the workplace.

Chanel wrote of this period: "I now had a clientele of active women. Active women need to feel comfortable in their dresses, they need to be able to pull up their sleeves" (in Bolt 2007: 22). Chanel, then, responded to the shifting spatial transformations in the nature of cultural, social, and professional space in regard to women and their reconceived, active place and position in the postwar society and culture of the modern world. If clothes act as a discourse of identity between the body and the outer world, the newly inhabited physical space by women allows their new public identities to be worn on their body. Women were now more active participants of a social, public, and professional space; a move away from the commodified, inactive form dressed for society, merely to be seen, during the nineteenth century. Women, through the shifting nature of clothing, in response to the changing nature of space, begin a transformation from the commodity to the buyers of it. In the wake of war, some women had greater autonomy over their own constructed image in the public eye, in space, and, importantly, to themselves. Significantly, fashionable women in this period wore their need to inhabit space on their bodies.

The flapper is often connected to ideas of the "roaring twenties," epitomizing modernity, fashion, status, and desirability; she is a fashionable embodiment of *the* feminine figure of the jazz age. As Martin Pumphrey puts it, the flapper embodies "unencumbered simplified clothing, short hair and boyish figure, rebellious lifestyle and pursuit of pleasure, [which] did genuinely challenge nineteenth-century constructions of femininity" (1987: 54). Flicking through copies of *Vogue* published during the 1920s, we see this "flapper girl" Pumphrey describes inhabiting the abstract cultural space of the gendered social psyche for women disseminated through magazine culture. She is a figure almost identical to Christie's depiction of Tuppence. Christie writes of the

> elfin lines of [Tuppence's] little face, with its determined chin and large, wide-apart grey eyes that looked mistily out from under straight, black brows. She wore a small bright green toque over her black bobbed hair, and her extremely short and rather shabby skirt revealed a pair of uncommonly dainty ankles.
>
> ([1922] 2016: 7)

This description reflects the essence of what Pumphrey encapsulates; Tuppence is "dainty" despite her shabbiness, which is presented as almost fashionable in its "unencumbered" essence, enabling free movement and enhancing the look or air of rebellion through the visible ankles. Moreover, our first meeting with Tuppence, as she gets off the train to meet Tommy, outlines her as the picture of feminine modernity. Christie's use of language allows us to read Tuppence's personality and flapper identity through the way she clothes her body in the wider cultural space of the twentieth century, marking clothing as being a spatial and gendered signifier, which contributes to the conception, creation, and examination of psychogeographical space.

Ole Reinsch observes that the multitude of women embracing these iconic fashion elements created a space for the rebellious young woman to inhabit in twentieth-century culture. He writes: "Young women in the years after the First World War who acted explicitly as apolitical individuals are, for instance, the so-called Flapper Girls. First and foremost, one associates a certain style of fashion with women during the twenties: the bob, rouge on the cheeks, powder on the knees, short skirts and 'objectively' cut clothing" (2012: 1). Here, Reinsch highlights the movement of women into the public sphere, marked by the corporeal ways in which they occupy both cultural and physical space. Attention to leg details marks the shift from the modest fashions of the *fin de siècle*, now dismantled, rejected, and subverted in order to paint a new picture of feminine rebellion and ownership over one's own image in the context of spaces of sociability. If, as Lefebvre suggests, *"(social) space is a (social) product"* ([1974] 1991: 26, emphasis original), then people produce space; a large part of the ways in which people produce (social) space lies in the ways in which clothing contributes to the signified/created space by its occupiers. What is important, then, are the ways in which women, en masse, inhabit spaces enacting and embodying the aesthetic of the flapper girl, and thus create a space and culture of feminine rebellion worthy of more critical examination, particularly when marked by the figure of a detective.

Tuppence, through her embodiment of the rebellious flapper, similarly responds to, and addresses, the ways in which a woman negotiates public, work, and city spaces. Christie's writing challenges patriarchal structures and reveals the presence of continuously ignored female psychogeography through the vehicle of detection. Christie writes of Tuppence wandering the city space in *The Secret Adversary,* as she considers her suspect:

> She walked as far as Kensington Gardens and then slowly retraced her steps, feeling infinitely better for the fresh air and exercise. [...] As she drew nearer and nearer to Hyde Park Corner, the temptation to return to south Audley mansions was almost irresistible. At any rate, she decided, it would do no harm just to go and *look* at the building. Perhaps, then, she could resign herself to waiting patiently for ten o'clock.
>
> (Christie [1922] 2016: 128–9, emphasis original)

Interestingly, Tuppence wanders the same topography as Clarissa Dalloway in Virginia Woolf's 1925 modernist novel, *Mrs. Dalloway.* With women wandering the same city space around the same time, both stories take place during the very early 1920s, and so the temporal space as well as the physical city space is similarly shared and inhabited. Moreover, the map Virginia Woolf chooses to place at the beginning of *Mrs. Dalloway* can be used to help trace Tuppence's whereabouts in relation to city space in this extract. This connection helps to highlight what Deborah L. Parsons suggests in relation to specifically feminine cartographies of viewing: "we are increasingly realizing the significance of the urban map as influential in the very structures of social and mental daily life. A city can be analysed demographically, economically, architecturally" (2000: 1).

We have, then, two superimposed, subjective *mental* maps, or cognitive maps, placed, traced, and plotted on top of the objective map of the city space; similar spaces wear the experience of the everyday for these different characters, and this similar space interacts with the character's thoughts, feelings, and behaviors individually. Both texts show that "the urban landscape needs to be studied as a feature that brings the psychological and the material in to collusion, in terms of theories and aesthetics that construct modern subjectivity and modern art from material urban experience," as Parsons suggests (2000: 1). While Clarissa Dalloway's plotted narrative is a stream of consciousness exposing the transformations in a woman's place in society and culture during the period, Tuppence's could best be considered as comparatively so; the end goal is importantly that of *detection*. This end goal further exposes the evil within and extends our understanding of a woman's place in society and culture beyond their imposed roles and into the world of choice: the detective, as an agent of space, can dismantle the status quo and make moral judgements.

Moreover, viewing the female detective as inherently psychogeographic allows us to further expose the active part women play in the social and cultural systems of the period; it exposes a women's active role in inhabiting these spaces, and the importance of their shifting social and cultural position. Elkin expresses that "with the large-scale entrance of women in to the work-force during the first world war, women's presence in the streets was confirmed" (2016: 15). However, Christie's writing of Tuppence articulates more than a woman's *presence* in the streets. In the above extract, Tuppence retraces her steps and finds it hard to "put the events of the evening out of her head." She is led by the dialogue existing between mental space and physical space; that two-way influence of mind and space, consequently, becomes naturally drawn toward the suspect's home: "it would do no harm to just go and *look* at the building." Tuppence's freedom to traverse the space and exploit the dialogue between mental space and physical space as an aid in her detection is an act of rebellion and records the rising freedom of women importantly freely inhabiting a myriad of spaces, including public space in the city.

It is a revolutionary act to freely walk, and by association think, as a woman, alone, inhabiting public space and by extension inhabiting the city streets as an owned space. The connection between thinking and walking is made by

Rebecca Solnit in *Wanderlust*. Solnit (2014) records the cultural meaning of women wandering alone through analyzing its significance in Austen's *Pride and Prejudice*.[1] Solnit suggests that protagonist Elizabeth's walk to Netherfield is "the first major demonstration of her unconventionality. [...] Elizabeth is likewise walking beyond the bounds of propriety for women of her class" (98). Solnit continues:

> Solitary walks express the independence that literally takes the heroine out of the social sphere of the houses and their inhabitants, into a larger, lonelier world where she is free to think, walking articulates both physical and mental freedom.
>
> (99)

Moreover, it is more than *walking* as Solnit and Elkin analyze. Existing, functioning, and having one's social identity constructed, influenced, and imposed by the physical space is significant for both Tuppence and Clarissa Dalloway here. Tuppence's freedom to roam the city space during this period enables a more extensive freedom; it offers her a means to think freely as a detective as she wanders, giving her further opportunity to experience the physical from a female perspective, thus exposing the hegemonic nature of the patriarchy layered within the physical space of the city. To walk is to think, and to experience physical space is to experience the dialogue between internal mental space (our thoughts and feelings), and external physical space (the layering of social, cultural hegemonic history, i.e., our performed and imposed social behaviors).

Christie exposes that dialectical nature between physical space and mental space; she exposes the symbolic nature of what the building means. As the wandering of the city space externalizes the thoughts and feelings of Tuppence, Christie writes that "the temptation to return to south Audley mansions was almost irresistible" ([1922] 2016: 128). It is the freedom she has to allow the space to wash over her thoughts, creating and structuring them, that leads her to the house. It is the ability she has to negotiate city space freely which also allows her to do so. Moreover, the freedom and influence of the physical space are key here to her detection. Christie continues: "what Tuppence had expected she hardly knew, but the sight of its red brick solidity slightly assuaged the growing and entirely unreasonable uneasiness that possessed her" (129). On seeing the tangible nature of the building, Tuppence is reassured, as though her internal worries have been suddenly physically externalized and symbolically reflected

---

[1]The comparisons we may draw between Christie and Austen do not end here; similarly satirical and ironic in tone, both authors present the issues surrounding a woman's place in society in a close community; a microcosm reflecting the bigger and wider issues for women within society and culture.

in the building. It is in *The Secret Adversary* that Tuppence first exploits the ways in which space imposes social identity, through constructing and layering her own superimposed space.

The second book in which Tuppence features, *Partners in Crime*, invites readers instantly into the domestic sphere. It is the influential nature of this particular space which Alison Light, in *Forever England*, suggests is of significant importance in terms of feminine modernity: "by exploring the writing of middle class women at home in the period [...] we can go straight to the centre of contradictory and determining tension in English social life in the period" ([1991] 2001:10). Light, then, sees the microcosm of the home or domestic sphere as a reflection of the bigger, more encompassing, macrocosm. It is in the domestic sphere that we get the metaphor of change and the energy of feminine modernity central to the zeitgeist of this era. We see how the suffocating space of the domestic sphere influences Tuppence's wish to rebel and take action. She is the very center of female modernity; our fashionable flapper from *The Secret Adversary*, now depicted just a few years later as a wife at home, but unsurprisingly wanting to rebel against socially and culturally imposed gender norms.

Via Tuppence, Christie writes of a woman's want to establish an owned sense of modernity during the period, of the kind Brigitte Søland proposes:

> women who came of age in the 1920s and 1930s [were] self-consciously seeking to take advantage of the social and sexual upheavals that characterized those years, to reshape female identities and gender relations, and to establish what they perceived to be "modern lives" for themselves.
>
> ([2000] 2021: 20)

Christie displays more than mere rebellion, though; Tuppence also challenges conservative notions of gender binary and the feminine being naturally or inherently parallel with the domestic, as we see her "[wish] that something would happen" (Christie [1929] 2016: 1), prompted by boredom in the enclosed space of the domestic sphere.

CLOTHING CULTURE AND SUBVERTING SPACES

As a female sleuth, Tuppence embodies the zeitgeist of post–First World War femininity, and, through the figure of the female detective as psychogeographer, articulates the transformations of a woman's place in society and culture. From the beginning of *The Secret Adversary*, Tuppence articulates this shifting social position of women in society in consequence of the war, and furthermore the changed nature of women more able to inhabit new physical spaces of the work place, as well as those spaces of sociability:

I had intended to become a land-girl, a post-woman and a bus conductress by way of rounding off my career—but the Armistice intervened! I clung to the office with the true limpet touch for many months, but, alas, I was combed out at last. (Christie [1922] 2016: 9)

Through Tuppence, Christie displays the transformed social position of women owing to the spatial restructures of war; women take on previously discouraged and/or unavailable work positions, which afford them more ease of entrance into previously less inhabited physical spaces of work, city, and sociability. It is Tuppence's blame of the Armistice that allows the reader an insight into the opportunities for women the war afforded. Her use of "intervened," suggesting the end of the war, was an inconvenience to her and, by extension, other young women's career endeavors, emphasizing the desperation of clinging to these new active, working positions held in society.

The attitude and desire of Tuppence to gain entrance to a wider range of career spaces further emphasize the transformation in the way women see their own potential and role in society. Arriving home, Tuppence deplores: "it's awful! All housework and mother's meetings! I have always been a changeling. I don't want to go back" (Christie [1922] 2016: 11). Labeling herself a "changeling," Tuppence articulates this fight for herself and, by extension, women more generally, against being reclaimed by the domestic sphere and its imposed social position and identity. Tuppence's agenda to maintain her place of entry into the public or working sphere emphasizes the reconceived spatial, social, and gendered identity of women during the period. Tied to her rejection of "going home" to daily domesticated life, Tuppence aligns the transformations in fashion with this new reconceived image of feminine identity in the interwar period: "Father's a dear [who thinks] short skirts and smoking are immoral. You can imagine what a thorn in the flesh I am to him! He just heaved a sigh of relief when the war took me off!" (11). Here, through both action and the autonomy over her own self-image, via clothing, Tuppence embodies the zeitgeist of postwar femininity: a want to disregard culturally inherited gendered patterns of behavior, which extends to the image of the self, as she aligns this image of being a "changeling" with the "shortness of skirt" and "smoking." Tuppence displays attributes of the flapper. It is transformations in the nature of the space, and the entrance of women into work spaces and spaces of sociability, which dictate the need for more liberating and functional clothes which, in turn, help Tuppence manipulate the image of the self in context of physical work space, for the benefit of detection.

The movement of women in cultural and societal space is mapped in Tuppence's clothing in the *Partners in Crime* short story "A Pot of Tea." Christie maintains the fashionable flapper image of Tuppence when she writes of her outfit in the guise of a secretary in a rather makeshift detective agency: "very neat and demure with smooth black head and dainty collars and cuffs" (Christie [1929] 2016: 17). Tuppence uses her costume to construct an image and space of professionalism in Blunt's Detective Agency; the agency which, the story highlights, is founded, in its new image, on female manipulation through the exploitation of Madame Violette's hat shop; Tuppence has an extended network of female friends hidden within the specific space of the hat shop, on whom she calls to manufacture a first case for the agency, so her navigation of the space enables the very plot of the short story. The absence of detail provided by Christie between the "cuffs" and "collars" draws attention to the suit-like quality of Tuppence's clothing and the move for women to more masculine clothing through suits, shirts, and businesswear. Through the ways in which Tuppence clothes her body, her suitability and performance of social identity within the context of the professional workspace are enhanced. The image of this new feminine modernity here is constructed through Tuppence, who uses her clothes to rebel, to make a statement of her place in the world and, more specifically, to inhabit the space of the workplace. Moreover, she goes on then to manipulate this, through exploiting the way the space imposes her perceived role as the secretary within the agency, against her actual role of detection.

Tuppence, as a part of her detection methodology, exploits the preconceived notion and structuralist concept that clothes equal identity. Instead, as an active detective who uses disguises, she recognizes the ways in which new, feminine modernity remaps and gives autonomy to women in the renegotiation and reconstruction of identity in the wider context of physical spaces, while also manipulating how new feminine modernity demands clothes suiting different spaces and the spatial creation of different types of women inhabiting previously uninhabited spaces. Furthermore, clothes become an essential part of a spatial performance of identity, and consequently a tool to aid manipulation in psychogeographic methods of detection.

Active and strong in her role as a female detective, her methods of detection respond to the transforming position of women in society and culture during the period. This exploitation of spatial influence of imposed spatial identities of women is displayed through Christie's attention to the controlled image of the self in social space, which Tuppence exploits through fashion in the text. Tuppence gains an extended network of surveillance through the use of Albert, a boy working in a suspect's building. Exploiting Albert's social position in this space, and manipulating him as an extension of the workplace, she learns intimate details of the space and persuades him to "mention that you'd got a young cousin, or a friend of yours [...], that might suit the place" (Christie [1922] 2016: 89). Here, Tuppence begins to implement her scheme of performing the part of a maid, through a spatial performance of identity. Instantly, then, we have a link between "place" and suitability.

The necessity for looking to be a part of, or extension of, the place, in order to "suit it," is essential for detection purposes in this instance. It is through a woman's ease of access into wider work spaces, which further enable her autonomy and ability to construct an image of the self in the work space, thus aiding Tuppence's detection. Christie writes:

> Starting with a cheap clothing store, and passing through one or two second-hand establishments, she had finished at a well-known hairdresser's. Now, in the seclusion of her bedroom, she unwrapped her final purchase. Five minutes later she smiled contentedly at her reflection in the glass.
>
> (90)

Clothes, here, are highlighted as being part of spatially performing social, cultural, and gendered identity. It is the reshaping of her spatially performed social and gendered identity that allows Tuppence to detect effectively. As Tuppence "smile[s] contentedly at her reflection in the glass," we see here her construction of the performed self, constructed specifically to "suit" a space as a maid, enabling her to shift through class boundaries as a part of her disguise. Tuppence exploits the way in which space attempts to claim identity, by subverting this process and manipulating the image of identity in the context of a physical work space.

As Tuppence stands before the glass, she acknowledges this performance "contentedly" in the mirror. Her creation of new identity signifies the autonomy she has over her perceived identity within a specific physical space. The autonomy over her own spatial identity reflects the way in which she views herself in society and culture and her shifting position as a more active woman partaking in everyday life. Here, the text articulates through the figure of the female detective, a woman's ability to perform other selves and manipulate the ways in which clothing restructures perceptions of identity within physical spatial contexts. Tuppence exploits the perception of clothing as signifying the identity of the wearer. She exploits the presupposed notion that outfit equals woman. As Roland Barthes argues,

> the term of reference [...] is no longer the spirit or style of a period, but the psyche of the person wearing the clothing: clothing is supposed to express a psychological depth. [...] We can see a dialectical nature of clothing, in which there seems to be an infinite and circular exchange from the wearer to the group and from the group to the wearer [...] clothing would seem to be [...] a form of communication.
>
> ([2004] 2013: 25)

However, Tuppence exploits the nature of imposed identity, wearing what Barthes terms "the Zeitgeist of a civilisation" (23). Tuppence rather manipulates the ways in which we can exploit spatially imposed identities through the use of clothing, further exploiting the notion that clothing is a "circular exchange." Tuppence, like Barthes, then, steps beyond the structuralist perception of clothes signifying the psyche of the wearer and reconstructs identity through clothing. The autonomy lies with the woman, but the identity lies with the clothing, exploiting spatially constructed self-image.

Here, then, clothes function as Daniel Miller observes: "On the surface, is found the clothing which may represent us and may reveal a truth about ourselves, *but it may also lie*" (2010: 13, emphasis original). It is her reconstructed self-image that allows her ease of access into the space of the suspect's home. That the clothes Tuppence buys are from "second hand establishments" reflects the fact that identity is *re*-created and also the repurposing of identities which the clothes carry from owner to owner. It is the relationships between clothes and body, and clothes and identity, that can be exploited and manipulated in order to detect. As Christie writes: "From hospital experience she knew only too well that a nurse out of uniform is frequently unrecognised by her patients" ([1922] 2016: 91). Tuppence exploits the culturally inherited relationship with clothing in spaces of sociability to create a self that will be welcomed in the space. The result is her ease of access in the space and her liminal social position within the house.

CONCLUSION

Clothes in both *The Secret Adversary* and *Partners in Crime* act as a communicator between identity, the body, and society. Tuppence, as a female detective and psychogeographer, recognizes spatial influences in re-creating and exploiting notions of feminine identity. Clothing in the texts negotiates and communicates the influential, dialectic nature of space. It acts as a discourse which materializes and inhabits the liminal space between body and the external world, between mental and physical space. Tuppence thus manipulates the ways in which clothes can embody spatial, cultural, and societal shifts, allowing the wearer to perform social identity in a post–world war society. It is this exploitation of spatially constructed ideals of feminine modernity that contributes to the psychogeographic nature of her detection.

The figure of the female detective and the methods of detection are rich landscapes which require continued attention and further exploration in Agatha Christie studies. The spatiality, fashion, and even gender construction of her specifically female detectives warrant closer examination than currently exists. As this chapter has addressed, there are examples where work into these subjects has begun, but many studies still fail fully to explore the significance of the very act of detection. Instead, focus has culminated on detective fiction as a whole, examining the position of a text and all characters, rather than focusing in on methods of detection or the very nature of criminality.

Moreover, there are rich theoretical frameworks emerging, such as psychogeographic theory as this chapter has illustrated, which have been too often claimed by the modernists, but which need to be extended in their application to detective fiction, and specifically detective fiction of the Golden Age. Theoretical frameworks such as material culture, ecocriticism, disability studies, and theories of trauma can intersect with psychogeography, too, through the differing ways in which different individuals experience, conceive, and inhabit physical and metaphysical spaces. There is, then, plenty of work still to be done.

REFERENCES

Auden, W. H. (1948), "The Guilty Vicarage: Notes on the Detective Story, by an Addict," *Harper's Magazine*, May: 407–12.

Barthes, R. ([2004] 2013), *The Language of Fashion*, trans. A. Stafford, London and New York: Bloomsbury Academic.

Bernthal, J. C. (2016), *Queering Agatha Christie: Revisiting the Golden Age of Detective Fiction*, London: Palgrave Macmillan.

Bolt, D. (2007), *Chanel: Collections and Creations*, London: Thames & Hudson.

Bright, B. (2015), *Beyond the Scene of the Crime: Investigating Place in Golden Age Detective Fiction*, PhD dissertation, Goldsmiths College, University of London.

Christie, A. ([1922] 2016), *The Secret Adversary*, London: Harper.

Christie, A. ([1929] 2016), *Partners in Crime*, London: Harper.

Debord, G. ([1955] 2016), "Introduction to a Critique of Urban Geography," trans. K. Knabb, in K. Knabb (ed), *Situationist International Anthology*, revised and expanded edn, 8–12, Berkeley: Bureau of Public Services.

Elkin, L. (2016), *Flaneuse: Women Walk the City in Paris, New York, Tokyo, Venice and London*, London: Chatto & Windus.

Goodman, S. (2015), *British Spy Fiction and the End of Empire*, New York: Routledge.

Grosz, E. (1995), *Space, Time, and Perversion*, New York and Abingdon: Routledge.

Hoffman, M. (2016), *Gender and Representation in British "Golden Age" Crime Fiction: The Female Detective*, London: Palgrave Macmillan.

Lefebvre, H. ([1974] 1991), *The Production of Space*, trans. D. Nicholson-Smith, Oxford and Cambridge: Blackwell.

Light, A. ([1991] 2001), *Forever England: Literature, Femininity, and Conservatism between the Wars*, London and New York: Routledge.

Makinen, M. (2006), *Agatha Christie: Investigating Femininity*, Basingstoke: Palgrave Macmillan.

Martin, S. (2018), "Psychogeography and the Detective: Re-evaluating the Significance of Space in Agatha Christie's *A Murder Is Announced*," *Clues: A Journal of Detection*, 36 (1): 20–9.

Miller, D. (2010), *Stuff*, Cambridge: Polity Press.

Parsons, D. L. (2003), *Street Walking the Metropolis: Women, the City and Modernity*, Oxford: Oxford University Press.

Pumphrey, M. (1987), "The Flapper, the Housewife, and the Making of Modernity," *Cultural Studies*, 1 (2): 47–62.

Reinsch, O. (2012), "Flapper Girls—Feminism and Consumer Society in the 1920s," *Gender Forum*, 40: 1–6.

Self, W. (2013), *Psychogeography*, London, New Delhi, and New York: Bloomsbury.

Søland, B. ([2000] 2021), *Becoming Modern: Young Women and the Reconstruction of Womanhood in the 1920s*, Princeton: Princeton University Press.

Solnit, R. (2014), *Wanderlust: A History of Walking*, London: Verso.

Tinkler, P. and C. Krasnick Warsh (2008), "Feminine Modernity in Interwar Britain and North America," *Journal of Women's History*, 20 (3): 113–43.

Tuan, Yi-Fu ([1979] 2012), "Place and Space: Humanistic Perspective," in S. Gale and G. Olssen (eds), *Philosophy in Geography*, 387–428, Dordrecht, Boston, and London: D. Reidell Publishing Company.

Wallach, J. (1998), *Chanel: Her Style and Her Life*, New York: Nan A. Talese.

Woolf, V. ([1925] 2000), *Mrs. Dalloway*, London: Penguin.

CHAPTER EIGHT

Christie's Contemporary Middle East

NADIA ATIA

In his memoir, *Princesses' Street: Baghdad Memories*, the Palestinian writer and translator Jabra Ibrahim Jabra devotes a chapter to his friendship with Agatha Christie. Jabra had arrived in Baghdad in 1948 "after the first *nakba* (catastrophe) of Palestine had come to a head" (Jabra 2005: 33). In this period of extreme turmoil and violence in the Palestinian territories, thousands of Palestinians were forcibly displaced. A highly educated man, Jabra was able to find work "at the higher institutes (that is, the university colleges) in Iraq" (33). He worked as a lecturer in English literature at the University of Baghdad. It was a chance meeting with a friend, the archaeologist Robert Hamilton, in a bookshop that brought Agatha Christie into Jabra's life.

Hamilton, who had recently joined the British Archaeological Expedition to Baghdad, invited Jabra to a gathering at Max Mallowan's home the following day. Jabra recalls meeting the woman he knew only as Mrs. Mallowan fondly. He remembers her as "a generous hostess," and was touched by her sincere desire to hear from him as an "eye witness" to what "exactly happened to our dear Jerusalem?" (37). Their long conversation about what Jabra describes as "the Zionist acts of killing, eviction, and land usurpation" ended with Christie's insistence that "[a]ll this must be known to the world … And in detail … Writers must write about these atrocities, about this inhumanity" and with her conclusion that "[t]he British Empire shouldn't come to an end like this" (37).

It would be over a year before Jabra finally discovered the amiable Mrs. Mallowan's full identity. When his friend and colleague, the writer Desmond Stewart, informed him that "Mrs. Mallowan is the mystery writer Agatha Christie" (40), Jabra was taken aback and clearly in awe. His affectionate hero worship does not seem to have waned over the many years of their acquaintance. In 1951, Jabra visited the Mallowans at Max's dig at Nimrud. Jabra's description of his time there suggests that he was as impressed by Mallowan's discovery of a "magnificent stela [...] a picture of Shalmaneser III, standing in his full height" (43), as he was fascinated by a glimpse into the "small room built of sun-baked mud bricks, which Agatha Christie had made into her study, tucked away amid the ruins, the statues of winged oxen, and the carved marble murals" (44).

Christie's study, affectionately called *beit Agatha* (Agatha's house) in Arabic, and labeled as such in cuneiform script (Christie 1978: 543), made such an impression that on a return visit to the site over thirty years later, in 1986, Jabra asked a guard to unlock a "crude wooden door" to reveal "Agatha Christie's same little room [...] preserved as it had been in the 1940s and the 1950s" (Jabra 2005: 44). *Beit Agatha*, Jabra recalls, was an "English room, including an English fireplace and its traditional mantelpiece"; it was in this tiny English haven in northern Iraq that Christie had written some of her most popular work (2005: 44). He ends his "Story with Agatha Christie" with a lovely anecdote in which he recounts a visit Christie made to Baghdad in the 1960s. As they chatted, the elderly Christie could not recall exactly how many novels she had written. She told him, laughing, that "when the number is over fifty, the figure no longer has any importance" (45). Christie asked Jabra, by then an established author and translator, how many books he had published, but he modestly demurred. As he concludes, "when one is speaking to a writer who stopped counting her books after fifty, it's probably a virtue to remain silent about one's own small achievements" (45).

Jabra's warmth and affection for Christie, like his admiration for her as a writer, are clear throughout the chapter, and are signaled as much by his choice to include a chapter on Christie at all as by that chapter's content. The young Jabra evidently venerates the older, more established, writer. "Was this really Agatha Christie, whose mysteries and detective novels I had read since my youth?" he asks (40). Jabra's star-struck disbelief reveals the importance of Christie's writing to him. Given that Jabra studied in the UK at the Universities of Exeter and Cambridge, taught English literature, and translated many texts from English into Arabic, we might attribute his love of Christie's writing to his attachment to English literature. However, we have evidence to suggest that a partiality for Christie's work was by no means limited to his particular tastes and experiences. Marcia Lynx Qualey (2016) has argued that "many Arab writers came of age reading translations of Christie's page-turning mysteries." She explains that Christie's novels circulated widely in the region but "because many appeared in unauthorized editions, the exact number [of Christie novels translated into Arabic] will remain a mystery." Using the evidence available, she concludes that "Christie vies with Shakespeare for the title of most-translated writer from English to Arabic." As Christiane-Marie Abu Sarah outlines, the 1940s and 1950s are seen by critics as the "Golden Age" of Arabic pulp fiction and of the popularity of crime writing, in particular; despite concerns about the morality of this type of *adab al-sha'b*, or popular literature, crime writing "remained an Egyptian national obsession in the forties and fifties" (Abu Sarah 2020: 6). Though the first translation of Agatha Christie's novels into Arabic officially dates to 1979, Abu Sarah insists that "readers [of this, much earlier, era] devoured Agatha Christie novels, Sherlock Holmes stories, Ponson du Terrail mysteries, and tales of detective Monsieur Lecoq" (6).

More broadly, critics have suggested that crime fiction had an important role to play in the emergence of the novel form in Arabic. Samah Selim shows that during the Arab novel's formative period, between 1835 and 1925, "the taste of both translators and audiences leaned decisively to popular nineteenth-century modes of the novel, particularly the massive French feuilleton and British (and to a lesser extent, American) detective fiction." Selim notes that these mostly unauthorized translations circulated widely. These texts were translations in the sense that the *Arabian Nights* stories were "translated" into European languages—part translation, part re-writing. They were "adaptations of some form or other, many with a shaky commitment to an 'original' text, where this text actually existed."

Jonathan Guyer, too, describes the slightly later period from the 1890s to the 1960s as the "golden age of illicit crime fiction translation" (Guyer 2014). He attributes the important influence of crime writing on the Egyptian literary scene in part to the wide proliferation of production of "thousands of unauthorized paperbacks, capped off with covers as lurid as their Western cousins." As Selim and Guyer highlight, largely unauthorized translations of European and American crime writing circulated widely in the Arab world, especially in Egypt, helping to create an eager reading public and an emerging cadre of authors and translators. Such was the attraction of translated texts that original texts written in Arabic were marketed as translations in order to appeal to an eager and growing audience of Arabic readers. Selim explains that "'European' or 'foreign' fiction was so popular among the new reading public that some Arab authors published their original work *as translations* of unattributed or falsely attributed European originals" (emphasis original). The detective novel, then, was integral to the early development of both writers and consumers of the novel in Arabic in the late nineteenth and early twentieth centuries.

Jabra Ibrahim Jabra was born to a poor, Christian family in Bethlehem in 1920. He moved to Jerusalem at the age of twelve and later won scholarships to study in the UK. In his earlier memoir, *The First Well*, Jabra describes himself as a student at the Rashidiyya School in Jerusalem. He was, he recalls, "obsessed with […] the reading of books, school texts as well as others. I filled my brains with Arabic and English words" (Jabra 2012: 161). His life was, literally and figuratively, miles away from the thriving Cairean literary scene that Selim and Guyer describe, yet he too was reading Christie's writing.

If Christie's novels had a bigger influence on the Middle East than even she probably realized, the Middle East certainly shaped Christie's life and work. In her autobiography, Christie recalls her first visit to Cairo with her mother—a money-saving location for Agatha to "come out." As she reflects, "if you were well off, your mother gave a dance for you. You were supposed to go for a season in London" (Christie 1978: 170), but "there could be nothing like that in [Christie's] life" (170). Instead, her mother chose to convalesce in Cairo where the young Agatha could "be familiarized with dancing, talking to young men, and all the rest of it" (1978: 172). The attractions of the city itself paled into insignificance when compared to dances and watching games of polo:

> the wonders of antiquity were the last thing I cared to see, and I am very glad [my mother] did not take me. Luxor, Karnak, the beauties of Egypt, were to come upon me with wonderful impact about twenty years later. How it would have spoilt them for me if I had seen them then with unappreciative eyes.
>
> (175)

Christie returned to the region in search of rest and recuperation after a difficult divorce from her first husband, Archie. She traveled to the Middle East in 1928 on a whim, changing her ticket for the Caribbean at the last minute after a chance conversation at dinner with Commander Howe, whose enthusiasm convinced her to travel by the Orient Express to Baghdad instead (Christie 1978: 372).

It was on that trip that she became friendly with the eminent archaeologist Leonard Woolley and his wife, Katharine, who was a fan of her crime writing. Christie returned to visit the couple at Ur in 1930, when she got to know Woolley's assistant, Max Mallowan. As Mallowan describes in his memoir, "Katharine Woolley in her imperious way ordered me to take [Agatha] on a round trip to Baghdad and see something of the desert and places of interest on the journey" (Mallowan 1977: 44). The pair visited Nippur, Diwaniya, Nejef, and Karbala "where we were to spend the night, visiting on the way the lovely Ummayad castle of Ukhaidir" (44). Afterward, they decided to bathe in a salt lake nearby, she in "a silk vest and double pair of knickers" and he "in shorts and a vest" (Christie 1978: 409). But as they were bathing, their car became stuck: "it had sunk gently into the sand and refused to move, and I now realized some of the hazards of desert driving," Christie reflected (409). It was,

Mallowan admits, Christie's stoic response to the disaster with the car that led him to conclude that "she must be a remarkable woman" (Mallowan 1977: 45), and as he told her later "it was that moment he decided I would make an excellent wife of him" (Christie 1978: 409). He proposed only a few months later, and the couple were married at St. Columba's Church in Edinburgh in September of that year. Throughout their married life, Christie accompanied Mallowan on almost all his excavations in Iraq, and later Syria. The couple had a house in Baghdad, and made temporary homes around the region as suited his digs. Charlotte Trümpler describes "the deep happiness [Christie] found living and travelling in eastern countries" (2001: 12). The Mallowans also traveled extensively "before and after their excavations, often visit[ing] other places of archaeological interest" (Korte 2000: 158). All this, as Barbara Korte reminds us, "had an impact on Christie's fiction" (158).

After realizing her full identity, Jabra Ibrahim Jabra pauses in his reminiscences to analyze two of Agatha Christie's "Iraqi novels," *Murder in Mesopotamia* and *They Came to Baghdad*. He concludes that "the atmosphere and the characters of both novels did not differ much from those of her novels set in England, except for her description of the markets of Basra in one and of the Zia Hotel and its owner in Baghdad in the other" (2005: 41–2). Jabra commends what he understands as the apolitical nature of Christie work, which "made no claim to be concerned with social, political, or documentary matters" (41–2). Like many critics of crime fiction since, Jabra insists that Christie's novels conform to the classic crime format in that they present the reader with a

> clever crime plot that required that she [Christie] move her characters within the confines of her basic intellectual creation. No importance is thus attached to the surroundings of the event other than the undefined background it offers to this game, which is almost purely mathematical in its logic and construction.
>
> (42)

Julian Symons echoes this view of Christie's writing, describing her work as "original in the sense that it is a puzzle story which is solely that" (1972: 100). As Christopher Prior has put it, "readers came to Christie's work for the puzzles, not the politics" (2018: 199). Christopher Baldick outlines "the conventions of the Golden Age detective puzzler, with its two-dimensional characters and its precisely specified times [...] and spaces" (2004: 278). He concludes that these rules "all quickly became matters of common knowledge and common amusement" (278). Simon Reeva Spector sees the formulaic nature of crime writing as part of what drives authors, such as Christie, to set their novels abroad. He suggests that "changes in location, setting, method of the murder, and ethnicity of the detective and the criminal are used to add spice to the script without boring [the] audience" (2010: 5). In particular he asserts that the Middle East, and especially archaeological digs—which feature heavily in Christie's writing set in the region—are attractive locations for murder mysteries "because of the confined nature of the sites. Egypt, Israel, Iraq, and Turkey—and cruise ships on the Nile, for that matter—have offered convenient backdrops for crime" (2010: 5).

In her preface to *Death on the Nile* (1937), Agatha Christie describes the novel tellingly as "one of the best of my 'foreign travel' ones," and declares that "if detective stories are 'escape literature' (and why shouldn't they be!) the reader can escape to sunny skies and blue water as well as to crime in the confines of an armchair" (2). Unsurprisingly, the novel evokes Egypt as an exotic travel location. The action begins in Britain, where the beautiful heiress Linnet Ridgeway steals her impoverished best friend Jacqueline de Bellefort's fiancé, Simon Doyle. Simon and Linnet marry and head to Egypt, but their honeymoon is dogged by Jaqueline, who seems to be following them, heartbroken, reminding them of their betrayal and ruining their honeymoon trip. When Linnet is murdered on a steamer travelling down the Nile, a holidaying Poirot is called upon to investigate. In *Death on the Nile*, Egypt is full of must-see sights "the Nile and the Pyramids and the sand" as Jacqueline declares to Simon when they are planning their own thwarted honeymoon (21). The characters stay at Mena House, take tea at the renowned Shepheard's Hotel, and rely on the services of the well-known travel agents Thomas Cook and Sons to arrange expeditions to "the Fayum," "Philae" or the "Second Cataract." Later, the cast of characters are gathered together on a cruise up the Nile to "Luxor and Assuan" (42). It is on this steamer that Linnet Ridgeway is murdered.

The people of Egypt themselves are part of the backdrop of this Euro-American touristic experience. The majority of Egyptians are merely anonymous servants: waiters, porters, cooks, and so on. At their most noteworthy, they are irritatingly persistent purveyors of souvenirs or travel experiences, which they aggressively try to sell to the foreign tourists. Christie describes for instance,

> Five watchful bead-sellers, two vendors of postcards, three sellers of plaster scarabs, a couple of donkey boys and some detached but hopeful infantile riff-raff closed in upon them. "You want beads, sir? Very good, sir. Very cheap … " "Lady, you want scarab? Look–great queen–very lucky … " "You look, sir–real lapis. Very good, very cheap … " "You want ride donkey, sir? This very good donkey. This donkey Whiskey and Soda, sir … " "You want to go granite quarries, sir? This very good donkey. Other donkey very bad, sir, that donkey fall down … " "You want postcard–very cheap–very nice … " "Look, lady … Only ten piastres–very cheap–lapis–this ivory … " "This very good fly whisk–this all-amber … " "You go out in boat, sir? I got very good boat, sir … " "You go back to hotel, lady? This first-class donkey … "
>
> (50, ellipses original)

Hercule Poirot's dismissal of what Christie describes as a "human cluster of flies" is evocative of their pestilential presence in the novel: their volume, their anonymity, and their status as practically subhuman. Egyptians are dirty, poor, and irritating to the tourists whose perspective Christie espouses. Described as "infantile riff-raff" (50), they are, as the secretly alcoholic author Mrs. Otterbourne announces, "local colour" (61). Even the children are "awful" according to the otherwise very likeable Mrs. Allerton. The "small black figures" are deeply irritating to her as they beg for "Backshish." "I thought they'd get tired of me," she explains to Poirot, but though she succeeds in shooing them away for brief periods, "they come back and stare and stare, and their eyes are simply disgusting, and so are their noses, and I don't believe I really like children—not unless they're more or less washed and have the rudiments of manners" (105). Deemed too dirty and poor to be likable children, the Egyptian "mob," as Christie describes the children, only "scattered and then reappeared, closing in once more" when Poirot attempts to disperse them (106).

Appointment with Death (1938) revolves around an American family ruled by a tyrannical stepmother, Mrs. Boynton. Poirot first encounters the Boyntons in Jerusalem, where they are all holidaying. The cast of European and American travelers meet while staying at the Solomon Hotel in Jerusalem, and later travel on to Petra in what would have been Transjordan in 1938. Christie stresses Jerusalem's religious significance, as well as the conflict between the various religious sects to whom the city is holy. As the British doctor Sarah King tells the French psychiatrist Dr. Gerard, "Religion is very odd!" (9). Gerard agrees, concluding that Jerusalem contains "[e]very imaginable sect squabbling and fighting!" (9). Christie's evocation of one of the most iconic cities of the Middle East is overtly touristic. The American traveler Jefferson Cope declares that he "hope[s] to have done Jerusalem thoroughly in a couple more days" (29). In an evocation of the quintessential modern tourist, Cope relies on his travel agents, "Cook's," to create "an itinerary ... so as to do the Holy Land thoroughly—Bethlehem, Nazareth, Tiberias, the Sea of Galilee" (29). Christie's Jerusalem and Palestine, more broadly, are entirely in keeping with a "backdrop" to her evolving crime scene, while the reader's focus is directed toward a wild psychological analysis of the Boynton family, and in particular of the damaging effects of Mrs. Boynton's parenting. Much of the plot is devoted to King and Gerard analyzing the potential damage being done to the children by their domineering stepmother, who seems to exercise as much control over her grown stepchildren as she did of the prisoners she oversaw as "wardress in a prison" (42). Meanwhile, Jerusalem is all sights to be ticked off a list in a guidebook, while "tourists passed by without disturbing the peace of the oriental atmosphere" (40).

As the action moves to Petra, Christie's narrative remains studded with familiar sights; the party's first halt is the Dead Sea, and they lunch at Jericho. Lady Westholme, a leading Tory MP who has joined the party, "armed with a

Baedeker" embarks upon a "tour of old Jericho" with "Miss Pierce, the doctor and the fat dragoman" (79). As before, the landscape, history, and culture of each place are reduced to the facile, but still exotic, tourist itinerary complete with the obligatory and classic guidebook, the Baedeker. Often, the reality of the place pales in comparison to its legend. Lennox Boynton declares "King David's city" to be "rather disappointing," for instance (28). The inhabitants of Jerusalem itself are few and far between in the first part of the novel, but in "the rose city" we encounter more Arab characters. Prominent among these is the long-suffering "dragoman," Mahmoud, who is in charge of the party's trip to Petra. Mahmoud is a fat, verbose, anti-Zionist, much to the chagrin of Lady Westholme. As Christie writes:

> The guide seemed the most exhausted of the three. He was quite subdued and hardly exuded any information on the way to Amman. He did not even mention the Jews. For which everyone was profoundly grateful. His voluble and frenzied account of their iniquities had done much to try everyone's temper on the journey from Jerusalem.
>
> (82)

Mahmoud is only made more ridiculous by his attempts to please his guests, for example by reciting English poetry badly in an attempt to show off his evidently wanting missionary education (184). Beyond the dragoman, the novel is full of insignificant and anonymous caricatures of non-white characters from the "strange wild-faced men" who crowd around the car as the tourists arrive in Jordan (85) to the "donkey boys and street touts" who so irritate Sarah King (17). At the camp where the murder of Mrs. Boynton takes place, the party is also served by a number of Arab "boys" whom only Mahmoud the dragoman calls by their names. Otherwise, Abdul, Mohammed, Aziz, and Aissa are interchangeable and anonymous servants to the tourists. Indeed, even the dragoman describes them as "very stupid Bedouin" (184).

I have written in more detail elsewhere about Christie's two Iraqi murder mysteries, *Murder in Mesopotamia* (1936) and *They Came to Baghdad* (1951) (Atia 2019). In *Murder in Mesopotamia*, the novel's narrator Amy Leatheran arrives in Iraq to care for the very nervous Mrs. Leidner, wife of the archaeologist Dr. Leidner. Shortly after Leatheran's arrival, however, Mrs. Leidner (who has been widely read as Katharine Woolley) is murdered at her husband's archaeological dig, and Poirot is called upon to investigate. *They Came to Baghdad* is a Cold War thriller concerned with solving an international criminal plot, and thus is quite different from Christie's traditional whodunits in many ways. It is, however, also set on an archaeological dig—that of the absentminded Dr. Pauncefoot Jones. In each of these novels, as well as in *Absent in the Spring* (1944), a mainstream novel written by Christie under the pseudonym Mary

Westmacott, the Middle East and Iraq specifically are evoked in predictably reductive terms. In Christie's Iraqi novels, British travelers arrive in search of the romantic allure they have come to associate with ancient Mesopotamia, but find in its place the *"dirt* and *mess"* that so appalls nurse Amy Leatheran (1936: 13, emphasis original).

The heroine of *They Came to Baghdad*, Victoria Jones, is equally disappointed to discover that far from the capital of the famed Abbasid Golden Age of Islam, the Baghdad of the 1950s is lamentably loud, modern, and still rather poor. She is appalled by the sight of "a crowded main thoroughfare thronged with people, cars hooting violently, people shouting, European goods for sale in the shop windows, hearty spitting all round her with prodigious throat clearing as a preliminary" (1951: 136). A very different kind of novel, *Absent in the Spring*, draws on the romantic tropes of the desert as a place to find oneself, and to seek enlightenment as well as recalling biblical stories of revelation, also set in the desert. Because Joan Scudamore's most notable journey in the novel is introspective, she reflects very little on the places she passes through, simply declaring Iraq "a horrible place ... Utterly horrible" (Christie [1944] 2009: 83). Her trip to Baghdad to support her daughter, Barbara, after the birth of her first child is far less significant than the mirage—"a queer watery effect" (176) that induces a journey of self-realization on her delayed journey home. The Arab and other non-white characters in the novel are peripheral to say the least. Joan Scudamore merely parrots familiar Orientalist views which caricature "Orientals" as lazy, fatalistic, and dirty. Despairing when her train is delayed, for example, Joan reflects that she was at the mercy of "Orientals" to whom "time means nothing" (52).

In all three novels, non-white characters conform to the worst traits ascribed to them by Orientalists. This is perhaps best encapsulated in the outward appearance and behavior of the Kim-like (Kipling 2011 [1901]) character of Harry Carmichael in *They Came to Baghdad*. Carmichael passes as an Arab by expressing his fatalism, and imitating uncouth, "native" manners. In one instance, "he hawked and spat, not too violently, just to be in the picture. Twice he blew his nose with his fingers" (64). These so-called oriental habits—sure to disgust the reader as much as the British characters in the novels themselves—are enacted only insofar as absolutely necessary to create the believable persona that enables Carmichael to pass as a genuine Arab, as so many of his Victorian and Edwardian predecessors had done. The city of Baghdad itself is most notable for "the filth of the streets and bazaars ... and the unhygienic rags the people wear," as Mrs. Hamilton Clipp informs Victoria on her arrival in the city (88). Even Mrs. Leidner's fondness for Arabs is construed in rather insulting terms in *Murder in Mesopotamia*. As Dr. Leidner tells Nurse Leatheran, "My wife likes Arabs very much—she appreciates their simplicity and their sense of humour" (24). Servants are "native boys" (14), and almost everything in Iraq is a disappointing version of the romance of the Orient that British characters hope to find in the country. In all three novels, the current reality of Iraq is a pale and disappointing imitation of the mythologies that British and European travelers had associated with the so-called cradle of civilization for centuries: the glittering minarets of the *Arabian Nights* stories, the idea of Mesopotamia as the seat of some of the ancient world's most impressive empires, and its associations with the Old Testament. As she approaches the town of Hassanieh, Amy Leatheran is pleasantly surprised to see a "very pretty" place, "standing up quite white and fairy-like with minarets." When she arrives at the town, however, she discovers that—much like Baghdad before it—Hassanieh only disappoints on closer inspection: "such a smell and everything ramshackle and tumble-down, and mud and mess everywhere" (33).

In short, every novel Christie sets in the contemporary Middle East represents the region and its people in ways familiar to her audience, echoing imperialist discourses of race that viewed the Middle East as inferior.[1] As such they stand out today as reductive or even offensive and racist portrayals of the people among whom Christie lived so much of her life with Max Mallowan. Blake Almendinger asserts that Christie "never questioned the notion of a racial hierarchy in her fiction, or the assumption of white authority made possible by British colonial rule" (2019: 62). Such a reading is difficult to deny, as many scholars have noted. How is it possible for the same woman who wrote with such warmth about the Middle East and its people in her life writing, and whom Jabra Ibrahim Jabra so admired and whose friendship he evidently valued, to present Middle Eastern characters in such a two-dimensional and reductive way in her fiction?

While many have read the Middle East in Christie's novels as she herself described it—a series of foreign backdrops to familiar and comforting mysteries that could just as easily have been set in St. Mary Mead—in recent decades, critics have read the choice of location in crime writing as more significant than simply a way to lend variety to a genre that might otherwise become rather repetitive. The argument that we should understand Christie's novels as more than just puzzles set in a variety of locations has perhaps been most persuasively made by Alison Light in her field-shaping analysis of Christie's writing: *Forever England: Femininity, Literature and Conservatism between the Wars*. Light reads Christie's detective fiction as a reflection of the anxieties of her era, and in particular as an antidote to the trauma and loss of the First World War, dubbing Christie's *oeuvre* a "literature of convalescence" (69). Light, Phyllis Lassner, and Susan Rowland have drawn our attention to the ways in which

---

[1]Though beyond the scope of this chapter, Christie's representation of an ancient Egyptian family in *Death Comes as the End* (1944) is notably more sympathetic, and human. For a longer discussion see, for example, Billie Melman (2020) and Waltraud Guglieimi's essay in Trümpler (2001).

Christie's seemingly simple whodunits reflect changing British society, and in particular Britain's diminishing role on the international stage and its waning imperial influence (Lassner 2009; Light 1991; Rowland 2000). Light maintains that Christie's novels always critique communities no matter their location, highlighting their dissolution and dissonance in the interwar years. "Whether in Mesopotamia or in St Mary Mead," she argues, in Christie's novels "society is a society of strangers" (93). Many critics have also noted Christie's choice of the Belgian, and rather effete, Hercule Poirot as a detective. Described by Christie herself as a "small dandified" man, "conceited" and sporting a "handsome moustache" (quoted in Curran 2012: 184), as Rowland has put it, Poirot is "most determinedly foreign [....] [a]n affront to English masculinity" (64). Meanwhile, Lassner has argued that Christie's use of "an alien to solve a mystery that threatens the cohesiveness of British identity highlights a relationship deeply embedded in Christie's Oriental plots of the 1930s, that is, between Britain and all those other nations that constitute its sphere of influence" (33).

More recently, Billie Melman has suggested that we should read Poirot in light of the region's interwar politics, which saw Britain and France take on League of Nations Mandates for Palestine, Iraq, Syria, and Transjordan—all formerly provinces of the Ottoman Empire. Designed by Woodrow Wilson as a means to avoid direct imperial rule, the mandates were supposed to act as a support system in order to enable the creation of strong, independent, postwar nations. In practice, however, mandated territories functioned as informal imperial territories by another name and were largely resented by a growing tide of Arab nationalism in the interwar years and beyond. Melman sees Poirot as a "mandatory trouble-shooter, scurrying from one mandate territory to another to solve murder cases and straighten up disorder that threatens the community of English and French people abroad" (2020: 198). However, though she notes the importance of his foreignness to the communities that Christie creates, Melman insists that Poirot is not "other" in Christie's writing. On the contrary, she argues that "it is precisely his blurred gender identity, asexuality, international tags, suavity [...] that make him a new imperial character" (199). For Melman, Poirot's alterity is "tolerated and [...] admired by readers because as in all of Christie's whodunits, a strong national identity is not presented as a value or praised" (199).

Tobias Döring reminds us that "the Golden Age of English mystery writing, occurred in the 1930s, [...] not long before the structure of the imperial world [...] began to crack and yield to decolonisation" (2006: 62–3). Analyzing Agatha Christie's "colonial novels" of the Middle East, Lassner insists that Christie uses the "inscrutable East" to throw light on the anxieties of Britons about their own status in the global economy and the shape of Britain's empire in the interwar years. Lassner maintains that far from presenting merely exotic backgrounds, Christie's Middle Eastern novels "reveal [...] the overweening imperial confidence that masks concerns about emerging imperial threats" (47). For Lassner, "Christie's archaeological metaphor," in particular, "shows that what is inscrutable is not the Oriental landscape, but the lessons of history that remain opaque to her victims and villains alike" (2009: 47). Melman, too, highlights the importance of the intersection between archaeology and empire in Christie's writing. She shows that in Christie's Middle Eastern novels "antiquity is ubiquitous and the remote past incessantly interferes with the present: it shapes the landscapes of Iraq, Syria, and Palestine" (200). As J.C. Bernthal has aptly summarized, even the so-called "pure whodunit is firmly in the territory of a small island losing its empire" (2018: 347). Read in light of this body of criticism, Christie's choice of location is not merely an exotic substitute for the quintessential English village, but also reflects the fissures in, and anxieties of, her contemporary society.

Agatha Christie's descriptions of the Middle East and its people conform closely to the expectations of her readership, and yet, beneath the veneer of the comfortingly touristic, there are subtle hints that the violence of empire is just beneath the surface. Among the touristic scenes are also uncharacteristic forays into the political realm. In *Appointment with Death*, Britain's role on the international stage is made central by Christie's inclusion of the dislikable and opinionated politician, Lady Westholme. In particular, as Melman has observed, Lady Westholme has very clear views on the controversial League of Nations of which she is "a fervent supporter" while "[Dr. Gerard] the Frenchman, on the other hand, chose to be witty at the League's expense" (83). As Christie describes, "from the attitude of the League concerning Abyssinia and Spain they passed to the Litvania boundary dispute of which Sarah [King] had never heard and from there to the activities of the League in suppressing dope gangs" (83). Melman argues that we must understand *Appointment with Death*, and especially its overt political references, in the context of the "anti-colonial Arab rebellion of 1936–9 in Palestine, at the time of a severe clash between Arab and Jewish nationalisms and the international crises that peaked in the failure of the League as arbitrator of conflicts, and the collapse of ideas of world peace" (196). When viewed in this light, Christie's repeated references to different religious and ethnic groups "squabbling" over Jerusalem take on a more substantive undertone. The word "squabbling" is used repeatedly by Sarah King to describe the escalating battles around control of Jerusalem, and Palestine more widely. Though the vocabulary undoubtedly infantilizes the feuding parties, reducing the conflict to the behavior of petulant children unable to share nicely, it is also an important reminder of the difficulties Britain faced in managing Zionist claims to a Jewish homeland in Palestine with the claims of the extant population. For Sarah King, these "fierce squabbling churches" obfuscate her connection with Jerusalem's genuine religiosity. If only she could "sweep all this away ... I might see Christ's quiet figure riding into Jerusalem on a donkey—and believe in Him," she reflects (47). Similarly, Mahmoud the Dragoman's repeated and voluble anti-Zionist sentiments arguably serve as a constant and (as the other characters complain), repeated reminder of attitudes toward escalating conflict in Palestine. Though often reductively described, the contemporary political struggles are evident in Christie's *Appointment with Death*.

Anonymous and often problematically described in terms that render them less than human, Christie's descriptions of the people of the Middle East also gesture toward the potential for violence in a region that had long been part of Britain's informal sphere of influence. Formally a part of the Ottoman empire for centuries, much of the Middle East was nevertheless also important to Britain, not least as part of the land route to India. Unusually, Egypt was brought under more direct British control in 1882 when British troops occupied it in part to ensure continued access to the Suez Canal. British troops remained in the country until the Suez crisis in 1954. As I've discussed, Britain took on the mandates for Iraq and Palestine in 1920. The tempestuous and uncertain nature of Britain's postwar control in the region is reflected in the number of uprisings British authorities had to subdue in the few months following Britain's acceptance of the mandates at San Remo. In the spring and summer of 1920, nationalist uprisings threatened British control over the newly created state of Iraq. Growing unrest, fed by an attempt by nationalists to occupy the city of Mosul in May 1920, festered into a widespread rebellion. Historian David Omissi argues that the uprisings "shook the very foundations of British rule in Mesopotamia" (1994: 22). In April of the same year, riots, rooted in growing tensions between different ethnic and religious groups over control of the city, erupted in Jerusalem during the festival of Nebi Musa. Only a few months earlier, the Egyptian Revolution of 1919 had seen nationwide protests against British occupation and the exile of the nationalist leader Saad Zaghloul, among others. Such conflicts continued to escalate throughout the 1930s and 1940s. Indeed, nationalist demands in Iraq resulted in the premature dissolution of the mandate and formal Iraqi independence in 1932, though Britain continued to exercise power in Iraq long after this date.[2] Christie was well aware of the geopolitical fault lines in the region, as her response to meeting Jabra Ibrahim Jabra in 1948 well illustrates. Her life with Mallowan was also directly affected by growing nationalism in Iraq. When a new antiquities law was introduced by the independent Iraqi government in 1935 which required 50 percent of archaeological finds and all unique artifacts to remain in Iraqi hands, like many archaeologists, Mallowan decided it was necessary to relocate to Syria the following season.

---

[2]For a general history of the region, see for example Eugene Rogan, *The Arabs: A History* (2018 [2009]).

Christie's sensitivity to the changing tide of politics in the region manifests itself in subtle allusions to thinly veiled violence in her seemingly benign mysteries. If we look more closely at Christie's descriptions of local people in *Death on the Nile*, we might recall that even the Egyptian children are described as a "mob" (105), a word often associated with threatening anti-imperial violence. The Egyptian landscape is also described as "savage" (115). Linnet and Simon Doyle declare the trip between the first and second cataracts on the SS *Karnak* less touristic, and therefore more authentic. Simon describes it as a trip to the "heart of Egypt" which Linnet declares is somehow "wilder" (116). Of course, in the context of the overt racial politics of the novel as a whole, these descriptions most obviously signal Egypt's status as a place populated by uncivilized and seemingly backward races, but Christie's language also suggests untamed and uncontrollable undercurrents beneath the façade of imperial control. The potential for violence is everywhere in Christie's colonial novels, and Arab sheikhs, as she reminds us in *They Came to Baghdad*, are "excitable and [...] love firearms" (80). Reinhold Schiffer argues that the anglophile character of Sheikh Hussein el Ziyara, a man "renowned [...] throughout the Moslem world, both as a Holy Man and a poet of renown [...] considered by many to be a Saint" (507) in *They Came to Baghdad*, "establishes a moral harmony between Arabs and Britons" (Schiffer in Trümpler 2001: 308). However, in contrast to Schiffer's conclusion that "searching for a political perspective on the Middle East in Christie ... would be futile" (308), I would argue that the figure of el Ziyara points us to the ongoing legacies of Britain's role in shaping the modern Iraqi state. "In favoring the shaikh," Toby Dodge has shown, "the British modernized his interaction with society based on revenue collection and land ownership, so imposing a new utilitarian dynamic between state and shaikh" (Dodge 2003: 120). If we read the apolitical and anglophile figure of Sheikh el Ziyara in light of this analysis, his combination of dignity but complete lack of agency or influence, as presented in the novel, speaks volumes about the role of sheikhs as key players in Iraq. Men like el Ziyara were given money and land by British officials in exchange for their suppression of nationalist sentiments and their collection of revenue for the state, but, Dodge shows, this came at the price of their political allegiance at a key nationalist moment in Iraq. Here, too, I would argue, Christie's evocation of the Arab sheikh is informed by her astute reading of the dynamics of Iraqi society and the ways in which it was shaped by imperial power structures.

As I have argued in a previous essay, and as Lassner's and Melman's work also highlights, Christie's reliance on the archaeological dig itself gestures toward the violence of empire (Atia 2019; Lassner 2009; Melman 2020). Well read and deeply invested (sometimes financially as well as emotionally) in Max Mallowan's archaeological career, Christie has been described as "of invaluable assistance to [Max's] archaeological team" (Trümpler 2001: 12–13 and 15; see also Joan Oates's essay in the same volume). Christie was more than cognizant of the fact that archaeological excavation had been entwined with imperial power since Napoleon's invasion of Egypt in 1798. As Donald Malcolm Reid summarizes, between Napoleon's conquest and the First World War, "archaeology and imperialism seemed to walk hand in hand" (Reid 2002: 2). While her fictional archaeologists are often likable, forgetful, insular academics seemingly far from imperial ciphers, Christie's careful twinning of murder and the archaeological dig also serves as a constant reminder of the discipline's reliance on the discourses and power of empire. The archaeological dig allows Christie to gesture toward the violence of empire, and indeed the violence of archaeology itself, while maintaining the façade of the benign, and commercially successful, whodunit. There is no denying that Christie's Middle Eastern novels recreate stereotypical colonialist ideas and discourses, the ideas and descriptions that her contemporary audience expected and that are so difficult for a modern reader to encounter. Yet her love for the region also shaped her writing. To read her novels at face value, one would never imagine that a proud Arab nationalist like Jabra could recall Christie and her writing with such affection. However, I would argue that, alongside the predictable, Christie's writing also contains an entirely different—but equally significant—set of clues inviting the reader to see beyond the puzzle in order to glimpse a fast-changing, unstable imperial world order, always threatened by violence.

In her classic analysis, Catherine Belsey shows that the novel always invites readerly interpretation, enabling a reader's "autonomous subjectivity" (1980: 56). As Belsey explains, realist fiction's "movement towards closure" precludes contradiction. "When contradiction exists in classic realism," Belsey argues, "it does so in the margins of the text" (68). However, the reader always has the ability to find the clues, evident only in the margins of the text, and in so doing to see beyond the main narrative strand in order to find hidden depths, otherwise obscured by the drive toward narrative closure. Often, as Belsey shows in a reading of Charles Dickens's *Bleak House*, texts contain an alternate narrative designed to be seen only through readerly intervention: "a reality which appears to be many-sided, too complex to be contained within a single point of view, but which is in fact so contained within the single and non-contradictory invisible narrative of the reader" (68). The overriding movement toward narrative closure that Belsey outlines is arguably all the more important in detective fiction, with its emphasis on the big reveal at the novel's close. In no other genre is the dénouement as crucial as that of the whodunit. In this sense we might read the detective novel, and particularly the puzzle-based form at which Christie excelled, as a particular extension of the dialogic relationship that Belsey outlines. As Ina Rae Hark has put it in a different context, "Christie's mysteries acknowledge themselves as not about crime-solving but about reading" (1997: 112).

"At the base of the whodunit," Tzvetan Todorov argues, "we find a duality." For Todorov, the detective novel "contains not one but two stories: the story of the crime and the story of the investigation" (1966: 140). Todorov's insistence on the duality of crime writing might also indicate a form that always demands detailed reading, and which expects an engaged and proactive close reader. Many critics of detective fiction since have reminded us that one of the most important aspects of the narratological puzzle at the heart of the murder mystery is to enable the reader to play along. As Stephen Knight explains,

> [t]he clue-puzzle [invites] the reader to participate, and many of its compulsive features emphasize this function: the need for "fair play," the reader-testing obsession with red herrings, the dropping of the intermediary Watson, the flat style and the two-dimensional characterization all create a space for the reader to encounter the author and construct a writerly self.
>
> (2003: 90–1)

Julian Symons cites Ronald Knox's rules for the Detective Club in the 1920s, which stressed that the detective novel should be understood as a game between "the author of the one part and the reader of the other part" (1972: 101). In other words, more than any other genre, the kind of narratological puzzles that Christie's writing exemplified *demand* that the reader engages in a process of deduction. This is not only the puzzle's purpose, but a prerequisite expected by readers themselves. Given this emphasis on readerly agency, Christie's subtle allusions to the violence of empire represent another strand of a two-way conversation between author and audience entrenched in the novel form, and especially in crime fiction. These allusions present an addendum to the main narrative, but one that is nevertheless firmly embedded in her Middle Eastern novels. To be sure, the focus of the vast majority of Christie's readers will always be on solving the mystery at the heart of the novel and nothing more. But in the final analysis—given the expectation of readerly engagement—Christie was able to exploit the crime novel's multiple narrative form to write with more depth, more nuance, and far more empathy, than we have hitherto acknowledged.

REFERENCES

Abu Sarah, C. (2020), "Golden Age of Crime," *ArabLit Quarterly*, 3 (2): 6–21.

Allmendinger, B. (2019), "The Erasure of Race in Agatha Christie's *And Then There Were None*," *ANQ: A Quarterly Journal of Short Articles, Notes and Reviews*, 32 (1): 60–4.

Atia, N. (2019), "Murder in Mesopotamia: Agatha Christie's Life and Work in the Middle East," in N. Atia and K. Houlden (eds), *Popular Postcolonialisms: Discourses of Empire and Popular Culture*, 89–107, London: Routledge.

Baldick, C. (2004), *Modern Movement, 1910–1940*, Oxford: Oxford University Press.

Belsey, C. ([1980] 2001), *Critical Practice*, London: Routledge.

Bernthal, J. C. (2018), "Detective Fiction: Resolutions without Solutions," in D. McNeill and C. Ferrell (eds), *British Literature in Transition, 1900–2000*, 331–47, Cambridge: Cambridge University Press.

Christie, A. ([1936] 2001), *Murder in Mesopotamia*, London: HarperCollins

Christie, A. ([1937] 1999), *Death on the Nile*, London: HarperCollins.

Christie, A. ([1938] 2010), *Appointment with Death*, London: HarperCollins.

Christie, A. ([1944] 2009), *Absent in the Spring*, London: HarperCollins.

Christie, A. ([1951] 2003), *They Came to Baghdad*, London: HarperCollins.

Christie, A. ([1978] 1993), *An Autobiography*, London: HarperCollins.

Curran, J. (2012), *Agatha Christie's Murder in the Making: Stories and Secrets from Her Archive*, London: HarperCollins.

Dodge, T. (2003), *Inventing Iraq: The Failure of Nation Building and a History Denied*, London: Hurst.

Döring, T. (2006), "Sherlock Homes—He Dead: Disenchanting the English Detective in Kazuo Ishiguro's *When We Were Orphans*," in C. Matzke and S. Muhleisen (eds), *Postcolonial Postmortems: Crime Fiction from a Transcultural Perspective*, 59–86, Amsterdam: Rodopi.

Guglielmi, W. (2001), "Agatha Christie and her Use of Ancient Egyptian Sources," in Charlotte Trümpler (ed), *Agatha Christie and Archaeology*, 351–90, London: British Museum Press.

Guyer, J. (2014), "The Case of the Arab Noirs," *The Paris Review*, August 20. Available online: https://www.theparisreview.org/blog/2014/08/20/the-case-of-the-arabic-noirs/

Hark, I. R. (1997), "Impossible Murderers: Agatha Christie and the Community of Readers," in J. H. Delamater and R. Prigozy (eds), *Theory and Practice of Classic Detective Fiction*, 111–18, Westport: Hofstra University Press.

Jabra, J. I. (2005), *Princesses' Street: Baghdad Memories*, trans. Issa J. Boullata, Fayetteville: University of Arkansas Press.

Jabra, J. I. (2012), *The First Well: A Bethlehem Boyhood*, trans. Issa J. Boullata, London: Hesperus.

Kipling, R. (2011 [1901]), *Kim*, London: Penguin.

Knight, S. (2003), "The Golden Age," in M. Priestman (ed), *The Cambridge Companion to Crime Fiction*, 77–94, Cambridge: Cambridge University Press.

Korte, B. (2000), "Agatha Was Here: Agatha Christie and the Orient—Criminology and Archaeology (Review)," *Public Archaeology*, 1 (2): 157–9.

Lassner, P. (2009), "The Mysterious New Empire: Agatha Christie's Colonial Murders," in R. Hackett, F. Hauser, and G. Wachman (eds), *At Home and Abroad in the Empire: British Women Write the 1930s*, 31–50, Newark: University of Delaware Press.

Light, A. (1991), *Forever England: Femininity, Literature and Conservatism between the Wars*, London: Routledge.

Lynx Qualey, M. (2016), "Agatha Christie's Love-Hate Story with the Arabs," *Al Jazeera*, January 12. Available online: https://www.aljazeera.com/opinions/2016/1/12/agatha-christies-love-hate-story-with-the-arabs/ (accessed December 1, 2021).

Mallowan, M. ([1977] 2001), *Mallowan's Memoirs: Agatha and the Archaeologist*, London: HarperCollins.

Melman, B. (2020), *Empires of Antiquity: Modernity and the Rediscovery of the Ancient Near East, 1914–1950*, Oxford: Oxford University Press.

Oates, J. (2001), "Agatha Christie, Nimrud and Baghdad," in Charlotte Trümpler (ed), *Agatha Christie and Archaeology*, 205–28, London: British Museum Press.

Omissi, D. (1994), *The Sepoy and the Raj: The Indian Army, 1860–1940*, Basingstoke: Macmillan.

Prior, C. (2018), "An Empire Gone Bad: Agatha Christie, Anglocentrism and Decolonization," *Culture and Social History*, 15 (2): 197–213.

Reeva Spector, S. (2010), *Spies and Holy Wars: The Middle East in 20th Century Crime Fiction*, Texas: University of Texas Press.

Reid, D. M. (2002), *Whose Pharaohs? Archaeology, Museums and Egyptian National Identity from Napoleon to World War I*, Berkeley: University of California Press.

Rogan, E. ([2012] 2018), *The Arabs: A History*, London: Penguin.

Rowland, S. (2000), *From Agatha Christie to Ruth Rendell: British Women Writers in Detective and Crime Fiction*, Basingstoke: Macmillan.

Schiffer, R. (2001), "Agatha's Arabs," in Charlotte Trümpler (ed), *Agatha Christie and Archaeology*, 303–34, London: British Museum Press.

Selim, S. (2017), "Translations and Adaptations from the European Novel, 1835–1925," in W. S. Hassan (ed), *The Oxford Handbook of Arab Novelistic Traditions*, no page numbers, Oxford: Oxford University Press, DOI. 10.1093/oxfordhb/9780199349791.013.6

Symons, J. (1972), *Bloody Murder: From the Detective Story to the Crime Novel, a History*, London: Faber and Faber.

Todorov, T. ([1966] 2000), "The Typology of Detective Fiction," trans. Richard Howard, in David Lodge and Nigel Wood (eds), *Modern Criticism and Theory: A Reader*, 225–6, London: Longman.

Trümpler, C. (2001), *Agatha Christie and Archaeology*, London: British Museum Press.

PART THREE

Christie and Society

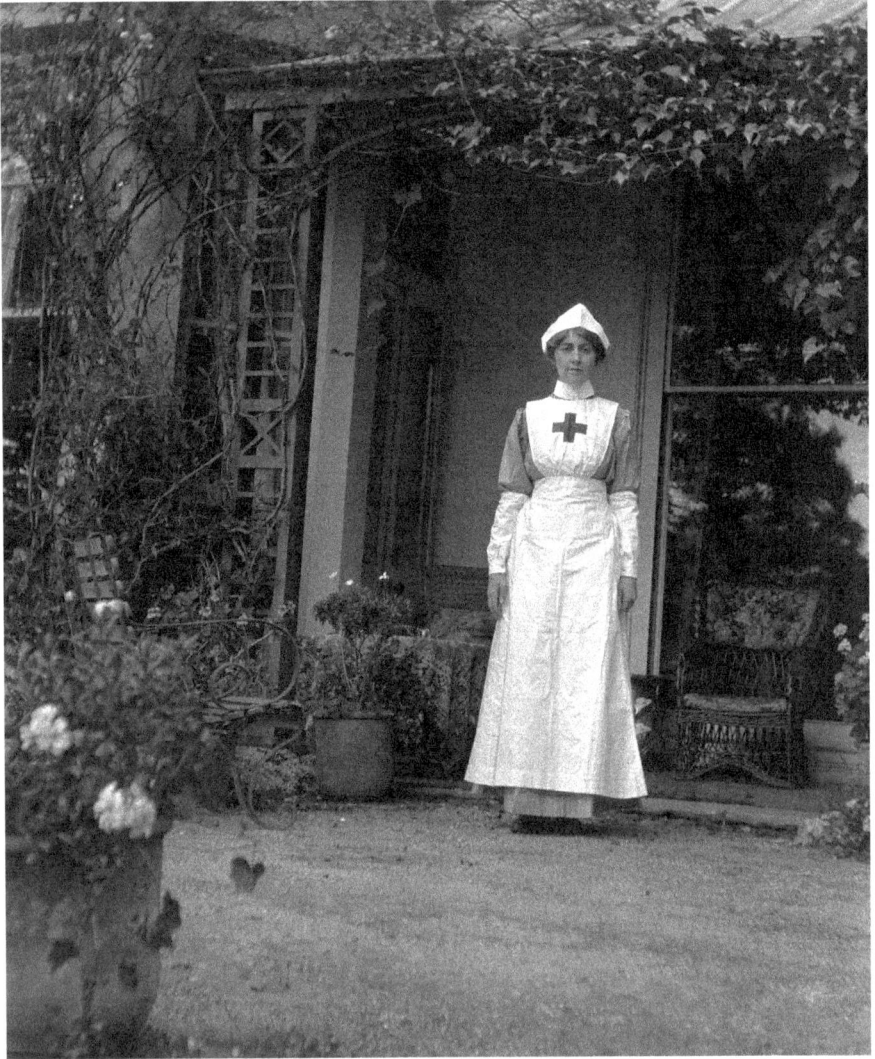

FIGURE 9.1 Agatha Christie dressed for work in the Voluntary Aid Dispatch in Torquay, *c*. 1915. Courtesy of The Christie Archive Trust.

CHAPTER NINE

Christie and the Carnage of War

J.C. BERNTHAL

INTRODUCTION

In 2020, as the world struggled to cope with the ravages of the Covid-19 pandemic, the British government evoked a "Blitz spirit," playing into a mythologized vision of Britons pulling together while isolated in the face of a global enemy. The idea of a "Blitz spirit" has always been controversial, but the underlying concepts of fear, isolation in the midst of traumatic surroundings, and the need to rethink community were well documented during the upheavals of the Second World War and again during the coronavirus pandemic. In 2020 and 2021, several newspapers, magazines, and online media outlets around the world published editorials with titles like "Killing time with Agatha Christie" (Daniels 2020). Some took the approach that "humans are connected" and a "detective story [...] reminds readers of this," while helping individuals "beat the boredom during the Covid-19 lockdown" (Peacock 2020), while a *New York Times* think piece posed the question: "People were dying all around me. So why was I escaping into tales of murder?" (Fisher 2021).

For scholars of twentieth-century literature and culture, this noticeable trend brings to mind reading habits during the Second World War, which are well documented in media accounts and—in Britain, at least—in materials collected for the Mass Observation Archive (MOA). An MOA report in 1944 found that, in the previous two years, during which the war was at its height, the number of self-described frequent readers had gone up from 40 percent of women and men to 59 percent of women and 56 percent of men ("Books and the Public": 1). It reported "an enormous increase in book sales and borrowing during the war" (54), just as booksellers reported a booming trade during the pandemic over seventy-five years later (Flood 2021): "The blackout has kept me indoors much more," one reader reported ("Books and the Public": 60). The MOA reported with some surprise that, while people in general were more aware of current affairs than during peacetime, this was not down to their increased reading habits; instead, "even really curious readers" preferred literature with a "strong conscious element of escape" (83).

The chief examples of this kind of literature, the MOA confirmed, were "detective stories," acknowledging for the first time that "[d]etective novels are read right up the scale of serious reading"—that is, by a wider range of readers—as opposed to the romance novel, which was then still the most widely read genre, and certainly offered escape, but was not elevated to the level of "serious" in the report (87). A range of responses identified crime fiction and Agatha Christie specifically on the grounds of "psychology" (90), but most referred to "escapism," "a break [...] from [...] the worries of the day," and "relocation" (90, 91). The MOA concluded that "light reading" which provided "information on life or people" could provide a serious lifeline during times of isolation and sacrifice (95).

A paradox of crime fiction research, and Christie research in particular, is that it has tended to run with this reading of the genre's enormous role and influence during the Second World War but failed to consider Christie or many of her peers as war writers. The idea of escapism seems like something worth talking about, but not like something that invites context. However, any escapist product is created in, tailored to, and honed by its own particular circumstances. The Second World War looms large in Christie's mid-to-late career, on and off the page, while other conflicts from the Anglo-Boer War to the Cold War are never far away.

BATTLES BEYOND BOOKENDS

In crime fiction scholarship, it is a truism that the genre's "Golden Age" can be bookended, roughly, by the two world wars. How this actually translates into dates or significant titles is more debatable. In her primer *Key Concepts in Crime Fiction*, for example, Heather Worthington puts the Golden Age between 1918 and 1930, that is, in the wake of the First World War (1914–18) and through to the end of the decadent subsequent decade (Worthington 2011: 13). Christie scholar and archivist John Curran attributes the Golden Age directly to the two wars, with 1918 as the kick-off point and the start of the Second World War (1939–45) as the end (Curran 2011: 14).

Such a reading positions Golden Age detective fiction as inherently both socially conservative and socially disengaged. John Scaggs writes, without textual evidence, that "the crime genre during this period was a particularly powerful ideological tool that consolidated and disseminated patriarchal power, and its voice was the rational, coolly logical voice of the male detective or his male narrator" (20). In these books, according to Scaggs, the corpse being investigated is "curiously sanitized and bloodless" because the reality of death and violence cannot be allowed to intrude (43). The idea here is that, after the First World War, readers were fed a steady stream of narratives where traditional authority figures could be seen and understood to return things to the way they were, and that this became increasingly unsustainable as economic conservatism bred into nationalism and fascism across Europe, with the result of what Christie called "a second and more desperate war" (1975: 5), where it became "natural to expect that you yourself might be killed soon" (1977: 489).

Meanwhile, Susan Rowland uses influential novels as her bookends, stating that the Golden Age can be said to run from the publication of Christie's debut in 1920 to that of Dorothy L. Sayers's last crime novel in 1937 (Rowland 2001: 3). Rowland focuses more on the texts than the stereotypes, reflecting on the importance of Christie's *The Mysterious Affair at Styles* (1920), which introduced many of the elements of the fairly clued, upper-middle-class closed-setting world of the Golden Age mystery, and Sayers's *Busman's Honeymoon* (1937), which problematizes the idea that these novels can bring closure or certainty in a morally upheaved world. However, this is not a warless characterization, since both these novels are hugely impacted by the reality/ aftermath and anticipation of international conflict, respectively. What the above definitions—and others with different, but similar start and end, points— have in common is an acknowledgment of the serious impact of war on creating a need for and then ending the easy answers of escapist puzzle-based fiction.

This assertion, though, risks sidestepping the fact that many Golden Age practitioners, Christie supreme among them, were more productive than ever during the Second World War. Christie, producing up to five books a year as well as articles, stories, and plays during the war years, commented on her prolific output during this period glibly: "I had no other things to do" (1977: 489).[1] More than this, though, as discussed above, detective novels were more widely read than ever during this time. However, the bulk of Christie's published fiction, at least, written and published during this period did not engage with war directly, for obvious reasons. Similarly, Christie at this time made the conscious decision to set many of her escapist novels in the 1930s—that is, the period between the wars, and the period seen now as her own golden age. These novels

---

[1]It is a misleading statement, since while Christie was away from much of her family and her usual archaeological adventures, she was active in the war effort, as she had been during the First World War. She lent out her holiday home, Greenway, to evacuees and American military personnel, and volunteered as a nurse at the University of London, as well as contributing articles, poems, and a recipe to various war initiatives.

still engage with war themes: notably, both *The Body in the Library* (1942) and *The Moving Finger* (1943) have characters irreparably wounded in airplane crashes, while later novels written in this period such as *The Hollow* (1946) are about trying to rebuild after big emotional upheavals. *Sparkling Cyanide* (1945), which deals with murders in the past and the "present," was originally titled *Remembered Death*, but Christie's UK publishers insisted on a jauntier, less resonant, title for wartime readers.

Christie did write about the war directly, however. Her 1941 mystery thriller *N or M?* concerns fifth columnists on a European holiday resort. Married adventurers Tommy and Tuppence discover a secret Nazi agent among the mostly British, mostly middle-class, guests on the island. Code-breaker Dilly Knox has provided the most enduring commentary on this novel, in his account of how it led to MI5, the British secret service, investigating Christie. *N or M?* features "a tiresome old major," Major Bletchley, which led some to believe she may be communicating secret knowledge about top-secret code-breaking exercises at Bletchley Park. Christie later told Knox that she had chosen the name because, stuck in a train station at Bletchley one day, "she found the place so boring she thought it would be the ideal name" (Smith 2013: 32).

Christie also penned a short story, "The Capture of Cerberus," designed to conclude a series of twelve, *The Labours of Hercules*, commissioned by *The Strand* in 1939. In this story, Poirot deals with the apparent assassination of a Nazi dictator known as August Hertzlein—the veil for Adolph Hitler could hardly be thinner. He reveals that Hertzlein's death was faked and that he was sequestered in an asylum. Poirot reveals that, having converted to Catholicism and vowed to bring about world peace, the dictator proved a threat to his followers and had to be martyred. As Merja Makinen points out, this story was penned during the "Phoney War," the period between Britain's declaration of war on September 3, 1939, and the evacuation of Allied Forces from Dunkirk in May 1940 when little was seen by the majority of Brits to be happening (Makinen 2020: 65). It manages to both chide "[c]ontemporary optimism that the war could be averted" (65) by showing that a dictator is a figurehead for an unstoppable movement and "allow [...] for a resolution of the threat to democracy" (66), as Poirot is able to use that figurehead as a figurehead of his own—for peace and reformation.

Unsurprisingly, the story was "repressed by her literary agent" (63) and not offered to *The Strand*, which ended up running with eleven *Labours of Hercules*. With a few exceptions,[2] Christie would not write directly about the

---

[2]These include *N or M?* (1941) and *Curtain: Poirot's Last Case*, a novel written around 1940 for publication after Christie's death (it was eventually published in 1975), which aims at timelessness but mentions the war and returns to the setting of her first war novel, *The Mysterious Affair at Styles*. Christie's wartime writing about war also includes some poems and articles, and a recipe for "Mystery Potatoes," which appeared in a celebrity cookbook, *A Kitchen Goes to War* (1940), to help the rationing effort.

war during the war. She famously turned down requests to write propaganda, knowing—likely guided by her publishers—that her readers wanted and needed to escape. However, war is insidious, and one cannot escape something without at least acknowledging it.

THE GREAT WAR, *THE MYSTERIOUS AFFAIR AT STYLES*, AND THE GOLDEN AGE

The bulk of research on Christie and war concerns the Second World War. However, the First World War has been widely discussed, especially in connection with Christie's debut, which was largely written in 1916. Christie served during the war as a Voluntary Aid Dispatch (VAD) in Torquay, where she acquired an extensive professional knowledge of poisons and pharmacy which provided a template for several (fictional) murders throughout her career, as detailed in Kathryn Harkup's contribution to the present volume. It was the war itself which led Christie to write a mystery. In 1941, Christie recalled, in Howard Haycraft's *Murder for Pleasure*, that "[t]oward the end of the [previous] war, [...] I had read many detective novels, as I found they were excellent to take one's mind off one's worries" but that, as her sister had lamented, "it was almost impossible to find a *good* detective story [...] I said I thought I could write one. She was doubtful. Thus spurred on, I wrote *The Mysterious Affair at Styles*" (in Haycraft [1941] 1974: 129). Although not published until 1920, *Styles* is essentially a wartime, not an interwar, novel, conceived, written, and set during the conflict, as a deliberate form of escape.

Despite its intended purpose to divert, and "take one's mind off one's worries," *Styles* engages directly with the war in ways that are not typical for Christie, at least as represented in most scholarship. First and foremost, it introduces the detective Hercule Poirot, who is in England purely because of the war. He is a Belgian refugee. While his sidekick, narrator Captain Hastings, is in the Essex village of Styles St. Mary because he has been "invalided home from the Front" (Christie 1921: 9), Poirot is staying there, with seven other Belgian "refugees from their native land," "by the charity of the good Mrs. Inglethorp" (35), a matriarch whose murder will spur the action in this novel.

Christie recalled creating Poirot from reality. Trying to decide on a detective, she recalls in her autobiography, "I remembered our Belgian refugees," specifically "quite a colony of Belgian refugees living in the parish of Tor [who] had been treated with loving kindness and sympathy when they arrived," although she notes "the usual reaction" of xenophobia in due course (Christie 1977: 256). "Why not make my detective a Belgian?" she concludes (256). These were refugees displaced by the German invasion of Belgium in 1914, at the start of the war. Poirot is something of an outsider in Styles, being eccentrically *different* and lodged with his countrymen in "a little house" on the edge of the village (Christie 1921: 35, 53). Anne Hart, in her biography of Poirot, notes that, while outsiders, Belgians were among the more welcome refugees at the time: "From the outset of the war the English had opened their hearts and homes to Belgian refugees. 'REMEMBER BELGIUM,' admonished enlistment posters" (1990: 19). Indeed, the choice to make Poirot Belgian has been broadly considered politically savvy. As Colin Watson points out, this made him less threatening to British readers than a French hero or one from any power that had not remained neutral and/or been invaded:

> The distinction was an important one in 1920. Not only had the British unaccountably neglected to coin a derogatory epithet for the inhabitants of Belgium but they were still inclined to thank of that country as the military propogandists of five or six years earlier had encouraged them to think— with indulgent sentimentality.
>
> ([1971] 1987: 166)

Christie's description of the Belgian refugees reflects, in fact, her own patronizing sympathy in her autobiography's remarks that the refugees were "poor things," "bewildered and in a strange country" (Christie 1977: 256). Poirot is a creation of war, but he stands outside of it, just as he is placed, geographically, on the edge of the village. Although he has a "military" bearing and a background in law enforcement, an initial description of his finicky habits is particularly revealing: "I believe," writes Hastings, "a speck of dust would have caused him more pain than a bullet wound" (Christie 1921: 35). In a novel written and set during an unprecedented period of gunfire, and published just after it, the imagery is telling—Poirot's priorities are order and method, and this is not going to be a story about the grim realities of war. Watson suggests that "in the context of 'gallant little Belgium'" (or, one might add, "plucky little Belgium"), Poirot's eccentricities, "which would have been deemed an odious affectation had he been one of the French," were endearing (166–7).

At the same time as endearing the readers, though, as Mark Aldridge points out, Poirot's "idiosyncrasies allow much of society to underestimate his powers of deduction" within the novel (2020: 7). These prejudices, fostered and conditioned during war, are exploited in two ways, then, by Christie and her character in *Styles*: Poirot can be trusted and unthreatening to the reader and the murderer, while underestimating him results in entertainment for the former and reckoning for the latter. Indeed, in this novel and subsequently, Poirot is considered with condescension by Britons who are his intellectual inferiors, and his self-importance in asserting this becomes part of the joke. Nonetheless, on introducing him, Hastings notes that "this quaint dandified little man who, I was sorry to see, now limped badly, had been in his time one of the most celebrated members of the Belgian police" (Christie 1921: 35). The unexpanded remark about the limp shows no intention of going into Poirot's backstory, but while viewing him as at best a curiosity Hastings also reveals his impeccable credentials. The idea that war could displace brilliant high-achievers, forcing them to take up roles in Britain that would be beneath them in their homeland, is an ever-relevant one, and Christie would return to it later in her career, with the figure of Mitzi, an eastern European economist-turned-domestic help in *A Murder Is Announced* (1950).

The household Poirot investigates is also entirely "a war household" (22). Not only has its matriarch taken in refugees, but she is spearheading community efforts to deal with the war, arranging charity events, reciting patriotic verses, and holding to the premise of "set[ting] an example of economy": "nothing is wasted," Mrs. Inglethorp tells Hastings. "[E]very scrap of waste paper, even, is saved and sent away in sacks" (22). This will become highly relevant to the mechanics of the plot later, when Poirot reveals that a love letter between Inglethorp's husband and his mistress was recycled as a spill above the fireplace.

Not spoken, but heavily illustrated, about the "war household" at Styles Court is the prominence of women within it. In *Queering Agatha Christie*, I pointed out that the household contains more and stronger women than men. As well as Emily Inglethorp, the matriarch,

> Emily's VAD protégée is "sharp and professional," and her [female] paid companion, with "manly," "stentorian tones" and a "hearty, almost painful" handshake, is a "Jack of all trades," helpful around the village and comradely with men. [...] Generally, the men are less robust and popular than the women: [a poet nephew] is "sickly"; Emily's husband is a brooding "outsider." "Women are doing great work nowadays," Poirot remarks of the VAD [...] He adds that this means women have access to deadly poisons and secrets— that is to say, they have power.
>
> (Bernthal 2016: 36–7)

The nephew is only there because he is "sickly"; the young, manly men are away at war. As a war novel, then, *Styles* is set in a world in which traditional gendered roles are both enforced and unended—an almost uncanny time. While some critics have pointed this out as a potentially feminist or proto-feminist move on the writer's part, Merja Makinen reminds readers in *Investigating Femininity* that it is more complex than that. Quoting the same line of Poirot's, "Women are doing great work nowadays," she notes that "[w]omen as working and efficient are portrayed as admirable" but cautions that such characters cannot be considered "'career women', since the jobs are a voluntary part of the war effort" (Makinen 2016: 81–2). She continues that Christie's work in "the late thirties" provided a more genuine arena to reflect and celebrate the advancement of "professional women" (82).

Although Christie's next novel, *The Secret Adversary* (1922), was a tale of espionage, and civil wars and revolutions bubble in the background of many of her 1920s short stories and novels, such as "The Kidnapped Prime Minister" (1924), *The Secret of Chimneys* (1925), and "The Rajah's Emerald" (1926), Christie did not make war a central focus in many of her 1920s and 1930s contributions, focusing instead on scenes from middle-class British society at home and abroad. To this end, British crime fiction and especially Christie's contributions to it in this period have widely been read as a literature of convalescence. In contrast to Dorothy L. Sayers, who gave her detective what was then known as shell shock, and dealt forthrightly with social issues arising from war such as "the problem of so-called surplus women" (James 2009: 99), crime writer P.D. James has upheld the idea that war in Christie is just something in the backdrop, almost ignored: "when a character in one of her books refers to returning from the war, [...] I have to look back to the date of publication to know whether he is referring to the Great War of 1914–1918 or the 1939–1945 conflict" (105).

However, underscoring these novels—especially those written in the late 1930s—is an awareness that the situation in Europe was darkening. *One, Two, Buckle My Shoe*, though published in 1940, was written before the war, and it features political unrest as a kind of backdrop and red herring, with the real murder for motive being both personal and political: a highly prominent financier wants to keep his bigamy secret so that he can retain money, power, and influence. When he tells Poirot that his livelihood and leadership is surely well-worth sacrificing a few worthless civilian lives in these dark times, Poirot chastises him heartily, reminding him that all life is sacred and no one is objectively more important than any other. In a letter to her agent, Christie referred to this as her "dragg[ing] the war in by the neck and crop" (in Aldridge 2020: 156). *And There Were None*, published in 1939, is marked by fear, unknowability, and nihilism as ten strangers—eight guests and two servants—are lured to a luxury island and promised a weekend of civilized decadence. On the first night, a disembodied voice on the gramophone accuses each in turn of having killed someone and gotten away with it, informing them that they will be punished. One by one, they die. As tension mounts and each character's backstory is revealed, it becomes clear that these are killings people knew about but no one talked about: a woman who drove her maid to suicide with religious intolerance, a playboy who ran over two children, a surgeon who killed a patient while drunk in the operating room, and so on.

The connection to war is oblique, except in the case of one character whose "crime" involved abuse of power in the First World War. Still, the idea of reckoning justice and the theme of unsustainable social norms and structures that permit injustice and are ultimately doomed to some form of destruction were highly topical. After all, when *And Then There Were None* was published,

Britain was heading straight into war, and this was, as Christie wrote in her autobiography, "not a war like the last one"; it was not out of the blue; people had known it was coming (Christie 1977: 482). Several critics and scholars have highlighted *One, Two, Buckle My Shoe* and *And Then There Were None* as war texts, including Katherine A. Miller in *British Literature of the Blitz: Fighting the People's War* in 2008 and Brittain Bright in "Writing through War: Narrative Structure and Authority in Christie's Second World War Novels" in 2020. Since the 2015 BBC television adaptation of *And Then There Were None*, which foregrounded its immediately prewar setting in dialogue, cinematography, and publicity, journals and edited collections devoted to popular fiction or culture have begun referencing it with a frequency that suggests it is becoming a standard text.

THE SECOND WORLD WAR, RADICAL DISPLACEMENT, AND *TAKEN AT THE FLOOD*

Christie's popularity during the Second World War has long been acknowledged, but its impact on her fiction remained bizarrely underexplored until the twenty-first century. Stephen Knight identified in Christie's work of the period "an Austenesque pattern of radical displacement, not recognizing the war as itself" but exploring the themes and issues; the "contemporary battles" brought up by it (Knight 1995: 163). Gill Plain has developed this concept of Christie's prose and plots "symboliz[ing], in manageable form, the alienating impact of war" (2013: 135), with neat escapist novels set generally in times before the war "firmly designed to assert stability in the face of change and to keep wartime trauma under control" (2010: 113). In 2020, Rebecca Mills and I published *Agatha Christie Goes to War*, an edited collection focused firmly on establishing Christie as a war writer, with specific reference to the Second World War. We included scholarship from Merja Makinen, looking directly at wartime thrillers like *N or M?* and the long-unpublished "The Capture of Cerberus" (Makinen 2020) alongside analyses of Christie's theatrical work and other titles that sought to offer escapism while remaining highly conscious of and shaped by the raging conflict (Green 2020). The volume also includes, however, several discussions of the aftermath and sweeping legacy of the Second World War in Christie's later fiction (Dalrymple 2020; Mills 2020).

The legacy of war runs strong in Christie, and it is in the years immediately following the Second World War that she dealt with it most directly in her fiction. Perhaps the most iconic of Christie's explicitly postwar texts is *The Mousetrap*, a stage play which has been running continuously in the West End since 1952—excluding government-mandated closures during the Covid-19 pandemic in 2020–1. It is firmly postwar, with early scenes reflecting food and coal rationing—an effort that had been ongoing throughout the war, the persistence of which showed that the disruption was far from over—and the difficulty of knowing who, what, or where one is after shared trauma. Of the eight characters, only two of whom know each other, none (including the police sergeant) is quite who they claim to be and, with echoes of *Murder on the Orient Express*, four have a strong connection to the same past murder case, which is the focus of the killer's efforts for revenge. However, despite the play's perennial presence, it was not extensively discussed as a war-conscious text until Jessica Gildersleeve's "'We're All Strangers': Post-war Anxiety in Agatha Christie's *The Mousetrap*" appeared in *Clues: A Journal of Detection* in 2014.

Gildersleeve's analysis maintains that *The Mousetrap* marks a break from "Golden Age" conventions and taps into "an anxiety present in Britain in the years of recovery following World War II" (2014: 115). It is, Gildersleeve points out, a play in which most characters are trying to escape their pasts, creating some form or other of new identities for themselves. Gildersleeve builds on Alison Light's argument in *Forever England* (1991) that Christie uses "the motif of shared destabilization" (Gildersleeve's term) to depict a society of individuals unknown and unknowable to one another, and links this to the ongoing trauma of murder but also of war (119). The play's focus on "the unknown" and "the presence of strangeness in plain sight," Gildersleeve suggests, "describes the destabilization of social structures and decorum at this time" (122). Federica Crescentini has provided a different perspective on the play—and the radio play and novella that inspired it—noting that the murderer's motive is based on a real-life story of child abuse that took place during the Second World War. Crescentini argues that the play engages directly with trauma, "mental health and memories" (2020: 119), as characters who are strangers come to realize that they knew one another in childhood. For Crescentini, the war in *The Mousetrap* is a destabilizing traumatic event; while it may have ended, the trauma of individuals and loss of essential identities have not. The play, Crescentini insists, "illustrate[s] fears, anxieties, and problems that are both real and contemporary" (122).

If Christie can be said to illustrate fears and anxieties, what contribution does she make to national efforts of recovery? Plain, one of the key voices for recognizing Christie as a war writer, has also argued that her "tangential negotiation of cultural anxieties" extended to "her novels of the post-Second World War period," which "register the effects of trauma and social change" (Plain 2020: 180). In particular, Plain's look at the immediately postwar novel *Taken at the Flood* (1948), as well as Rebecca Mills' analysis of the same text in "Detecting the Blitz: Memory and Trauma in Christie's Postwar Writings," will now inform our second case study.

While it is a Poirot mystery, Poirot himself takes something of a back seat to the family drama in *Taken at the Flood*. The protagonist is Lynn Marchmont, returning home after serving in the Women's Royal Naval Service (so, as a

WREN) in the Second World War. She is to marry her old fiancé and first cousin, Rowley Cloade, who has waited for her and, much to her alarm, seems not to have changed at all. His life on the family farm continued largely as usual during the war while hers changed considerably. The family is dealing with a bigger problem, though: a threat to its livelihood. Wealthy patriarch Gordon Cloade—their grandfather—has died in an air raid, one of the few survivors of which was his new much younger wife, Rosaleen. Rosaleen is arriving to meet the family for the first time, with her aggressive Irish brother, David Hunter, who is determined to stop the family getting any of Gordon's money out of her. Three deaths follow: that of a stranger in the village who may have been able to disprove Rosaleen's claim to inherit, that of a retired major who verified some of the stranger's claims, and that of Rosaleen herself. Meanwhile, Lynn is torn between pursuing adventure with the dark and dangerous David and the banal comfort of the familiar with Rowley.

The bulk of the action seems to be set in 1946. A prologue takes place two years earlier, during the war, in a gentlemen's club where the only indication of war is the presence of Major Porter, formerly of the Indian Army. Christie writes that time is standing still here, "and the fact that an Air Raid was in progress made no difference to normal procedure"—that procedure being the major's rambling (Christie 1948: 7). Already, as Mills observes, Christie is interacting directly with the idea of storytelling as escapism during war, and confronting the "escapist and insulating" unreality of her own genre (Mills 2020: 147). The major's story, which falls mostly on deaf ears, is in fact that of the air raid that killed Gordon Cloade, and is how Poirot first hears about the Cloade family. He talks almost entirely about the people involved, but descriptions of the bombing and its aftermath trickle through and emerge later.

The "blast" Porter describes "[b]lew the basement" of Gordon and Rosaleen Cloade's residence "and ripped off the roof" but the "[f]irst floor practically wasn't touched" (Christie 1948: 7). As Mills (2020: 143) points out, this directly mirrors an account in Christie's autobiography of a bomb's impact on her own London property in 1940: "The effect it had on 48 Sheffield Terrace was to blow up the basement [...] and to damage the roof and top floor, leaving the ground and first floors almost unharmed" (Christie 1977: 486). David Hunter, who was in the house when it blew up, survived because he slept, apparently dangerously, on the first floor rather than in the seemingly safe basement—a habit Christie also formed (Mills 2020: 144). This kind of insight is so counter-logical that, in a highly rational detective novel, it can only come from real life. The novel confronts the unreality of escapism in the prologue, then, but also grounds itself in an authentic and realistic, in the truest sense of the word, account of living through war.

Lynn's dilemma is not about bombs but it is about war. Coming home to safe, predictable Rowley, she feels herself inhabiting "[a]n aimless, formless method of living," and has to confront, already, "nostalgia [...] for those war days. Days when duties were clearly defined, when life was planned and orderly—when the weight of individual decisions had been lifted from her" (Christie 1948: 80). It is, ostensibly, having to make the decision to marry or leave Rowley that worries her and makes her miss military service, but it is also something else. Perhaps it is not the sense of purpose or duty, the respectable reasons to miss the war, that fuels Lynn's nostalgia, but excitement and danger. She is confused and frustrated by her growing attraction to David: "Why did this man attract her so?" (85).

David is unpredictably aggressive and highly masculine. "He is the archetype of the dysfunctional veteran," Plain points out, with "a war neurosis that is easily comprehensible to her" (Plain 2020: 188). With his Irish accent and "bronzed," "unhappy and defiant and slightly insolent" face (Christie 1948: 36, 37), he also represents the allure of the vaguely exotic and worldly. In short, David represents the war—not its sense of purpose, but its sense of the unknown. At one point in the narrative, Lynn chooses to run away with David. However, her mind is changed when Poirot reveals that David is a murderer. The allure of danger works better in principle than in practice—although when Lynn does end up with Rowley, as discussed below, she is by no means shirking the unknown.

David commits the third "murder" in the book, which is, according to Poirot, the only real one. The stranger who came to the village is an actor employed by the family to discredit Rosaleen, who is killed accidentally in a fight with Rowley. Major Porter, bribed to corroborate the actor's story, dies by suicide. Rosaleen, however, is murdered by David. She was not really Rosaleen, but a maid in Gordon Cloade's service. After the bomb, David manipulated her, using his charms, into pretending to be the late Rosaleen in order to acquire the money. Afraid she will talk, David kills her. Here, Christie negotiates the realities of war in two ways: as a crime writer planting clues and as a novelist dealing with psychology. Throughout her deception, Rosaleen finds herself unable to give full color to her accounts of life with and marriage to Gordon—because she is not really Rosaleen. She is kept from speaking, understandably given the truth, by David, who explains that she is traumatized by having survived the bombing. That, he tells Lynn, is why Rosaleen seems so afraid of the Cloades and the police: "Fear isn't logical. When you've suffered from the blast—" at which point Lynn apologizes (82).

This device is open to two interpretations as to how authentically the novel engages with war. At this stage in Christie studies, it should come as no surprise that the same passages and themes can be open to multiple readings: that, after all, is part of the recipe for Christie's near-universal appeal and endurance, discussed in the introduction to the present volume. For Plain, the use of blitzes and blackouts as a device to keep Rosaleen from revealing details she cannot know is evidence that "Christie's narrative takes her to the place of wartime trauma, but she will not admit its substance, using it rather as a device enabling conventional plotting" (Plain 2020: 187). However, for Mills, it is evidence of engagement with trauma playing out in the novel. Mills contrasts Rosaleen to Lynn: while the latter is "struggling with peacetime," the former "remains temporally and mentally caught within the epicenter of the horror" (Mills 2020: 146). Her nervousness may have to do with her deception, but they are also to do with the site of that deception, the place where she had lost her identity just two years previously in an air raid. "[T]he bombs were there—the bombs," she remembers in a private conversation with her "brother." "I'll never forget—*never* ... " (Christie 1948: 44, emphasis original).

Despite the gentlemen's club in the prologue seeming to suggest escape and insularity, bombs still rage outside it. The war, though theoretically over, is living out in every character's psyche in *Taken at the Flood*, as some struggle to rebuild themselves, others struggle to remold themselves, and others struggle to put an end to the horrors they still live with. This complicated mess of intentions and outcomes is mirrored in the novel's unique three-pronged solution, where the deaths are explained as accident, suicide, and murder. It is the generically prescribed tidy resolution, but it is not a neat or entirely satisfactory one.

Similar things can be said of the conclusion to Lynn's arc. When she learns that Rowley punched the actor, fatally, because he was acting in bad faith, and sees Rowley try to murder David, who has now been outed as a villain, Lynn falls back in love with him—she is drawn to the danger. It is a problematic conclusion, and generations of critics have chosen to ignore it, quietly, but Plain links it to "Christie's fantasy of postwar construction":

> Postwar society, suggests Christie, has an unhealthy fascination with danger, but rather than suggesting that this can be repressed or forgotten, she concludes that it has to find an outlet somewhere; and so, rather uncomfortably, she brings it into the bedroom.
>
> (Plain 2020: 189)

Plain acknowledges that "Rowley—like many actual veterans guilty of domestic violence in the aftermath of the war—is treated remarkably leniently" and notes that his greater narrative role here is to "re-insert Lynn into normative, domestic femininity: an ideal that is now explicitly underpinned by violence" (189). It is difficult to argue with this conclusion, which understands the novel as foremost a conservative, formulaic detective story. However, it is also one thoroughly and emotionally alive to the enduring destructions wrought by war.

SPIES AND SUPERMEN IN *PASSENGER TO FRANKFURT*

The conversation on war in Christie is far from over. With some exceptions, little work has been done on Christie's engagement with conflicts beyond the two world wars. Most notably, the Cold War (1947–91) is a strong, but underexamined, presence in her later work. Subtitled "An Extravaganza," *Passenger to Frankfurt* was published in 1970, and marketed—disingenuously— as the author's eightieth book for her eightieth birthday. It is less a traditional detective novel than a deeply paranoid spy narrative with mystery elements. Although people around Christie, her publishers, and early critics were "dismayed [and] feared the book would be a disaster" (Morgan [1984] 1997: 364), there is some evidence that it was a story Christie had been wanting for many years to tell.

Christie's notebooks show that she had been planning the details for this story at least as early as 1963 (Curran 2011: 378; Morgan [1984] 1997: 362) and that she returned to the idea again and again throughout the 1960s (378–81). Christie took the unusual step of writing an introduction to this title, explaining that the "Extravaganza" is like all good creative writing grounded in everyday reality: "Real people, real places. A definite place in time and space" (Christie 1950: 13). One of her mission statements, she writes, is to "[h]old up a mirror to 1970 in England" (13), and she describes seeing terrifying things in the newspapers every day, including murder, gangs, unrest, and mobilization, "all growing stronger" (14). "Fear is awakening—fear of what may be," she writes (13). Noting "worship of destruction, pleasure in cruelty," she asks, "What does it all mean?" (14). Defending the novel as something Christie felt it necessary to write, biographer Janet Morgan has pointed out it was "confused but published at a time when everything seemed upside down" ([1984] 1997: 364).

The novel features a diplomat, Sir Stafford Nye, who unwittingly enters a global conspiracy, the figurehead of which is said to be Adolf Hitler's secret son, conceived after the German dictator faked his own death during the Second World War. The conspiracy centers around the resurgence of Nazi ideas, a mind-control drug, and a cult of youth. It has been called "a farrago" (Osborne 2000: 341) and an "incomprehensible muddle" (Barnard 1980: 230), and above I used the term "deeply paranoid." However, what this reflects is a sense of uncertainty and fear that also marked the years leading up to the Second World War. While the novel has been—frequently—cited as an example of the author's failing cognitive abilities, in its Cold War context, it makes a serious effort not only to change with the times but also to illustrate the cyclical nature of conflict and the lessons of history.

These echoes are made explicit early in the text. Sir Stafford has noted "a general kind of discontent" in the world, but his Great Aunt Matilda, who acts as his voice of reason throughout, tells him to take this more seriously: "[p]eople are worried" and "[t]here are things going on" (Christie 1950: 75, 76). At this point, what is happening is unclear, but Matilda notices that whatever movement is going on is centered on youth—or, rather,

> They—whoever *they* are—work through youth. Youth in every country. Youth urged on. Youth chanting slogans, slogans that sound exciting, though they don't always know what they mean. So easy to start a revolution. That's natural to youth. All youth has always rebelled.
>
> (76, emphasis original)

In this way, Matilda—and Christie—position the messages and mechanics of political revolution as less relevant, and certainly less terrifying, than the individuals behind them. Young people, who appear to be threatening the established orders, are conceived here as *part* of the established order, being exploited in order to be overthrown. "What's going to come next?" she asks, rhetorically. "And who [...] is behind them, urging them on? That's what's frightening about it" (76).

While Sir Stafford tries to dismiss Matilda's "extraordinary fancies," she explains that the current moment is nothing new: "They are not only fancies [...] That's what people said about Hitler. Hitler and the Hitler Youth. But it was a lot of careful preparation. It was a war that was worked out in detail" (76–7). She goes on to explain that, while young people in 1970 are protesting for something quite new, they are really being worked to bring about the same thing the Hitler Youth was groomed for: preparing the world for "the supermen" (77). Lost, her great-nephew asks who is grooming people now— "the Chinese or the Russians? What do you mean?" (77). Matilda dismisses both of these very topical perceived threats to Western democracy and says she cannot name the forces behind the movement. However, she is frightened that, despite apparently different ideologies, everything goes back to the same archetypes that structured Nazi thought in the build-up to the Second World War: "The young hero, the golden superman that all must follow," she says, represents "[h]istory repeating itself" (77).

There is much to unpack here. On the one hand, Great Aunt Matilda's observations drive the plot, as discussed below, by introducing to the novel a direct Nazi theme. However, they also reflect some of the ideas in Christie's earlier thrillers, such as *They Came to Baghdad* (1951) and *Destination Unknown* (1954), and even her first such book, *The Secret Adversary* (1922). In those books, individual villains, involved in politics or finance, work behind the scenes to manipulate enthusiastic followers into embracing what they think is a fresh ideology but which actually means power for the mastermind at the expense of whole communities or even countries. That idea is similarly echoed in more conventional detective novels such as *One, Two, Buckle My Shoe*, discussed above, and *Hallowe'en Party* (1969), which is more about religious cultish behavior than about politics or war. In both *Baghdad* and *Destination*, the villain plays multiple political angles, uniting his followers by virtue of their conditioned fanaticism, so communists and fascists walk arm in arm to bring about his unclarified vision. *Passenger to Frankfurt*, then, is in a Christiean tradition of illustrating political and revolutionary movements as mechanisms for individual power plays.

Matilda's remarks also reflect and perhaps allow us to reframe comments Christie made in her autobiography, which was published after her death. Discussing thriller plays, she wrote that they shared similar plots:

> all that alters is the Enemy. There is an international gang *à la* Moriarty— provided first by the Germans, the "Huns" of the first war; then the Communists, who in turn were succeeded by the Fascists. We have the Russians, we have the Chinese, we go back to the international gang again, and the Master Criminal wanting world supremacy is always with us.
>
> (Christie 1977: 434)

That passage was written at some point between 1950 and 1965, and is echoed in Matilda's comments about the generalities and the names, and even the detailed trappings, but not the fundamental specifics of war changing. Matilda even dismisses explicit references to "the Russians" and "the Chinese." She is not a writer discussing the mechanics of plot, of course, and with her dialogue Christie goes beyond the process of writing to ask what is underneath. In the quest for meaning raised in her introduction, she identifies a single force behind all threats to order—the "Master Criminal" who has many faces but "is always with us."

Matilda concludes her remarks with a reference to "the young Siegfried" (77), which prompts Sir Stafford to listen, finally, to her. He has heard this expression before. It was an aria from Wagner's *Siegfried* (originally titled *Der Junge Siegfried*), remarked on by a mysterious woman, that got him into his current amateur investigation of the "general rest." That opera, in which the eponymous hero learns that he was predestined to slay a dragon and various enemies of a suppressed race, famously impacted Adolf Hitler who was declared "a new Siegfried," a Wagnerian hero ready to march Germany to glory (Michaud 2004: 58). It is also being applied to a non-specific figure in some circles of political unrest in *Passenger to Frankfurt*. "The Young Siegfried" is the nearest thing to a name that one agent can put to the threat (64).

Later, it becomes apparent that the Young Siegfried referred to is Franz Joseph, rumored to be the illegitimate son of Adolf Hitler, who has secretly survived the Second World War. He is to lead a fascist revolution and herald the arrival of a third world war and a new world order. It is an outlandish idea but not an unprecedented one, and taps into the popularity of alternate history novels such as Philip K. Dick's *The Man in the High Castle* (1962), which imagines a contemporary world in which the Axis Powers had been victorious against the Allied Powers. It also preempts several later works of fiction in which Hitler's progeny tries to continue his legacy, such as Irving Wallace's *The Seventh Secret* (1986). However, in *Passenger to Frankfurt*, it is highly unlikely that the highly Aryan Franz Joseph is anything but an orphan who has been groomed and conditioned into his current position. As in *Destination Unknown*, where communists and fascists are able to fight together against diametrically embodied enemies because the real enemy is the world at peace, Christie shows a figurehead without substance or knowledge that or why he is being used.

As mentioned, the context for *Passenger to Frankfurt* is the Cold War, as well as the many social and sexual revolutions of the 1960s that saw young people becoming, apparently, more openly hedonistic and aggressive. In the years after the Second World War as Britain's hold on its empire weakened and fell, and Russia gained power with the ever-looming and ever-increasing threat of nuclear war between it and the United States, several forms of fiction began to reflect the contingent anxieties and uncertainties. The spy novel in particular gained traction, as secrets and unclear, even existential, threats bred confusion: a spy can be an embodiment of secret intelligence and as a fictionalized hero, antihero, or villain is necessarily to some extent a comforting presence in an unknowable world. Ian Fleming's James Bond (first novel appearance in 1953, first serious film appearance in 1962) and John le Carré's George Smiley (first appearing in 1961) were British literary products of the Cold War, "figure[s] designed to resist the threat to empire" (Black [2000] 2005: 4). However, in her Cold War books where the enemy changes from fascist to communist to non-specific, Christie indicates that the threat is not *to* forces currently in place, but *from* them.

A villain in *Passenger to Frankfurt*, who is also a tool of the greater powers in charge, is the fantastically wealthy Gräfin Charlotte von Waldsausen, whose family name is Krapp (a "scathing pun" on Krupp, the family that manufactured weapons for Germany in both world wars; Lassner 2017: 237). The Gräfin is decidedly a fascist who longs for more holocausts, and she is a gargantuan, sedentary figure who exerts global influence by virtue of her wealth. She is obsessed with youth and beauty and plans to rule the world, flanked by young Adonises. An embodiment of excess and hypocrisy—deriving power from the beauty, action, and destruction of others while doing nothing, which is made possible because of money she has gained unethically—mirrors the paranoia about new excesses in young drug-taking, partying socialists and rebels. However, her excesses, enabled and reinforced by her wealth, are more enduring than any character or conflict in the novel. It is greed, not individual people or wars, that endures without end.

In a welcome re-evaluation of *Passenger to Frankfurt*, Phyllis Lassner has argued that Christie was part of a mid-twentieth-century move from women writers to "revise [...] the conventions of crime and detective fiction to construct a hybrid, fluid, intermodern fiction," and that this book should be considered in the context of "John le Carré's Cold War novels" (Lassner 2017: 228). According to Lassner, the novel "dramatise[s] how Cold War tensions, the Vietnam War, and prevailing fears of the resurgence of Nazi power conjoin to inspire revisionary spy fictions" (228), and suggests that one of the reasons Christie's—and other women's—spy fiction has been critically neglected is because "they question the genre's constructions of gender," translating as they do "the genre's conventional dismissal of women's domestic disappointments into political analysis and activism" (228).

To expand on this point, Lassner considers three women on whom much of the narrative centers and notes that, while the chief villain, the chief investigator, and the scientist who saves the world are all men, it is women who spur all of these to action and actively translate their ideas or ideals into realization (234). Indeed, Agent Mary Anne, who is also known as Daphne Theodofanous, performs a great deal of the action in the novel undercover, sometimes in disguise as Sir Stafford Nye himself—this is, certainly, a direct inversion of older war narratives and then-contemporary spy stories in which the male hero would be the one to infiltrate and deceive, very occasionally having to cross-dress. In this way, for Lassner, the novel makes a contribution to the fiction of war and espionage while presenting space for women to "embody and activate [the traditionally masculine] mythic archetypes of wisdom, villainy, and heroism" (234).

However, *Passenger to Frankfurt* does still fit conventions of Cold War British spy narratives. The protagonist is very much a middle-aged man, who informs the much younger Mary Anne that he will marry her at the end, without giving her so much as a chance to flirt: her intelligence and activity avoiding a global disaster constituted her flirting. It is undeniably a conservative, regressive conclusion to an ambitious narrative. An epilogue informs readers that, having halted the global conspiracy, Sir Stafford is preparing for his marriage to Mary Anne. The apparent son of Hitler has been reformed and is now an organist at his wedding. An even more unsettling part of this apparently happy ending concerns a secret mind-control drug, "Project B," which has floated in the background as a source of suspense and uncertainty. The scientist who invented it previously destroyed it to stop it falling into the wrong hands, and then suffered a paralyzing stroke. "B" stands for "Benvo" or "Benevolence"; it forces those who take it into altruistic compliance, with serious risks of brain damage. The happy conclusion to that strand of the story is that, following a miraculous recovery, the scientist resolves to finish work on it, so that it can be used to tame all the young revolutionaries. In all, this ending is a cruel fantasy of easy answers in the face of convoluted issues and wide-reaching misdirection, and perhaps it should be read as such.

DIRECTIONS FOR FUTURE RESEARCH

Reading *Passenger to Frankfurt* as a war novel means grappling with uncomfortable conclusions and contradictions. The novel's ending seems to contravene much of its messaging, not least the idea that, while political movements come and go, the people who exploit them, their pawns, and their victims do not change. That is a strong and consistent theme across Christie's later works, and, as discussed, can be traced as far back as her second novel. Moreover, as the research of Gill, Plain, and Lassner demonstrates, war affords an opportunity to popular writers to re-examine and renegotiate gendered roles and expectations in a society under threat. However, to understand the full nuances of Christie as a war writer, it is essential to examine her own prejudices.

Christie has, for example, a complicated relationship with anti-Semitism, which was documented as early as 1987 by Jane Arnold, who concluded that it was a dangerous part of her use of stereotypes (280). However, while more recent analyses of Christie's work have uncovered a strategic and significant deployment of stereotypes, the tendency has been to sidestep the uncomfortable issue of anti-Semitic stereotyping or to qualify it as a product of its time. There is a myth here that, after the Second World War, Christie suddenly woke up to the dangerous ideas she was perpetuating, and stopped writing negatively about Jewish characters altogether. However, a Holocaust survivor is presented as a figure of fun in *A Murder Is Announced* (1950). As Shane Brown has noted, "sensitivities regarding these issues were not what they are today, but how can one excuse the ridicule of a refugee character who has witnessed Nazi atrocities in a book written just a few years after the end of the war?" (Brown 2020: 78). It is an uncomfortable area but one that needs to be explored and historicized, in the context of social and political change and in the context of Christie's writing career.

Another area that would warrant further exploration in terms of Christie and war is the role of adaptations in how these books are consumed, understood, and even analyzed. As discussed above, screen adaptations have been enormously influential in our understanding of Christie as a nostalgic novelist, then as a psychological novelist, and their presentation of Britain at war has varied too. This relationship is one that could reward thorough scrutiny.

Christie was a complex writer, and her legacy is far from unilateral. War was something of a structuring principle in her life and career, and her prominence as a voice in the literature of war is finally being recognized. It is imperative that future scholarship continues to challenge easy answers and thoroughly interrogate the many factors in play with Christie's presentation of nostalgia, war, and identities—individual, national, and international.

REFERENCES

Aldridge, M. (2020), *Agatha Christie's Poirot: The Greatest Detective in the World*, London: HarperCollins.

Barnard, R. (1980), *Agatha Christie: An Appreciation*, London: Collins.

Bernthal, J. C. (2016), *Queering Agatha Christie: Revisiting the Golden Age of Detective Fiction*, London: Palgrave.

Black, J. ([2000] 2005), *The Politics of James Bond: From Fleming's Novels to the Big Screen*, Lincoln: University of Nebraska Press.

"Books and the Public: A Report for the National Book Council" (1944), Mass Observation, February.

Bright, B. (2020), "Writing through War: Narrative Structure and Authority in Christie's Second World War Novels," in R. Mills and J. C. Bernthal (eds), *Agatha Christie Goes to War*, 46–62, London and New York: Routledge.

Brown, S. (2020), "'Scoring Off a Foreigner?' Xenophobia, Antisemitism, and Racism in the Works of Agatha Christie," *Clues: A Journal of Detection*, 38 (1): 70–80.

Christie, A. (1921), *The Mysterious Affair at Styles*, London: The Bodley Head.

Christie, A. (1948), *Taken at the Flood*, London: Collins.

Christie, A. (1950), *Passenger to Frankfurt*, London: Collins.

Christie, A. (1975), *Curtain: Poirot's Last Case*, London: Collins.

Christie, A. (1977), *An Autobiography*, London: Collins.

Crescentini, F. (2020), "'There are Things One Doesn't Forget': The Second World War in 'Three Blind Mice' and *The Mousetrap*," in R. Mills and J. C. Bernthal (eds), *Agatha Christie Goes to War*, 109–24, London and New York: Routledge.

Curran, J. (2011), *Agatha Christie's Murder in the Making: Stories and Secrets from Her Archive*, London: HarperCollins.

Dalrymple, R. (2020), "'The Thrill When It Suddenly Went Pitch Black!': Blackout Cultures in *A Murder Is Announced* and *The Mousetrap*," in R. Mills and J. C. Bernthal (eds), *Agatha Christie Goes to War*, 155–67, London and New York: Routledge.

Daniels, A. (2020), "Killing Time with Agatha Christie," *The New Criterion*, November. Available online: https://newcriterion.com/issues/2020/11/killing-time-with-agatha-christie (accessed October 31, 2021).

Fisher, J. (2021), "The Mystery of My Obsession with Agatha Christie," *The New York Times Magazine*, July 27. Available online: https://www.nytimes.com/2021/07/27/magazine/agatha-christie-books-death.html (accessed October 31, 2021).

Flood, A. (2021), "Book Sales Defy Pandemic to Hit 8-Year High," *The Guardian*, January 25. Available online: https://www.theguardian.com/books/2021/jan/25/bookshops-defy-pandemic-to-record-highest-sales-for-eight-years (accessed October 31, 2021).

Gildersleeve, J. (2014), "'We're All Strangers': Postwar Anxiety in Agatha Christie's *The Mousetrap*," *Clues: A Journal of Detection*, 32 (2): 145–23.

Green, J. (2020), "'A Worrying, Nerve-Wracked World': Agatha Christie's Emergence as a Playwright during and after the Second World War," in R. Mills and J. C. Bernthal (eds), *Agatha Christie Goes to War*, 95–108, London and New York: Routledge.

Hart, A. (1990), *The Life and Times of Hercule Poirot*, London: Sphere.

Haycraft, H. ([1941] 1974), *Murder for Pleasure: The Life and Times of the Detective Story*, New York: Biblo and Tannen.

James, P. D. (2009), *Talking about Detective Fiction*, Oxford: Bodleian Library.

Knight, S. (1995), "Murder in Wartime," in P. Kirkham and D. Thoms (eds), *War Culture: Social Change and Changing Experience in World War Two*, 161–72, London: Lawrence & Wishart Ltd.

Lassner, P. (2017), "Double Trouble: Helen MacInnes's and Agatha Christie's Speculative Spy Thrillers," in C. Hanson and S. Watkins (eds), *The History of British Women's Writing, 1945–1979*, 227–40, London: Palgrave Macmillan.

Makinen, M. (2016), *Agatha Christie: Investigating Femininity*, Basingstoke: Palgrave Macmillan.

Makinen, M. (2020), "Taking on Hitler: Agatha Christie's Wartime Thrillers," in R. Mills and J. C. Bernthal (eds), *Agatha Christie Goes to War*, 63–80, London and New York: Routledge.

Michaud, E. (2004), *The Cult of Art in Nazi Germany*, trans. J. Lloyd, Oxford: Oxford University Press.

Miller, K. A. (2008), *British Literature of the Blitz: Fighting the People's War*, Basingstoke: Palgrave.

Mills, R. (2020), "Detecting the Blitz: Memory and Trauma in Christie's Postwar Writings," in R. Mills and J. C. Bernthal (eds), *Agatha Christie Goes to War*, 137–54, London and New York: Routledge.

Morgan, J. ([1984] 1997), *Agatha Christie: A Biography*, London: HarperCollins.

Osborne, C. (2000), *The Life and Crimes of Agatha Christie*, revised edn, London: HarperCollins.

Peacock, J. (2020), "Five Detective Novels You Can Read to Beat the Boredom during the Covid-19 Lockdown," *Scroll.in*, April 7. Available online: https://scroll.in/article/958285/five-detective-novels-you-can-read-to-beat-the-boredom-during-the-covid-19-lockdown (accessed October 30, 2021).

Plain, G. (2010), "'A Stiff is Still a Stiff in this Country': The Problem of Murder in Wartime," in P. Rau (ed), *Conflict, Nationhood and Corporeality in Modern Literature: Bodies-at-War*, 104–23, London: Palgrave Macmillan.

Plain, G. (2013), *Literature of the 1940s: War, Postwar and "Peace,"* Edinburgh: Edinburgh University Press.

Plain, G. (2020), "'Tale Engineering': Agatha Christie and the Aftermath of the Second World War," *Literature & History*, 29 (2): 179–99.

Rowland, S. (2001), *From Agatha Christie to Ruth Rendell: British Women Writers in Detective and Crime Fiction*, Basingstoke: Palgrave Macmillan.

Scaggs, J. (2005), *Crime Fiction*, London and New York: Routledge.

Smith, M. (2013), *Bletchley Park: The Code-Breakers of Station X*, London: Shire.

Watson, C. ([1971] 1987), *Snobbery with Violence: English Crime Stories and Their Audience*, London: Methuen.

Worthington, H. (2011), *Key Concepts in Crime Fiction*, London and New York: Routledge.

CHAPTER TEN

Of Race, Law, and Order: Colonial Ghosts

META G. CARSTARPHEN

Her voice rings with familiarity for any fan who has heard recordings of the acclaimed author Agatha Christie speaking. In this instance, she narrates her remembrances in an audio version of her autobiography, mixing bits of her lived experience with insights about the craft behind her beloved works. And in Chapter 7, with the ease and analytical tones of a supremely skilled and confident artisan, she opens: "I wrote the book, *Ten Little N*****s*,[1] because it was so enormously difficult to do. The idea was fascinating [...] and I was pleased with what I was able to do" (Christie [1977] 2011: 471). It is one of the most celebrated mystery stories written by one of the most renowned mystery writers in the world. Published in 1939 in the UK under its original, racially offensive title, that title was modified that same year for US readers.

In 1944, *And Then There Were None* debuted as a play based upon the novel.[2] This title has remained since, extending to plays and movie versions of the story, as well as to reprints of the original novel.[3] The haunting narrative

---

[1]The novel, *And Then There Were None*, was originally published with a title using a racial epithet, which is the focus of this chapter. I choose not to elevate this racially offensive term by repeating it, so I use it sparingly, and only as a matter of historical accuracy. Hereafter, I will refer to this work directly by its current name.

[2]See Craig A. Warren's "Gender and Moral Immaturity in Agatha Christie's *And Then There Were None*," where the decision to substitute "Indians" for the original racial slur generated new criticisms. By 2004, Warren notes, Christie's estate changed the Island's name from "Indian Island" to "Soldier Island" (52).

[3]An exception was in the UK, where print editions with the original title continued to be published until 1985. See Blake Allmendinger (2018: 60).

sketches out a truly horrific scenario. Ten strangers watch as each slowly dies in horrible ways. All of the deaths eerily match a childhood nursery rhyme and the deaths match the details and spirit included in the verses. Tracing the contexts of this story's original title, and subsequent revisions, reveals a complicated history of literature, performance, and social stratification.

COUNTING RHYMES AND MINSTRELSY

A central conceit of *And Then There Were None* is the sinister countdown to the deaths of each of its ten characters. And for every adult reader, the overarching structure may resonate with familiar childhood rhythms of early literacy rituals, including learning our numbers and learning how to count. Well before Christie wrote her novel and named it, generations of children's rhymes and a century of an Americanized version of folk songs imbued a familiar song with racial and social resonances.

Nursery rhymes represent a familiar, even sentimental, part of our shared literary canon. Global examples with long histories include Japanese lullabies, Bengali rhymes, Romanian folktales, and English songs and poems. Their survival over centuries owes much to vibrant oral traditions with the earliest evidence recording such tales in the sixteenth century and their subsequent publication in the eighteenth century (Maiti and Naskar 2017). Using simple imagery, repetitive words, and rhyming sounds, these children's tales were designed to serve dual purposes, as historians and literary scholars have uncovered. One purpose was entertainment, in the sense that children's rhymes persisted throughout countless generations as poems and songs before being recorded in print. Another was indoctrination, with the nursery rhymes often hiding messages bearing "the toxic scars of history" (28). For example, the English rhymes about "Three Blind Mice" refer to the persecution of Protestant priests under the brief rule of the Catholic Queen Mary I (28), while "The Old Woman Who Lives in a Shoe" reflects the grim realities of poor women and prostitution (29).

Christie's reputation as an internationally lauded author grew, in part, due to the enormous popularity of this book. From its initial publication, through to its current iteration, the novel's suspenseful tension hinges upon the unfolding drama of a children's nursery rhyme. The numeral 10, central to all versions, begins a slow countdown to the inevitable "none" represented in the current title. But the activity of counting backward, with its attention to rhythm, rhyme, and narrative, serves a utilitarian purpose—teaching a numerical literacy. Learning numbers backward requires a mental agility that, captured in a rhyme, can captivate the youngest of listeners. This childhood association—numerical literacy with a game wrapped in song—has complicated adult listeners' relationship to the text, particularly those who learned racially offensive versions of these rhymes as children without the cultural context to understand their meaning.

Kristin Loftsdóttir examines this duality more explicitly when noting the popularity of this Christie novel in Iceland, citing adult readers who saw the book as "having nothing to do with racism" (306) or their own current racial attitudes. The poem at the center of Christie's novel was published in 1922 in Iceland as *The Negro-Boys* (301). A version of this poem resurfaced in Iceland in a 2007 republication of this book, featuring a familiar rhyme:

> *Ten little Negros went out to dine;*
> *One chocked his little self and then there were nine.* (295)

Sparked by the republication, an Icelandic newspaper published an article featuring interviews with moms who feared that their children with mixed ethnicities would face heightened harassment in schools (296). Loftsdóttir noted that this, in turn, generated days of media attention and public debates about censorship, Icelandic identity, and racism, including the social significance of these rhymes attributing their origin to an "American Frank J. Green in 1864" (296). In fact, according to another source, Septimus Winner wrote an adapted version of the counting song called "Ten Little Indians" in 1868, which Green adapted in 1869 (Allmendinger 40). Still, like many contemporary readers, much of the Icelandic public sentiment expressed by the media attributed racist consciousness to an individual choice, ignoring a connection to what Loffsdóttir describes as a shared "racist imaginary" (303). And the construction of a racial hierarchy really becomes spotlighted in the origins of the childish rhyme that animates this story.

Pinning down an exact date for the origin of counting rhymes like this migrates through the history of centuries-old counting games, and the distortion of African American culture through song, dance, and comic performances known as minstrelsy. Acted out by White performers, this version of entertainment spread rapidly starting in the 1820s and hinged upon deliberate misrepresentations of "Black culture ... almost entirely grounded in racist stereotypes" (Bloomquist 411). Concurrently, the historical, global tides of colonialism, wars with Indigenous peoples in the Americas, and the growing African slave trade converged in the British colonies.

The American minstrel tradition, when located within US-based theatrical history, emerged in the late 1820s, combining blackface with musical farce (Jones 26). One of the early boosters of southern-style minstrels was Daniel Decatur Emmitt, recognized as one of three white musicians who founded the "Virginia Minstrels" ("Daniel Decatur Emmitt" 2013). Originally popularized on the stage, blackface featured White actors who darkened their faces and hands with makeup and performed stereotypes of African Americans featuring outrageous gestures and exaggerated movements. All of these broad, ridiculous movements and dialects were part of the unique theatrical style of minstrelsy, underscored by nonsensical songs (Jones Jr. 33). Coinciding with the rise of minstrelsy were robust waves of Irish immigrants to the United States. Among them were performers, such as Thomas Dartmouth Rice and George Washington Dixon, who popularized minstrel performances throughout the southern states and abroad (Nowatzki 162). Also, English theater had its own variations of blackface in theater, with performances in such dramas as the 1605 Ben Jonson's *Masque of Blacknesse*, and the 1688 novel Aphra Behn's *Oroonoko* (165). However, the key elements of the US version of minstrelsy—white performers in blackface, musical melodies, and memorable, if nonsensical, lyrics—helped ensure that this contrived view of Black culture would be consumed devoid of serious political or social contexts (Jones Jr. 2013: 35).

Still, the 1836–7 expansive tour by White minstrel performer Thomas Rice in English and European assembly halls led to an explosive popularity for this type of blackface theater (Nowatzki 165). An example of the popularity—and profitability—of the traveling minstrel show was revealed in the documented earnings of one of the most prominent troupes. With admission prices of only twenty-five cents, The Christy Minstrels earned nearly $318 million after 2,792 performances in the late nineteenth century (Moody 326). As a benchmark comparison, based upon data from the US Bureau of Labor Statistics' Consumer Price Index (CPI), 1 million dollars in 1890 would be worth about $30,144,000 in 2021 currency (Webster 2021).

Even as the stage minstrel era faded in the early twentieth century, supplanted by the growing popularity of film, the rhyme persisted. So-called trench newspapers, written by active-duty servicemen and specifically with soldiers in mind, circulated a rhyme called "Ten Little Soldier Boys":

Ten little soldier-boys tried to form a line,
One formed aéchelon, and then there were nine,
Eight little soldier-boys thought it wasn't heaven,
One told the sergeant so, and then there were seven. (Anderson 2018: 136)[4]

These rhymes proliferated during the First World War and became known for their apparent nonsensical verses and comic sensibilities, even when cloaked in violent depictions. Such verses could also be seen as ironic representations of the violent horrors these soldiers witnessed and experienced with regularity. Andersen's interpretation of these poems reveals a "dissident quality" in the humor, suggesting narratives that contrasted sharply with the more somber,

[4]See Emily Andersen's " 'There was a young girl of the Somme,/Who sat on a number five bomb': The Representation of Violence in First World War Trench Newspaper Nonsense Rhymes" (2018). This excerpt shows how soldiers adapted existing traditions of nursery rhymes and nonsensical verses to the real-life horrors they faced on the battlefields.

heroic literature of the time (142). In other words, trench newspaper rhymes mocked the very ideology of the First World War as the emblem of a great military effort being fought by intrepid heroes, suggesting just the opposite. The unpredictable ways in which soldiers faced death and injury could have heightened their sense of objectification. Situated within the craft of this story, a soldier could easily stand in for a racialized other.

AGATHA CHRISTIE AND IMPERIAL CONTEXTS

In her original version, ten strangers—all White—meet on an isolated island also named with the same epithet as in the original title. In later versions, their address becomes "Soldier Island." Even as they represent a mix of social classes, these individuals reflect jobs that are as seemingly nondescript as their lives:

- Vera Claythorne, an ex-governess
- Philip Lombard, described as an ex-soldier-of-fortune
- Lawrence Wargrave, a retired judge
- John Gordon MacArthur, a retired First World War general and well-regarded hero
- Ethel Rogers, a timid cook
- Thomas Rogers, her domineering husband and a butler
- Emily Brent, a single, never-married woman of a certain age and rigid moral beliefs
- Anthony Marsden, a youthful, but irresponsible, heir to his family's wealth
- Edward Armstrong, a surgeon with an alcoholic past
- William Blore, a retired police inspector and private detective

They are all guests of a mysterious host, "U.N. Owen," who remains as "unknown" as his cryptic pseudonym. Although they are guests at a stately and aristocratic mansion, the island itself boasts of nothing more than an isolated location, rocky cliffs, a lonely beach, and watery horizons. As Alison Light observes, the location and original name of this island speak to the "otherness" of both the characters and their social status. Their physical isolation displays the insularity and uncertainty of an emerging social class attempting to find its place in an otherwise clearly stratified British society. Such a juxtaposition of physical isolation yet connection with England "could have evoked so many of the shared anxieties which the differently respectable could feel about social belonging" (1991: 99). Thus, although these murders take place on a fictitious island, the symbolic location could also represent the social and emotional isolation of modern society.

If this is so, none of this estrangement can be understood without recognizing the inherent stratification British colonialism imposed on its colonies. In this view, Christie's work is explicitly racist. But after two world wars, former British colonies, such as countries on the continent of Africa and the country of India, for instance, marked their new status with orchestrated separation ceremonies from the British government and monarchy, beginning the process of cracking open this imposed stratification. For those who shared Christie's high regard for an earlier generation of imperial servants, her low regard for Indigenous peoples, and her displeasure at a younger generation of men supposedly emasculated by a welfare state, making the connection between morality and the decline of the empire required "no great leap of imagination" (Prior 2018: 208). He continues in this analysis of the "Golden Age" of crime fiction in British literature, led by Christie's work, that finds parallels between the rhetorical and narrative arc of her crime fiction and the dismantling of the British Empire after the Second World War. As the size of empire measurably declined, Christie's finely crafted mysteries assured all that, despite chaos, reassuring order would return in triumph. Considered to be apolitical in her art, Christie allowed politics to intrude subtlety in her works, according to one critic who felt that her "thrillers attempted to exploit the fears and concerns most pronounced in her most conservative readers" (Prior 199). *And Then There Were None* navigates through the fears of losing control and power, which were especially pronounced among her more conservative readers, for potent effects.

All of the murders in *And Then There Were None* are driven by a peculiar morality as uneven as the victims' offenses. The crime of only one character, Philip Lombard, overtly invokes a racial bias, as he admits to leaving twenty indigenous Africans to starve in exchange for his own life. None of the other nine, however, stands accused of mass murder. By making Lombard's willful murders the equivalent of everyone else's single act, this detail actually diminishes, not accentuates, the horror of Lombard's remorseless act. Consistent with colonial-driven views about whose lives matter, Lombard makes an easy equivalency that would have seemed logical to many readers as long as it was unknown. In this telling, Lombard's murders, long hidden, become criminally tinged once his actions become known and publicly shared among his contemporaries.

At the same time, the murderer makes a telling comment in a final note of confession discovered after all are dead:

> The order of death upon the island had been subjected by me to special thought and care. There were, I considered, amongst my guests, varying degrees of guilt. Those whose guilt was the lightest should, I decided, pass out first, and not suffer the prolonged mental strain and fear that the more cold-blooded offenders were to suffer.
>
> (Christie [1939] 1967: 199)

Indeed, the reference to being cold-blooded closely reflects the manner in which Lombard relates his decision to abandon Africans to save his own life. He never reflects emotional distress about his choice, and the lack of remorse seemed to have accounted for his extended punishment on the island as one of the last two surviving victims. And yet, as one of the last two surviving characters, Lombard becomes, over the course of the narrative, heroic in the readers' eye—handsome, courageous, and intelligent. As readers, are we being conditioned to regard his crime as one youthful deviation from an otherwise worthy character? If Christie allows us to entertain this view, our perspective must change by the story's end, when Lombard dies and the murderer reiterates the crime for which he is condemned. It is a delicious complexity, one of many, that compels readers to return to this story again and again.

Still, the casual, matter-of-fact manner in which Christie takes Lombard's crime and equates it to those of his ill-fated companions may reflect what Carolyn Betensky describes as a "casual racism" that looms frequently in Victorian-era literature (2019: 743). Evidence of these racially tinged perspectives surfaces in pejorative language, identity slurs, and negative comments about the character traits of those "Others." Betensky's argument is that such instances have meaning even when they are clearly not the dominant concern of the texts in which they appear. Or, in other words, she asks how should we, as readers and critics, "remark the unremarkable?" (725). Her commentary and analysis argue strongly that every instance of expressed racism has meaning, not only within its original text, but increasingly so for the contemporaneous readers of these words. And as those meanings shift, those of us who teach should be prepared for new discussions about familiar themes.

Such is the case for *And Then There Were None*. The novel, in its original presentation, so off-handedly uses a racial slur for its title and as the name of its island-prison. Subsequent versions retitled it as "Soldier Island," adding more complexity, perhaps, about her authorial intentions. I believe one commonality throughout every iteration is the recurring theme of isolation coupled with a calculated disregard for human life. Whether the subjects of the pivotal nursery rhymes are nameless Africans, Indians, or infantrymen, Christie's essential narrative framework never wavers. Metaphorically speaking, even when the organizing rhymes evoke uncelebrated racialized others or obscure soldiers, the sequential construct of *And Then There Were None* holds us captive as if we ourselves were ensnared on an inescapable island. And, while this Christie novel situates itself in the relative modernity of the interwar era of the twentieth century, it simultaneously offers contexts that reflect Victorian-bound notions of order, morality, and privilege. All of these tensions combined—a shift to modernity, a questioning of hierarchies, and the untidiness of warfare—provided a perfect mix in which social class and race could reverberate throughout the story without overtly centering them.

In her autobiography, Christie shares how she felt unnerved when she discovered in 1932 that a married couple—friends of hers and her husband—were fiercely loyal Nazis. Describing a scene where the well-regarded German physician and husband was playing classical music for his guests, she quotes his assertion that their Jews "should be exterminated" because they pose "a danger" (Christie [1977] 2011: 465). And even as she defines that moment, in hindsight, as a harbinger of horrors to come, Christie asserts that the German resolve to murder Jews represented "for ordinary people ... a complete lack of fore-knowledge" (466). One could read this as her confession of true unawareness of the deadly Nazi agenda.

Another view could be that this masterful storyteller was controlling the narrative of her own life as carefully as she plotted her fictional works. Despite this protestation—or because of it—Christie's failure to disavow evil when she saw it (or heard it) asks us to ignore it too. Then, we too can glide over the material fact that someone with elite status asserted that the marginalized "other" must die, becoming complicit intellectually, if not emotionally. We all know the ambiguity of knowing what is right and doing what may be wrong. At its heart, *And Then There Were None* captures perfectly the spirit of this conundrum. People can be disposable when needed to uphold the larger order of things—African Americans, Indigenous people, and even infantry soldiers.

RHETORICAL RACISM: SYMBOLIC SUBSTANCES

Widely read and broadly translated, the contentious original title has also undergone revisions in other languages. For instance, one scholar notes four Italian renditions that include (in translation) "And Then There Was No One Left," "Ten Little Black Boys," and "Ten Little Indians" (Percec and Punga, 246). In tracing these changes through the UK variations, Christie's twenty-sixth novel changed names to "avoid a title that might be regarded as racially offensive" (248). Finally, in comparing this change to decisions made by US-based publishers, Percec and Punga attribute the choice to "political correctness" (248).

By the end of *And Then There Were None*, we learn that the murderer is a self-confessed sadist and a deluded moralist. There is a delicious double irony in this characterization, as readers are forced to confront what it means to think of oneself as morally righteous, yet capable of committing cruel acts without so much as a trace of remorse. Once again, this ending captures the recorded histories of imperial conquest across the globe. The victorious nation-state characterizes its quest as a righteous one, even at the deadly expense of the "Other."

CONCLUSION

As the famed author reminisced about her career, she was clearly proud of the story she crafted now known as *And Then There Were None*, writing that it "set me on the path of being a playwright, as well as a writer of books" ([1977] 2011: 472). But in the early years, she recognized this taut mystery for its enormous impact upon her work in fiction and in drama. She helped to translate her novel to the stage, preparing it for the television and film adaptations to come later. The simple counting song from which the novel derived its inspiration took on social significance as it was revised through the lenses of slavery and socially constructed hierarchies. Minstrelsy then exported this song and its variants to stages throughout Great Britain and Europe in the nineteenth and early twentieth centuries. The song was famous. Christie's novel, with such a deliberately chosen title, followed the trail of its popularity. Only imagine the incongruity when readers discovered that all of the characters were White.

Was Agatha Christie a racist? Certainly, she was a woman of her time and station. Her parentage combined the mixed legacies of the British colonial experiences and the colonial expansion of the United States of America. She lived her life in comfort, and her success as a writer catapulted her to superstar status and financial riches. Today, *And Then There Were None* remains as a compelling, chilling narrative. Its many iterations—as a novel, play, game, and movie—show that its central premise still has the power to fascinate and frighten us. *What if a group of us was being murdered, without any apparent reason?* And what if there appeared to be little that any one member of the group could do to fight against random annihilation?

Apart from Christie's motivation for conceiving such a horror, today's readers can marvel at the resonance of this storytelling in contemporary times. *Amaud Aubery. George Floyd. BreAnna Taylor. Botham Jean. Trayvon Martin. Luis Rodriguez.*[5] Add the seemingly daily acts of genocide against powerless, socially marginalized peoples in countries throughout the world. *What if a group of us was being murdered, without any apparent reason?*

The real horror of Agatha Christie's masterpiece is not that this work published in 1939 survived and thrived under clearly racially belittling names. The real horror is that, with only the slightest meditation upon repeated, contemporary, and violence-charged racial incidents, we can see uncomfortable parallels between imagined dread and real, lived terror.

---

[5]These names represent a small sample of unarmed people of color, as covered by various US media reports, who were killed by law enforcement. Numbers of police killings in countries like Germany, the United Kingdom, and Japan are low compared to police officers in the United States, who shoot and kill hundreds of people every year.

REFERENCES

"And Then There Was None," *Agatha Christie Wiki*, Fandom Books Community. Available online: https://agathachristie.fandom.com/wiki/And_Then_There_Were_None (accessed December 1, 2021).

Allmendinger, B. (2018), "The Erasure of Race in Agatha Christie's *And Then There Were None*," *ANQ: A Quarterly Journal of Short Articles, Notes, and Reviews*, 32 (1): 60–4.

Anderson, E. (2018), "'Who Sat on a Number Five Bomb': The Representation of Violence in First World War Trench Newspaper Nonsense Rhymes," *Literature & History*, 27 (8): 8.

Anderson, Tiffany M. B. (2019), "'Ten Little N*****s': The Making of a Black Man's Consciousness," *Folklore Forum: The Open-Access Journal of Trickster Press*, May 1. Available online: https://folkloreforum.net/2009/05/01/%E2%80%9Cten-little-niggers%E2%80%9D-the-making-of-a-black-man%E2%80%99s-consciousness/ (accessed April 4, 2022).

Ardolino, F. (2001), "Deceptive and Deadly Numbers and Letters in Christie's Double Versions of *Ten Little Indians* and *Witness for the Prosecution*," *Journal of Evolutionary Psychology*, August. 98. Available online: https://link.gale.com/apps/doc/A83038232/LitRC?u=anon~f748aa8e&sid=googleScholar&xid=916eb68a (accessed December 1, 2021).

Betensky, C. (2019), "Casual Racism in Victorian Literature," *Victorian Literature and Culture*, 47 (4): 28.

Bloomquist, J. (2015), "The Minstrel Legacy: African American English and the Historical Construction of 'Black' Identities in Entertainment," *Journal of African American Studies*, 19 (4): 410–25.

Borroff, E. (1984), "Origin of Species: Conflicting Views of American Musical Theater History," *American Music*, 2 (4): 101–12.

Britannica, T. Editors of Encyclopaedia. (2021), "Daniel Decatur Emmett." *Encyclopedia Britannica*, October 25. Available online: https://www.britannica.com/biography/Daniel-Decatur-Emmett (accessed December 1, 2021).

Byrd, J. (2009), "Whitewashing Blackface Minstrelsy in American College Textbooks," *Popular Music and Society*, 32 (1): 9.

Christie, A. ([1939] 1967), *And Then There Were None*, New York: Berkley Books.

Christie, A. ([1977] 2011), *An Autobiography*, London: Harper.

Cockrell, D. (1999), "Christy, George N. Harrington (1827–1868)," in *American National Biography*, Oxford and New York: Oxford University Press.

Hanes, V. L. L. (2018), "The Retitling of Agatha Christie's *Ten Little N*****s* in Anglophone and Lusophone Markets," *Translation and Literature*, 27 (2): 10.

Jones, D. A. (2013), "Black Politics but Not Black People: Rethinking the Social and 'Racial' History of Early Minstrelsy," *TDR (1988-)*, 57 (2): 21–37.

Lakoff, R. T. (2000), *The Language War*, Berkeley: University of California Press.

Lassner, P. (2009), "The Mysterious New Empire: Agatha Christie's Colonial Murders" in H. Robin, F. Hauser, and G. Wachman (eds), *At Home and Abroad in the Empire: British Women Write the 1930s*, 31–50, Newark: University of Delaware Press.

Light, A. (1991), *Forever England: Femininity, Literature and Conservatism between the Wars*, New York: Routledge.

Loftsdóttir, K. (2013), "Republishing 'The Ten Little Negros': Exploring Nationalism and 'Whiteness' in Iceland," *Ethnicities*, 13 (3): 19.

Lynn, J. L. (1985), "Runes to Ward Off Sorrow: Rhetoric of the English Nursery Rhyme," *Children's Literature in Education*, 16 (1): 3–14.

Maiti, A. and D. Naskar (2017), "Of Deception and Dogma: The Delusive History Behind Nursery Rhymes," *European Journal of English Language and Literature*, 5 (4): 27–52.

Moody, R. (1944), "Negro Minstrelsy," *Quarterly Journal of Speech*, 30 (3): 321–8.

Moore, J. R. (1999), "Christy, Edwin Pearce," in *American National Biography*, Oxford and New York: Oxford University Press.

Nowatzki, R. (2006), "Paddy Jumps Jim Crow: Irish American and Blackface Minstrelsy," *Eire-Ireland*, 41 (3): 162–84.

Percec, D. and L. Pungă (2019), "They Do It with Nursery Rhymes.: The Mystery of Intertextuality in Agatha Christie's Detective Fiction from a Literary Critic's and a Translator's Perspective," *British and American Studies*, 25 (1): 10.

"Police Killings by Country 2021" (2021), *World Population Review*, Walnut: World Population Review.

Prior, C. (2018), "An Empire Gone Bad: Agatha Christie, Anglocentrism and Decolonization," *Cultural and Social History*, 15 (2): 197–213.

Viezzi, M. (2014), "The Italian Titles of Agatha Christie's Novels," doctoral thesis, University of Trieste, 2014.

Ware, T. (1998), "Race and Conflict in Garner's 'One-Two-Three Little Indians' and Laurence's 'The Loons'," *Studies in Canadian Literature/Études en littérature Canadienne*, 23 (2): 71–84.

Warren, C. A. (2010), "Gender and Moral Immaturity in Agatha Christie's 'And Then There Were None'," *CEA Critic*, 73 (1): 51–63.

Webster, I. (2021), "1,000,000 in 1890 — 2021/Inflation Calculator," in *CPI Inflation Calculator*, San Mateo: Official Data Foundation/Alioth LLC.

CHAPTER ELEVEN

Christie and the State

MARY EVANS

The title of this chapter may astound readers, given that the many works of Agatha Christie are generally presented on television and film in terms of the sunniest, most affluent, most charming aspects of the British past. In this past, the state has little or no explicit presence other than that of an occasional incompetent policeman. Not for the program makers of Christie any suspicion that it rains in the UK, or that the decades of the 1920s and the 1930s were periods when poverty dominated the lives and the landscape of the country. Thus, no smoking chimneys or groups of clearly poor people are to be seen. There are certainly servants and people with little or no money in Christie's work, but these are the exceptional cases, the people who have a part to play in the plots of the novels rather than as representatives of particular groups.

However, in drawing attention to these media interpretations of Christie, it must also be said that a considerable scholarship about Christie has now engaged with her work's relationship with the social worlds that her work spanned, and the changes within them. Given that she published from 1920 to her death in 1976, a time span that covered the impact of the First World War, the poverty of the years both before and after the Great Crash of 1929, the emergence of modern consumerism, the enfranchisement of women, and the erosion of British Imperial political authority, her work has become a rich vein for scholarship on the UK in the twentieth century. Alison Light, Gill Plain, Marion Shaw, Sabine Vanacker, and Christopher Prior are among those many writers who have found in Christie's work complex themes that transcend assumptions about the limitations of crime fiction (Light 1991; Plain 2001; Prior 2019; Shaw and Vanacker 1997).

The argument here is not one based on the various films and television productions of Christie but one that follows those many critics who have drawn from a reading of Christie rather than from the various visual meanings and interpretations that have been imposed upon her. From this reading, a particular focus is on the role of the state, and the variety of ways in which the state does, or does not, intrude on the worlds which Christie creates. Some of the ways in which the state appears in Christie (e.g., the friendly, if ineffectual, village policeman) have become part of that nostalgic re-creation of her work which may seem to support the conservative reading of it. Yet, at the same time, other indications and themes in her writing suggest a more problematic attitude to the question of the relationship between the individual and the state than that which is generally assumed. Overall, the re-creation of Christie has placed her in a created world which has been widely used as an embodiment of all that is stable and ordered, in which hierarchies of class, gender, and race are all accorded respect and value. Individuals may disturb and even threaten the social order but through specific individual talents—intuition and social perception in the case of Jane Marple, cerebral and organized logic in the case of Hercule Poirot—individuals restore that social harmony. The state, in the sense of an organized bureaucracy which directs the lives of its citizens, is apparently distant and only evident in its resources for punishment and policing. But that distance of the state is central to Christie's world, in that it provides little or no assistance for its fictional citizens.

The absence of the state as a source of material support for its citizens is central to that theme of classed precarity and instability which is central to Christie's work. As her biography demonstrates, her own world had all the superficial appearance of the prized genteel stability of the white middle-class world, but much of her early life was riven by the very financial fragility which is often denied in visual interpretations of her work. The recognition of this uncertainty, not just in Christie's own life but also in the lives of her created characters, has an important bearing on the ways in which we think of the term "middle class." Often assumed to be associated with stability, reliable prosperity, and a permanent state of social and material predictability, that world is often one that is very different. It is today, and across the many decades in which Christie was writing, a place that can be one of anxiety and concern about both the present and the future, concerns related to both the material and the psychosocial worlds.

The various insecurities of the middle-class world which provided the background to the work of Christie in the 1920s and 1930s were vividly captured in George Orwell's novel of 1935, *A Clergyman's Daughter*. In this novel the middle-aged daughter of an Anglican clergyman fights to maintain both a material and social status quo which is no longer viable (Orwell 1935). What this work of fiction and the many nonfictional reports of living conditions in Britain in these years demonstrated was that the British state provided little or no support for those living in poverty. Indeed, the implementation of the May Report in 1931 on unemployment relief not only decreased financial support for the unemployed but was accompanied by the Means Test, which became a hated symbol of the state's attitude to long-term poverty (Ward 2013).[1] It is thus one of the singular paradoxes of the British political and literary imagination that Christie, a writer so aware of conditions of precarity, should be so often presented as the embodiment of social and material stability. In the period prior to the Second World War, and certainly before the impact of rearmament began to decrease the rates of unemployment, it was the absence of a secure income that impacted people across both the working and the middle classes. In the 1950s and the 1960s, both of them decades of rising prosperity and low rates of unemployment, material insecurity did not wholly disappear but other forms of the insecurity of the person began to emerge. These took the form of changing perceptions of the possibilities and the definitions of class, gender, and race: "angry" young men challenged the assumptions of an older male generation, while decolonization began to shift racial expectations from those about subjects of the empire to self-defining subjects.[2] These themes, most generally about differences between the "modern" and the "traditional," all find their place in Christie and were reflected in wider political debates of the 1950s and 1960s.

BIOGRAPHY

Two initial questions that need investigation are those of Christie's own relationship to the state and of the presence of the state in her own life. A simple reading of her biography would suggest a straightforward progress from middle-class girlhood to a first unfortunate marriage and then a second very happy marriage accompanied by an increasingly successful writing career. This was not quite the reality, either in Christie's early life or in that of many other women in the decades between the end of the First World War and the beginning of the Second World War, when the question of the relationship of women to the state continued to be contested. Christie was certainly born into the English provincial middle class, but the death of her father plunged her mother into poverty, a poverty which bordered on the "just about" genteel. Christie herself wrote of the consequences of this moment:

---

[1]The May Report on unemployment assistance was published in 1931 by the National Government. The introduction in that year of the Means Test led to the resignation of the Labour Party from the Government. The impact of the test was most acutely felt by the long-term unemployed, many of them in Wales and northern counties of the UK.

[2]The "angry young men" were novelists and playwrights (John Braine, Arnold Wesker, John Osborne, and Kingsley Amis) associated with various forms of radical ideas (Kroll 1961: 157–66).

Life took on a completely different complexion after my father's death. I stepped out of my child's world, a world of security and thoughtlessness, to enter the fringes of the world of reality. I think there is no doubt that from the man of the house comes the stability of the home [...] You accept it all unquestioningly.

(in Thompson 2007: 85)

Christie and her mother managed to stay on in that existing, formerly stable home, named Ashfield, but their lives were now precarious. What Christie describes here as the "world of reality" is a world that was shared by millions of her fellow citizens.

It was in Ashfield that Christie grew up, a loved child in the provincial calm of late Victorian England. At an early age, she began to write but it was not until the years after the First World War that her writing career began. Christie had served (like her contemporaries Vera Brittain, E.M. Delafield and Enid Bagnold) in the Voluntary Aid Detachment, an organization initially designed to support, through nursing and domestic work, hospitals for the wounded. Initially confined to the UK, the women who belonged to this organization were eventually sent overseas and to hospitals and field hospitals closer to the front line. Christie never went to work in these overseas contexts, but she did have the experience of nursing severely injured men and seeing at first hand the human injuries of war. Her further major experience in this period of her life was her marriage in 1914 to Archie Christie, a man who became a member of the emergent Royal Air Force. The marriage was not to last, and it would appear that it resulted in the emotional turmoil that led in 1926 to the single lasting mystery of Christie's life, her disappearance for eleven days. Already a well-known author, Christie appeared to vanish without trace, reappearing to say only that she had lost her memory. But prior to that disappearance, Archie Christie had asked for a divorce, a divorce which was granted in 1928.

Here, at the beginning of a career that was to take Christie to global fame and considerable fortune, were two major interventions by the state in her life. The first was that of war, leaving her with a firsthand knowledge of its appalling consequences. Christie was clearly not alone in this experience since the First World War decimated a generation of men and left thousands of others throughout Europe with the psychological consequences which were only just beginning to be understood. That impact, the difficulty of recovering from the brutality of war, is to pervade, as we shall see, Christie's fiction. Men were expected to return to "normal," whatever their physical or psychic injuries, but her work depicts men who do not find this easy or, in some cases, even possible. There is in Christie, as in Virginia Woolf's *Mrs. Dalloway*, a literary reminder that the consequences of the war are not just those of general political change, of victory or defeat, but of the devastation of individual lives. The suicide of Septimus Smith in *Mrs. Dalloway* is one instance of the permeation of the literary imagination by the horrors of the First World War; in Christie, that recognition is a vivid presence in her work.

A second, much more personal, aspect of the part that the English state played in the lives of its citizens was that of its regulation of marriage. Until 1923, a woman could not divorce her husband on the single grounds of adultery; what was required was one of several other causes, such as cruelty. In 1923, the Matrimonial Causes Act allowed women, like men, to cite the single reason of adultery for a marriage to end. This is what Agatha Christie was able to do, so that by 1928 she had divorced Archie Christie, although she was to retain his name for the rest of her writing career. Archie Christie was anxious to end the marriage since he was determined to marry another woman, and he willingly colluded with the then-general practice of a fictitious act of adultery. Agatha Christie, like Archie, was to remarry: her second husband was the archaeologist Max Mallowan. With a somewhat unnerving perception, Agatha Christie had chosen a partner whose work, like hers, was primarily about the unearthing of mysteries.

These two circumstances, the psychic consequences of the First World War and the presence of the state in the private lives of its citizens, bring Christie closer to the direct experience of the state than is often supposed. It is also worth noting in these initial remarks about Christie's biography that, at the time of the writing of her first major novel (*The Mysterious Affair at Styles* in 1920), women under the age of thirty could not vote and the explicit sexual double standard of divorce had not changed. The stigma of divorce, even if a woman was the so-called innocent party, was considerable. It was not until 1928 that women over the age of twenty-one were given the vote and all property qualifications were abolished for both women and men. Among the many other forms of sexual discrimination existing at that time were those of equal pay and entry to many professions (Ferguson 1965: 55–68). Christie lived and worked, it is essential to recognize, in a world that neither assumed nor implemented twenty-first-century expectations of gender and racial equality. Even though there were active and articulate campaigns for change on both issues, the policies of the British state, for several decades of Christie's life, did little to alter or question profound inequalities. It is this state, a state supporting imperial and patriarchal power, which is implicitly re-created in many of the renderings of Christie's work. In the following sections, I will show that such representations are, at best, an interpretation of Christie; at their worst, they are a determined re-creation of a culture of privilege and authority.

THE DOMESTIC STATE

As every reader (or watcher) of Christie knows, the two major characters in her fiction are Miss Jane Marple and Monsieur Hercule Poirot, one a spinster and the other a Belgian refugee. In these creations, Christie gave her two central characters the personal characteristics of two of the most problematic identities of the twentieth (or indeed the twenty-first) century. Jane Marple belongs to a generation of women who were generally defined as a problem: the "surplus" women who would be unable to find husbands as a result of the deaths of young men in wars during the late nineteenth century and extending through the First World War. The social question of "surplus" women has a long history in the politics of Britain from the mid-nineteenth century onwards (Levitan 2008: 359–78). By the 1870s, emigration societies of various kinds had begun the work of assisting young, unmarried women to travel to various parts of what was then the British Empire in order to provide them with paid work. The issue, for these societies, was that unmarried women could not be supported within the domestic economy of the UK and that, crucially, there was no "respectable" work for these women. It was taken for granted that the ideal situation for every adult woman was that of wife and mother; should this not be possible, then solutions had to be found. This "problem" did not go away. The women's magazine *Home Notes* published a long article in 1898 headed "A Million Spinsters and What to Do with Them" (Home Notes 1898). The language and the title of this article were part of the culture into which Christie was born, and it is important to note here that, although the loss of male lives in the First World War gave new vigor to the social concern about the loss of the prospect of marriage for millions of women, the preoccupation was not a novel one. The nineteenth-century concerns did not arise out of the consequences of war but from a lasting concern that women without male financial support would be paupers. Christie's own mother was left virtually penniless on the death of her husband; the young Agatha had to find either "respectable" paid work or a husband. Agatha Christie was to find both, but Jane Marple found neither.

The social assumption of the world in which Jane Marple lived would have been that as a single woman she had little or no part to play in that married world of provincial middle-class sociability. Social life for the conventional middle class was organized around heterosexual married couples; to be unmarried or widowed was to be put apart from the usual round of invitations and social participation. Jane Marple belonged, again in common with Agatha Christie, to a generation of middle-class women for whom war had radically altered their prospects of marriage. In large part, this was due to the deaths of large numbers of young middle-class men, many of whom had been early volunteers (Winter 1977: 449–66). Marple's unmarried state and the many social assumptions that accompanied it were a fictional testament to the impact of a military state.

Jane Marple lived comfortably enough, always able to employ a servant and occupy a comfortable home. But with that went the patronizing attitudes to her which accompanied elderly women with no husband, the view that "Aunt Jane" would be invited as a social obligation.

The first full-length novel in which Miss Marple appears is *The Murder at the Vicarage* (1930), although she had previously appeared (and was to appear again) in various short stories. In her literary incarnation, Jane Marple is slight and elderly; she is not the exuberant, untidy, or physically large person sometimes portrayed in televised reincarnations. On the contrary, she is a person of restraint and self-containment, sure of her own judgment. Although others might see her as a person whose thinking is slightly muddled, Jane Marple is given, from her first appearance, access by Christie to determinedly categorical statements. To speak with this degree of authority cuts across gendered expectations of the way in which women speak. Jane Marple sometimes speaks in ways which to many of her listeners are typical of "feminine" speech, a series of apparent *non sequiturs* and references to matters outside the immediate concerns of the conversation.

But to assume, as many listeners to Jane Marple have done, that this necessarily indicates confusion of thought is entirely mistaken. Here is Jane Marple, speaking of a character in *The Murder at the Vicarage* with utter confidence: "'He had always struck me a rather a stupid man,' said Miss Marple, 'the kind of man who gets the wrong idea into his head and is obstinate about it'" (Christie 1930: 28). Later, in the same novel:

> "Dear Vicar," said Miss Marple, "You are so unworldly. I'm afraid that observing human nature for so long as I have done, one gets not to expect very much from it. I dare say that idle tittle-tattle is very wrong and unkind, but it is so often true, isn't it?"
>
> (Christie 1930: 29)

Here, Christie is arguing for the voice of women. The term "finding our voice" has been applied from the latter half of the twentieth century to women, to African Americans, to all marginalized ethnic and social groups, but here, in 1930, is a very clear female voice. What is important here are two issues: the first is that in that year we have to remember that women were excluded from anything but the most junior positions in those English institutions, the law and the Church of England, most obviously associated with the enforcement and the articulation of social morality. There were no female judges in the English legal system until Rose Heilbron was appointed as a judge in the English county courts in 1962, and women were not allowed full ordination in the Church of England until 1992. Christie is writing, for the major part of her career, of a world in which, as Emmeline Pankhurst had remarked in her autobiography, women had to live by the moral order made by men (Pankhurst 1914: 268).

The certain tone and absolute authority of the remarks by Jane Marple quoted above are replicated in the other Christie novels in which she appears. In all these cases what Jane Marple is doing is speaking not "for women" in any explicitly feminist sense but for the public recognition of what is revealed about people in that domestic world which women inhabit and for which women are assumed to be responsible. The home is, literally, the world of women and it is in this home that women learn, as Jane Marple has done, to observe the private habits and the often-relevant body language of its inhabitants. So, what Jane Marple sees are those patterns of what will come to be recognized in theoretical terms in the late twentieth century as the gendered power relations of the home: who controls money, who defines relations with the public world, and, most importantly, who is able to exercise power. One of the most dramatic of Jane Marple's comments on society occurs at the conclusion of *4.50 from Paddington* (1957): "'So you see,' said Miss Marple, 'it really turned out to be as I began to suspect, very, very, simple. The simplest kind of crime. So many men seem to murder their wives'" (Christie [1957] 1974: 217).

As considerable research has demonstrated since, this is not a matter of fiction but of fact. The domestic world, for Christie as much as in the twenty-first century, is one that is all too often dangerous, if not deadly, for women. Crucially, however, that danger has been too little recognized and acted upon. When Christie wrote *4.50 from Paddington*, crude judgments about "nagging" wives still informed public statements; the legal recognition of "coercive control" was only brought into legal parlance in England in 2019 (Elliott 2008; UK 2017).[3] Christie, like many women but unlike much conventional wisdom, did not see the home as a safe place.

AMATEURS AND PROFESSIONALS

Both Hercule Poirot and Jane Marple are amateur sleuths, in a tradition which includes Sherlock Holmes and Lord Peter Wimsey. But while these latter gentlemen belong to the white, upper middle, and aristocratic classes, Poirot and Marple belong to the much lowlier marginal categories of, respectively, refugee and spinster. Moreover, Poirot earns money for his work.[4] Apart from this distinction, what this tradition collectively endorses is the general incompetence of the organized police force. Although both Christie and Sayers acknowledge that many policemen, particularly the higher ranks, may be

---

[3]Legal judgments which invoked assumptions about "nagging" wives and provocation were first fully reviewed for English law in the *Law Commission's Report No. 304, Murder, Manslaughter and Infanticide* (2006).

[4]Entry to many professions, and the higher education necessary for qualification, remained largely dominated by white, middle-class men in the inter-war years. The numbers of women employed in service/clerical work went up, but professional work remained largely a male preserve (Ferguson 1975: 55–68).

perfectly nice people—"good chaps" in the language of the time—they are not blessed with the powers of intellect or imagination with which Poirot and Jane Marple are blessed. It would seem that Christie is saying that to be part of a bureaucracy is to lessen the human ability to imagine: all too often Poirot and Jane Marple have to point the police toward the right suspect and divert police attention from false arrest.

This tradition of the opposition between the amateur and the professional is not one which was only to be found in British crime and detective fiction in the interwar years. The same was true of the United States where the independent sleuths, the "private eyes" of Raymond Chandler and Dashiell Hammett, upheld standards of honesty and competence seldom present in the official police force. The disjunction between crime and its supposed opponents was, in the United States, one widely recognized as the corruption of the police force. In the main, the fiction of Hammett and Chandler saw this in terms of the willingness of the police to accept bribes and to overlook the crimes of the powerful. What was seldom observed in crime fiction of the time were the racial politics of policing in the United States, politics which were to become a matter of central concern later in the twentieth and twenty-first centuries.

In Britain, there is little suggestion in fiction that the police were corrupt in the same way as in the United States. The charge against them was one of limited intelligence; most particularly the inability to think outside the narrow boundaries of given stereotypes. It is perhaps this which gives Christie some claim for upholding the importance of giving credence and respect to the socially marginal. The servant, the person with little or no money or secure social position, and the young person attempting to find a place in the world are all given a place. At the other end of the social continuum, the rich and socially privileged are not depicted as free from evil or murderous intent.

For the outsiders, the Hercule Poirots of the world and, to a lesser extent, the Jane Marples, it is the rich and the powerful who are going to make decisions about both their lives and the lives of others. Being "independent," free from the constraints of the everyday world of paid employment and the expectations of deference and obedience, gave to Poirot and Jane Marple the intellectual space to consider possibilities which to others (including representatives of the state) seemed impossible: that a beautiful young woman (in *Death on the Nile*) should be a partner in murder and that an apparent pillar of the community (the doctor in *The Murder of Roger Ackroyd*) should be a killer. To consider these possibilities is to abolish conventional social wisdom. It is the "how" of this ability which is part of the intrigue of Christie's work.

If we turn to look at the decades of the 1920s and 1930s in Britain, there are two themes which potentially relate to the ways in which Jane Marple and Poirot can think so independently of the assumptions made around them. The first is that of income. Both have incomes sufficient to maintain immediate domestic worlds for themselves which are entirely to their own liking; they are subject to no external authority and live lives of great decorum and order. In this, both Poirot and Jane Marple are typical of other middle-class people of their time, living in what the social historian Ross McKibbin has described as decades of a "golden" age for much of the middle class (Winter 1977: 449–66). But in the same discussion, he also points out that these decades were very much not the same for working class people. He writes that

> the 1920s experienced more severe class conflict than at any other time in modern British history; and this produced powerful ideological antagonisms and stereotypes that long survived the decade.
>
> (McKibbon 1998: 54–9)

McKibbin's qualification of the condition of the British middle class in the interwar years is important here, in that although he fully documents the ways in which the majority of the middle class enjoyed material security and prosperity in these years, they did so in the context of two changes which are relevant to Christie's work. The first is that for a section of the middle class (e.g., some professions such as the law and that of the established church) incomes did not keep pace with the cost of living. Although taxes for the middle class did not rise in these years, a common assumption was that individuals in various professions would be supported by private incomes. The second is that, for all middle-class people, there was an inevitable experience of living in a deeply divided country: one divided by place and occupation.

In the leafy shire villages and towns where Christie placed many of her novels, there was little engagement with the world that George Orwell and other writers in the 1920s and 1930s described. But what underpinned the poverty of millions of people was the refusal of governments of the time to engage actively or effectively with any programs for the relief of poverty. On the contrary, after the May Report of 1931, the British government cut unemployment benefits by 10 percent and instituted the hated Means Test, by which claimants for benefits could be investigated in terms of any other assets. These assets were generally small (items of furniture for example), but nevertheless were seen as items of potential income.[5] Thus, while the middle classes generally, if not universally, could live in some degree of prosperity, millions of others, distant through geography or circumstance from the world of Jane Marple, could not.

The refusal of successive governments in the 1920s and the 1930s to engage with questions of poverty and inequality was not, however, because they lived in a world without advice, analyses of alternative policies, and considerable

---

[5]In 2017, the concept of "controlling" behavior was recognized for English law in *Controlling or Coercive Behaviour in Intimate Family Relations* (United Kingdom Crown Prosecution Service 2017).

evidence about deprivation and disadvantage. These decades saw the emergence of the social sciences, the growing impact of Fabian ideas and, perhaps most significantly in terms of the long-term impact of its ideas, the publication in 1936 of John Maynard Keynes's *The General Theory of Employment, Interest and Money*. These sources were producing a consensus that governments could intervene in ways that could regulate the uncertainty of capitalist markets and that it was possible for governments to plan the conditions in which their citizens lived. Despite the evidence, the experts, and the many alternatives possible for governments, the British government continued with policies that protected the pound (and hence the value of middle-class incomes and investments) and punitive policies towards the unemployed. In this, it is possible to see what might be described as an amateur state, one which refuses to consider possibilities, rejects analysis, and follows views derived from a highly singular and unexamined class position.

The work of the Fabian Society, the growing expertise of social investigation, and the various engagements by individuals such as Leonard Woolf and Kingsley Martin were all a testament to the expertise which did exist, but was seldom utilized (Addison 1975).[6] In short, Jane Marple was able to recognize the *professional* possibilities of her limited experience of the world; the Conservative politicians of the 1930s were not. From this, Jane Marple could be considered as the professional, the person who has considered her position and assessed evidence in the world outside herself. The British state of the time was run by those significantly lacking in the ability that became known in the late twentieth century as "reflexivity."

The ability to think outside an individual's given world brings us to Christie's other major character: Hercule Poirot. Here is someone who is not afraid to make it clear to the world that he believes in the power of rational thought, the exercise of those famous "little grey cells." Of the many interesting characteristics that Christie gives to Poirot, two stand out: his frequent refusal to take things as they appear and the second, no less significant, the organization of his own life. While we can see Jane Marple at home among the inherited furniture and the chintz of many middle-class homes, Poirot lives in a way which relates to Le Corbusier and the Bauhaus. In 1927, Le Corbusier famously remarked that a "house is a machine for living in"; a look at a picture of his 1931 house Villa Savoye shows the kind of house of which Poirot would approve. More importantly, these tastes and habits associate Poirot with a world outside the UK, a world of European modernism in taste and design. In the decade of the 1930s, when many of the new suburbs around major British cities were being

---

[6]The various "experts" putting forward plans for new forms of Keynesian economics, largely endorsed in the Labour Government of 1945, are discussed by Paul Addison in *The Road to 1945: British Politics and the Second World War* (Addison 1975).

built, a singular characteristic, indicative of different kinds of associations, was what is described as "mock Tudor." Sections of the country embraced the idea of recalling a world in which sewage ran in the streets and houses were subject to frequent infestations of various forms of vermin. Poirot emphatically did not. He admired the organized, the thought-through, the designs which served a purpose rather than sentimental recall.

Marple and Poirot are two detectives on the fringes of society. In their different ways, they represent forms of professional competence which are recognized in the worlds in which they live. Clearly, both are outside those expectations of training and career progression which we associate with professional work. But in a different way, they both represent forms of expertise which come to be recognized later in the twentieth century. With Jane Marple, this is of understanding and giving a place to domestic and emotional experiences of the social world; the concealed motives and what come to be described as the "hidden agendas" of everyday life. Hercule Poirot is an avowed exponent of rational thought, believing that the social world can be understood and that it is not a matter of allowing taken-for-granted stereotypes to overcome further rigorous investigation. Agatha Christie is not simply presenting us with slightly eccentric characters. She is presenting us with people who in different ways appeal to our wishes both to understand the world and to extend that understanding to others.

IMPERIAL JOURNEYS

A division between the experiences of Hercule Poirot and Jane Marple is that the former travels outside the UK and the latter seldom ventures far from St. Mary Mead. Poirot's overseas travel appears to have been largely in western Asia, the part of the world which Christie herself knew well through her various visits with her second husband to archaeological sites in the area. Max Mallowan became a distinguished figure in his work, and he was one of those responsible for the establishment of the major museum in Baghdad. This was a couple who knew and experienced other cultures. At the same time both Mallowan and Christie lived in decades in which the part that women might play in both the British Empire and in countries associated with British interests was a contested issue. As Penelope Tuson has pointed out, there were voices that called for women to be engaged in matters of the overseas British state; others, such as the onetime Viceroy of India Lord Curzon regarded any form of engagement by women with the state as possibly leading to the "disruption and even the ruin of the Empire" (Tuson 2008: 11). Crucially, what these voices were challenging was the expectation that forms of female emancipation in the UK could be translated to the countries of the empire.

Western Asia was one of the regions with which the British state was most centrally involved in the years between the First and the Second World Wars, not least because of its oil reserves and its location in terms of access to India (Anderson 2013; Cottingham-Rolls 2005; Murphy 2008). It was the world of T.E. Lawrence, as well as of the excavation of the ancient civilizations of the area. Between these various activities, there were close connections, some of which involved Christie and her husband. Max Mallowan had been the assistant to the archaeologist Leonard Woolley, a man who was also a colleague of Lawrence and with him a major informant on the area for the British Foreign Office. Leonard Woolley's wife, Katharine, was known to Christie and was the inspiration for the murdered character Louise Leidner in *Murder in Mesopotamia* (1936). The central characters in this world were all well connected with various British elites. (Woolley, for example, had a long correspondence with Charlotte Shaw.)

Over and above these biographical connections, what Christie was part of was a world which was, through the writings and lectures of Lawrence and others, rapidly acquiring a reputation that became known as "Orientalism," a construction portraying Asian cultures as sensuous, secretive, and deeply seductive (Said 1978). Moreover, at this point in history, it appeared that this culture remained friendly to the British, as opposed to those locations, most importantly India, which were becoming increasingly vocal in demands for freedom from colonial rule. (The Indian Congress Party had been established in Mumbai in 1885 and by the time that Mallowan and Christie arrived in the Middle East, there was a growing awareness of the problematic status of the British Empire.) So Christie wrote about a place that was still assumed to be sympathetic to the British, but is nevertheless one that is best not regarded through the romantic and problematic gaze of Orientalism. Hercule Poirot embodies this less than enthusiastic view: he does not comment on the politics of western Asia, but he dislikes the heat, the food, and the flies. More crucially he is also someone who is not, unlike some of the other characters in Christie's novels located in the area, at all seduced by foreign places and cultures. "Abroad" and imperial projects, in general, do not provide characters in Christie with necessarily positive outcomes. Indeed, these are places where violence and murder still stalk individual lives.

One of the consistent visitors to the Middle East in Christie's novels is Captain Hastings, the ex-army officer who accompanies Poirot in seven novels. Hastings has served and worked in the Middle East, although his final career destination is a ranch in Argentina. What Hastings embodies is the idealization of the "good" colonialist, the eminently fair and judicious imperial administrator who brings the expectations of British justice to distant parts of the world. It is a figure not altogether different from the real-life character of Leonard Woolf, husband of Virginia, who served for seven years as a colonial administrator in what was then known as Ceylon (Woolf 1913). He, like Hastings, was a model of probity and honesty. But for both men, and for Christie, the right of the British to administer anywhere outside the British Isles was in question and becoming more problematic, not just in the countries themselves but in domestic politics. It is this uncertainty that Christie acknowledges through her depiction of those who return from Imperial locations and find it hard to re-adjust to British life. Their homes, as she points out, are frequently replete with artifacts from the part of the empire in which they have lived and their incomes, which might have provided them with secure and prosperous lives abroad, are now inadequate. For some characters (such as Thomas Eade in *4:50 from Paddington*), the colonies are the place in which white men can make a fortune. The same novel includes a reference to the character of Ronnie Wells, a character known by Jane Marple from St. Mary Mead and representing another side of the possible fortunes of the empire: Mr. Wells lost all his money (Christie 1957: 219).

Concluding a detailed analysis of Christie's relationship to the empire, Christopher Prior writes:

> Christie's overarching conclusion is clear. The colonies—both the old "white dominions" and otherwise—have failed to contain threat. They lack a younger generation with both sufficient powers of vigilance and a willingness to be vigilant [...] The scale of the problem was indicated by the fact that the empire was now not simply home to individual criminals but the cradle of larger global conspiracies.
>
> (Prior 2019: 197–213)

The empire, arguably, was the major intervention in global politics of the British state. It has had consequences which continue to this day and remains a battleground of competing political views. Christie might be placed on the side of those for whom the empire was positive, but in other ways she has a sense of the problems that its racialized politics and systems of exploitation and control produced, as much as in a general structural sense as in terms of individual experiences. It is always men who are associated with the empire in Christie's novels and that explicit bias should alert us to her assumption, which takes for granted the right of men to rule. Of the many characters who appear in Christie's novels, a wider social remit than is often supposed, the exclusion of one figure stands out: a woman in a position of political power. Neither the empire nor any other state was run by a woman; in reality as well as in Christie's fiction only rarely did women, such as the British MP in *Appointment with Death*, exercise political power.

The white male figures who run the empire are divided by Christie into good and bad. On the side of the good are those like Leonard Woolf who see imperial administration as positive, as taking British values of justice to other cultures. On the bad side are those who see the countries of the empire as a place for personal enrichment. This disjunction makes clear, through the context of the politics of the empire, a central point in Christie: she has neither respect nor liking for those who see making money as a positive way of life. Her respect is for what she sees as "honest" work, a definition which for subsequent generations concerned with the politics of the empire is more than slightly problematic. But it puts Christie far from enthusiasm for a spirit of exploitation and entrepreneurship, a position which the British state has increasingly come to adopt with explicit enthusiasm. To quote Christopher Prior again:

> Agatha Christie's immensely popular crime novels [...] constructed a narrative of British decline rooted in a sense of departure from pre-war ideals of imperial masculinity, but whose Anglocentrism nevertheless offered up the potential for imperial renewal pending a "rediscovery" of such characteristics.
>
> (Prior 2019: 209)

The British state, and indeed the empire, could not maintain any form of legitimacy without the moral characteristics exemplified by the fictional Hastings and the real-life Leonard Woolf. The state, Christie implicitly recognized, needed human beings who shared values that she considered positive. But for Christie, as for subsequent generations well into the twenty-first century, finding such people who were also prepared to countenance active memory in aspects of British consciousness and political life proved impossible. If her novels are simply read as paeans to the empire and the state undergirding it, they ignore this recognition of the complexity of its human servants. The social and political relations of the British Empire became increasingly impossible. Thus, Christie's discussion of the empire is always elegiac.

CONCLUSION

Christie was complex. A brilliant storyteller, her work contains much that would now be read as offensive. On race and class, though arguably less on gender, she exhibits many of the prejudices of the world in which she grew up and for which she was writing. But throughout her work two themes stand out: that the world (contrary to visual reenactments of her novels) does not and cannot avoid social change. The second that she gives to both her central characters is the strength of the marginal: of seeing the world less in terms of its surfaces as portrayed by conventional wisdom, and more in terms of hidden motives, concealed fears, and disguised antagonisms.

In this context, she has to be regarded as one of the most radical writers of her time, in that she allows outsiders to demonstrate understanding and comprehension. Very few writers of her generation did this and it was not until the 1970s when "outsider" detectives became commonplace in crime fiction that the tradition was continued. In a world in which both women and refugees are still refused the same voice as white English men, that core of her work remains a critical one.

REFERENCES

Addison, P. (1975), *The Road to 1945: British Politics and the Second World War*, London: Jonathan Cape.

Anderson, S. (2013), *Lawrence in Arabia: War, Deceit and Imperial Folly and the Making of the Modern Middle East*, New York: Doubleday.

Bargainnier, E. F. (1980), *The Gentle Art of Murder: The Detective Fiction of Agatha Christie*, Bowling Green: Popular Press.

Christie, A. (1930), *The Murder at the Vicarage*, London: Collins.

Christie, A. (1936), *Murder in Mesopotamia*, London: Collins.

Christie, A. (1938), *Appointment with Death*, London: Collins.

Christie, A. ([1957] 1974), *4:50 from Paddington*, London: Pan.

Cottingham-Rolls, S. (2005), *Steel Chariots in the Desert*, London: Leonaur.

Elliott, C. (2008), "Men Shouldn't Get Away with It," *The Guardian*, July 25.

Ferguson, N. A. (1975), "Women's Work: Employment Opportunities and Economic Roles, 1918–1939," *Albion*, 7 (1): 55–68.

Keynes, J.M. (1936), *The General Theory of Employment, Interest and Money*, London: MacMillan.

Kroll, M. (1961), "The Politics of Britain's Angry Young Men," *Social Science*, 36 (3):157–66.

Levitan, K. (2008), "Redundancy, the 'Surplus Woman' Problem and the British Census. 1851–1861," *Women's History Review*, 17 (3): 359–76.

Light, A. (1991), *Forever England: Femininity, Literature and Conservatism between the Wars*, London: Routledge.

McKibbon, R. (1998), *Classes and Culture: England 1918–1951*, Oxford: Oxford University Press.

Murphy, D. (2008), *The Arab Revolt: 1916–1918*, London: Osprey Books.

Orwell, G. (1935), *A Clergyman's Daughter*, London: Gollancz.

Pankhurst, E. (1914), *My Own Story*, London: Eveleigh Nash.

Plain, G. (2001), *Twentieth Century Crime Fiction: Gender, Sexuality and the Body*, Edinburgh: Edinburgh University Press.

Prior, C. (2019), "An Empire Gone Bad: Agatha Christie, Anglocentrism and Decolonisation," *Cultural and Social History*, 15 (2): 197–213.

Said, E. (1978), *Orientalism*, New York: Pantheon.

Scaggs, J. (2005), *Crime Fiction: The New Critical Idiom*, London: Routledge.

Shaw, M. and Vanacker, S. (1997), *Reflecting on Miss Marple*, London: Routledge.

Thompson, L. (2007), *Agatha Christie: A Mysterious Life*, London: Headline.

Tuson, P. (2008), *Playing the Game: Western Women in Arabia*, London: I.B. Tauris.

United Kingdom Crown Prosecution Service (2017), *Controlling or Coercive Behaviour in Intimate Family Relations*, June 30. Available online: https://www.cps.gov.uk/legal-guidance/controlling-or-coercive-behaviour-intimate-or-family-relationship (accessed June 30, 2017).

United Kingdom Parliament (2006), *Law Commission's Report No. 304, Murder, Manslaughter and Infanticide, Project 6 of the Ninth Programme of Law Reform: Homicide*, London: House of Commons.

Ward, S. (2013), *Unemployment and the State in Britain: The Means Test and Protest in South Wales and North East England*, Manchester: Manchester University Press.

Winter, J. M. (1977), "Britain's 'Lost Generation' of the First World War," *Population Studies*, 13 (3): 449.

Woolf, L. (1913), *The Village in the Jungle*, London: Edward Arnold.

FIGURE 12.1 Agatha Miller at a house party in Petersfield for the Goodwood Races. Date unknown. Courtesy of The Christie Archive Trust.

CHAPTER TWELVE

House and Home: The Country House

BRITTAIN BRIGHT

A casual mention of "the house" in Agatha Christie's detective novels probably does not, for most readers, bring to mind the Gothic house in *One, Two, Buckle My Shoe* or Daisymeade in "The King of Clubs." Instead, the image usually evoked is that of the "country house," full of servants and guests, secret passages and motives. Certainly, Christie's houses inherit characteristics from those in earlier English literature, including the Gothic and the Romantic, and it cannot be denied that they play a part in generating stereotypes of the house in detective fiction. However, Christie's house is actually a surprisingly complex and flexible place. While it relates to the country house form that evolved in the hands of many Modern novelists, Christie's particular notion of the house is focused on domestic pressures, social expectations, and, particularly, family. The scholarly assessment of place in general, and the house in particular, in Christie's work has evolved dramatically as both detective fiction and fictional place have received more critical attention. This chapter situates Christie's houses in relation to theoretical ideas about place, examines the assumptions that lead to misinterpretation of her work, and details an evolving understanding of the house or home in Christie's work.

Place in fiction acts as a framework for both the composition and the interpretation of the text. Simply put, the places in a novel largely determine what kind of novel it is. It is no coincidence that Raymond Chandler and W.H. Auden both use spatial-environmental models to discuss the detective novel: Chandler contrasts "Cheesecake Manor" to his "mean streets" ([1944] 1992: 222–37), and Auden details a formula in which the appropriate "milieu" is the first requirement of the whodunit (1948: 406–12). In Christie's work, the connection between stories and their environments is essential. However, before the 1990s, fundamental errors plagued critical approaches to the house, as they did other aspects of detective fiction. Today, though the study of place is receiving increased critical attention, scholars still combat conventional interpretations, and a powerful network of assumptions still surrounds the crime and detective genre, Christie's work in particular.

Readers of Christie's time would have understood her houses very differently than do readers of the present. After Christie's death, as Alison Light (1991: 63) notably observes, she and her places were firmly assimilated into the heritage industry. While twenty-first-century scholarship has revolutionized the analysis of crime and detective fiction, there are few detailed assessments of place therein. Some scholars who view Christie in Modernist terms, notably Light, Margaret Boe Birns, Nicholas Birns, and J.C. Bernthal, consider the role of the house in Christie's worldview. In addition, many of the new conceptual frameworks illuminate that most Christie-an environment. "After all," said Christie herself, "one has to be concerned with houses. It's where people *live*" (in Wyndham 1966: 2, emphasis original).

Christie had a personal and fictional preoccupation with houses: she owned a number of houses in her lifetime, some of which appear in her novels (most notably her Dartmouth home Greenway, which is the focal point of *Dead Man's Folly* [1958]). Her fictional houses reveal a concentrated and consistent attention to national preoccupations such as work, status, modernity, and domesticity. Christie's ascendancy as a writer of the house exists in part because of her timing—*The Mysterious Affair at Styles* (1920) capitalized on an existing notion of the country house, and its success established the house as a quintessential setting for the postwar detective novel boom—and in part because she used the place repeatedly. The house, in various guises, dominates a catalogue of her places during the 1920s, and again throughout the 1940s and 1950s. Overall, twenty-five of Christie's novels, and many short stories, are centered around a house.

PLACING THE HOUSE

The house, particularly the "country house," has appeared in detective fiction since Wilkie Collins's *The Moonstone* (1868), often considered the first detective novel. The country house is ineluctably associated with the "long weekend" glamour of the interwar period, as in the work of novelists from P.G. Wodehouse to George Bernard Shaw, and its apotheosis in detective fiction corresponds. Many Golden Age writers tried a country house mystery, probably because of the proven appeal of the setting: Philip MacDonald's *The Rasp* (1924), Anthony Berkeley's *The Layton Court Mystery* (1925), Margery Allingham's *The Crime at Black Dudley* (1929), Gladys Mitchell's *Speedy Death* (1929), and Ngaio Marsh's *A Man Lay Dead* (1934) are all country house debuts, most from authors who rarely revisited the setting. The country house novel has been parodied by some novelists, including Leo Bruce (*Case for Three Detectives*, 1936) and James Anderson (*The Affair of the Blood-Stained Egg Cosy*, 1975), and reconsidered by more contemporary ones, including Stuart Turton (*The Seven Deaths of Evelyn Hardcastle*, 2018) and Lucy Foley (*The Hunting Party*, 2018). The country house detective narrative also takes other guises, in game form as Cluedo (first released 1949) and as escapist fantasy in "murder mystery" weekends. Other art forms have also commented on it, in such works as Tom Stoppard's play-within-a-play *The Real Inspector Hound* (1964), Robert Altman's film *Gosford Park* (2001), and Henry Filloux-Bennett's multimedia production *What a Carve-Up* (2020, based on the novel by Jonathan Coe).

Despite its sustained popularity, the critical discussion of the country house detective story has not evolved significantly since Chandler and Auden. George Grella, typifying an outdated critical approach, writes, "[t]he typical detective story presents a group of people assembled at an isolated place—usually an English country house—who discover that one of their number has been murdered" (1970: 30). More recently, Blake Morrison has demonstrated the enduring power of the country-house stereotype, writing in the *Guardian*'s review supplement that "few plots in fiction are as familiar as a murder committed during a country house weekend" (2011). The common, reductionist misinterpretation of "a posh and stylized milieu" in "a calm and virtually unruffled world" (Grella 1970: 33) exemplifies the assumptions that prevail about the house in detective fiction. This generalization is employed by other late twentieth-century scholars including (but far from limited to) Robert S. Paul in *Whatever Happened to Sherlock Holmes?: Detective Fiction, Popular Theology, and Society* (1997), James E. Bartell in "The Bureaucrat as Reader" (1997), and the otherwise insightful Patricia D. Maida and Nicholas B. Spornick in *Murder She Wrote: A Study of Agatha Christie's Detective Fiction* (1982).

That the "country house party" is considered a quintessential setting for the detective novel, from Collins to Foley, exemplifies a critical tendency to overlook the work of place in the text. Some detective novels do feature social events in country houses, but it does not follow that all houses in all detective novels conform to such a pattern. The interwar Golden Age of detective fiction, the beginning of which is usually marked by the publication of *The Mysterious Affair at Styles*, was an extraordinarily fruitful period for many themes in detective fiction; however, few Golden Age novels actually revolve around shooting parties and bizarrely diverse gatherings, and Christie's never do. Instead, Christie develops an entirely different set of possibilities, which evolve over the course of her career. For Christie, the house represents not visitors, but inhabitants. Light's *Forever England*, one of the first treatments of twentieth-century fiction to deal with the intersections of high- and low-brow forms, stresses that "[w]hen she does use big houses, they are seldom described as repositories of national character or a lost civility; it is their character as private homes which appeals to her" (1991: 81). Thus, rather than styling the places in these texts as "country houses," it is more relevant to consider them as "family houses."

In most studies of her work, Christie's novels have been considered primarily in sociohistorical terms, to which place might seem extraneous. However, the paramount social questions of Christie's work—those of class, social roles, modernity, and, most particularly, personal, familial, and national identity—develop further through their relationship with place. Light observes how changing perception of Christie's cultural place obscures the meaning of her work:

> Ironically, that which is now peddled as "Olde England" appeared in a form originally seen as cheapskate, felt to be new and as intrusive as the loudspeaker, wireless, or film. Christie's kind of detective story began life as one of many new varieties of a commercial culture whose expendability and temporality [...] offended those who preferred nineteenth century forms.
>
> (Light 1991: 64)

As contemporary interpretation of detective novels has changed, so has that of its characters, plots, and, consequently, houses. Light points out that contemporary assumptions about Christie are "historically contingent," illustrating the essential linkage between a text and its environment, and, by extension, between time and place. It is essential to contextualize Christie's novels in their own times, as Light and Bernthal do, in order to fully understand her places.

But what is place, in fact or in fiction? Despite the apparently tangible nature of "the house," the very idea of space/place bears investigation: the "spatial turn," geocriticism, and ecocriticism all consider how use and cultural practice define places. Philosopher Edward S. Casey observes that "just because place is so much with us, and we with it, it has been taken for granted" (1997: x). The "spatial turn" in contemporary thought was not a rejection of the idea of history, but an acknowledgment that spaces might affect history as much as they were created by it. Marxist theorist Henri Lefebvre writes in *The Production of Space*, "a spatial code is not simply a means of reading or interpreting space: rather it is a means of living in that space, of understanding it, and of producing it" ([1974] 1991: 47–8). Space and place, then, are not simply a background to the action of history, but a vital part of it.

Lefebvre argues that the meaning of a space is established through use: "Representational space is alive: it speaks. It has an affective kernel or center: Ego, bed, bedroom, dwelling, house; or: square, church, graveyard. It embraces the loci of passion, of action and of lived situations" (16). My own work centralizes the word "place" (as opposed to "space," "location," or "setting") largely because it connotes relationships and belonging, and implies a specific characterization. How any place may be defined depends not only on where it is, but also when, or by whom, it is perceived or described. Geographer Tim Cresswell writes:

> the word *place* turns up in common phrases such as: a place for everything and everything in its place" or "know your place" or "she was put in her place." In these expressions the word *place* clearly refers to something more than a spatial referent. Implied in these terms is a sense of the proper. Something or someone *belongs* in one place and not in another.
>
> (1996: 3, emphasis original)

Place, he contends, "is not just a thing in the world, but a way of understanding the world" (Cresswell 1994: 11). Light also touches upon place's implication of relative value, observing in Christie's description of her own society the English "need to 'place' people as groups or individuals" (Light 1991: 87). Dwellings, of course, are essential indicators of "place" in society as well as place in geography and time, with place in a family or class system often an important factor in Christie's stories. In the detective novel, the obvious question may be, *who was in what place?* but equally important is, *who is in place, and who is out of place?*

The meanings attributed to an individual place, or a type of place, are composed both culturally and individually, superimposing meaning onto the material, and making "place" out of the juncture between the two. To complicate matters further, a physical place may contain both an assumed (socially accepted) use and an active (individualized) use, as is common in the detective novel—hence the inherent shock of a phrase like "the body in the library." In addition, the way a place is understood, as Cresswell observes, is both preexisting and evolving. The notion that various places have a commonly understood meaning and use allows an author to evoke what literary theorist Leonard Lutwack calls an "elemental orientation" (1984: 37), but at the same time to undermine the stability of accepted "spatial practice." One of Christie's lasting contributions to the detective genre is a disruption of the traditional meanings of such presumably intelligible places as the house and the village.

"Sense of place" transcends the real world, and literary critics have been equally conflicted about its definitions. Wesley A. Kort asserts that "The various locations of a narrative can be read as constituting a kind of 'geographical synthesis' in the narrative analogous to the kind of synthesis of actions and events we refer to as the narrative's plot " (2004: 15). Kort's *Place and Space in Modern Fiction* is, along with Lutwack's *The Role of Place in Literature*, one of the most thorough explorations of place and space in literature. For Lutwack,

> [p]lace gets into literature in two ways, as idea and form: as attitudes about places and classes of places that the writer picks up from his social and intellectual milieu and from his personal experiences, and as materials for the forms he uses to render events, characters, and themes.
>
> (1984: 12)

Kort and Lutwack focus broadly on English literature, but this study narrows to a particular genre and place type, which, as Lisa Fletcher suggests, "approach popular genres as complicated systems of meaning, which have an immeasurable impact on our spatial awareness and imagination" (2016: 3). Despite, or perhaps because of, its codifications, the detective novel's use of place is at least as complex as in less genre-specific narratives.

CHRISTIE'S CHARACTERIZATION OF PLACE

Fictitious places, even more than real ones, *seem* to be readily understood. Patricia Maida and Nicholas B. Spornick comment, with some credulity, that "the reader moves easily into [Christie's] milieux because they are so disarmingly simple" (1982: 170). The knowability of these places is both facilitated and hindered by Christie's descriptive style. Douglas McManis, in one of the only articles to specifically address place and Golden Age detective fiction, calls Christie "the mistress of thumbnail characterization, a stylistic feature that applies to her settings as well as to her characters" (1978: 321). R.A. York comments that "the very fact that she is easy to read and enjoy suggests that her writing takes for granted a mass of assumptions about the relationships and acts that appear in stories" (2007: 1). These assumptions are actually a large part of the creation of place for Christie herself, who felt that "writing plays is much more fun than writing books, because you haven't got to bother about long descriptions of places and people" (Christie 1955). In truth, even short descriptions are rare in her work. She maintained that places must seem familiar: "it must be a background that readers will recognize, because descriptions are so boring" (in Wyndham 1966).

The fact that readers feel they *do* understand these places bespeaks rich implications, muddled assumptions, or both. McManis notes that "[Christie] was apt to bring the reader to the door and usher him inside quickly, with only the briefest mention of identifiable or distinguishing characteristics" (1978: 326). Styles Court, the first house that Christie created in text, is generically described as "fine," "glorious," and "beautiful" (Christie 1921: 14, 27, 57), but its period, style, and size remain unclear. Other houses are barely described with even such indeterminate adjectives. Maida and Spornick point out Christie's "economy of detail": "when she wishes to convey a family's financial difficulty, she focuses on a specific area such as the weeds in the garden or the dilapidated shutters on the house [...] Her method is like the poet's use of synecdoche" (Maida and Spornick 1982: 171).

There is rarely much description beyond a basic introduction, such as that in *4:50 From Paddington*: "The house was desperately cold inside. Her guide led her along a dark hall and opened a door on the right. Rather to Lucy's surprise, it was quite a pleasant sitting-room, with books and chintz-covered chairs" (Christie 1957: 39). The impressionistic quality of such descriptions recalls Rainer Maria Rilke's memory of a house: "it is not a building, but quite dissolved and distributed inside me: here one room, there another, and here a bit of corridor which, however, does not connect the two rooms, but is conserved in me in fragmentary form" (Bachelard 1994: 57). This technique belies another presumed chestnut of the genre, the map or plan. Maps are frequently presumed to have risen to prominence in the Golden Age: numerous studies include confident statements such as "plans of the house were an indispensable aid to the aspirant solver of detective stories" (Barnard 1980: 24). Christie used maps and plans in several early works, but rather than placing evidential value in a map or plan, she always places it in individual perception. By contrasting ways or means of seeing, her novels continually emphasize perspective.

Christie's house, like those of philosopher Gaston Bachelard, "constitutes a body of images that give [...] proofs or illusions of stability" (Bachelard 1994: 17). Through these images, she used places to generate meaning for plots and characters. Dorothy L. Sayers protested against settings "put in only for picturesqueness and forming no integral part either of theme or plot. To make an artistic unity it is [...] essential that the plot should derive from the setting, and that both should form part of the theme" ([1937] 1992: 217). Christie herself contended that "real people, real places. A definite place in time and space" were essential to her work, and which she based in "the fantastic facts of daily life" (1970: xi, xiii). She clearly thematizes place types and their intrinsic cultural concerns, manipulating assumptions and subverting expectations. Lutwack observes:

> Repeated association of some generic places with certain experiences and values has resulted in what amounts almost to a system of archetypal place symbolism. Thus, mountains have come to represent aspiration and trial; forests and swamps, peril and entrapment; valleys and gardens, pleasure and well-being; deserts, deprivation; houses, stability and community; roads

or paths, adventure and change. From these basically concrete associations more specialized meanings are generated to form materials for literary genres like the pastoral, medieval romance, and Gothic novel, in which there is a steady relationship between settings and literary form.

(1984: 31)

The recurrence of certain kinds of places in fiction, specifically in genre fiction, generates a meaning for these places that can, thus, signify to a reader what to expect. As a corollary to that idea, the fictional meanings of a place evolve continuously, to contribute to a set of expectations dependent on previous fictional characterizations of that place. Nicholas Birns and Margaret Boe Birns, whose groundbreaking essay "Agatha Christie: Modern and Modernist" first assessed Christie in Modernist terms, point out the "tropological density" of the classic detective novel (1990: 129). Tzvetan Todorov develops the idea of typology: "The text is both the product of a system of pre-existing literary categories, and the transformation of this same system; the new text modifies the very combination-reservoir of which it is the product" (1977: 239–40). Umberto Eco also acknowledges the increased specificity of this process to genre fiction, observing that "frequently the reader, instead of resorting to a common frame [derived from experience], picks up from the storage of his intertextual competence already reduced intertextual frames" (1979: 21). Furthermore, within the place-tropes of the genre, there is an individual author's place-typology, which builds upon itself to form a specific set of expectations. Place acts as a lexicon, a framework for the composition and interpretation of the text.

Christie's novels and stories, though they take place in a variety of actual locations, are largely divisible into place-types. Earl F. Bargainnier identifies five "principal settings: foreign, in transit, London, the village and the country house" (1980: 22). Heta Pyrhönen also points to Christie's "typical settings: the manor house, the country village, the fashionable city dwelling, the holiday resort, the exclusive girls' school, or the train," though she uses this example to illustrate the theatricality of Christie's places as opposed to their typological distinctions (1999: 191). My own categories are more functional: the house, the village, London, and the holiday (Bright 2015: 53). These distinct types, though similar, are far more revealing than the "closed societies" W.H. Auden suggests in "The Guilty Vicarage":

(a) the group of blood relatives (the Christmas dinner in the country house); (b) the closely knit geographical group (the old world village); (c) the occupational group (the theatrical company); (d) the group isolated by the neutral place (the Pullman car). (1948: 407)

The closed circle device, common to many classic detective novels, has often been interpreted as part of an underlying social agenda, variously illustrating both its conservatism and its innovation. David Lehman remarks on the genre's "fixed limits and closely defined relationships," and calls murder "an exceptional but finally temporary violation of the social order" (2000: 109–10), and Robert S. Paul emphasizes class, calling "the English country-house murder" a "gilded cage" (1997: 89). On the other hand, Birns and Boe Birns remark that Christie "is less probing the souls of her characters than involving them in carceral circumstances that are sometimes apprehended as 'criminal,' sometimes not" (1990: 122–3), and Light argues that "Christie modernises the detective story by domesticating it, bringing it firmly inside the respectable classes. For Conan Doyle and many of Christie's own contemporaries, the criminal by definition could only be 'one of them'; for Christie, as her characters must always realize with alarm, the criminal is first of all 'one of us'" (1991: 94).

Place, however, is often far more than a plot-based limitation. For Kort,

> The language of place becomes even more determining when [...] action or characters are restricted to a particular place. Characters are thrown or held together by the confines of the space, and they are forced by place not only to deal with one another but also with the spatial concerns that they share.
>
> (2004: 16)

The house necessarily brings characters into intimate contact, the discomfort of which is particularly evident in novels that concern an extended family, some of whom are returning home. The centrality of houses to Christie's work indicates they have an important role, but their very ubiquity, like that of place itself, undermines clarity of understanding. While all places are loaded with meaning, Auden's passing reference to "blood relatives" is insightful. Each of Christie's types develops a distinct set of assumptions, both within itself and with respect to other texts, and one of the most important themes of the house is a problematic restructuring of family. Houses, which Lutwack cites as places of "stability and community," may indicate class, socioeconomic status, or history. More essentially, however, nearly all houses are rooted in a concept of family, and it is in this respect that Christie's houses are most distinctive.

Why, then, do contemporary audiences have such powerful ideas about the "country house" in Christie and her contemporaries? Light hints at an answer when she observes that an "Agatha Christie television bonanza" made the author seem "the high priestess of nostalgia" (1991: 62). Light refers to the 1980s, but the enduring appeal of Christie makes her work a continual victim of widely distributed misinterpretation. It is revealing, in this study, that adaptations rarely portray houses as they are in the source text: in a recent instance, Gilles Paquet-Brenner's "sumptuous fifties adaptation" (O'Donovan 2017) of *Crooked House* was filmed at Minford Manor in Hampshire, the high Victorian country house standing in for the suburban Three Gables, "a Greek restaurateur's idea of [...] an Englishman's home" (Christie [1949] 1986: 29). When, in the post–Second World War novel, the narrator Charles Hayward sees it for the first time, he finds it visually disorienting:

> The curious thing was that it had a strange air of being distorted—and I thought I knew why. It was the type, really, of a cottage; it was a cottage swollen out of all proportion. It was like looking at a country cottage through a gigantic magnifying glass. The slantwise beams, the halftimbering, the gables—it was a little crooked house that had grown like a mushroom in the night!
>
> (Christie [1949] 1986: 29)

The house is explicitly *not* grand: though it is disproportionately large, it is awkward, laughable rather than impressive. In altering the character of the house, the adaptation loses that of patriarch Aristide Leonides—unconventional, not quite honest, verging on ridiculous, but unique, and supremely confident. Although he never appears in the text, Leonides's powerful personality keeps his family in discomfiting closeness after his death, and dictates the action of the novel. In a different, decidedly less "crooked," house, this inevitably becomes a different kind of story.

It is an irony that Christie's continued popularity has made her writing, in some ways, less legible to successive generations. Light refers to Chandler, who, as early as 1949, misinterprets (perhaps purposefully) Christie's "'suburban idiom' [which some critics of her time] found offensively modern"; she suggests that Christie "is to be understood not as the *doyenne* of country house fiction but as queen of the 'middlebrow'" (1991: 75). Light observes, "When [Christie] does use big houses, they are seldom described as repositories of national character or a lost civility; it is their character as private homes which appeals to her" (1991: 81). The house in Christie is not a destination for a weekend party, but a locus of the problematic family. In another break from popular assumption, the inhabitants of these houses are not aristocrats; though the families are wealthy enough to maintain large houses, they range from middle-class professionals to wealthy widows to self-made men.

FAMILY HOUSES AND UNCANNY HOMES

Christie consciously adopted existing thematic structures around the house, even as she evolved her own concepts. Jonathan Culler suggests why a "known" place might be particularly useful for the detective novelist: "[p]recisely because the reader expects to be able to recognize a world, the novel [...] becomes a place in which models of intelligibility can be 'deconstructed', exposed and challenged" (2002: 222). The house, specifically the country house, has a distinct character in English literature. Since Ben Jonson's "To Penshurst," the country house has been used as a powerful image of class, heritage, and England itself. As Richard Gill writes, "Jonson does more than describe the house; he transforms its whole style of life into a symbol of humane order and true community" (1972: 227). Gill's identification of "order" and "community" is particularly salient: those ideas are reshaped over time, yet they also retain a strong, and perhaps misleading, association with that original context. The same notions are essential, and as often misunderstood, in the detective novel.

In the twentieth century, as M.M. Kelsall observes, "the apparent demise of the country house in the real world as a subject of modern fiction [was] its salvation in the world of the imagination. The house, separated from the social order which once sustained it, [becomes] a pure symbol" (1993: 161). The symbolism of the house pulls in multiple directions: Gill notes that "[n]ot only identifiable symbolists like James, Forster, and Virginia Woolf, but documentary realists like Wells and Galsworthy, as well as satirists like Huxley and Waugh, have all found in the country house a means of embodying the qualities and values of community, whether in a state of decay, transformation, or renewal" (1972: 14). Christie joins a long line of authors employing the house to consider transformations of society and family, firmly inserting herself among the Modernists, whose approach to the country house, as Gill writes of Vita Sackville-West's *The Edwardians*, lacks "pensive nostalgia," and "assumes a perspective which leaves no room for either moral earnestness or antiquarian sentimentality" (1972: 144).

The outline of the noble house is sometimes still evident in Christie, particularly before the Second World War, and the family therein may act the part of the local aristocracy. However, Christie uses the connotations of these houses to emphasize the differences between the people who might be *expected* to live there and the people who *do* live there, a tension promptly established in *The Mysterious Affair at Styles*: John Cavendish complains that Styles "should be mine now by rights, if my father had only made a decent will" (Christie [1920] 2001: 27). The narrator Captain Hastings observes, in a moment of uncharacteristic perspicacity, that Cavendish would like "to have a home of his own. [His stepmother] however, [...] expected other people to fall in with [her wishes], and in this case she certainly had the whip hand, namely: the purse strings" (11). Rather than the hereditary "rights" of the aristocracy, the power of the middle class is exerted through money, and this shift creates new hazards: if the family were aristocrats, John Cavendish would be his father's heir, and his stepmother a dependent, so the fortune-hunter Inglethorpe would not have conspired to marry, and murder, her.

Christie's private homes are, almost without exception, identified with the power of a central figure: some notable examples, besides Emily Inglethorpe and Aristide Leonides, are Nick Buckley (*Peril at End House*, 1932), Emily Arundel (*Dumb Witness*, 1937), Simeon Lee (*Hercule Poirot's Christmas*, 1938), Gordon Cloade (*Taken at the Flood*, 1948), Rex Fortescue (*A Pocket Full of Rye*, 1953), Luther Crackenthorpe (*4:50 From Paddington*, 1957), and Rachel Argyle (*Ordeal by Innocence*, 1958). While some of these characters are colorfully drawn through a whole novel, others only appear in the memories or words of others, or are present in the text very briefly; all, however, exert a lasting influence that is in many ways expressed by their houses. Lutwack notes, "a habitation is not only an expression of the person living in it but a condition influencing his life" (1984: 69), and Malpas remarks on "the specific dependence of self-identity on place" (2007: 177). One might say that, in Christie, the house is the expression of one person who influences the lives of all others under its roof—or in its purview, as the house does not cease to influence those who attempt to separate themselves from it.

Christie not only uses houses as settings, but gives them leading roles. As she developed her own set of meanings for the place, it became a powerful theme that references not only preexisting ideas about the house, but the developing idea of *Christie's* house. Kort observes that the balance of place with character and plot can influence the narrative style and tone significantly:

> The language of place in a narrative is often subordinate to the language of character, as when descriptions of a room or house serve to indicate a character's personality, tastes, or social standing. The language of space can also be subordinate to plot, as when it provides places where events can occur. However, the language of space begins to dominate character and plot when it *determines the kind of characters that are likely to appear in certain locations or the kinds of events that occur.*
>
> (2004: 16, emphasis added)

Houses like Styles Court, Three Gables, Yewtree Lodge, and Sunny Point reflect aspects of their inhabitants or creators. In a plot-oriented view, as mentioned above, they often represent a situation in which one person uses financial power to manipulate others. An imbalance of power is often used to sustain a false family structure, such as that of the Fortescue family in *A Pocket Full of Rye*: the patriarch exercises complete control over the lives of his adult children. In this he is similar to Mrs. Inglethorpe; to Aristide Leonides, who is unfailingly generous but certain that he is "the best judge of anybody in this house" ([1949] 1986: 140); and to Rachel Argyle in *Ordeal by Innocence*, who smothers her adopted children with her devotion. All of these characters dominate the lives of their adult children and dependents, in what Bernthal has called the "smothering and toxic nature of tradition, observed or created" (2016: 190). By exerting financial control, they attempt to reconstruct an ideal family, but in fact create a perversion of the domestic ideal that infantilizes the economically subservient.

Christie's house, though often referred to as "home," is distinctly separate from the idea of home as a place of belonging, comfort, and security. "House" and "home" seem, at least in English, to be nearly equivalent terms, but the gulf between the two is notable in Christie's work. Members of the Lee family in *Hercule Poirot's Christmas* variously define themselves and others through relationship to "home," whether they are "coming home," "leaving home," or "staying at home" (Christie [1938] 2001: 64, 157, 59). Patriarch Simeon Lee sows division and motives for his own murder through apparently welcoming language when he tells his family, "Pilar will make her home here, naturally. And Harry is home for good" (Christie [1938] 2001: 83). Few of the characters in these novels feel a genuine sense of belonging in the family house, whether they reside there as adults or not. The question arises again, of what it means to be "in place," and whether being "out of place" might, in itself, be a motive for crime.

Indeed, Christie's houses, even when they are secondary settings, are nearly always more indicative of concealment than of comfort. They often evoke a sense of what Sigmund Freud famously terms "The Uncanny." Freud's argument refers to an earlier essay by Ernst Jentch, for whom:

> every language [...] provides particular instances of what is psychologically correct or at least noteworthy in the way in which it forms its expressions and concepts. With the word *unheimlich* ["uncanny"] the German language seems to have produced a rather fortunate formation. Without a doubt, this word appears to express that someone to whom something "uncanny" happens is not quite "at home" or "at ease" in the situation concerned, that the thing is or at least seems to be foreign to him.
>
> ([1906] 1996: 7)

Freud's investigation of the *unheimlich* considers that the word *heimlich*, as well as its accepted meaning, "belonging to the house, not strange, familiar, tame, intimate, friendly, etc." ([1919] 2001: 222), contains a secondary meaning: "concealed, kept from sight, so that others do not get to know of or about it, withheld from others" (223). He continues: "*heimlich* is a word the meaning of which develops in the direction of ambivalence, until it finally coincides with its opposite, *unheimlich*. *Unheimlich* is in some way or other a sub-species of *heimlich*" (226). This duality of meaning, which emphasizes the unavoidable presence of the uncanny within the "home-like," is particularly resonant in a consideration of the domestic in the detective novel; instead of indicating the familiar, the home suggests concealment or duplicity. The ideas of "home" and, by extension, of "family" become increasingly complex, often mysterious in themselves. In *Hercule Poirot's Christmas*, Poirot comments on the butler's experience of *déjà vu*: "No wonder Tressilian felt confused when he had answered the door to not two, but *three* men who resembled each other closely" (Christie [1938] 2001: 320). The repetitions that seem uncanny and inexplicable are, in fact, the solution to the puzzle.

Even novels that do not center around a house can use its structure of meaning. For instance, the entitled references to the Gothic House in *One, Two, Buckle My Shoe* (1940) are a hint that not all is at seems with the family therein; the house itself—luxurious, well positioned, respectable—serves as part of a disguise that depends, above all, on reputation. The house also contains powerful connotations, if not of heritage, then of heirs and (not always monetary) inheritance. Nick Buckley, for example, commits murder for money, but not because she wants money for its own sake; the stolen inheritance will save End House, her family home, and make her the true heir of her devilish grandfather, Old Nick. There are instances in which the centrality of the house itself implies that, despite initial appearances, family and inheritance are critical: in *Dead Man's Folly*, Nasse House has apparently been sold out of the family after the death of the heirs, but as the ferry man declares meaningfully, "Always Be Folliats at Nasse" (Christie [1958] 1970: 46). In Christie's later work, houses do not even always contain families: in *They Do It with Mirrors* (1952), a Victorian estate has been converted into a home for delinquents, and in *Cat among the Pigeons* (1959), the house has become a school. However, the solutions to both novels revolve around inheritance and heredity. The house, simply by *being a house*, reveals.

IN PLACE, OF PLACE, OR SUBJECT TO PLACE?

McManis observes that "Christie's penchant for houses became one of her trademarks [...] In some stories the role of house was so significant to the plot that the house became part of the title" (1978: 325). Early in Christie's career, names are straightforward: Mrs. Inglethorpe almost literally "holds court" at Styles Court, while End House proves the end of its owner. Kort suggests that "personal spaces [...] not only acquire qualities from the persons who inhabit them, but also bring out those qualities" (2004: 84). Many of Christie's novels suggest that as much as the house is an expression of the householder, it is also an influence on his or her personality. Over time, the house names become more nuanced, satirical, and illuminating; even when the name of the house is not that of the novel, names are essential and revealing. Some, like Sunny Point, are pointedly ironic:

It was *her* [Rachel Argyle] called the house that—in the war. It were a new house, of course, only just been built—hadn't got a name. But the ground 'tis built on [...] Viper's Point, that is! But Viper's Point wouldn't do for *her*— not for the name of her house. Called it Sunny Point, she did.

(Christie 1958: 3, emphases original)

The ominous place name is contradicted by the house itself, "a well-built, modern, characterless modern house, gabled and porched. It might have stood on any good-class suburban site, or a new development anywhere" (Christie 1958: 4). However, this apparent contradiction does not nullify the initial information: vipers are most certainly at Sunny Point.

A Pocket Full of Rye reconstructs the "country" house as a suburban villa. Easily accessible from the City and surrounded by golf courses, Yewtree Lodge belies its name. Inspector Neele is struck by the disjuncture:

Call it a lodge, indeed! [...] The house was what he, Inspector Neele, would call a mansion. He knew what a lodge was. He'd been brought up in one. [...] But this place, this pretentiously named Yewtree Lodge was just the kind of mansion that rich people built themselves and then called it "their little place in the country." It wasn't in the country, either.

(Christie 1953: 2, 4)

As Kathy Mezei and Chiara Briganti note, "symbolic *names* signifying social status and genealogy or, equally, aspirations to social status, are [...] easily recognizable signs of one's place in English society" (2002: 841, emphasis original). Yewtree Lodge holds no claim to heritage, only money. Like its suburban location, the name simultaneously mocks the idea of the country house and reminds the reader of that basis for comparison; the people who named it, Christie implies, do not know the difference, and do not care. The incongruity of the name and the place, like the duality of Viper's Point and Sunny Point, suggests the increasing disjuncture between what the house is supposed to be and what it is.

A Pocket Full of Rye is another noteworthy example of Christie's fondness for nursery rhyme references. Light observes that the author "plays deliberately with the metamorphosis of the everyday and the comfortable into the unfamiliar and the sinister," which emphasizes "the unsteady boundary between the homely and the malevolent" (1991: 88). The nursery rhyme echoes the house itself by evoking the comfort and apparent security to be found in traditional forms, while exposing the hollowness of such forms by using them to define a murder plot. In addition, the simple fact of their *being* nursery rhymes alludes to the dangerous infantilization of the economically constructed family.

Casey declares, "we are not the masters of place, but prey to it; we are subjects of place, or, more exactly, *subject to place*" (2001: 415), and Gill observes, "characters reveal themselves in their attitudes toward the house" (1972: 137). Examples of this process can be found in nearly all of Christie's novels, even the most unexpected. *Death on the Nile* begins with Linnet Ridgeway's plans to transform Wode Hall into her "real idea of a country house" (Christie [1937] 2001: 29), plans which are, for all her charm, absolute, autocratic, and destructive. In other novels, the notion of the house seems to overpower the characters. Birns and Boe Birns note that in *The Hollow* (1946), the title

> refers to the name of the estate where the novel takes place, but hollowness is also an abstract theme in this novel [...] This "hollow" quality of the characters reverberates back on to the estate, which is a hollow not only in name, but in fact: 'The Hollow' is doomed to take perpetual second place in the hearts of the Angkatell family to Ainswick.
>
> (Birns and Birns 1990: 127)

The novel's "hollow" is also structural: Ainswick, the house around which characters' memories and desires revolve, is not actually in the novel. The house, in this case, is not *the* house.

Christie's novels observe, even anticipate, the increased social mobility of the interwar years and the upheaval that followed the Second World War. Class and spatial divisions become increasingly complex, and, in later works, the notions of "home" and "family" become increasingly tenuous. The house, while it continues to evoke the English country house, has either declined or been remade, and much of its inherent structure has vanished. As Bernthal points out, insisting on the thematic development so often neglected, the family "cannot be the same across time and space" (2016: 200). Light argues that throughout,

> [f]ar from suggesting a world in which every person knows their place, and in which values are firm and fixed, the fiction explores the difficulty of social belonging in a modern world in which the very idea of social status has something dramatic and impermanent about it.
>
> (1991: 97)

Traditional spatial distinctions, writes Victoria Rosner in *Modernism and the Architecture of Private Life*, "helped to manage the diverse household community, creating a domestic space that stratified the many different social groups that lived in such close proximity" (2005: 64). The idea of the "traditional" or "country house" evokes master–servant relationships, as well as a gendered understanding of spaces like the "study" or the "morning room." Even within the house, there is a concern that everyone should be "in place."

However, characters frequently fail to fulfill their structural roles: from the rule-breaking *The Murder of Roger Ackroyd* (1926), in which the parlor maid Ursula is actually married to the heir, to *Ordeal by Innocence*, in which adopted child Micky clings to his previous identity. Questions of identity are frequently thematized in detective fiction, but are uniquely fraught in the house novel. Conflicting and hidden identities are often red herrings, but they further destabilize the concept of "home." The notion of being "in one's place" is thoroughly dissolved by characters such as Mary Dove in *Pocket Full of Rye* and Lucy Eyelesbarrow in *4:50 From Paddington*. While Merja Makinen and York mention these two characters in the same capacity, and though both are resourceful young women who turn a shortage in the labor market into an opportunity, they perform very different roles. Mary, whose perfect composure and "butter wouldn't melt" appearance make her an ideal criminal, is obviously "playing a part [...] not the part of a housekeeper, but the part of Mary Dove" (Christie 1953: 72, 26). Lucy, while she is also playing a part, is emphatically a detective heroine, an Archie Goodwin to Miss Marple's Nero Wolfe.

In taking a position at Rutherford Hall "undercover," Lucy creates a bridge between the detective and the family, but also between the detective and the domestic. Anna Marie Taylor comments on the "authorization of the domestic and the positive value placed on feminine talk" in Christie's work (1990: 143), but Lucy's unique role demonstrates a new permeability of boundaries. Hidden identifications create questions around access and knowledge: the conclusion of *Hercule Poirot's Christmas* re-identifies no fewer than three characters, and changes the structure of the "family" each time. Pilar Estravados appears to belong, but is revealed as an impostor, whereas Superintendent Sugden seems to be an outsider, but is in fact a blood relation. Christie continued to invent new ways to destabilize the comfortable and traditional, and her rewritings of the home and the family reminded her reader that the places that seem most familiar may be the least understood.

Eric Prieto proposes that place is "useful as a kind of ideological lens—a way to bring into focus and illuminate both the unspoken assumptions and the ideological objectives that bring people to the place" (2013: 15). Detective stories seem, by their form, to bring order to chaos; indeed, numerous critics assert, in the words of James E. Bartell, that "[m]urder is a momentary expression of the breakdown of the rules that tie a social class together. It is assumed that the principles that govern this class are generally viable and work to produce a basic social harmony" (1997: 183). However, Christie insists on the essential and hazardous normality of the criminal, who necessarily "belongs." Crime is not a breakdown of societal norms in her work, but a confirmation of them, and Christie stresses that such possibilities lurk in all families, and in all houses.

Agatha Christie's house is only occasionally a country house, and rarely is it truly a home. Instead, her deconstructed house represents the infinite entanglements of family and dependence. Christie questions whether it is possible to escape these ties, but the only time she explicitly addresses the question is in *Crooked House:* Aristide Leonides believes that "someone must be my successor, must take upon him or herself the burden of responsibility for the rest of the family" (Christie [1949] 1986: 159). The patriarch leaves his fortune, and his power, to his granddaughter Sofia, but at the conclusion of the novel she agrees to marry the narrator and to "forget the little Crooked House [...] Don't worry about them any more" (223). Sofia's implied refusal of family duties demonstrates that it is possible to break the dangerous pattern of dependence that characterizes Christie's families, and it is revealing that she does so by agreeing to forget the *house.* The house, through all its manifestations, engaged Christie throughout her career. Her ominous figuration of the unhomelike house refuses to provide the reassuring stability of tradition or the comfortable security of family; instead, she insists that this most recognizable place, in fact, shelters the most dangerous unknowns.

REFERENCES

Auden, W. H. (1948), "The Guilty Vicarage," *Harper's Magazine*, 196 (1176): 406–12. Available online: https://harpers.org/archive/1948/05/the-guilty-vicarage/ (accessed January 15, 2021).

Bachelard, G. (1994), *The Poetics of Space*, trans. M. Jolas, Boston: Beacon Press.

Bargainnier, E. F. (1980), *The Gentle Art of Murder: The Detective Fiction of Agatha Christie*, Bowling Green, OH: Bowling Green University Press.

Barnard, R. (1980), *A Talent to Deceive: An Appreciation of Agatha Christie*, New York: Dodd, Mead.

Bartell, J. E. (1997), "The Bureaucrat as Reader," in J. H. Delamater and R. Prigozy (eds), *Theory and Practice of Classic Detective Fiction*, 177–92, London: Greenwood Press.

Bernthal, J. C. (2016), *Queering Agatha Christie*, London: Palgrave Macmillan.

Birns, N. and M. B. Birns (1990), "Agatha Christie: Modern and Modernist," in R. G. Walker and J. M. Frazer (eds), *The Cunning Craft*, 120–34, Macomb: Western Illinois University.

Bright, B. (2015), "'You'd be surprised if you knew how very few distinct types there are': Agatha Christie's Typologies of the House, the Village, the City, and the Holiday" in "Beyond the Scene of the Crime: Place in Golden Age Detective Fiction," 51–116, doctoral thesis, Goldsmiths, University of London. Available online: http://research.gold.ac.uk/id/eprint/11637/ (accessed January 12, 2021).

Casey, E. S. (1997), *The Fate of Place: A Philosophical History*, Berkeley: University of California Press.

Casey, E. S. (2001), "Body, Self, and Landscape," in P. C. Adams, S. Hoelscher, and K. E. Till (eds), *Textures of Place: Exploring Humanist Geographies*, 403–23, Minneapolis: University of Minnesota Press.

Chandler, R. ([1944] 1992), "The Simple Art of Murder," in H. Haycraft (ed), *The Art of the Mystery Story*, 222–37, New York: Carroll & Graf.

Christie, A. ([1920] 2001), *The Mysterious Affair at Styles*, London: HarperCollins.

Christie, A. ([1923] 1998), "Christmas Adventure," in *While the Light Lasts*, London: HarperCollins.

Christie, A. ([1937] 2001), *Death on the Nile*, London: HarperCollins.

Christie, A. ([1938] 2001), *Hercule Poirot's Christmas*, London: HarperCollins.

Christie, A. ([1949] 1986), *Crooked House*, New York: Pocket.

Christie, A. (1953), *A Pocket Full of Rye*, London: Collins.

Christie, A. (1955), interview, BBC radio, February 13.

Christie, A. (1957), *4:50 from Paddington*, London: Collins.

Christie, A. ([1958] 1970), *Dead Man's Folly*, London: Fontana.

Christie, A. ([1958] 1959), *Ordeal by Innocence*, New York: Dodd, Mead.

Christie, A. ([1960] 1999), "The Adventure of the Christmas Pudding," in *Hercule Poirot: The Complete Short Stories*, London: HarperCollins.

Christie, A. (1970), "Introduction," in *Passenger to Frankfurt*, London: Dodd, Mead.

Cresswell, T. (1994), *Place: A Short Introduction*, London: Blackwell.

Cresswell, T. (1996), *In Place, Out of Place: Geography, Identity, and Transgression*, Minneapolis: University of Minnesota Press.

Culler, J. (2002), *Structuralist Poetics: Structuralism, Linguistics, and the Study of Literature*, London: Routledge.

Eco, U. (1979), *The Role of the Reader*, Bloomington: Indiana University Press.

Fletcher, L. (2016), *Popular Fiction and Spatiality: Reading Genre Settings*, New York: Palgrave.

Freud, S. ([1919] 2001), "The 'Uncanny,'" trans. J. Strachey, in A. Freud (ed), *Complete Psychological Works of Sigmund Freud*, vol. XVII, 217–56, London: Vintage, 2001.

Gill, R. (1972), *The English Country House and the Literary Imagination*, New Haven, CT: Yale University Press.

Grella, G. (1970), "Murder and Manners: The Formal Detective Novel," *NOVEL: A Forum on Fiction*, 4 (1): 30–48.

Jentsch, E. ([1906] 1996), "On the Psychology of the Uncanny," *Angelaki*, 2 (1): 7–15.

Kelsall, M. M. (1993), *The Great Good Place: The Country House and English Literature*, United Kingdom: Harvester Wheatsheaf.

Kort, W. A. (2004), *Place and Space in Modern Fiction*, Gainesville, FL: University Press of Florida; London: Eurospan.

Lefebvre, H. ([1974] 1991), *The Production of Space*, trans. D. Nicholson-Smith, Oxford: Blackwell.

Lehman, D. (2000), *The Perfect Murder: A Study in Detection*, Ann Arbor: University of Michigan Press.

Light, A. (1991), *Forever England: Femininity, Literature, and Conservatism between the Wars*, London: Routledge.

Lutwack, L. (1984), *The Role of Place in Literature*, Syracuse, NY: Syracuse University Press.

Makinen, M. (2006), *Agatha Christie: Investigating Femininity*, Basingstoke: Palgrave Macmillan.

Maida, P. D. and N. B. Spornick (1982), *Murder She Wrote: A Study of Agatha Christie's Detective Fiction*, Bowling Green, OH: Bowling Green University Press.

Malpas, J. (2007), *Place and Experience: A Philosophical Topography*, Cambridge: Cambridge University Press.

McManis, D. R. (1978), "Places for Mysteries," *Geographical Review*, 68 (3): 319–34.

Mezei, K. and C. Briganti (2002), "Reading the House: A Literary Perspective," *Signs*, 27 (3): 837–46.

Morrison, B. (2011), "The Country House and the English Novel," *Guardian*, June 11. Available online: http://www.theguardian.com/books/2011/jun/11/country-house-novels-blake-morrison (accessed January 10, 2021).

O'Donovan, G. (2017), review in *The Telegraph*, December 17. Available online: https://www.telegraph.co.uk/tv/2017/12/17/agatha-christies-crooked-house-sumptuous-fifties-adaptation/ (accessed January 12, 2021).

Paul, R. S. (1997), *Whatever Happened to Sherlock Holmes?: Detective Fiction, Popular Theology, and Society*, Carbondale: Southern Illinois University Press.

Prieto, E. (2013), *Literature, Geography, and the Postmodern Poetics of Place*, New York: Palgrave Macmillan.

Pyrhönen, H. (1999), *Murder and Mayhem: Narrative and Moral Problems in the Detective Story*, Toronto: University of Toronto.

Rosner, V. (2005), *Modernism and the Architecture of Private Life*, New York: Columbia University Press.

Sayers, D. L. ([1937] 1992), "Gaudy Night," in H. Haycraft (ed), *The Art of the Mystery Story*, 208–21, New York: Carroll & Graf.

Taylor, A. M. (1990), "Home Is Where the Hearth Is: The Englishness of Agatha Christie's Marple Novels," in I. A. Bell and G. Daldry (eds), *Watching the Detectives: Essays on Crime Fiction*, 134–48, London: Macmillan.

Todorov, T. (1977), *The Poetics of Prose*, Oxford: Blackwell; Ithaca, NY: Cornell University Press.

Wyndham, F. (1966), "The Algebra of Agatha Christie," *Sunday Times*, February 17: 25.

York, R. A. (2007), *Agatha Christie: Power and Illusion*, Basingstoke: Palgrave Macmillan.

CHAPTER THIRTEEN

Agatha Christie, the Law, and Justice

MARY ANNA EVANS

THE LITERATURE OF JUSTICE

Crime fiction could be, and I would argue that it should be, called the literature of justice. Every crime story begins with a disturbance of justice: someone has broken one or more of their society's laws, usually the law proscribing murder.[1] These works center on the survivors'—and the reader's—desire for the killer to bear the consequences of murder. Christie addresses the tension between this desire and a recognition of the need for societal and legal norms to govern it, even by an individual willing to act on a thirst for revenge, when she puts these words into the mouth of Colonel Arbuthnot, her "honourable, slightly stupid, upright" but vengeful "Englishman" in *Murder on the Orient Express*: "Well, you can't go about having blood feuds and stabbing each other" (Christie 1934a: 133, 131).

Crime fiction resonates with our need to believe that justice can be done after a violent disruption, and it investigates the question of what, exactly, constitutes justice in such cases. In this chapter, I will discuss current scholarship on the relationship between crime fiction, the law, and this desire for justice, suggesting areas where further investigation would be valuable and presenting

---

[1] For the purposes of this discussion, I will focus on the fictional treatment of murder, particularly the pursuit of justice by the work's characters in a case of murder. The percentage of detective novels and stories that do not involve a murder is so small that this plot element often makes them famous. An example of this phenomenon would be Dorothy L. Sayers' *Gaudy Night* (1935).

case studies on justice as explored in two of Agatha Christie's most famous works: *Witness for the Prosecution* and *Murder on the Orient Express*.

To begin, it is worth considering the definition of the word "justice." Wai Chee Dimock opens *Residues of Justice: Literature, Law, and Philosophy* with a useful and succinct overview of historical philosophical approaches to the concept of justice, beginning with Aristotle's rather mathematical view in *Nichomachean Ethics* that justice is a "species of the proportionate," a virtue "that not only covers all agents and events but 'weighs' each in turn, resolving each of them into a common measure of right and wrong, merit and desert, obligation and entitlement." Dimock goes on, however, to observe that Aristotle's "working definition" of justice is more modest. Setting aside the ideal that "in justice is every virtue comprehended," he says that "all events what we are investigating is the justice which is a *part* of virtue," and as for "the justice, then which answers to the whole of virtue, we may leave [it] on one side" (qtd in Dimock 1997: 3–4).

Dimock then traces an erosion over time in this limited approach, marked by an ascendancy of justice as a philosophical concept that owes much to John Rawls's *A Theory of Justice* (1971), which she compares to *Nichomachean Ethics*. Rawls presents justice as "analogous to truth," "an absolute ideal," "an ontological given," "an objective reality," and an "axiomatic expression of human reason itself" (4). She sees this understanding as one that is not limited to philosophers but is in fact the "commonsensical understanding" of the general public (4). In more common terms, it is human nature to believe that finding just solutions to conflict is simply a matter of common sense. In our hearts, we believe justice is immutable and that it will prevail. Or, if it does not, then it should. Christie speaks to this ontological view in *Death Comes as the End*: "Justice is justice, in this world and the next, a business that moves slowly but is adjusted with righteousness in the end" (1944: 192), yet her words in *Sparkling Cyanide*—"You can't play safe and take care of your own skin when it's a question of justice" (1945: 247)—do not suggest a passive, fatalistic acceptance that justice will inevitably be done. For Christie, active pursuit of justice is laudable; her characters recognize that the pursuit can fail.

Dimock's approach to recognizing that justice can, and does, fail is to acknowledge those failures as the "residues of justice" for which she titles her book. These residues include the losses that occur when real-life conflicts are adjudicated (5). It is my position that all crime fiction engages with questions of justice, but there is a distinction between works which suggest that justice is satisfied when the perpetrator of a crime is punished and works which recognize that residues of injustice invariably remain. In crime fiction that deals with murder, as most crime fiction does, there is the inarguable fact that the victim remains dead and their loved ones remain bereaved; complete justice would require restoring the victim to life and, thus, a residue of justice not achieved will always remain, and the thoughtful author will acknowledge this. There is also the inarguable fact that courtrooms sometimes render decisions that violate the public's "commonsensical understanding" of justice. It is in this liminal space between justice and injustice that Christie did some of her most creative and influential work, going far beyond tales of open-and-shut cases where the just outcome is obvious. Critics who consider her stories formulaic often ignore her forays into the realm of ambiguity in stories that ask, "What is the just outcome in this situation?" and then leave the reader to ponder. A famous example of a critic who willfully overlooks this subtlety is Raymond Chandler in his commentary on *Murder on the Orient Express* in "The Simple Art of Murder":

> M. Poirot decries that nobody on a certain through sleeper could have done the murder alone, therefore everybody did it together, breaking the process down into a series of simple operations, like assembling an egg-beater [...] Only a halfwit could guess it.
>
> (in Haycraft [1946] 1975: 230)

By focusing on the justifiably famous twist ending without acknowledging the moral ambiguity behind the conspirators' actions, Chandler denies the boldness with which Christie asks her readers to meditate on what they consider to be a just outcome in this situation.

When twelve bereaved survivors of an unpunished murder band together on the Orient Express as a jury unsanctioned by law to execute a killer who has escaped a courtroom unpunished, they are intent on sweeping away a residue of injustice, but can they be successful when their vigilantism leaves its own residue? When a retired judge enacts vigilante justice in *And Then There Were None* (1939), then uses suicide to administer the same punishment to himself, has he truly swept up residual injustice? When three murderers who had previously escaped punishment come to grief in *Cards on the Table* (1936), without the truth of their crimes becoming public, is that justice? When Poirot decides for himself in *Curtain* (1975) that he must kill an Iago-like sociopath who drives others to murder in ways so diabolical that Poirot does not believe the man will ever be punished, is there no element of injustice to his unilateral decision? As J.C. Bernthal has written of Poirot's actions in *Curtain*, "If the detective—the symbol of law and order—cannot be trusted to be readers' moral compass, whom or what can be trusted?" (33). Are the efforts of these characters to right wrongs akin to the physical concept of an entropic process that accomplishes the work that was its goal, yet invariably results in losses to the system's capacity to do work? In these texts and others, Christie explores the consequences of humans' imperfect attempts to enact justice.

CHRISTIE, CRIME FICTION, AND JUSTICE IN THE LITERATURE

Scholarly work that directly addresses Christie's treatment of justice is comparatively scant. Work addressing justice in crime fiction in general exists, but the topic is more often addressed as part of a discussion focused elsewhere. However, two papers that do have a primary aim of investigating Christie's portrayal of justice were published in recent issues of *Clues: A Journal of Detection*: "Killing Innocence: Obstructions of Justice in Late-Interwar British Crime Fiction" by J.C. Bernthal (2019: 30–9), and a 2010 article on "Transforming Justice? *Murder on the Orient Express* 1934–2010," by Merja Makinen and Patrick Phillips (2016: 41–51). In addition, a 2010 book, *Revenge versus Legality: Wild Justice from Balzac to Clint Eastwood and Abu Ghraib* by Katherine Maynard, Jarod Kearney, and James Guimond (2010), includes a discussion of *Murder on the Orient Express* as part of its exploration of the law and the human desire for retribution.

Bernthal's essay on justice in late-interwar British crime fiction addresses Christie's *And Then There Were None* and Raymond Postgate's *Verdict of Twelve*, considering the broader social contexts of two novels that center on failures of the British legal system to convict murderers. He presents the resolution of *And Then There Were None* as an invitation for readers to consider that "a gross perversion of legal justice might have been necessary to expunge threats that are woven into respectable British society," stating the root cause of this necessity clearly: "The law—the current state of authority and security—is not enough" (794/3272).

Makinen and Phillips, writing on another of Christie's books centered on vengeance as a means to right a justice system's perceived wrong, are less willing to consider an act of retribution "necessary." They rightly point out that *Murder on the Orient Express* (1934) "explores the theme of justice in relation to three categories: retribution, what is legally possible, and what is morally right" (1145/4067). They point out that "Cassetti's murder is positioned as a morally just execution precisely because of the excessive but precise number of stab wounds—12," saying that Christie "is very careful to cast the murder of Cassetti as justice and neither savage nor intemperate" (1151–1155/4067). More willing than Bernthal (and this author) to criticize Christie's implicit approval of her vigilante characters' act of retribution, they state the conundrum at the center of the novel thus: "[E]veryone has done it. Even more outrageously, the victim is transposed into the villain, and the deliberate, calculating murderers are recast as piteous victims and allowed to go free" (1093/4067).

Maynard, Kearney, and Guimond devote a full section of their chapter on revenge and the detective tradition to Christie. Like Makinen and Phillips, their discussion focuses on *Murder on the Orient Express*. They compare it to Arthur

Conan Doyle's "Charles Augustus Milverton," emphasizing the importance of masking and concealed identities in both texts. In addressing the conflict between the conspirators' act, a murder committed as an act of retribution, and their victim's act, a child-murder committed as part of a crime of extortion that resulted in the deaths of three other innocent parties, they quote the conspirators' leader as she justifies the murder, then accept her explanation by saying that it "is in a factual sense a confession, but in a moral sense it is the justification for what she and the other passengers have done as a group" (36). They suggest that Christie successfully justified the unlawful revenge taken by the passengers on the Orient Express, emphasizing Poirot's use of the word "honour" in the final sentence of the book when he says that he has the "honour to retire from the case" (Christie 1934a: 264); then they make this suggestion explicit by writing that "[r]evenge and homicide—for the right reasons—will be just, and truth and the law will be ignored" (37).

Unlike the Makinen and Phillips paper and the work of Maynard, Kearney, and Guimond, Stuart Sim's *Justice and Revenge in Contemporary American Crime Fiction* (2015) addresses crime fiction in general, rather than Christie in particular, which is to be expected, as she is not an American author nor did she write in the late-twentieth-century period that is the book's focus. However, it is worth considering this book here, because the hallmarks of the darker view of justice seen in the late twentieth century that Sim discusses in this book are visible in Christie's much earlier work. He sees a dark turn in American crime fiction near the end of the twentieth century as a response to "a culture in which moral values are in decline" (2), resulting in a world where "[d]etectives find themselves compelled to commit criminal acts in order to punish criminals, since the justice system can no longer reliably guarantee that this outcome will occur" (3). I do not argue with his conclusion that a distrust of the justice system can generate stories of retribution aimed at enacting the kind of "absolute justice" written about by James Ellroy, which Sim defines as "bypassing the judicial system and taking the law in one's own hands" (18).[2] However, I do think it noteworthy that Christie's published work shows a deep interest in extrajudicial justice far earlier in the twentieth century that the period Sim is discussing.

In a key conversation in *Murder on the Orient Express* during which Princess Dragomiroff alludes to the vengeance plot at its heart, Christie uses the phrase "strict justice" (1934a: 229), but this is by no means a new concept for her. She uses the phrase significantly earlier in a letter written during her world tour in 1922. In this letter, she writes of a pictorial history made by Indigenous Tasmanians who had documented both the execution of an Indigenous man for

---

[2]In Ellroy's *LA Confidential* ([1990] 2013), the phrase "absolute justice" appears fourteen times, used in much the same way that Christie had used the phrase "strict justice" (229) in *Murder on the Orient Express* (1934) fifty-six years before.

killing a White man and the hanging of a White man for killing an Indigenous Tasmanian, and she says that this is done "in accordance with strict justice" (Prichard 2012: 166). Her long-standing interest in "strict justice," which dates, as these quotes show, at least to 1922 and 1934, and Ellroy's interest in "absolute justice," seen in *LA Confidential* in 1990, are related to the "wild justice" that Susan Jacoby explores in her book of that name, which takes its title from Francis Bacon's essay "Of Revenge": Revenge is a kind of wild justice, which the more man's nature runs to, the more ought law to weed it out (1: 1983). Jacoby posits that "The proper relationship between justice and revenge has been a major preoccupation of literature, religion, and law" (4), a preoccupation that Christie, Ellroy, and the late-twentieth-century authors discussed by Sim used literature to explore.

My intent here is not to contradict Sim. His conclusion is apt that there is a subversive quality to the work of the authors whom he highlights. What is more, he acknowledges the popularity of the crime fiction genre, while refusing to suggest that this necessarily means that the works within the genre are insubstantial, a position with which I concur. Rather, he credits them with intellectual depth that can be a "powerful social critique" that "deserves to be prized as such" (118). My purpose here is to claim this depth for Christie's work, particularly those texts that address extrajudicial justice. Sim discusses authors of early hardboiled detective fiction like Raymond Chandler and Dashiell Hammett in his introduction (1–14), but sets them apart from the later writers highlighted in the book because of his position that characters of their era retain the status of "moral exemplar" (2). He specifically gives Chandler's Philip Marlowe as an example of a protagonist who is "a heroic figure no matter how corrupt the society around him may turn out to be" in tales where "[c]losure of some kind is always achieved" (2). However, Christie did not always give her detectives the status of "moral exemplar," nor did she always give them closure, and she was inarguably a contemporary of Chandler and Hammett. She made her authorial debut two years before Hammett and twelve years before Chandler and she continued to publish throughout both their careers, sometimes in the same publications. Thus, it is noteworthy that she was willing to take her "heroic figure," Hercule Poirot, into murkier moral waters.

For example, in *Murder on the Orient Express* (1934), Poirot allows twelve premeditated murderers to walk free without even a court trial. *Curtain*, in which she places Poirot in the precise position described by Sim—"compelled to commit criminal acts in order to punish criminals, since the justice system can no longer reliably guarantee that this outcome will occur" (3)—was written in the early 1940s, decades before the late-twentieth-century period that Sim explores. Specifically, Poirot commits premeditated murder himself in *Curtain* for complicated reasons that leave him saying, "I do not know Hastings, if what I have done is justified or not justified" (214). In these and other texts, Christie can rightly be seen as a progenitor of the authors whom Sim discusses. Like them, she approached the question of justice with the skeptical eye that Julian Symons described in *Bloody Murder* when he wrote that the social attitude of the crime novel is "often radical in the sense of questioning some aspect of law, justice or the way society is run" (Symons 1985: 163).

Turning to works of crime fiction scholarship that, though not focused on matters of justice, do address the topic as part of their argument, Susan Rowland's *From Agatha Christie to Ruth Rendell: British Women Writers in Detective and Crime Fiction* (2004) makes the essential point that "crime fiction, when defined as *fiction*, is offering the story that the laws cannot or will not tell [...] that there is more to crime than the institutionalised stories told in courts and police stations" (17). She also addresses the problematic interface between women and the laws that govern them, saying, "What the anti-heroic feminised detective discovers is that the law is not a stable, infallible system for administering justice, and that its instabilities are often bound up with formations of gender" (21).

Barnard, too, considered justice in his analysis of some of Christie's most well-known works in his *A Talent to Deceive: An Appreciation of Agatha Christie* (1980). In discussing the community-destabilizing situation of an unpunished murderer, he said of *Murder on the Orient Express*, "They had rid the world of a monster the law could not reach, and they are therefore not punished. This is a natural extension of Christie's respect in the thrillers for people who take the law into their own hands—and in its turn it is pushed to its logical conclusion in the solution to *Curtain*" (1980: 41–2). Elaborating on his position that Christie's personal opinions are not always evident in her treatment of issues like justice, he said that "[o]ne of the few Christie opinions which come over strongly from the books is one in favor of capital punishment." Supporting this view, he cites this statement by Miss Marple in *4:50 from Paddington* (1957): "I am really very, very sorry [...] that they have abolished capital punishment because I do feel that if there is anyone who ought to hang, it is Dr. Quimper" ([1957] 2011: 270). By contrast, he states that she offers a less conservative view of law enforcement in *Five Little Pigs* (1942) that acknowledges the tension between the idealized and actual operation of any real world justice system: "All the images, taken together, suggest very effectively, even scathingly, the moral duality of law and its enforcement [...] leaving the spectator not exhilarated, as after an apparently equal fight, but nastily conscious of the eye-for-an-eye aspects—as well as the hypocrisy—of the judicial process" (Barnard 1980: 85).

In *The Imagination of Evil: Detective Fiction and the Modern World* (2011), Mary Evans (no relation to the author) considers crime fiction's interface with social structures related to justice, writing that "crime fiction has an honourable history of maintaining a social presence for radical views about crime and punishment" (3). She goes further, emphasizing the widespread desire for stories that explore issues of justice, noting that "crime fiction, therefore, can satisfy public demand for fiction which provides the reassurance of capture and disclosure, but it can also provide something of an imaginative bulwark about facile judgements of guilt and innocence familiar to many discussions of crime in the real world" (12). Evans, a sociologist, offers in this text a perceptive analysis of the intersection between crime fiction and crime in the material world.

Crime fiction's capacity for such critique makes it well suited to the approach used by scholars of law and literature, as laws provide the framework for a society to administer justice. The laws governing the society that experiences the murder in a work of crime fiction are essential scaffolding supporting the author's work, and they are generally modeled on real-life laws. Thus, it is appropriate to consider work published in the field of law and literature as an extension of the literature relating crime fiction to justice, despite the fact that scholars of law and literature rarely address crime fiction works that are, like Christie's, aimed at popular audiences, a category of texts that I will refer to here as "genre crime fiction." Dimock, whose theories of "residues of justice" I have used as a springboard for this discussion, develops her thesis that seeking justice leaves insoluble residues by applying it in most cases to works by writers like Melville, Chopin, and Whitman whose works are considered part of the literary canon, without considering works of genre crime fiction (Dimock 1997). A review of recently published work in law and literature shows that this exclusion of popular fiction is common in that field.

While *Fatal Fictions: Crime and Investigation in Law and Literature* (2017), one in a series of edited collections on the topic, states that it is specifically intended to present "scholarly investigation of the law and literature of crime" (LaCroix, McAdams, and Nussmann 2017: xv),[3] the volume is less useful to scholars of crime fiction as a genre than might have been hoped. Despite a statement that its topics span genres "from tragedy to science fiction, lyric poetry, and mystery novels" (xvi), crime fiction that was published as such receives little attention. While essays that analyze classic works by canonical authors like Shakespeare (Strier and McAdams 2017: 111–38; Foa 2017: 139–48) and Aeschylus (Telech 2017: 15–40) are valuable, as is an analysis of Supreme Court justice Clarence Thomas's self-identification with the also-canonical James Baldwin's character Bigger Thomas (Driver 2017: 159–76), genre crime fiction is only represented in an informal essay by best-selling crime novelist Scott Turow (1–12) and in a single critical chapter by Steven Wilf on

---

[3]This is the fourth in a series of volumes emerging from conferences on law and literature at the University of Chicago Law School. I chose this volume for consideration based on the editors' observation that crime had been a recurring theme in the earlier collections, "even though the organizing topic was not crime, which suggests that criminal fiction deserves some sustained attention of its own" (xv).

historical devices in detective fiction (275–99) that includes discussions of work by Dorothy L. Sayers, Sarah Caudwell, and Batya Gur. A similar volume with a focus on the analysis of genre crime fiction by law and literature scholars would tap the potential of their methodologies for providing insight into the work of writers of popular crime fiction who, like Christie, spend their careers examining crime in society. In fact, Christie engaged so thoroughly and so frequently with her country's legal system and with the concept of justice that an entire volume approaching her work from a law and literature standpoint would be worthwhile.

Saul Levmore and Martha C. Nussbaum's *American Guy, Masculinity in American Law and Literature* (2014) and Maria Aristodemou's *Law & Literature: Journeys from Her to Eternity* (2000)—two volumes that provide an entry point to law and literature for those working on gender studies—also exclude genre crime fiction in favor of authors like William Faulkner, Ossie Davis, Ernest Hemingway, Harper Lee, Philip Roth, and Herman Melville. For Christie scholars, the topic of *Masculinity in American Law and Literature* is less immediately useful to the study of the literary works of a British woman, but *Law & Literature: Journeys from Her to Eternity* includes an introduction that gives a useful overview of the field's philosophical underpinnings, highlighting language, law, and literature as sites of struggle (Aristodemou 2000: 1–28).

Kieran Dolan, writing in *A Critical Introduction to Law and Literature* (2007), chooses a historical frame for introducing the field to his readers, paying more attention than the other texts discussed here to legal documents as literature, with correspondingly less attention paid to fiction and no attention paid to genre crime fiction. However, the chapter on Victorian women's issues is of use in contextualizing Christie's portrayal of women in terms of the laws of the society in which she was born. The chapter on modernism, which defines modernism as "a cultural movement critical of modernity," is helpful in placing the cultural critique seen in her fiction, particularly in the Westmacott novels, squarely within the modernist movement.

Law and Literature, the flagship journal for the field of law and literature, also focuses on canonical and literary texts. Although it has in the past published articles on genre crime fiction, including essays on the work of Chester Himes (Cavallaro 2007) and on history and narrative conventions in hardboiled detective narratives (Sargent 2010), Christie and most of her peers have been neglected. Within the five-year period 2016–21, articles on topics in other subcategories of genre fiction including legal form in speculative fiction (Hourigan 2018), the political aspects of movies based on comic books (Davison-Vecchione 2017), and literary aspects of horror fiction (Sollazzo 2017) were published, as were reviews of books on graphic storytelling (Davison-Vecchione 2017) and on science fiction (Gandorfer 2019), but those exceptions only call attention to the absence of commentary on genre crime fiction, which has evident links to the journal's theme. The only published work listed in the tables of contents for those five years that is clearly related to genre crime fiction is a review of *Holmes Reads Holmes: Reflections on the Real-Life Links between the Jurist and the Detective in the Library, in the Courtroom, and on the Battlefield* (Butler and Rains 2021). During that five-year period, a journal focusing on a subspecialty within law, *Entertainment and Sports Law Journal*, did publish work on Christie, an essay titled "'Bad Business': Capitalism and Criminality in Agatha Christie's Novels" (Nicol 2019). This essay, although it was focused more on economics than the law, argued that Christie's frequently negative portrayal of financiers reflected a society more critical of capitalism during the interwar and postwar periods. An expansion of this analysis to consider Christie's portrayal of laws, their limitations, and their enforcement during the same period would be useful.

In two books entitled *Law and Literature*, Richard A. Posner ([1988] 2009) and María José Falcón y Tella (2016)[4] present analyses of many works of fiction, most of them considered to be literary fiction, but they do both consider a relatively recent book of popular crime fiction, John Grisham's *The Firm* (1991). While discussing Grisham's work in general and *The Firm* in particular, Posner opens the door to serious analysis of genre crime fiction, writing that "[p]opular novels about law, [...] some of which have shaded into or become classic works of literature, can profitably be studied as literature," although he judges that they are "unlikely to attain classic status" (55).[5] He calls *The Firm* "an allegory of professional greed and amorality" that "is better read as an engaging potboiler" (56), but concludes his discussion of Grisham's work by writing, "Popular literature can supplement journalism in prompting social reform" (60), a position with which I concur. Posner's section on the law in popular culture (51–60) goes beyond fiction on the printed page to embrace fictional stories in television and film, offering commentary on *The Bonfire of the Vanities*, *The Caine Mutiny*, *My Cousin Vinny*, and *Rumpole of the Bailey*. Falcón y Tella limits her discussion of genre crime fiction to *The Firm*, faintly praising Grisham's work as "not always superficial" (2016: 221) and drawing a conclusion that "*The Firm* can be seen as a kind of allegory of the 'aprofessional professional'" that can be read as a "simple page-turner" (222), which tracks Posner's words rather closely. Falcón y Tella's opinion that *The Firm* is a

---

[4]Falcón y Tella's book is of interest as a work written in Spanish but available in English that offers a viewpoint from someone living in a country with a legal system that differs from the more-commonly-written-about British and American systems.

[5]His definition of classic status cites George Orwell, Samuel Johnson, and David Hume as background for a criterion that "a work of literature can be judged great only by its ability to survive in competition with other works, not only works of literature but other cultural products as well" (22). I find this definition limited for reasons that include its reliance on literature's worth being judged by its success in the marketplace, but it must be noted that it does not exclude Christie's work, which is still widely read after a century.

"genuine treatment of legal sociology, which describes in fairly detailed fashion the way in which large law firms [...] use all kinds of influences and pressure, legal ruses and tricks, to deprive the law of all its meaning, purpose and justice" (221), aligns with my thesis that the engagement of popular crime fiction with serious issues including justice is worthy of study.

The value of more dialogue between scholars working in crime fiction intended for popular audiences and those working in law and literature seems evident, given their common interest in the intersection between art, society, and the laws that govern society. I look forward to seeing more cross-fertilization between the fields, and I suggest that Christie's large body of work written over a half-century and still read after a century in print, all of it engaging with the law to some degree, offers rich opportunities for such interdisciplinary study.

"I DON'T KNOW A THING ABOUT LEGAL PROCEDURE": CHRISTIE'S OWN VIEW OF HER WORK'S RELATIONSHIP TO THE LAW IN *WITNESS FOR THE PROSECUTION*

It is worth considering Christie's own thoughts about the relationship between legal matters in her fictional world and the laws governing the real world in which she lived. Her autobiography details significant efforts that she made to ensure verisimilitude in her portrayal of her own society's legal system in action, and it indicates that this necessity caused her some anxiety. When asked by producer Peter Saunders to adapt her short story "The Witness for the Prosecution," originally published as "Traitor Hands" in 1925, into the stage play ultimately titled *Witness for the Prosecution* (1953), she said, "I didn't want to write it; I was terrified of writing it [...] I don't know a thing about legal procedure. I should make a fool of myself" ([1977] 2012: 514). Implicit in her words is a desire to portray legal procedures accurately, and her concern that errors in portraying them would make her look like "a fool" shows that she believed that the play's audience would expect that accuracy.

She did agree to write the adaptation, preparing by reading about famous trials, speaking with solicitors and barristers, and sitting in on courtroom trials, all in the name of accuracy ([1977] 2012: 515). This anxiety may have been partly rooted in criticism she received more than thirty years before, recorded in an undated, typed note signed LDH held in the files of her first publisher, The Bodley Head. Written while The Bodley Head was deciding whether to publish her debut, *The Mysterious Affair at Styles* (1920), the note conveys very specific criticism, intimating that the courtroom scene was poorly written and that the reviewer suspected that this was the case because the writer was a woman. A handwritten message of encouragement on the typed note suggests that Christie was intended to see this criticism or a copy of it (LDH). This disparagement of her ability to write such a scene also played out during her first meeting with John Lane, founder of The Bodley Head, when he told her that she would need to rewrite the final chapter or find someone to help her with its legal aspects. In her autobiography, she described this meeting, stating, "I had written it as a court scene, but it was quite impossible written like that. It was in no way like a court scene—it would be merely ridiculous" (276).

Her attention to verisimilitude in the courtroom scene in *Witness for the Prosecution* is evidence of her concern, and her publishers' concern, that the systems intended to ensure justice in society be accurately rendered.[6] A particularly intriguing instance of her attention to the smallest details of courtroom verisimilitude can be seen in two passages found in the script for *Witness for the Prosecution*. One of those passages relates to the jurors, only three of whom she directs to be present onstage. In her instructions, Christie specifically notes that one of the three jurors should be a woman.[7] There is no such specification in the original short story, "Traitor Hands" (1925), in the slightly different version of the story published as "The Witness for the Prosecution" (1933), or in the draft typescript held by The Christie Archive Trust (*c.* 1953). There is no plot-driven reason for the specification that a juror be female, other than to provide the opportunity for a barrister to wish that there were more women on the jury to feel sympathy for his charming client (*Witness* 83). While the ability of both the accused killer Leonard Vole and his common-law wife Romaine to manipulate others with their sex appeal is an important part of the storyline, this barrister's line would have been as true if the jury had included no women. (Or eleven.) When considering Christie's desire to realistically depict a courtroom, the key point to be made about the barrister's statement is his—and Christie's—implicit acknowledgment that gender remained a consideration in jury selection in 1953. This was a real-world aspect of the English justice system that she intentionally included in her text.

This stage direction can be seen as simple verisimilitude, a recognition that a female juror was possible and even likely in 1953 that shows concern for accurately portraying a courtroom of the day. A study of female jury participation at the time "Traitor Hands" was written found that the average jury included

---

[6] So, too, is the alternate American ending of *Three Act Tragedy* (1934b), published in the United States as *Murder in Three Acts* (1935), in which the murderer's motive is changed in recognition of the two countries' differing laws governing the legality of divorcing a mentally ill spouse.

[7] Not all of the secondary characters are specified by gender in the stage directions, but her intentions can be inferred for almost all characters by pronouns used to reference them (Greta, Janet MacKenzie, Usher, Judge's Clerk, Inspector Hearne, Dr. Wyatt, Carter), gender-specific descriptive nouns (The Other Woman, Alderman, Policeman), and/or gender-specific titles (Mr. Justice Wainwright, Mr. Mayhew, Foreman of the Jury, Alderman, Policeman). Only Plainclothes Detective, Warder, and Court Stenographer have no gender that can be extrapolated from the text.

women, but in a distinct minority (Crosby), and that all-male juries were still possible. In fact, a drawing of a courtroom published in the same 1925 magazine as "Traitor Hands" shows no female jurors (Reeve). Female jury participation had increased substantially by the play's 1953 premiere, and Christie's direction that one female juror be cast may well have been rooted in her desire for her fictional courtroom to reflect reality.

We know that she considered the appearance of the jury on stage, consulting with Saunders in their correspondence by asking "Have you any strong feelings about including the jury on stage? Does it worry you if the judge and counsel address the audience who would be the jury?" (in Green 346). We also know by her reference to "visible" members of the jury (*Witness* 40), by her stage directions advising directors of low-budget productions that audience members could be invited on stage so that the audience doesn't "lose the benefit of the spectacle of a lot of people in the court scene" (*Witness* 7), and by the staging of the play to include the audience as the unseen members of the jury, that she put considerable thought into the layout of the courtroom and the placement of the people in it while working with Saunders on plans for the play's visual layout. Considering the weight she put into these matters, it seems unlikely that her specifications that a juror should be female was a throwaway decision.

Another stage direction pertinent to Christie's desire for control over the presentation of her fictional courtroom is her instruction that one of the six barristers be a woman. Other than Robarts and the prosecutor Myers, the barristers do not speak, and there is no plot-based reason to specify that they should not all be male. Verisimilitude could again be the reason for this instruction, but if the courtroom in 1953 had become a bastion of gender equality casting both women and men would have been a natural occurrence, and there would have been no need for Christie to direct it specifically.

An intriguing exchange recorded in Christie's correspondence with Saunders includes her flippant remark responding to his suggestion that a woman be cast in the star role of Sir Wilfred—"I know there are women barristers but one always feels that they are rather a joke (343)"—that is hard to reconcile with the fact that she purposefully put a female barrister in her fictional courtroom in a role that is small but is in no way a joke (in Green: 360). The presence of this woman onstage gives context that pushes back against her own statement that she found women in that role ludicrous, opening up the possibility that the joke was a way of shutting down a discussion that was not productive. As Green says, "Romaine makes unashamed use of her sexuality to bamboozle the self-satisfied and easily led male lawyers, and the focus of the play would have changed beyond recognition if the barrister had been a woman" (343).

The presence of women in Christie's 1953 courtroom, especially in places of responsibility where no woman had been acknowledged to be present in the 1925 and 1933 versions, has the appearance of an acknowledgment that the world and its halls of justice had changed. The fact that Christie specifically instructs that they be cast in the minority suggests that her intent was to mimic the real-world courtrooms where women were still making inroads. These women are evidence that Christie, in her fiction, intentionally engaged with the social and legal structures intended to administer justice in the real world.

MURDER ON THE ORIENT EXPRESS: WHAT HAPPENS WHEN THE LAW FAILS?

Christie returned time and again to the question of failed justice, asking the reader to consider the consequences when a murderer walks free. In *Witness for the Prosecution*, Leonard Vole escapes the noose in a miscarriage of justice orchestrated by his common-law wife Romaine, but only for a moment before she transmutes into his executioner when she discovers his treachery toward her. This is far from the only time in Christie's fiction that an unpunished-by-the-law murderer receives punishment, and perhaps justice, sometimes at the hands of characters who act as vigilantes and sometimes at the hands of fate, and Christie is not shy about asking the reader to consider whether this outcome was truly just. For example, *And Then There Were None*, perhaps her most famous novel, revolves around a character's plan to serve as executioner for ten people whom most people would consider to be morally culpable for the death of innocent people, even though circumstances put them outside the reach of the law and allowed them to walk free. This character, a retired judge, credits himself with "a strong sense of justice," claiming to "have always felt strongly that right should prevail" and inviting the reader to agree with him that justice required that his victims (and, in the end, he himself) be punished for their crimes (251). In *Curtain*, Poirot weighs the consequences of killing a man responsible for a long string of deaths who has escaped justice because he has accomplished the killings by manipulating others to do them for him. By killing this man who would likely have always evaded the law, Poirot believes that he has "saved other lives—innocent lives" (214), but this invitation to credit him with a just action is undercut, because he is not as sure as the killer in *And Then There Were None* that he has done the just thing. He questions his actions, saying, "I do not know Hastings, if what I have done is justified or not justified [...] I am very humble and I say like a little child, 'I do not know'" (214).

This is by no means the first or only time that Poirot engages with the question of extrajudicial acts of justice in a way that questions whether they can be used to truly address injustice. In *Cards on the Table*, published in 1936, Superintendent Battle says to Poirot and Ariadne Oliver, "You can't have human beings judging other human beings and taking the law into their own hands," and Poirot answers only, "It happens, Battle. It happens" (163).[8] Pushed to

---

[8]Christie actually includes a spoiler for *Murder on the Orient Express* in *Cards on the Table*, an interesting detail that further connects these two thematically linked works.

elaborate on this statement by Oliver, Poirot says, "You do not comprehend. It is not the victim who concerns me so much. It is the effect on the character of the slayer" (163). These are only some of the most famous examples of works in which Christie questions the ability of a legal system to deliver justice reliably.

In contrast to these statements of doubt concerning acts of vigilantism, Christie expresses an ontological view of justice in a very different setting, ancient Egypt, in *Death Comes as the End* (1944). In this passage, spoken by a female servant to a man of power, she suggests that the destiny or the gods, rather than a human-made court system, push human events toward a state of justice: "Justice is justice, in this world and the next, a business that moves slowly but is adjusted with righteousness in the end" (192). It is important to emphasize that this is a view that does not deny the possibility of justice being achieved by individual extrajudicial acts. It is akin to Dimock's description of Rawls's presentation of justice as "analogous to truth," "an absolute ideal," "an ontological given," "an objective reality," and an "axiomatic expression of human reason itself" (4). Pitting Christie's presentation of Poirot's doubts about extrajudicial justice against her simpler "Justice is justice" commentary puts her in dialogue with herself on this issue. Nowhere is this dialogue more evident than in *Murder on the Orient Express*.

In *Murder on the Orient Express*, Christie creates a situation that speaks to the "commonsensical understanding" of justice described by Dimock (4). A horrific set of crimes—kidnapping, attempted extortion, and the murder of a child—has been committed. The effects of these traumatic events have rippled outward, first consuming the child's mother and unborn sibling through complications of grief-induced premature labor and then triggering her father's grief-stricken suicide. Another innocent party, the child's nursery maid, then committed suicide when wrongly accused of the crime, and it is important to distinguish between the causes of these deaths. The bereaved parents die as a direct result of the actions of the child's murderer, but the nursery maid dies due to a failure of the justice system to identify the guilty party.

Christie does not leave the identity of the guilty party in doubt, nor does she leave any doubt as to the "commonsensical understanding" of the general public that his crime merited a capital punishment that they would have delivered in an act of extrajudicial justice if they had been able; she states that "he would have been lynched by the populace had he not been clever enough to give them the slip" (70). Yet he has evaded any apparent punishment, remaining free and living on an ample income:

Cassetti was the man! But by means of the enormous wealth he had piled up and by the secret hold he had over various persons, he was acquitted on some technical inaccuracy. Notwithstanding that, he would have been lynched by the populace had he not been clever enough to give them the slip [...] Since then he has been a gentleman of leisure, travelling abroad and living on his *rentes.*

(71)

Thus, Christie is invoking both the justice system's futile attempt to bring Cassetti to justice and the failure of the populace to enact an extrajudicial execution. When twelve co-conspirators kill him on the Orient Express, they are doing precisely what the members of little Daisy Armstrong's community had intended for its justice system to do, if Cassetti had not used his wealth and influence to subvert its intent, and what they themselves would have done if he hadn't escaped. But does Christie distinguish their illegal act from the retribution that would have been taken by an angry lynch mob if he had been caught? The conspirators' clear intent to function as a jury shows that their motive was to justify the killing of Cassetti, even if only to themselves, by styling his death as a quasi-legal execution following societally agreed-upon rules for dealing with murder, rather than as a bloodthirsty act of retribution.

Was this Christie's attempt to justify their actions as just? This is not as clear. Makinen and Phillips claim: "Retribution is raised briefly in the novel, but it is linked lexically to personal vengeance and intemperate 'blood feuds'" (1152/4056). This observation is related to John D. Niles's work on feuds and revenge in Anglo-Saxon England, in which he states that "[o]ne of the chief functions of the law codes of the Anglo-Saxons was to distinguish illicit acts of revenge from their lawful counterparts, thereby sanctioning vengeance as a recourse to injury as long as certain rules of engagement were observed" (165). In *Murder on the Orient Express*, Christie marks its cast of conspirators, led by well-known actress and grandmother of the murdered child Linda Arden, as descendants of this tradition, as they strive to distinguish their killing of Cassetti from an illicit act of revenge by cloaking it in modern-day rules of engagement. However, Arden's offer to accept the blame during the final encounter between the twelve executioners and Poirot—"If it must all come out, can't you lay the blame on me and me only?"—signals that she, and by extension her co-conspirators, had not expected their self-identification as an arm of the justice system necessarily to be accepted by a court in whichever country ended up trying the case.

The very proper Colonel Arbuthnot, who had been, according to Arden, "very keen on having twelve of us" (263), is marked by Christie as intent on constructing a plan reflecting a trial by jury that approximated British or American legal procedure. He states his belief in this system explicitly in answer to a pointed question from Poirot—"In fact, Colonel Arbuthnot, you prefer law and order to private vengeance?"—when he says, "Well, you can't go about having blood feuds and stabbing each other like Corsicans or the Mafia [...] Say what you like, trial by jury is a sound system" (131). Later, Poirot incorporates this statement into his explication of the murder plot:

> I remembered a remark of Colonel Arbuthnot's about trial by jury. A jury is composed of twelve people—there were twelve passengers—Ratchett [Cassetti's alias] was stabbed twelve times [...] There was no question as to his guilt. I visualized a self-appointed jury of twelve people who condemned him to death and were forced by exigencies of the case to be their own executioners.
>
> (257–8)

This excerpt makes it clear that Poirot believes Arbuthnot, as a male conspirator, is heavily invested in his society's rules distinguishing justice from vengeful blood feuds. Niles's discussion mentions damage found on male skeletons from Anglo-Saxon England as providing insight into the historical practice of vengeance (165–6). This presumption that revenge is a male act stands in contrast to the fact that Christie addresses, and indeed emphasizes, women's desire for revenge in *Murder on the Orient Express*, as well as in other works including *The Mirror Crack'd From Side to Side* (1962). Her portrayal of female revenge is particularly notable in *Murder on the Orient Express*, as it is framed as the act of an extrajudicial jury in a society where women were still partially excluded from service in courtrooms when the book was published in 1934 (see Crosby (2017) and Anwar (2017)). Based on the longstanding view of vengeance as male and on the contemporaneous exclusion of the women from participation in their society's structures for administering justice (Niles 165–6), the fact that Arden, the child-victim's grieving grandmother, takes leadership in the planning of the revenge/justice plot, along with the fact that five of the twelve conspirators who participated in its enactment were female, displays a criticism of the status quo that is, I argue, far from her reputation as conservative on matters of gender, although it does hew closely to the approval for capital punishment that we have seen she espoused in Miss Marple's voice in *4:50 from Paddington*: "I do feel that if there is anyone who ought to hang, it is Dr. Quimper."

Arbuthnot is the character who is vocal about crafting the conspirators' revenge to imitate the actions of legally sanctioned retribution, whereas the conspirators' female ringleader, Arden, considers that the verdict has already been decided and there is nothing left to do but act: "[Y]ou can't quite imagine what it was like—that awful day in New York. [...] We decided then and there—perhaps we were mad—I don't know—that the sentence of death that Cassetti had escaped had got to be carried out" (262). Arden is old enough to have been well into adulthood before American society recognized her right to vote and, more to the point, sit on a jury (Adams 2014), and this is a personal history that could contribute to some skepticism as to whether what is legal is equivalent to what is just. Dragomiroff, who is portrayed as elderly and thus would have been an adult in the nineteenth century at a time when women in her native Russia also had a limited voice in their society, makes explicit her perception of a separation between what is legal and what is just when she says of Cassetti's murder, "In this case I consider that justice—strict justice—has been done" (229). With lines like these, the reader is asked to conclude, along with Arden and Dragomiroff, that twelve premeditated murderers should evade punishment. They are asked to conclude that it is right for the dead child and her family to receive justice, even though it could be argued that it is denied to her killer. It is as if Christie leads each reader by the hand to this conclusion, while in the end allowing Poirot's final encounter with the killers to acknowledge the insoluble moral conflict embedded in his decision to let them get away with murder. Then, along with her detective, she ends her narrative and leaves the final decision with her reader, as Poirot states that, "having placed my solution before you, I have the honour to retire from the case" (264).

REFERENCES

Adams, J. (2014), *Women and the Vote: A World History*, Oxford: Oxford University Press.

Anwar, S., P. Bayer, and R. Hjalmarsson (2017), "A Jury of Her Peers: The Impact of the First Female Jurors on Criminal Convictions," *The Economic Journal*, 1–48. Available online: https://onlinelibrary.wiley.com/doi/epdf/10.1111/ecoj.12562 (accessed September 5, 2021).

Aristodemou, M. (2000), *Law & Literature: Journeys from Her to Eternity*, Oxford: Oxford University Press.

Aristotle (2009), *The Nicomachean Ethics*, W. D. Ross and L. Brown (eds), Oxford: Oxford University Press.

Barnard, R. (1980), *A Talent to Deceive: An Appreciation of Agatha Christie*, New York: Dodd, Mead.

Bernthal, J. C. (2019), "Killing Innocence: Obstructions of Justice in Late-Interwar British Crime Fiction," *Clues: A Journal of Detection*, 37 (2): 30–9.

Butler, W. E. and R. E. Rains (2021), Review of *Holmes Reads Holmes: Reflections on the Real-Life Links between the Jurist & the Detective in the Library, in the Courtroom, and on the Battlefield*, R. E. Davies and M. H. Hoeflich (eds), *Law and Literature*: 547–50. Available online: https://doi.org/10.1080/153568 5X.2021.1930890

Cavallaro, R. (2007), "Chester Himes's Cotton Comes to Harlem: A Reparations Parable," *Law and Literature*, 19 (1): 103–37. Available online: https://doi-org. ezproxy.lib.ou.edu/10.1525/lal.2007.19.1.103 (accessed October 13, 2021).

Chandler, R. ([1946] 1974), "The Simple Art of Murder," in H. Haycraft (ed), *The Art of the Mystery Story*, 222–37, New York: Biblo & Tannen.

Christie, A. (1925), "Traitor Hands," *Flynn's Weekly*, January 31: 273–83.

Christie, A. (1933), "The Witness for the Prosecution," in *The Hound of Death*, 115–40, London: Odham's Press.

Christie, A. ([1934a] 2003), *Murder on the Orient Express*, New York: HarperCollins, ebook.

Christie, A. ([1934b] 2011), *Three Act Tragedy*, New York: HarperCollins, ebook.

Christie, A. ([1936] 2011), *Cards on the Table*, New York: HarperCollins, ebook.

Christie, A. ([1939] 2009), *And Then There Were None*, New York: HarperCollins, ebook.

Christie, A. ([1942] 2013), *Five Little Pigs*, New York: HarperCollins, ebook.

Christie, A. ([1944] 2012), *Death Comes as the End*, New York: HarperCollins, ebook.

Christie, A. ([1945] 2012), *Sparkling Cyanide*, New York: HarperCollins, ebook.

Christie, A. ([1957] 2011), *4:50 from Paddington*, New York: William Morrow.

Christie, A. ([1962] 2011), *The Mirror Crack'd from Side to Side*, New York: HarperCollins, ebook.

Christie, A. ([1975] 2011), *Curtain: Poirot's Last Case*, New York: HarperCollins, ebook.

Christie, A. ([1977] 2011), *Agatha Christie: An Autobiography*, New York: William Morrow.

Christie, A. (n.d., believed *c*. 1953), *Hostile Witness/Witness for the Prosecution*, Typescript. The Christie Archive Trust.

Christie, A. (n.d., believed *c*. 1953–1963), *Witness for the Prosecution*, First performance, Winter Garden Theater, London, Directed by Peter Saunders, New York: Samuel French.

Crosby, K. (2017), "Keeping Women Off the Jury in 1920s England and Wales," *Legal Studies*, 37 (4): 695–717.

Davison-Vecchione, D. (2017), "How Is the EU Like the Marvel Universe? Legal Experientialism and Law as a Shared Universe," *Law and Literature*, 30 (2): 185–220. Available online: https://doi.org/10.1080/1535685X.2017.1379743 (accessed October 13, 2021).

Davison-Vecchione, D. (2018), Review of *Graphic Justice; Intersections of Comics and Law*, *Law and Literature*, 12 (1): 143–8. Available online: https://doi.org/10.1080/1 7521483.2018.1464247 (accessed October 13, 2021).

Dimock, W. C. (1997), *Residues of Justice: Literature, Law, and Philosophy*, ACLS Humanities E-Book (Series), Berkeley: University of California Press.

Driver, J. (2017), "Justice Thomas and Bigger Thomas," in A. Lacroix, R. McAdams, and M. Nussbaum (eds), *Fatal Fictions: Crime and Investigation in Law and Literature*, 159–76, Oxford: Oxford University Press.

Dolan, K. (2007), *A Critical Introduction to Law and Literature*, Cambridge, UK: Cambridge University Press.

Ellroy, J. ([1990] 2013), *LA Confidential*, New York: Grand Central Publishing. Ebook.

Evans, M. (2011), *The Imagination of Evil: Detection Fiction and the Modern World*, New York: Continuum International Publishing Group.

Falcón Ytella, M. J. (2016), *Law and Literature*, Leiden, the Netherlands: Brill Nijhoff.

Foa, P. (2017), "What's Love Got to Do With It? Sexual Exploitation in *Measure for Measure*," in A. Lacroix, R. McAdams, and M. Nussbaum (eds), *Fatal Fictions: Crime and Investigation in Law and Literature*, 139–56, Oxford: Oxford University Press.

Gandorfer, D. (2019), Review of *Living in Technical Legality: Science Fiction and Law as Technology* by K. Tranter, *Law and Literature*, 32 (1): 185–8. Available online: https://doi.org/10.1080/1535685X.2019.1635357 (accessed October 13, 2021).

Green, J. (2015), *Curtain Up: Agatha Christie: A Life in the Theatre*, New York: HarperCollins.

Hourigan, D. (2018), "On the Possibility of Legal Form in Mieville's Speculative Fictions," *Law and Literature*, 30 (2): 167–84. Available online: https://doi.org/10.1080/1535685X.2017.1370800 (accessed October 13, 2021).

Jacoby, S. (1983), *Wild Justice: The Evolution of Revenge*, New York: Harper and Row.

Lacroix, A., R. McAdams, and M. Nussbaum, eds. (2017), *Fatal Fictions: Crime and Investigation in Law and Literature*, Oxford: Oxford University Press.

Levmore, S. and M. C. Nussbaum, eds. (2014), *American Guy: Masculinity in American Law and Literature*, Oxford: Oxford University Press.

Makinen, M. with P. Phillips (2016), "Transforming Justice? *Murder on the Orient Express* 1934–2010," *Clues: A Journal of Detection*, 1 (34): 41–51.

Maynard, K. K., J. Kearney, and J. Guimond (2010), *Revenge versus Legality: Wild Justice from Balzac to Clint Eastwood and Abu Ghraib*, Oxford: Birkbeck Law Press.

Nicol, D. (2019), "'Bad Business': Capitalism and Criminality in Agatha Christie's Novels," *Entertainment and Sports Law Journal*, 17 (1): 6. Available online: https://doi.org/10.16997/eslj.230 (accessed October 13, 2021).

Niles, J. D. (2015), "The Myth of the Feud in Anglo-Saxon England," *The Journal of English and German Philology*, 2 (114): 163–200.

Posner, R. A. ([1988] 2009), *Law and Literature*, Cambridge, MA: Harvard University Press.

Prichard, M., ed. (2012), *Agatha Christie around the World with the Queen of Mystery: The Grand Tour*, London: HarperCollins.

Rawls, J. (1971), *A Theory of Justice*, Cambridge, MA: The Belknap Press of Harvard University Press.

Rowland, S. (2004), *From Agatha Christie to Ruth Rendell—British Women Writers in Detective and Crime Fiction: S. Rowland: Palgrave Macmillan*, London: Palgrave Macmillan.

Reeve, A. B. (1925), "Craig Kennedy and the 'Six Senses—Sight'," *Flynn's Weekly*, January 31: 195–209.

Sargent, N. C. (2010), "Mys-Reading the Past in Detective Fiction and Law," *Law and Literature*, 22 (2): 288–306. Available online: https://doi-org.ezproxy.lib.ou.edu/10.1525/lal.2010.22.2.288 (accessed October 13, 2021).

Sayers, D. L. (2012), *Gaudy Night*, New York: Harper.

Sim, S. (2015), *Justice and Revenge in Contemporary American Crime Fiction*, London: Palgrave Macmillan.

Sollazzo, E. (2017), "'The Dead City': Corporate Anxiety and the Post-Apocalyptic Vision in Colson Whitehead's *Zone One*," *Law and Literature*, 29 (3): 457–83. Available online: https://doi.org/10.1080/1535685X.2017.1327696 (accessed October 13, 2021).

Strier, R. and R. H. McAdams (2017), "Cold-Blooded and High-Minded Murder: The 'Case' of *Othello*," in A. Lacroix, R. McAdams, and M. Nussbaum (eds), *Fatal Fictions: Crime and Investigation in Law and Literature*, 111–38, Oxford: Oxford University Press.

Symons, J. (1985), *Bloody Murder: From the Detective Story to the Crime Novel*, New York: Viking.

Telech, D. (2017), "Mercy at the Areopagus: A Nietzschean account of Justice and Joy in the Eumenides," in A. Lacroix, R. McAdams, and M. Nussbaum, (eds), *Fatal*

Fictions: Crime and Investigation in Law and Literature, 15–40, Oxford: Oxford University Press.

Turow, S. (2017), "On My Careers in Crime," in A. Lacroix, R. McAdams, and M. Nussbaum (eds), *Fatal Fictions: Crime and Investigation in Law and Literature*, 1–12, Oxford: Oxford University Press.

Wilf, S. (2017), "Slouching toward Bethlehem: Oxford's Tamar, Jerusalem's Ohayon, and Historical Devices in Detective Fiction," in A. Lacroix, R. McAdams, and M. Nussbaum (eds), *Fatal Fictions: Crime and Investigation in Law and Literature*, 275–99, Oxford: Oxford University Press.

CHAPTER FOURTEEN

Christie and Christianity

J.C. BERNTHAL

INTRODUCTION

Crime fiction has a complex relationship to religion. As a genre, it inevitably deals with transgression, judgment, and metaphysical questions of good and evil, which are also, in several contexts, religious terrains. Although a devout Christian, Agatha Christie rarely introduced overt religious conversations into her detective narratives. However, readings of Christie as a religious writer, or one who writes about religion, have increased steadily in the twenty-first century. This is, perhaps, symptomatic of the loosening hold of a once ubiquitous religious framework in everyday Britain that underpins the world Christie depicts. It is no longer as easy as it once was to read religion and society's presumed structural underpinnings as part of the background, because fewer and fewer readers are likely to take it for granted that British society is an innately Protestant Christian one.

This chapter outlines Christie's Christian background and biographical relation to religion, before examining theologically and biblically informed analyses of crime and detective fiction, with special attention to readings of Christie. While outlining existing conversations, this chapter considers references in Christie's life writing and crime fiction to God, the Bible, and theology as well as the formal similarities between crime fiction and the Christian gospels. A case study considers Christianity in Christie's non-detective fiction—stories collected in *Star over Bethlehem* in 1965 manifest a theology of humanity as the living incarnation of religious gospel—providing an indicative look at her underexplored religious literature. Ultimately, this chapter outlines possible future directions for research in considering Christianity or religion more generally in this extremely popular author's complex and socially engaged literary landscape.

CHRISTIE'S CHRISTIAN LIFE

A woman of faith, Agatha Christie was raised in the Church of England with a "simple-hearted orthodox Christian" father, an imaginative mother who dabbled in several faiths, and a nonconformist, Sabbatarian "Bible Christian" for a governess (Christie 1977: 25). "Nursie," as Christie called her, was strictly opposed to any form of secular activity on the Sabbath, which led the young Agatha Miller to worry for her father's immortal soul when she observed him playing croquet on a Sunday (25). A limited range of approaches, then, influenced her in childhood, leading to strong biblical literacy and an awareness that there was more than one way to "do" faithful Christianity. However, it is a fundamentally British, Protestant range and that limited worldview, albeit one that is cognizant of diversity, plays into Christie's prose. Biblical quotations appear with regularity in her publications, as do Shakespearean quotations and other literary references, but they are not necessarily tied to faith, which is presented if at all as something personal, not derived solely from the Bible but reflected in one's acts.

Christie read religious literature beyond the Bible throughout her life. Until her death, she slept beside her mother's copy of Thomas à Kempis's *The Imitation of Christ*, a fifteenth-century mystical devotional work that instructs the reader in cultivating a holy inner life through pious devotion and withdrawing from the secular standards and judgments of the world. On the flyleaf of her mother's book, Christie had written: "Who shall separate us from the love of Christ?" (in Thompson [2007] 2008: 30), a quotation from Romans 8.35 in the King James Version. The handwritten verse reflects a tenet in Christie's life, that the cultivation of an inner spiritual life was only possible because of the unconditional "love of Christ," and values in Christ could be at odds with worldly ones.

Nonetheless, Christie lived as a worldly woman, embracing the pleasures of life without esoteric withdrawal, but underpinned by a resounding faith. This was a faith that saw its share of guilt. As an Anglican, she believed in the sanctity of marriage, and famously resisted her first husband's requests for a divorce in 1926. After the marriage became irretrievably broken and the divorce was finalized in 1928, Agatha Christie refused to participate in Holy Communion for several years. While the Church of England has traditionally stigmatized divorce less than the Roman Catholic Church, it was not unusual for Anglican divorcees to refuse or be denied communion in the first half of the twentieth century, and the point was still sufficiently contentious to cause a minor stir when the monarch's grandson married a divorced woman in an Anglican ceremony with Mass in 2018 (Booth and Adam 2018). Christie was a woman of faith conventional to her time and class, then, but also one who took her religious convictions seriously and thought about them. Throughout her life, Christie was a conscientious churchgoer who was involved in church life: as is often remarked, her 1956 mystery *Dead Man's Folly* started life as a novella written to raise funds for a church window (Christie 2014).

In her lifetime, Christie also made an impact on the Roman Catholic Church. The "Agatha Christie Indult" is the informal name given to a holy decree from Pope Paul VI allowing Catholic churches to perform the full Tridentine Mass in Latin. In 1971, Christie was among signatories of a petition to the papacy, calling for it to reconsider replacing the Tridentine Mass with the Pauline Mass (now called the Ordinary Mass), a more accessible form in vernacular translations. Christie's husband Max Mallowan also signed the petition, as did multiple high-profile cultural individuals, including Cecil Day-Lewis, Yehudi Menuhin, Nancy Mitford, and Iris Murdoch. Almost as soon as the pope bowed to demands to allow Catholic churches to perform the Latin service, his decision became known as "The Agatha Christie Indult": of all the signatories to the petition, Christie's name struck a chord with the general public.

The indult's moniker can be connected with the love of tradition for its own sake. Even toward the end of her lifetime, Christie was seen by many as a conservative relic, who transported her readers to a vanished, genteel, and very proper world. Professor of Theology David Grumett has used the word "traditional" to describe Christie's novels and the appeal to her of the Latin Mass (Grumett 2017: 298). Even more than "establishment" names like poet laureate Day-Lewis and the iconically aristocratic Mitford, Christie was seen to stand for formality and vanishing ways of life. However, Grumett has also connected Christie's involvement with the idea of "mysteries": the Latin language adds an extra layer of mystery and interpretation to the sacred rite, which Grumett has linked to the mysteries Christie wrote about in her professional life (298).

The petition is specifically framed as "ecumenical and non-political" and makes clear that its signatories are not talking about religious faith:

We are not at this moment considering the religious or spiritual experience of millions of individuals. The rite in question, in its magnificent Latin text, has also inspired a host of priceless achievements in the arts—not only mystical works, but works by poets, philosophers, musicians, architects, painters and sculptors in all countries and epochs. Thus, it belongs to universal culture as well as to churchmen and formal Christians.

("1971 Statement")

So, it is not a religious argument, but what it does point out is the importance of religious traditions and rituals in daily and artistic life. We see this in *By the Pricking of My Thumbs*, published in 1968, in which Tuppence, the middle-aged daughter of a clergyman, laments on the decline of the King James Version of the Bible: "I was brought up properly and I used to know my bible quite well, as any good clergyman's daughter should. But now [...] they don't read the lessons properly any more in churches. They give you some new version where all the wording, I suppose, is technically right and a proper translation, but sounds nothing like it used to" (Christie [1968] 1977: 175). It is not so much about the meaning—the "proper translation" is eschewed—but about keeping things as they "used to" be.

Religion in Christie's life, then, served an important structuring principle, with long-standing forms of organized Christianity providing a backbone for social and cultural ways of living. In trying to keep things "traditional," Christie evidently promoted the irreligious value of religious texts. But this does not mean she wanted to move away from a model of religion that is grounded in actual faith. Separately, personal devotion for Christie was rooted in living in "the love of Christ," and acting accordingly. Her upbringing showed her the value of a range of approaches to what are essentially the same tenets: the same God, the same savior, and the same scripture. Although in her life, she valued religion for its personal accessibility, her involvement late in life in this call to preserve an archaic Catholic service shows that she saw value in divine religious mysteries, not just the mysteries of interpretation and not, as has been traditional, the idea of keeping things in Latin to keep them out of the vocabulary of the general populace. Faith for Christie was a living thing, related to but separate from religious observation—and this translates into her fiction, where the formal murder mystery structure enables an understated but probing dialogue on the dynamics of good and evil.

CRIME FICTION AND CHRISTIANITY IN SCHOLARSHIP

While crime fiction is a fairly secular genre, there has long been a link between the classical, traditionally British, "whodunit" school of crime writing and theology. Some of the early twentieth century's leading British crime writers, including G.K. Chesterton (1874–1936), Ronald Knox (1888–1957), and Dorothy L. Sayers (1893–1957), were also theologians or clergy, while some preservers of the mystery tradition such as P.D. James (1920–2014) provided overtly religious framing for their mysteries. The ascendance of crime fiction to chart-topping popularity in the interwar years coincided with organized religion losing some of its hold and authority, over the British especially, and these points have been linked.

W.H. Auden wrote about detective fiction in specifically biblical terms in his 1948 essay "The Guilty Vicarage." Opening with a "confession" that he is addicted to detective stories, "like alcohol or tobacco," Auden analyzes very specifically the "Whodunit" model of crime writing as opposed to psychological or literary treatments of crime and mystery (1948: 406). Auden notes that, in murder mysteries, there is a basic formula: idyllic order is broken by murder—and it is nearly always murder—and, after an investigation, that order is restored. For this to work most effectively, Auden writes, the setting must start out "appear[ing] to be an innocent society in a state of grace" (407–8), which is to say, resembling the Garden of Eden in Genesis, the first book of the Bible, which exists as a paradise before the introduction of sin. Indeed, "the more Eden-like it is, the greater the contradiction of murder" (408). Murder, of course, is widely regarded as the ultimate sin. With the identification and apprehension of the criminal, Auden notes, "innocence is restored" (408), enabling a fantasy of returning to Eden.

Writing in 1948, Auden was addressing a readership widely impacted by the incomprehensible trauma of the Second World War. His reading of mystery-based detective fiction emphasizes its escapism and its psychological and spiritual importance as a literary genre offering comfort in the face of broader, inexplicable mysteries. Moreover, taking issue with the assumption that reading murder mysteries lets readers indulge their secret sadistic sides, Auden asserts that these books derive their value from "the illusion of being dissociated from the murderer" (411–12): the murderer is expelled from society as presented in the narrative, allowing "innocence which is discovered to contain guilt" to be transformed via the detective's "divine intervention" into true, untainted innocence (412). Auden concludes that "the detective story addict indulges [a] phantasy of being restored to the Garden of Eden, to a state of innocence" (412) at a time when, in real life, innocence is unachievable.

Auden's essay has influenced an array of approaches to the study of detective fiction, many of which see the genre taking over the role of mass comforter and ethical stay as the appeal of organized religion began noticeably to wane. The interwar years had been marked in British religious circles by at least the perception of a decline in faith and church attendance: "suddenly, it seemed as if no one wanted to go into a church," writes S.J.D. Green ([1996] 2002: 366), adding that "a crisis of faith [was] observed by experienced contemporaries [and] experienced by everyone" (375). Senseless death had diminished trust in the Church, and in the powers and hierarchies in whose names so many lives were lost. The result has been understood as, in Charles N.M. Baldock's terms, "a religious gap at the heart of the population" (2009: 80). Certainly, detective fiction enjoyed mass appeal, and many readers were more devoted to what Penguin Books founder Allen Lane called "my weekly blood" (in *Agatha Christie Close Up*) than to their daily devotions. This is reflected in the jokey

"Ten Commandments" for crime writers that Catholic priest and crime writer Ronald Knox produced in 1928.

The idea that whodunits have taken the place of religion, with detectives becoming godlike figures, remained a hot one throughout the twentieth century. In 1993, John Wren-Lewis published "Adam, Eve and Agatha Christie: Detective Stories as Post-Darwinian Myths of Original Sin," arguing that, in a secular society, the works of Christie, Chesterton, and Sayers provide a Christian moral framework for readers who are looking for it, presenting clear distinctions between good and evil without the obvious trappings of religion (Wren-Lewis 1993). Robert S. Paul's *Whatever Happened to Sherlock Holmes?* (1991) is subtitled *Detective Fiction, Popular Theology, and Society*. In it, Paul argues that "the writer of detective fiction, without conscious intent, appeals directly to those moral and spiritual roots of society unconsciously affirmed and endorsed by the readers" (7), a similar point to that made later by Wren-Lewis. Paul also suggests that detective fiction arose from the Enlightenment and bifurcated in terms of its approach to society: endorsing the status quo, where it takes the place of organized religion in the twentieth century, and resisting it, where it comes into dialog with personal faith and philosophy. He suggests that "the humanized" detective in late-twentieth-century whodunits, as opposed to the "infallible" sleuths of the Golden Age, helps marry these strands, putting the genre in more of a dialog than competition with religion (186).

Many of these readings have been rightly challenged for their reliance on stereotypes. In the case of Christie, often taken as the figurehead of the interwar British whodunit school of crime writing, for instance, Marty S. Knepper has pointed out, the narratives "are not so morally simple or predictable; neither are her characters and settings innocent" (2021: 20). Nonetheless, the general principle has survived into more nuanced readings in the present century. Peter C. Erb has argued that the problems of faith are not puzzles like those confronted by the detectives and readers of fiction but divine "mysteries," "never expendable and never concluded" (2004: 26). Comparing crime writers to the authors of letters collected in the Christian New Testament, Erb suggests that they too answer some questions but pose bigger, less soluble ones, that is, engaging with social evils, and offer comfort but equally engage with the pervading sources of the original discomfort (27).

Crime writer P.D. James once asserted, following Dorothy L. Sayers's lead, that detective fiction started life in the Jewish Bible, with the murder of Abel by his brother Cain in the Book of Genesis (James 2009: 11). Noticing that a large number of the most prominent English-language crime writers have traditionally been prominent members of Christian churches, Suzanne Bray argued in 2013 that "[t]he typical golden age detective novel" favors a setting that "resembles the Garden of Eden," but that the "appearance of innocence [...] is deceptive" since, even before the crime occurs, evil is already present (2, 3). Bray argues that Christie's (and Sayers's and Chesterton's) detective fiction does not offer escape so much as force the reader to confront evil in the world, in order to process and deal with it. She quotes Chesterton: "Things must be faced, even in order to be forgiven" (10) and concludes that detective fiction is a kind of popular theology that reminds readers of the presence of ultimate justice and of individual responsibility; that "every individual is personally and morally responsible for his acts" (13).

Bray engages more explicitly with the (detective) texts than many of her predecessors, and the result is a more nuanced and convincing argument, even along similar lines. More recent work has granted the genre the dignity of further direct engagement. For example, in 2019, Caroline Blyth and Alison Jack published *The Bible in Crime Fiction and Drama*, which analyzes explicit and implicit biblical references across the field of crime fiction. Two of the chapters, which focus on Christie, are discussed in more detail below. Going on an "intertextual journey," Blyth and Jack insist that "the ancient biblical search for justice in a violent and chaotic world" is essentially the same quest shared by the authors, characters, and readers of crime fiction (2019: 3, 7).

CHRISTIEAN THEOLOGY?

Notably, these conversations around detective fiction and theology, though they occasionally namecheck Christie in their titles, rarely actually cite her work. In her analytic biography, Gillian Gill wrote that "religion is a subject rarely discussed in Christie's mystery novels [but that it] provides the framework for all her writing" (Gill [1990] 1991: 92), but discussions of Christie and Christianity have traditionally focused on the biographical elements highlighted above. In particular, a wealth of informal articles have highlighted the "Agatha Christie Indult" (Grumett 2017; Marquette 2021).

There have been exceptions. While "Agatha Christie" has been used as shorthand for "detective fiction" in several of the pieces emphasizing the genre's focus on guilt, innocence, and morality without necessarily engaging with her actual work, Heta Pyrhönen devoted a full chapter of *Mayhem and Murder: Narrative and Moral Problems in the Detective Story* (1999) to "The Anatomy of Good and Evil in Agatha Christie." Pyrhönen looks at role-playing and relationship triangles in *Evil Under the Sun*, the title of which is a paraphrase of a quotation found in Ecclesiastes 9.3 and applies the philosophies of Slavoj Žižek to close-read other biblically allusive works, concluding that Christie presents human morality as a balancing act between divine good and innate evil (Pyrhönen 1999: 227).

Indeed, Christie's use of the Bible in her writing goes beyond quoting or evoking it in titles such as *Evil Under the Sun* and "Butter in a Lordly Dish." A close reading of Christie's texts shows an interest in religion and faith, and especially a fascination with how people read the Bible. It is true that clergymen rarely develop beyond the stereotype of the benevolent patriarch or muddled do-gooder in her books, and vicars or priests can rarely be found quoting the scriptures. However, other characters do—and they do not tend to be the most sympathetic ones. Murderers in "The House of Lurking Death" and *By the Pricking of My Thumbs* both wreak havoc convinced in their own heads that they are fulfilling the orders of God, acting as his instrument on earth. In both cases, their conduct is explained, or in the characters' views informed, by close, repeated, and obsessive, reading and quotation of the Bible. In *And Then There Were None*, the monstrous Emily Brent eschews human company, "[e]nveloped in an aura of righteousness" (Christie [1939] 2015) as she clutches her Bible on the train. She never actually opens it in the course of the novel, but is normally seen with it, and is known to quote carefully selected passages in order to convince herself that she is in the right, no matter how much misery she inflicts on others (160). These characters are at best self-deceiving hypocrites, and Christie clearly presents Christian values as something in opposition to biblical religiosity in all of these cases.

Since 2009, most explorations of Christie and Christianity (or, indeed, Christie and religion more generally) have taken their lead from Nick Baldock's "The Christian World of Agatha Christie," an online article arising from his doctoral thesis on theology and interwar detective novelists (Frye 2013; Freeman 2021). For Baldock,

> [t]he plain fact is that detective fiction is a distinctively moral genre; indeed, a distinctively theological genre. Questions of guilt and justice are inherent within even the most implausible and incredible whodunit. The world of Agatha Christie was a Christian world. The assumptions, morality and society are Christian.
>
> (Baldock 2009)

Baldock reads Christie, then, as a *Christian* writer, both in background and in content, building on the work of Auden and his successors to dig into the actual texts. Examining passing references to God in texts such as *Cards on the Table* and *Taken at the Flood*, he notes an apparent theology of the sanctity of life and notes that such references "appear throughout her work," while their understatedness is deliberate, to avoid "being overstated or didactic" (Baldock 2009).

Leonard Freeman in particular has developed Baldock's ideas with more close reading to propose a theology of "human nature" that he credits as a major part of her extreme commercial success. Freeman holds that Christie's metaphors and characters represent, consistently, the presence of sin behind, or even on, idyllic facades. For example, he cites bindweed, an oft-repeated metaphor covering the family homes in Christie, and moral ambiguities exhibited by Hercule Poirot and Jane Marple. Noting the detectives' "fallibility," Freeman suggests that they are theologically significant not because they are divine omnipotent figures but because they are human and flawed. They demonstrate the failings of human morality even as they succeed. Freeman argues that, in Christie's work, Original Sin is a real and pervading presence, and the detectives help the reader "recognize [them]selves" in Christie's fictional world: "broken yet searching for, and trusting in, redemption and *le bon dieu*" (Freeman 2021).

As the *"bon dieu"* allusion suggests, Hercule Poirot has taken center stage somewhat in text-based analyses of Christie and Christianity. Poirot is, after all, canonically a Catholic. While his faith is more central to his character in some of the television adaptations than in the books, Poirot certainly confronts it in-canon. It is more cultural knowledge than religious knowledge that allows him to know in *Lord Edgware Dies* that an Anglo-Catholic luminary cannot marry a divorced woman, but he does evoke and emulate Catholic rites on multiple occasions. Most commonly, he incites vulnerable characters to confess their sins to him, even calling himself "Papa Poirot," a domesticated form of the Catholic priestly "Father": in *Taken at the Flood*, a flustered woman meets him in a church, worried that she is "cut off from the mercy of God," which he assures her is not the case, encouraging her "to confess [her] sins" and receive "comfort" (Christie 1948: 231–2).

He also seems to confront the idea both proposed and argued against in texts cited above, that a Golden Age detective is a secular god, on several occasions. For instance, in *One, Two Buckle My Shoe*, he tells the murderer that no one life is more important than any other, and that it is for God, not man, to judge humanity (Christie 1940: 254–6). In his last case, Poirot remarkably commits the final murder: he executes his greatest nemesis, whom the law cannot touch. Echoing his own criticisms of a murderer who "usurped the functions of *le bon Dieu*" in *Cards on the Table* (Christie [1936] 2001: 203), Poirot shoots a man directly in the center of the forehead, reminding Hastings, who sees the body, of "the brand of Cain" (Christie 1975: 221), that is, the mark left by God on the first biblical murderer. Poirot notes in his confession: "I have always been so sure—Too sure … I prefer to leave myself in the hands of the *bon Dieu*. May his punishment, or his mercy, be swift!" (220, ellipsis original). It makes sense, then, that those looking at Christie's literary theology or reading her work as religious writing have tended to focus on Poirot.

However, as its title suggests, Poirot is not the focus of Isabel Anders's *Miss Marple: Christian Sleuth*. Configuring Marple as a Christian hero, Anders argues that the character's enduring appeal lies in espousing the teachings of Jesus, especially the commandment to love one's neighbor, and putting those teachings into practice. Anders argues that Marple is not *innocent* but is *good*, and that she like anyone else has to follow the teachings of Christ rather than having all the holy qualities innate within herself. In Anders's reading, Marple emerges as a figure who uses biblical teachings in order to arrive at solid, provable truths in the form of solutions to crimes. St. Mary Mead, the apparently idyllic village where several murders fail to spoil the picturesque view, emerges as a Garden of Eden where serpents dwell and breed. Marple is, for Anders, "a woman for others": one who represents "danger" for antisocial forces, and one who "recognizes the God-given value in other people and sees them as her neighbors for whom she bears responsibility" (Anders 2013: 4).

Two chapters in Blyth and Jack's edited collection, *The Bible in Crime Fiction and Drama*, focus exclusively on Christie. Hannah M. Strømmen's "Poirot, the Bourgeois Prophet: Agatha Christie's Biblical Adaptations" makes the case for Christie as a popularizer of biblical narratives. Focusing on Christie's Golden Age texts, Strømmen notes that Poirot is presented as "unswerving in his belief that justice must be put first" (Strømmen 2019: 153), and argues that "visionary justice" is presented in Christie in "secularized" terms (157). However, refreshingly, Strømmen does not pretend that Poirot is presented as a flawless and traditionally godlike hero, but that he is the kind of person many of Christie's contemporary readers would have looked down on. Like Freeman, Strømmen argues that the books do not merely offer escape, then, but for the religious reader are clearly situated in the real world. The restoration of order at the end of a Poirot case, she contends, mirrors the delivery of prophetic knowledge in the Bible because, just as sin remains with us, we know at the end of a Christie book that another one, and therefore another murder, is just around the corner.

My own contribution to Blyth and Jack's volume is "'A Dangerous World': The Hermeneutics of Agatha Christie's Later Novels." In this, I seek to broaden the approach to religion and biblical metatext in Christie's fiction by moving away from the detectives themselves. Instead, that chapter focuses on the end of the world and what might come later as presented in Christie's more mature, experimental works. Highlighting a certain level of biblical literacy expected of the reader, as well as a knowledge of William Shakespeare, I look at how Christie presents charming, beautiful false prophets and an increasing awareness that biblical evil is internal: not just in society, but within the human soul, as the author and her readers were confronted with "an increasingly secular" world (Bernthal 2019: 182). Like all the approaches discussed in this section, that chapter focuses on Christie's detective fiction, underpinned by biographical, societal, and theological insights. What it does not do is look at Christie's overtly religious writing, of which many readers remain unaware. To this end, Christie's "Christmas stories," which are unapologetically grounded in the Bible, reward academic scrutiny.

DIVINE MYSTERIES IN "THE ISLAND"

The stories collected in *Star over Bethlehem* are overtly religious. One, "The Naughty Donkey," is clearly written for children, but the others could have been written for any age group. Like her peer Dorothy L. Sayers, Christie wrote theological fiction for all ages: Sayers's Christian fiction takes the form of accessible dramatic work, while her only stories for children, collected as *Even the Parrot* (1944), are highly moralistic but not religious in tone.[1] Christie's book, published in 1965 under the name Agatha Christie Mallowan, was publicized as a "little book [to] celebrate Christmas" (1965: dustjacket). The only other book published under that name, *Come, Tell Me How You Live*, two decades earlier, had also introduced by its author as a "little book" ([1946] 1999: 18): the suggestion is that these books are not supposed to be taken too seriously, but it is also a strategy of the detective novelist, reassuring readers that this departure from the norm does not mark a career shift. A "little book" is not to be taken, the author suggests, as part of their main body of work.

Notwithstanding the assertions that *Star over Bethlehem* is not part of the author's main canon, it handles many of the same themes and ideas as Christie's detective fiction: death, guilt, the highs and lows of human emotion, and questions about moral absolutes. The biblical mysteries become, in essence, Agatha Christie mysteries, as well-known stories from the Christian tradition are retold in human terms, either in cautionary tales about twentieth-century characters ("The Water Bus"), future-gazing depictions of prophecy coming to be ("Promotion in the Highest"), or stories set thousands of years in the past ("Star over Bethlehem"). It is not simply that biblical themes and characters are integrated with the mundane; they are presented as already part of it.

In "The Island," Mary, slowly revealed to be the biblical mother of Christ, gossips with other mothers and remembers a wedding she attended with her son many years before. When her friends complain that the wine always runs out at ceremonies and they have to drink water, she replies, "We did not drink water at this wedding" (Christie Mallowan 1965: 72). This is an early clue to her identity, for those readers with existing knowledge of Christian narratives. According to the Bible, Jesus attended a wedding at Cana, where he turned water into wine: this is his first miracle in the Gospel of John (Jn 2.1-12). Like any Christie clue, it works as a statement in its own right—the wedding Mary attended was so lavish the hosts never ran out of wine—but has another meaning when extra knowledge is applied. In detective fiction, this knowledge comes from the story's hidden narrative, that of the crime itself, while in Christian fiction it comes from the bible and its traditions. The religious story, then, becomes the mystery element in "The Island."

---

[1]Although Sayers also wrote theological essays and treatises for adults.

It grows darker when the other mothers ask Mary what happened to her son. They have heard that he was executed as "a criminal." Mary agrees that he was found to be "a criminal" by "[t]hose that should know" but points out that he "loved people, good and bad" (73). These are not obviously the words of a divine and canonized individual, as Mary is in many religions, but those of a law-abiding mother who still loves her publicly disgraced son. For example, the mother of a man imprisoned for 99 years for assaulting an officer wrote in 2020 that she had "made peace" with the sentence and described her son as "an obedient, polite, and non-violent son" (Slaymaker 2020). Like this mother, Mary in "The Island" respects or at least does not dispute the law but takes pains to emphasize the good in her criminal son. By now, the clue element is working in reverse: the text assumes that readers will have worked out the identity of Mary's son; that they will be at least glancingly familiar with the story of Jesus, whose gospel of love caught the attention of Roman authorities, with "[t]hose that should know" sentencing him to death. The surprise, then, is that the mother of God incarnate—as Christians believe Jesus to be—should be a normal mother, whose love for her son is unconditional while acknowledging the reality of what happened to him, in the worldly world. She does add that her son "is well [now], thanks be to God" (Christie Mallowan 1965: 73).

The next lines spell it out clearly, when another mother comments that Mary "must be proud" because her son is said to be "a Holy Man." Mary responds: "He is a good son [...] And, as you say, a very Holy Man" (73). Again, she is prioritizing her role as the mother of a man, not the mother of Christ: the "good son" comes first, and embellishing her friend's words—"a *very* Holy Man"—can be read theologically as a reminder that Christ is about as "Holy" as it is possible to be but also as maternal pride in action. It is not unheard of for parents to emphasize their offspring's exceptionalness when describing their achievements. Mary is presented as, in her own words, "a very ordinary woman" (77), whose life happens to have been affected by a major talking point—not dissimilar to the way that Agatha Christie presented herself in interviews, perhaps disingenuously: as "an ordinary successful hard-working author—like any other" (in Morgan [1984] 1997: 358).

When Mary leaves the scene, it becomes clear that the other women, at least, were talking about two sons: one who died, and the other, still living, who is a "Holy Man." They "nod" and "cluck" in the "pleasure" of gossip (74), recalling how the holy son is a blessing while the other "went wrong" (73). Another mystery, never outright framed as such, opens up: who is this sibling of Jesus, and what is going on? A mystery reader will likely be trained by now to assume that the "criminal" and the "holy man" are one and the same after all—that the one who died and, in Christian tradition, rose again is living with his mother under the guise of a brother who never existed. Indeed, convenient siblings' identities are assumed in several Christie novels, including *Peril at End House*, *A Murder Is Announced*, and by Hercule Poirot himself in *The Big Four*.

However, when the holy son is introduced, he is more devoutly pious than he is messianic. He will not eat and ignores Mary's feelings until she directly tells him that eating is a holy thing to do. He is too abstracted with metaphysical questions, but she reminds him of his worldly needs. That is, the need to eat and drink and live in the world, in a community symbolized by the gossiping villagers who open the story. Two strangers arrive, looking for a place "among these islands" where the "Queen of Heaven" dwells (75). Mary's son tells them to worship God alone—or God's son—and no heathen goddess. When Mary apologizes for him, one of the strangers tells her she is a woman of unusual beauty. This is not in her face, he says, but "beneath the skin [...] In the bone, and [...] in the heart" (78). Mary returns to her son and finds he has grown weak: "the strangers had made him restless" (78). She notes that, while he feels the need for a direct spiritual connection with God, her memories are blessing enough for her. In Christie's theology, and in the stories collected in *Star over Bethlehem*, the Christian gospel is to be lived more than it is to be studied.

The twist occurs when another stranger arrives with a boat. Mary recognizes the boat, then recognizes him: he is the son that died (so, now readers know that the "Holy Man" is indeed someone else). She tells him:

> I have done as you asked me—I have looked after John—He has been as a son to me. I am not clever—I cannot always understand his high thoughts and his visions, but I have made him good food, and washed his feet, and tended to him and loved him ... I have been his mother and he has been my son ... ? (80, ellipses original)

The question mark shows that she is looking to the newcomer for guidance. It is the equivalent of a criminal's confession, unraveling for the reader our mistaken presumptions about who was who, in a crime story, while the punctuation shows that there are no complete answers but a higher authority that must be appealed to. The Son ("Son" is capitalized in the text from this point) says she has done well, but that he is taking her home. As they walk across water to an unclear destination, Mary remembers with laughter the strangers who were looking for "the Queen of Heaven" and her son replies that "they did not know her when they saw her" (81).

The story ends with John, the "Holy Man," writing of "a new heaven and a new earth" (81). The final lines are taken from the prophecies of John in the final book of the Christian Bible, Revelation. Again, to make sense of what has happened, the reader needs some biblical knowledge. They need at least to be able to recognize "a new heaven and a new earth" or "I am the Alpha and the Omega" (81) and to know "John" is the prophetic voice of Revelation. The solution is as concise as that of any whodunit, but once again it relies on outside cultural knowledge, and insists on a certain transformative way of processing that knowledge. In "The Island," Mary is a humble and "ordinary" woman whose intense beauty is spiritual. She lives and remembers the gospel. John, a divine prophet, is clearly an important man but he does not understand the topic in which he is a divinely recognized authority, because he thinks about it more than he lives it. He is not a force for evil, like the scripture-quoting Emily Brent whose biblical fundamentalism drives a girl to suicide in *And Then There Were None*, nor for pity like the old lady who becomes convinced that she is an instrument of God's retribution in "The House of Lurking Death," but simply flawed.

Like theologian Karl Barth, Christie seems here to be saying that God's plans, motives, and self are ultimately "inconceivable" (Barth [1949] 2020: 46). Barth wrote: "We know that God is He whom we do not know, and that our ignorance is precisely the problem and the source of our knowledge" ([1933]1968: 45) and Christie has Mary assert her normality but paradoxically her profundity by stating: "I do not know myself what is right or wrong. I am too ignorant" (Christie Mallowan 1965: 73). We return, then, to the divine mysteries, which, unlike murder mysteries, are not meant to be solved.

CONCLUSION

The present chapter contains one of the few extended studies of Christie's religious writing; it is undoubtedly a neglected area of her work that warrants further attention. Christie was a devoutly religious woman, and her major works strike a balance between being molded in the context of received Protestant Christianity and maintaining universal appeal in a range of religious and secular contexts. Scholarship in this area has traditionally highlighted Christie's Christian biography or the formal parallels between Christian mysteries and murder mysteries, but at a textual level, discussions are only just getting started.

Another area that would warrant further scrutiny, and one which has not been touched on here, is Christie's awareness of and interaction with other religions. As an active member of an archaeological team, and a widely traveled woman, she was in respectful contact with people from a range of faiths in and beyond the Middle East, and these faiths are reflected in her fiction. In any discussion of this work, it is essential to draw on the literature of race and colonialism, and to point out inaccuracy and stereotyping. However, Christie's Christian writing demonstrates the importance of humanity, compassion, and community as the tenets of the Christian gospel, and there is in her religious and secular work an overriding theme of respect, humility, and the divine authority that comes with living one's faith.

REFERENCES

"1971 Statement by Scholars, Intellectuals, and Artists Living in England" (1971). Formerly available online via *The Institute of Christ the King Sovereign Priest*. Available online: http://www.institute-christ-king.org/uploads/main/pdf/england-statement.pdf (accessed May 29, 2017).

Agatha Christie Close Up: An Investigation into the Queen of Crime ([1955] 2017), BBC Physical Audio, compact disc.

Anders, I. (2013), *Miss Marple: Christian Sleuth*, Winchester and Washington: Circle Books.

Auden, W. H. (1948), "The Guilty Vicarage: Notes on the Detective Story, by an Addict," *Harper's Magazine*, May: 407–12.

Baldock, N. (2009), "The Christian World of Agatha Christie," *First Things*, August 4. Available online: https://www.firstthings.com/web-exclusives/2009/08/the-christian-world-of-agatha-christie (accessed December 1, 2021).

Baldock, C. N. M. (2009), "The Religious Imagination in British Popular Fiction and Society, 1900–1945," doctoral thesis, University of Cambridge.

Barth, K. ([1933] 1968), *The Letter to the Romans*, 6th edn, trans. E. C. Hoskins, London, Oxford, and New York: Oxford University Press.

Barth, K. ((1949) 2020), *Dogmatics in Outline*, trans. G. T. Thomas, New York: Harper Touchstone.

Bernthal, J. C. (2019), "'A Dangerous World': The Hermeneutics of Agatha Christie's Later Novels," in C. Blyth and A. Jack (eds), *The Bible in Crime Fiction and Drama: Murderous Texts*, 167–82, London and New York: T&T Clark.

Blyth, C. and A. Jack (2019), Introduction to *The Bible in Crime Fiction and Drama: Murderous Texts*, 1–8, London and New York: T&T Clark.

Booth, W. and K. Adam (2018), "How the Church of England Has Shifted on Divorce, from Henry VIII to Meghan Markle," *The Washington Post*, May 15. Available online: https://www.washingtonpost.com/world/how-the-church-of-england-has-evolved-on-divorce-from-henry-viii-to-meghan-markle/2018/05/15/85ca3388-4d6c-11e8-85c1-9326c4511033_story.html (accessed November 30, 2021).

Bray, S. (2013), "First Steps towards a Theology of English Detective Fiction," in S. Bray and G. Préher (eds), *Fatal Fascinations: Cultural Manifestations of Crime and Violence*, 1–14, Newcastle-upon-Tyne: Cambridge Scholars Publishing.

Christie, A. ([1936] 2001), *Cards on the Table*, London: HarperCollins.

Christie, A. ([1939] 2015), *And Then There Were None*, London: Harper.

Christie, A. (1940), *One, Two, Buckle My Shoe*, London: Collins.

Christie, A. (1948), *Taken at the Flood*, London: Collins.

Christie, A. ([1968] 1977), *By the Pricking of My Thumbs*, Glasgow: Fontana.

Christie, A. (1975), *Curtain: Poirot's Last Case*, London: Collins.

Christie, A. (1977), *An Autobiography*, London: Collins.

Christie, A. (2014), *Hercule Poirot and the Greenshore Folly*, London: HarperCollins.

Christie Mallowan, A. ([1946] 1999), *Come, Tell Me How You Live: An Archaeological Memoir*, London: HarperCollins.

Christie Mallowan, A. (1965), *Star over Bethlehem*, London: Collins.

Erb, P. C. (2004), *Murder, Manners, and Mystery: Reflections on Faith in Contemporary Detective Fiction*, London: SCM Press.

Freeman, P. (2021), "The Theology of Agatha Christie," *The Living Church*, March 2. Available online: https://livingchurch.org/2021/03/02/the-theology-of-agatha-christie/ (accessed December 1, 2021).

Frye, C. (2013), "Agatha Christie," *Hollow Verse*, January 20. Available online: https://hollowverse.com/agatha-christie/#identifier_2_9701 (accessed December 1, 2021).

Gill, G. ([1990] 1991), *Agatha Christie: The Woman and Her Mysteries*, London: Robson Books.

Green, S. J. D. ([1996] 2002), *Religion in the Age of Decline: Organisation and Experience in Industrial Yorkshire, 1870–1920*, Cambridge, NY: Cambridge University Press.

Grumett, D. (2017), *Material Eucharist*, Oxford: Oxford University Press.

James, P. D. (2009), *Talking about Detective Fiction*, Oxford: The Bodleian Library.

Knepper, M. S. (2021), "Contemporary Cozy Mysteries, Agatha Christie and the 1990s: Six Steps towards a Definition," in P. M. Betz (ed), *Reading the Cozy Mystery: Critical Essays on an Underappreciated Subgenre*, 17–48, Jefferson: McFarland.

Marquette, K. (2021), "How Agatha Christie Saved the Latin Mass," *Born of Wonder*, October 9. Available online: https://www.bornofwonder.com/home/how-agatha-christie-saved-the-latin-mass (accessed December 1, 2021).

Morgan, J. ([1984] 1997), *Agatha Christie: A Biography*, London: HarperCollins.

Paul, R. S. (1991), *Whatever Happened to Sherlock Holmes?: Detective Fiction, Popular Theology, and Society*, Carbondale and Edwardsville: Southern Illinois University Press.

Pyrhönen, H. (1999), *Mayhem and Murder: Narrative and Moral Problems in the Detective Story*, Toronto, Buffalo, and London: University of Toronto Press.

Slaymaker, S. (2020), "My Son Is in Prison for Life," *Prison Writers*. Available online: https://prisonwriters.com/my-son-is-in-prison-for-life/ (accessed December 1, 2021).

Strømmen, H. S. (2019), "Poirot, the Boregious Prophet: Agatha Christie's Biblical Adaptations," in C. Blyth and A. Jack (eds), *The Bible in Crime Fiction and Drama: Murderous Texts*, 149–66, London and New York: T&T Clark.

Thompson, L. ([2007] 2008), *Agatha Christie: An English Mystery*, London: Hodder Headline.

Wren-Lewis, J. (1993), "Adam, Eve and Agatha Christie: Detective Stories as Post-Darwinian Myths of Original Sin," *The Chesterton Review*, 19 (2): 193–9.

CHAPTER FIFTEEN

Poison in Golden Age Detective Fiction

KATHRYN HARKUP

INTRODUCTION

Commonly recognized defining features of Golden Age detective fiction include the dominance of women writers, domestic settings, and private detectives. However, there is one aspect of this large volume of work that perhaps receives less attention than it deserves, considering that it is the weapon used to kill so many fictional victims in this era—poison. As a method of murder, it is staggeringly pervasive in the works of the "Queens of Crime": a third of the books produced by Dorothy L. Sayers and Ngaio Marsh feature poisons prominently in their plots and Margery Allingham was just as keen. However, none of these literary giants used poison more prominently, more accurately, or as often as Agatha Christie. Over two-thirds of her books include some reference to poison, and it was the cause of approximately two-fifths of the deaths of her main characters (Gambrell 2020). She used over thirty different toxic compounds, all with impressive attention to medical detail and scientific accuracy (Gwilt 1978: 572).

The dominance of poisons in Christie's work is hardly surprising. Her knowledge and background are often noted, and any biography of the author would be incomplete without covering Christie's work as an apothecary's assistant and her training with the pharmacist Mr. P, who would later be reimagined in *The Pale Horse* (Christie [1961] 1977: 254–61). Her knowledge of potentially toxic compounds and the dangers of an overdose would have been an important part of her training, but her use of toxic compounds in her crime fiction went far beyond what she learned as an apothecary's assistant (Curran 2011: 323). Curran has detailed her collection of toxicology books and consultations with experts to expand her knowledge and check her facts. However, the significance of the use of poisons in her plots and in the stories written by the other Queens of Crime does not often feature prominently in the books and articles written about her. There have been few in-depth academic studies of Christie and her preoccupation with poison with the exception of Gerald's *The Poisonous Pen of Agatha Christie*, which includes a comprehensive list of every biologically active chemical featured in a Christie story, and Harkup's *A Is for Arsenic*, which takes a detailed look at just fourteen poisons. A comprehensive analysis of how poisons fit into the world of detective fiction as a whole is noticeably absent from the literature.

Poisonings have always held a fascination for readers of factual and fictional crime. In his essay "The Decline of the English Murder," George Orwell commented that in "the 'perfect' murder [... t]he means should, of course, be poison" (Orwell 1946). The prominence of poisons in Golden Age fiction would support Orwell's assertions. There are also many nonfiction books for the popular market on toxicology, poison, and poisoners, suggesting considerable public enthusiasm for the subject. These books sometimes reference fictional poisonings and authors such as Christie and Sayers, but it is usually a short chapter or an occasional comment within a book that spans a broad range of topics. For example, in his book *The Elements of Murder*, Emsley gives just a few paragraphs to Christie and her use of thallium in *The Pale Horse*.

One aspect of academic interest is the range of compounds used in detective novels. Arsenic has become strongly associated with Golden Age detective fiction, perhaps through its common use in real-life cases in the past and the prominence of a few particularly well-known plots such as Sayer's *Strong Poison*, or films such as *Arsenic and Old Lace*. It might be thought arsenic would therefore dominate the plots of these stories but this does not appear to be the case. In a survey of 187 fictional works, toxicologist John Trestrail III found sixty-three different compounds, although there is some potential duplication where the same active ingredient is operating under a different name (Trestrail 2000: 94–5). In Trestrail's survey, cyanide topped the list for popularity with twenty-five references, followed by mushrooms with fifteen. Arsenic was tied in third place with "unknown poison." Trestrail's survey is limited in that it is a simple tally with no indication of what works of detective fiction were scrutinized, but it is nevertheless a useful indicator of trends. What it clearly shows is that, in a world of fiction and creativity, a surprising number of genuine toxic compounds were thoroughly researched and written about in impressive detail. This attention to chemical fact is found with many fictional works, but Christie is exceptionally good at weaving such details into her plots.

Poison is a defining feature of Golden Age detective fiction and dates the books written in this era just as much as the dialogue or descriptions of cars and clothes. Just as some of the language and attitudes expressed in some of Christie's later novels seem very outdated, so too does her persistent use of medicines and remedies that had long fallen out of medical favor (Gerald 1992: 100). As just one example, in *4:50 From Paddington* (or *What Mrs. McGillicuddy Saw!*), aconitine is put into pills to kill one of the characters. It is explained that it is normally used for external application (Christie 1957: 173), but even this use would have fallen out of favor by the time the novel was written. The tonics and tinctures that often crop up in Christie's works were largely abandoned by the medical profession as the twentieth century progressed. There are almost no examples of cutting-edge medicines being employed in Christie's plots, and she relied heavily on compounds that would have been familiar to her from training as a dispenser in the 1910s. Many have a mental image of Christie's work as all being set in the 1930s and 1940s, in part due to the popularity of the television adaptations set in that era, but perhaps also thanks to her continued reference to old-fashioned medicines and poisons.

To include many of these substances in a modern crime novel would be almost unthinkable. The medical prescriptions and household items that contained potentially lethal substances would be unfamiliar to readers today, and these antiquated applications would stand out as glaring anachronisms. Thus, the types of compounds used in poisoning plots have changed, along with the settings in which they are used. Prominently reported poisonings have moved from domestic cases, such as Florence Maybrick accused of poisoning her husband in the nineteenth century, to hospitals and anonymous poisoning by those like Harold Shipman with access to lethal compounds, and the world of international spies and espionage, where the Markov and Litvinenko murders attracted headlines around the world.

A common theme running throughout the history of poisoning is the misuse of medicines. Medical professionals featured prominently as murderers in the Golden Age (Gerald 1991: 31–2) but the medicines they could use to kill differed enormously from today's pharmacopeia. Strychnine would not be available from a pharmacy today as it was in the nineteenth century, and barbiturate poisonings could not have been carried out before their invention in the twentieth century. Other well-known poisons are simply much more difficult to get hold of in the modern world.

What is particularly noticeable in Golden Age detective fiction is how often the poison is chosen to suit the plot, or how well the plot supports the chosen poison. Christie was particularly good at selecting compounds that would give the right information to the reader. Well-known symptoms of familiar poisons like cyanide or arsenic were used to raise suspicions about a sudden death, for example, the smell of bitter almonds in *The Secret Adversary* (Christie 1922: 202). More obscure poisons could be used to disguise crimes and suspects as shall be seen in this chapter.

With some exceptions, poisons used in Christie's work can be grouped into a few broad categories: home (e.g., pesticides and cleaning products), garden (plants and fungi), and medicinal (prescriptions, tonics, and remedies). The majority of these compounds were relatively commonplace substances at the time. Christie and her contemporaries rarely resorted to exotic imports, new compounds devised by scientists, or invented substances. The concept of an untraceable poison is something of a myth (Harkup 2018: *The Guardian*). They may be a very convenient plot device, but they stretch credibility. Several lethal substances can test the limits of detection by forensic techniques, but as the science has advanced over the decades the number of these substances has shrunk dramatically. Also notable is the attention to detail displayed by the Queens of Crime (Christie, Sayers, Allingham, and Marsh). All four thoroughly researched the use of poisons. However, there are notable differences in how they presented their research to the reader and Christie in particular set herself apart from her contemporary crime writers in this field of expertise.

The following case studies focus on three poisons—thallium, nicotine, and arsenic—and six novels. These three toxic substances range from the well-known to the obscure and cover the three categories—home, garden, and medicinal—outlined above. Christie's approach to each poison is compared to examples from, in order, Marsh, Allingham, and Sayers. The discussion is intended to facilitate future research into this rich, but much overlooked, aspect of crime fiction.

THALLIUM

Thallium is an obscure poison. It is an element in the periodic table that today is scarcely known outside specialist settings. Its rarity in terms of both legitimate applications and illegal abuse by poisoners would seem to make it an unusual choice of murder weapon for crime fiction writers. With few real-life cases to draw on, and little in the way of accessible texts written about the effects of thallium on the human body, beyond a few key symptoms, research would have been difficult. However, Christie and Marsh chose this poison in their respective novels, *The Pale Horse* (1961) and *Final Curtain* (1947).

In *Final Curtain*, the mystery centers around whether Sir Henry Ancred, a celebrated actor, died of natural causes. His exhumed body is said to show signs of thallium poisoning and this is indeed revealed to be the case after Inspector

Alleyn explains the process of detecting the poison in the body. Clues that indicate "howdunit" come from observations of children being treated for ringworm using thallium acetate.

Thallium was chosen as a treatment for skin conditions because it would cause the hair to fall out and the underlying ringworm (a fungal infection) could be treated more easily (Emsley 2005: 323). Hair loss, the classic sign of thallium poisoning, is a desirable effect in terms of medical treatment, but also a sign of damage to the human body and, in the context of the novel, a clue that Sir Henry was deliberately poisoned. That the same effect could be seen as detrimental and beneficial at the same time is fairly common up until the early twentieth century, but Marsh's novel brings this contradiction into particularly sharp focus.

Marsh notes in the text that thallium was an unusual prescription for ringworm and the oral doses described in the novel were certainly falling out of favor at the time the novel was written. If thallium were to be employed at this date, it would more likely have been formulated as a cream that was rubbed on the skin rather than a solution to be swallowed (Emsley 2005: 329). Using direct application of a cream meant the thallium dose could be considerably lower, and only a small area of hair would fall out, rather than the whole head of hair—but thallium creams present considerable logistical problems for poisoners, even fictional ones. Rather than having to find a convoluted reason for the victim to be smothered in cream, or even swallow it, Marsh took the much easier plot route of having everyone take their thallium orally. It also served the purposes of detection because the unusual way thallium is prescribed is the key to solving the crime.

Fourteen years later, thallium was pressed into service by a fictional poisoner in Agatha Christie's *The Pale Horse*. The novel sees a series of unrelated deaths, all initially explained away by natural causes, but later found to be murders committed under contract. The Pale Horse organization arranges for the timely demise of individuals so that inheritances can be gained or inconveniences removed by request, in exchange for payment of a sum of money. The organization is fronted by a trio of "witches," who use flamboyant rituals to give the illusion of dark powers or mysterious action at a distance.

Similarly to *Final Curtain*, the clue to solving the mystery is seeing someone administering thallium to treat ringworm. This time, the thallium is formulated as a cream but, by the 1960s the use of thallium-based creams was also falling out of favor, something that Christie acknowledges in the novel. The severe toxicity of thallium was of serious concern in over-the-counter remedies. In this novel, the only ones receiving legitimate thallium treatments in creams are dogs. Christie could take advantage of thallium's increasing obscurity to avoid revealing too much to her audience too soon. As thallium fell out of use, it was less likely her readers would know about the effects of the element and it, therefore, became harder to spot the signs of poisoning. Hints about hair falling out could be dropped into the text regularly before suspicion would be aroused. Christie has her character Ariadne Oliver describe examples of thallium's use from her childhood to introduce the relevant information to the plot, simultaneously acknowledging its old-fashioned status and introducing important scientific details.

Both Marsh and Christie chose thallium as an obscure poison. Had a more well-known poison been employed, such as arsenic or cyanide, the symptoms would have been easy to recognize and it would have been much clearer much earlier on that the police should be involved, bringing a whole different pattern to the way the novels would proceed. Even Christie's hints at supernatural forces in *The Pale Horse* become credible in the context of the novel because of the poor knowledge of thallium and how it can be administered and act on the body.

Thallium also has particular advantages for both plots because, aside from hair falling out, the number and variety of symptoms it produces means it is commonly misdiagnosed as a wide range of natural causes (Holden 1995: 185), as Christie points out in her novel. The misdiagnoses in her fictional victims run to quite a list: pneumonia, cerebral hemorrhage, brain tumor, gallstones, polio, toxic polyneuritis, encephalitis, influenza, gastroenteritis, bulbar paralysis, epilepsy, paratyphoid, and alcoholic neuritis. Marsh did not have the same luxury of extravagant diagnoses, having only two victims in *Final Curtain*, but she was certainly accurate in describing the initial symptoms of an acute dose of thallium—vomiting and diarrhea. Vomiting and diarrhea are common symptoms in poisoning by a wide variety of compounds, as well as food poisoning. The situation for Sir Henry is complicated by his existing gastric ulcers, weak heart, and tendency to fly into a rage, a constellation of factors that ultimately leads to his death being initially attributed to heart failure. Any heavy metal compound, and several other plant or organic poisons, would have served the purpose here. Marsh's focus on thallium's properties lies elsewhere and reliance on symptoms in her plot is minimal compared to Christie.

Christie made the most of thallium's unusual characteristics. She describes the range of symptoms her victims suffered; the effects might begin with diarrhea, vomiting, then progress to intoxication, pain in the limbs, and sometimes pigmentation of the skin. Fevers, sore throats, aching, agonizing pain when anything touches the body, and difficulty breathing can also occur. Christie distributes these symptoms among her many victims. As is well known, her detailed descriptions are credited with saving two lives (Gerald 1993: 194). One case involved a young girl who mistakenly ate thallium rat poison, whose strange symptoms were recognized as signs of thallium poisoning by the nurse on her ward after she read *The Pale Horse*. There was also a case of deliberate poisoning in South America that was prevented when someone spotted the symptoms described in Christie's novel and intervened.

In *The Pale Horse*, Christie, as is common in her poisoning stories, is symptom-led. The majority of her clues are delivered in terms of the victim's health. She comments in detail on what the poisons are normally used for and how they might be obtained. However, forensic analysis is hardly ever mentioned in her novels and not at all in *The Pale Horse*. Pathologists almost never appear on her pages, or they are mentioned as characters off-stage who deliver confirmation of what was suspected all along. In this respect, the technical knowledge required to solve the crime is not restricted to specialists.

All the knowledge needed to identify the cause of the varied symptoms and unravel the mystery of the Pale Horse organization is delivered by Mark Easterbrook, a historian with no obvious background in science, who discovers information on thallium by chance in a magazine, and the aforementioned Ariadne Oliver, a novelist. It is an excellent way for Christie to reassure readers that they need no more or less specialized knowledge than her protagonists and have just as much chance of solving the puzzles put before them. It is also a more subtle way of presenting clues than calling in experts when scientific detail needs to be imparted to make the plot comprehensible.

In *Final Curtain*, when the remains of Sir Henry are exhumed, the body shows the classic symptom of thallium poisoning: the hair has fallen out. Inspector Alleyn goes into considerable detail about the forensic processes that will be carried out on the body and what he expects them to show. He names the Marsh-Berzelius test, usually used to detect arsenic, but which will also extract other heavy metals from human remains. Further tests are needed to identify exactly which heavy metal has been extracted. Alleyn cites the Fresenius process, a technique that can distinguish between arsenic and antimony (the next likely suspect in cases of deliberate heavy metal poisoning). He goes on to talk about "your ammonium chloride and your potassium iodide" that would eliminate more heavy metals sometimes used in criminal poisonings, and finally, "your Bunsen flame and your platinum wire. And look for the pretty green line" (Marsh 1947: 263) that would unequivocally identify thallium. However, at no point in this lengthy monologue about chemical processes does he mention thallium. All the details are scientifically accurate, and Alleyn is discussing the case with a doctor who obviously understands the references, but it is of no help to the non-chemist reader in understanding what is really going on. Christie also presents technical clues but in a much more accessible way. Her list of misdiagnoses in *The Pale Horse* is a long list of conditions, many of which are rare and unlikely to be known to the average reader and are unlikely to help the reader guess *how*dunit. It could feel that Christie is cheating the reader out of the chance to work out *who*dunit for themselves before the detectives, but the clues are all there and fairly presented for the careful reader.

In the final pages of *Final Curtain*, Marsh clears up any confusions and explains how her murderer administered the thallium intended to treat ringworm. It was a straightforward swap of the contents of one medicine bottle into another. Christie's methods of administration, on the other hand, though always creative, are particularly so in *The Pale Horse*. Knowing thallium can be absorbed through the skin, it is added to everyday products like soap or shampoo in appropriate concentrations to bring about a slow or more rapid end to the victim, tailored to the specific requirements of the contract drawn up with The Pale Horse organization. Marsh's deaths, by contrast, are rapid, particularly that of Sonia Orincourt, who takes an improbably short forty minutes to die.

Both authors show a remarkable attention to detail and thorough research but in very different aspects of thallium poisoning. Christie's extensive knowledge of therapeutic compounds and their effects on the body really comes to the fore in *The Pale Horse*. Marsh shows impressively detailed knowledge of forensic toxicology, but it comes with little explanation as to why the multiple tests she names will help the investigation. Christie's focus is very much on her reader and helping them to understand the plot, whereas it feels that Marsh is showing off her detailed research.

NICOTINE

In a similar vein, nicotine presents multiple possibilities for the crime writer. Unlike thallium, it is a very familiar substance and, though widely recognized as detrimental to health, few realize how potently toxic it is. Its wide availability but scarce use as a murder weapon leaves a knowledge gap that would seem ripe for exploitation in crime novels, yet it has only been used in six of the 137 plots on Trestrail's list.

Nicotine is, of course, the key ingredient in tobacco products that keeps smokers going back for more. The addictive qualities of nicotine are difficult to separate from social and habitual influences on smoking habits, but it is certainly an important factor in addiction to tobacco products. While the dangers of smoking are well known, the health issues like chronic obstructive pulmonary disease and lung cancer that most people are familiar with are not due to nicotine; this does not make nicotine innocent of harm. Nicotine is a powerful neurotoxin with differing effects on the body depending on dosage and previous exposure to the compound (Waring 2002: 170–1). In the 1930s and 1940s, nicotine was also commonly used in the garden in extremely high concentrations as an insecticide (McNally 1923: 83–5). Given nicotine's abundance and ready availability, it is surprisingly rare in mystery narratives.

It would have been clear to a 1930s reader that nicotine could be harmful. Its wide use as an insecticide in the first half of the twentieth century showed it could kill insects easily and accidents in handling insecticides, both commercial products and home-made recipes, showed that it also threatened the lives of humans (McNally 1920: 213–17). Nicotine-based insecticides are now banned (replaced by less toxic neonicotinoids in the 1980s), but in the early twentieth century, when these products were commonly used, the toxic properties of nicotine were better, or more widely, known than they are today.

As with many other toxic compounds in the first half of the twentieth century, there seems to have been a disconnect between the known toxic properties of nicotine and its acceptability for everyday use in potentially lethal quantities (Whorton 2010: 194). This disconnect is exploited by Christie in *Three Act Tragedy* (1935) and Allingham in *Death of a Ghost* (1934).

Allingham's 1934 novel centers around the legacy of a renowned artist John Lafcadio. The artist left behind a series of works to be unveiled one a year after his death. The suspects are a group of family, friends, and acquaintances who guard the artist's legacy and benefit from it. A series of murders is carried out to cover up the fact that some of the legacy works are forgeries. Several methods are used to dispatch the victims, but the murder of Clare Potter, a former model for Lafcadio and an artist in her own right, involves nicotine.

The death is treated as suspicious from the outset. A graphic description of the appearance of the body, particularly the face, suggests asphyxiation but with no obvious sign of how it occurred. Campion and Inspector Oates speculate that the murderer had probably hoped it would be attributed to natural causes and that "if that young doctor hadn't been particularly honest, or even if he hadn't had his suspicions aroused by the Dacre business [another murder], it's a hundred to one he'd have called it heart failure" (Allingham 1934: 159). An autopsy is ordered and Inspector Oates puts his faith in the pathologist and Home Office analysts to determine the true cause of death. Oates's trust of the scientific skills of the professionals is well founded. Their tests reveal that nicotine has been used. A detailed discussion of its toxicity, availability, and previous use as a murder weapon follows. The murderer is later revealed to have given the victim the dose of nicotine in a bottle of spirits.

Christie's nicotine-based novel was published just a year after Allingham's, in 1935. She may or may not have read Allingham's novel before starting her own, but given her extensive knowledge and varied use of poisons, she may have chosen it independently. There are several similarities with *Death of a Ghost*, but Christie's use of nicotine is more extensive. Three people are poisoned by nicotine in *Three Act Tragedy*: a vicar, a doctor, and a patient in a sanatorium. Two receive their fatal dose in an alcoholic drink and one via a chocolate liquor. Their deaths are all rapid, reflecting reality. The first death is attributed to natural causes. The second death occurs in similar circumstances (after taking a drink at a dinner party) and the parallels between the two make both deaths suspicious. Post-mortem analysis confirms that nicotine poisoning was the cause of death in both cases.

Both novels utilize the fact that nicotine deaths could be misinterpreted as due to natural causes and it is their coincidence with earlier deaths arouses suspicions. The symptoms Allingham describes have to be extrapolated from the evidence found at the scene of the crime, because her victim dies alone. Christie has more detailed descriptions of symptoms and how quickly the poison kills because all three deaths happen in front of multiple witnesses. It is a bold approach, making it difficult to obscure telltale facts and not give away too much information. It is mainly because of nicotine's rarity as a murder weapon that Christie's audience is unlikely to spot obvious clues.

The appearance, smell, and taste of nicotine are discussed in accurate detail in both novels. The distinctive taste and smell of the compound, even diluted in alcoholic drinks, would raise suspicions and so the sources of the nicotine, the poisoned drinks, have to be disposed of and both authors go to pains to explain that this is done. With no obvious clues as to cause of death from any of the bodies, and with all the poisoned drinks destroyed, autopsies are needed to determine causes of death.

In *Three Act Tragedy* and in *Death of a Ghost*, the cause of death is established via forensic analysis. Allingham goes into the details of the process used: Stas-Otto, the standard method for extracting plant alkaloids like nicotine from human remains (Thorwald 1969: 54). Identifying which alkaloid has been extracted can be more difficult, but nicotine's characteristic smell may offer clues. At this point Allingham describes in considerable detail the appearance and availability of nicotine, all of which can be delivered in fairly dry factual terms because it is in relation to a forensic report. Allingham's details, while medically insightful, offer no real insights into the murder investigation or clues as to the murderer's identity. In Christie's novel, the revelation that nicotine has been used in the first two murders is given during an inquest, but with no technical details as to how this conclusion was reached. Christie's characters discuss how easy it would be to find nicotine in a body after it had been buried for some time, as well as complications from the fact that one of the victims was a smoker who would have naturally had nicotine in their body. However, the technical details of how the nicotine would be extracted and analyzed are not discussed at all.

The confirmation of nicotine poisoning comes as a surprise in both novels. Both authors stress how rare nicotine poisoning is in criminal cases, but only Allingham offers real-life examples. She even has footnotes on the first-known nicotine poisoning case as proof of her research into the subject. Once nicotine poisoning is confirmed, attention turns to how the murderer might have got hold of it. Christie mentions tobacco products and insecticides, offering a tantalizing hint about a character seen using rose spray early on in the novel. Allingham includes only tobacco products in her brief discussion about obtaining nicotine, but does say that a box of cigars would be sufficient for a lethal dose and the means of extracting it easy. (This offers no insight into the murder being investigated.)

Both authors demonstrate an extensive knowledge of nicotine. Allingham, with only one nicotine murder, divulges most of her research in a few pages, which are heavy on detail but short on useful information in terms of "whodunit." Christie drops nuggets of information throughout the novel, something she is able to do because there are three nicotine-related deaths scattered throughout. There are no superfluous details at any point in *Three Act Tragedy*. Technical language barely exists, but Christie conveys the important features of nicotine as a poison. As an example of the two authors' distinct approaches, when talking about the lethal dose, one uses everyday language while the other uses specific numbers and measurements. Christie states that "a few drops" are all that is necessary (Christie 1935: 61), but Allingham is more specific, citing 10–20 milligrams (Allingham 1934: 142). This is certainly accurate for the time of writing; it is now believed that more is needed to kill, though the lethal dose is still frighteningly small (Waring 2002: 171).

Christie's approach to poison is more sophisticated than Allingham's. Details and clues are embedded into the text subtly, whereas Allingham presents extensive research in a technical way. The murder of Clare Potter in *Death of a Ghost* could have been carried out with a number of other poisons that were only marginally more difficult to get hold of in 1934. Allingham's use of nicotine is thoroughly researched, but not critical to her plot. Christie, however, tailors her plot to her poison or her poison to her plot. Nicotine is not as pivotal to the plot, nor are the characteristics of nicotine poisoning used as fully as thallium is to *The Pale Horse*. However, the ordinariness of nicotine is useful. It is a familiar substance but not in the context of murder. When it is revealed as the murder weapon in both stories, it produces an unsettling moment for the characters involved as well as the reader.

ARSENIC

The use of a wide range of poisons in detective fiction helps keep stories fresh and the use of well-known substances in a new context provides a novel twist. Nonetheless, there is something comforting and reassuring about the appearance of an old favorite, even when it is a highly toxic substance with a long history of murder behind it.

Arsenic is the gold standard of chemical killing and a byword for murder and poison. Arsenic poisoning may seem virtually synonymous with Golden Age crime fiction, but it is not nearly so abundant as one might expect. Trestrail's survey reveals only thirteen uses of arsenic in 187 works of fiction. It was certainly a popular choice, but considerably overshadowed by cyanide. Even mushrooms and unknown poisons feature more often in Trestrail's list than arsenic.

Overfamiliarity with the poison may have put off many authors from including it in their stories. At a time when arsenic compounds were still readily available in shops and prominent arsenic poisoning cases were common in newspapers, authors may have feared a lazy choice. Many readers would have been familiar with real-life high-profile arsenic murderers, or suspected murderers, such as Seddon, Smith, and Maybrick. These names appear in Christie's stories as asides or throwaway comments and without any explanation, because none was needed at the time of publication. Equally, important clues would be all too easy to spot. Still, this familiarity could work to the author's advantage, giving the opportunity to drop subtle hints for the many readers who understood the references. It also forced a more creative use of the poison, in order to maintain originality, while still letting readers indulge the comfort of the familiar, as they recognize the stages and symptoms of arsenical poisoning.

Arsenic also had many advantages that other poisons simply did not offer. It was, for example, easy to obtain; paint, wallpaper, flypapers, cosmetics, and medicines could all provide the necessary killer ingredient (Whorton 2010: x). Arsenic has no noticeable taste to warn the victim and it dissolves well in water, particularly hot drinks, so the typically English cup of tea provided ample opportunity for means of delivery. The symptoms of arsenic poisoning are similar to gastroenteritis and could be attributed to food poisoning or contagious disease, diverting suspicion of foul play (Emsley 2005: 140). A long history of classic cases could also provide sources of inspiration. Christie fully embraced the historical and cultural baggage that came with using arsenic in her plots, using it several times, though with relatively few fatalities (Gwilt 1978: 572–3). Christie's 1953 novel, *After the Funeral*, and Dorothy L. Sayers's *Strong Poison*, published in 1930, both use arsenic in classic pieces of misdirection. Their murderers deliberately poison themselves to be eliminated from the list of suspects. Christie, writing more than twenty years after the publication of Sayers's novel, even admits that it is an old trick (Christie 1953: 200).

Christie often made the poison central to the plot, such as cyanide in *Sparkling Cyanide*, thallium in *The Pale Horse*, and nicotine in *Three Act Tragedy*, but her use of arsenic is notably different. She never used arsenic for her "main" murders, but it often appears in cameos, and her references to the poison are subtle. By contrast, Sayers's *Strong Poison* gives arsenic a central role, with a staggering amount of detail about the poison conveyed in one short novel. Christie had no less knowledge than Sayers, but it was spread out over multiple novels. The plot of *After the Funeral* not only features arsenic poisoning but also parallels *Strong Poison* in both method of administration and motivation.

The premise of Christie's novel is a series of murders for financial gain. The culprit diverts attention from the true crime by setting up a false trail. The murderer tries to suggest that she herself is the target rather than the culprit by staging a self-poisoning. After adding arsenic to a slice of wedding cake, she eats part of it, taking care to consume a small enough amount to avoid a fatal dose, ensuring that there is a witness to her actions to divert suspicion.

The wedding cake makes the murderer very ill with the classic arsenic symptoms: vomiting and abdominal pain. It results in her hospitalization, but she survives. By not eating the whole slice, she avoids real danger of dying and leaves a clue for forensic analysis to confirm the source of the arsenic and bolster the evidence for a malicious attack by persons unknown. Arsenic poisoning is suspected as soon as the doctor arrives to treat the victim, and is confirmed in hospital, though there are no details of what tests or how much arsenic was consumed, only that it was not enough to be fatal. *After the Funeral* is sparse on details about the properties of arsenic, such as where it could be found, what it could be used for, or exactly what constitutes a fatal doses, presumably to avoid distracting from the plot.

By contrast, in Sayers's *Strong Poison*, there is a tremendous amount of accurate detail about arsenic, which is used to poison Phillip Boyes. Boyes dines with his cousin before visiting his ex-girlfriend Harriet Vane for a cup of coffee. On the journey home, he falls ill and his condition deteriorates until he dies a few days later. That Boyes was killed by arsenic poisoning is known almost from the first page of the novel, the mystery being who administered it and how.

The setup in *Strong Poison* allows a thorough exploration of all things arsenic in relation to poisoning cases. The sequence of events on the evening of the poisoning allows an exploration of when arsenic could have been administered in order for symptoms to appear when they did, and establishes what the symptoms were that clearly indicated arsenic poisoning: vomiting and severe abdominal pain. The food and drink served to the victim over the course of the night can be thoroughly scrutinized. The opening of the novel concerns Vane's trial for the murder of Boyes, enabling a detailed discussion of forensic tests carried out to confirm death by arsenic poisoning. The assumption of poison, and particularly arsenic, being a woman's weapon is played up to the hilt but ultimately proved to be a tired cliché when the true killer is revealed to be a man.

Vane's defense relies on her occupation as a writer. Her explanation for purchasing so many different poisons under false names is that she was conducting research for a novel by finding out how easy it is to obtain toxic substances. The different applications of arsenic are explored (rat poison and weed killer), as well as the legal requirements of selling these products. During Lord Peter Wimsey's investigation to prove Vane innocent, he reads up on previous poisoning cases, allowing Sayers to name-drop a long list of arsenic murderers, several of whom are also mentioned in *After the Funeral*. The other suspect in the investigation is Boyes' (male) cousin, eliminated early on because he ate exactly the same food as the victim on the night of the poisoning with no ill effect. However, Wimsey realizes that the killer deliberately ate the same poisoned food as his victim to eliminate himself from the inquiry. This ploy enables an in-depth discussion of how eating small amounts of arsenic is, in the context of 1930, believed to help the body develop a resistance to the poison (Sayers 1930: 218). In fact, it takes thousands of years and many generations to build up a tolerance to arsenic, not a few grains a day over a few weeks (Apata 2017: 192–9). However, what Sayers wrote was accurate for the time she was writing (Parascandola 2015).

Strong Poison provides extensive information about arsenic and many of its uses, not just in criminal poisonings. It shows that Sayers's research was detailed and comprehensive and is perhaps the most successful example of a compelling crime narrative that includes a huge amount of the factual information discussed in this chapter. It is surprising that Christie never devoted a single novel to arsenic in the way she did for other poisons. The prominence and success of *Strong Poison* may go some way toward explaining why Christie did not believe it was necessary. All the information Sayers describes can be found in Christie's works, but spread out over several titles and not always as explicitly stated as in *Strong Poison*. Christie had a broad knowledge of poisons she could draw on to avoid clichés and the detailed knowledge and skill to acknowledge those clichés as she does in *After the Funeral*.

CONCLUSIONS

The evidence of the six novels discussed here clearly demonstrates extensive research into toxic compounds. There was evidently a willingness to explore unusual poisons, such as thallium, or familiar substances not often associated with murder, as in the case of nicotine, on the part of all of the authors discussed here. Even familiar poisons are given new twists or used with a nod and a wink to a well-informed audience. Of the four authors discussed, Agatha Christie wore her learning lightly, something that possibly acted both to her advantage and disadvantage. The lack of technical detail and explicit demonstration of her in-depth knowledge make her stories more accessible, but can also be interpreted as a lack of substance, belying her intense research. This attitude has traditionally pervaded Christie scholarship, despite the considerable skill and understanding required to weave salient details into a plot so effectively that they almost go unnoticed.

Christie's focus on methods of administration and symptoms is in stark contrast to her contemporaries who tended to concentrate on forensic processes of detection. Christie was able to tailor her poison to her plot, and vice versa, far more successfully than her contemporaries, with the possible exception of Sayers. Future scholarship could examine the extent to which specific poisons influenced plots or plots determined the poisons. Little academic work has been done on the methods of murder in Golden Age crime fiction more generally, and this is a vacuum that warrants further attention. The dominance of poison in this small niche of crime writing is striking, and the reasons behind it are still to be investigated. The cultural, historic, and scientific context of Christie's use of poisons specifically merits a closer look.

REFERENCES

Allingham, M. (1934), *Death of a Ghost*, London: Heinneman.

Apata, M., B. Arriaza, E. Llop, and M. Moraga (2017), "Human Adaptation to Arsenic in Andean Populations of the Atacama Desert," *American Journal of Physical Anthropology*, 163 (1): 192–9.

Christie, A. (1922), *The Secret Adversary*, London: Bodley Head.

Christie, A. (1935), *Three Act Tragedy*, London: Collins.

Christie, A. (1953), *After the Funeral*, London: Heinneman.

Christie, A. (1957), *4.50 from Paddington*, London: Collins.

Christie, A. ([1961] 1977), *The Pale Horse*, London: Collins.

Curran, J. (2011), *Agatha Christie's Murder in the Making: More Stories and Secrets from Her Archive*, London: HarperCollins.

Emsley, J. (2005), *The Elements of Murder*, Oxford: Oxford University Press.

Gambell, D. (2020), "Who Did What in Every Agatha Christie Murder Novel," *Bloomberg*, February 7. Available online: https://www.bloomberg.com/news/features/2020-07-02/who-did-what-in-every-agatha-christie-murder-mystery-novel (accessed December 1, 2021).

Gerald, M. C. (1991), "Agatha Christie's Helpful and Harmful Health Providers: Writings on Physicians and Pharmacists," *Pharmacy in History*, 33 (1): 31–9.

Gerald, M. C. (1992), "Agatha Christie's Drugs and Disease," *Pharmacy in History*, 34 (2): 95–107.

Gerald, M. C. (1993), *The Poisonous Pen of Agatha Christie*, Austin: University of Texas Press.

Gwilt, P. R. and J. R. Gwilt (1978), "Dame Agatha's Poisonous Pharmacopoeia," *Pharmaceutical Journal*, 28 (30): 572–3.

Harkup, K. (2015), *A Is for Arsenic: The Poisons of Agatha Christie*, London: Bloomsbury.

Harkup, K. (2018), "From Spy Novels to Skripal, the Myth of the Untraceable Poison," *The Guardian*, March 8. Available online: https://www.theguardian.com/science/blog/2018/mar/08/from-spy-novels-to-skripal-the-myth-of-the-untraceable-poison (accessed November 1, 2021).

Holden, A. (1995), *The St Albans Poisoner*, London: Corgi Books.

Marsh, N. (1947), *Final Curtain*, London: Collins.

McNally, W. D. (1920), "A Report of Five Cases of Poisoning by Nicotine," *Journal of Laboratory and Clinical Medicine*, 5: 213–17.

McNally, W. D. (1923), "A Report of Seven Cases of Nicotine Poisoning," *Journal of Laboratory and Clinical Medicine*, 8: 83–5.

Orwell, G. (1946), "Decline of the English Murder," *Tribune*, February 15.

Parascandola, J. (2015), "The Arsenic Eaters of Styria," *Hektoen International: A Journal of Medical Humanities*, 7 (2). Available online: https://hekint.org/2017/01/30/the-arsenic-eaters-of-styria/ (accessed December 1, 2021).

Sayers, D. L. (1930), *Strong Poison*, London: Gollancz.

Thorwald, J. ([1966] 1969), *Proof of Poison*, London: Pan.
Trestrail, J. H. (2000), *Criminal Poisons: Investigational Guide for Law Enforcement, Toxicologists, Forensic Scientists, and Attorneys*, New Jersey: Humana Press Inc.
Waring, R. H., G. B. Steventon, S. C. Mitchell, eds. (2002), *Molecules of Death*, London: Imperial College Press.
Whorton, J. C. (2010), *The Arsenic Century: How Victorian Britain Was Poisoned at Home, Work, & Play*, Oxford: Oxford University Press.

PART FOUR

Beyond the Crime Novels

CHAPTER SIXTEEN

Hiding in Plain Sight: Mary Westmacott

MERJA MAKINEN

INTRODUCTION

Between 1930 and 1956, Agatha Christie published six novels under the pseudonym of Mary Westmacott that ignored the crime genre for a wider literary narrative that allowed her to critique social and cultural concerns about familial relationships, husbands and wives, mothers and daughters, and love and sex outside of conventional marriage. These six pseudonymous novels have been largely ignored by Christie scholars, since they add little to crime theory, and this has necessitated a slightly different focus to this particular chapter. Since it cannot explore the current critical discussions on these novels, my chapter seeks to instigate such a debate and to indicate a fruitful theoretical positioning of the novels within both autobiografiction and gendered historical analysis. While the Westmacott novels add little to our knowledge of Christie's crime tropes, they give insight into the detective fictions' social critiques. The first two, *Giant's Bread* (1930) and *Unfinished Portrait* (1934), have a bildungsroman format, causally linking the mature protagonists to their childhood experiences and containing similar events to some of those found in Christie's 1977 *Autobiography*. Her next two novels, *Absent in the Spring* (1944) and *The Rose and the Yew Tree* (1947), are the most artistically successful and objectively distanced. The first examines with a tight focus the role of the social wife and mother, while the second has a wider historical and geographical focus, exploring the place of a young marriageable woman as the khaki election of 1945 sweeps away the accepted Edwardian mores for a chaotically unknown modernity.

The final two, *A Daughter's a Daughter* (1952) and *The Burden* (1956), were published after the press had revealed the pseudonym. Christie complained to her literary agent, "The people I really minded about knowing were my friends. Cramping to one's subject matter. It's really all washed up" (Gill [1990] 1992: 156). Given the close mining of her personal life in exploratory, critical, and often unexpected fictional representations, anonymity was essential to her literary freedom. The two final novels, written in the 1950s after her identity was publicly exposed, are both the thinnest and the most didactic presentations of the theme developed in all the Westmacott novels: real love is about leaving the other alone, not interfering or trying to possess, because everyone is essentially unknowable. The uncovered Christie loses the delight not only in the subject matter but also in the bolder literary exploration. *A Daughter's A Daughter* is an adaptation of a play written in 1939 destined for production but abandoned because of the onset of Britain entering the Second World War (Green 2020: 98), and the tight structure appropriate for the initial genre gives a certain glibness to the literary version thirteen years later. After the publication of the novel, the play was revised to situate the time at the close of the war, allowing it to "add a sense of postwar displacement to the characters' efforts to redefine themselves in a period of accelerated social change" (Green 2020: 105). Produced in 1956 as a play by Mary Westmacott, the run was not successful (Green 2020: 105–6). This history of the transformations seems to point to the energy lying in it as a play rather than a novel, adding to the concept that the loss of the pseudonym limited the novelist's experimentalism.

The first Westmacott novel, the sprawling *Giant's Bread*, is the only one to have a male protagonist as it charts the genius composer Vernon Deyre's difficult path to forge the modernist "music of tomorrow" (Westmacott [1930] 2001b: 169). Despite two others, *Unfinished Portrait* and *The Rose and the Yew Tree*, having a flawed male narrator, all the following five novels focus on a female protagonist and the complex identities of the feminine self in conflict and complicity with social expectations and pressures of the family. Only in this first assay into the more literary format does Christie feel the expectation to focus on a male artist. In her youth, Christie had tried to become a professional musician, but lacked the necessary public persona (Christie [1977] 1993: 167), perhaps a further indication of the crucial need for her of a pseudonym when exploring the personal.

Writing as Mary Westmacott, Christie had the freedom to explore and comment in depth on femininity in relation to contemporary cultural expectations from the 1930s through to the 1950s in a way that her detective format could not fully allow. Each of the Westmacott novels of the 1930s and the 1940s is different in its structure, format, and narrative, also allowing

Christie to expand her literary potential, while the two 1950s novels return to a similar theme that is explored through differing but more conventional narratives. *Absent in the Spring*, written in the white heat of creativity in three days, remains an astonishingly accomplished modernist masterpiece of a woman's self-delusion of happy respectability and was "the one book that satisfied me completely" (Christie [1977] 1993: 516). The novels circulate around a number of tropes: sheltered childhoods that damage an adult's ability to cope with vicissitude, the damage inflicted by possessive love, and the inability to know how life can transform others, linked to the inalienable difficulties of knowing oneself.

Sadly, all the Westmacott novels have been critically neglected, and, while some biographers have mined them for biographical relevance, few have realized their accomplishment as novels in themselves. In "Agatha Christie in Dialogue with *To the Lighthouse: The Modernist Artist*," I began the recuperation of Westmacott by comparing the *Giant's Bread* modernist composer to Christie's modernist sculptor in *The Hollow* and Virginia Woolf's modernist painter in *To the Lighthouse* (Makinen 2016). The Westmacott novel tackles equally complex, gendered, and societal questions to Woolf's text, if in a less accomplished mode. Indeed all six texts composed under the pseudonym explore dynamic feminine passions, both sexual and familial, and argue that the greatest journey is to acknowledge the truth of oneself, in all its tenuous complexity, and to follow courageously wherever that truth leads. Writing as Westmacott, Christie declares that clinging safely and blindly to cultural norms and external social positions is cowardly and results in an inauthentic feminine self. In one sense, the Westmacott books are fictional speculations on what might have been if her life had been otherwise; the distancing effect of the pseudonym allowed Christie to mine the personal experience of being a lover, wife, and mother to create differing scenarios of the feminine real. Their gendered focus on social analysis is one of their main claims to continued notice, and it is therefore surprising that they have been overlooked by the "middlebrow" critics, for they fit so perfectly within their theoretical focus: "middlebrow English novels of the interwar years, a body of work that inhabits, epitomizes and anatomizes middle-class English social mores" (Hinds 2009: 294).

LIFE WRITING ANALYSIS

Almost all discussion of the Westmacott novels comes from Christie's biographers, predominantly using *Unfinished Portrait* as the unmediated memoir of the novelist's childhood and first marriage. Janet Morgan's official biography, *Agatha Christie: A Biography*, states:

Unfinished Portrait [is] the novel in which two of the principal characters, Celia and Dermot, derive from Agatha herself and from Archie. Agatha was now sufficiently secure to be able to reflect more calmly on her first marriage.

(Morgan 1984: 207)

Morgan mines the novel for factual descriptions of the author's life—"Reggie, who is the model for Peter Maitland in *Unfinished Portrait*" (Morgan 1984: 57)—or detailing Agatha's dash to say farewell to Archie as he returns to war, "a trail vividly described in *Unfinished Portrait*" (Morgan 1984: 65). Treating the text as a *roman à clef*, a novel where real people and events are portrayed with fictitious names, she presents the work as useful mainly for its facticity. Andrew Norman amends the novel's title to claim the significance of his own biography, *Agatha Christie: A Finished Portrait*, but continues the simplistic treatment of the novel as unmediated fact. "Ostensibly fiction, this in reality, is the story of Agatha herself, in all its harrowing and lurid detail" (Norman 2006: 10):

The sentiments expressed above by Celia are, in reality, an in-depth description by Agatha of this unhappy period, and a far more candid one than is provided by her autobiography.

(Norman 2006: 69)

The interrelationship of fact and fiction in life writing needs a more subtle touch, one that Laura Thompson's *Agatha Christie: A English Mystery* in 2007 allows. While again reading *Unfinished Portrait* as exploring the writer's emotions more fully than Christie' restrained *Autobiography*, written decades later, Thompson's biography acknowledges the more complex negotiations needed for fiction. *Unfinished Portrait* is "a hymn to the past" where "she wanted [...] to revisit memory" (Thompson 2007: 304), both "hymn" and "revisit" pointing to a more complex creativity. While biography will always focus primarily on the facts, Thompson acknowledges that this also should encompass the facts of writing secretly under a pseudonym. This act, she suggests, allowed Christie a freedom that kept her hidden from public view:

she had felt an absolute freedom writing those books. She could go wherever she wanted, into every idea that had ever fascinated her, even into the recesses of her own past [... a door] that opened into her most private and precious imaginative garden.

(Thompson 2007: 366–7)

Perhaps the most successful life writing analysis to date comes from Gillian Gill's *Agatha Christie: The Woman and Her Mysteries*, Gill's gendered focus allowing for a sensitive critique of both the life and the novels. Her chapter on *Absent in the Spring* and *The Rose and the Yew Tree*, informed by Christie's reading of Thomas à Kempis, argues for the unknowability of the self and others as stemming from religious mysticism as much as from a modernist aesthetic. For Kempis, we ultimately exist and have meaning only in the mind of God. Gill reads Isabella as exemplifying the unknowable, inward-turning mystic whose death inspires the worldly John Gabriel to Christian activism. While still wedded to the authorial analysis of biography, and reading Isabella and John Gabriel as Christie's rewriting of the inexplicable power of sexual desire between such different people as herself and Archie, Christie's exploration of her religious views and quest for a Christian activism enlightens the novels. Linked to intentionalism, as life writing must be to some extent, the analysis of these "mature novels" is nuanced, illuminating, and exploratory. Gill's analysis of the first two Westmacotts is less so. Like the other biographers, she reads *Unfinished Portrait* as a *roman à clef*, interesting for its revelation of what happened and for how Christie felt. However, she is aware that the facts need to be interrogated. Examining the chapter where Dermot asks for a divorce, Gill comments:

> Agatha's portrait of Archie at this point is devastating. It is also one-sided and shaped by the writer's disillusionment and resentment. One of the twentieth-century's most expert writers of dialogue is at work here, crucifying her husband with words that seem to come from his mouth—and perhaps did!
>
> (Gill [1990] 1992: 106)

Analyzing life writing is not just about the extraction of the facts and a simple discussion of the interpretation and self-censorship of the facts, because facticity is slippery.

The autobiography shows that the Westmacott novels do, at times, mine Christie's past experience for their material, but they are, first and foremost, novels. For the literary critic, their literariness also needs attention. Life writing is certainly a valid and fascinating way of reading the novels, as a form of autobiographical fiction or autobiografiction, but recent life writing criticisms such as Liz Stanley's *The auto/biographical I* and Max Sanders's *Self-Impression: Life-Writing, Autobiografiction and the Forms of Modernist Literature* remind us that we need to consider memory and fictionality as complex and slippery formats. Memory is not fixed in the past and stable; it is in constant renegotiation with the changing present self. That past, refracted through the present viewpoint, is actively reconstructed to give some form of meaning or story (since lived life is plot-less until recounted). When refracted memory is maneuvered to serve the generic demands of a novel, its relevance and meaning will shift even further. Laura Marcus in *Autobiography: A Very*

Short Introduction reminds us that writing about the self is complicated both by the refracted nature of the self and by the viewpoint of the narrator:

> Yet autobiography also asks of its readers that they be open to the complexities of truth. These include the work of memory and the gaps produced by forgetting the distinctions between experience revived (as if, for example, from the child's point of view) and recalled (from the perspective of the adult narrator); the conception of the self from the "inside" and from the "outside" as reflected back to us by others.
>
> (Marcus 2018: 4)

This is a list that would function effectively in an analysis of *Unfinished Portrait,* with its alternate "outside" narrator, Larraby, Celia's lengthy childhood memories commenting upon her present view of herself, other characters' reported disparate views of her, and Larraby's inability to narratively grasp her character. Marcus further explains how as in the twentieth century psychoanalysis affected the life writing genres, the concept of repression on characterization and also the awareness that the multiple self can be "divided and/or unified by patterns established in the early years of life" emerged (Marcus 2018: 59). Both Celia and Larraby point to the early Edwardian, sheltered childhood as leaving the protagonist vulnerable to the harsher modern vicissitudes she encounters, and this psychoanalytic premise to some extent justifies the extended representation within the structure of the novel. Crucially, Marcus delineates autobiographical fiction as, rather than something to be valued for its facticity, a vehicle to explore and represent the process of subjectivity, identity, and self-formation.

> Autobiographical fiction, with its possibilities for multiple perspectives on characters and situations, answered to the need to represent complex, composite and divided selves, creating the most appropriate vehicles for identities that can never be fully known.
>
> (Marcus 2018: 112)

Unfinished Portrait is narrated by a disabled painter, unable to paint, who instead turns to the unfamiliar medium of words to "paint" his portrait of Celia, and it is clear that he has a divided narrative:

> I've seen her you know from two angles. First from my own. And secondly ... I've been able—at moments—to get inside her skin and see her from her own. And the two don't always agree. That's what's so tantalizing and fascinating to me!
>
> (Westmacott [1934] 2009: viii)

The vagaries of memory, in relation to Celia's incomplete reminiscence, are made overt as Larraby exhorts the reader to question the concept of self-formation and identity while simultaneously undermining the value of Celia's remembrance.

> It's an odd question, when you come to think of it, the things we choose to remember. For choice there must be, make it as unconscious as you like. Think back yourself—take any year of your childhood. You will remember perhaps five—six incidents. They weren't important, probably; why have you remembered them out of those three hundred and sixty-five days? Some of them didn't even mean much to you at the time. And yet, somehow, they've persisted. They've gone with you into these later years.
>
> (Westmacott [1934] 2009: 16)

As the "outside" view, Larraby believes he can see a "pattern" to Celia's experiences that she is unaware of, and he gives an adult modern critique of the Edwardian child's evaluations. However, he also acknowledges that the characters he re-presents from her memories have become his own fictional possessions, thereby questioning his own veracity as narrator: "That's how I see it. But perhaps I invent … These people have, after all, become my creations" (Westmacott [1934] 2009: 105). Indeed, this portrait remains partial, "unfinished" in a number of ways, only one of which is Celia's departing without our knowing what will happen. "That's how I see it. It is my fixed belief that Celia went back into the world to begin a new life" (Westmacott [1934] 2009: 400), but Larraby is a novice narrator, flawed, and questioning the medium. Moreover, like Hugh Norreys, the disabled narrator of *The Rose and the Yew Tree*, he is a conventional man incapable of properly comprehending real, unconventional femininity. Implicitly, gender queries and queers what we are shown and told about Celia. The autobiographical genre is problematized in one further way when Celia's publisher tells the fledging writer to ignore "facts" because readers "want fiction—which is plausible untruth" (Westmacott [1934] 2009: 327). *Unfinished Portrait* is unmistakably published as fiction, questioning the reception of the text as simple autobiography.

In the tensions between fact and fiction, when reading *Unfinished Portrait* as a mirror for Christie's traumatic divorce, biographers would do well to consider Jeanette Winterson's explanation for the glaring inconsistencies between her 1985 autobiografiction *Oranges Are Not the Only Fruit* and her autobiography *Why Be Happy When You Could Be Normal?* written twenty-six years later. The novel, she explains, was a "cover version" because "I wrote a story I could live with. The other was too painful. I could not survive it" (Marcus 2018: 75). Life writing analysis needs a sensitive touch. The Westmacott novels can be read as what-might-have-been novels, explorations of alternate narratives on her life fashioned into fiction to allow her to say things about living as a woman in her contemporary society. But the connections between life and art are always complex and tenuous, even when they seem most clear, and genre will always be relevant to the reading.

Around the time that Westmacott was creating her künstelroman *Giant's Bread* (1930) and her autobiografiction *Unfinished Portrait* (1934), a number of modernist writers were exploring the genre. Two decades before, D.H. Lawrence's *Sons and Lovers* (1913), Dorothy Richardson's novel sequence *Pilgrimage* begun in 1915, and James Joyce's *Portrait of the Artist as a Young Man* (1916) had all questioned the narrativity of autobiografiction. Indeed, *Unfinished Portrait*'s opening section of Celia as a baby echoes Joyce's "appropriate language" trope in narrating the baby's viewpoint using childish, limited semantics. But the most relevant context for *Unfinished Portrait* starts with Virginia Woolf's essay "The New Biography" published in 1927 and the parodic novel *Orlando*, subtitled "A Biography," in 1928, both questioning the patriarchal dominance within the genre. Further, the two most subversive novelized autobiographies of the 1930s, Woolf's *Flush* (the biography of Elizabeth Barrat Browning's spaniel) and Gertrude Stein's *The Autobiography of Alice B. Toklas* (written by Stein purporting to be by Toklas on her life with Stein), were both published in 1933, the latter becoming an immediate bestseller in May. Both "experiments in displaced autobiography" (Sanders 2010: 357) are engaged in what Linda Anderson delineates as "the problem of writing women's lives" (Anderson 2002: 92).

Christie composed *Unfinished Portrait* at the very end of 1933, having already completed four other texts that year (*Murder on the Orient Express*, *Why Didn't They Ask Evans?*, and the short story collections *Parker Pyne Investigates* and *The Listerdale Mystery*). Was it just coincidence that Christie decided to write her own autobiografiction at the close of the same year that saw the publication of these two feminist modernist challenges and chose to displace the narrative by giving it a male narrator only partially capable of comprehending its female subject? The chronology is tantalizing, although there is no overt connection between the publications earlier in the year and Christie's decision to start writing. What is indisputable is that she wrote *Unfinished Portrait* during a period of cultural debate about the genre. As Max Sanders argues, the 1930s saw a regrowth and reinvention of the biography: "The rise in popularity of biographies was linked to the perception that biography had been reinvented for the twentieth century, requiring a new level of critical self-awareness" (Sanders 2010: 451). It is this critical generic self-consciousness that needs to be acknowledged when analyzing autobiografication from the 1930s. *Unfinished Portrait* is a much more complex, gendered questioning of the genre, along the lines of *Flush* and *The Autobiography of Alice B Toklas*, than simple readings of it for its autobiographical facts have so far given it credit.

FEMININE MIDDLEBROW ANALYSIS

The most appropriate analysis for the six Westmacott novels is the body of criticism looking at "middlebrow" novels (defined as neither "highbrow" or "serious" literature nor "popular" formulaic fiction). Frustratingly, some of the middlebrow critics do include Christie's detective novels, but the general neglect of Westmacott obscures these works from their view. Hilary Hinds points out that while a general middlebrow will include "the detective fiction of Chesterton, Christie, and Sayers," Nicola Humble's conception of "feminine middlebrow" is of novels "written by women and aimed at a female readership" (Hinds 2009: 293), citing Richard Dyer's view that these texts formed "a cultural framework in which women spoke to women" (Dyer 1993: 40). Nicola Humble's influential *The Feminine Middlebrow Novels 1920s to 1950s: Class, Domesticity and Bohemianism* does use a number of Christie's detective fiction works to illustrate her thesis, *Crooked House* in particular but also *The Hollow, Appointment with Death*, and *The Murder of Roger Ackroyd*. Humble categorizes feminine middlebrow novels as "redefining the significance of the home and of reading for the middle-class woman and [in] actively revising conceptions of class politics, gender roles, and sexuality" (Humble 2001: 149). This is a definition that goes right to the heart of *The Rose and the Yew Tree*, in particular, but encompasses all the Westmacott novels because, as Humble delineates, the feminine middlebrow characteristically interrogates the normative middle-class family, with

> its sense of the family as a profoundly eccentric organization. Repeatedly, a particular sort of family is foregrounded and emerges under the spotlight as a bizarre institution—idiosyncratic rather than normative; a place where social values are challenged rather than inculcated. The family becomes a profoundly ambivalent space, functioning for its (largely female) members as a source of both creative energies and destructive neuroses, simultaneously a haven and a cage.
>
> (Humble 2001: 149)

From *Giant's Bread* to *The Burden*, Westmacott too during this same historical period, the 1930s to the 1950s, interrogates the feminine roles of lover, wife, and mother by turning conventional family milieus strangely eccentric.

An examination of the six differing novels uncovers a consistent critique of both the feminine self, in all its unknowable transience, and the pressures to fit conventional expectations. Conforming to cultural roles is positioned as inhabiting an inauthentic false self and a form of bad faith. A naming of the experiential real therefore ensues, as opposed to the conventional sentimental assumptions, a re-writing of feminine experience to acknowledge the radical and the problematic, as a lover/wife, mother, or a woman pursuing choice, desire, and pleasure otherwise than via the middle-class heteronormative expectations of her time. What distinguishes all of the six Westmacott novels is the desire to unpack the dream or the fairytale heteronormative myth to explore the real experiential darker emotions involved. Alongside this rejection of the conventional comes an argument for freedom of the feminine self to make its own choices and for those choices to ignore the conventional expectations of behavior.

REFIGURING MARRIAGE AND SEXUAL RELATIONSHIPS

All six novels position the concept of marrying and living happily ever after as a fairy tale, and hence unreal. Living within such a myth creates a character that is accused of lazy thinking rather than acknowledging the harder truths of life and sexual relationship. *Giant's Bread* (1930) has the obnoxious, weak Nell as the conventional wife, described as "empty-headed" and a "coward" who "sees things as they have been shown to her and she hopes that they are" (Westmacott [1930] 2001b: 328). Vernon gives up his musical vocation for her, but she won't give up her luxurious, bigamous second marriage for Vernon, lying to keep herself within the safety of convention. In contrast, Jane, Vernon's lover, and Joe, his cousin, are clear-eyed, courageous, and adventurous, risking their singing voice or their social acceptance to follow their sexual attraction and love outside of marriage. The words "courage" and taking "risks" are always important in the Westmacott novels, and Jane's emotional intelligence and clear, straightforward gaze accepts that life is "a difficult, dangerous but endlessly interesting adventure," and that she won't turn her "back on life" ([1930] 2001b: 312).

Following the Westmacott credo of facing reality "with your chin up and your eyes steady" (Westmacott [1930] 2001b: 312), Jane embraces her life as Vernon's mistress and as a vocalist in bohemian Moscow. Notably, the attractive characters have sexual desire met outside of marriage; the coward clings to the conventions of a passionless wedlock. *Giant's Bread* introduces a triptych of feminine roles that circulate throughout the *oeuvre*: the frightened, frigid woman who lazily allows convention to think for her (Nell), the brave woman who acknowledges her own sexual needs but allows desire to overrule sense and makes a series of socially disastrous choices (Joe), and the clear-sighted woman who courageously refuses to have convention prevent her living a balanced, fulfilling life with the man she loves (Jane).

Two years later, Westmacott extends the exploration of how a conventional Edwardian upbringing ill prepares a woman for the modern realities of marriage, in *Unfinished Portrait* (1934). The novel depicts the happy childhood of Celia as allowing her to be cushioned and too happy, unprotected from the realities of life and particularly the reality of men. Celia has been brought up to believe that marriage means happily ever after. She begins to be disabused of this notion by her husband's dislike of certain aspects of her behavior and his lack of physical affection. Her desire for an affectionate marriage is textually linked to Victorian notions imaged as "clinging ivy" (Westmacott [1934] 2009: 289), not appropriate for postwar independence. She acknowledges that they are relative strangers to each other, even when deeply in love, and when he leaves, the cruelty of his behavior is carefully delineated. Marriage can be a place of real loneliness and cruelty, a contrast to the cultural ideal of suffocating togetherness. Rather than blame the husband, Celia blames herself for being emotionally stupid, explaining that it is unfair to trust people too much, or to try to put them "on pedestals" (Westmacott [1934] 2009: 387). Castigating the conventional beliefs of marriage and wifely subservience as outmoded, she contemplates suicide since she is irretrievably damaged by the experience— "nobody can hurt you except a husband—no-one's near enough" (Westmacott [1934] 2009: 391) and is unable to contemplate a life of meaningless affairs, since the novel assumes her sexual desire will still need to be met. Using the triptych of femininity introduced in *Giant's Bread*, Celia is a more likeable but equally flawed conventional Nell figure, terrified of becoming a Joe figure in the future and contemplating suicide. The intervention of Larraby extends hope of a more clear-sighted Jane self-formation, but the novel never clarifies whether Celia succeeds. It is, after all, an "unfinished" portrait of a woman ejected from her role within marriage.

Ten years later, Westmacott returns to the focus of marriage and its limitations for feminine desire in *Absent in the Spring* (1944), again concentrating on the "Nell" figure, but a much less sympathetic version than Celia, despite an even more internalized viewpoint. Joan is positioned as a conventional woman smugly self-satisfied with her life as an apparently successful wife and mother, whom the novel positions as in cold storage, turning her back on life as "a horribly smug creature" (Westmacott [1944] 2001a: 137). Stranded in the desert without distraction for a couple of days, Joan is forced to face her true self and acknowledge the cowardly failures of her past role as wife and mother. Described as "cold as a fish" (Westmacott [1944] 2001a: 9), "straight-laced" (Westmacott [1944] 2001a: 10) and as someone who "always play[s] the game" (Westmacott [1944] 2001a: 11), her sexual desire is minimal and her focus on social position is everything. In contrast, the sympathetic women who shoulder social disasters to follow their desire are given the accolades of "brave" and "courageous."

Blanche (the Joe figure), an old school friend, has been through a series of spectacular affairs and marriages with increasingly lower-class men, but has been happy and has notably refused to steer her men to financial success, allowing them to fulfill their own ambitions even when she knows these will be unsuccessful. In contrast, Joan controls her husband, "deciding she must be wise for two of them" (Westmacott [1944] 2001a: 26), and steers him away from his passion, farming, and into a half-life as a successful solicitor where she can have a better social position. Joan is shown to be selfishly ruthless in pursuing the conventional myth: to marry Rodney, to have children and a comfortable home "[a]nd to live happily ever afterwards, world without end" (Westmacott [1944] 2001a: 15).

Joan believes she has this mythical happiness, and it takes the desert vigil for her to recognize her true self, through the contrast of her own life with her memory of the courageous Lesley (the Jane figure), who cares for her husband and children's inner lives and braves social ostracism when her husband embezzles and is sent to prison. As Westmacott says, "She walked through disillusionment and poverty and illness like a man walks through bogs and over plough and across rivers, cheerfully and impatiently" (Westmacott [1944] 2001a: 161). The reality is that Joan's husband loves the now-deceased Lesley and Joan's children hate their mother for her interference. Joan comes to acknowledge that it is she who is not "real" (Westmacott [1944] 2001a: 63) and recalls her wise headmistress's exhortation: "[D]on't just accept things at face value—because it is the easiest way, because it may save you pain—life is meant to be lived! Not glossed over" (Westmacott [1944] 2001a: 70). Joan clearly has not lived her life. She has buried herself in "the cotton wool" of accepting conventional myth, and she is horrified by the self that she has become. Her children blame her for their father's unhappiness: "[D]on't you know anything about father?"; her husband pities her for her frigidity: "[D]on't you know anything about love?" (Westmacott [1944] 2001a: 91). Despite the clarity of Joan's desert vision, returning to England means a return to her old, false, conventional self. But the days in the wilderness have allowed Westmacott to deliver another blistering denunciation of living conventionally within marriage, accepting the lazy thinking of the sentimental cultural expectations. Again, the brave women who embrace life in all its vagaries and acknowledge their own passionate natures successfully exist outside of marriage or, when within the convention, live it alternatively, thereby "othering" the social conventions.

The final challenge to conventional marriage as the ideal role for women comes three years later in *The Rose and the Yew Tree* (1947). Positioned from the viewpoint of an uncomprehending male, the novel views externally the enigmatic Isabella, brought up to marry the returning Lord Rupert and live happily ever after in the Castle at Loo. The novel characterizes this as another fairy-tale scenario, which the iconoclastic Gabriel refers to as "gingerbread" (Westmacott [1944] 2001a: 596) to reinforce the unreality. Despite Isabella's childhood desire for such a happy ending, and Rupert's resolution that "we would marry and live here for the rest of our mortal lives" (Westmacott [1944] 2001a: 593), the clear-sighted Theresa insists that the fairytale atmosphere is too dreamlike. Hugh, the narrator, is astonished when Isabella elopes with the working-class opportunist and womanizer, John Gabriel, the prospective Conservative candidate in the 1945 election. But the text develops the ways in which the narrator is incapable of seeing Isabella clearly. Isabella has had a modern schooling, excelling at mathematics and astronomy, but the narrator refuses to comprehend this, and insists on viewing her falsely as an enchanted maiden from the medieval fairy tale age. This is explained as the viewer noticing only the characteristics relevant to the viewer; "you pick out of everything the things in it which are significant to *you*" (Westmacott [1944] 2001a: 552).

Gabriel's obsession with Isabella is tied up with his class hatred and sexual desire, two things which Hugh denounces as he recounts how Gabriel has sadistically burned her arm with a cigarette then made brutal love to her in the garden and now, unaccountably, on the eve of her marriage to Rupert, Isabella flees to Paris and then Belgrade to live with Gabriel in squalor and degradation. Gabriel has rudely declared that the paraplegic Hugh is unable to understand the power of sexual desire, but he is also unable to comprehend Isabella's viewpoint, blinded by his conventional mystifying of femininity. We only ever get an external view of Isabella. The internal is denied the reader, except through Hugh's baffled reporting of her speech and her calm impenetrability.

Hugh obviously positions Isabella as a Joe figure, but Isabella herself claims the Jane role. Westmacott perfected the implicit narrative behind the narrator's overt ignorance and repression in *Absent in the Spring* and returns to it in *The Rose and the Yew Tree*, with a more gendered slant. Visiting Belgrade, Hugh sentimentalizes her as the captive maid in an ogre's tower. Isabella acknowledges that she is not happy now, and that she had been happy in St. Loo with Rupert, but she will not leave Gabriel and does not expect him to marry her. Happiness, it turns out, is not the important focus, but grasping at life and experience is. She is, the text explains, "[l]iving through a deep and poignant experience" as an "uncompromising realist" (Westmacott [1947] 2001c: 633). Neither Gabriel nor Isabella really comprehends the other, but even the knowledge that they are strangers to each other does not affect the power of her love. To both the narrator and Gabriel, Isabella has been an enigma, and the sacrificial proof of her absolute love turns Gabriel, the man who believed himself base and unlovable, from a political opportunist into the courageous and saintly Father Clements, and an "incredible life of heroism, endurance, compassion and courage" (Westmacott [1947] 2001c: 478) in war-torn eastern countries.

Isabella's selfless sacrifice allowing her loved one to fulfill his true purpose thereby confirms her Jane role within Westmacott's feminine scenario. Jane in *Giant's Bread* knowingly sacrifices her singing voice to enable Vernon to become the great modernist composer and Isabella braves her phobia of death in stopping the bullet aimed at Gabriel, thereby proving to him his essential lovability and pushing him into being the courageous righter of social wrongs to which his earlier political aims only paid lip service. These courageous women who face life clearly, live it to the full, eschew convention, and love to the hilt, whether Jane, Leslie or Isabella, all die early, but this novel tries to explain Westmacott's ascetic sense of time to evaluate their worth. Life is judged by its depth rather than its length.

> "Five minutes and a thousand years are equally significant" [Theresa] quoted softly, "The moment of the Rose and the moment of the Yew Tree are of equal duration ... "
>
> [...] "You persist in seeing Isabella's life as a thing cut short, twisted out of shape, broken off ... But I have a strong suspicion that it was a thing complete in itself ... "
>
> "The moment of the Rose?"
>
> (Westmacott [1947] 2001c: 641)

The quotation comes from Christie's favorite poem, T.S. Eliot's *The Four Quartets* (1941), and seeks to validate Isabella's life despite its inscrutability for masculinity. *The Rose and the Yew Tree* is a complex novel that does indeed, to repeat Nicola Humble's description of the feminine middlebrow, engage "in actively revising conceptions of class politics, gender roles, and sexuality" (Humble 2001:149). The novel clearly delineates that the conventional fairy tale, marriage and living happily ever after, is not enough for Isabella in the real postwar world. Instead her choice to embrace the importance of darker, sexual desire within a bohemian relationship grants her a deep emotional experience. The justness of her choice is validated by Gabriel's apotheosis. The power of unrestrained, real femininity changes lives for the good, although it is also notable that Westmacott cannot configure these passionate women continuing within the everyday, as if the contemporary has as yet no place for them to inhabit.

Over eighteen years, Agatha Christie, hiding in plain sight behind the pseudonym Mary Westmacott, wrote four novels that challenged conventional marriage as unreal and inadequate for women's emotional experience of life and feminine desire, advocating following passion wherever it led in order to live life to the full. These books show that the social expectation of the wife as a support to her husband and the perception of marriage as a fairy tale incarcerate women within these conventions, stifling their lives, preventing them from understanding men, and leading to an unreal and damaging bad faith toward their own inner selves.

FAMILY LIFE

The final two novels, *A Daughter's a Daughter* (1952) and *The Burden* (1956), focus on uncovering the selfish and damaging realities within families, continuing to explore how selfishness and even hatred lurk behind the myths of maternal and sibling relationships. The real focus, as in the earlier novels, is the idea that we should never choose to impose our wishes on other women, since everyone is an unknowable stranger, and that the height of love is to stand back and refuse to interfere. In *A Daughter's a Daughter*, the mother sees her daughter off for a three-week holiday, and steps out of her maternal role to rediscover her own feminine needs. Anne is attracted to and becomes engaged to Richard, embracing what the wise Dame Laura calls her "second blooming [...] of the mind and spirit" (Westmacott [1952] 2009: 18). Post-motherhood, women have a chance to spread themselves, "grow wider," and become "interesting" (Westmacott [1952] 2009: 18). The daughter, on her return, jealously breaks up the relationship, by playing on her mother's maternal conventions. Despite everyone warning her not to interfere—"I wouldn't go monkeying about with other people's lives" (Westmacott [1952] 2009: 108)—Sarah selfishly persists and in consequence, earns the mother's hatred for her lost possibility of happiness.

Engineering Sarah's marriage to a cruel, licentious, and rich older man, as an unacknowledged revenge, Anne is unable to live with herself and inhabits an inauthentic self, as a gay society partygoer suffering from nerves. Only with the mother and daughter's voicing of their mutual, repressed undercurrent of hatred can they find a way forward to forgive each other: "You hate me for spoiling your life, Mother. Well, I hate you for spoiling mine" (Westmacott [1952] 2009: 274). Westmacott unpacks the vicious and selfish undercurrents in a mother–daughter relationship, stripping the myths of love to explore the vengeful resentment between the two still sexually active women.

The Burden, published four years later, focuses equally on familial resentment and hatred. Conventionally "loving parents" unfairly favor some of their children over the others, wishing the plain Laura had died instead of their beloved son Charles. The young unloved Laura's reaction to a new baby being preferred to her is murderous. Alongside this unpacking of conventional familial happiness comes the plea not to interfere in others' lives. Young Laura has an elderly confidant who echoes the wise Dame Laura in the previous book, when she argues that Laura should not interfere in her sister's choices: "Nothing is your business but yourself" (Westmacott [1956] 2009: 46) and "You can't run other people's lives for them. Young Shirley has got her own row to hoe" (Westmacott [1956] 2009: 115). Laura falls passionately in protective love with her sister and the text argues that extreme love is a smothering burden. Shirley makes a poor marriage, and her socially unsuccessful husband contracts polio. Laura poisons him to free her sister from the unhappy situation. The text, however, suggests, again, that conventional comfort is not the purpose of a woman's life and that our knowledge of others is always only partial. Where Laura mistakenly sees her younger sister as weak and needing protection, Shirley is "a brave, gallant, adventurous young woman" (Westmacott [1956] 2009: 292) living a "difficult but passionately worth while" life (Westmacott [1956] 2009: 293).

Potentially another Leslie/Jane figure, Laura's interference forces Shirley into a Nell role but without Nell's comfortable ignorance. With her first husband's death, Shirley accepts the protective love of her second husband, and is thrust back into the "layers of cotton-wool and soft wrapping, and anxious love" (Westmacott [1956] 2009: 293) that drive her to alcohol until her untimely death. Laura's sibling/maternal loving interference proves to be her sister's destruction because she has a limited understanding of Shirley's reality, and indicts her own need to see herself as acting for the best. Both novels of the 1950s uncover the darker and more violent emotions present in family life between parents and children and sibling. Women making choices for other women, whether really or only superficially out of love, are equally damaging. The height of love, and of respect for the feminine, is to leave them alone to make their own decisions and mistakes and to live their own lives.

In conclusion, these six novels composed under the Westmacott pseudonym explore dynamic feminine passions, both sexual and familial, and argue that the greatest journey is to acknowledge the truth of one's self, in all its tenuous complexity, and to follow it courageously wherever it leads. Clinging safely and blindly to cultural norms and external social positions is cowardly and results in an inauthentic cultural half-self. These are speculative novels; the distancing effect of the pseudonym allows Christie to mine close personal experience to create differing scenarios of the feminine real. As such, their main interest lies is in their social analysis of how abnormal the conventional institutions of marriage and family can be and what hotbeds of selfish possessiveness, hatred, and suffocation they can become beneath the veneer of normality. As Nicola Humble reiterated in 2013 of feminine middlebrow fiction:

> Dealing mostly in conventional "feminine" subjects, such as home, romance, marriage, motherhood and the family, it remakes the everyday into something strange, slightly off-centre. Closely attuned to the shifting demands of its readers, it is subtle and flexible, renegotiating changing social structures and ideologies, balancing the conservative and the radical.
>
> (Humble 2013: 110)

Mary Westmacott's oeuvre surely demands to be included within the framework of this continuing analysis of feminine middlebrow writers to bring it out of obscurity to stand alongside the works of Rosamund Lehmann, Elizabeth

Taylor, Stella Gibbons, Nancy Mitford, Elizabeth Bowen, and Ivy Compton-Burnett. And, when these books are analyzed as life writing, the analysis needs to be both more critically sensitive and more generically aware to appreciate just how questioning the works are in relation to the self and to the presentation of a life. Taken alongside the more famous crime fiction, these literary novels expand our understanding of Christie's literary ambitions and her achievements.

REFERENCES

Anderson, L. (2002), *Autobiography*, London: Routledge.

Christie, A. ([1977] 1993), *An Autobiography*, London: HarperCollins.

Dyer, R. (1993), *The Matter of Images: Essays on Representations*, London: Routledge.

Gill, G. ([1990] 1992), *Agatha Christie: The Woman and Her Mysteries*, Toronto: Free Press.

Green, J. (2020), "A Worrying Nerve-Wracked World: Agatha Christie's Emergence as a Playwright during and after the Second World War," in Rebecca Mills and J. C. Bernthal (eds), *Agatha Christie Goes to War*, 95–108, London and New York: Routledge.

Hinds, H. (2009), "Ordering Disappointments: Femininity, Domesticity, and Nation in British Middlebrow Fiction, 1920–1944," *Modern Fiction Studies*, Summer, 55 (2): 293–320.

Humble, N. (2001), *The Feminine Middlebrow Novels 1920s to 1950s: Class, Domesticity and Bohemianism*, Oxford: Oxford University Press.

Humble, N. (2013), "The Feminine Middlebrow Novel," in M. Joannou (ed), *The History of British Women's Writing*, Vol. 8, 97–111, London: Macmillan.

Makinen, M. (2016), "Agatha Christie in Dialogue with *To the Lighthouse*," in J. C. Bernthal (ed), *The Ageless Agatha Christie: Essays on the Mystery and Legacy*, 11–28, Jefferson: McFarland.

Marcus, L. (2018), *Autobiography: A Very Short Introduction*, Oxford: Oxford University Press.

Morgan, J. (1984), *Agatha Christie: A Biography*, London: HarperCollins.

Norman, A. (2006), *Agatha Christie: A Finished Portrait*, London: Tempus.

Sanders, M. (2010), *Self-Impression: Life-Writing, Autobiografiction and the Forms of Modernist Literature*, Oxford: Oxford University Press.

Stanley, L. (1992), *The Auto/Biographical I: The Theory and Practice of Feminist Auto/Biography*, Manchester: Manchester University Press.

Thompson, L. (2007), *Agatha Christie: An English Mystery*, London: Headline.

Westmacott, M. ([1944] 2001a), *Absent in the Spring* in *Absent in the Spring and Other Novels*, 1–162, New York: St, Martin's Minotaur.

Westmacott, M. ([1930] 2001b), *Giant's Bread*, in *Absent in the Spring and Other Novels*, 163–405, New York: St. Martin's Minotaur.

Westmacott, M. ([1948] 2001c), *The Rose and the Yew Tree*, in *Absent in the Spring and Other Novels*, 469–644, New York: St. Martin's Minotaur.

Westmacott, M. ([1956] 2009), *The Burden*, London: Harper.

Westmacott, M. ([1934] 2009), *Unfinished Portrait*, London: Harper.

Westmacott, M. ([1952] 2009), *A Daughter's a Daughter*, London: Harper.

FIGURE 17.1 Agatha Christie broadcasting for the BBC, 1937. Credit: BBC, Reference No. 1263787—Yellow Iris.

CHAPTER SEVENTEEN

Christie's BBC Radio Broadcasts, 1930–55

VIKE MARTINA PLOCK

INTRODUCTION

Agatha Christie and the BBC are products of the interwar period. In 1922, a year after Christie's first novel, *The Mysterious Affair at Styles*, was published in the UK, the British Broadcasting Company (later the British Broadcasting Corporation) took up its task to "inform, educate and entertain" the country's population ("Broadcasting"). A first Royal Charter consolidated the Corporation's independence as public service broadcaster in 1927, meaning that the BBC once more trailed Christie, who had achieved another significant career highlight with the publication of *The Murder of Roger Ackroyd* the previous year. Whereas the interwar period was one of experimentation and gradual consolidation for both the writer and the broadcaster, their parallel history during and after the Second World War sees the BBC and Christie rise to iconic status at home and abroad. Until the arrival of commercial television in 1956, the BBC had a monopoly on electronic communication transmission in the UK. In the same decade, Mark Aldridge suggests, Christie, "the writer slowly morph[ed] into 'Agatha Christie' the brand," showing how she "had come to dominate the crime fiction market so absolutely" (2020: 235). By mid-century, Christie and the BBC had also begun to wield soft power like few other British cultural exports, helping to establish positive, often idealized, images of Britishness in countless countries around the globe.

While it might seem little productive to read the career and reputation building of a twentieth-century woman novelist alongside the BBC's institutional history—there is no evidence that Christie was, at any point in her life, affected or impressed by the Corporation's rise to cultural authority—this chapter will show that occasional collaboration marked the early phase of their professional acquaintance and allowed Christie and the BBC to develop a relationship of mutually beneficial promotion. In the 1920s and 1930s, Christie's gradual emergence as a successful writer was based on experimentation, leading directly to some of her most famous challenges to the crime fiction genre. With no established formula to fall back on and before any kind of audience research project was begun in earnest, editors at the BBC had also to rely on trial-and-error approaches in programming in these early decades of broadcasting. It was in these years that the relationship between Christie and the BBC was the most direct and often the most productive. While she would remain a staple on the British radio schedule long beyond this initial phase of direct collaboration, Christie accepted her last BBC commission in 1954 when she delivered the manuscript for the radio drama *Personal Call*. After the formation of Agatha Christie Ltd in 1955, her appearances on BBC airwaves were all but confined to newly commissioned adaptations of her work with which she was not directly involved.

This chapter returns to the early years of the BBC–Christie collaboration to examine how Christie drew creative inspiration and learned from the advent of radio technology in the first decades of her writing career. In revisiting materials from the BBC Written Archives Centre (BBC WAC) and the Hughes Massie Archive at the University of Exeter, it will also show that Christie's professional confidence and her willingness to make concessions for BBC demands became inversely proportional as she began to manage her career more determinedly and effectively. As such, the discussion of Christie's work for the BBC is significant for two reasons. It illustrates her resourcefulness as a writer whose work was responsive to the cultural atmosphere of its time.[1] But Christie's occasional dealings with the BBC also tell the story of a female writer who held her own in male-controlled professional networks in charge of disseminating culture in the first half of the twentieth century.

CHRISTIE AND THE WIRELESS

Christie was no fan of other people's attempts to adapt her work for another medium. Aldridge notes that she "made no secret of the fact that she did not care for television" and that there "were no television series based on her

---

[1]Christie's "adaptive ability, and her responsiveness to the cultural climate" have been analyzed by Gill Plain (2020: 182) in relation to the postwar period.

work" during her lifetime (2016: 35). Julius Green agrees, stating that Christie "had absolutely no interest in film or television" and "disliked the majority of film adaptations of her work that she saw" (22). A cursory look through surviving archival records suggests that she was equally contemptuous of radio adaptations, of broadcasting in general and of the BBC's version in particular. In the 1940s, a series of Poirot adaptations was broadcast on the radio in the United States. But Christie recoiled from the thought of undertaking similar experiments to home: "Perish the thought that I should ever have a synthetic Poirot on the wireless in this country," she wrote to her agent in 1947 (Christie 1947a; 1947b).[2] In 1948, an article in *The Observer* must have claimed that she was "violently allergic to the B.B.C." When the Head of the BBC Talks Department invited her to "give a 15 minute talk in the Third Programme saying why [she] felt so strongly about broadcasting," Christie declined his "sporting offer," clarifying that she did not "do much on the B.B.C. because [she was] allergic to its remuneration" (Christie 1948; Luke 1948).[3] While her biographer Janet Morgan argues that "relations with the BBC were not always prickly" and that Christie "liked working for the wireless" (304), Laura Thompson claims that the "BBC was not really Agatha's kind of set-up; she never liked anything state-controlled, and she certainly disliked low wages" (165). Christie's BBC engagements were undoubtedly few and far between, beginning with the collaboratively penned serial *Behind the Screen* in 1930 and culminating with *Personal Call* in 1954. Unlike her fellow crime-writer Dorothy L. Sayers, who scripted the controversial BBC radio series *The Man Born to Be King* (1941–2) during the Second World War (see Goody 2014: 79–96), Christie never committed herself to any kind of continuous broadcasting work.

For this reason, it is little surprising that criticism focusing on Christie's radio work is sparse. Alison Light is one exception, pointing out an obvious relationship between the wireless and Christie's detective novels. As "new variants of a commercial culture" signifying "expendability and temporality (such novels could be read in one sitting)," Christie's fiction, Light argues, would have been considered "as intrusive as the loudspeaker, wireless or film" by readers "who preferred nineteenth-century forms" (64). In the interwar period, many of Christie's intellectually minded contemporaries would instinctively

---

[2]Christie was keener on radio adaptations of her work if they were based on her lesser-known characters and if they were to be broadcast abroad. "I think Parker Pyne an excellent subject for a Radio programme—much more suitable than Poirot," she said of a suggested US radio series involving one of her other creations (Christie 1947b).

[3]Edmund Cork, Christie's agent, was equally clear when Val Gielgud, the Head of BBC Television Drama, approached her in 1948 with the request to write another radio play. Cork explained that Christie "has on two occasions written plays specially for broadcasting, but in each case there has been a special consideration, and in light of the large prices she obtains from other markets," he continued, "it is unlikely that the fees which the Corporation could offer her would prove very attractive" (in Aldridge 2016: 44).

associate her work with the broadcasts of the BBC, dismissing both as conveyers of culture for people with middlebrow tastes. In 1925, *Punch* had famously satirized the Corporation's commitment to educational uplift: "The BBC claim to have discovered a new type, the 'middlebrow,'" the magazine announced. "It consists of people who are hoping that some day they will get used to the stuff they ought to like" (*Punch* 1925: 673). While not directly aligning Christie's work with BBC broadcasts, Nicola Humble suggest that both were of value to ambitious social climbers. She sees Christie's books as examples of feminine middlebrow novels, which "had a significant role in the negotiation of new class and gender identities in the period from the 1920s to the 1950s." By the same token, she notes that the "careful diction and received pronunciation of the BBC announcers of the period" disseminated the linguistic signifiers frequently associated with the cultural hegemony of the upper classes in Britain (5, 86).

To date, Aldridge offers the most useful and detailed discussion of Christie's involvement with BBC radio broadcasting. His *Agatha Christie on Screen* recovers the story of her professional association with the Corporation (2016: 35–8, 42, 44, 65), but as the title of his monograph suggests, her UK radio work is considered only within the debate of screen adaptations with which his work is principally concerned.[4] This chapter makes Christie's radio presence in Britain in the first half of the twentieth century its focus, assessing how she adjusted her work to fit the requirements of BBC broadcasting projects. As she would have learned early on in her dealings with the Corporation, the medium demanded scripts that conveyed the spontaneity of informal storytelling if it was to be read by one person. In radio plays, dialogue was prioritized. Description was actively discouraged. Working within the parameters of an exclusively aural medium was new to Christie when she agreed to her first commissions in the 1930s. But as her radio plays from the postwar period illustrate, she was adept in dealing with these new challenges. The four-scene radio drama *Butter in a Lordly Dish* (1948), for instance, is composed entirely of fast-paced dialogue and makes exemplary use of sound effects. This chapter will chart what I call Christie's apprenticeship in writing for a new type of market: interwar and mid-century radio audiences also courted by the BBC. As Christie would have known, even if fees were decidedly unattractive, it was in her interest to broker occasional deals with the Corporation. Exposure on the airwaves would raise her visibility as a writer of detective novels and could boost sales figures of new books. Broadcasting her work on the BBC, *News Talks* editor J.R. Ackerley reassured her in 1932, would "not steal the thunder from a subsequent publication, but will in all probability enhance the value" (Ackerley 1932b). BBC producers were

---

[4]Peter Haining's *Agatha Christie: Murder in Four Acts* (1990), a beautifully illustrated coffee table book dealing with film, TV, radio and stage adaptations of Christie's work, contains a detailed, at times incorrect account of her appearance on BBC airwaves (54–67).

also keen to remind Christie that, "bare broadcasting rights" aside, she would retain all other copyright for pieces written for the Corporation (Ackerley 1934a). In the case of *Three Blind Mice*, a radio drama originally written in 1947, Christie was able to exploit the commercial advantages of copyright deals agreed with the BBC. While she donated her broadcasting fee (100 guineas) to the Southport Infirmary Children's Toy Fund, she adapted the radio drama into a short story that was published in the United States in 1948. More importantly, she also turned it into *The Mousetrap*, which became the longest-running play on the British stage.[5]

In keeping with her well-established status as professional author, Christie nonetheless kept the financial viability of projects firmly in sight when dealing with the BBC. Patronizing requests from male producers to "please be nice and kind and say that [the suggested fee] will do" would, for good reasons, have fallen on deaf ears.[6] At the BBC, this "approach" was quickly decried as "commercial": "Why should I exhaust a good idea in a broadcast for a few guineas when I could make thousands out of it in a book" was one producer's summary assessment of Christie.[7] Ackerley, who worked with her several times in the 1930s, privately called her "surprisingly good looking and extremely tiresome." He noted in a memo addressed to a BBC colleague that she was "always late sending in her stuff, very difficult to pin down for engagements, and invariably late for them" while he rated her broadcasting abilities as no more than "adequate" and perhaps "a little on the feeble side" compared with "the terrific vitality, bullying and bounce of that dreadful woman Dorothy L. Sayers."[8] But in the male-dominated world of broadcasting, governed by "the 'public school' atmosphere and 'old boys' networks," women and their demands for professional recognition could easily get sidelined. As Kate Murphy has shown, while women occupied a range of different positions within the BBC, only "[t]hree women held Director-Level posts" before 1950 (6, 2–3). If it was unusual for a busy woman writer such as Christie to demand that she be paid properly for her labor and normal for (male) BBC producers to respond dismissively to these requests, then it is vital to call attention to Christie's professional experiences with the BBC. They show us how little cultural value

---

[5]In the case of *The Yellow Iris*, first transmitted by the BBC on November 2, 1937, a short story seems to have preceded the broadcast: "Yellow Iris" had been published the previous year in the *Strand Magazine* and the *Chicago Tribune*. However, Aldridge argues that "the history of the *The Yellow Iris* is difficult to untangle," coming to the conclusion that "both radio and print version were written more or less concurrently" (2020: 118). In 1945, the material was re-purposed again for Christie's novel *Sparking Cyanide*.

[6]"The truth of the matter is that I hate writing short things and they really are <u>not</u> profitable," Christie wrote in response to this particular plea to accept an unacceptable fee for writing a series of short radio plays. See Ackerley 1932b; 1936.

[7]BBC Internal Memo, October 5, 1948, BBC WAC, Agatha Christie, Talks File 1: 1930–58.

[8]BBC Internal Memo, August 15, 1939, BBC WAC, Agatha Christie, Talks File 1: 1930–58.

was attached to women's creative work in the early decades of the twentieth century. They also show that women who had, like Christie, a good sense of how much their work was worth were frequently derided by the men with whom they were forced to discuss the price of their creative labor.

Irrespective of fee disputes, Christie seems to have been a fan of radio broadcasting. Even at the BBC, she left the impression that "she is quite happy to listen."[9] Aspects of her creative output show that she was also aware of the cultural debates accompanying radio's establishment as a mass communication medium in the interwar period. This interest in broadcasting is visible in one of her early short stories. In September 1925, Christie published "Wireless" in Britain in the *Sunday Chronicle Annual*.[10] The story deals with Mary Harter, an elderly widow with a heart condition, who is talked into the purchase of a radio by her young nephew. Initially dismissive of "these new-fangled things" and worried about the effect of "the electric waves" on her health (Christie 2008: 145), Mrs. Harter is soon won over and begins to enjoy her new purchase. One evening she begins to receive strange messages from the wireless. A voice professing to be that of her deceased husband seems to be calling her from the afterlife. Increasingly worried, Mrs. Harter begins to prepare for an impending death.

In penning this story, Christie responded to contemporary debates aligning new communication technologies with spiritualism. As Pamela Thurschwell has shown, it was not uncommon at the turn of the twentieth century to associate paranormal phenomena that had become the subject of psychical research with new technologies that were now used for communication transmission. "Teletechnologies such as the telegraph and the telephone," she explains, "suggested that science could help annihilate distances that separated bodies and minds from each other. When these new technologies begin suffusing the public imagination from the mid-nineteenth century on," she continues, "they appear to support the claim of spiritualist mediums; talking to the dead and talking on the phone both hold out the promise of previously unimaginable contact between people" (3). In Christie's story, it seems as if the difference between technological and occult transmission collapses when Mrs. Harter receives her first personalized message over the ether.

In the end, "Wireless" opts for a non-spiritualist explanation. Even so, it shows that technological knowledge of "bright-emitter valves, of dull-emitter valves, of high frequency and low frequency, of amplification and of condensers" could simulate experiences that have all the appearance of paranormal events (Christie 2008: 145). It was written at the time when Christie's work repeatedly turned to the exploration of parapsychological

---

[9]BBC Internal Memo, October 5, 1948, BBC WAC, Agatha Christie, Talks File 1: 1930–58.
[10]Publication date and context as stated in "Appendix: Short Story Chronicle" (Christie 2008).

phenomena. Short stories such as "The Red Signal" (1924) and "The Fourth Man" (1925) involve an "alienist" and a "mental specialist" respectively and in both cases the plot hinges on the exploration of events that range from the "purely pathological to the super-psychological" (Christie 2008: 31, 185, 186). In the latter story, the scientific and the paranormal coalesce when a psychiatrist revisits a famous case of personality dissociation only to have the scenario reinterpreted as a particular sinister form of transmigration by a layman's eye witness account. Less ambiguous but also more disturbing is the Gothic story "The Last Séance" (1926). Here, the supernatural is more readily identified as the cause for a medium's gruesome death. "Wireless," in other words, was written at a time when Christie's fiction consciously experimented with exploring correspondences between the scientific and the supernatural that fascinated and disturbed many of her contemporaries. Collectively, these stories show that Christie was, in the early years of her career, by no means set on the whodunit plot. Versatile and creatively adventurous, she tried her hand at writing in different genres and in different voices. It is hardly surprising that she readily accepted the first commission to contribute to a radio series when the BBC reached out to her in 1930. Not only would this engagement give Christie the opportunity to capture a new market of readers, it would also give her the chance to test her skills in writing for a medium to which many of her contemporaries assigned an almost magical quality.

THE CHRISTIE–BBC COLLABORATION

In the 1930s, Christie's work began to feature regularly and often prominently on BBC airwaves. Recently published novels received occasional mention by Vita Sackville-West and E.M. Delafield in the Corporation's "New Novels" review broadcasts;[11] John Maynard Keynes broadcast a general endorsement in a talk in June 1936 (Keynes 1936); and in August 1938, *The Listener* printed a short piece by Christie explaining her reasons for the "adoption of a writing career." It appeared in a series entitled "I Became an Author" to which W.B. Yeats had previously contributed (Christie 1939). Also in 1938, the BBC broadcast an adaptation of a Poirot story. *The Incredible Theft* was transmitted in the *Detective in Fiction* series on May 10 on the National Programme.[12] But it was early on in the decade, in 1930, that Christie was asked to write a piece especially for broadcasting. In April, she had received a letter from Hilda Matheson, the

---

[11]See, for instance, *The Mysterious Mr. Quin* reviewed by West on April 28, 1930 and *Three Act Tragedy* reviewed by Delafield on January 9, 1935. *The Listener*, May 7, 1930: 822; January 23, 1935: 165.

[12]The story was adapted for broadcasting by playwright and BBC producer Leslie Stokes ("BBC Genome"). In the same year, the BBC also televised a dramatic adaptation of Christie's story "Love from a Stranger" (Aldridge 2016: 40–1).

BBC's first Director of Talks, inviting her to "join in a mystery serial" which was scheduled for broadcasting "on succeeding Saturdays during May and June." Christie was asked to write "an instalment of, roughly, 1800 words" to be transmitted alongside those of other "leading detective story-writers" such as Ronald Knox, Dorothy Sayers, and E.C. Bentley (Matheson 1930a).

This "co-operative serial detective story for broadcasting," appropriately termed an "experiment" by Matheson, was to become *Behind the Screen* and Christie was assigned the second slot on the schedule (Matheson 1930b). Overall, she must have been pleased with this first experience of broadcasting on the national airwaves. She had been invited to dine with Matheson at the Savoy to talk about the project and her voice test, which occurred three days before her microphone appearance on May 21, had been enthusiastically received at the BBC. But writing for the wireless also came with challenges. Before the event, Matheson reminded Christie to time herself carefully when reading her installment so as not to "overrun the period of twenty minutes allotted." Broadcasting schedules required punctuality, as Matheson explained, with "subsequent items" being "thrown sadly out of gear if timing is not rather strictly watched" (Matheson 1930c). Equally important was continuity between installments, and Matheson politely but firmly requested that Christie eliminate a number of small inconsistencies between her own and Hugh Walpole's installment, which had gone out the previous week. This, a later BBC letter to Christie explained, was essential to avoid confusion with the listener who, unlike "the reader of a published story [who] has leisure to study it […] has no such opportunity except to read later on in <u>The Listener</u> what his ear has failed to catch or his mind to follow during the actual transmission" (Ackerley 1930).

The fact that *Behind the Screen*, this "serial detective story," had multiple authors added layers of complexity. Even so, Christie would have noticed during this first encounter with radio work that any kind of broadcasting project was—unlike writing fiction—a collaborative task and that BBC editors frequently intervened in the preparation of broadcasting scripts. The "microphone does need," as they were keen to point out, "a special technique" (Ackerley 1932a). In addition to the importance of timing, they were acutely aware of and adamant that the ephemerality of the live broadcast had to be taken into account when penning and reading radio scripts. Simplicity, directness, and economy were repeatedly identified in correspondence with Christie as the goalposts for broadcasting. For scriptwriting this meant that "characters in the story should be kept down to a minimum" and "[d]ialogue should be written in such a way that the listener is never in doubt as to who is speaking" (Ackerley 1930).

Frequently curbing her creative freedom, BBC producers edited Christie's scripts to make them more easily digestible for a listening public. They would also insist on properly rehearsing so-called outside artists such as Christie, making significant demands on her time. Additionally, Christie could not have failed to notice that the BBC had, by the 1930s, become an increasingly bureaucratic apparatus with interconnected divisions that made professional engagements laborious and time-consuming. While commissions were initially agreed with BBC editors who advised on manuscript delivery, the talks booking department was in charge of organizing the broadcasting schedule. The finance department issued contracts and organized payments while the editorial team of *The Listener* would have needed print versions in good time before live transmissions went out on the airwaves to make sure these print versions could be included in forthcoming magazine numbers. It is understandable that Christie, a hardworking author with a busy schedule, would have thought twice about accepting a great deal of BBC commissions in a period of her life when she also began to travel extensively. While she often claimed that she could write her novels anywhere, needing only a table, a typewriter, and occasionally a Dictaphone, early experiences with broadcasting had shown her that it could be creatively and geographically restricting.

On Sayers's insistence, Christie wrote two installments for the second Detection Club radio serial, *The Scoop*, which was broadcast by the BBC on Saturday evenings from January to April 1931. Fittingly, Freeman Wills Crofts's penultimate installment had members of the BBC's Music Department assist the investigating officer in the dismantling of a suspect's alibi. This second attempt at collaboration between the BBC and member of the Detection Club turned out to be extremely exhausting for everyone involved (see Morgan 195–9). But Christie was still intrigued enough by the experience of speaking on the wireless to joke with her husband about putting in "a suitable plug" for him (in Morgan, 197). Max Mallowan was in Iraq at the time of her *The Scoop* broadcasts and had to face a horse ride across the desert in the attempt to find a radio with sufficient signal strength to receive BBC transmissions. Given the enthusiasm and excitement with which both spouses commented on the possibility of exchanging secret messages over the wireless, it is tempting to suggest that the opportunity to use the radio to speak to a loved one abroad was one reason why Christie accepted her second commission from the BBC.

In 1932, Christie declined another request to write a series of short detective stories for broadcasting, citing time constraints and inadequate remuneration as reasons for her decision. But as a letter from Christie's secretary, Charlotte Fisher, to Ackerley suggests, she was intrigued by his suggestion of short plays featuring Miss Marple (Fisher 1932). In his letter, Ackerley had acknowledged that the BBC had learned lessons from earlier experiments with detective fiction broadcasting. They were now "considering getting stories written completely in dialogue or of broadcasting a complete murder trial [...] specially written for [the BBC]" (Ackerley 1932a). This shift in dramaturgy must have appealed to Christie, who would state her preference for writing plays over novels in the BBC broadcast *Close-Up* in 1955 (Christie [1955] 2016). When she received Ackerley's offer in 1932, she would also have remembered the pleasure it had given her to see her first play, *Black Coffee* (1930), performed on the stage.

Understandably, the suggestion to write dialogue-based radio plays might have been of interest to her. It is certainly significant that all but one of the subsequent Christie-authored BBC broadcasts adopted a dramatic form, showing that the author and the Corporation had settled on a broadcasting format that worked best for everyone involved.

Before this shift from straight talk to dramatic feature was realized with the production of *The Yellow Iris* in 1937, the Corporation commissioned one more Christie broadcast that was read by the author herself. Over the next couple of years, Ackerley sent more requests to Christie to submit material for broadcasting, first in May 1933 and then again in February 1934. His tenacity, a good bit of flattery and, above all, his shrewdness in letting Christie suggest a suitable fee finally paid off. For a payment of thirty guineas Christie agreed to write a short story for broadcasting. As Ackerley was keen to stipulate at this point, the BBC were trying to implement a shift in broadcasting technique toward a "revival of story telling as distinct from story writing." This, he noted in a letter to Christie, required a "definite change of technique on the part of writers." It can "be assumed," he continued, that "quoted speech" was "wrong," because it "immediately gives the impression that the story is being read and not told." What the BBC had in mind was a manuscript for a story that could be read as if "told across a dinner table" (Ackerley 1934a). Once more, he noted how suitable the stories in *The Thirteen Problems* (1932) would be for this purpose. In 1927, Miss Marple had made a first appearance as sleuth in the short story "The Tuesday Night Club." It had morphed into a collection of thirteen stories dealing with "[u]nsolved mysteries" that are discussed by a handful of people gathered in Miss Marple's living room (Christie 2008: 304).

On March 14, 1934, Ackerley, who was keen to generate publicity for the event, asked Christie for a title for her forthcoming broadcast. Christie submitted her manuscript, *In a Glass Darkly*, two days later, prompting the *Radio Times* to announce that her talk was scheduled for Friday, April 6 at 10:35 pm (National Programme) as the first in a series of short story broadcasts. Reminding potential listeners that "this new series" was as much as the *Behind the Screen* serial "an experiment in technique," the *Radio Times* announcement also declared that this time "the short story is to be experimented with." Reminiscent of Ackerley's letters, it noted the BBC's newfound interest in presenting the medium as a vehicle for story-telling: "[O]nce upon a time, when there were no books to read, no films to see, no wireless sets to switch on, people told each other stories, and listeners were absorbed." Associating modern technology with prehistoric communication transmission, it promised listeners a broadcast that "will appeal to an audience that depends upon the ear alone" (1028). Given the effort the BBC had invested in contracting, setting up, and advertising Christie's broadcast, it must have been devastating when *In a Glass Darkly* turned out to be unsuitable for broadcasting. Although Christie had used a first-person narrator for her story about an uncanny premonition, it seemed over-engineered and did not meet the requirements for spontaneous narration identified in Ackerley's letters as a priority for specially commissioned BBC talks.

Even if she was privately annoyed, Christie responded professionally to what might have easily been seen as an unforgivable rebuff. She went straight to work on an alternative story to be broadcast on a later date. She also made good use of the fact that the BBC had only bought broadcasting rights for *In a Glass Darkly* and had the story published in *Collier's Weekly* in the United States (July) and in the *Woman's Journal* in the United Kingdom (December). The Corporation similarly sprang into action, asking Christie's approval of an adaptation of "The Tuesday Night Club" that they decided to broadcast in the spot previously reserved for *In a Glass Darkly* if no other original story could be commissioned from another source (Ackerley 1934b). In the meantime, they also awaited the arrival of Christie's new manuscript, which they were to receive in late April. It is possible that the BBC were preparing for a repetition of the first unsuccessful attempt to broadcast Christie. This time, the prosaically titled "Miss Marple Tells a Story" was accompanied by a significantly reduced amount of fanfare, receiving only minimal mention in the *Radio Times*. Scheduled for Friday, May 11, 1934 at 9:20 pm (National Programme), it was advertised as a "short story" by Agatha Christie in a barely visible program note (394).

In spite or probably because of its plainness, "Miss Marple Tells a Story" was considered "a great success" at the BBC. Ackerley told Christie that it was "an excellent story for our purposes" (Ackerley 1934c). It can easily be seen why this was the case. The story assumes the appearance of a fireside chat among Miss Marple, her writer nephew Raymond West, and his partner Joan, a modernist painter. While "Miss Marple" does all of the talking, she repeatedly addresses the other two, so as to give the broadcast the impression of a spontaneously conduced conversation. An atmosphere of quaint homeliness is also evoked early on when Miss Marple identifies herself as a relic of the Victorian period, confessing her admiration for nineteenth-century painters such as Lawrence Alma-Tadema and Frederic Leighton. Christie even slips in a note of realist mis-en-scène when she has Miss Marple state her preference for "sitting in the dining room because in early spring I think it is so wasteful to have two fires going" (Christie 2008: 591).

At this juncture, it is worth noting that radio had turned into a mass domestic medium in the 1930s. By the end of the decade, millions of households in Britain had bought licenses and gained access to cheaper and easier-to-operate wireless sets. As such, radio was at the heart of intersecting debates about domesticity and gender. Because the medium was discursively tied to the domestic sphere, the activity of listening to the wireless became stigmatized as the recreational habit of women. Radio was seen to work in support of traditional gender ideologies. At the same time, and somewhat contradictorily, the development of broadcasting was apprehensively observed by those who opposed women's demands to gain access to the male-coded public sphere. The wireless, as

Maggie Andrews explains, was "a symbol of modernity" and easily "crossed the boundaries between public and private, masculine and feminine spheres." With the help of their radios, women listeners suddenly "found themselves engaging with politics; gaining a familiarity with and experiencing the public world, from the 'safety' of their homes" (6). Paradoxically, the radio was regarded as both a domesticating and an emancipatory medium, confirming but also upsetting traditional notions of gender.

The fact that many BBC programs of the interwar period opted for an atmosphere of feigned domesticity would have further unsettled contemporary observers regarding broadcasting with apprehension. On the one hand, cookery talks and other programs explicitly designed for women must have aggravated female listeners with emancipatory agendas. Throughout the 1930s, female broadcasters in the BBC's *Household Talks* series "were constructed—as on the boundary between 'ordinary housewife' and 'extra-ordinary broadcaster'—as they adopted a discursive position of 'a friend at the fireside'" (Andrews 2012: 44). A barely concealed patriarchal agenda dominated the delivery of these programs, which aimed to replicate the domestic setting through the use of an informal and conversational broadcasting style. On the other hand, the so-called fireside chat had, in this decade, become associated with none other than Franklin D. Roosevelt, who had begun to broadcast politically focused evening talks in 1933. At the BBC, many broadcasters similarly aimed for performances of "scripted impersonality," speaking to "an audience in their home while conjuring up images of the home" (Andrews 2012: 69). It can easily be seen why the fireside format was met with suspicion by opponents of women's rights activists: by adopting a personal, conversational demeanor, the broadcaster gained access not just to the home but also to the heart of the listener. In this manner, the boundary between the public and the private further disintegrated in programs that introduced (female) listeners to new and potentially radical ideas about their roles and responsibilities.

Miss Marple's fireside chat with Raymond and Joan is responsive to these debates about broadcasting and gender. Prompted by Ackerley, who had repeatedly confessed how much the Tuesday Night Club stories had pleased him, Christie must have realized the appeal of her "fluffy old lady" for the BBC. Miss Marple's "intimate style" met the new emphasis on story-telling they preferred (Christie 2008). As the story unfolds, a fireside atmosphere is easily created by Miss Marple's conversational demeanor, with carefully inserted moments of digression in relevant places. Most importantly, however, "Miss Marple Tells a Story" seems to reinforce traditional gender roles while simultaneously subverting them. As already stated, the character presents herself as a relic of the Victorian period whose sitting room "with broad beams across the ceiling" and its "good old furniture" meets Raymond's "approving glance" at the beginning of another story (Christie 2008: 304). But as many

Christie readers would have known at the time of the broadcast's transmission, this image of domesticated femininity is a red herring. Here as elsewhere, Miss Marple's shrewdness and knowledge of human nature outwit the professionally trained law enforcers assigned to the case. Her tendency of "coming out on top," as Ackerley once described it (1932a), is emasculating. It undermines male authority while pretending to be in its spell. At the same time, the discussion of brutal murder clearly undermines the atmosphere of cozy domesticity initially created in the program.

While it might take matters too far to suggest that Miss Marple, in this 1934 radio program, acted as focalizer for controversies about broadcasting, domesticity, and gender, her first appearance on the airwaves is an invitation to consider the liminal status of radio technology in the 1930s. Potentially challenging to social orthodoxies, broadcasting affected an air of domesticity in many of its programs to alleviate fears about the medium's transgressive potential. As a regular listener to radio programs, Christie might have been familiar with these debates about the new communication technology in the second decade of its official existence in Britain. When challenged, she was able to learn quickly and deliver a manuscript that met but also undermined BBC attempts to present the medium as reassuringly familiar. "Miss Marple Tells a Story" marks a significant moment in Christie's professional engagements with the Corporation. As an example of productive collaboration, it was created at a time when the writer and the broadcaster keenly sought to consolidate their reputation as suppliers of scripts that were entertaining, informative, and at times extremely unsettling.

FUTURE LISTINGS: CHRISTIE'S PRESENCE ON AIRWAVES AROUND THE WORLD

On June 18, 1937, the BBC transmitted *The Wasp's Nest*, its first televised Christie play. The script was based on a short story published in 1928. By the end of the 1930s, Christie's BBC radio commissions had also moved away from the original talks format. She was now submitting dramatized radio plays. The first one, *The Yellow Iris*, was transmitted on Tuesday, November 2, 1937, on the National Programme. Designated as a "musical radio play" by the BBC the next year (*Radio Times* 1938: 39), it was a complex production and required Christie's presence at rehearsals (Figure 17.1). Based on the BBC's idea for an experimental format interspersing the detection plot with musical interludes, she wrote a dramatic piece for broadcasting that was deemed too confusing by many reviewers (Aldridge 2020: 119–29). After this first experience with radio drama writing, Christie would submit only three other original plays for broadcasting. In 1947, she contributed *Three Blind Mice* to an evening program celebrating

Queen Mary's eightieth birthday,[13] *Butter in a Lordly Dish* was broadcast as part of a series of plays by Detection Club members one year later, and, in 1954, Christie wrote her last BBC radio drama, *Personal Call*. In all three cases, manuscripts are dialogue-based and use sound effects sparsely, showing that Christie had learned to use her creative talents to meet the medium's particular demands. Although Aldridge is correct in stating that Christie, who had asked the Corporation to send her sample scripts for perusal, "felt that she was still learning the form" (2016: 42), surviving manuscripts and recordings suggest that she was beginning to master the art of writing scripts for radio in this phase of her career. The use of the telephone as a central plot device in *Personal Call* was particularly adept.[14] By the mid-1950s, Christie was clearly able to write scripts that played to the strengths of an exclusively aural medium.[15]

While Christie's own professional engagements with the Corporation came to an end in the mid-1950s, she continued to have a permanent presence on BBC airwaves. Many abridged readings of her books were transmitted on *Woman's Hour* on the Light Programme,[16] suggesting that associative connections between femininity, broadcasting, and light entertainment continued to flourish at mid-century. In 1953, a thirteen-part BBC radio series, *Partners in Crime*, starred Richard Attenborough and Sheila Sim as Tommy and Tuppence Beresford. Sim and Attenborough had been part of the original cast of West End production of *The Mousetrap* (1952). For this reason, they would have been an obvious choice for this new radio production. The BBC could rely on the fact that many listeners would already associatively connect these two actors with Christie's work.[17] In February 1956, the BBC also launched an *Agatha Christie Season*

---

[13]"I was attracted by the idea" to write a "short radio play for a programme they were putting on for some function to do with Queen Mary" were Christie's own comments about the genesis of *Three Blind Mice* as a BBC radio drama (Christie [1977] 2010: 510).

[14]Christie's adaptive talent for writing for different outlets is confirmed by J. C. Bernthal, who suggests that *Personal Call* is one of "Christie's most concise pieces of dramatic writing," "modelled on the kinds of thirty-minute plays being broadcast in the United States in series such as *Suspense!*" (2022).

[15]Scripts for *The Yellow Iris*, *Three Blind Mice*, *Butter in a Lordly Dish*, and *Personal Call* can be consulted in the BBC Written Archives Centre (microfilm). *Butter in a Lordly Dish* and a 1960s recording of *Personal Call* have been made available on CD. See *Agatha Christie: The Lost Plays* (BBC, 2015).

[16]The Light Programme was the renamed Forces Programme launched as part of a postwar stratification of BBC services alongside the Home Service and the newly developed Third Programme. As its name suggests, broadcasts focused on entertainment for a mass audience. But as Director-General William Haley's broadcasting model of cultural uplift demanded, they were meant to create appetite for the more instructive and intellectually challenging programs transmitted on the BBC's other broadcasting channels.

[17]Surviving archival material relating to the 1953 *Partners in Crime* radio production once more shows how little value was attached to women's creative and cultural labor in mid-century Britain. While Attenborough and Rex Rienits, the freelance writer who had adapted Christie's stories for broadcasting, were to be paid £42 per broadcast, the two women equally responsible for making the project a success were to receive far less. Sim was to receive a fee of £26 5s. for each production, while Christie's copyright fee was £21 per broadcast ("Cost of 'Partners in Crime'").

with seven new adaptations. Given its sparsely documented history, there is considerable scope for future scholarship exploring the production of these broadcasts that followed in the wake of the BBC–Christie collaboration begun in the interwar period (see Table 17.1). The BBC Written Archives Centre has preserved many of the scripts for these Christie adaptations with several

TABLE 17.1 Christie's BBC Commissions (1930–55)

Date of First Transmission	Broadcast	Comments
June 21, 1930	*Behind the Screen* (9:25–9:40 pm, National Programme)	Radio serial written co-operatively by Detection Club Members (Christie wrote and read the second installment)
Jan 17 and Jan 31, 1931	*The Scoop* (9:20–9:45 pm, National Programme)	Radio serial written co-operatively by Detection Club Members (Christie wrote and read the second and fourth installments)
May 11, 1934	*Miss Marple Tells a Story* (9:20–9:40 pm, National Programme)	Christie specially wrote this short story for the BBC and read it herself (*Radio Times* had originally advertised *In a Glass Darkly* for April 6, 1934, but this story was deemed unsuitable for broadcasting.)
Nov 2, 1937	*The Yellow Iris* (8–9 pm, National Programme)	Radio drama (with musical interludes) written specially for broadcasting
Aug 11, 1938	*I Became an Author*	Print version published in *The Listener* (pp. 275–6) but there is no record in the BBC WAC, BBC Genome, or *Radio Times* of a live transmission of this talk
May 30, 1947	*Three Blind Mice* (8–8:30 pm, Light Programme)	Radio drama specially written for BBC as part of an evening program celebrating Queen Mary's Eightieth Birthday
Jan 13, 1948	*Butter in a Lordly Dish* (9:30–10 pm, Light Programme)	Radio drama written specially for broadcasting as part of a series of plays by Detection Club members
May 31, 1954	*Personal Call* (8:30–9 pm, Light Programme)	Radio play written specially for broadcasting
Feb 13, 1955	*Agatha Christie in Close-Up* (6–6:30 pm, Light Programme)	Portrait including interviews by Christie, Richard Attenborough, Sir Allen Lane, Margaret Lockwood, Peter Saunders, Francis L. Sullivan, Sir Mortimer Wheeler (included extract from Ambassador Theatre production of *The Mousetrap*)

Programme, Talks, Copyright, and Scriptwriter files offering insights into the planning of these broadcasts. Equally fascinating would be the retrieval of archival material relating to the history of further Christie projects considered but ultimately rejected by the Corporation. Critical attention should also be paid to Christie's appearance on radio programs abroad.

As one of Britain's most successful cultural exports, it is to be expected that her work will have been frequently and enthusiastically adapted into foreign languages for dissemination by a medium that was, as Christie's own works were, extremely capable of transcending national borders. This chapter was written to generate interest in the still under-researched topic of Christie's presence on BBC airwaves. Hopefully, it can clear the way for subsequent inquiries into other aspects of Christie's appearance on radio programs in Britain and in other places around the world.

REFERENCES

Ackerley, J. R. (1930), "Letter to Agatha Christie, December 19, BBC WAC, Agatha Christie," *Talks File,* 1: 1930–58.

Ackerley, J. R. (1932a), "Letter to Agatha Christie, September 12, BBC WAC, Agatha Christie," *Talks File*, 1: 1930–58.

Ackerley, J. R. (1932b), "Letter to Agatha Christie, October 20, BBC WAC, Agatha Christie," *Talks File*, 1: 1930–58.

Ackerley, J. R. (1934a), "Letter to Agatha Christie, February 23, BBC WAC, Agatha Christie," *Talks File*, 1: 1930–58.

Ackerley, J. R. (1934b), "Letter to Agatha Christie, March 28, BBC WAC, Agatha Christie," *Talks File*, 1: 1930–58.

Ackerley, J. R. (1934c), "Letter to Agatha Christie, April 20, BBC WAC, Agatha Christie," *Talks File*, 1: 1930–58.

Ackerley, J. R. (1936), "Letter to Agatha Christie, October 26, BBC WAC, Agatha Christie," Talks File, 1: 1930–58.

Aldridge, M. (2016), *Agatha Christie on Screen*, London: Palgrave Macmillan.

Aldridge, M. (2020), *Poirot: The Greatest Detective in the World*, London: HarperCollins.

Andrews, M. (2012), *Domesticating the Airwaves: Broadcasting, Domesticity and Femininity*, London: Continuum.

"BBC Genome" [nd], "British Broadcasting Corporation." Available online: https://genome.ch.bbc.co.uk/ (accessed April 6, 2021).

Bernthal, J. C. (2022), *Agatha Christie: A Companion to the Mystery Fiction*, Jefferson: McFarland.

"Broadcasting: Copy of Royal Charter for the Continuance of the British Broadcasting Corporation" (2016), Secretary of State for Culture, Media and Sport. Available online: http://downloads.bbc.co.uk/bbctrust/assets/files/pdf/about/how_we_govern/2016/charter.pdf (accessed April 7, 2021).

Christie, A. (1939), "I Became an Author," *The Listener*, August 11: 275–6.

Christie, A. (1947a), Letter to Edmund Cork, January 27, 1947, Hughes Massie Archive, University of Exeter (EUL MS 99/1/1947/).

Christie, A. (1947b), Letter to Edmund Cork, September 17, 1947, Hughes Massie Archive, University of Exeter (EUL MS 99/1/1947/).

Christie, A. (1948), "Letter to N.G. Luker, 1948, October 14, BBC WAC, Agatha Christie," *Talks File*, 1: 1930–58.

Christie, A. ([1955] 2016), *Agatha Christie Close Up: A Radio Investigation into the Queen of Crime*, BBC Audio.

Christie, A. ([1977] 2010), *An Autobiography*, London: Harper.

Christie, A. (2008), *Miss Marple and Mystery: The Complete Short Stories*, London: Harper.

"Cost of 'Partners in Crime'" (1953), March 6, BBC WAC, Partners in Crime, R119/890.

Fisher, C. (1932), "Letter to J.R. Ackerley, September 13, BBC WAC, Agatha Christie," *Talks File*, 1: 1930–58.

"In a Glass Darkly," *Radio Times*, March 30, 1934: 1028.

Goody, A. (2014), "Dorothy L. Sayers's *The Man Born to be King*: The 'Impersonation' of Divinity: Language, Authenticity and Embodiment," in M. Feldman, E. Tonning, and H. Mead (eds), *Broadcasting in the Modernist Era*, 79–96, London: Bloomsbury.

Green, J. (2018), *Agatha Christie: A Life in Theatre*, London: HarperCollins.

Haining, P. (1990), *Agatha Christie: Murder in Four Acts*, London: Virgin Books.

Humble, N. (2001), *The Feminine Middlebrow Novel, 1920s to 1950s: Class, Domesticity, and Bohemianism*, Oxford: Oxford University Press.

Keynes, J. M. (1936), "On Reading Books," *The Listener*, June 10: 1126.

Light, A. (1991), *Forever England: Femininity, Literature and Conservatism between the Wars*, London and New York: Routledge.

Luker, N. G. (1948), "Letter to Agatha Christie, October 6, BBC WAC, Agatha Christie," *Talks File*, 1: 1930–58.

Matheson, H. (1930a), "Letter to Agatha Christie, April 17, BBC WAC, Agatha Christie," *Talks File*, 1: 1930–58.

Matheson, H. (1930b), "Letter to Agatha Christie, May 1, BBC WAC, Agatha Christie," *Talks File*, 1: 1930–58.

Matheson, H. (1930c), "Letter to Agatha Christie, June 19, BBC WAC, Agatha Christie," *Talks File*, 1: 1930–58.

"Miss Marple Tells a Story," *Radio Times*, May 4, 1934: 394.

Morgan, J. ([1984] 2014), *Agatha Christie: A Biography*, London: HarperCollins.

Murphy, K. (2016), *Behind the Wireless: A History of Early Women at the BBC*, London: Palgrave Macmillan.

Plain, G. (2020), "'Tale Engineering': Agatha Christie and the Aftermath of the Second World War", *Literature & History*, 29 (2): 179–99.

Punch (1925), December 23, "Punch Historical Archive, 1841–1992." Available online: https://www.gale.com/intl/c/punch-historical-archive (accessed April 4, 2021).

Thompson, L. (2007), *Agatha Christie: A Mysterious Life*, London: Headline.

Thurschwell, P. (2001), *Literature, Technology and Magical Thinking, 1880–1920*, Cambridge: Cambridge University Press.

"The Yellow Iris," *Radio Times*, May 10, 1938: 39.

FIGURE 18.1 St. Martin's Theatre, London, in May 2021, during the week *The Mousetrap* reopened after a fourteen-month closure in its sixty-eighth year. Courtesy of J.C. Bernthal.

CHAPTER EIGHTEEN

Christie and the Theater

BENEDICT MORRISON

AGATHA CHRISTIE AS PLAYWRIGHT

Agatha Christie was a prolific playwright. In 1977, in an appreciation of her work for theater, J.C. Trewin calculated that she had written "twelve full-scale plays [...] and three in a single act" (1977: 133). Such a substantial body of work would have been remarkable enough but, nearly forty years later, Julius Green's *Agatha Christie: A Life in Theatre* uncovered a wealth of other scripts in archives, raising the total to twenty-one full-length and eleven one-act plays, a third of which remain—extraordinarily—unperformed and unpublished.[1] This prolificacy does not result from Christie's rehashing of a reliable formula ad infinitum; the thirty-two plays consist of such diverse dramas as *Akhnaton* (written in about 1937) about the politics of appeasement in ancient Egypt, *Witness for the Prosecution* (1953) about the operation of justice and the complex question of guilt, and *Verdict* (1958) about the dangers of idealism in contemporary Britain. As Green argues, when people talk about a "typical Christie play," they are often thinking of a set of clichés that she did not create. Christie coupled this range with enormous commercial success, and *The Mousetrap*'s sixty-eight-year run, interrupted only when its temporary closure was forced by the Covid-19 pandemic, qualifies it for legendary status.

Nevertheless, criticism has largely ignored Christie's plays. Penetrating and wide-ranging histories of the British stage routinely snub her; Christopher

---

[1]This total does not include adaptations of Christie's fiction by other playwrights. There is no time to discuss these adaptations in this chapter, although they would certainly welcome further study.

Innes's *Modern British Drama: 1890–1990* overlooks Christie's plays altogether and Richard Eyre and Nicholas Wright, in *Changing Stages*, manage only snide comments about "monotonous, uninflected sentences that dribble purposelessly off the stage like ping-pong balls falling on a wet carpet" (2000: 339). With strange contempt for a major art form, Eyre and Wright also disparagingly liken the artifice of *The Mousetrap* to Kabuki theater, failing to recognize that artifice is a major theme in the play. Biographers have not offered much more, tending to privilege Christie's triumphant work on the page over her triumphant work for the stage. Some, including Laura Thompson in her authorized biography, have been openly hostile; Thompson argues that Christie's plays were "lightweight things" (2007: 360) and that her stage adaptations of earlier novels "leech all the subtlety from the originals" (360) and are "stranded, like a jiggling skeleton, bereft of what gives it artistic life" (459–50). While the phrasing may be dynamic, the analysis is unconvincing.

The relatively few pieces of constructive writing on the plays almost invariably begin by expressing regret at this lack of academic attention and affection: Green argues that Christie's theatrical work has been "overlooked" (2015: 1), Beatrix Hesse describes critical coverage of these texts as "minimal" (3), Jessica Gildersleeve comments on how there "has been little discussion" even of a play as famous as *The Mousetrap* (2014: 115), and Christine Marie suggests that "recent criticism [...] doggedly disregards her plays" (2014: 48). This chapter provides a survey of the slim but growing body of critical work that aims to address this oversight. In order to give shape to the discussion, I shall focus particularly on how two of the works for theater have been approached by critics. *The Mousetrap*, adapted by Christie from a radio play and short story entitled "Three Blind Mice" and in continuous production since 1952, is a record-breaking icon of West End Theater. Regularly ridiculed by detractors impervious to its subtleties and playfulness, the drama is set in an isolated boarding house in which an unknown murderer continues a campaign of revenge against those responsible for his infant brother's death years before. The whodunit—with its effective twist that the fake policeman is the killer, calling notions of realness into question—climaxes in a thwarted attack on the heroine and a final two-page comic coda. It is the most written about of Christie's plays, although commentaries often extend no further than discussion of its staggering longevity. My second case study, *Rule of Three*, is a trio of plays, first performed in 1961, consisting of *The Rats* (a claustrophobic tale of three unpleasant people caught up in a grim narrative of revenge-through-framing), *Afternoon at the Seaside* (a light comedy set amongst beach huts the day after a jewel robbery), and *The Patient* (a whodunit featuring the attempted murder of a woman who has apparently been left paralyzed). *Rule of Three* has been largely dismissed as a failure or ignored by scholars. In her autobiography, Christie wrote that writing for the stage was a "glorious gamble" (1977: 475) because there was no way of predicting whether a play would be a success. This history of unaccountable hits and misses is represented by *The Mousetrap* and *Rule of Three*—Christie's greatest commercial triumph and a flop that is perhaps ripe for rediscovery—and tracking them allows insight into the range and scope of criticism on Christie's theater.

THE YEARS OF NEGLECT

Even in the years in which criticism routinely overlooked Christie's work for theater, some writers did consider the plays. J.C. Trewin's 1977 account of the writer's "Midas Gift to the Theater" remains enjoyably irreverent and witty. The gift of the title lay in the fact that "nobody sustained a problem as [Christie] did, or solved it so quickly without a tedious explanatory huddle" (Trewin 1977: 133) making her "Britain's most popular dramatist" (134). Trewin is interested in the plays as plays, speculating on what quality makes them "magnetic in performance" (139); uninterested in Christie as a stylist, Trewin focuses his analysis instead on her ability to create theatrical moments that grip the audience and create atmosphere. He references each of Christie's plays, but so short a survey can give them only superficial coverage. He describes *The Mousetrap* as a "closely-manoeuvred puzzle" (142), but predominantly offers a series of speculative musings on the play's enduring appeal and some interesting photographs of the original publicity and cast. Trewin's evaluation of *Rule of Three* as a mixed bag of one hit (*The Rats*) and two misses (the "unexciting" (152) *Afternoon at the Seaside* and *Patient*, dull until its final curtain) is too brief to be really nourishing. Nevertheless, Trewin's work marks the beginning of criticism's engagement with Christie's plays. His observation that her work has "outlived new waves and second waves and trickling fashions" (150) distances Christie decisively from the Royal Court writers who were revolting in the years following 1956, a maneuver echoed decades later in Green's work. Somewhat contradictorily, Trewin also notes that "she knew about plays of menace before the tag was modish" (154), suggesting a family resemblance between her work and Harold Pinter's comedies of menace and Joe Orton's sinister farces, an idea that could yet be developed into a major re-evaluation of Christie's plays.

Five years later, in 1982, criticism on Christie took a stride forward with the publication of Charles Osborne's *The Life and Crimes of Agatha Christie*. Uniquely, Osborne gives equal attention to her novels and dramatic writings. The style of the work is not academic and it offers enjoyable, if underdeveloped, anecdotal accounts of the plays (including a prison escape from Wormwood Scrubs during a performance of *The Mousetrap*). Quoting liberally from contemporary reviews, Osborne gives a snapshot of each play's first production. The account of *The Mousetrap* combines details of the partnership between Christie and her regular producer Peter Saunders with a discussion of the play's unique longevity and its lavish anniversary parties. Osborne's detailed plot summaries are occasionally embellished with critical observations; of *The Mousetrap*, he remarks that "[a]s always with Agatha Christie at her best, the dénouement is startling and the end, thereafter, comes with the brutal swiftness of an early Verdi opera" (Osborne 1982: 222), but this is a rather lightweight analysis of the tonal complexities of the play's ending. He concludes his discussion of the play with a rather underwhelming (even if, in part, ironic) reference to the "monstrously unfair success of the undaring, non-experimental, but entertaining *Mousetrap*" (225). Later critics have uncovered the play's daring, experimental qualities. Osborne briefly addresses each of the plays of *Rule of Three*, suggesting that *Afternoon at the Seaside* is the weak link, although offering little beyond a vaguely defined "weakness of construction" (1982: 266) to support his judgment. Overall, Osborne's book marks a critical recognition of the significance of the plays, although contextual production details eclipse analysis.[2]

The detail in Trewin's and Osborne's accounts is richer than that in Peter Haining's *Murder in Four Acts* (1990). His chapter on Christie's theatrical works is a charming celebration of the plays but lacks any critical edge. The discussion of *The Mousetrap* is most concerned with the records broken by, parties held in honor of, and horse races named after the play. *Rule of Three* is acknowledged as an "experiment" but one that came after Christie's "reign as the undisputed ruler of London theaterland [had come] to an end" (Haining 1990: 35). The one-sentence summary of the three plays fails to capture their strangeness or to offer any insight into their origin, production, or textual qualities. The work is a useful summary of the chronology of Christie's plays, but it offers little additional insight.

JULIUS GREEN AND *A LIFE IN THEATRE*

It is appropriate that an account of critical work on Christie's plays should concentrate especial attention on the work of Julius Green. *Agatha Christie: A Life in Theatre* is the pivot around which criticism of Christie's theatrical works revolves; there is before Green and there is after Green, and it is hard to imagine that any serious criticism on the subject could be written in the future without a rigorous engagement with this book. It is a project marked by intricate research and illuminating insights into the conditions within which the plays were written and produced. In a frank introduction, Green establishes the book's scope precisely: a piece of rigorous popular scholarship which surveys "the journey that each of Agatha Christie's plays took from page to stage in their original productions" (Green 2015: 24). All the key players from Christie's theatrical

---

[2]Osborne has also adapted three of Christie's plays as novels: *Black Coffee* (1998), *The Unexpected Guest* (1999), and *Spider's Web* (2000).

career pass through the book's over 600 pages. While inevitably the narrative orbits Christie, other figures (among them producer Peter Saunders, director Hubert Gregg, and stars Richard Attenborough and Margaret Lockwood) feature prominently and the research into their contributions is detailed and generous. Green is aware of both the scale and the novelty of his project: "[h]ere, for the first time, we see the story as it unfolded from the point of view of those responsible for the staging of Christie's work: literary licences, theatre and artiste contracts, publicity material, budgets, accounts, and lively correspondence with directors, designers and Christie herself, including handwritten missives from her about script changes and casting" (25). Measured against the (considerable) ambition to tell this particular story, the book scores impressively.

Much of Green's commentary is informed by a claim which is first established in the clear and wittily provocative sentences of the book's opening: "This is the story of the most successful female playwright of all time. She also wrote some books" (1). This is the beginning of a catalogue of similar evaluations that pulse through the book as a reminder of why it matters that theater history has ignored Christie. Green describes her at various points as the "unassailable [...] Queen of the West End" (26), "the people's playwright" (173, 498), "the undisputed Queen of the West End" (249), able to "boast of being 'by Royal Appointment'" with great appeal "to the widest possible market" (371), and "a true playwright, fully engaged with her art on all levels" (375). Green sidesteps any accusations of hyperbole by matching these claims with fuller details of Christie's achievements. He returns more than once to the fact that "[s]he not only holds the record for the world's longest-running theatrical production, but is also the only female playwright to have had three of her works running in the West End simultaneously" (1), namely, *The Mousetrap*, *Witness for the Prosecution*, and *Spider's Web* from 1954 to 1956. He balances this tale of success with a frank account of Christie's struggles to achieve and then maintain her firm foothold in the monopolistic and fickle world of postwar theater. Green writes elegantly and makes the most of the page-turning qualities of a career in which "there were to be some bitter disappointments before her position as the most successful female playwright of all time became unassailable" (193).

Green relies heavily on the critical voices of others, quoting extensively from contemporary reviews of the plays. His engagements with more recent criticism are often less happy. Green states that "the significance of [Christie's] contribution to theater has been largely overlooked by historians" (1) and he positions his own work as a challenge to critical snobbery about the popular mainstream: "royal endorsement, of course, wins you no friends amongst the chroniclers of post-war theatre history. And, ironically, neither does successfully appealing to the widest possible market" (371–2).[3] He reserves particular scorn

---

[3]This snobbery may stem, in part, from unfair derision at the continued popularity of Christie's plays with amateur acting groups.

for feminist academics. He offers the controversial view that "[g]ender history is a fascinating subject, but the problem with it is that it tends to be written by gender historians" (15), claiming that the charge of such historians that Christie's plays reinforce patriarchal systems of thought is "based on a comprehensive misreading of a small number of the later works, and seems to be a common misapprehension amongst academics" (15). This attitude resounds through the book, born of a frustration that "[a]cademics can sometimes forget that plays are written for performance rather than reading" (473). While Green offers some limited rebuttal of such charges in his discussion of particular plays, and especially *Verdict*, there remains an important project for future scholars to develop the re-evaluation of gender politics in Christie's theater.

Green also emphasizes how much Christie loved writing for the theater. Novel writing is repeatedly referred to (drawing from Christie's own words) as her "day job" (1). In the 1950s, when "some commentators believe [...] that her creative output was slowing down," she was, Green suggests, really enjoying her freedom "to spend time on the work that she really enjoyed and found fulfilling" (414). Christie herself wrote that her pleasure in writing plays was "simply because it wasn't my job" and that they were "much *easier* to write" (Christie 1977: 473–4). These explanations do not entirely support Green's claims that "she found true creative fulfillment in her work for the stage" (Green 2015: 1) or that "playwriting was her true vocation" (2). At moments, Green's enthusiasm becomes a (partially) veiled criticism of Christie's other writing: "[w]hilst the received wisdom is that Christie's novels are to a certain extent formulaic [...] the same most definitely cannot be said of her work as a playwright, and it almost seems that she found herself enjoying greater freedom of expression as a writer in this genre" (8). Criticism on Christie's fiction has often demonstrated how her fiction complicates as much as replicates formulas. Despite this bias, Green's book offers a crucial challenge to the critical assumption that Christie's plays are peripheral to the canon of her work. He champions them as major achievements. Although he does not develop these points at length, he downplays the mechanics of whodunit plotting and credits instead her "exploration of the human condition and the dilemmas faced by her characters" (9). He urges those "commentators who regard her primarily as a constructor of plots, and dismiss her characters as stereotypes, [...] to study her plays in more detail" (327).

Green's approach to researching and recording the history of Christie the playwright is at its most revealing when he presents previously unpublished archive material. His access to such material allows him to compare *Love from a Stranger* (1936), Frank Vosper's adaptation of the story "Philomel Cottage," and Christie's own unperformed and unpublished version, entitled *The Stranger*. Green quotes substantially from nine other unperformed, unpublished early works; he writes that his long quotation from *Someone at the Window* is "for no other reason than that it is a wonderfully well-written and witty piece of theatrical dialogue and, as nobody has ever seen it performed on a stage, it seems a shame not to share it" (129). Alongside these rescued titles, Green includes copious textual variants from early or discarded versions of Christie's classic stage thrillers, including differences between the published version of *And Then There Were None* (1943) and the copy submitted to the Lord Chamberlain's Office for approval (175–7), alternative endings for 1944's *Murder on the Nile* (200–3), and the original prologue to *The Mousetrap* as an "experiment with form and content" (306–10). These variants offer glimpses into Christie's writing process, as well as the historical processes of production and censorship.

There are, nevertheless, omissions and oversights in the book. Green, never less than frank, prepares the reader for this in his introduction, in which he not only sets out what the book does but also what it does not do; he is clear that the book "is not a biography" (27), "is not a book about Christie's imaginary world" (28), "neither is it a 'reader's companion'" (28), and "is definitely not about [...] detectives" (29). Most strikingly, he acknowledges that the book "is not a literary analysis; there is no point at all in engaging in the long-running debate between the 'highbrow' and the 'middlebrow' when it comes to popular culture. I have neither the vocabulary nor the patience for it" (28).

By omitting literary analysis, Green leaves some of the claims he makes unsubstantiated. Too much work is performed by undefined terms such as "theatricality" (175) and "dramatic" (201). Despite his use of long quotations from the plays, he often offers no detailed commentary. When he suggests that *The Hollow* (1951) "clearly has a lot more to say" (259) than the average whodunit and that its "portrayal of a crumbling aristocracy in a time of rapid social change could easily take its cue from Chekhov" (262), he does not substantiate the claim or develop the analysis further. The full discussion of Christie's relationship to other playwrights remains a question for other scholars to take up.

Green's study is certainly the most wide-ranging account of Christie's theatrical works. The production histories of *The Mousetrap* and *Rule of Three* each receive detailed attention, as do those of every other Christie play. Uniquely in studies of Christie's theater, *The Mousetrap* is not allowed to dominate. The chapter on Christie's most famous play chronicles the cavalcade of directors associated with the original production: Hubert Gregg, John Fernald, and Peter Cotes. Green tracks the passing of responsibility through autobiographies and production documents. Alongside this history, Green places the play firmly in its historical context, arguing that it "subtly captur[es] the spirit of the age" (304). The historical material allows new critical approaches to the text, even in the fleeting snapshots of peripheral events, such as the London Council for the Promotion of Public Morality's reluctance for children to see the play (327).

Green, as a defender of Christie's theatrical work against its detractors, affords the play serious intentions:

> The play's subject matter is as hard-hitting as its setting is contemporary, exploring as it does the long-term consequences of child abuse, and inspired by the case of the two O'Neill brothers who were placed under the care of Reginald and Esther Gough of Bank Farm by Newport Borough Council in 1944.
>
> (305)

Other possible routes to arguing that the play deserves serious attention, however, are missed. The play's manifold metatheatrical gestures (which include its play with performance and self-reflexivity) are addressed only fleetingly:

> "The Mousetrap" is the title flippantly given by Shakespeare's Hamlet to a play performed by a group of strolling players for his uncle, Claudius [...] The new title resonated with Christie's play on a number of levels. Not only did it fit neatly with the theme of "Three Blind Mice" (as the killer refers to their potential victims), but Christie's policeman has the suspects re-enact the murder at Monkswell Manor in much the same way that the players [*sic*] performance in effect reconstructs the murder of Hamlet's father. The re-enactment in Christie's play, however, results in the trapping of the next intended victim rather than the murderer.
>
> (315)

This fails to address the layers of complex metatheatricality at work that have proven to be such an inspiration to other scholars. If *The Mousetrap* is reimagined as a revenge drama, the parallels with *Hamlet* become richer than Green allows. Hamlet and Trotter are victim/avenger/killer, and Claudius and Mrs. Boyle are killer/victim. Mollie, who is the "next intended victim" of the vengeful Trotter, is, in fact, an innocent, but one suspected of complicity in the earlier death of the child. The concept of murder as execution, in both *Hamlet* and *The Mousetrap*, represents a significant disturbance of conventional ethical schemata.

Green presents far and away the most detailed account of *Rule of Three* yet produced. He situates the play squarely within the tradition of Grand Guignol, spine-tingling and rather lurid theatrical programs leavened with inserted "short comedy plays" designed to provide "some light relief from the horrors" (503). Green attributes *Rule of Three*'s commercial and critical failure to the fact that "Christie's younger producer and his team did not fully appreciate" her particular theatrical exercise. Interestingly, rather than identifying ways in which *Rule of Three* is more modern than others have realized—finding parallels with Joe Orton's fun and games with Grand Guignol motifs, for example—Green is content to assert that "if elements of *Rule of Three* appear to be old-fashioned then I have no doubt that Christie had very deliberately crafted them to be so" (505). This lapse into unsubstantiated authorialism does not seize the chance to resuscitate interest in this trio of plays. Green does, however, describe and commend the abandoned original conceit of dropping the curtain at the end of *The Patient* without revealing the killer's identity. Indeed, Green surveys how "none of the three plays was presented as Christie herself had originally envisaged" (526). The most striking of *The Rats'* daring Grand Guignol flourishes—the onstage stabbing and implied suicide—were cut; the playful comedy of *Afternoon at the Seaside* was coarsened by director Hubert Gregg into the kind of seaside postcard humor that was more at home in the new series of *Carry On* films; the experimental ending for *The Patient* had been replaced with a conventional reveal. "As was so often the case," Green suggests, "Christie's own theatrical imagination displayed a far more intriguing frame of reference than that of those responsible for delivering her work" (526).

The coverage of *Rule of Three*'s history is substantial and intriguing. There are, nevertheless, missed opportunities. Green credits Christie with a daringly direct presentation of homosexuality in the figure of "nasty piece of work" (507) Alec in *The Rats*. A great deal of energy within queer criticism has devoted itself to tracing the controversial but significant links between queerness and criminality, both as pejorated objects of historical discourse and as parallel projects in destabilizing normative values. Green does not pursue this line and settles instead for concluding that "Christie's point is that crimes of passion are not a heterosexual preserve" (8). While Green's book succeeds as a compelling history of the original productions of Christie's works for theater, its partial coverage of key critical concerns must be taken as invitations to other scholars to respond to and elaborate on its insights.

A WIDENING CRITICAL LANDSCAPE

Green focuses largely on Christie's popular and commercial success and attends relatively little to other, more qualitative measures. His praise for Christie's ability to transform aspects of the period in which she lived into theater "in a manner acceptable to the censor, palatable to West End family audiences of the early 1950s and within the considerable constraints of the 'whodunit' format" (306) is focused principally on broad appeal rather than aesthetic achievements. When he discusses her major themes, it is typically in broad strokes, as when he loosely references "the familiar Christie themes of guilt and the nature of justice" (179). At around the same time that Green's history was published, however, a number of other critics began to produce work which responded to Christie's plays with a kind of scholarly rigor more regularly applied in recent years to her fiction. These responses fall loosely into two categories: studies of the plays as adaptations and as social commentary. The categories are not watertight, and there is significant overlap between them. Nevertheless, they help to clarify the emerging debates around Christie's dramatic works.

Adaptation studies have provided a firm foundation for recent criticism, although it does prevent discussion of original plays such as *Black Coffee*, *Spider's Web*, *Verdict*, and my case study *Rule of Three*. Preeminent among the studies of Christie's adaptations are those by Caroline Marie, who focuses on what she describes as the poetics of Christie's work. She concentrates on the role of form and genre in Christie's short stories and plays, both critically overlooked modes. Marie argues that careful attention reveals radical play with "generic and modal assumptions" (2014: 48) and a Modernist handling of time and space. She explores the operation of key generic signifiers (and especially objects-as-clues), and her witty and sensitive approach to *The Mousetrap*'s use of repetition, redundancy, and excess (which have often been mistaken for bad writing) allows a new appreciation of Christie's skill as a playwright. Using the theories of Jacques Rancière, she reflects on how the drama is not "efficiency-oriented" but, instead, "a poetical, meta-theatrical reflection on what theatre is" (Marie 2015: 189).

This analysis is underpinned by a concept of *theatrical embryos*, elements in narrative fiction which seem to be especially suitable for dramatic adaptation. Marie argues that Christie's adaptations defy expectation through a "poetical recreation" (2014: 49) in which the seemingly obvious theatrical elements of prose fiction are resisted and revised rather than reproduced. A theater-appropriate vocal clue in "Three Blind Mice," for example, is translated into a gestural clue in *The Mousetrap*; in the former, Trotter's real identity is signified when "the tone of his voice alters" (Marie 2014: 55), and in the latter his real identity is uncovered when he plays with his hair as he did as a child. This marks what Marie describes as "a qualitative rupture" (55) between story and play in which "the written text plays on the reader's illusion of language's transparency, and the play on the false equivalence between stage, visibility, and truth" (52).

The Mousetrap is defined, for Marie, by such ruptures. The play generates a tension between the jarring modes of detective drama and farce, the latter "work[ing] both within the detective plot and against it" (Marie 2015: 196). The different temporalities of these modes—future-oriented mystery, past-oriented detection, and in-the-moment farce—collide. For Marie, the second act is slow and repetitive, redundantly describing *and* re-enacting the murder in Act One, a doubling up which creates a "tension [...] between the purposeful temporality of the detective frame [...] and the aimless temporality of theatre, the rhythm of simply pacing the stage, which is irreducible to the linear, unifying logic of the first—a tension that is not to be found in the short story" (2014: 60). This is very different from Green's description of *The Mousetrap* as "lean and efficient" (2015: 310) and is, for Marie, the secret of the play's modernity and of Christie's metatheatrical poetics. The second act's inefficient repetitions are "a gratuitous act of pleasure, a space for the theatrical mode to break free of the storyline" in a display of repetition for the sake of repetition, linking the play's fun with the audience's fun and, subversively, with the "mischievous one-sided fun enjoyed by Trotter" (Marie 2014: 59). Marie compares this gratuitousness, undetermined by narrative, to structural *flâneurism* in Fritz Lang's 1931 film *M* and Victor Hugo's *Les Miserables* (1862). Trotter becomes a kind of aesthete, manipulating time and space (through the reconstruction) as an act of jouissance.

Unlike Green's rather cursory acknowledgment of *The Mousetrap*'s metatheatrical title, Marie pursues this line of enquiry further. The play's drawing attention to its own construction questions its status (as crime drama or parodic farce) and reinforces the narrative conceit "that identity is an essentially fictional construct" (Marie 2015: 193). This, in turn, queries theatrical systems of knowledge, complicating the categories of visibility/ knownness/security. In Act Two, when Trotter tricks and traps Mollie, visible stage space becomes as dangerous as dark non-stage space during Mrs. Lyon's murder at the beginning of Act One and dark stage space during Mrs. Boyle's murder at the end of Act One.

Marie argues that the play first creates and then confuses an "illusory equivalence between visibility and protection and invisibility and danger" (2014: 58) and that it is this poetics of epistemological confusion that makes "Agatha Christie [...] modern, rather than [...] thematic reasons, such as the sociological depiction of interwar England" (59).

Beatrix Hesse also writes within the field of adaptation studies, and her study of *The English Crime Play in the Twentieth Century* builds on the premise that crime on stage—"in which living bodies utter living, spoken language" (Hesse 2015: 1)—has fundamentally different conventions from crime on the page. Although Christie is jostling for position in the book with a huge number of notable writers, she is the only author to have a chapter devoted entirely to her work, and more precisely to the stage adaptations of her fiction. It is a shame that this book should have come out at the same moment as *Agatha Christie: A Life in Theatre*, because the two works could have been in productive dialogue with each other. Hesse relies instead on Osborne's *Life and Crimes of Agatha Christie*. She has a more rigid view of the modal differences between detective fiction and crime play than Marie and suggests fewer ways in which Christie subverts assumptions. Addressing such a broad range of texts in the book leads to some schematic approaches to the use of a linear structure, repetition, and dramatic irony. Hesse argues, for example, that "[i]n detective fiction, the detective knows more than the reader, which produces surprise, while in drama, the audience knows more than the characters, which creates suspense"

(2015: 200), not accounting for a play such as *The Mousetrap* which is not particularly predicated on dramatic irony.

Hesse's analysis of *The Mousetrap* brings its parodic elements to the fore, revealing it to share a knowingness with later parodies by Stoppard and Orton, suggesting that this "self-ironic streak may help to account for the play's phenomenal success" (Hesse 2015: 55). A brief consideration of the play's broader historical concerns with postwar anxiety about demobbed soldiers is followed by an analysis of *The Mousetrap*'s origins as a radio play, a legacy which she argues the play clearly reveals in its opening "audiodrama relating the discovery of the initial murder" (Hesse 2015: 54). Hesse's detailed account of the adaptation process, unlike Marie's, concentrates on the play's "impeccably classic [...] construction" (54) and its strict adherence to convention, glossing over the play's "slightly unconventional ending" (54). Although Hesse passes between plays swiftly, her arguments are most penetrating when focused on precise achievements. A broad point about the use of *doppelgänger* motifs is made theatrically concrete when it is tethered to the symbolic use of the Dresden lamps in Leslie Darbon's 1977 adaptation of *A Murder Is Announced* (Hesse 2015: 211). However, in a book with such a broad remit, it is inevitable that many plays are treated superficially and many omitted altogether. The sheer range of Hesse's research and knowledge remains invaluable, contextualizing Christie's work within the wider tradition of crime plays within which they played so important a part. And every Christie fan will be grateful to discover Tudor Gates's "highly metatheatrical two-hander" (81) *Who Killed "Agatha" Christie*, in whose parodic experiments with the genre a murder play becomes the weapon.

Since 2015, other writers in adaptation studies have attempted to develop these arguments, although their work has tended to be overshadowed by the theoretical rigor of Marie's work and the scale of Hesse's survey. It is unfortunate, perhaps, that scholars such as Anita Neira Tiemann continue to focus their studies on *The Mousetrap*. While it is a text of enormous cultural significance, Christie's other plays could also offer opportunity for original scholarship. Tiemann uses Roland Barthes's theory of semiotic codes to underpin an interesting discussion of Trotter's triple role within the play: he is "the detective-reader trying to find the criminal, the murderer-author who, as disguised reader, has led us astray all along, and the murderer-reader" (Tiemann 2019: 5) trying to discover who his third victim should be. However, Tiemann's innovations would be more keenly felt if applied to other, less familiar works.

Alongside this work on the poetics and practices of adaptation, a significant strand of criticism has developed on Christie's drama as social commentary. This strand has also concentrated its attentions on *The Mousetrap*, with very little focus on other plays, including *Rule of Three*. Jessica Gildersleeve's work on postwar anxiety in *The Mousetrap* explores how identity becomes unreliable as part of "the destabilization of structures of authority and social decorum at this time" (Gildersleeve 2014: 122). She recruits *The Mousetrap* (singling out the play as exceptional rather than more generally representative) as a complication of the image of Christie's "conventional and highly moral texts" (117). Gildersleeve's work is interested in the play's presentation of "the menacing figure of 'the stranger'" (116) who was "the result of, or enabled by, the relative distraction of wartime and the era of reinvention that followed it" (116). This historical approach is markedly different from Green's. Gildersleeve's focus is intently on a single play, but her analysis could be extended to aspects of other plays (including slippery identity and culpability in *Witness for the Prosecution*, ideology in *Verdict*, and guilt in *The Rats*), as would postwar novels, including *A Murder Is Announced* (1950).

Gildersleeve develops her analysis with a particular focus on how this environment makes women vulnerable "without the knowledge, support, or capacity for surveillance offered by an extended familial or social network" (116). This is an important area for study, although its exclusion of other forms of vulnerability is unfortunate given the play's interest in the complex gender performances of Christopher Wren and Miss Casewell, the immigrant status of Mr. Paravicini, and a historical narrative of child abuse. Even Giles becomes vulnerable through being unknown; the suspicions leveled at him by Trotter and Mollie because he has no family to support his claims mean that he can never be trusted. Gildersleeve's concentration on vulnerable women prevents full engagement with these issues, but it does permit a fresh analysis of how the play's "performance of a comedic conclusion masks a deeper anxiety about the potential for continued violence as a result of our failure to know" (119). The bathos of Mollie and Giles's exchange of anniversary gifts and Mollie's panic about her burning pie spectacularly fail to compensate for the anxiety that the play has produced up to this point. This uncomfortably rushed comic ending may be read in parallel with the kind of comedy of menace that Pinter became famous for. Six years before *The Birthday Party* discomforted London audiences, *The Mousetrap*, as read by Gildersleeve, offered a comparably unsettling image of unresolved social anxiety. At the curtain call, when the actor who plays Trotter asks the audience to keep the secret of the solution, "his direct address to the audience [...] reaches outside the boundaries of the stage, spilling his potential for danger into the 'real world' and making the audience complicit with his crimes" (120). Gildersleeve's combination of historical survey of postwar cultural anxiety and detailed textual analysis concludes that the play's epilogue (rarely written about by critics except as a kind of joke) "establishes the basis for secrecy and deception beyond the realm of the play itself, characterizing postwar Britain as a site of ignorance, duplicity, and danger" (120).

In 2020, Rebecca Mills and J.C. Bernthal edited a new collection entitled *Agatha Christie Goes to War*. Of its ten essays, three were entirely or largely about theatrical works. In his essay, Julius Green picks up (and, indeed, quotes directly) several key ideas from his earlier book. With characteristic authority, Green argues that Christie scholars have misunderstood the effect of the Second World War on the writer's imagination because of their lack of attention to the plays. Green's notion of Christie as a writer of "'immersive' theater" for "wartime audiences [sitting] in their seats in fear that they might themselves at any moment become victims of an unseen enemy" (Green 2020: 105) remains compelling. According to this logic, 1943's *And Then There Were None* offers both a morale boosting happy ending and a thrillingly unsettling staging of its audience's ongoing experiences of air raid shelters and enemy voices broadcast into their homes. This immersive style, Green argues, shows how Christie "experimented radically" (106) with theatrical forms.

Roger Dalrymple, in his essay on blackouts in Christie's postwar writing, economically presents the separate histories of wartime blackouts and the use of sudden darkness in gothic and sensational fiction. Dalrymple offers the intriguing suggestion that blackouts in Christie's works are a source of surprising comfort because, after the years of state-imposed darkness, they "reclaim individual agency and moral responsibility" (Dalrymple 2020: 155). An identifiable and punishable killer who flicks a light switch is of more comfort than an enemy state which plunges a nation into darkness. While this argument is compelling, it does not entirely resolve the discomfort that remains at the end of *The Mousetrap*. If Trotter is read as a product of trauma, the blackout that he instigates in order to kill Mrs. Boyle is not a straightforward indication of individual agency but, arguably, the collective failure to support those damaged by war (including Trotter's abused and murdered infant brother). Dalrymple suggests that a sense of the ludic (arising from the wartime games that made the enforced blackout tolerable) makes the play's darknesses comforting. Read as postmodern, this ludicity may instead mark the site of an uncomfortable collapse of meaning, identity, and security. Dalrymple argues that in *The Mousetrap* "the specific motif of the darkness-plunge is tamed" (164), but perhaps it also retains some of its wildness.

Federica Crescenti's essay is commended by Green for exploring *The Mousetrap* as social commentary, considering its presentation of the war's effects on material life, social identity, and mental health. The essay shares many of its concerns with Gildersleeve's work, unpacking the text's presentation of the figure of the stranger as a symptom of postwar disruption. The net, however, is cast wider than in Gildersleeve's work, and Crescenti productively discusses Paravicini's status as immigrant and Wren's and Trotter's wartime traumas. Perhaps most significantly, Crescenti's work combines its social commentary with an interest in adaptation, offering detailed discussions of how the text-based suggestions of postwar privation in "Three Blind Mice" are realized on stage through mise-en-scène, taking advantage of theatrical opportunities for visual cues (and clues). Crescenti's account of strangeness is character-based, and it would be useful to see some of her insights developed in an analysis of form, genre, and mode, with the unresolved/resolved ending a potentially productive area for analysis. The conclusion that the play is not as much concerned with whodunit as with who is responsible for Trotter's condition is humane and, crucially, insists that the play be taken more seriously than a modest piece of disposable entertainment that has enjoyed an inexplicable level of success.

CONCLUSION

Recent moves in Christie criticism to embrace and celebrate the theatrical works—as complex, subtle adaptations and as illuminating, surprising social commentaries—are heartening. They think beyond the logic that Christie's success is fundamentally commercial and that *The Mousetrap*'s significance can be boiled down to its incredibly long run. The growing number of critical responses allows productive dialogue: Crescenti references Gildersleeve and Hesse, Green references Crescenti, Tiemann references Marie, and so on. Nevertheless, despite these developments, there seems to be an eternal return to *The Mousetrap* (with occasional glances at the almost-as-famous *Witness for the Prosecution*). New insights are certainly still emerging about the famous play, but it is regrettable that so many of Christie's dramatic works continue to be neglected. They are not worth dismissing simply because they are not as *successful*. A more inclusive approach could profitably contribute to a broader discussion of what cultural *success* is. If success is conceived as the satisfaction of a number of cultural criteria, an exploration of *failure* could expose many of the assumptions and prejudices that underpin reception and interpretation. *Rule of Three*, for example, perhaps fails only if it is measured against a preexistent notion of what plays—and Agatha Christie plays in particular—should do. Its failure to measure up to this arbitrary standard may in fact offer some indication of how daring, unsettling, and queer a piece of theater it is. For a production to succeed, it may need to recalibrate its audience's understanding of what a successful Agatha Christie play looks like.

Christie wrote in a letter to her husband Max Mallowan that Shakespeare "saw a play as a series of scenes [...] [r]ather like beads on a necklace—the thing to him remained always individual beads strung together" (quoted in Green 2015: 11). Christie is describing a kind of bricolage, a formal arrangement predicated on variety and the collision of discrete "'turns'—like the music halls" (quoted in Green 2015: 11). Green quotes this early in his book as evidence of Christie's shrewd understanding of theater. He does not, though, draw a connection with the string-of-beads structure of *Rule of Three*. The claustrophobia of *The Rats* is theatrically centripetal, drawing attention inward to the chest in which the body is concealed, as Sandra and David become rats in a trap. *Afternoon at the Sea*, conversely, is centrifugal, with an extraordinary development of a threatening offstage world, never discussed by any critic as far as I am aware, in which unseen children bawl, dogs bark and bite, stones are thrown, and from which beach balls suddenly irrupt and strike sunbathers; here the mildly diverting action onstage is encased in a soundscape that draws the mind to the dangers beyond, marked by characters' risky movements beyond the proscenium world of the stage. *The Patient* is, once again, centripetal, focused on the paralyzed patient, the anxious suspects, and the ultimately cornered killer as the onstage world closes in. Scholarship could help to give *Rule of Three* a new lease of theatrical life by observing qualities such as this rhythmic fluctuation between a contracting and expanding stage world.

The *Rats*, in particular, continues to feel strikingly contemporary. It remains a stepping-stone between Patrick Hamilton's *Rope* (1929) and Joe Orton's *Ruffian on the Stair* (1964) and *Loot* (1965). It is archly, cruelly funny in a way that is ripe for rediscovery, enjoying a playful sense of irony. Its depiction of an anti-normative, anti-relational queerness-as-criminality would have been at home in the New Queer Cinema of the 1990s. In challenge to Green's repeated insistence that Christie "remained delightfully untouched by the Royal Court revolution" (2015: 3), John Orr makes the startling claim that "[t]hree plays in particular foreshadow the disruptive poetics of paranoia in the work of Pinter, Tom Stoppard and Joe Orton which are the key to English theater in the sixties and the early seventies. These are *Night Must Fall* (1935), *An Inspector Calls* (1946) and *The Mousetrap* (1952)" (Orr 2008: 21). For Orr, like so many critics, *The Mousetrap* dominates, but *Rule of Three*, along with her 1967 novel *Endless Night*, indicates how Christie was not constrained by the dated conservatism that some commentators insist characterizes her work. Criticism has begun to embrace Christie's work for the theater; now it has only to free itself from its mousetrap, to embrace failure, and to open up new perspectives on Christie's other plays.

REFERENCES

Christie, A. (1957), *Spider's Web*, New York: Samuel French.

Christie, A. (1963), *Rule of Three (The Rats, Afternoon at the Seaside, The Patient)*, New York: Samuel French.

Christie, A. ([1973] 2009), *Akhnaton*, London: HarperCollins.

Christie, A. (1977), *An Autobiography*, London: Collins.

Christie, A. (1993), *The Mousetrap and Other Plays*, London: HarperCollins.

Crescenti, F. (2020), "'There Are Things One Doesn't Forget': The Second World War in 'Three Blind Mice' and *The Mousetrap*," in R. Mills and J. C. Bernthal (eds), *Agatha Christie Goes to War*, 109–23, New York: Routledge.

Dalrymple, R. (2020), "'The Thrill When It Suddenly Went Pitch Black!': Blackout Cultures in *A Murder Is Announced* and *The Mousetrap*," in R. Mills and J. C. Bernthal (eds), *Agatha Christie Goes to War*, 155–66, New York: Routledge.

Eyre, R. and N. Wright (2000), *Changing Stages: A View of British Theatre in the Twentieth Century*, London: Bloomsbury.

Gildersleeve, J. (2014), "'We're All Strangers': Postwar Anxiety in Agatha Christie's *The Mousetrap*," *Clues: A Journal of Detection*, 32 (2): 115–23.

Green, J. (2015), *Agatha Christie: A Life in Theatre*, London: HarperCollins.

Green, J. (2020), "'A Worrying, Nerve-Wracked World': Agatha Christie's Emergence as a Playwright during and after the Second World War," in R. Mills and J. C. Bernthal (eds), *Agatha Christie Goes to War*, 95–108, New York: Routledge.

Haining, P. (1990), *Murder in Four Acts*, London: Virgin Books.

Hesse, B. (2015), *The English Crime Play in the Twentieth Century*, London: Palgrave Macmillan.

Innes, C. (1992), *Modern British Drama 1880–1990*, Cambridge: Cambridge University Press.

Marie, C. (2014), "When Page Won't Go to Stage: Adaptation-Resistant *Embryos of Theatricality* in Agatha Christie's 'Three Blind Mice' and 'Witness for the Prosecution,'" *Adaptation*, 7 (1): 47–61.

Marie, C. (2015), "Agatha Christie's *Mousetrap* and Tom Stoppard's *Real Inspector Hound*: Playing Cat and Mouse with Farce, Mystery, and Meta-Theatricality," in C. Cothran and M. Cannon (eds), *New Perspectives on Detective Fiction*, 189–208, New York: Routledge.

Morgan, J. (1984), *Agatha Christie: A Biography*, London: HarperCollins.

Orr, J. (2008), "Pinter and the Paranoid Style in English Theatre," *Instants de Théâtre Cycnos*, 12 (1): 21–30.

Osborne, C. (1982), *The Life and Crimes of Agatha Christie*, Chicago: Contemporary Books.

Thompson, L. (2007), *Agatha Christie: An English Mystery*, London: Headline Review.

Tiemann, A. N. (2019), "Agatha Christie's *The Mousetrap*: Adaptation and the Repeat (Murder) Performance," *English Studies in Latin America* (16): 1–20.

Trewin, J. C. (1977), "A Midas Gift to the Theatre," in H. R. F. Keating (ed), *Agatha Christie: First Lady of Crime*, 131–54, New York: Weidenfeld & Nicolson.

CHAPTER NINETEEN

Film and TV Adaptations of Christie

MARK ALDRIDGE

INTRODUCTION

Agatha Christie's plots have been interpreted for the screen for nearly a century and, just as the creators of those films and television productions have found different approaches to their adaptations, so too must the analysis of them be tailored to take into account their particular contexts and aims. Although widely discussed informally by fans and in the media, scholarship surrounding Agatha Christie on film and television is a limited, but growing, field of discourse. My own *Agatha Christie on Screen* (2016) is an overarching history that establishes relevant biographical and industrial contexts which may serve as a springboard for further debates. One aim of the book was to establish the sheer breadth of adaptations since 1928, and some of the most substantial recent scholarship surrounding screen adaptations of Christie has further tapped into those areas that have previously received little attention. For example, I.R. Smith's "Bollywood Adaptations of Agatha Christie" (2016) draws attention to a vibrant and active area of Christie film adaptations that has been little more than a footnote in previous discussions. Such an analysis is a positive sign for the slow, but definite, growth of Agatha Christie screen studies. In this chapter, I suggest ways in which analyses of Christie adaptations can be situated within adaptation studies, and offer some case studies that show how discussions of these screen productions may be informed by important biographical and industrial contexts and their associated scholarship.

Agatha Christie sits slightly awkwardly within the world of adaptation studies, although as a frequently adapted author she is often featured in the roll call of familiar names whose work has transferred to screen. Films and television productions based on her books are the type of adaptation that James Naremore says are typically dismissed as "belated, middlebrow, or culturally inferior" (Naremore 2000: 6). Contemporary discussions within adaptation studies tend to stem from dismay at what Linda Hutcheon calls "the constant critical denigration of the general phenomenon of adaptation," which is prominent in older analyses (Hutcheon 2012: xiii–xiv). Such dismissal has been widespread, but Hutcheon also asks: "If adaptations are, by this definition, such inferior and secondary creations, why then are they so omnipresent in our culture and, indeed, increasing steadily in numbers?" (Hutcheon 2012: 4). Certainly, Christie screen adaptations are as popular as ever; prominent and commercially successful examples include the recent BBC and Amazon co-productions, which sit alongside the big-budget spectacle of Kenneth Branagh's films of *Murder on the Orient Express* (2017) and *Death on the Nile* (2022) for 20th Century Studios, now part of Disney. Adaptations have often required defense in both scholarly and popular discussions, and ongoing interrogation in the likes of the journal *Adaptation* show how discussion surrounding adapted texts has moved on from straightforward questions of fidelity (and, especially, the alleged relationship between it and quality).

However, in general discussions beyond academia, Christie adaptations are yet to fully escape questions of faithfulness to the original text. In his article "Twelve Fallacies in Contemporary Adaptation Theory," Thomas M. Leitch argues that

> Fidelity to its source text—whether it is conceived as success in re-creating specific textual details or the effect of the whole—is a hopelessly fallacious measure of a given adaptation's value because it is unattainable, undesirable, and theoretically possible only in a trivial sense. Like translations to a new language, adaptations will always reveal their sources' superiority because whatever their faults, the source texts will always be better at being themselves.
>
> (Leitch 2003: 161)

A scholar's "fan brain" (for surely most Agatha Christie scholars must also be fans, of some description) may instinctively try to prioritize fidelity as a barometer of an adaptation's success but, as Leitch indicates, adaptation studies have long since reduced the importance of such discussion. Nevertheless, the question of "truthfulness" in relation to the original text has been an important part of popular discussion of Christie adaptations since 1928's *The Passing of*

Mr. Quinn, a film that bore little resemblance to Christie's original story. More recently, there have been mainstream media discussions about changes made by screenwriter Sarah Phelps in her adaptations for the BBC, which ranged from hyperbolic tabloid articles—"'It's beyond arrogant to think you can do better than Agatha Christie!' *Ordeal By Innocence* viewers slam ending of BBC drama as the killer is unmasked ... but NOT the one from the book," screamed the *Daily Mail* (McDermott 2018)—to trending Twitter hashtags (with expletives in 2020's *The Pale Horse* leading to a #SwearyChristie meme).

When it comes to Christie, there is the further complicating factor that most adaptations in the last forty years have featured the author's name prominently, either above the title or in publicity material. As a result, there is not merely (for example) a new adaptation of *And Then There Were None*—we have a new adaptation of *Agatha Christie's And Then There Were None*, so the original author is still expressing posthumous ownership of the story.[1]

The links between the author's name and apparent fidelity are then easily confused when we consider the likes of the long-running series *Agatha Christie's Poirot* (ITV, 1989–2013), which offered faithful retellings of some stories (such as *The Mysterious Affair at Styles*) alongside others that were nearly complete inventions (such as "The Case of the Missing Will," ostensibly based on a very short story that would barely fill fifteen minutes of screen time, and so expanded to the extent that it is essentially an entirely new mystery). No matter how close (or not) each episode may be to Agatha Christie's original, her name remains important. Unlike many other frequently adapted authors, Christie's works remain in copyright, so there is still a sense of overall authorship—or, at the very least, permission—stemming from the Agatha Christie estate, which has been largely controlled by her family (first her daughter Rosalind Hicks and grandson Mathew Prichard, and now his son James Prichard).[2] This means that adapting Agatha Christie is an entirely different prospect than with many other frequently adapted writers such as Shakespeare, Austen, Dickens, or Doyle—all of whom have had their works reinvented in radical ways, from *Pride and Prejudice and Zombies* to *The Muppet Christmas Carol* and *Sherlock Holmes in the 22nd Century*, with creative teams freed from having to seek permission from owning parties.[3]

---

[1]The most common exceptions are usually unlicensed non-English-language adaptations. A rare licensed exception is the 2001 American television movie of *Murder on the Orient Express* starring Alfred Molina as Hercule Poirot; the modernization of the story meant that it was given the awkward credit "from Agatha Christie." For reasons of brevity and readability, with the exception of long-running series, I have generally dropped the "Agatha Christie's ... " prefix in this chapter.

[2]Her books are slowly falling out of copyright in the United States, when 95 years have passed since publication. Under current rules in Britain, her published writings remain in copyright until 70 years after her death.

[3]The precise copyright status of Sherlock Holmes and the stories featuring him has been the subject of legal debate at times, and several stories remain in copyright in the United States.

Such an issue of authorship would matter less were it not for a general sense that the original remains the superior version, in almost any scenario. Leitch argues that "[t]he tenacity of the prejudice in favor of novels and against films is due no doubt in part to the impossibility of refuting it," and that "films, as many commentators realized long ago, can contain quite as many telling details as novels" (Leitch 2003: 155). Along similar lines, Hutcheon says that "[o]ne lesson is that to be second is not to be secondary or inferior; likewise, to be first is not to be originary or authoritative" (Hutcheon 2013: xv). However, this is a problem when Agatha Christie's name and often her signature are displayed prominently, placing the literary origins in front of the filmic experience. The presence of the signature and name is not a surprise when Agatha Christie maintains an active literary "brand" that continues to enjoy excellent sales that can be linked to the publicity surrounding screen projects, something borne out when Kenneth Branagh's 2017 film of *Murder on the Orient Express* catapulted the original novel back on to the bestseller lists. Christie herself never fully came to grips with the idea that adaptations by others were anything more than secondary, as she generally perceived fidelity to be the most important issue regarding whether they could be considered a success or not, something that explains her horror when she realized the freedom that MGM had been granted when adapting her works in the 1960s: "I held out until seventy but I fell in the end," she wrote regretfully (in Aldridge 2016: 104).

However, despite her reservations when it came to adaptations, Christie liked Billy Wilder's 1957 film, *Witness for the Prosecution*. Wilder took the core plot beats from the original play (itself Christie's own adaptation of a short story) and, arguably, managed to improve on them through the addition of humor and additional characterization that transformed a courtroom drama to a mystery thriller. That Christie felt positively toward Wilder's additions shows she understood that a cinematic artistic vision needed to work alongside her own storytelling for there to be a successful transition of her stories to the screen. Certainly, she noticed when films were aesthetically lacking, as she dismissed the first of MGM's films of the 1960s as looking like a television production (Aldridge 2016: 96), a more potent criticism in 1961 than in 2021. Leitch alludes to the problems of multiple creative voices, as he points out that "Everyone knows, for example, that movies are a collaborative medium," before asking, "but is adaptation similarly collaborative, or is it the work of a single agent—the screenwriter or director—with the cast and crew behaving the same way as if their film were based on an original screenplay?" (Leitch 2003: 150). We may get some sense of how other Agatha Christie productions responded to this question by noting how often her name features prominently in pre-publicity and cast interviews, whatever the truth of the film's relationship with the source text. For example, the trailer for *Murder She Said* (1961), starring Margaret Rutherford as Miss Marple, claims that "only" Agatha Christie "can mix murder and mirth with such hilarious abandon" as the film apparently features. This is a description that, on the one hand, pays tribute to the author of its source material (the novel *4.50 from Paddington*) but also reveals to any reader of Christie that the filmmakers are looking to present the story in the most commercially attractive manner, regardless of the source material's actual tone and narrative.[4]

The popularity of Agatha Christie's work as the source of so many adaptations brings its own problems. Many of her mysteries have been produced for the screen multiple times, and so each new version must compete with (or complement) the memory of not only the source text, but also previous adaptations. The most frequently adapted Christie title is the 1939 novel *And Then There Were None* (and Christie's own subsequent stage play version), which has not only received five major "official" English-language screen adaptations (in 1945, 1965, 1974, 1989, and 2015) but also dozens more on television and internationally, as well as scores of pastiches. As Leitch points out, the existence of precursor texts only complicates adaptation analysis (Leitch 2003: 150), something especially pertinent when considering that elements introduced in the 1945 adaptation were reused in some later screen versions, but reviews of these adaptations tend to be more straightforward, as they almost always draw negative comparisons with earlier versions of the story. Such dismissal is not true of all audiences, however, as Hutcheon describes "repetition with variation" as being part of the pleasure of new adaptations, "from the comfort of ritual combined with the piquancy of surprise. Recognition and remembrance are part of the pleasure (and risk) of experiencing an adaptation; so too is change" (Hutcheon 2012: 4). This may help answer the question of why we apparently need two high-budget, high-profile, and star-studded takes on *Murder on the Orient Express* (1974 and 2017). Perhaps this is in part because the audience's pleasure in revisiting a known story sits alongside the pleasure of differentiation (plus, of course, the classic Hollywood marketing staple of revisiting old stories for new generations of filmgoers, who can now watch their own era's all-star cast play out the mystery on screen). Finding new ways to tell old stories may be seen "as a process of creation," Hutcheon writes. "[T]he act of adaptation always involves both (re-)interpretation and then (re-)creation; this has been called both appropriation and salvaging, depending on your perspective" (2012: 8).

For the rest of this chapter, I will look at case studies of various screen adaptations and suggest particular biographical and industrial contexts that may need to be considered as part of an analysis. I have taken a chronological approach, largely because it allows the story of the films' developments to become clear as they are informed by changing contexts (such as the developing

---

[4]Although she often features witty and lighter moments; perhaps her most explicit foray into comedy on any grand scale was in the semi-farcical mystery play *Spiders Web* (1954).

roles of Christie, her family, and the company that bears her name—as well as the industry at large), and because existing scholarship can be grouped neatly by era. However, this historical approach is only one of many, and there is as much value in considering the existing scholarship in terms of themes such as stardom, genre, and national cinemas. The chosen examples demonstrate the importance of establishing and understanding wider aims of the adaptations, especially considering that they have often been closely monitored by Agatha Christie and her estate, while still adhering to the creative and financial desires of film and television producers. These two "pulls" have often been in conflict, and potentially differing desires for the end product have often underpinned the perspective and style of any given film or television production based on Christie's works.

EARLY SCREEN ADAPTATIONS OF AGATHA CHRISTIE

The conflict between the aims of Christie and her estate and of the aims of film and television producers was clear from some of the earliest film adaptations, such as *The Passing of Mr. Quinn* (1928), which was followed by Austin Trevor starring as Poirot in *Alibi* (1931), *Black Coffee* (1931), and *Lord Edgware Dies* (1934). Meanwhile, in Germany, there was an adaptation of the Tommy and Tuppence thriller *The Secret Adversary* (*Die Abenteuer GmbH*, 1929). These productions did not aim to find exciting ways to bring Christie's stories to the screen, but instead tapped into her usefulness as a British author with a range of tightly plotted and usually small-scale stories in the era of the "quota quickie." In *Quota Quickies: The Birth of the British "B" Film*, Steve Chibnall explains the rise of these features, which resulted from the 1927 Cinematograph Films Act, a piece of legislation that forced distributors to adopt a minimum quota of British films. The result was a range of cheaply made pictures that were usually shown in support of more expensive efforts (often from Hollywood). As a British writer, Christie was a useful source of material, who helped the distributors to satisfy the requirements. Chibnall specifically mentions the Poirot films in relation to the "quota quickies" tariff, although the apparently slightly larger budget for *Lord Edgware Dies* may mean it "had pretensions to co-feature or first feature status" (Chibnall 2007: 26).

These early screen adaptations also demonstrate the range of approaches to bringing Agatha Christie to the cinema screen. *The Passing of Mr. Quinn* elected to invent an almost entirely new story for the now-missing film that can now only be experienced through a contemporary novelization (by the pseudonymous G. Roy McRae, reprinted in 2017). Contemporary criticism and the surviving third film indicate that the three Hercule Poirot adaptations were static and soulless affairs, shunning atmosphere and exciting cinematography in favor of straightforward condensed retellings of Christie stories, the first two of which were already taken from stage adaptations, with the films making little attempt to shake off their obvious origins.

The filming of stage plays became the most common form of Agatha Christie screen adaptation during the 1940s and 1950s. On television, for the most part there was barely any adaptation at all, as live performances of the likes of Christie's 1943 play *And Then There Were None* (based on the novel) became commonplace on both sides of the Atlantic. Some stories were given original adaptations on television, including "The Case of the Missing Lady" in 1950 (which co-starred Ronald Reagan), *They Came to Baghdad* in 1952 (an ambitious production for live television, considering the novel's international settings), and several productions of "The Witness for the Prosecution." The latter was adapted for television before Christie reworked the short story for the stage herself, raising the possibility that it was interest in the story from others that helped Christie to see its potential. On cinema screens, Christie's stage successes were largely well received, including the films of *And Then There Were None* (1945) and *Witness for the Prosecution* (1957), while *Love from a Stranger* made it to the big screen twice, in 1937 and 1947.

THE 1960s: BRITISH TRADITIONS

In 1960, Agatha Christie signed a deal to allow MGM to adapt her works for both film and television. Despite extensive plans, television productions were limited to a single pilot for a Poirot series in 1962. However, there was more activity (and success) on cinema screens, and this is where the importance of both biographical and industrial contexts comes into play, as they establish the background that underpins the choices made for adaptations at this time, which must be considered in any further analysis. One important personal influence was that of Christie herself, as well as her daughter and son-in-law Rosalind and Anthony Hicks, who soon became distressed when they saw the extent to which MGM was reinterpreting the books to become comedic romps first and foremost (Aldridge 2016: 95–109; Morgan [1984] 1997: 327–37; Thompson 2008: 430–3). This approach was also informed by the personality of the main star of these MGM productions, Margaret Rutherford.

Rutherford starred as Miss Marple in four films between 1961 and 1964, and also made a cameo appearance in the fifth MGM film, *The Alphabet Murders* (1965), which starred Tony Randall as Poirot. The character actress herself supplied important influences on the films, as explored by Sarah Street in her essay "Margaret Rutherford and Comic Performance." Street points out that Rutherford's reluctance to dabble with crime on screen due to her own distaste toward such matters was assuaged only when she was convinced that murder was seen more as a game, or a puzzle to be solved, than a serious and affecting piece of criminality (Street 2012: 96). "It was important to Rutherford that her character possessed her own sense of moral integrity" (Street 2012: 96), Street writes, highlighting the fact that Rutherford was more than just a choice of actress; she brought with her a personal set of expectations regarding how the character of Marple might work. She was already well known as "a quintessential British character actress" (Street 2012: 89), who took on roles that "provided scope for embellishment" (Street 2012: 90). Rutherford's previous screen appearances certainly informed expectations of how she would handle the character, and these Marple films may be seen as broadly continuing the Ealing comedy tradition. Street points out that Rutherford only appeared in one Ealing comedy, *Passport to Pimlico* (1949), but their essence is certainly retained for her Marple pictures. Looking at the comedy films made by Ealing Studios between 1947 and 1957, Tim O'Sullivan has described them as offering "conventionalised projections of 'Britishness'" (O'Sullivan 2012: 66), as well as other qualities including a sense of mischief with a subversive edge and juvenile energy, both of which appear throughout the Marple pictures starring Margaret Rutherford.

Claire Mortimer has drawn comparisons between Rutherford as Marple and an important earlier role that she played, stating that her performance "centred on her aberrant qualities, established by her role as the medium Madame Arcati in *Blithe Spirit*, the part which lifted her to star status and sealed her persona" (Mortimer 2016: 312). Mortimer also highlights the films' own mischievous and subversive edges by looking at Rutherford's Marple as a "trickster," which is accentuated in these films compared to the novels, especially when Rutherford's Marple happily disguises herself as a railway workman and a maid: "Rutherford's performance as Miss Marple uses comedy to further cultivate the sense of mischief and chaos at the heart of the trickster" (2016: 317). As with many commentators, both Street and Mortimer have discussed Rutherford's physical attributes, including the way she uses her body and especially her face for comedy, something often mentioned in contemporary reviews. The attention that such physicality inevitably receives from the audience means that this iteration of Miss Marple is not the reserved character of Agatha Christie's novels and short stories: "Rutherford's performance of old age dispenses with the physical shackles which hold Christie's Marple back, making the character central to almost every scene of the film as compared to the withdrawn elderly figure in the book" (Mortimer 2016: 319). In short, these films from MGM demonstrate the fact that these adaptations (with their links to Christie that could be loose or almost non-existent) were the result of wider film industry attempts to tap into known quantities popular with audiences. In this case, the important elements were Margaret Rutherford's screen persona and British film's postwar comedy tradition, with Agatha Christie's stories in a secondary position. So keen was Christie to keep her own Miss Marple separate from Margaret Rutherford's portrayal that not only did she write her own disclaimer for the opening titles of 1964's *Murder Ahoy*, which followed the screenwriters' credit for their mostly original story ("Based on their interpretation of Agatha Christie's Miss Marple"), but a similar note appeared in Christie's novel *A Caribbean Mystery* published the same year—"Featuring Miss Marple, The Original Character as created by Agatha Christie."

THE 1970s: BECOMING HERITAGE

While Tony Randall had offered a lighter take on Poirot for MGM's *The Alphabet Murders*, Albert Finney's performance of the character in 1974's *Murder on the Orient Express* is very different, as befits a much more serious production. One template for this change may have been the likes of *Rosemary's Baby* (1968) and *The Exorcist* (1973), which had taken genre literature (horror) and adapted the novels for the screen in a way that broke out of typical conventions.[5] Both films emphasize characterization and human responses to horrific scenarios, treating the source material with the utmost seriousness. Sidney Lumet's film of *Murder on the Orient Express* does much the same thing, only this time with crime fiction. Paul Dehn's script follows Christie's original novel closely (and such adherence was a key factor in the film being made at all, as Christie was not inclined to allow film adaptations by this point—see Aldridge 2016: 122–5), and Lumet imbues the all-star production with a sense of style and melancholy, maintained alongside the central mystery—the exact opposite to the knockabout fun of the MGM pictures a decade earlier. As an example of this change of approach, in an essay looking at the relationship between love and crime in Agatha Christie adaptations, I have argued that the placement of a dramatic flashback to the kidnapping of a baby at the beginning of the film "emphasizes the emotive issue of revenge from the very beginning, rather than Christie's original emphasis on the puzzle of the conflicting witness statements and the unusual manner of the stab wounds" (Aldridge 2012: 85).

Even at the time, scholarly response to the film marked it out as a special and distinctive adaptation of a mystery novel. In a 1975 edition of *Literature/Film Quarterly*, Irene Kahn Atkins drew attention to the fact that the film was pleasing more than just established Agatha Christie fans: "Acclaimed by most reviewers and doing healthy business throughout the United States and Great Britain, *Murder on the Orient Express* has found a satisfied audience, not necessarily the same personae as the Christie readers, but an enthusiastically responsive group" (Atkins 1975: 206), she wrote. After classifying it as a "civilized mystery" (1975: 208), Atkins also describes the film as "slightly

---

[5]Both films were part of the Hollywood New Wave, aka New Hollywood, which saw films liberated from the censorious Production Code. They show influences from more thoughtful and avant-garde European influences, as well as sex and violence. See Biskind (1999) for more on this era.

old-fashioned" (1975: 208), but this is not intended as a criticism, as she clarifies that this makes the film "more solid, more substantial and carefully thought-out than many products of today's shoddy workmanship" (1975: 208). Although the film taps into some sense of nostalgia with its period setting (and accordingly glamorous mise-en-scène), Atkins points out that the ending would not have been acceptable under the censorious production code that was enforced in Hollywood from the early 1930s to the mid-1960s, as it concludes with happy murderers toasting their success (1975: 212). Atkins argues that the film's mixture of diversion and nostalgia, within a story that could now be told in full without censorship, was right for the 1970s: "I don't wish to deprecate the film as a polished entertainment, but I believe that it *is* helped by its timing" (1975: 212).

Despite the critical acclaim that Atkins discusses, some have been more dismissive of the overall quality of Agatha Christie adaptations, even when it comes to one of its most consistently acclaimed mainstays. In his discussion of Agatha Christie as the *"locus classicus"* of the "cosy, reassuring" image of Britain so frequently seen on film and television screens, Barry Forshaw places the 1974 *Murder on the Orient Express* alongside later adaptations from the same producers, John Brabourne and Richard Goodwin (namely *Death on the Nile* [1978], *The Mirror Crack'd* [1980], and *Evil under the Sun* [1982]), and describes them as "journeyman efforts due to the workmanlike (and rarely inspired) directors" (Forshaw 2012: 53). Forshaw argues that adaptations of Christie's work have generally had what he calls a "parodic pitch" (2012: 53), "with all elements of social observation ruthlessly expunged" (2012: 54). Forshaw does not separate the rather darker Lumet film of *Orient Express* from the undoubtedly lighter later films from the producers, writing that "Albert Finney and Peter Ustinov propel their broad-brush Poirot characterisations in the direction of caricature and comedy" (2012: 54) and, more generally, "[t]he endless TV and film adaptations have created a series of ineluctable images in the public mind of unrealistic picture-postcard English villages" (2012: 54–5). This judgment speaks to an implicit sense among some critics and scholars, especially in the past, that screen adaptations of Agatha Christie adaptations exist outside of the real world, being situated in a timeless rural fantasy instead—although some more recent adaptations, such as 2015's *And Then There Were None* and 2018's *The ABC Murders*, certainly emphasize real-world brutality and emotional complexity far removed from the gentle village life alluded to by Forshaw.

In her discussion of changing approaches to adapting Agatha Christie on screen, Sarah Street cites *Murder on the Orient Express* as an influence on the heritage-themed films that would become an increasingly significant part of British film industry in the 1980s (Street 2008: 114), a movement that included the likes of *Chariots of Fire* (1981) and *A Room with a View* (1985). Street points out the extent to which changes in the film industry made an impact on the differing approaches toward Christie adaptations, including such unglamorous, but important, elements as sources of funding, distribution deals, and tax breaks. When considering Christie films as an influence on these later heritage pictures, Street states that, as with the later Brabourne and Goodwin pictures, *Murder on the Orient Express* features a plot "about middle- and upper-middle-class people who are frequently not what they seem" (Street 2008: 114). She goes on to argue that the films present "hyper-stylised representations of the past":

> As examples of "international" productions registered as British films that frequently featured foreign locations, actors and personnel from different countries, they have been rather overlooked by critics and scholars. The neglect is undeserved, since they exemplify the pressures towards co-production and demonstrated some of the pleasures and pains of adapting such a popular novelist's work for the screen. *Murder on the Orient Express* represents the high point of this experiment.
>
> (Street 2008: 115)

Although Christie was still alive when *Murder on the Orient Express* was released, her 1976 death meant that she did not see Brabourne and Goodwin's subsequent films. However, in the early 1980s, David Grossvogel argued that they were an important contribution to her legacy. In his 1983 essay "Death Deferred: The Long Life, Splendid Afterlife and Mysterious Workings of Agatha Christie," Grossvogel discusses how the Brabourne films featured "old-time actors now seldom seen on the screen," and that "these actors represent the cinema of a shinier moment, over a third of a century ago, before they were swept away by the new forms of the present cinema" (Grossvogel 1983: 13). This shows us that heritage and nostalgia were present in discussions of these films not long after their release and just as the heritage film boom was starting to ascend to its peak.

THE 1980s AND 1990s: QUALITY TELEVISION

On the small screen, the 1980s saw the arrival of what has been called "quality television," a concept that still struggles to have a unifying definition. In commercial markets the idea of "quality television" has been linked to wider efforts to aim programs at the "right" audience—usually of upper socioeconomic classes, who are attractive to advertisers who will pay handsomely for access to them, even if the total number of viewers is lower than other programming. It has also become a term for American serial television that has a complex narrative and cinematic visuals, but in 1990 Charlotte Brunsdon helped to define and problematize use of the term for British programming. Citing

Granada Television's lavish productions of *Brideshead Revisited* (1981) and *The Jewel in the Crown* (1984) as "the acme of British quality," Brunsdon listed expected features for these "quality" programs. They included the program having a literary source, "Best of British" acting, a large budget (by television standards), and its use as a heritage export (Brunsdon 1990: 85–6). It may fairly be said that both the BBC's *Miss Marple* (1984–92) and the series of Poirot adaptations for ITV (1989–2013) satisfy this set of definitions.

The BBC's approach to the Marple adaptations starring Joan Hickson was certainly rooted in this rapid expansion of interest in high-quality literary adaptations that *Brideshead Revisited* had spearheaded (itself tapping into the rise of heritage cinema). The program went beyond the mostly studio-bound efforts that had been the vogue for British television to that point (as had recently been seen in London Weekend Television's series adapting some of Agatha Christie's Tommy and Tuppence mysteries, *Partners in Crime*, shown on the ITV network across 1983–4). In the UK, the BBC also has to satisfy its public service remit; by the 1980s its attitude toward Christie was less dismissive than had been the case in earlier decades, and she could now take her place alongside the likes of Dickens, Austen, and Shakespeare as a writer of importance, whose works were expected to feature on the country's public service television. The fact that a production of Marple mysteries that was made on film with a healthy budget was also easily exportable and desirable to international broadcasters was an attractive, but secondary, point that happened to boost the coffers of the corporation's commercial arm.[6]

While the BBC worked on its own Marple series, in the United States a series of television movies included stand-alone Christie titles (such as *Murder Is Easy* [1982] and *Sparkling Cyanide* [1983]) as well as two Marple novels that starred Helen Hayes (*A Caribbean Mystery* [1983] and *Murder with Mirrors* [1985]) and a host of well-known character actors. However, the highlight (and most overt link with the lavish heritage films from producers Brabourne and Goodwin) was Peter Ustinov, who returned as Hercule Poirot in three adaptations (*Thirteen at Dinner* [1984], *Dead Man's Folly* [1985], and *Murder in Three Acts* [1985]). For reasons of economy, on television the period setting was now removed, as Ustinov's Poirot solved these crimes in the present day— something immediately established when *Thirteen at Dinner* opens with Poirot on a David Frost chat show for television. Alistair Rolls has commented that

> The 1986 film adaptation of Agatha Christie's *Dead Man's Folly*, starring Peter Ustinov, is to some extent a folly in its own right. Ustinov is still the same Hercule Poirot of *Death on the Nile* (1978) and *Evil under the*

---

[6]Indeed, the Miss Marple adaptations were presold to an Australian broadcaster, which gave the Seven Network a co-producer credit.

Sun (1982) and thus perhaps much like Dame Margaret Rutherford in her famous portrayals of Miss Marple—"larger than life." Yet this film made for television has none of the star power of Ustinov's previous Poirot outings.

(Rolls 2016: 52)

Rolls further points out that the modernized adaptation does provide points of interest for the Agatha Christie legacy: "Lackluster though it may seem, the film does more than simply trade on Ustinov's stage presence and Christie's enduring success; indeed, it presents a case of 'living on' (in the words of Jacques Derrida's essay of the same name)" (2016: 52). While not given the critical acclaim of most of the British Marple and Poirot adaptations of the 1980s and 1990s, for the scholar the American television movies are a striking deviation from what was becoming a heritage-based pattern.

Agatha Christie's Poirot, starring David Suchet and broadcast on ITV over twenty-four years from 1989, was probably the most visible example of Christie screen adaptations during this period. Following on from Brunsdon's links between "quality television" and its exportability value, Mary F. Brewer has looked at the Poirot series within the context of it being seen as a "safe bet" (Brewer 2016: 169), stating that "it seemed that anywhere the little Belgian detective travelled, tall profits were sure to follow" (2016: 170). Brewer cites specific instances that showed *Agatha Christie's Poirot* to be particularly popular as an export to international broadcasters, including an unusual sale to Italy, while arguing: "One element that makes ITV's *Poirot* stand out from other adaptations is the series' heightened degree of fidelity to Christie's vision of the character and his world" (2016: 171). For Brewer, this "world" is not only important to the international success but also integral to the series itself. "The England presented to viewers represents a social idyll, one that is defined by archaic class hierarchies that represent continuity and security for the upper-classes" (2016: 174), she writes:

The model of national identity we see in Poirot resembles what Stephen Haseler describes as "theme-park Englishness" (1996: 57). This is the "English product" that is sold around the world, and is favoured especially by American audiences. The idea that such a contrived replica of English political and social mores resonates with contemporary American audiences appears aberrant when this brand of conservatism is compared to the values that allegedly uphold the American way of life—democratic and egalitarian. However, it looks less unusual if, following Haseler, one understands Englishness within the context of the televisual heritage industry as principally about lifestyle and status[.]

(Brewer 2016: 177)

Merja Makinen and Patrick Phillips have explored the series' 2010 adaptation of *Murder on the Orient Express* as part of a discussion linking the story to questions of justice. They point to the importance of this screen treatment appearing after Suchet had inhabited the role for more than two decades:

> This episode took the opportunities provided by a long-running series, scheduled to come to an end in another seven episodes, with an actor who had inhabited the role for 20 years and the additional budget and prestige associated with a Christmas-night broadcast slot, to interrogate the character of Poirot. Poirot has been shocked out of his professional complacency, his too-convenient position on the relationship among guilt, the law, and the exercise of justice. At the end he is conflicted, and so is the audience. This adaptation as rewriting is a one-off insertion into the comforts of a long-established series to confront the taken-for-granted and force key issues into consciousness.
>
> (Makinen and Phillips 2016: 41)

Along similar lines, I have argued that Albert Finney's Poirot of the 1974 film adaptation of the story was almost as much a stranger to the audience as the suspects, and that Suchet's "emotional response can only have real resonance in the television series, where the audience has had over 20 years with the character and actor and are fully aware of the importance of the truth to him whatever the implications" (Aldridge 2012: 86).

Such was the ubiquity of Suchet's characterization of Poirot during this time (and arguably beyond, given the frequency of repeats) that, as Serena Formica has pointed out, by the time the series concluded with an adaptation of *Curtain* in 2013, Suchet and Poirot were almost inseparable for many, perhaps including the actor himself. Referring to a documentary that coincided with the program's finale, Formica highlights Suchet's meeting with Sten Lauryssens, a Belgian crime writer, in which she says that "Suchet thinks of himself as Poirot. Suchet is not Belgian, yet, when Lauryssens refers to Belgians as good looking, Suchet thanks him. What is happening here is a transfer of personas: The fictional persona of Poirot is being transferred to the real persona of Suchet to an extent that they merge into one" (Formica 2015: 114). Formica's article highlights the difficulty for both parties (Suchet and the character of Poirot) once the relationship reached its inevitable end, perhaps because Suchet "has turned Poirot into a celebrity" (Formica 2015: 115). However, whatever the era, there is always a new incarnation of Poirot waiting in the wings.

NEW APPROACHES IN THE TWENTY-FIRST CENTURY

In the twenty-first century, domestic Agatha Christie adaptations started to move away from what had become the traditional quality mold (especially in the British sense). One of the most prominent examples of this was the ITV series *Agatha Christie's Marple*, which strove to be different from the BBC's adaptations two decades earlier (Aldridge 2016: 318–9). One area of differentiation that immediately attracted attention was its sometimes radical (re)interpretation of characters, especially when it came to depictions of homosexuality. In his queer reading of Agatha Christie, J.C. Bernthal states that "[w]hen characters in *Marple* (and in later episodes of *Poirot*, such as *Hallowe'en Party* (2010)), are presented as homosexual, the presentation will be inspired by something in the source text" (Bernthal 2016: 239). Although much fan and press discussion has focused on the series' opening adaptation of *The Body in the Library*, where a reader would have to dig quite deeply to find the source inspiration for the presented gay relationship, the sense that the series depicts not just "real life" but also brings out the implicit in Christie's stories is, Bernthal points out, most obvious in the likes of *A Murder Is Announced*. Christie's original novel features a very clearly coded prominent lesbian couple, whose relationship is presented overtly in the adaptation. Discussing remarks by Christie's grandson Mathew Prichard, Bernthal points out that

> The couple's on-screen kiss is configured as a natural extension of its "patently obvious" subtext, although it is also a kind of progression, as their relationship is moved from subtext to text. Significantly, the kiss occurs in the couple's farmyard: outside. Appearing in a conservative 1950s village with Miss Marple, a character who "doesn't judge them for it", the women appear to come out of their literary closet.
>
> (Bernthal 2016: 239–40)

This principle that screen productions can make explicit issues that were only implicit in the original text has been further explored by Sarah Phelps, who adapted five Agatha Christie novels for the BBC, broadcast between 2015 and 2020. To date, scholarship on these productions is limited, but Phelps's emphasis on the dark underbelly of society is sure to become a cornerstone of how Christie adaptations are discussed.

This likely future trajectory of scholarship may also draw attention to the way in which Kenneth Branagh's 2017 film of *Murder on the Orient Express* similarly questions the relationship between trust and background (particularly class, religion, and race), an issue that Christie herself was no stranger to invoking, often for use as a red herring. Branagh's near-classical take on the story, shot on the expensive and high-quality 65mm film format like a Hollywood epic of the 1950s or 1960s (and now little used), certainly invites comparisons with previous takes on Agatha Christie, while adding elements that speak to blockbuster trends, such as an incongruous and narratively circular chase sequence. In his review for *Adaptation*, Wieland Schwanebeck goes as far as to argue that audiences "are invited to view 2017's *Murder on the Orient Express* through the prism of the 1974 version" (2017: 97). Such is the specter of the earlier film version that, as Schwanebeck points out, audiences may consider the 2017 film to be less an adaptation of a 1934 novel, and more a remake of the 1974 film (2017: 97). This points to the strength of the Agatha Christie screen legacy, an overlapping and contradictory universe of adaptations that continues to pivot in different directions as demands of producers and audiences change, and where the reality of the relationship between source text and adaptation is of varying importance to those making use of the Christie name and texts.

REFERENCES

Aldridge, M. (2012), "Love, Crime, and Agatha Christie," in K. Ritzenhoff and K. Randell (eds), *Screening the Dark Side of Love*, 83–94, Basingstoke: Palgrave Macmillan.

Aldridge, M. (2016), *Agatha Christie on Screen*, Basingstoke: Palgrave Macmillan.

Atkins, I. K. (1975), "Agatha Christie and the Detective Film: A Timetable for Success," *Literature/Film Quarterly*, 3 (3): 205–14.

Bernthal, J. C. (2016), *Queering Agatha Christie*, London: Palgrave.

Biskind, P. (1999), *Easy Riders, Raging Bulls*, London: Bloomsbury.

Brewer, M. F. (2016), "Exporting Englishness: Agatha Christie's Poirot," in R. McElroy (ed), *Contemporary British Television Crime Drama*, 169–83, London: Routledge.

Brunsdon, C. (1990), "Problems with Quality," *Screen*, 31 (1): 67–90.

Chibnall, S. (2007), *Quota Quickies: The Birth of the British "B" Film*, London: BFI.

Formica, S. (2015), "The Importance of *Being Poirot*: A Critical Examination of 'Curtain' as Seen on ITV," *Journalism and Mass Communication*, 5 (3): 112–18.

Forshaw, B. (2012), *British Crime Film: Subverting the Social Order*, Basingstoke: Palgrave Macmillan.

Green, J. (2018), *Agatha Christie: A Life in Theatre*, revised edn, London: HarperCollins.

Grossvogel, D. I. (1983), "Death Deferred: The Long Life, Splendid Afterlife and Mysterious Workings of Agatha Christie," in B. Bernstock (ed), *Essays on Detective Fiction*, 1–17, Basingstoke: Palgrave Macmillan.

Haseler, S. (1996), *The English Tribe: Identity, Nation and Europe*, Basingstoke: Palgrave Macmillan.

Hutcheon, L. (2012), *A Theory of Adaptation*, London: Routledge.

Leitch, T. (2003), "Twelve Fallacies in Contemporary Adaptation Theory," *Criticism*, 45 (2): 149–71.

Makinen, M. and P. Phillips (2016), "Transforming Justice? *Murder on the Orient Express* 1934–2010," *Clues: A Journal of Detection*, 34 (1): 41–51.

McDermott, K. (2018), "'It's beyond arrogant to think you can do better than Agatha Christie!'," *Daily Mail*, April 16. Available online: https://www.dailymail.co.uk/femail/article-5620299/BBCs-Agatha-Christie-adaptation-different-ending-book.html (accessed December 1, 2021).

McRae, G. R. (2017), *The Passing of Mr. Quinn*, London: HarperCollins.

Morgan, J. ([1984] 1997), *Agatha Christie: A Biography*, London: HarperCollins, 1997.

Mortimer, C. (2016), "Cheating Death: The Potency and Perversity of Margaret Rutherford as Miss Marple," *Social Semiotics*, 26 (3): 311–24.

Naremore, J. (2000), *Film Adaptation*, New Brunswick, NJ: Rutgers University Press.

Nowell-Smith, G. (2013), *Making Waves: New Cinemas of the 1960s*, New York: Bloomsbury.

O'Sullivan, T. (2012), "Ealing Comedies 1947–57," in I. Q. Hunter and L. Porter (eds), *British Comedy Cinema*, 66–76, London: Routledge.

Rolls, A. (2016), "Agatha Christie's *Dead Man's Folly*: Stagnation, Negation, and Adaptation," *Clues: A Journal of Detection*, 34 (1): 52–62.

Schwanebeck, W. (2018), "*Murder on the Orient Express* (2017): A Return Ticket," *Adaptation*, 11 (1): 96–100.

Smith, I. R. (2016), "Bollywood Adaptations of Agatha Christie," *Alluvium*, 5 (4): Web.

Street, S. (2008), "Heritage Crime: The Case of Agatha Christie," in R. Shail (ed), *Seventies British Cinema*, 105–16, Basingstoke: Palgrave Macmillan.

Street, S. (2012), "Margaret Rutherford and Comic Performance," in I.Q. Hunter and L. Porter (eds), *British Comedy Cinema*, 101–11, London: Routledge.

Thompson, L. (2008), *Agatha Christie: An English Mystery*, London: Headline.

FILMOGRAPHY

The ABC Murders (2018), [TV program] BBC One, December 26–28.

Agatha Christie's Marple (2004–13), [TV program] ITV, December 12, 2004–December 29, 2013.

Agatha Christie's Miss Marple (1984–92), [TV program] BBC One, December 26, 1984–December 27, 1992.

Agatha Christie's Partners in Crime (1983–4), [TV program] ITV, October 9, 1983–January 14, 1984.

Agatha Christie's Poirot (1989–2013), [TV program] ITV, January 8, 1989–November 13, 2013.

Alibi (1931), [Film] Dir. Leslie S. Hiscott, UK: Julius Hagen Productions.

The Alphabet Murders (1965), [Film] Dir. Frank Tashlin, UK: MGM.

Black Coffee (1931), [Film] Dir. Leslie S. Hiscott, UK: Julius Hagen Productions.

Blithe Spirit (1945), [Film] Dir. David Lean, UK: Two Cities Films.

Death on the Nile (1978), [Film] Dir. John Guillermin, UK: EMI.

Death on the Nile (2021), [Film] Dir. Kenneth Branagh, UK/USA: 20th Century Studios.

Endless Night (1972), [Film] Dir. Sidney Gilliat, UK: British Lion.

Evil Under the Sun (1982), [Film] Dir. Guy Hamilton, UK: EMI.

Lord Edgware Dies (1934), [Film] Dir. Henry Edwards, UK: Real Art Productions.

The Mirror Crack'd (1980), [Film] Dir. Guy Hamilton, UK: EMI.

The Muppet Christmas Carol (1992), [Film] Dir. Brian Henson, US: Jim Henson Productions.

Murder on the Orient Express (1974), [Film] Dir. Sidney Lumet, UK: EMI.

Murder on the Orient Express (2017), [Film] Dir. Kenneth Branagh, UK/USA: Twentieth Century Fox.

Murder Ahoy (1964), [Film] Dir. George Pollock, UK: MGM.

Murder She Said (1961), [Film] Dir. George Pollock, UK: MGM.

Ordeal by Innocence (2018), [TV program] BBC One, April 1–15.

The Pale Horse (2020), [TV program] BBC One, February 9–16.

The Passing of Mr. Quinn (1928), [Film] Dir. Julius Hagen and Leslie S. Hiscott, UK: Julius Hagen Productions.

Passport to Pimlico (1949), [Film] Dir. Henry Cornelius, UK: Ealing Studios.

Pride and Prejudice and Zombies (2016), [Film] Dir. Burr Steers, UK/US: Lionsgate/Sony.

Sherlock Holmes in the 22nd Century (1999–2001), [TV program] ITV May 6, 1999–July 21, 2001.

Ten Little Indians (1989), [Film] Dir. Alan Birkinshaw, USA: Cannon.

And Then There Were None (1945), [Film] Dir. René Clair, USA: Twentieth Century Fox.

And Then There Were None [aka *Ten Little Indians*] (1965), [Film] Dir. George Pollock, UK: Tenlit Films.

And Then There Were None [aka *Ten Little Indians*] (1974), [Film] Dir. Peter Collinson, UK et al.: Filibuster Films.

And Then There Were None (2015), [TV program] BBC One, December 26–28.

Witness for the Prosecution (1957), [Film] Dir. Billy Wilder, USA: MGM.

CHAPTER TWENTY

Legacies

BARBARA PETERS, WITH MARTIN EDWARDS, RHYS BOWEN,

RAGNAR JÓNASSON, AND L. ALISON HELLER

EDITORS' PREFACE

In these, the concluding pages of a volume dedicated to scholarship that investigates the work of the bestselling and, we would argue, most influential crime novelist of the twentieth century, we turn to people crafting crime fiction for the twenty-first century. We have asked Barbara Peters, founder and editor-in-chief of Poisoned Pen Press and founder of The Poisoned Pen Bookstore, to contribute her own thoughts on the ongoing influence of Agatha Christie's work on modern crime fiction and to invite commentary from this generation of authors following in Christie's footsteps.

After careers at the Library of Congress and in law, Peters founded The Poisoned Pen Bookstore in 1989 as a not-for-profit corporation. It continues today as one of the leading mystery specialty bookstores in the United States. In 1997, she and her husband Robert L. Rosenwald founded Poisoned Pen Press, now the mystery imprint at Sourcebooks, and Peters served as editor-in-chief for its entire history. She was a finalist for the 1998 Edgar Allan Poe Award in the Critical/Biographical category, and she has received the Mystery Writers of America's Raven Award for book-selling and Ellery Queen Award for editing. Bouchercon, Left Coast Crime, and Malice Domestic mystery conventions have all accorded her Lifetime Achievement honors.

In this chapter, Peters has shared Christie's influence on her as a reader, a bookseller, and a traveler who has followed in many of her footsteps, and she has invited essays from Martin Edwards, Rhys Bowen, Ragnar Jónasson, and L. Alison Heller about Christie's influence on them as authors. Edwards is recipient of the Crime Writers' Association's Diamond Dagger, the highest honor in UK crime writing, and he follows Christie as current president of the Detection Club. Bowen is the *New York Times* bestselling author of more than forty novels, and she is the winner of the Left Coast Crime Award for Best Historical Mystery Novel, of the Agatha Award for Best Historical Novel, and of multiple Agatha, Anthony, and Macavity Awards. Jónasson, an internationally best-selling author, has translated fourteen Agatha Christie novels into Icelandic beginning at the age of seventeen, and his own novels have been named among the Top 100 Best Crime Novels and Thrillers since 1945 by *The Times* (*The Darkness*) and the Top 100 Works of Crime Fiction of All Time by Blackwell's (*Snowblind*). L. Alison Heller is the author of three books, including *The Neighbor's Secret*, which received starred reviews from *Booklist* and *BookPage*.

Peters, Edwards, Bowen, Jónasson, and Heller offer perspectives on Christie's role as a formative influence in the world of mystery writing, publishing, bookselling, editing, and translating. More than a hundred years after Agatha Christie made her debut in that world, these writers' thoughts offer a look at her influence on the literature of this century.

AGATHA CHRISTIE: PERSONAL ENCOUNTERS

Barbara Peters

I have been privileged to lead a long life. Along the way, first as a reader, then as a librarian turned bookseller, and especially as a traveler, I've encountered Agatha Christie across seven decades and numerous countries, although never in person. There is much to be said about the sales, reach, and influence of Agatha and her books, but nothing beats experiencing them in the real world in real time.

Encountering Agatha as a Reader

I was a reader at a very young age, cutting my teeth on my beloved Oz books and various children's classics. By age ten, I'd graduated to more adult fare and, my mother being a mystery addict, I was given Agatha Christie as a perfect gateway into fiction. *Murder at the Vicarage* (1930) became my introduction into the British village cozy and remains among my favorites with its lively characterizations, romance, humor, and the puzzle to solve. I'm pleased to see that my longtime friend, author Val McDermid, expresses her own delight in *Murder at the Vicarage* in this volume. By now it's become a British historical cozy, but it was a contemporary case when Agatha published the book in 1930 with Miss Jane Marple, British spinster, as the sleuth. It was Miss Marple's debut in a novel, but she was a character Agatha had earlier created for short stories eventually collected and published as *The Thirteen Problems* (1932).

I lean on the word "puzzle" when I discuss Agatha's work, because she excelled at creating them. In rereading *Mallowan's Memoirs* (1977), the autobiography penned by her second husband, the archaeologist Sir Max Mallowan, I take note that he comments on her mathematical and puzzle-making prowess, which was a kind of recreational activity as well as a literary one for her. Several times, he underscores his belief that Agatha benefited from having what was essentially home schooling, rather than being sent to a formal English boarding school for education. He believed that this allowed her imagination to roam unfettered. You can see this in play in her own autobiography (Christie 1977), a treasure I have read several times, mainly for its portrait of middle-class Victorian life, a world now long gone, and of the shaping of Agatha's creative powers. Yet my favorite Christie is her memoir of her second marriage, *Come Tell Me How You Live* (Christie 1946).

Appreciating puzzles, as do most readers of detective fiction as opposed to thrillers and perhaps novels of suspense, I read on from *Murder in the Vicarage* and discovered *The Murder of Roger Ackroyd* (1926), an early and justifiably famous example of the unreliable narrator so popular today in books like *Gone Girl* or *Girl on the Train* and their ilk. This was far from her only work that has influenced authors over the decades, including those writing now. Her *Hercule Poirot's Christmas* (1938) offers a classic take on the country house mystery structure, but she went further in *Murder on the Orient Express* (1934) and *Death on the Nile* (1937) and translated the familiar tale to a train and a boat. These stories of limited casts in constrained circumstances, and many others, have influenced scores of contemporary authors like L. Alison Heller, who has contributed to this chapter, and Ruth Ware. *And Then There Were None* (1939) is a variation on the locked-room mystery, which has seen a real vogue lately in works by authors including J.T. Ellison and Rachel Howzell Hall. And *The ABC Murders* (1936) displays a serial deaths structure I enjoyed seeing reappear in thriller ace John Sandford's 2018 Lucas Davenport investigation, *Holy Ghost*.

Hercule Poirot and Jane Marple are her best-known sleuths, but Agatha also created Harley Quin and his friend Mr. Satterthwaite, and the married couple Tommy and Tuppence Beresford, who are sometimes overlooked in favor of her more famous detectives. I am not one to overlook them or her plays. While *The Mousetrap* (1952) is known for its performance longevity on London's West End, from 1952 until an only-temporary hiatus when the Covid-19 pandemic shut London theaters in 2020, with attendance being a kind of rite-of-passage moment for so many, I think *Witness for the Prosecution* (1953) is her best. Who of my age can forget the shock value of the 1957 movie and the performances by Charles Laughton, Marlene Dietrich, Tyrone Power, and Laughton's wife Elsa Lanchester? The 2016 TV mini-series does not deliver the same experience. The plot and its twist(s) are classic Christie. No wonder the play won the 1953 Edgar Allan Poe Award from the Mystery Writers of

America for Best Play. In her autobiography, Agatha wrote, "Plays are much easier to *write* than books, because you can *see* them in your mind's eye, you are not hampered by all that description which clogs you so terribly in a book and stops you from getting on with what's happening" (Christie 1977: 474, emphases original).

And when I was a young reader, I felt, even at an inexperienced age, that the romances by Christie writing as Mary Westmacott revealed much about the author. We can glimpse her in these six novels. Playwright Kirt Shineman, author of *The Mysterious Disappearance* (2020), his interpretation of events in her life, agrees that the Westmacott stories, not leaning on puzzle/plot, express her imaginative side best. Interestingly, a journalist outed her identity as Westmacott, a sensation recently repeated when J.K. Rowling's identity as the crime writer Robert Galbraith was leaked.

Encounters with Agatha as a Bookseller

As a bookseller, I suggest to my customers that they read Agatha Christie for her own sake and as a springboard to modern treatments of her constructs, which adds an extra element of fun or challenge for the reader. For example, you have only to read John Banville's 2020 mystery *Snow* to see the Christie country house murder design still flourishing and garnering award nominations. Readers grounded in classic crime gain extra joy by identifying variations and tributes composed by modern authors.

I encourage young readers to dip into her short stories, which are less daunting for many to tackle than a novel. But another strength of her work for teens is that she took care to keep her novels short so the reader would not put them down and lose the plot. Ideally a person could pick up and complete a Christie mystery between dinner and bed, it was said.

Encountering Agatha as a Traveler

I come now to my central reason for this essay and that is to touch on how Agatha's influence and imprint have popped up as I have traveled, underlining both the global nature of her fame and how well she took advantage of the opportunities that travel, especially to archaeological sites with Mallowan, provided for her writing. Without him there would be no *They Came to Baghdad* (1951), for example.

London: As a lover of travel for its own sake, and later as a necessity for a bookselling/publishing professional, I have made many visits to London. Lucky me to have been invited as a guest to meetings of The Detection Club. This august group is not to be confused with the Crime Writers Association, of which I am a member. It is a social group, a club in the British sense, accepting members only by invitation, with officers and bylaws and rituals. Several distinguished figures in the world of British mystery have served sequentially as presidents who take office with arcane and secret rituals. Everyone has a terrific time. My first attendance as a guest first occurred some twenty years after Christie's tenure. H.R.F. Keating was the president at that time, to be followed by Simon Brett at my second visit. Today it is Martin Edwards.

I am able to quote from an address given to the Dorothy L. Sayers Society by the distinguished crime writer, Diamond Dagger Award winner Peter Lovesey, on Agatha's swearing-in ceremony:

> She was co-president of the Detection Club from 1958 to her death in 1976. Agatha Christie was an obvious choice, but, notoriously shy as she was, she would only take on the role if someone else would wear the cloak and perform the ceremonies. Lord Gorell had been a member since 1930 and did the honors. All the paraphernalia came out again for his installation. It was said to have been full of high drama, with a lugubrious piano introduction and mock-Shakespearean lines spoken by a dozen voices. Whether the Warden of the Firearm actually pulled the trigger, I cannot say.

Harrogate: This spa town in Yorkshire is perhaps best known to the mystery community as the scene of the annual Theakston Old Peculier Crime Writing Festival. Attending the Festival, as I have, inevitably reminds one that the Hydro Spa Hotel in Harrogate is the place where Agatha was found in December 1926, after her sensational eleven-day absence. She was registered under the surname of her husband's mistress Nancy Neele.

Much has been speculated, written, and produced about the "mysterious disappearance." My theory accords with that of many, which is that Agatha, raised in a middle-class bubble with a Victorian-era nursemaid, experienced profound trauma akin to PTSD—not just at Archie Christie's affair but at the shock and scandal of the prospect of divorce coming on the heels of the loss of her mother. I have never viewed her actions as deliberately engineered for purposes of punishment or publicity, as some have. In her *Autobiography* she dismisses the divorce in a few words: "There is no need to dwell on it" (Christie 1977: 353).

In my opinion the divorce, despite her severe emotional distress, was Agatha's lucky break. Archie's addiction to golf (Max says that Agatha made him promise never to take up the game when she accepted his marriage proposal) (Mallowan [1977] 2001: 199), and likely his addiction to risk for he was a war hero, made him a very poor bet as a supporter of her writing career. He wanted to hang out with the sports-minded. I can't see him as the happy husband of a woman who would become much more famous, and wealthier, than he. No, divorcing Archie enabled her to share the life of a renowned archaeologist whose career provided her with experiences and landscapes for many of her books. Which takes us to … *Turkey*, in particular Istanbul and the Pera Palace Hotel, at the terminus of the Oriental Express. Agatha always stayed in Room 411. It is rumored that she wrote *Murder on the Orient Express* in Room 411. Certainly, her travels on the famous train inspired the novel. Today Room 411 retains its original furniture and has materials saluting Agatha, including books by her published in several languages, and a replica of the typewriter she used. Agatha wrote with a view that faced Tepebaşi.

While I did not follow in Agatha's steps as she took the Orient Express on her way to Baghdad in 1928 where she became friends with "modern" archaeologist Sir Leonard Woolley and his wife Katharine, I wish I had, because the wars since in Iraq have been so destructive to its archaeological sites. Her luck was that the Wooleys invited her back in 1930, where she was introduced to Max Mallowan who, in December of that year, married her, as recounted in her *Come Tell Me How You Live* and his *Mallowan's Memoirs*. Despite the thirteen-year age difference, she being the older, their union continued until her death in 1976. Agatha traveled with Max to many places to assist with excavations including Tell Brak, Nineveh, and Nimrud, setting up her own work room at one of Max's digs where she could bang away at her writing, putting the words directly onto the typewritten page for she had brought a machine along.

This is worth noting: Out to reveal the identity of the murderer in *Death on the Nile*, Poirot credits his experience at an archaeological site, recounted in *Murder in Mesopotamia*, with developing his methods in detection. He muses:

> Once I went professionally to an archaeological expedition—and I learnt something there. In the course of an excavation, when something comes up out of the ground, everything is cleared away very carefully all around it. You take away the loose earth, and you scrape here and there with a knife until finally your object is there, all alone, ready to be drawn and photographed with no extraneous matter confusing it. This is what I have been seeking to do—clear away the extraneous matter so that we can see the truth.
>
> (Christie [1937] 2011: 306)

While a traveler is in Istanbul trailing Agatha Christie, another stop to make is at the Sirkeci railway station built in 1890 by the Oriental Railway as the eastern terminus of the Oriental Express. Travelers like Agatha would disembark at the station, which is just next to the Golden Horn, and be driven to the Pera Palace. When last I was in Istanbul, the station was a performance venue for Whirling Dervish dancers of the Mevlevi Dervish order, as the famous train had stopped running in 1977. In *Mallowan's Memoirs*, Sir Max Mallowan devotes a chapter to the Express and to the background of her writing the book, which she dedicated to him, including the information that she once slipped on its icy platform and fell beneath the train—but was rescued in time by a porter.

Egypt: While traveling in Egypt in December 2019 on a research trip with author Dana Stabenow, we flew from Cairo to Aswan and checked in at the

Old Cataract Hotel. This is a luxury resort built in 1899 by Thomas Cook, the British pioneer of tourist travel. Agatha set portions of *Death on the Nile* here, then sending her characters traveling up river, or south, on a steamer. Like the Pera Palace, the Old Cataract Hotel has undergone restorations, the last in 2011, so staying there today is an upgrade from Christie's time. But you can still have an English tea on the terrace, admire the same views of the Nile and of Elephant Isle, and understand the literary inspiration of her time there. Who could not visit the marvelous temple Abu Simbel while in the region? In *Death on the Nile*, the river steamer *Karnak* stops there where various sinister incidents occur. And I love this: an image of the temple appears on the dust jacket of the first UK edition of this novel.

Torquay: This town in Devon where Agatha, younger than her siblings, spent much time on her own in the house and gardens of Ashfield, the family home, was host to the 1990 Christie Centenary. I was a new member of the British Crime Writers' Association, having opened The Poisoned Pen in 1989, and, enamored with Christie's *Autobiography*, was eager to spend time in this town on the English Riviera.

Being new to crime my husband and I did not appreciate our fabulous fortune in being seated at the dinner with H.R.F. Keating, author, bibliographer, scholar, and for many years the crime critic for the *Times*, and his wife Sheila; Peter Lovesey, multi-award winner, and his wife Jax; the late Robert Barnard, like Peter a Diamond Dagger Award winner, and his wife Louise; and CWA Chairman Robert Richardson, winner of the John Creasey (first crime novel) Dagger and his wife Sheila. This was indeed British mystery royalty—royalty that was very kind to us.

But first, there was a slate of activities organized for the celebration. On the first night was the chance to attend a performance of Christie's play *Spider's Web* at the Princess Theatre or to visit the Agatha Christie exhibition opened at the Torquay Museum. We did attend the play and judged it dated—it is a comedy mystery, and in my experience comedy does date. Two others of her plays were also performed in Torquay during the celebrations: *The Unexpected Guest* and *Verdict*, both produced by Charles Vance.

On the Saturday, we learned that the banquet was to be black tie. While men can rent formal clothes with ease, and indeed my husband whipped out and did so in a local shop, women have a harder row … luckily, I had packed well. This was a good thing as the evening developed. But first, as part of the celebration it had been arranged that David Suchet, renowned for his role as Hercule Poirot in the television adaptations of his investigations at the time, and Joan Hickson, famed as Miss Marple (I loved Margaret Rutherford as Miss Marple but her outsized personality was not as well suited to the character as that of Hickson), would arrive at the local train station aboard a special branch of the Orient Express and be honored at the banquet.

On September 15, Christie's birthday, we all trooped down to the station with its open-air platform and waited excitedly for the train to arrive. When it did, one car door opened and Mr. Suchet, dressed impeccably as Poirot and flourishing a bouquet, alighted. From a separate compartment descended Miss Hickson, garbed as Miss Marple. Mr. Suchet crossed to her, flourished the bouquet, bowed over her hand, and said, "At last we meet." Sensation. Christie had never brought her two most famous sleuths together in a book. Here was a true first. I was sorry she was not there to enjoy this historic meeting.

Then it was back to the banquet at the English Riviera Centre. We worked to keep up our end of the conversation in such august company. We were obliged to join the dancing. Most of the attendees were people I knew from reading their books but not from life, so I was a little shy. But then my cup overflowed for David Suchet stepped up, bowed over my hand, and asked me to dance. I am a short person, not quite five foot three, and Sir David as he is now known is five foot seven. We were well-matched and able to carry on a conversation. While he is six years my junior, in his Poirot personality he felt senior, so we were quite a staid dancing couple. To this day I cannot remember what conversation I was able to muster.

On the Sunday, a double treat. First, a flower show arranged at a church in Brixham, St. Mary the Virgin, Churston Ferrers. Owning Greenway made Agatha automatically a governor of Churston Primary School, a role she was said to have taken very seriously. Max donated a memorial classroom to the school the year after Agatha's death, but Agatha had earlier donated a stained-glass window to St. Mary's in colors she approved of. I still have the program issued by the Churchwardens detailing the September 13–16 programming which included an organ recital of hymns and a concert by the Brixham Orpheus Male Voice Choir, as well as a reminiscence that the Christies' daughter Rosalind Hicks supplied for the printed program. Included in that reminiscence was a line appropriate for the historic church and its liturgical music: "Agatha Christie was christened at Tor Mohun Church which she attended with her father. She loved the Old Testament, which she thought had rattling good yarns for children" (Hicks 1990).

So, what is a flower show? This one was themed; the flower arrangement entries by the parish ladies each were created to depict a Christie mystery. We had the program guide I cite, but the point was to wander along and "Guess the book titles." I believe looking back that there was a prize for the most correct answers. We did not win. I most clearly recall the arrangement illustrating Miss Marple's investigation, *The Mirror Crack'd from Side to Side* … the mirror in the arrangement was a dead giveaway.

And then came our afternoon at Greenway House, the country home of the Mallowans overlooking the River Dart, organized as part of the CWA's annual conference which had been scheduled to coincide with the Centenary. We had a hired car. Following directions, we arrived early at Greenway and parked on the verge of the estate road leading into the extensive property. Pulling out an edition of *Bridge World* (we were tournament bridge players in those days), we were practicing bidding when a car rolled up, the door opened, and a large man stepped to the window. We explained we were not trespassers but early for the CWA reception. "Follow me," he said and drove away. So we did.

The man turned out to be Matthew Prichard, Christie's only grandson, the producer of *Poirot* and at that time the chairman of Agatha Christie Limited, a position filled today by his son James. Matthew and his elegant wife invited us into the mansion and gave us a personal tour. It was home to Christie's only child Rosalind Hicks and her husband Anthony Hicks, who came to live there after Christie's death, filled with family possessions and mementos. Walking sticks. Boxes. Books. Of particular note, highlighted still today, was the collection of ceramics and of Christie's inherited collection of European porcelain which came to Greenway when she bought it in 1938. Rosalind and Anthony had assembled a growing collection of studio pottery. And of course, there were relics of Max's archaeological excavations not otherwise preserved at the British Museum in London or elsewhere.

We then went out to join the arriving crime writers assembling in extensive grounds, gardens, and woodlands that I believe were largely under Anthony Hicks's care. Eventually the author Catherine Aird welcomed the group into Greenway. Among the highlights was a look at the frieze painted by a US Coast Guardsman stationed at Greenway during preparations for D-Day. Today Greenway is owned by the National Trust as gifted by the Prichards after Rosalind died in 2004 and was designated a World Heritage Site in 2004. Good news: Christie's many fans can now arrange visits to the estate rather than being private guests and elect to stay at one of four holiday cottages on the grounds. Christie was known to have called Greenway "the loveliest place in the world." It also is said to have inspired at least one of her works, *Dead Man's Folly*.

A final note: at some point in the weekend, very likely on the Friday afternoon, a cruise down the River Dart for CWA members had been arranged. I clearly remember the author Caroline Graham, whose debut mystery *The Killings at Badger's Drift* had been a recent sensation, saying bemusedly that it had been bought for television by one Anthony Horowitz (then already a key dramatist on *Agatha Christie's Poirot*). Little did we realize then that *Midsomer Murders* would still be playing into the 2020s, not likely to set a performance record like that of *The Mousetrap*, but one impressive in the world of television; a world where, as with films, Agatha's work is continually presented, often with new interpretations.

AGATHA'S ENDURING INFLUENCE

Martin Edwards

The world has changed out of all recognition during the hundred-plus years since Agatha Christie published her first detective novel. Yet, at the time of this writing, Golden Age detective fiction is enjoying a renaissance following decades of critical neglect. A striking number of present-day bestsellers display the influence of Christie and her peers, not least in the plethora of modern variations on the premise of that classic "who will be next?" mystery *And Then There Were None*.

Christie has been a major influence on my own work. My first series, set in Liverpool and featuring the lawyer Harry Devlin, was conceived as an attempt to marry a gritty modern urban setting with twisty puzzles in the Christie vein. The only trouble was that, in the 1990s, classic detection was so far out of fashion that not a single review commented on the plentiful nods to the Golden Age; the critics were benevolent, but their interest lay in the characters and the locale. Critical attitudes are different now. The Devlin books are enjoying a new lease on life, and while my latest series has a kind of "great detective" in Rachel Savernake, the innumerable connections to Christie and the Golden Age have not been missed this time around.

A key component of Christie's legacy, one which I—like so many others—find inspiring, is that she demonstrated, time and again, the endless potential of the genre. This matters, because over the years many commentators have suggested that the well of ideas for detective writers is likely to run dry. As early as 1928, Dorothy L. Sayers, an influential scholar of the genre as well as one of Christie's most gifted literary colleagues, said when introducing her first anthology of crime fiction that: "There certainly does seem a possibility that the detective-story will some time come to an end, simply because the public will have learnt all the tricks" (Sayers 1928: 44). Christie's career might be seen as dedicated to proving that there was nothing whatsoever for Sayers to worry about.

Take, for instance, the possibilities of the memorable detective. Christie's most interesting creation is surely Jane Marple, whose laser-like focus on the common characteristics of human behavior not only explains her brilliance as a sleuth (admittedly one who is sometimes over-reliant on intuition rather than evidence) but also the breadth of Christie's appeal. Whatever your background, wherever you come from, Christie's insight into the way people tick is likely to strike a chord.

Interestingly, critics were slow to understand why Marple is such a superb creation. Ronald Knox described her in an anthology of 1929 as "the stupidest member" of the Tuesday Night Club, while two years later, in *Masters of*

Mystery, H. Douglas Thomson opined: "one cannot help thinking that she is not of the stuff of the great detectives [...] Moreover, Miss Marple can only hope to solve murder mysteries on her native heath" (1930: 211). But Christie refused to be deterred by these supposed limitations, and over the next forty years or so, Jane Marple solved mysteries in a London hotel, on a coach tour, and even in the Caribbean.

Christie's ability to see the infinite potential of detective fiction took many forms, extending beyond questions of content to encompass the often-underestimated craft of story structure. She was, for instance, acutely aware of the crucial importance of choices of narrative viewpoint. Unreliable narrators are enjoying a vogue at present, but none is more famous than Dr. Sheppard, who recounts *The Murder of Roger Ackroyd*. The novel has often been hailed as a story of breathtaking originality, but (even if we leave aside earlier examples of a comparable storytelling device from writers from outside Britain such as Anton Chekhov and Norway's Stein Riverton) Christie had already experimented with an unreliable narrator in *The Man in the Brown Suit*. Astonishingly, she played the same trick yet again more than forty years later in *Endless Night*; by writing in an unfamiliar voice and presenting the puzzle in a fresh way, she managed once again to conjure up a stunning surprise. That the plot also owes a good deal to an earlier Miss Marple story, "The Case of the Caretaker," is simply one more example of Christie's mastery of literary disguise.

Today, the classic tropes of detective fiction are being reworked by writers as different as Ruth Ware, Shari Lapena, Stuart Turton, Janice Hallett, and Alex Pavesi, but Christie was doing this during the Golden Age. In a foreword to *The Body in the Library*, she explained that for years she had toyed with the central idea of that novel, writing a mystery which took as its starting point a tired cliché of the genre, the discovery of a murdered corpse in a library, and did something new with it.

Similarly, twenty-first-century authors are producing historical mysteries in industrial quantities, but as long ago as 1945, Christie had the audacious idea of setting a "fair play" whodunit in Thebes 4,000 earlier. What is more, *Death Comes as the End* conforms to the conventions of the Golden Age whodunit, one more example of the timelessness of the human motivations in which Christie trades.

Throughout her career, she juggled "least likely culprits" with remarkable skill, her murderers including a child, a Marple-like spinster, a police officer, and even Hercule Poirot himself. Nevertheless, in a preface to *Cards on the Table*, published in 1936, she announced: "*this is not that kind of book*. There are only *four* starters and any one of them, *given the right circumstances*, might have committed the crime. This knocks out forcibly the element of surprise [...] The deduction must, therefore, be entirely *psychological*" (Christie [1936] 2005: 5–6, emphases original). She was by no means the first Golden Age writer to emphasize the importance of psychological detection—Anthony Berkeley, whom she much admired, famously did so in his preface to *The Second Shot* six years earlier—but her focus on psychology in crime fiction, even if elementary, helped to point the way for the future.

There are plenty of illustrations of this, but I'd like to highlight one in particular: her empathy with people who are falsely suspected. This issue crops up explicitly in the 1930 short story "The Four Suspects," when Sir Henry Clithering, late of Scotland Yard, says: "it isn't really guilt that is important—it's innocence [...] some people may go through a lifetime crushed by the weight of a suspicion that is really unjustified" (Christie 1932: 163). More than a quarter of a century later, she developed this theme so that it became the driving force (and even the title) of a full-length novel, *Ordeal by Innocence*, in which Hester Argyle echoes Sir Henry, stating that it is the innocent, not the guilty, who matter. This was unquestionably a long-term preoccupation of Christie's. My guess is that it sprang from the hurtful public criticism directed at her around the time of her disappearance in 1926, but that is beside the point. The impact of suspicion on the innocent, or apparently innocent, remains fertile ground for novelists concerned with the impact of crime on everyday lives. This timelessness is a fundamental constituent of Christie's fiction and is why her influence endures.

WHY HAS AGATHA CHRISTIE ENDURED THIS LONG?

Rhys Bowen

I read an article recently by Sophie Hannah (who is continuing to write Agatha Christie books) in which she called Agatha Christie a genius. She said:

> Anyone who suggests that Agatha Christie's actual writing or prose style or novelistic ability is anything other than top-notch is a crazy fool! Not only is she a brilliant plotter and entertainer; she is also a writer of unparalleled excellence! No, not just a great storyteller—actually a great writer in a literary sense! Like Virginia Woolf! Like Charles Dickens! Like Shakespeare!
> (Hannah 2021)

I think some of us may be laughing by now or shaking our heads. She was no Pat Conroy or Louise Penny, or even Dennis Lehane, or Reginald Hill whose novels still haunt me. Her writing is spare, not rich in vocabulary or description. She told a good tale. She kept me guessing until the end. But that was about it. Great books to read on a plane or a beach. You are never going to pause and savor an Agatha Christie turn of phrase or poetic description.

Her characters are usually rather one-dimensional. Poirot is vain and boastful. We never know what makes him tick, whether he has ever been in love, wept, mourned. Miss Marple is more complicated and, I think, Christie's most interesting character. But the others can be summed up in two words: nosy spinster, bad son, domineering father. We know that the son is bad because he forged checks and therefore is a suspect in a murder, but we never know why he turned out that way. Was he sent off to boarding school at seven, rejected by his mother, kept short of cash by a controlling father? There are some exceptions. I recently reread *The Hollow*, which has a completely character-driven plot.

The stories are always *whodunnit* and never *whydunit*. The crime writing field has moved into richer, more multilayered stories in which we are involved in the private lives and histories of the sleuth and the characters and their relationships. The best mysteries today relate the personal life of the sleuth to the crime he or she has to solve. For some reason it becomes personal to them—wanting to atone for a past misstep or wanting justice when someone they loved was given none. We see none of this in Agatha. We are told the tale. It ends. We close the book.

She does not always play fair. *The Murder of Roger Ackroyd* is considered a clever, innovative novel, but there is an inherent unfairness to it. The narrator only tells you what he wants to and can withhold what he wants to.

We have little sense of place in her books. The village. The market town. The big country house. But that is about it. We rarely know what plants are blooming, what birds are in the garden, what the air smells like, whether the scenery is wild and remote or soft and gentle. People do not stop to notice their surroundings unless there is a clue to be had. We know there are cliffs because someone is going to fall off. We know there is a causeway to an island because the characters are going to be trapped there by high tide. The old boathouse had its door open. The rooks were cawing suddenly. The books do not touch our emotions. Nobody weeps for the body in the library. Nobody is sad when the tormented murderer is apprehended. We remain detached observers to a crime and its solution.

I think the same is true to a certain extent with the other ladies of the Golden Age. Ngaio Marsh. Margery Allingham. Dorothy L. Sayers' Lord Peter Wimsey is rather one-dimensional, but Harriet Vane is more interesting. Josephine Tey becomes more nuanced in a couple of novels like *The Daughter of Time*. It seems that these ladies allow chinks of their own character and humanity when they create female characters but have little clue about the complexities of a male sleuth. Poirot is boastful, self-satisfied, and patronizing to the point of being annoying. If I were Hastings, I would have bopped him one on the chin.

And yet there must be something. Agatha Christie has sold more books than any other novelist ever. That is a remarkable achievement. And confession time: I own every book she wrote. If I am stressed or overworked, I take one of her books off the shelf to read. Comfort reading—because I know what I'm going to get. It is not going to touch my emotions or leave me tense and upset.

One of the reasons I believe that the books remain popular now is that these stories are safely removed from our own time and place. In the same way that we go to London as tourists and watch the changing of the guard at Buckingham Palace because it is quaint and different, we enjoy the Christie novels because we'd like to spend time in a village with thatched cottages and a dotty vicar. We enjoy stepping back in time to meet dazzling and dangerous countesses and lords of the manor. We enjoy going to house parties with servants and to fancy hotels where there are handsome young men to be dancing partners.

She really created the so-called cozy mystery. The bloodless sort of crime within a genteel setting. And in a way it should be more shocking to us that murder occurs where all appears to be safe and serene. In the hardboiled mystery set in the backstreets of a city one expects to encounter evil. Not in the cottages of a peaceful village.

Her plots and characters are enduring. Her characters might have been living in 1930s England but we recognize them. We have all witnessed the dysfunctional family dynamics that she portrays. The gossip within an enclosed society. The jealousy and insecurity. Her characters are, to an extent, everyman.

Another reason is that she was clever. It is very rarely that I have outguessed her sleuth. Her murders are never the basic shot or stabbed variety. Her knowledge of poisons from when she worked in a hospital dispensary during the First World War gives the stories a feeling of veracity. We know that murders in real life are mostly sordid and ordinary affairs. Domestic violence or robberies gone wrong. Tawdry affairs, not worthy of being captured in literature. So we applaud the clever murders, the supposedly locked door, the cry from a locked room that couldn't have happened. One of my favorites was not a Marple or Poirot but a novel called *The Pale Horse*. She strings the reader along into believing in witchcraft only to reveal that it was a clever use of poison.

I like the way Miss Marple uses village parallels to solve her crimes. Hers is a character that one can relate to. One feels that in another era she would have had opportunities to go to university and use her brain. Also, an opportunity to marry. But the Great War had killed off a whole generation of young men leaving too many spinsters like Miss Marple with too much time on their hands and not enough outlets for their energy and brainpower.

I also enjoyed Tommy and Tuppence (Christie's married detectives) because they were bright and hopeful, although they did put themselves into stupidly dangerous situations. But *By the Pricking of My Thumbs*, the book where Tuppence is old and gets herself into a difficult situation, was one of the few moving stories. Christie herself would have been realizing as she wrote it that she was old and could no longer do what she used to. And then there is *Curtain*, the final Poirot mystery that she would allow to be published before her death. I would not read it for ages, not wanting to experience the end of Poirot, but when I did, I was touched that she finally managed to give him the humanity he had avoided until then.

And so we continue to pick up an Agatha Christie book knowing that we cannot be shocked or repulsed. We will not get nightmares from it. We will enjoy a sojourn in a country house or a village cottage and have a chance to eavesdrop on a group of suspects and, if we are lucky, will figure out whodunit before Poirot or Miss Marple. We'll be surprised but not horrified or shocked. We will want to turn the pages to come to the truth. Justice will be served and we can fall asleep, content. Isn't that what you really want from a crime novel?

But oh, how we have evolved. The best crime writing today can be truly called great literature. Complex characters, multiple timelines, incredible sense of place, nuanced feelings of right and wrong. Moreover, we have plots and climaxes and we don't end our books walking down a beach in Maine wondering about the meaning of life as in so-called literary novels. But I wonder if any of us will endure in the way that Agatha Christie has. Only time will tell.

AND THEN THERE WAS CHRISTIE

Ragnar Jónasson

I first came across Agatha Christie's work at around the age of ten. There was a Christie film on television, *The Seven Dials Mystery*, and almost immediately I felt that this was something special, such a clever twist at the end. A year or two later, my cousin told me that he had started reading Christie's books and praised them highly, so I thought I might give them a chance. I remember that the first one I read was *Evil under the Sun*, in Icelandic translation. A wonderful read, so I kept going. I went to my local library, and lots of other libraries nearby, and borrowed all the translated Christie books I could find and read them as quickly as I could get my hands on them. (I even started writing my own "detective stories" at that age, handwritten in a notebook, set in the London fog, very Christie-esque, not realizing that many years later I would actually be writing my own mystery novels.)

And then, suddenly, I ran out of books to read. Not all of Christie's books had been translated into Icelandic, and not all of the translations were widely available. The next stop on my journey was the National Library of Iceland, one of the most majestic buildings in Reykjavik, opened to the public in 1909, located in the center of town, a truly lovely place to sit and read books. The problem for me was that the great Reading Hall in the National Library was not open to anyone under the age of sixteen at the time, so I had to almost sneak in there with my father, who was doing research there. We spent every Saturday morning there, a day when the library was open and I was not at school. The memories from there are really wonderful: reading old, out-of-print translations of Agatha Christie novels in such amazing surroundings, including what is now my favorite Christie, *The Murder on the Links*. And then, I ran out of books at the National Library as well! So I ventured into unknown territory, and started reading Christie's books in their original English, enjoying more of her masterpieces.

In Iceland, we have a lovely tradition of giving each other books for Christmas, and then reading our favorite new book on Christmas Eve, by candlelight, into the night. As a result of this, most books in Iceland are published in the months leading up to the holidays, and when I was growing up, an Icelandic publishing house made sure that, each Christmas, readers had a new Christie translation to enjoy. One summer, when I was seventeen years old, I had a crazy idea—that I could possibly translate an Agatha Christie book, as I had translated a few of her short stories for a local magazine. My mother drove me to the publishing house, as I did not yet have a license to drive, and I met with the publisher. Surprisingly, he knew who I was, because he realized that I was the boy who had been calling the publishing house every year to enquire which Christie book they were going to publish in translation that year. He greeted me warmly and said that he would give my suggestion some thought. I honestly never expected to hear back from him, but he called me back and said that he would give me a chance. I could pick any title, and would need to have a translation ready by Christmas. I rushed to my bookshelves and picked the shortest novel I could find, *Endless Night*, and that turned out to be my first Christie translation.

Translating Christie was a wonderful experience. I carried on translating one Christie per year through college, law school, and even after I had graduated and started working as a lawyer. Translating gave me insight into her methods and her magic, and also presented me with memorable puzzles of its own. One clue was so difficult (and in the end, really impossible) to translate, that I postponed translating that book for ten years. I will not give away which title, but the clue has a lot to do with the English language, as it relates to a word which has a completely different meaning if one letter is added to it. I looked at other Nordic translations, searching for clues on how translators had gone about making this work in a Nordic language, but to no avail. In the end, I still translated the book, and had to stick to the English words to explain Christie's trick.

There were other interesting challenges for an Icelandic teenager in translating Christie's novels in a pre-Google era. For example, I kept wondering why her characters kept walking out of windows, until I realized the true meaning of "French windows."

All joking aside, the translations provided me with invaluable experience for my writing career. When I wrote my first crime novel, I had translated fourteen of Christie's books. To this day, my novels tend to be around the same length as an average Christie book, and that is no coincidence. I also tried to learn as much as I could from her. She created the most beautiful plots, always with a twist at the end. Her detectives were ever so memorable, and her use of setting was unparalleled; the river Nile, the Orient Express, an English manor in the snow, the scene was set for a first-rate mystery, and the setting usually played an important part in the story.

Some people say that Christie took all the best plots away from other authors, and to an extent there is probably some truth in that, although the rest of us keep trying to surprise our readers. A friend of mine, John Curran, who has written extensively about Christie, maintains that the secret of her plots was how simply they could be explained, perhaps in one word or sentence only, yet the readers were almost always taken by complete surprise. I keep rereading Christie; it is impossible not to, if not for the plots (some of which are hard to forget, of course), then simply for the atmosphere she conjures up, transporting the reader to a different place, reminding me of the young boy who sat in the National Library on Saturday mornings, enjoying a great book.

MISS MARPLE MEETS SUBURBIA

L. Alison Heller

What do a cozy English village and a modern suburb have in common? Thanks to Agatha Christie's influence, both serve as a showcase for human foibles and local secrets, as well as a natural place to hide a dead body or two.

For nearly a century, Christie's village mysteries have offered readers Swiss-timepiece plotting and a romp through English life. Chatty and humorous, they are as concerned with the quotidian tensions and familiar characters of the small towns in which they are set as they are with solving murders. In addition to introducing Miss Marple, who, ninety years after her first appearance, remains a mainstay of page and screen, Christie's village mysteries have a legacy beyond the picturesque British countryside. Look at any of the popular suburban mysteries published this century, and you will find elements of Christie.

First: an amateur detective, someone of the affected community, is pressed into investigation by a personal connection to the crime. In Megan Miranda's *Such a Quiet Place* (2021), Harper Nash is inspired to dig through her neighborhood's secrets after her roommate is arrested for murdering a couple on their block. Nora, the amateur sleuth in Chandler Baker's *The Husbands* (2021) is a lawyer contemplating a move to Dynasty Ranch, when she's hired to investigate a suspicious fire. Joshilyn Jackson's Amy (*Never Have I Ever* [2019]) meets the blackmailing criminal who will upend her life—unless she fights back—at her neighborhood book club. Their progenitor, Miss Marple, is similarly compelled into service by the proximity of a dead body found next door to her home in *Murder at the Vicarage*.

While there might be an official detective on the scene as well—and he or she may range from skilled to hapless and overly enamored with red herrings—ultimately, the salaried sleuth is window dressing. There is no solving the crime without the amateur, whose success rate is, like Miss Marple's, 100 percent. The amateur detective is not in it for professional accolades, which is good, because even after Marple has racked up an unimpeachable crime-solving record, the detectives in search of her guidance chalk up her abilities to intuition, rather than skill or experience. As contrasted with Poirot, the self-described "greatest detective in the world" (Christie 1928: 143), Miss Marple considers herself an "ordinary rather scatty old lady" (1971: 50). In *Murder at the Vicarage* (1930), she downplays her talents as follows:

> living alone as I do, in a rather out-of-the-way part of the world, one has to have a hobby. There is, of course, woolwork, and Guides, and Welfare, and sketching, but my hobby is—and always has been—Human Nature. So varied—and so very fascinating. And, of course, in a small village, with nothing to distract one, one has such ample opportunity for becoming what I might call proficient in one's study.
>
> (Christie [1930] 2005: 323)

There is an argument to be made that Marple's modesty, agreeability, and relative invisibility as a woman of a certain age reflects outdated values about femininity (especially when contrasted to Poirot's bluster). But perhaps Marple was the most commercially palatable way for Christie to expand the mystery genre. Certainly, Marple's village mysteries rely on the trope of an underestimated woman going head-to-head with—and running circles around—the hard-boiled male detectives. And in Christie's books, female criminals are every bit as greedy and craven as their male counterparts.

The modern suburban murder mystery remains largely concerned with female amateur sleuths, some of whom work outside the neighborhood like Baker's Nora and some of whom are stay-at-home parents. In their modern iterations, these characters are allowed to fall short of Miss Marple's reliable consistency. They have dark secrets, like *Never Have I Ever*'s Amy. They are messy and struggle with addiction like Paula Hawkins's Rachel in *The Girl on the Train* (2016). They lie to save their own skin, like Jenny in Michele Campbell's *It's Always the Husband* (2017). They also, like Miss Marple, live in small communities that can swing from cozy to suffocating. In Marple's St. Mary Mead, everyone "knows exactly where you keep your toothbrush and what kind of tooth powder you use" (Christie [1930] 2005: 225–6).

Another crucial element of the village mystery is how this familiarity breeds a false sense of security. In picturesque Clipping Cleghorn, when an announcement is placed in the local paper that a murder will take place

6:30 p.m., on Friday, October 29, at Little Paddocks, the community members show up in droves, assuming it will be a role-playing game, thus delivering themselves for the killing in *A Murder Is Announced*. Naturally, Miss Marple's services are required.

Christie's juxtapositions—of grisly murders in vicarages, libraries, and pubs—echo throughout the modern suburban mystery. When writing *The Neighbor's Secret*, I used cul-de-sacs and book clubs as the symbols of community comfort zones, but I strove to scratch the same veneer of safety that Christie does.

Ultimately, in both the village mystery and its modern iteration, it is the community's whisper network, along with the amateur detective's doggedness, that solves the crime. It's how Miss Marple learns, while calling on her neighbors, the dishy nugget that one potential suspect was seen painting another in her bathing dress (*The Murder at the Vicarage*). What starts out as harmless gossip becomes crucial evidence upon which the neighborhood sleuth builds her case.

That sense of intimacy is the largest through line between the village and the modern suburban mysteries, with dangers and resolutions as relatable—and close—as possible. A crime of the domestic sphere is solved by a local amateur who has as little detective training as the presumptive reader. *This could be you*, Christie and her literary heirs beckon, *living somewhere not quite as safe as you think*.

REFERENCES

Baker, C. (2021), *The Husbands*, New York: Flatiron.
Campbell, M. (2017), *It's Always the Husband*, New York: St. Martin's.
Christie, A. (1923), *The Murder on the Links*, New York: Dodd Mead.
Christie, A. (1924), *The Man in the Brown Suit*, London: The Bodley Head.
Christie, A. (1926), *The Murder of Roger Ackroyd*, London: Collins.
Christie, A. (1928), *The Mystery of the Blue Train*. London: Collins.
Christie, A. ([1930] 2005), *The Murder at the Vicarage*. London: Harper.
Christie, A. (1932), *The Thirteen Problems*, London: Collins.
Christie, A. (1934), *Murder on the Orient Express*, London: Collins.
Christie, A. (1936a), *The ABC Murders*, London: Collins.
Christie, A. (1936b), *Murder in Mesopotamia*, London: Collins.
Christie, A. ([1936] 2005), *Cards on the Table*, London: Harper.
Christie, A. ([1937] 2011), *Death on the Nile*, London: Collins.
Christie, A. (1938), *Hercule Poirot's Christmas*, London: Collins.
Christie, A. (1939), *And Then There Were None*, London: Collins.
Christie, A. (1941), *Evil under the Sun*, London: Collins.
Christie, A. (1942), *The Body in the Library*, New York: Dodd Mead.
Christie, A. (1944), *Death Comes as the End*, New York: Dodd Mead.
Christie, A. (1946), *The Hollow*, New York: Dodd Mead.
Christie, A. ([1950] 2011), *A Murder Is Announced*, New York: William Morrow.
Christie, A. (1951), *They Came to Baghdad*, London: Collins.
Christie, A. ([1954] 1957), *Spider's Web*, New York: Samuel French.

Christie, A. (1956), *Dead Man's Folly*, New York: Dodd Mead.

Christie, A. (1958a), *Ordeal by Innocence*, London: Collins.

Christie, A. (1958b), *The Unexpected Guest*, New York: Samuel French.

Christie, A. (1958c), *Verdict*, New York: Samuel French.

Christie, A. (1961), *The Pale Horse*, London: Collins.

Christie, A. (1962), *The Mirror Crack'd from Side to Side*, London: Collins.

Christie, A. (1968), *By the Pricking of My Thumbs*, London: Collins.

Christie, A. (1967), *Endless Night*, London: Collins.

Christie, A. (1971), *Nemesis*, New York: HarperCollins.

Christie, A. (1977), *An Autobiography*, London: Collins.

Christie, A. (1978), *The Mousetrap and Other Plays*, New York: G. P. Putnam's Sons.

Christie, A. (n.d., believed circa 1953–1963), *Witness for the Prosecution*. New York: Samuel French.

Christie Mallowan, A. (1946), *Come Tell Me How You Live*, London: Collins.

Flynn, G. (2014), *Gone Girl*, New York: Crown.

Graham, C. (1987), *The Killers at Badger's Drift*, London: Century

Hannah, S. (2021), "Sophie Hannah on the Literary Side of Agatha Christie: 'Her Style is Not Simplistic but, Rather, Beautifully Simple'," *Crimereads*. Available online: https://crimereads.com/sophie-hannah-agatha-christie-literary-style/ (accessed November 21, 2021).

Hawkins, P. (2016), *The Girl on the Train*, New York: Riverhead.

Heller, L. A. (2021), *The Neighbor's Secret*, New York: Flatiron.

Hicks, R. (1990), *Essay in Program for Agatha Christie Centenary*, Brixham: Churchwardens of St. Mary the Virgin, Churston Ferrers.

Horowitz, A. (1997), *The Midsomer Murders* [television series], London: Bentley Productions.

Horowitz, A. (1989), *Agatha Christie's Poirot*, [television series], London: ITV.

Jackson, J. (2019), *Never Have I Ever*, New York: William Morrow.

Mallowan, M. ([1977] 2001), *Mallowan's Memoirs: Agatha and the Archaeologist*, London: HarperCollins.

Miranda, M. (2021), *Such a Quiet Place*, New York: Simon & Schuster.

Thomson, H. D. (1930), *Masters of Mystery*, London: Collins.

Sandford, J. (2019), *Holy Ghost*, New York: G.P. Putnam & Sons.

Sayers, D. L. (1928), Introduction to *Great Short Stories of Detection, Mystery and Horror*, 9–47, London: Victor Gollancz.

Tey, J. (1951), *The Daughter of Time*, London: Peter Davies.

LIST OF CONTRIBUTORS

Mark Aldridge is an Associate Professor in Film and Television at Solent University, Southampton, UK. He is the author of *Agatha Christie on Screen* (2016), *Agatha Christie's Poirot: The Greatest Detective in the World* (2021), and *The Birth of British Television: A History* (2011).

Nadia Atia is a Senior Lecturer in World Literature at Queen Mary University of London. Her research examines Britain's ever-evolving relationship with Iraq, and the ways in which Iraq and its people are represented in contemporary Iraqi literature available in the UK. She is the author of *World War I in Mesopotamia: The British and the Ottomans in Iraq* (2015) and coeditor with Kate Houlden of *Popular Postcolonialisms: Discourses of Empire and Popular Culture.*

J.C. Bernthal is a Visiting Fellow at the University of Suffolk. He is the author of *Queering Agatha Christie* (2016) and *Agatha Christie: A Companion to the Mystery Fiction* (2022). He has previously edited *The Ageless Agatha Christie* (2016) and, with Rebecca Mills, *Agatha Christie Goes to War* (2020). In 2020, he received the Popular Culture Association's George N. Dove Award for encouraging the serious study of crime fiction.

Brittain Bright is an independent scholar of detective fiction. Her research focuses on place and narratology, and she has published articles on the work of Agatha Christie, Dorothy L. Sayers, Gladys Mitchell, and Rex Stout.

Meta Carstarphen is a Professor at the University of Oklahoma, where she holds a Gaylord Family Professorship. Her research explores how media can affect social change. She is the author of five books, including *Race, Gender, Class,* *and Media: Studying Mass Communication and Multiculturalism*, and she is currently at work on *Writing Home: Race, Newspapers and the Culture of Place in Oklahoma*.

Mary Evans is a Visiting Professor at the London School of Economics. Her work has included studies of feminist and gender theory, as well as studies of literary genres (detective fiction) and writers (Jane Austen and Simone de Beauvoir).

Mary Anna Evans is an Associate Professor in Professional Writing at the University of Oklahoma. Her fourteen crime novels have received recognition including the Benjamin Franklin Award, the Oklahoma Book Award, and the Will Rogers Medallion Award. Her research focuses on the portrayal of women's lives by women crime novelists and, in particular, on the evolution over her long career of Agatha Christie's portrayal of women's interactions with the law and their experiences with justice.

Kathryn Harkup is a writer and science communicator. Her interests are in anything gothic, gory and geeky, and preferably all three. As well as *A Is for Arsenic: The Poisons of Agatha Christie*, she has written several other books on the crossover between science, history, and literature, including *Making the Monster: The Science of Mary Shelley's Frankenstein* (2018), *Death by Shakespeare: Snakebites, Stabbings and Broken Hearts* (2020), and *Vampirology: The Science of Horror's Most Famous Fiend* (2021).

Michelle M. Kazmer is a Professor in the School of Information at Florida State University. Her research includes qualitative and mixed-methods studies of distributed knowledge in settings associated with health and learning, and she maintains an active research agenda applying information science theories to Golden Age detective fiction. She has authored and co-authored more than fifty peer-reviewed publications, including a book chapter on Miss Marple as examined through the lens of Information Worlds Theory.

Merja Makinen retired as Director of Communication and Culture, Middlesex University, UK, and now works as a freelance reader and writer. Her research interests include gender in twentieth-century fiction, including Angela Carter, Jeanette Winterson, and gender aspects of popular genre fiction, including Agatha Christie. Her publications include "Taking on Hitler: Agatha Christie's Wartime Thrillers" (2020) and *Agatha Christie: Investigating Femininity* (2006).

Rebecca Mills is a Lecturer in Communication and English at Bournemouth University, UK. Her research interests include women's crime writing, gothic communities and landscapes, and celebrity culture. Recent projects include

Agatha Christie Goes to War (2020), which she co-edited with J.C. Bernthal, and an article titled "'A Pleasure of That Too Intense Kind': Women's Desires and Identity in Stella Gibbons's Gothic London" in *Studies in Gothic Fiction* (2020).

Benedict Morrison is a Lecturer in Literature, Film and Television at the University of Exeter, UK. His research interests include queer theory, British and European film, radical televisual form, and critical animal theory. He has recently published a book called *Complicating Articulation in Art Cinema* (2021) and is currently researching and writing a book on queer theoretical approaches to post-War British cinema.

Barbara Peters is the founder of The Poisoned Pen Bookstore, one of the leading mystery specialty bookstores in the United States, and co-founder of Poisoned Pen Press, now the mystery imprint at Sourcebooks. She has received the Mystery Writers of America's Raven Award for bookselling and Ellery Queen Award for editing. Bouchercon, Left Coast Crime, and Malice Domestic mystery conventions have all accorded her Lifetime Achievement honors.

Mathew Prichard, CBE, DL, is the former CEO of Agatha Christie Limited. He is the editor of *The Grand Tour: Letters and Photographs from the British Empire Expedition* (2013). The son of Hubert Prichard and Rosalind Hicks, he is the only grandchild of Agatha Christie.

Vike Martina Plock is a Professor of Modern Literature and Culture at the University of Exeter. She is the author of *Joyce, Medicine, and Modernity* (2010), *Modernism, Fashion and Interwar Women Writers* (2017) and, most recently, *The BBC German Service during the Second World War: Broadcasting to the Enemy* (2021). She is co-editor of *Literature & History* and an associate editor of the *James Joyce Quarterly*. She is currently working on a new research project on the dissemination of early-twentieth-century writers and intellectuals as Penguin paperback authors.

Susan Rowland is Core Faculty, and Advisor in Research and the Humanities in MA Depth Psychology and Creativity, as well as teaching in the Doctoral Program in Jungian and Archetypal Studies. She is the author of two books on women's detective fiction—*From Agatha Christie to Ruth Rendell* (2000) and *The Sleuth and the Goddess* (2015)—as well as books on Jung, literary theory, and ecocriticism such as *The Ecocritical Psyche* (2012). She also writes the Mary Wandwalker mysteries.

ACKNOWLEDGMENTS

We have worked to ensure that a broad selection of Christie's crime novels, short stories, literary novels, dramatic adaptations, and more have been examined through case studies, and that her life and ongoing legacy have been considered. We are grateful to acknowledge the access given by Mathew Prichard and The Christie Archive Trust to scholars who contributed to this book, as well as their kind provision of photographs included here, and we are grateful to the British Broadcasting Corporation for access to its archives and for a photograph of Christie at the microphone. The University of Reading Special Collections and the University of Exeter's Special Collections kindly provided access, and the Penn Museum provided a photograph of Christie and her husband Max on an archaeological dig, long hidden in their files because Christie was identified only as Mrs. Mallowan.

Additionally, we would like to thank Ben Doyle, Laura Cope, and the team at Bloomsbury for their assistance throughout the editorial and production process, as well as David Avital for first approaching Mary Anna with the idea of editing this volume. Working transatlantically throughout the Covid-19 pandemic has presented a unique set of challenges, and we are grateful to all contributors. They were able to rise, brilliantly, to these challenges.

We acknowledge, gratefully, our colleagues, families, and loved ones who provided supportive frameworks that enabled us to get on with the work. Mary Anna is grateful to her husband Tony for his loving encouragement throughout the process of tackling this exciting-but-daunting opportunity. She would also like to thank Dr. Lisa Smithstead for her gracious support in helping a crime fiction practitioner learn to see the field through a scholar's lens. Jamie (J.C. Bernthal) is grateful to his spouse Alan who has been an absolute rock throughout the process, with unfathomable stores of patience and listening power. Jamie would also like to thank his long-suffering co-editor, Mary Anna Evans, who has been a pleasure to work with on this two-year labor of love, and who will be pleased to know he is finally spelling "labor" the American way. Mary Anna would like to thank Jamie for the depth and breadth of his knowledge on all things Agatha and for his kindness in sharing it; she feels that the spelling of "labour/labor" is immaterial when one is rightly calling this book a labor of love. Creating it has been a fascinating journey, and Jamie has been the ideal traveling companion.

INDEX